MULTIPLE-CHOICE AND FREE-RESPONSE QUESTIONS IN PREPARATION FOR THE AP ENGLISH LITERATURE AND COMPOSITION EXAMINATION

(EIGHTH EDITION)

By

DR. RICHARD VOGEL

Edited and Introduced by Sally Pfeifer

D&S MARKETING SYSTEMS, INC.
1205 38th Street Brooklyn, NY 11218

w w w . d s m a r k e t i n g . c o m

ISBN # 978-1-934780-18-3 / 1-934780-18-9

INTRODUCTION

I began using D&S Marketing's *Multiple-Choice Questions in Preparation for the Advanced Placement English Literature & Composition Examination* in the early 1990s. At that time, as a relatively new AP English teacher, I was looking for some concrete help with the multiple-choice section of the exam, a section that seemed to baffle and frustrate teachers and students alike. I quickly discovered that practice with multiple-choice samples was limited by the few practice tests and sample passages available. D&S Marketing's AP English texts helped fill that void. As the years progressed and I gained experience, I learned that teaching my students close reading skills and giving them practice with the types of multiple-choice questions that appear on the exam proved a good tool. My subsequent experiences as a Reader and Table Leader at the exam grading and as a member of the Test Development Committee helped me to understand the construction of the exam and the skills it assesses. Thus, when fellow AP colleague Rich Vogel asked me to review and edit his latest edition, I was excited to use my experience and knowledge to help make this text a dynamic and usable tool for students and teachers of AP English Literature.

With that in mind, I would like to suggest some ideas or methods for using this edition in the AP classroom. This new edition has been expanded to include not only sample exams with multiple-choice and free-response questions, but useful preparatory guides for the poetry, prose and free-response sections as well, in addition to explications, rubrics, student samples and assessments of student responses. There are extensive explanations for each multiple-choice and free-response question. Rich has worked diligently to deliver great pieces of literature with solid and provocative questions, and though you may or may not agree with the answer to a given question, you will be able to see and understand the thought process behind it. I suggest that you try not to criticize a particular question, but instead come to an understanding of it with your students, enjoying a "teachable moment."

Though there are many ways to use this wealth of materials and expertise in your classroom, here are a few suggestions:

1. Don't ask your students to take every test "cold." Rather, work backward on a few of the samples first. Read the piece, than the explication, and, in the case of the essays, review the scoring guide and student samples if included. Discuss the piece, then try the questions as a class, in small groups or individually.

2. Try small "chunks" at first. For example, after studying some poetry or a novel, complete one of the multiple-choice pieces on a poem or prose passage. Work up to the "whole exams" slowly—there are four complete exams included in this edition in addition to the two contained in the Prepping for Poetry, Prepping for Prose, and Prepping for Literature sections.

3. Read a poem or prose passage together and speculate about questions that might be asked; then, see what questions actually appear.

In other words, let this book "work" for you. Incorporate the poetry, prose selections and open questions into your syllabus. Remember: if you bring your students your "best game"—a love of literature and the skills of reading and responding to it—this book will serve you well.

Thank you to Rich Vogel and David Lederman for the opportunity to play a small part in this edition.

Sally Pfeifer

ACKNOWLEDGMENTS

No work of literature is a solitary effort, even if it is written by a single author, and the 8th edition of *Multiple-Choice and Free-Response Questions in Preparation for the Advanced Placement English Literature & Composition Examination* is no exception. I would like to express my gratitude to David Lederman of D&S Marketing who has supported my efforts since the first edition of this text appeared in the mid-1980s. Though I am sure I have on occasion exasperated him with revisions to the text, I think he has grown to understand that the same ambiguity of literature that permits multiple interpretations of *Hamlet* bedevils the creator of multiple choice questions who must try to eliminate all potential challenges to the correctness of a right answer while still creating a choice or two that may serve as a reasonable distractor. And though I doubt he will ever understand that the search for the great passage (one that will yield a dozen or more multiple choice questions) or a great essay prompt often rivals Ahab's search for the white whale, he has nevertheless shown an amplitude of patience in our mutual endeavor to produce the best possible AP English text. Seldom have I been asked to forego a piece that I really thought would add quality to the book despite, I am sure, the considerable royalty some contemporary pieces command. For this unflagging support I am forever grateful.

As for my editor and back-reader, Sally Pfeifer, I cannot begin to express my appreciation for the long hours she has contributed, the literary insights she has shared, and the rigid standards to which she has held me during the arduous gestation of this book. She has provided the most useful feedback, whether it be suggesting potential authors or passages, offering an alternate perspective on a particular text, or deterring the wrong-headed foray of which I am sometimes capable. All of these she has done with an admirable mixture of professionalism and affability that has made a process that can easily become turbulent a smooth and enjoyable ride. A comrade and dining companion from my days as a Reader and Table Leader in San Antonio, Daytona and Louisville, Sally has been an invaluable resource and someone whom I have been fortunate to have had working with me on this new edition.

I would be remiss not to mention our typesetter, Chaya Pruzansky, whose patience during the long process of fashioning early drafts into a refined final product, as well as her tolerance for the multiple emendations this process entails, has been boundless. I am deeply appreciative of her efforts in making the presentation of the material on the page both accurate and visually attractive.

I would also like to thank the AP English students at Croton-Harmon High School and at Wilton High School whose essays appear in this book for so generously sharing their time and talent. In joining them in our mutual exploration of literature, I have been humbled daily by their bright minds and engaging personalities.

Lastly, I would like to thank the present and former members of the English Department at Wilton High School. Being surrounded daily by such diverse, fecund and idiosyncratic minds is a continued source of inspiration to me, and the insights you have shared on particular passages and your proffered words of perseverance and encouragement have provided the last gust to guide this bark into its harbor. I am blessed to call you colleagues, even more so to call you my friends.

Richard Vogel

All communications concerning this book should be addressed to:

D&S Marketing Systems, Inc.
1205 38th Street
Brooklyn, NY 11218
www.dsmarketing.com

TABLE OF CONTENTS

Prepping for Poetry: How to Achieve Success on the AP Multiple-Choice and Free-Response Poetry Questions

"Poetry. I, too, dislike it: there are things that are important beyond all this fiddle."

—from "Poetry" by Marianne Moore

The sentiment expressed by Marianne Moore is unfortunately shared by too many high-school students who approach poetry with the apprehension of a hobbit entering Mordor. Sadly, the AP English Literature Examination—to be fair, *any* examination—will do little to mitigate this trepidation. Reading and enjoying poetry is a reflective act, one best carried out curled up in an easy-chair or leisurely sprawled in a field of grass, not a task carried out under the severe auspices of a ticking clock. That said, the exam is what it is, and students who score well must be able to read poetry efficiently—for theme, for diction, for figurative language, for syntax and for tone, not to mention to have some awareness of the rhythmic and aural devices of the poem and even its historical context.

Even so, the task for students need not be an onerous one. Approach it as you would a sport or a trip. In the former case, recognize that repeated instances of practice—of reading and interpreting poems of different periods and styles; of recognizing interesting word choices, striking images, figures of speech, and syntactical constructions; of pondering how these elements contribute to the poem and why they have been elected over others; and of (for essay questions) organizing your thoughts in a rough outline that responds to the demands of an AP prompt—will help develop skills of analysis and synthesis in much the same way as dribbling or shooting a basketball will enhance your ability to play the sport. As to the latter, think of the exam as a weekend getaway rather than six months' abroad and pack light. For example, one does not need a suitcase full of literary terms; a satchel will do just fine.

When I work with my own students on poetry, I have very simple goals in mind. First and foremost is to dispel any fears they have developed from previous exposures to poetry. It is important for them to understand that *economy*—unless you've decided to write an epic—is an important feature of poetry. Novelists have several hundred pages in which to convey their message; a poem often has less than a page. Therefore, *words matter*, and it is important to recognize that in good poetry they are not chosen arbitrarily. Now I am not being condescending. Clearly, it does not take the greatest of efforts to pen a four-line verse for a greeting card, but to write a serious poem demands a meticulous attention to detail. So we work, as I call it, "at word level," working our way up from word, to phrase, to clause, to line, to stanza. Many students can understand the big ideas of a poem rather handily, but it is learning to manage the elements that combine to advance those big ideas—the *language* of the poem—that decisively captures the flag. For example, most students have either read or are familiar with "The Road Not Taken" by Robert Frost, and most students can understand without too much difficulty that the poem involves a choice. We are more interested, however, in subtleties, lines such as

I shall be telling this with a sigh
Somewhere ages and ages hence:
Two roads diverged in a wood and I—
I took the one less traveled by,
And that has made all the difference.

1

Why, for example, is he telling this with a "sigh?" What does that word connote? Is it a sigh of relief, or a sigh of disappointment? What does the speaker mean by the words "that has made all the difference?" Is the "difference" something positive, or something negative? The difference between his being a success, or his being a failure? Granted, this is a simple poem with simple diction, but the same skills and approach are what we take with us to a harder piece. Consider the opening stanza of Sylvia Plath's "Daddy:"

> You do not do, you do not do
> Any more, black shoe
> In which I have lived like a foot
> For thirty years, poor and white,
> Barely daring to breathe or Achoo!

When we go to work on an intellectually challenging piece such as this, we take out the hammer and crow-bar and deconstruct a little, starting with the simple question "What do you see in the stanza?" Now from year to year the order of the response may differ, but students usually observe the following things:

- The speaker feels confined. She feels like a foot in a shoe.

- She is totally paranoid, afraid to even breathe or sneeze.

- She has endured this situation for a long time: thirty years to be exact.

- Her situation is no longer acceptable: the shoe "does not do" anymore.

These are all accurate and merit-worthy observations about the opening five lines, but we are still on "idea level." My job is to bring my class back down to "word level" through such questions as:

- "Do you notice anything about the relationship between the foot and the shoe?" (Students may notice a color relationship, black-white)

- "Have any of you seen this idea of living in a shoe before? (Students may recognize the allusion to a children's poem, "There was an old woman who lived in a shoe.")

- "What is the effect of the repetition in the first line?" (Most students, even in AP, may not yet recognize the authoritarian, scolding voice of the father; that's where my job begins).

- "Why do you think the speaker says "Achoo" rather than "sneeze?" (Sometimes someone recognizes it as a sound, but rarely does someone realize its onomatopoeic potential.)

- "Does the rhyme remind you of anything?" (Some students will say a nursery rhyme; this comes in handy later when we start to see similar references such as the allusion to Humpty Dumpty.)

We continue this progression throughout the poem until we are ready to try to put all these pieces together and reach a coherent impression. You can, too.

Prose is sometimes defined as "the language of direct communication" or "the ordinary language people use to communicate with each other." The lion's share of what you read, hear in the media, or speak to others around you falls in this category, and while it would be over-simplifying and somewhat silly to label poetry the "language of *indirect* communication," that's sort of what it is. Poets are not necessarily interested in serving you the meaning of their poems on a plate. Rather, they communicate through image and symbol, through comparisons such as similes and metaphors, through playing something up (hyperbole) or playing something down (understatement), through making connections to older things in literature, history, religion and other subjects (allusion). This latter technique is hardest for students to recognize because of the limited scope of their reading, and I can assure you it can be just as hard for your teachers. An enormous amount has occurred and been written over the last two millennia, and everyone sooner or later has to rely on footnotes or conduct a little research. If for students poetry appears harder, this is one of the reasons—because, save for some elementary poetry, one never gets things delivered directly. This and the other obvious problematic factor—the archaic language of most things written prior to the mid-nineteenth century—can make poetry frustrating, but with some help from a competent teacher, you can learn to read and hopefully appreciate poetry of all ages and cultures.

This being a preparation book for the AP English Literature exam, I cannot break poetry down into all of its various parts. As someone who has read the poetry question many times at the annual AP English Literature Exam grading, I can, however, give you some basic advice, advice that will be equally helpful in the multiple-choice and essay sections:

1. Focus on close reading.

Students who gloss or scan a poem seldom write anything profound. You must, as has been advised earlier in this essay, get down to "word level." Now there is a difference between vocabulary and diction. The former, a more comprehensive term, is defined as "all the words in a language," the latter, a more specific term, as the "choice of words in speech and writing." The key word here is "choice." Poets many times choose words with multiple connotations. Much like allusions, connotations open up new avenues of thought, giving the poem a richer texture. Consider these four stanzas which follow consecutively in Sylvia Plath's "Daddy:"

> You stand at the blackboard, daddy,
> In the picture I have of you,
> A cleft in your chin instead of your foot
> But no less a devil for that, no not
> Any less the black man who
>
> Bit my pretty red heart in two.
> I was ten when they buried you.
> At twenty I tried to die
> And get back, back, back to you
> I thought even the bones would do.
>
> But they pulled me out of the sack,
> And they stuck me together with glue.
> And then I knew what to do.
> I made a model of you,
> A man in black with a Mein Kampf look

And a love of the rack and the screw.
And I said I do, I do.
So daddy, I'm finally through.
The black telephone's off at the root,
The voices just can't worm through....

Now since I have not explicated the entire poem in this essay, I need to fill in a couple of blanks for you. The speaker in Plath's poem, denied the affection of her father first by his cold aloofness and second by his premature death, has no practical way to resolve her psychological issues, no tangible hope of reconciliation. Ten years after her father's death, she attempts to reunite with him in death, if not in life, but her suicide attempt is thwarted. Unable to reconnect with her father in either way, she does the next best thing: marries a man just like him. This, she believes, will resolve her dilemma for good.

Now let's look at this at "word level." The first two stanzas do not offer much in this respect, other than the word "cleft," a physical depression in her father's chin which the speaker associates with the cloven foot of a devil. "Daddy" is also a black man who "Bit [her] pretty red heart in two," an action that associates him with a vampire. Stanza three is a bit more fecund, yielding the aforementioned Humpty Dumpty allusion in the line "stuck me together with glue," as well as an allusion to Hitler, another male tyrant, in the reference to "Mein Kampf." Stanza four, however, offers fascinating diction. The man she marries has "a love of the rack and the screw," which on one level calls to mind medieval torture devices but on another enhances this with an intriguing sexual connotation, "rack" being slang for bed and "screw" slang for fornication. Saying "I do, I do," words that are the inverse of the "You do not do, you do not do" that opens the poem, the speaker mirrors the traditional wedding vow. Believing she has finally achieved psychological closure, she "hangs up" on Daddy, noting that "The black telephone's off at the root" and that "The voices just can't worm through." Here diction assumes great importance, in particular the words "root" and "worm." Though one expects "hook" instead of "root," the choice of the latter creates an incongruous marriage of technology and nature, suggesting that since daddy is interred, communication is done by root, not by wire. The word "worm," which also has associations with dirt, further connotes something small and narrow enough to crawl through a root. To cite a line from another notable American poetess, Emily Dickinson, what the speaker in Plath's poem desires is to "close the valves of her attention like stone;" to once and for all lay the specter of her father to rest. Close reading requires paying attention to diction, figurative language, syntax, choice of detail and tone. Its end is to collect enough "evidence" to support whatever conclusions you have made about the poem in response to a given prompt and to anticipate the kind of multiple-choice questions that test-makers have created. This is the single most important skill for success on the examination.

2. Travel light.

This idea was introduced earlier, but I will expand upon it in greater specificity here. There is really no need to encumber your mind with dozens of literary terms when mastery of a select few will do. I have found the following "select seven" to be the most useful:

Personification

Metaphor (both stated and implied) and **Simile**

Hyperbole and its antithesis, **Understatement**

Irony

Allusion (Biblical and classical, to the extent that you are able)

Of course, there are others you should know the meaning of in the event they surface in a multiple choice question, but **Oxymoron** and **Paradox** come up infrequently, **Metonymy** and **Synecdoche** are many times treated as subsets of metaphor, and **Onomatopoeia** is easy to remember (sound and meaning the same) but troublesome to spell. Familiarity with these terms is to be encouraged, but mastery of the "select seven" is a must.

As for aural aspects of the poem, things such as **Rhyme**, **Alliteration**, **Assonance** and **Consonance**, these I generally downplay. There has yet to be an essay that focuses exclusively on the sound aspect of a poem, and while discussion of these can sometimes enhance an essay, papers that do so are more rare than essays scoring a 9. Moreover, there is precious little that can be said about the first two other than to restate the obvious: that the words rhyme or begin with the same consonant sound. In this regard, onomatopoeia is more valuable in that the sound can often reinforce an emotion or an action.

As for **Meter**, consider this fact: there is generally one, if any, question on meter asked per exam, and spending hours learning to recognize dactylic tetrameter seems counter-productive. What is important is being able to identify the number of stresses in a given line of poetry, and knowing what prefixes such as tetra- and penta- mean. Many times if you can figure out that the lines all have three stressed syllables, only one answer will have that choice of meter in it. Of course, you should, having likely studied a Shakespearean Play, be able to recognize **Blank Verse** (unrhymed iambic pentameter), and **Free Verse** (no regular rhythm, no pattern of rhyme), as well as to understand a term such as **Enjambment** (the overflow of one line of poetry into subsequent lines). However, students in my class averaged over 4.7 on the exam last year, and this is pretty much all that we traveled with.

In terms of knowing the characteristics of the poetry of various periods, this can only help. This is one of the advantages of having an anthology of literature in an AP English class since it usually offers summaries of both the era and the manner in which the historical and literary climates affected the poetry produced in those periods. A student, for example, who knows the influences of the Romantic period upon both content and style can more readily explain the differences between the poetry of William Blake and the poetry of John Keats. Having similar familiarity with the Metaphysical school, the sonneteers, the Victorians and moderns, etc. can only make a good essay a better one. And speaking of sonnets, inasmuch as the dense and compact form of this fourteen-line poem makes it a favorite choice for the examination, students should certainly be familiar with both the **Petrarchan** and the **Shakespearean** forms of the sonnet as well as with its later diversifications (by this I am referring to its shift from a traditional love poem to a poem exploring a wide variety of subjects in addition to changes in its physical appearance on the page).

3. For essays: Respond to the <u>entire</u> question.

Many times essays on a poem will ask you something about the poem's *meaning* as well as something about the *language* of the poem. Sometimes they will list particular elements for you to consider. These lists are never prescriptive, and you can certainly use something that is not listed there, but know this: if it *is* listed as something for you to consider, it usually figures prominently in the poem. It is a good habit to circle or underline the essential parts of the question so you do not inadvertently omit something you have been asked to discuss.

4. Also for essays: Frame a thesis and make a rough outline.

Readers, new and old, are always reminded to treat each paper as a rough draft. All readers know that students have roughly forty minutes to read a prompt and a passage, then write a response that addresses the question provided. Thus, they are not expecting perfection. Though they are trained to follow rubrics for each question, they are also schooled in the following golden rule: essays scoring 5 or above have insight, development, support and fluency, and essays scoring below a 5 lack these qualities. Thus, using your close reading skills to come up with a plausible interpretation and supporting it with convincing detail is paramount, and rendering that response in organized, fluent prose is as well.

Toward that end I have always found papers which frame a thesis to be very helpful—provided, of course, they support it convincingly with textual evidence. Your thesis need not be a work of art, but it needs to be more than a parroting of the question. You have read enough of Plath's "Daddy" to weigh in on these:

Thesis One: "Sylvia Plath's 'Daddy' depicts her difficult relationship with her father through strong diction, allusion and metaphor."

Thesis Two: "Sylvia Plath's 'Daddy' examines the speaker's attempt to resolve acute psychological problems caused by a lack of attention and affection from her father and by his premature death when she was ten. Plath uses diction and metaphors that portray her father as a stern, authoritarian figure, as well as a Nazi and a vampire who tormented her emotionally."

In the first case, the student suffers from what I call 'Empty Thesis Syndrome.' She uses a generic word like "difficult" which does little to explain the specific psychological issues that the speaker suffers in trying to resolve her relationship with her father. She compounds this shortcoming by merely repeating literary elements that were likely listed in the prompt. In the second, the student clearly identifies the nature of the psychological issues that are plaguing the speaker, then clearly identifies the nature of the diction and metaphors she will later discuss. The key difference here is that in the first case the reader is no further along when he starts the body of the essay than he was when he started the introduction. In the second example the reader knows exactly where the paper is headed; he can relax and look for evidence that supports these claims.

The thousand college and secondary school teachers who rate the AP exam in June collectively have to read over a million essays in less than a week. It is grueling work which takes a physical toll—on attention span, on posture, on endurance, but especially upon the eyes. Papers which feature a clear, if roughly framed thesis, make a reader relax. There is no need to wade through the entire paper, trying to uncover its main claim; it is there up-front, directing the action. A good rule to remember is ***concise but precise***. I drill this into my own students. Don't take forever to make your point, but make sure it is specific rather than vague or generic.

As for outlining, there is not much to say in this regard that is not obvious. Clearly, a paper which has a plan and a progression will read more effectively than one which features haphazard and disorganized ideas. In forty minutes there is no time to be creating a Harvard outline, but there is ample time to sketch out a rough one. Of the three free-response questions, the poetry is many times the lowest scoring question and the one that averages the shortest response. The literature question scores the highest and generally produces the longest essays, and the prose is usually in the middle (though it can occasionally challenge poetry as the hardest). Inasmuch as students do not have to read a poem or a passage to complete the Literature essay, I often tell my students that they can "borrow" five minutes from this question to use as their outlining time. The payoff lies in better organization, better clarity, and better fluency, all of which can only abet a good analysis.

5. The Last Word

In the subsequent pages, you will be put through a gauntlet of poems from different cultures, epochs and gender perspectives. These have been designed to help you develop the types of skills that have been discussed in the previous pages for both the multiple-choice and essay formats. They are not a substitute for your Advanced Placement English curriculum, but a complement to it. It is my hope that, together, they may combine to make you a more confident and more accurate reader of poems.

A Primer for Poetry: W.H. Auden's "Funeral Blues"

This first poem, W. H. Auden's "Funeral Blues," is a good poem with which to begin your preparation for poetry, and it will serve as a primer for the remainder of the tasks in the poetry section. Unlike other explanatory materials in this book, this one will not give you all the answers; rather, it is designed to initiate your journey through certain aspects of the poem, so that when you try the questions, you will approach with some prior knowledge of theme and technique. To begin, read the poem to yourself carefully.

Funeral Blues

Stop all the clocks, cut off the telephone,
Prevent the dog from barking with a juicy bone,
Silence the pianos and with muffled drum
Bring out the coffin, let the mourners come.

(5)   Let aeroplanes circle moaning overhead
Scribbling on the sky the message He is Dead,
Put crepe bows round the white necks of the public doves,
Let the traffic policemen wear black cotton gloves.

He was my North, my South, my East, my West,
(10)   My working week and my Sunday rest,
My noon, my midnight, my talk, my song;
I thought that love would last for ever: I was wrong.

The stars are not wanted now: put out every one;
Pack up the moon and dismantle the sun;
(15)   Pour away the ocean and sweep up the wood;
For nothing now can come to any good.

—W. H. Auden

"Funeral Blues" is a special type of poem, a poem of mourning (the term for which, if you don't already know, you will learn later). Its title is also worth taking time to consider. Ask yourself whether it can possibly function on more than one level. These are the first two things you should consider.

Moving on to the poem itself, you can tell right away that the poet is doing something interesting with his verbs in the first two stanzas. "Stop" (line 1), "cut off (line 1), "Prevent" (line 2), "Silence" (line 3), "Let" (line 5), "Put" (line 7) and "Let" again (line 8) —what type of verbs are these? What do they all have in common? Do you know the name for this type of verb? If not, you will have to wait for the explication, or skip ahead to the "Prepping for Prose" section. Now take a look at the direct objects of these verbs. What do "clocks" (line 1), "the telephone" (line 1), "the dog" (line 2), "pianos" (line 3) and a "drum" (line 3) have in common? If you have an answer, put your thoughts together. What does the speaker demand happen in stanza one? If you know, you're ready to move on.

Stanza two is a little different in terms of what the speaker is asking the "aeroplanes" (line 5), people and "traffic policemen" (line 8) to do. What "message" (line 6) does he want the planes to "[scribble] on the sky" (line 6)? Why do you think two of the words, "He" and "Dead" (line 6), begin with upper-case letters? What do you make of the imagery in lines 7 and 8? (Make sure you are looking at the right words!) What is the purpose of these images? Connect your thoughts on stanza two with your explication of stanza one.

Ah, stanza three: do you sense a change in focus? What is the speaker speaking about now? What figure of speech is occurring when the speaker begins with "He was," then makes a comparison? If you look carefully, you'll see he is making multiple comparisons. To what is he comparing his dead friend? Can you suggest reasons why he is making those comparisons?

Line 12 is comprised of two sentences that are separated by a colon. What kind of sentences are these? If you don't know, you can either wait for the explication or look it up in the "Prepping for Prose" section as well. However, breathe easy. Once you are familiar with these terms and devices, you'll find they work just as well in poetry as they do in prose—and vice versa. You don't need to worry about this issue now. However, when you do learn what type of sentence this is, you'll be able to say something profound about why it is particularly appropriate in this instance.

One stanza to go, so let's begin by asking ourselves some simple questions. First, has the focal point changed in this stanza? What type of things are now being discussed? Take a quick look at the verbs: see anything familiar? By now you should be able to figure out what the speaker is saying in this stanza, and if you can figure out the meaning of the final line, you'll be able to determine why he is saying it as well. However, before we go on to the questions, I'd like you to think about one more thing—and that's lines 13-15. Do you notice anything odd about the verbs and their objects? Compare, for example, "Stop all the clocks" (line 1) with "Pack up the moon" (line 14). If you see it, but don't know how to articulate it, don't worry. Right now seeing it is progress enough.

What you have just done is engaged the text in the way all competent readers do. In time, this will come more naturally for you. Now, if you are ready, let's move on to some questions.

Questions 1-10. Refer to the following poem.

Funeral Blues

Stop all the clocks, cut off the telephone,
Prevent the dog from barking with a juicy bone,
Silence the pianos and with muffled drum
Bring out the coffin, let the mourners come.

(5)   Let aeroplanes circle moaning overhead
Scribbling on the sky the message He is Dead,
Put crepe bows round the white necks of the public doves,
Let the traffic policemen wear black cotton gloves.

He was my North, my South, my East, my West,
(10)   My working week and my Sunday rest,
My noon, my midnight, my talk, my song;
I thought that love would last for ever: I was wrong.

The stars are not wanted now: put out every one;
Pack up the moon and dismantle the sun;
(15)   Pour away the ocean and sweep up the wood;
For nothing now can come to any good.

—W. H. Auden

1. "Funeral Blues" is BEST classified as a(n)

   (A) sonnet
   (B) ode
   (C) elegy
   (D) ballad
   (E) dramatic monologue

2. Which of the following is a plausible interpretation of the poem's title?

   I. A reference to the depression that the speaker feels over his friend's untimely death.
   II. A reference to mournful music that typically characterizes a funeral service.
   III. A reference to the poem itself.

   (A) I only
   (B) II only
   (C) I and II
   (D) I and III
   (E) I, II and III

3. To augment the dramatic imperative that opens the first stanza, the poet employs which of the following?

   (A) an iamb
   (B) a trochee
   (C) a dactyl
   (D) an anapest
   (E) a spondee

4. The death of his friend prompts the speaker to demand all of the following EXCEPT

   (A) the muting or elimination of all sounds
   (B) an opportunity for solitary mourning
   (C) a public acknowledgment of the deceased's passing
   (D) an extinguishing of celestial objects
   (E) a forfeiture of nature

5. The mournful nature of the occasion is aurally reinforced by the

   (A) ticking of the clocks
   (B) ringing of the telephone
   (C) baying of the dog
   (D) music from a piano
   (E) droning of the aeroplanes

6. The third stanza differs MOST from the other three stanzas in its

   (A) subject
   (B) tone
   (C) perspective
   (D) rhyme
   (E) figurative language

7. Of the following, which BEST describes the nature of the contrast between the first and fourth stanzas?

   (A) activity to inertia
   (B) sound to light
   (C) temporal to cosmic
   (D) mourning to celebration
   (E) secular to spiritual

8. The word which BEST describes the speaker's feelings for his now-dead friend would be

   (A) platonic
   (B) collegial
   (C) fraternal
   (D) distant
   (E) reverential

9. All of the following are used as metaphors in the poem EXCEPT

   (A) a musical instrument
   (B) a pad or billboard
   (C) a compass
   (D) a time of day
   (E) a candle

10. The MOST unique aspect of Auden's poem is its

    (A) use of the imperative mode
    (B) metrical structure
    (C) distortion of nature
    (D) symbols of mourning
    (E) use of antithesis

Précis and Explication of W.H. Auden's "Funeral Blues"

Auden's "Funeral Blues" is an elegy, a poem of mourning, in this case for a recently deceased friend. Its title has multiple meanings. It alludes perhaps to the music played at New Orleans funerals, it reflects the "blues" that the speaker himself is experiencing over this sudden and painful loss, and it references the poem itself, the expression of sadness through words, meter and rhyme. As a whole, the poem pays tribute to an individual who was the center of the speaker's affection and conveys the emotional devastation of loss and the disillusionment with life that often accompanies it.

The poem begins with a series of imperatives in which the speaker demands that all mundane noises—ticking clocks, ringing telephones, and barking dogs be silenced. The use of a spondee (/ /) makes the initial command even more passionate, reflecting the speaker's determination that this otherwise ordinary day be a singularly solemn one. Even the funeral music, the "pianos" and "muffled drum" (line 3), are intentionally muted. This is no occasion for joyous or frivolous sound. In the second stanza the speaker bids "aeroplanes" circling overhead to "[Scribble] on the sky the message He is Dead" (line 6). Here the sky becomes a giant billboard or writing pad on which the dolorous pronouncement of his friend's death is made, the upper-case lettering in the message implying the deity-like status of this friend in the speaker's eyes. In what is almost a pathetic fallacy, the planes are heard "moaning" (line 5), keening in the sky above in response to the grim news. The speaker continues the imperatives, insisting that "crepe bows" be placed around the "white necks of the public doves" (line 7) and that traffic policemen "wear black cotton gloves" (line 8). In this way white, the symbolic color of innocence, is either muted or replaced by black, the traditional color of mourning and one that reflects a public acknowledgment of death (much like the black band worn by athletes on their uniforms on similarly mournful occasions).

Stanza three marks a shift in the poem as the speaker switches to a more personal, first-person perspective, acknowledging in lines 9-12 that the deceased was

> ....my North, my South, my East, my West,
> My working week and my Sunday rest,
> My noon, my midnight, my talk, my song;
> I thought that love would last for ever: I was wrong.

The stanza is replete with metaphor, the speaker comparing his beloved friend to a compass, a calendar week, times of day, conversation and song, showing how all-encompassing was his affection for and involvement with his friend. The two declarative sentences that close the stanza state a romantic belief, then cruelly and bluntly dispel it with a grim reality. People die. Love dies. That is life.

The concluding stanza of Auden's poem offers the most interesting language. So complete is the speaker's despair that no celestial body—not stars, not moon, not sun—can offer any hopeful light. Rather, the speaker dismisses the stars, saying they are "not wanted now" (line 13) and, returning to the imperative, demands of God or the universe to "put out every one" (line 13) like so many celestial candles, another metaphor. The language that follows is incongruous, linking large natural bodies such as the sun, moon, ocean and forest, with small ordinary actions such as packing a box, taking something apart, pouring something out, or sweeping something up. The verbs here, again all imperatives, suggest discarding, disposal, as if nothing beautiful in nature can ever make him happy again.

Auden's poem simply and eloquently captures the pain of loss that all humans experience—and the disconsolation and disillusionment that such loss can bring about. Written in primarily masculine rhyme in lines that vary from tetrameter to hexameter, it is a perfect example of how a gifted poet can effect complex things within a simple poetic structure.

1. "Funeral Blues" is BEST classified as a(n) **(C) elegy**.

   An elegy is a poem of lamentation, of mourning. The title, "Funeral Blues," is actually sufficient to determine this as one, but the content of the poem—the speaker's request that all things be muted or silenced in honor of the passing of his friend—fully confirms it as such.

2. Which of the following is a plausible interpretation of the poem's title?

     I. A reference to the depression that the speaker feels over his friend's untimely death.
     II. A reference to mournful music that typically characterizes a funeral service.
   III. A reference to the poem itself.

   (E) I, II and III.

   As was suggested in the overall explication of the poem, the "blues" in the title, a slang term for moroseness or depression, implies an association with the sadness the speaker feels over his friend's decease (I). In addition, the title perhaps alludes to the traditional New Orleans "jazz funeral," the march through the streets to the cemetery with the mourners accompanied by a jazz combo. While this allusion is not specifically defensible from the poem's content, the more general idea of a requiem or even any type of music played at a funeral is certainly a reasonable connection to draw from the title (II). Finally, the title references the poem itself, both in the instruments mentioned in line 3 which seem to be accompanying the funeral procession in line 4, and the overall "music" created by the words, rhythm and rhyme of the poem (III); thus, the selection of E as the best answer.

3. To augment the dramatic imperative that opens the first stanza, the poet employs which of the following? **(E) a spondee**.

   A spondee is a metrical foot consisting of two stressed syllables (/ /). The order to stop everything that opens the poem is aurally reinforced by the meter.

4. The death of his friend prompts the speaker to demand all of the following EXCEPT **(B) an opportunity for solitary mourning**.

   The silencing of the clocks, phone and dog confirm A while the aeroplane writing "He is dead" in the sky and the white gloves of the policemen support C. The instruction in stanza four to extinguish the stars and put away the moon and sun defends D while the pouring out of the ocean and sweeping up of the forest confirm E. Choice B receives no support from the poem.

5. The mournful nature of the occasion is aurally reinforced by the **(E) droning of the aeroplanes**.

   The planes are said to be "moaning" (line 5) in a circle overhead. This gives them a pathetic fallacy-like quality in that their engines are responding to the human death below in an expression of sorrow or pain.

6. The third stanza differs MOST from the other three stanzas in its **(C) perspective**.

The imperatives of the first two stanzas, while giving orders, do not readily identify the relation of the speaker to the deceased. In the third stanza, however, the speaker comes out from a shield of anonymity to reveal that the deceased was his love (perhaps lov-er). In a series of metaphors he compares him to everything from a compass (figuratively showing the totality of his devotion by citing all four directions on it), to a song (suggesting something uplifting and inspirational). His extensive use of the possessive pronoun "my" conveys that he has lost a truly "personal" possession. He then switches fully to the first-person "I," declaring romantically "I thought that love would last for ever" and then dispelling that fantasy with the brutally laconic "I was wrong" (line 12). Choice C captures this best.

7. Of the following, which BEST describes the nature of the contrast between the first and fourth stanzas? **(C) temporal to cosmic**.

The things the speaker mentions in the first stanza—clocks, a telephone, the dog—are all worldly possessions. The fourth stanza, however, focuses more on celestial objects: the stars, the moon and the sun. This perhaps reflects the change of status of the deceased from a temporal existence to some other consciousness. This is the logic behind the selection of C.

8. The word which BEST describes the speaker's feelings for his now-dead friend would be **(E) reverential**.

Lines 9-11, "He was my North, my South, my East, my West, / My working week and my Sunday rest, / My noon, my midnight, my talk, my song…", capture the totality of the impact of the speaker's friend upon his existence. So important is he that he is all four points of the compass, both work and rest, both the height of day and the depth of night. Choice E offers the best expression of this sentiment.

9. All of the following are used as metaphors in the poem EXCEPT **(A) a musical instrument**.

The celestial surface on which the aeroplanes scribble confirms B, the points of the compass in line 9 defend C. The words "noon" and "midnight" in line 11 attest to D, the "putting out" of the stars in line 13 supports E. Neither the "pianos" nor "muffled drum" in stanza one are intended as metaphors.

10. The MOST unique aspect of Auden's poem is its **(C) distortion of nature**.

Certainly other poems have featured imperatives (A), a free-verse metrical structure (B), black gloves and symbols of mourning (D) and antitheses such as midnight-noon, North-South, and talk-song (E). What is most singular in this poem is the distortion of nature that occurs in stanza four. Here the moon and sun, massive celestial objects, are "pack[ed] up" and "dismantle[d]" like a stage set; the distant stars are "put out" like so many bedside candles. A similar distortion is found in the Book of Revelation, in the account of the Apocalypse or end of days: things such as the sun going out, the sea turning to blood. Here the speaker may be suggesting that the death of his beloved friend is of apocalyptic proportion; that it has essentially shattered his world. This is the reasoning behind the selection of answer choice C.

Questions 11–19. Refer to the following poem.

Sparkles from the Wheel

Where the city's ceaseless crowd moves on the livelong day,
Withdrawn I join a group of children watching, I pause aside with them.

By the curb toward the edge of the flagging[1]
A knife-grinder[2] works at his wheel sharpening a great knife,
(5)   Bending over he carefully holds it to the stone, by foot and knee,
With measured tread he turns rapidly, as he presses with light but firm hand,
Forth issue then in copious golden jets,
Sparkles from the wheel.

The scene and all its belongings, how they seize and affect me,
(10) The sad sharp-chinn'd old man with worn clothes and broad shoulder-band of leather,
Myself effusing and fluid, a phantom curiously floating, now here absorbed and arrested,
The group, (an unminded point set in a vast surrounding),
The attentive, quiet children, the loud, proud, restive[3] base of the streets,
The low hoarse purr of the whirling stone, the light-press'd blade,
(15) Sparkles from the wheel.

—Walt Whitman

---

[1] flagstones—flat stones used for paving

[2] knife-grinding was a trade brought to America by Italian immigrants; it involved sharpening a knife against a

"grindstone" usually by employing a system of pedals and wheels

[3] restless

11. The overall purpose of the poem is to

(A) deride the materialistic rat-race of urban living
(B) bemoan the desperation of the aged poor
(C) explore the cosmic purpose behind a quaint instance of local color
(D) decry the social conditions that compel the knife-grinder to such harsh labor
(E) acknowledge the importance of Old World craftsmanship in America

12. The syntax of the opening stanza emphasizes which of the following?

(A) the haste and bustle of urban life
(B) the duration of the day
(C) the populous nature of the city
(D) the attentiveness of the children
(E) the autonomy of the speaker

13. The speaker's description of the knife-grinder seems MOST intent on establishing which of the following?

(A) his impoverished attire
(B) his indefatigable nature
(C) his expert craftsmanship
(D) his lapsing concentration
(E) his dolorous mien

14. The phrase "measured tread" (line 6) refers to the

(A) intent focus with which the knife-grinder labors
(B) precise force with which the knife-grinder depresses the pedal
(C) detached manner in which the knife-grinder observes the crowd
(D) continuous passings of the blade over the grindstone
(E) constant pressure the knife-grinder applies to the great knife

15. The phrase "copious golden jets" (line 7) suggests all of the following EXCEPT

    (A) the hazardous nature of the flying sparks
    (B) the font-like outpouring of sparks
    (C) the colorful stream of the glowing sparks
    (D) the speed with which the sparks emanate from the grinding wheel
    (E) the volume of the sparks

16. One reason that the speaker repeats the phrase "Sparkles from the wheel" (line 8) again in line 15 is to

    (A) identify the source of the "copious golden jets" (line 7)
    (B) mark the continuous friction caused by the metal striking the stone
    (C) reinforce the arresting impact of the knife-grinder's activity
    (D) warn of the potential danger inherent in sharpening knives
    (E) show how easily young children can be distracted

17. Which of the following capture(s) the intent of the parenthetical phrase in line 12, "(an unminded point set in a vast surrounding)?"

    I. It deplores the lack of supervision of the neighborhood children.
    II. It connects the knife-grinder and the bystanders with the larger cosmos.
    III. It points out the otherwise unheeded nature of the street scene.

    (A) II only
    (B) III only
    (C) I and II
    (D) II and III
    (E) I, II and III

18. Which of the following contributes LEAST to the climactic image of the knife-grinder in lines 14-15?

    (A) fireworks-like images
    (B) the trio of participles
    (C) the use of trochees
    (D) onomatopoeic diction
    (E) enjambment

19. Of the following words, which BEST captures the effect of the street scene upon the speaker?

    (A) interesting
    (B) distracting
    (C) boring
    (D) mesmerizing
    (E) touching

Précis and Explication of Walt Whitman's "Sparkles from the Wheel"

Anyone familiar with *Leaves of Grass* knows of Whitman's predilection for studying scenes of Americana in intimate detail, and his short poem, "Sparkles from the Wheel," contains a similarly intense focus. In the poem a somewhat anonymous speaker—all we know of him is that he is a more reflective member of "the city's ceaseless crowd" (line 1)—stops to watch a knife-grinder plying his trade in front of a group of mesmerized children. The knife-grinder, likely an immigrant who is supporting his New World existence with an Old World skill, offers a snapshot of urban local color, an image of concentrated industry reminiscent of some scene from a Norman Rockwell painting. Thematically, the poem offers little beyond the fact that much of the world seems too preoccupied with where it has go or what it has to do to notice this simple but fascinating scene, and Whitman seems more intent in creating a tableau or a visual image similar to, but more expansive than, those provided by imagistic poets such as Ezra Pound or William Carlos Williams.

The street scene in the poem has four distinct elements: the knife-grinder at his wheel, the fascinated group of street urchins, the sea of faces that pass without pause, and the speaker who sets himself apart from the "ceaseless crowd" (line 1) by saying that he has "Withdrawn" from the mob and "pause[d]" alongside the children (line 2). The second stanza is devoted solely to the spectacle of the knife-grinder who near the edge of the flagstone curb meticulously works at "sharpening a great knife" (line 4). The speaker describes the attention and the precision he devotes to his task, noting how he bends over the grinding wheel, "carefully hold[ing] [the knife] to the stone" (line 5) with his foot and knee. His "measured tread" (line 6) turns the wheel at the proper speed, and his equally measured touch "presses with light but firm hand" (line 6) as "copious golden jets" (line 7), the "Sparkles from the wheel" (line 8), pour forth like Fourth of July fireworks. The description is at once a paean to Old World craftsmanship and a strikingly beautiful visual image that arrests the reader as much as it does the children that are watching it.

The third and concluding stanza offers little that is new other than the speaker's admission of how the "scene and all its belongings…seize and affect [him]" (line 9). His focus becomes tighter, and the reader becomes aware of the knife-grinder's sadness, his angular features, his worn clothes and "broad shoulder-band of leather" (line 10); of the "attentive, quiet children" (line 13) and the "low hoarse purr of the whirling stone" (line 14); and, again, of the scintillating "Sparkles from the wheel" (line 15). Calling himself "a phantom curiously floating" (line 11), the speaker almost appears to have an 'out-of-body' experience, some sort of quasi-spiritual reaction to this "unminded point set in a vast surrounding" (line 12). The human equivalent of Williams' red wheelbarrow, the knife-grinder says nothing but nevertheless speaks volumes about immigrant work ethic, craftsmanship, focus and perseverance. Frozen in activity 'midst a crowd of captivated youths, he becomes an enduring and iconic symbol of Americana. Whitman also uses the circular motion of the wheel as a symbol which connects past to present, human to human, human to nature, and earth to cosmos. The microcosm of the street scene thus becomes a mirror of the macrocosm of the universe.

11. The overall purpose of the poem is to **(C) explore the cosmic purpose behind a quaint instance of local color**.

    Though on the simplest level the poem depicts a late 19th century immigrant street scene, there are hints of the author's greater purpose. One, the knife-grinder is a somewhat singular attraction, enough to make the speaker separate himself from the "ceaseless crowd" (line 1) and pause enraptured. The fantail of sparks generated by the pressing of blade to grinding wheel is almost like mini-fireworks, and both the speaker and the crowd of children he joins stand mesmerized by the light show. So riveting is the scene that the speaker almost seems to have an out-of-body experience, describing himself as "effusing and fluid, a phantom curiously floating" (line 11). This "ironic point of light," as Auden might call it, is but one speck in the great dark cosmos, but like the world of which it is a part, it is a scintillating one. This is the rationale behind the selection of C as the correct answer.

12. The syntax of the opening stanza emphasizes which of the following? **(E) the autonomy of the speaker**.

    The placement of the participle "Withdrawn" (line 2) at the beginning of the main clause establishes a key disparity between the speaker and the "ceaseless crowd" (line 1). Moreover, its inherent sense of movement, as a verbal, suggests agency, a deliberate choice by the speaker to be apart and to "pause aside with [the children]" (line 2). Though A and C deserve some consideration because of the phrase "ceaseless crowd" (line 1), this is less a function of syntax than it is a function of diction. The same may be said of D which is predicated upon the participle "watching" in line 2. This is the rationale behind the choice of E as the answer.

13. The speaker's description of the knife-grinder seems MOST intent on establishing which of the following? **(C) his expert craftsmanship**.

    The knife-grinder is depicted bending over the grinding wheel and holding the great knife to the stone "carefully" (line 5) with his foot and knee, in itself an act of dexterity. He is said to turn the grinding wheel rapidly with "measured tread" (line 6) and to press the knife to the stone "with light but firm hand" (line 6). This suggests both a deftness of touch and control. Choice C is the choice that captures this.

14. The phrase "measured tread" (line 6) refers to the **(B) precise force with which the knife-grinder depresses the pedal**.

    Since the word "measured" suggests a control of force and "tread" is a word associated with the feet, choice B seems most logical here. The craft of sharpening a blade is dependent upon the grinder's exerting just the right amount of pressure, much as shaving with a razor requires a certain measure of delicacy.

15. The phrase "copious golden jets" (line 7) suggests all of the following EXCEPT **(A) the hazardous nature of the flying sparks**.

Since one of the meanings of the noun "jets" is "spouts" (such as you might find in a jacuzzi), choice B has validity. The word may also mean a "stream," and this, along with the adjective "golden," gives C credibility. Since the word "jets" also connotes speed, choice D is confirmed while choice E is supported by the adjective "copious." Nothing, however, points to the sparks posing a danger, making A the exception.

16. One reason that the speaker repeats the phrase "Sparkles from the wheel" (line 8) again in line 15 is to **(C) reinforce the arresting impact of the knife-grinder's activity**.

The "Sparkles from the wheel" are clearly the sparks caused by the friction of the metal knife on the rotating stone. The repetition of and isolated placement of this phrase seem intended to reinforce the mesmerizing impact of the knife-grinding upon both children and speaker, a captivation reinforced by the attentiveness and silence of the children. The phrase itself connotes a mini-display of fireworks, a sort of street-side 'light show.' The diction—words such as "watching" (line 2), "seize" (line 9), "absorbed and arrested" (line 11), and "attentive" (line 13)—confirms that C is indeed the best choice.

17. Which of the following capture(s) the intent of the parenthetical phrase in line 12, "(an unminded point set in a vast surrounding)?"

    I. It deplores the lack of supervision of the neighborhood children.
    II. It connects the knife-grinder and the bystanders with the larger cosmos.
    III. It points out the otherwise unheeded nature of the street scene.

(D) II and III.

The selection of D is based upon diction. The word "unminded," in this context, is best defined as "unwatched" or "unheeded." In short, the knife-grinder carries out his trade in relative anonymity, ignored by the "ceaseless crowd" which all day moves to other destinations in the "vast surrounding" of the city. This confirms the validity of III. As was suggested in the overall explication and in the explanation of question #11, the singular "point" is set against a "vast surrounding." This suggests that the microcosm of the street scene has significance in the macrocosm of the cosmos (II).

18. Which of the following contributes LEAST to the climactic image of the knife-grinder in lines 14-15? **(D) onomatopoeic diction**.

Not only is the phrase "Sparkles from the wheel" reiterated in the poem, but it is also designated as the title. This and the colorfully arresting nature of the image give credence to A. The trio of appositives—"The low hoarse purr of the whirling stone, the light press'd blade, / Sparkles from the wheel"—all ostensibly clarify the "scene and all its belongings" (line 9), giving B plausibility. The trochees "whirl-ing," and "light-press'd" create an interesting, upbeat aural effect that emphasizes sound and movement while the enjambment of lines 14-15, like that of the entire final stanza, creates a fluid blend of all the disparate elements of the scene. While the grinding stone does "purr" under the knife-grinder's pressure, this has the least impact upon the poem's climax.

19. Of the following words, which BEST captures the effect of the street scene upon the speaker? **(D) mesmerizing**.

As has been suggested in the explanation of question #15, this is determined by the diction. Words such as "watching" (line 2), "seize" (line 9), "absorbed and arrested" (line 11), and "attentive" (line 13) make D the best choice here.

Questions 20–33. Refer to the following poem.

Vanitie

The fleet Astronomer can bore,
And thred the spheres[1] with his quick-piercing minde:
He views the stations, walks from doore to doore,
    Surveys, as if he had design'd
(5) To make a purchase there: he sees their dances,
      And knoweth long before
Both their full-eyed aspects,[2] and secret glances.

    The nimble Diver with his side
Cuts through the working waves, that he may fetch
(10) His dearly-earned pearl, which God did hide
    On purpose from the ventrous[3] wretch;
That he might save his life, and also hers,
      Who with excessive pride
Her own destruction and his danger wears.

(15)   The subtil Chymick[4] can devest
And strip the creature naked, till he finde
The callow[5] principles within their nest;
    There he imparts them to his minde,
Admitted to their bed-chamber, before
(20)   They appeare trim and drest
To ordinarie suitors at the doore.

    What hath not man sought out and found,
But his deare God? Who yet his glorious law
Embosomes in us, mellowing the ground
(25)   With showres and frosts, with love and aw,
So that we need not say, Where's his command?
      Poore man, thou searchest round
To finde out death, but missest life at hand.

— George Herbert

---

[1] the ancients believed each planet revolved around a sphere

[2] faces, looks

[3] hazardous; audacious; adventurous

[4] chemist or alchemist, though here most likely a physician

[5] not yet developed; hidden away

20. The title of the poem, "Vanitie," abets its central theme in which of the following ways?

   I. It reveals man's secular focus and his pride both in himself and in his capabilities.
   II. It suggests, via pun, the ultimate futility of man's quest for total knowledge.
   III. It bemoans man's mortality and the ephemeral nature of human existence.

(A) I only
(B) III only
(C) I and II
(D) II and II
(E) I, II and III

21. The word "fleet" (line 1) is BEST interpreted as

(A) nimble
(B) perceptive
(C) assiduous
(D) transient
(E) visionary

22. The professions represented in the first three stanzas are linked by the

(A) education required to attain them
(B) lucrative compensation they command
(C) search and exploration that preface significant discovery
(D) measure of celebrity that accompanies each occupation
(E) potential each has for enhancing the public good

23. In depicting the astronomer and the celestial object of his study—the stars, planets, et al.—the speaker makes use of all of the following EXCEPT

(A) verbs that emphasize the astronomer's intellect and reflection
(B) a simile that compares the astronomer to a prospective buyer
(C) diction that personifies the stars as awestruck and coy
(D) an allusion to a literary soothsayer
(E) a metaphor that compares the movements of heavenly bodies to dance

24. The Diver's effort to recover a valuable underwater pearl differs MOST significantly from the Astronomer's survey of the heavens in that it

(A) demands laborious effort
(B) takes more time
(C) has more tangible worth
(D) requires assistance from others
(E) involves moral consequence

25. The actions of the Astronomer, Diver and Chymick seem progressively more

(A) reticent
(B) degrading
(C) exciting
(D) elaborate
(E) invasive

26. The extended metaphor in the third stanza implies that the chemist's exploration of the human body is which of the following?

   I. An incursion essential to the development of medical knowledge.
   II. A violation of intimacy and privacy afforded him by his skill and position.
   III. A cruel exploitation without true scientific merit.

(A) I only
(B) III only
(C) I and II
(D) II and III
(E) I, II and III

27. In lines 15-17, "The subtil Chymick . . . within their nest," the poet might be accused of which of the following writing flaws?

(A) excessive elaboration
(B) faulty parallelism
(C) mixed metaphor
(D) malapropism
(E) misplaced modifier

28. In practical terms the "ordinarie suitors at the doore" (line 21) are most likely

    (A) visitors or relatives of the deceased
    (B) medical colleagues
    (C) additional cadavers
    (D) student interns
    (E) members of the media

29. All of the following represent important stylistic changes in the concluding stanza of the poem EXCEPT

    (A) a shift in focus from the human to the divine
    (B) a movement from declarative to interrogative sentence structure
    (C) alterations in versification and meter
    (D) a change in tone from the laudatory to the sympathetic
    (E) a concluding poignant irony

30. In light of the overall schema of the poem, lines 23-26 –"Who yet his glorious law . . . . Where's his command?"– are primarily intended to

    (A) celebrate the bountiful benevolence of the Creator
    (B) imply than man is inherently moral, good and altruistic
    (C) suggest that the omnipresence of divinity makes it easily overlooked
    (D) allude to the Ten Commandments
    (E) debunk the earlier accomplishments of the Astronomer, Diver and Chymick

31. The title and content of the poem suggest that its overall tone is

    (A) ironic
    (B) elegiac
    (C) nostalgic
    (D) condescending
    (E) reverential

32. Which of the following does NOT contribute to the structural unity of the poem?

    (A) an interlocking pattern of rhyme
    (B) a juxtaposition of persons who seek things hidden by nature
    (C) an unusual blend of trimeter, tetrameter and pentameter
    (D) imperatives that imply these invasive investigations are wrong-headed and self-destructive
    (E) verbs that emphasize examination and discovery

33. In light of its content and structure, this poem is BEST classified as

    (A) Metaphysical
    (B) Elizabethan
    (C) Romantic
    (D) Neoclassical
    (E) Modern

Précis and Explication of George Herbert's "Vanitie"

Those familiar with George Herbert's poetry who expect in "Vanitie" a metaphysical and spiritual bent will not be disappointed since the first three stanzas of Herbert's poem present a series of men whose professions focus on discovery or inquiry—an Astronomer, Diver and Chymick—and a culminating fourth stanza that contrasts the productive pursuits of these individuals with man's frustrated search for the divine. The title, "Vanitie," both suggests man's hubris in thinking that he can actually accomplish this as well as the fruitlessness of such a 'vain' endeavor. As the speaker in Herbert's poem ultimately (and ironically) concludes, the presence of the divine is so immanent both in humanity and in the natural world that man's quest is a needless one, a search for something that is ubiquitous and evident: "Poore man, thou searchest round / To finde out death, but missest life at hand" (lines 27-28).

In the first three stanzas of the poem Herbert presents the reader with three different individuals whose professions involve probing the sky, sea and human body respectively in search of greater knowledge. The Astronomer in stanza one "can bore, / And thred the spheres with his quick-piercing minde" (lines 1-2) and, through this meticulous scrutiny, "knoweth long before / Both their full-eyed aspects, and secret glances" (lines 6-7). The diction in the first two lines—"bore," "thred," "quick-piercing"—emphasizes the probing depth of the sky-watcher's perception as he "views the stations" (constellations) in line 3 from horizon to horizon like a man gauging the merits of a piece of property.

The second stanza moves from the heavens to the depths of the ocean, where a Diver "Cuts through the working waves, that he may fetch / His dearly-earned pearl" (lines 9-10). However, while the Astronomer's pursuit seems justified by the subject of his scrutiny, the Diver's quest seems materialistic and the object of it, a valuable pearl, a treasure "which God did hide / On purpose from the ventrous wretch" (lines 10-11). Moreover, not only is the Diver seen as the instrument of his own moral destruction but also as the corruptive agent of the female beneficiary of the lovely pearl who, because she wears it with "excessive pride," is herself put in moral danger (lines 13-14).

Stanza three presents a "Chymick," a scientist or physician, who, similar to someone conducting an autopsy, "can devest / And strip the creature naked, till he finde / The callow principles within their nest" (lines 15-17). Though the lack of agreement in number ("Creature"/"their") and the complex conceit ("Creature"/"nest") that uses the physical to suggest the temporal make comprehension more difficult, the depiction of the "Chymick" reinforces the theme of inquiry established in the previous stanzas of the poem. Here, however, the investigations seem even more intrusive since the Chymick is "Admitted to their bed-chamber, before / They appear trim and drest / To ordinarie suitors at the doore" (lines 19-21), permitting him to see them in a state of exposure, even nakedness, that the public does not.

Stanza four, however, functions in much the same summative manner as a Shakespearean couplet, first asking in rhetorical wonder "What hath not man sought out and found" (line 22), then answering in the concluding part of the question "But his deare God?" (line 23). According to the speaker, man has discovered both celestial secrets and underwater treasures, and even explored the inner workings of the human and animal body, but he has failed to recognize the immanence of the deity in the world around him, the God whose "glorious law / Embosomes in us, mellowing the ground / With shoures and frosts, with love and aw, / So that we need not say, Where's his command?" (lines 23-26). The concluding lines present an irony, lamenting "Poore man, [who] searchest round / To finde out death, but missest life at hand." In some ways the situation depicted in Herbert's poem is reminiscent of that described in Henry Vaughn's "Man:"

Man hath still either toys, or care;
He hath no root, nor to one place is tied,
But ever restless and irregular
　　　About this Earth doth run and ride.
He knows he hath a home, but scarce knows where;
　　　He says it is so far,
That he hath quite forgot how to go there.

Ultimately, Herbert's poem implies that mankind's Faustian pursuit of secret knowledge and riches—and perhaps the fame that such discoveries often bring—is a road that leads to spiritual death; that true knowledge comes from recognizing and acknowledging the powerful presence of the divine in ourselves and in the world around us. Thus such pursuits as are displayed in the poem are 'vain' in both senses of the word.

20. The title of the poem, "Vanitie," abets its central theme in which of the following ways?

    I. It reveals man's secular focus and his pride both in himself and in his capabilities.
   II. It suggests, via pun, the ultimate futility of man's quest for total knowledge.
  III. It bemoans man's mortality and the ephemeral nature of human existence.

(C) I and II.

The first three stanzas of the poem mirror each other in that they depict individuals who probe nature, be it sky, sea, or the human body, in search of its hidden wealth or secrets. In each case, the Astronomer, Diver or Chymick invasively probes into the heart of things, laying its secrets bare. This seeming paean to man's capacity for divining knowledge in Mother Nature, however, is contrasted in the fourth stanza by his inability to find God: "What hath not man sought out and found / But his deare God?" (lines 22-23). Man is so engrossed by his scientific or materialistic pursuits that he fails to perceive the immanence of the deity in the world around him, how "his glorious law / Embosomes in us, mellowing the ground / With shoures and frosts, with love and aw" (lines 23-25). The speaker reveals this futility in the concluding, ironic observation, "Poore man, thou searchest round / To finde out death, but missest life at hand" (lines 27-28).

Choice C is the selection here because I draws support from the extremely secular focus of the three professionals and the vanity they display in carrying out their explorations while II is defended by the dual meaning of the title: "vain" as in "conceited" and "vain" as in "futile." Though the poem suggests in its closing lines that all men die, there is no excessive dwelling upon either mortality or the brevity of existence.

21. The word "fleet" (line 1) is BEST interpreted as **(B) perceptive**.

Since the adjective "fleet" refers to the Astronomer's ability to "bore, / And thred the spheres with his quick-piercing minde" (lines 1-2), his ability to survey the constellations "And knoweth long before / Both their full-eyed aspects, and secret glances" (lines 6-7), B seems the best choice. Though the usual meaning of the word is "quick" (as in "fleet of foot"), the context in which it is used is a mental one, not a physical one, eliminating A. Choice E has a greater sense of this, but suggests a longer, future view that the context will not allow. And while choice D, "transient," means "brief" or "impermanent," it also lacks the intellectual sense that this usage demands. Choice C, meaning "hard-working," is simply inappropriate.

22. The professions represented in the first three stanzas are linked by the **(C) search and exploration that preface significant discovery**.

The "fleet Astronomer. . . . bore[s] / And thred[s] the spheres" (lines 1-2), surveys the constellations from "doore to doore" (line 3), or horizon to horizon, witnesses their "dances" (line 5) or movements in the night sky and comes in time to know "Both their full-eyed aspects, and secret glances" (line 7). The phrase "full-eyed" perhaps refers to the moon when it is at its fullest, the "secret glances" to objects that are obscured or hidden by clouds or perhaps by an eclipse. In either case, the words suggest that the Astronomer has derived a complete knowledge of the heavens.

Similarly, the Diver and Chymick both probe hidden realms which yield singularly appropriate treasures: the ocean, with its "dearly-earned pearl" (line 10), and the human or animal body, with its "callow principles within their nest" (line 17). Both treasures appear to be somewhat taboo, stanza two suggesting that the pearl "God did hide / On purpose from the ventrous wretch" (lines 10-11), stanza three that in exploring the innermost recesses of the body the Chymick has been "admitted to their bed-chamber, before / They appear trim and drest / To ordinarie suitors at the doore" (lines 19-21).

23. In depicting the astronomer and the celestial object of his study—the stars, planets, et al.—the speaker makes use of all of the following EXCEPT **(D) an allusion to a literary soothsayer**.

Choice A is apparent in verbs such as "bore" (line 1), "thred" (line 2), "views" (line 3) and "Surveys" (line 4). Choice B is validated by lines 4-5, "as if he had design'd / To make a purchase there." Choice C is supported by the implied metaphor in line 7, "their full-eyed aspects, and secret glances," choice E by the end of line 5. There is nothing that supports choice D.

24. The Diver's effort to recover a valuable underwater pearl differs MOST significantly from the Astronomer's survey of the heavens in that it **(E) involves moral consequence**.

The speaker first notes that God has hidden the pearl "On purpose from the ventrous wretch" (line 11), suggesting the Diver's pursuit of riches is an immoral one. Later, both the Diver and the woman to whom he presents the pearl are censured, the former for his greed, the latter for her vanity. Lines 12-14 suggest that God had deliberately concealed the pearl underwater "That he might save his life, and also hers, / Who with excessive pride / Her own destruction and his danger wears." Thus, by eschewing riches we "save" ourselves from damnation. One is reminded here of the proverb cited by Chaucer's Pardoner: "*Radix malorum cupiditas est*," or "Avarice is the root of all evil." As a result, choice E seems best.

25. The actions of the Astronomer, Diver and Chymick seem progressively more **(E) invasive**.

As has been suggested by the overall explication of the passage and in the commentary on several earlier questions, the actions of the three individuals seem to become progressively invasive. While the Astronomer's exploration of the heavens seems reasonably benign, the Diver's recovery of the pearl seems taboo in that God has deliberately hidden it from his "ventrous" (line 11) grasp. Moreover, the Chymick seems, in his exploration of the body, to have violated the "bed-chamber" (line 19), the individual's most private and personal space; to have seen them in their nakedness "before / They appear trim and drest / To ordinaire suitors at the doore" (lines 19-21). In the case of doctor, this suggests he has a more intimate access to their bodies. In the case of an autopsist, this suggests the body has been "tidied up" for viewing by members of the immediate family.

26. The extended metaphor in the third stanza implies that the chemist's exploration of the human body is which of the following?

   I. An incursion essential to the development of medical knowledge.
   II. A violation of intimacy and privacy afforded him by his skill and position.
   III. A cruel exploitation without true scientific merit.

   (C) I and II.

   The Chymick is complimented as "subtil" and for his ability to "devest / And strip the creature naked, till he finde / The callow principles within their nest" (lines 15-17). Clearly, his examination of the body yields important medical knowledge (I). At the same time, the metaphor of the bedchamber suggests that his work exposes the most intimate and private secrets of his subjects (II), even if it is carried out in the name of science. Nowhere, however, is there any suggestion of exploitation or a lack of scientific merit (III), making C the best answer.

27. In lines 15-17, "The subtil Chymick . . . within their nest," the poet might be accused of which of the following writing flaws? **(C) mixed metaphor**.

   The Chymick is said to "strip the creature naked" (line 16), words which imply an anatomical procedure, perhaps even an autopsy. The use of the word "nest" (line 17), an implied metaphor, connotes birds. Though Herbert is likely developing a complex conceit here, to some this may seem anomalous; thus, the selection of C as the answer.

28. In practical terms the "ordinarie suitors at the doore" (line 21) are most likely **(A) visitors or relatives of the deceased**.

   The word "ordinarie" suggests that these "suitors" lack the authority of the Chymick who gains ready and intimate access to the body before all others. If they are visitors, they cannot be admitted until the residents are dressed. If they are cadavers, they must be "trim and drest" (line 20) before they are presented to the family. In light of this, choice A seems reasonable.

29. All of the following represent important stylistic changes in the concluding stanza of the poem EXCEPT **(C) alterations in versification and meter**.

   The fourth and concluding stanza introduces in its opening question, "What hath not man sought out and found, / But his deare God?" (lines 22-23), both a switch from a secular search to a spiritual one and a movement from the declarative to the interrogative modes (A and B). No longer does the speaker compliment the ingenuity of man in uncovering secrets; rather, he suggests he is "Poore" (line 27) in that he cannot see the presence of the divine right under his nose (D). Furthermore, the concluding lines, "Poore man, thou searchest round / To finde out death, but missest life at hand" (lines 27-28), present an irony that questions the greatness of man's accomplishments (E). The verse form and meter remain consistent throughout the four stanzas, making C the exception.

30. In light of the overall schema of the poem, lines 23-26 —"Who yet his glorious law . . . . Where's his command?"—are primarily intended to **(C) suggest that the omnipresence of divinity makes it easily overlooked**.

   In these lines the speaker suggests that God is present within man ("Embosomes in us") and in the natural world around him ("mellowing the ground / With shoures and frosts, with love and aw"). This immanence of the deity makes man's endless quest for knowledge cruelly ironic in that the greatest knowledge—that of his origin, his Maker, and his salvation—lies right under his nose without his being conscious of it: "Poore man, thou searchest round / To finde out death, but missest life at hand" (lines 27-28).

31. The title and content of the poem suggest that its overall tone is **(A) ironic**.

   The word "Vanitie," here in its 17th century spelling, connotes both conceit and also hopelessness. The accomplishments of man in delving the secular mysteries of the sky, sea and human body are ultimately seen as fruitless, even insignificant. Though they potentially result in fame and fortune, they yield no self-knowledge. Despite these acquisitions man knows no more about who he is, whence he derives, and where he is bound. Ultimately, man is seen as "Poore" (line 27) because he has failed to seek out and find his "deare God" (line 23). He is spiritually bereft, caught up like Chillingworth and other Hawthorne characters in a world of scientific scrutiny that cannot possibly bring him closer to salvation. Such investigations are "vain" in both senses of the word: egocentric and futile. The speaker in Herbert's poem is censuring such wrong-headed pursuits.

32. Which of the following does NOT contribute to the structural unity of the poem? **(D) imperatives that imply these invasive investigations are wrong-headed and self-destructive**.

   Herbert's poem features an intricate, interlocking seven line rhyme scheme: ABABCAC, DEDEFDF, GHGHIGI, JKJKLJL (A). As has been previously suggested, the trio of Astronomer, Diver and Chymick unite the poem by the inquiry that is characteristic of their professions (B). The poem features an interlocking metrical pattern as well, a series of 4-5-5-4-5-3-5 stresses that repeats in each of the four stanzas (C). Similarly, verbs that emphasize examination and discovery—"bore" (line 1), "thred" (line 2), "views" (line 3), "Surveys" (line 4), "Cuts through" (line 9), "devest" (line 15), "strip" (line 16), "finde" (line 16), "sought out" (line 22)—pervade the entire poem (E). There is, however, no justification for the claim made in choice D.

33. In light of its content and structure, this poem is BEST classified as **(A) Metaphysical**.

   The highly intellectual nature of the poem, its elaborate conceit of inquiry from Astronomer to Diver to Chymick, its clearly archaic language, and Herbert's status as one of the premier metaphysical poets make A the logical choice here.

Questions 34–47. Refer to the following poem.

Terminus

It is time to be old,
To take in sail:—
The god of bounds,
Who sets to seas a shore,
(5) Came to me in his fatal rounds,
And said: 'No more!
No farther shoot
Thy broad ambitious branches, and thy root.
Fancy departs: no more invent;
(10) Contract thy firmament
To compass of a tent.
There's not enough for this and that,
Make thy option which of two;
Economize the failing river,
(15) Not the less revere the Giver,
Leave the many and hold the few.
Timely wise accept the terms,
Soften the fall with wary foot;
A little while
(20) Still plan and smile,
And, —fault of novel germs,[1]—
Mature the unfallen fruit.
Curse, if thou wilt, thy sires.
Bad husbands of their fires,
(25) Who, when they gave thee breath,
Failed to bequeath
The needful sinew stark as once,
The Baresark marrow[2] to thy bones,
But left a legacy of ebbing veins,
(30) Inconstant heat and nerveless reins, —
Amid the Muses, left thee deaf and dumb,
Amid the gladiators, halt and numb.'

As the bird trims her to the gale,
I trim myself to the storm of time,
(35) I man the rudder, reef[3] the sail,
Obey the voice at eve obeyed at prime:
'Lowly faithful, banish fear,
Right onward drive unharmed;
The port, well worth the cruise, is near,
(40) And every wave is charmed.'

—Ralph Waldo Emerson

---

[1] Perhaps suggestive that the speaker's decline is mysterious and without cure

[2] Anglo-Saxon variation of "berserk;" in this instance, doughty; hardy

[3] To reduce the size of a sail by tucking it in

34. In light of the content of the poem, its title—"Terminus"—may be said to allude to which of the following?

    I. Physical death.
    II. The cessation of creative and procreative endeavors.
    III. The spiritual goal of an afterlife or heaven.

    (A) I only
    (B) II only
    (C) I and II
    (D) I and III
    (E) I, II and III

35. The declarative statement, "It is time to be old, / To take in sail" (lines 1-2), that opens the poem conveys the speaker's

    (A) insufferable hubris
    (B) consciousness of finitude
    (C) *carpe diem* philosophy
    (D) lack of remorse
    (E) sense of injustice

36. The phrase "take in sail" (line 2) is a metaphor for

    (A) taking stock of one's accomplishments
    (B) making amends for one's misdeeds
    (C) slowing down one's pace
    (D) being more frugal with one's money
    (E) attending to one's will

37. The primary rhetorical characteristic of the monologue (lines 6-32, 37-40) delivered by the "god of bounds" is

    (A) a contrast between the speaker's endeavors and his achievements
    (B) an admonitory tone that chastens the speaker for his moral failings
    (C) eschatological imperatives that instruct the speaker how best to ready himself for death
    (D) an extended metaphor that compares the speaker's tenure on earth to a binding contract
    (E) wry understatement that directs the blame at the speaker's parenting

38. The initial words of the "god of bounds" in lines 6-9 are BEST described as

    (A) wistful and nostalgic
    (B) exasperated and irate
    (C) desperate and imploring
    (D) resigned and submissive
    (E) imperious and unequivocal

39. The metaphors contained in lines 6-11 imply that the speaker must

    (A) limit his outdoor activities
    (B) scale down his creative undertakings
    (C) stop traveling and stay in one place
    (D) prepare his last will and testament
    (E) abandon his family

40. The "'terms'" (line 17) may be interpreted as which of the following?

    I. The life-span that the speaker has been given.
    II. The imperatives delivered by the "god of bounds."
    III. The incurable disease from which the speaker suffers.

    (A) I only
    (B) III only
    (C) I and II
    (D) II and III
    (E) I, II and III

41. The "god of bounds" suggests that the speaker's impending demise is a result of a

    (A) profligate lifestyle
    (B) genetic deficiency
    (C) calamitous event
    (D) spiritual bankruptcy
    (E) material obsession

42. The phrase "'unfallen fruit'" (line 22) exemplifies which of the following literary techniques?

    (A) allusion
    (B) metonymy
    (C) paradox
    (D) understatement
    (E) onomatopoeia

43. By suggesting that the parents of the speaker have been "'Bad husbands of their fires'" (line 24), the "god of bounds" accuses them of

    (A) neglecting their parental duties
    (B) displaying weak survival skills
    (C) committing rampant infidelity
    (D) failing to pass on a hardy constitution
    (E) lacking vigilance

44. The references to the Muses and to the gladiators (lines 31-32) are intended as

    (A) ironies that reflect the speaker's flawed condition
    (B) paeans to the speaker's literary and physical accomplishments
    (C) metaphors that clarify the "broad ambitious branches" (line 8) that the speaker has put forth
    (D) allusions to other notables that have peaked and faded
    (E) antitheses that mirror the choice the speaker must make between "'this and that'" (line 12)

45. In the final eight lines of the poem, the speaker

    (A) seeks to avoid his untimely end
    (B) distracts himself with physical labors
    (C) acquiesces to the will of the divine
    (D) questions the unfairness of his lot
    (E) prays for a convalescence

46. Ultimately, the change effected in the speaker from the first to the second stanza is BEST expressed as

    (A) hesitation to determination
    (B) stasis to flight
    (C) rejection to acceptance
    (D) arrogance to humility
    (E) epiphany to action

47. The poem's literary devices include all of the following EXCEPT

    (A) an apostrophe in which he addresses his creator
    (B) a personification of the imagination
    (C) diction that accents his physical weaknesses and shortcomings
    (D) classical allusions
    (E) a conceit drawn from seafaring

Précis and Explication of Ralph Waldo Emerson's "Terminus"

"Terminus," as its title suggests, is about the end of days—at least on a personal level. Written in 1866, just prior to the period in which Emerson began to suffer from aphasia (acute memory loss), the speaker in the poem acknowledges in the opening two lines that "It is time to be old, / To take in sail," figuratively suggesting that he has reached a point in life where he needs to slow down, to take in sail and hence to slacken pace. The speaker depicts an imaginary visit from the "god of bounds, / Who sets to seas a shore" (lines 3-4) who instructs him in a series of a dozen imperatives to cease his creative activity and prepare for his end. With an dramatic "'No more!'" (line 6), this divinity instructs him to "'No farther shoot / Thy broad ambitious branches, and thy root'" (lines 7-8), implying both creative ("'ambitious branches'") and procreative ("'root'") activities. The speaker is told "'no more invent'" (line 9) and, in a striking spatial image, to "'Contract [his] firmament / To compass of a tent'" (lines 10-11). The "'firmament,'" traditionally being the sky, is here a metaphor for the speaker's ambitions on earth, suggesting that his tenure there is limited by death. Time being short, the "'god of bounds'" further instructs the speaker to simplify his life by choosing between two options, whether they be tasks ("'this and that'") or people ("'Leave the many and hold the few'"). The contract of his life being up, the speaker is asked to "'Timely wise accept the terms'" (line 17). And though there is yet "'A little while / Still [to] plan and smile'" (lines 19-20)—some time to "'Mature the unfallen fruit'" (line 22) or bring to fruition the things on which he is working—the end is unequivocally near.

In lines 23-32 the tone of the "god of bounds'" monologue noticeably changes, and the speaker is told he has no one to blame but those who created him, "'Who, when they gave [him] breath / Failed to bequeath / The needful sinew…'" (lines 25-27) but instead "'left a legacy of ebbing veins, / Inconstant heat and nerveless reins…'" (lines 29-30). This indicts his sires for endowing him with whatever genetic deficiencies have led to this premature decline. Calling them "'Bad husbands of their fires'" (line 24), the "god of bounds" figuratively suggests that it was their carelessness that was responsible for the fire of the speaker going out. Lines 31-32, "'Amid the Muses, left thee deaf and dumb, / Amid the gladiators, halt and numb,'" not only convey a sense of abandonment but also a cruel paradox since the speaker lacks the necessary intellectual and physical tools to compete successfully in either arena.

The brief, eight line stanza which concludes the poem returns once more to the title and the poem's opening metaphor in that the speaker compares his life's journey to a sea voyage into the "storm of time" (line 34). Here, however, having resigned himself to approaching death, he acts with agency, manning the rudder and trimming the sail and harking now, in his twilight hour, to the voice obeyed at "prime" (line 36), or at the beginning. Here the "god of bounds" once more reminds the speaker to "'…banish fear / Right onward drive unharmed; / The port, well worth the cruise, is near, / And every wave is charmed'" (lines 37-40). The seafaring conceit that closes the poem—to a degree reminiscent of extended metaphors used by Wyatt and other sonneteers to depict the lover's frustrated pursuit of his beloved—here takes on a more spiritual context, the port being the final solace of death or perhaps the afterlife. Emerson's poem also bears similarity to Milton's "On His Blindness," in which the speaker comes to grips with a loss of vision at the height of his creative powers. Though the speaker in that sonnet ultimately concludes "Those also serve who only stand and wait," the speaker in Emerson's poem takes peremptory action, suggesting perhaps that he wants to insure his salvation, not leave it to divine discretion.

34. In light of the content of the poem, its title—"Terminus"— may be said to allude to which of the following?

    I. Physical death.
    II. The cessation of creative and procreative endeavors.
    III. The spiritual goal of an afterlife or heaven.

(E) I, II and III.

The word "Terminus," derived from Latin, literally means "an end." Since the speaker announces in lines 1-2 that "It is time to be old. / To take in sail:—," choice I is immediately validated. Choice II is supported by lines 6-9—"'No more! / No farther shoot / Thy broad ambitious branches / and thy root. / Fancy departs; no more invent.'"—which suggest that the "god of bounds" has decreed that the speaker may no longer pursue creative ("'ambitious branches'") or procreative ("'thy root'") endeavors. Choice III does not gain credibility until the final four lines in which the "god of bounds" urges the speaker (and all humanity) to "'Right onward drive'" towards the "'port'" that is "'well worth the cruise'" (lines 38-39). This directive, and who delivers it, suggest that the "port," or "terminus," is ultimately a metonymy for heaven or the afterlife; thus, the choice of E as the best answer.

35. The declarative statement, "It is time to be old, / To take in sail" (lines 1-2), that opens the poem conveys the speaker's **(B) consciousness of finitude**.

The speaker's declaration that "It is time to be old" (line 1) immediately admits his awareness of aging, of reaching a definitive milestone, the end of the journey or race. The metaphor "To take in sail," drawn from seafaring, suggests an attempt to slow down, to concede that the end is nigh. Choice B reflects this best.

36. The phrase "take in sail" (line 2) is a metaphor for **(C) slowing down one's pace**.

As was suggested in the explanation of question #35, taking in sail would be to reduce the area of sail that the breeze would affect, thereby slowing the vessel down. This is most accurately captured by choice C.

37. The primary rhetorical characteristic of the monologue (lines 6-32, 37-40) delivered by the "god of bounds" is **(C) eschatological imperatives that instruct the speaker how best to ready himself for death**.

All told, there are a dozen imperatives: "'No farther shoot'" (line 7); "'no more invent'" (line 9); "'Contract thy firmament'" (line 10); "'Make thy option which of two'" (line 13); "'Economize the failing river'" (line 14); "'Not the less revere the Giver'" (line 15); "'Leave the many and hold the few'" (line 16); "'Timely wise accept the terms'" (line 17); "'Soften the fall with wary foot'" (line 18); "'Still plan and smile'" (line 20); and "'Mature the unfallen fruit'" (line 22), in addition to "Obey the voice at eve obeyed at prime" (line 36), "'banish fear'" (line 37) and "'Right onward drive, unharmed'" (line 38). All of these comprise the last instructions given to the speaker by the "god of bounds."

38. The initial words of the "god of bounds" in lines 6-9 are BEST described as **(E) imperious and unequivocal**.

The series of imperatives, cited in the explanation of question #37, conveys clear directives to the speaker as to what he must do in the closing moments of his existence. Choice E reflects this best.

39. The metaphors contained in lines 6-11 imply that the speaker must **(B) scale down his creative undertakings**.

Both metaphors, drawn from nature, suggest constriction, a cutting back. In terms of "'thy broad ambitious branches, and thy root'" (line 8), the "god of bounds" declaims "'No more!'" (line 6), forbidding their expansion. In terms of the directive to "'Contract thy firmament / To compass of a tent'" (lines 10-11), the limitless expanse of the heavens is reduced to the area of a camping tent. In both cases, downsizing is the order of the day; thus, the choice of B.

40. The "terms" (line 17) may be interpreted as which of the following?

   I. The life-span that the speaker has been given.
  II. The imperatives delivered by the "god of bounds."
 III. The incurable disease from which the speaker suffers.

(C) I and II.

The word "'terms,'" in its legal sense, means conditions, and these conditions have been laid out in the series of twelve imperatives delivered by the "god of bounds." This validates II. Since the word "'terms'" bears close similarity to the title, it also suggests the ultimate condition—death—that the speaker has come to realize is proximate. III, however, gains no credibility since there is no evidence in the poem that the speaker has an incurable disease.

41. The "god of bounds" suggests that the speaker's impending demise is a result of a **(B) genetic deficiency**.

This is derived from lines 23-32 which suggest that the "'sires'" of the speaker have left him ill-equipped to survive in a highly competitive world: "'Failed to bequeath / The needful sinew…'" and "'…left a legacy of ebbing veins, / Inconstant heat and nerveless reins'" (lines 26-27, 29-30). This blames his predecessors for his current failings. This is reflected by choice B.

42. The phrase "'unfallen fruit'" (line 22) BEST exemplifies which of the following literary techniques? **(B) metonymy**.

Fruit that is "'unfallen'" is still ripe and on the tree. Since lines 7-9 suggest "'No farther shoot / Thy broad ambitious branches and thy root. / Fancy departs; no more invent,'" the speaker seems to be a writer or similarly creative spirit. Thus, the "'unfallen fruit'" would be works that he has not yet brought to full fruition, making the phrase a metonymy.

43. By suggesting that the parents of the speaker have been "'Bad husbands of their fires'" (line 24), the "god of bounds" accuses them of **(D) failing to pass on a hardy constitution**.

The word "'husbands,'" in this usage, probably derives from the verb "to husband," meaning "to conserve" or "to economize." In terms of a fire, the implication would be that they have not conserved the wood and, as a result, have let the fire burn out. Metaphorically, this means they have used up all of the "'needful sinew'" (line 27) and "'Baresark marrow'" (line 28), leaving the speaker "'a legacy of ebbing veins, / Inconstant heat and nerveless reins…'" (lines 29-30). Choice D reflects this most accurately.

44. The references to the Muses and to the gladiators (lines 31-32) are intended as **(A) ironies that reflect the speaker's flawed condition**.

That he is left deaf and speechless among the classical font of inspiration, the Muses—who were called upon by playwrights, poets and historians for literary inspiration—and that he is left limping and unresponsive amid the barbarous gladiators who fought, most often to the death, for the amusement of the Emperor— implies that he is unfit for either creative or physical accomplishments. Since the diction ("'deaf and dumb,'" "'halt and numb'") is antithetical to the skills most apt for these two professions, this appears ironic, making A the best choice here.

45. In the final eight lines of the poem, the speaker **(C) acquiesces to the will of the divine**.

This is derived directly from lines 36-40, "Obey the voice at eve obeyed at prime: / 'Lowly faithful, banish fear, / Right onward drive unharmed; / The port, well worth the cruise, is near, / And every wave is charmed.'" Whereas "eve" clearly is symbolic of the twilight of the speaker's life and career, "prime" seems perhaps to allude not merely to birth but to Creation and the Garden. Thus, the speaker metaphorically embarks on a spiritual journey toward a distant port, likely the afterlife or heaven.

46. Ultimately, the change effected in the speaker from the first to the second stanza is BEST expressed as **(E) epiphany to action**.

Whereas the opening stanza began with the speaker's experiencing the epiphany that "It is time to be old, / To take in sail" (lines 1-2), the second sees him taking decisive action: "As the bird trims her to the gale, / I trim myself to the storm of time, / I man the rudder, reef the sail, / Obey the voice at eve obeyed at prime" (lines 33-36). The simile which begins these lines shows a bird adapting to the fiercer winds of a gale; so the narrator must adapt himself to the "storm of time."

47. The poem's literary devices include all of the following EXCEPT **(A) an apostrophe in which he addresses his creator**.

In line 9 "'Fancy'" is said to "'depart,'" a human action; the "god of bounds" describes the speaker's constitution with phrases such as "'ebbing veins, / Inconstant heat and nerveless reins'" (lines 29-30) and figuratively depicts him as "'deaf and dumb…halt and numb'" (lines 31-32); allusions are made in lines 31-32 to the Muses and to the gladiators; and lines 1-2 and 34-40 feature an extended metaphor drawn from seafaring. This confirms choices B, C, D and E. There is no apostrophe in the poem; rather, the "god of bounds" addresses the speaker through an interior monologue.

Questions 48-60. Refer to the following poem

An Arundel[1] Tomb

Side by side, their faces blurred,
The earl and countess lie in stone,
Their proper habits vaguely shown,
As jointed armour, stiffened pleat,
(5)   And that faint hint of the absurd—
The little dogs under their feet.

Such plainness of the pre-baroque
Hardly involves the eye, until
It meets his left-hand gauntlet,[2] still
(10)   Clasped empty in the other; and
One sees, with a sharp tender shock,
His hand withdrawn, holding her hand.

They would not think to lie so long.
Such faithfulness in effigy
(15)   Was just a detail friends would see:
A sculptor's sweet commissioned grace
Thrown off in helping to prolong
The Latin names around the base.

They would not guess how early in
(20)   Their supine stationary voyage
The air would change to soundless damage,
Turn the old tenantry away;
How soon succeeding eyes begin
To look, not read. Rigidly they

(25)   Persisted, linked, through lengths and breadths
Of time. Snow fell, undated. Light
Each summer thronged the glass. A bright
Litter of birdcalls strewed the same
Bone-riddled ground. And up the paths
(30)   The endless altered people came

Washing at their identity.
Now, helpless in the hollow of
An unarmorial age, a trough
Of smoke in slow suspended skeins
(35)   Above their scrap of history,
Only an attitude remains:

Time has transfigured them into
Untruth. The stone fidelity
They hardly meant has come to be
(40)   Their final blazon,[3] and to prove
Our almost-instinct almost true:
What will survive of us is love.

—Philip Larkin

[1] A town in Southern England that is the site of a medieval castle

[2] A protective glove

[3] Coat-of-arms; heraldry

48. The opening two lines of the poem establish an important contrast between which of the following?

    (A) tranquility and turmoil
    (B) permanence and impermanence
    (C) clarity and obfuscation
    (D) company and solitude
    (E) proximity and distance

49. All of the following help to establish the physical erosion of the couple's stone effigies EXCEPT

    (A) "blurred" (line 1)
    (B) "vaguely shown" (line 3)
    (C) "empty" (line 10)
    (D) "Washing at their identity" (line 31)
    (E) "Only an attitude remains" (line 36)

50. The phrase "proper habits" (line 3) likely refers to the couple's

    (A) features
    (B) behavior
    (C) titles
    (D) epitaphs
    (E) attire

51. The BEST equivalent for the word "involves" (line 8) would be

    (A) concerns
    (B) attracts
    (C) troubles
    (D) requires
    (E) damages

52. The "sharp tender shock" (line 11) to which the speaker refers is a reaction to which of the following?

    (A) the unadorned nature of the tomb's design
    (B) the eroded condition of the Arundel tomb
    (C) the absence of the earl's sword
    (D) the earl's devoted clasping of his wife's hand
    (E) the inclusion of the little dogs

53. By "faithfulness in effigy" (line 14) the speaker is referring to which of the following?

    I. The accuracy of the couple's countenances.
    II. The incongruous sculpting of the joined hands.
    III. The visits to the tomb by tenants on the couple's estate.

    (A) I only
    (B) II only
    (C) I and II
    (D) I and III
    (E) I, II and III

54. Lines 16-18—"A sculptor's sweet commissioned grace / Thrown off in helping to prolong / The Latin names around the base"—imply that the detail of the clasped hands was included as a(n)

    (A) original part of the couple's design for their tomb
    (B) traditional depiction of husband and wife
    (C) extraneous gratuity to encourage commission for more ornate details
    (D) personal expression of the sculptor's gratitude for the couple's patronage
    (E) saint-like depiction of secular personages

55. In the fourth stanza (lines 19-24), the speaker captures the couple's passage through time by means of a(n)

    (A) oxymoron
    (B) understatement
    (C) allusion
    (D) simile
    (E) personification

56. The speaker implies all of the following about the people who succeed the "old tenantry" (line 22) EXCEPT

    (A) that they belong to later centuries
    (B) that they no longer have a personal connection to the deceased
    (C) that they come to the tomb with a tourist's curiosity, not a serf's devotion
    (D) that they have contributed to the erosion of the couple's monument
    (E) that they continue to work the land for their new owners

57. The speaker likely coins the word "unarmorial" (line 33) in order to

    (A) accent the vulnerability of the monument to weather and time
    (B) commend the peacefulness of contemporary times
    (C) imply how obsolete the couple would feel if alive in this age
    (D) show how death conquers all, even the powerful
    (E) condemn the vandalism of the memorial

58. By "Time has transfigured them into / Untruth…" (lines 37-38), the speaker is implying which of the following about the earl and countess?

    (A) That the sculpted impression of their appearances no longer does them justice.
    (B) That they have been canonized by the church.
    (C) That they have been ironically memorialized as a perpetually devoted couple.
    (D) That their identities have been worn from the monument.
    (E) That they are more celebrated in death than they had been in life.

59. The "almost-instinct" (line 41) to which the speaker alludes is the human desire to

    (A) survive
    (B) be known forever
    (C) retain youth and beauty
    (D) sustain love
    (E) leave a legacy

60. Which of the following phrases exemplifies the literary technique known as synecdoche?

    (A) "stiffened pleat" (line 4)
    (B) "soundless damage" (line 21)
    (C) "succeeding eyes" (line 23)
    (D) "Bone-riddled ground" (line 29)
    (E) "unarmorial age" (line 33)

Précis and Explication of Philip Larkin's "An Arundel Tomb"

Philip Larkin's poem "An Arundel Tomb" responds to the sarcophagus of a medieval earl and countess in Chichester Cathedral, which depicts them in traditional attire, resting side by side as if for perpetuity. The poem focuses on a minor incongruous detail—the fact that the left hand of the earl is depicted clasping the hand of his wife in a display of spousal affection—a detail that the poet sheepishly admitted he got wrong, misremembering the correct hand. The speaker wryly notes that "Time has transfigured them into / Untruth" (lines 37-38) in that this display of fidelity, unlikely in their life together, has been ironically preserved for all time by the sarcophagus. Thus, visitors to their weathered tomb perceive the relationship of the long-dead pair in quite a different manner than their contemporaries would have.

The opening six lines of this seven-stanza poem present the visual image that inspired the poem: "Side by side, their faces blurred, / The earl and countess lie in stone, / Their proper habits vaguely shown…" (lines 1-3). Words such as "blurred" (line 1) and "vaguely shown" (line 3) attest to the weathered nature of the tomb while "proper habits" (line 3) refers to the ceremonial garb in which each has been depicted: he the "jointed armour" (line 4) of a medieval knight, she the "stiffened pleat" (line 4) of a formal dress. The "little dogs under their feet" (line 6) hint at the domestic world of which they were a part in life and add a touch of levity to what is otherwise a somber pairing. The speaker remarks in the second stanza how "Such plainness of the pre-baroque / Hardly involves the eye…" (lines 7-8), meaning the less than ornate depiction (a characteristic of the pre-Baroque period) lacks any arresting quality—that is, until "It meets his left-hand gauntlet, still / Clasped empty in the other; and / One sees, with a sharp tender shock, / His hand withdrawn, holding her hand" (lines 9-12). For the speaker this display of marital fidelity and spousal affection rendered in stone by the sculptor is inconsistent with the nature of the deceased couple whom he says in line 13 "would not think to lie so long." The phrase "lie so" is particularly intriguing in that it simultaneously yields the interpretation "maintain this position" and "maintain this façade," as well as to do both of these for such a long time. This intimate gesture "Was just a detail friends would see" (line 15), not something intended to be memorialized for the ages. Lines 16-18, "A sculptor's sweet commissioned grace / Thrown off in helping to prolong / The Latin names around the base," seem to imply that the sculptor "threw in" the detail in an effort to extend his commission (the word "prolong" means "drag out," and the "Latin names around the base" seem to be something ornamental and extraneous).

Stanza four moves away from description and toward the emergence of the poem's message. The speaker somewhat musingly observes how the couple "would not guess how early in / Their supine stationary voyage / The air would change to soundless damage, / Turn the old tenantry away…" (lines 19-22). Here the oxymoronic "stationary voyage" (line 20) captures the incongruity of their fixed, supine position and the spiritual journey of their souls to the afterlife. That "The air would change to soundless damage" (line 21), when coupled with the phrase "Turn the old tenantry away" (line 22), seems to imply that the people who worked on the estate and who would be most prone to pay their respects stopped coming, and the "soundless damage" (line 21) was the weathering wreaked by the elements. The "succeeding eyes" (line 23), a synecdoche which clearly refers to visitors of later years, now "begin / To look, not read" (lines 23-24) because the inscriptions carved in the stone have faded, or perhaps because, lacking any personal connection to the deceased, the couple's tomb has become less an object of veneration than a tourist spot. Still, "Rigidly they / Persisted" (lines 24-25), this stone couple, through changes in season and year marked by changes in weather, light and fauna while still "up the paths / The endless altered people came / Washing at their identity" (lines 29-31). The participle "Washing" not only metaphorically associates the crowds of people with waves or a tide, but also connotes the gradual erosion of the tomb, perhaps by people touching it. The steps of Canterbury Cathedral, for example, a popular visiting spot for pilgrims since the assassination of Thomas Becket in 1170, have been made perilously navigable by the millions of feet that have passed over them in a millennium.

The most difficult lines to parse are lines 32-36:

> Now, helpless in the hollow of
> An unarmorial age, a trough
> Of smoke in slow suspended skeins
> Above their scrap of history,
> Only an attitude remains.

For one, these lines are syntactically difficult. The words "helpless in the hollow of / An unarmorial age" appear to be a participial phrase modifying an understood "they," while the phrase, "a trough / Of smoke in slow suspended skeins / Above their scrap of history," seems an appositive to "they," followed by four prepositional phrases. In terms of meaning, the "unarmorial age" clearly refers to the era of the speaker's visit, a relatively contemporary one in light of the date of the poem's composition (1964). This phrase also connotes vulnerability and exposure, consistent with the physical erosion of the tomb. The word "hollow," here a noun meaning a topographical depression like a vale, nevertheless conjures thoughts of T.S. Eliot's "hollow men" and the twentieth century wasteland. However, it is the words "a trough / Of smoke in slow suspended skeins / Above their scrap of history," which create the densest image. The word "trough," often a term for a stone receptacle for water or feed for animals, may be mocking the erosion of the effigies—no Grecian urn here (Keats' romantic *object d'art* which forever preserved youth and passion).

However, this heavy stone object is incongruously matched with "slow suspended skeins [of smoke] / Above their scrap of history." This image—an ephemeral and ethereal one—suggests impermanence, something that might dissipate momentarily. Perhaps they are deliberately meant to be antithetical, a wry reminder of the impermanence of stone, marble and gilded monuments noted earlier by Shakespeare in Sonnet 55: "When wasteful war shall statues overturn / And broils root out the work of masonry...". Or perhaps this "trough / Of smoke" is yet another wasteland symbol, the residue of war and conflagration that drifts ominously above their "scrap of history." The choice of the word "scrap" again connotes insignificance but also disposability. Whatever they were, whatever image they wished to present in perpetuity, "Only an attitude remains" (line 36).

The seventh and concluding stanza of the poem cements the poem's central irony: that the "faithfulness in effigy" preserved is not characteristic of the people who lived; that "The stone fidelity / They hardly meant has come to be / Their final blazon..." (lines 38-40). This irony, however, was apparent as early as stanza three. The more important content here lies in the remaining two-and-one-half lines: "...and to prove / Our almost-instinct almost true: / What will survive of us is love." These lines, reminiscent of Auden's "You will love your crooked neighbor / With your crooked heart," comment on human fallibility and weakness. We would like to believe the best of us survives, and we have filled museums and time-capsules to ensure it. Yet though the earl's gesture of fidelity endures, it represents something ingenuine—and if so, how can it be significant? On the other hand, perhaps the statement being made is that love endures in spite of our foibles and fallibility. And that would be comforting.

48. The opening two lines of the poem establish an important contrast between which of the following? **(B) permanence and impermanence**.

The phrase "Side by side," not only depicts the position of the countess and earl on the monument slab, but it suggests an enduring bond, a love that will last for all time. The "faces blurred," however, suggests just the opposite: features that have been eroded by weather and time. Choice B represents this best.

49. All of the following help to establish the physical erosion of the couple's stone effigies EXCEPT **(C) "empty" (line 10)**.

As was noted in the explanation of the previous question, the word "blurred" (line 1) shows the physical deterioration of the couple's effigies as does "vaguely shown" (line 3), which does the same to the armor and dress in which they are attired. "Washing at their identity" (line 31) is an implied metaphor comparing the crowds which visit the memorial to a tide that gradually erodes the surface on which it washes up. Similarly, line 36, "Only an attitude remains," implies that there is only a vestige of the details of the original effigies. Choice C is the exception because the word "empty" refers specifically to the discarded glove that the other armored hand is holding.

50. The phrase "proper habits" (line 3) likely refers to the couple's **(E) attire**.

The choice of E as the correct answer is determined by the remainder of line 3 "vaguely shown / As jointed armour, stiffened pleat...", which refers to the clothing that the couple is wearing (The word "habit" meant clothes in that time period).

51. The BEST equivalent for the word "involves" (line 8) would be **(B) attracts**.

This is largely determined by context. The speaker says "Such plainness of the pre-baroque / Hardly involves the eye" (lines 7-8), which implies that there is nothing especially appealing about the style of the monument. The word "attracts" fits this interpretation best.

52. The "sharp tender shock" (line 11) to which the speaker refers is a reaction to which of the following? **(D) the earl's devoted clasping of his wife's hand**.

The speaker notes nothing particularly interesting about the effigies until the detail of "His hand withdrawn, holding her hand" (line 12). Here "withdrawn" means "taken out of the glove," and it is this unexpected depiction of the earl's affectionate grasp that sparks the "tender" shock that the speaker experiences; thus, the selection of D as the correct answer.

53. By "faithfulness in effigy" (line 14) the speaker is referring to which of the following?

   I. The accuracy of the couple's countenances.
  II. The incongruous sculpting of the joined hands.
 III. The visits to the tomb by tenants on the couple's estate.

(B) II only.

Though the phrase "faithfulness in effigy" steers one immediately to I, the phrase is really only intended to connote II. The key here is line 15, which reveals that it was "just a detail friends would see," not something intended to proclaim a mutual fidelity for all time. This is further supported by the speaker's affirmation in lines 38-40 that "The stone fidelity / They hardly meant has come to be / Their final blazon…".

54. Lines 16-18—"A sculptor's sweet commissioned grace / Thrown off in helping to prolong / The Latin names around the base"—imply that the detail of the clasped hands was included as a(n) **(C) extraneous gratuity to encourage commission for more ornate details**.

As was explained in detail in the overall explication of the poem, the phrase "thrown off" seems to be an equivalent for "thrown in" or "added," the word "grace" suggests a kindness or favor, and the mention of 'prolonging' the Latin names along the base appears to be a reference to more ornate detailing for which the sculptor was vying. This explains the selection of C as the proper answer.

55. In the fourth stanza (lines 19-24), the speaker captures the couple's passage through time by means of a(n) **(A) oxymoron**.

This is quite straightforward in that the phrase "stationary voyage" (line 20) is self-contradictory, simultaneously suggesting stasis and movement. By definition, an oxymoron (A) combines such opposites.

56. The speaker implies all of the following about the people who succeed the "old tenantry" (line 22) EXCEPT **(E) that they continue to work the land for their new owners.**

Since the word "succeed" means to "follow" or "come after," A is validated. The fact that these successive generations "begin / To look, not read," suggests that they have no personal connection to the individuals memorialized by the monument (B) but have 'washed' up the paths to the tomb with a tourist's curiosity (C). As was noted in both the overall explication and the explanation of question #49, the implied metaphor comparing these people to a tide also connotes erosion, in this case the wearing down of the monument (D). Only choice E does not garner any support from the passage.

57. The speaker likely coins the word "unarmorial" (line 33) in order to **(A) accent the vulnerability of the monument to weather and time**.

Armor by nature shields and protects. The fact that this is an "unarmorial age" suggests that the monument is exposed and vulnerable, one of the reasons its faces have blurred and its "proper habits" (line 3) been dulled to vagueness. Choice A captures this best.

58. By "Time has transfigured them into / Untruth…" (lines 37-38), the speaker is implying which of the following about the earl and countess? **(C) That they have been ironically memorialized as a perpetually devoted couple**.

    As has already been established, the couple's "stone fidelity" (line 38) was "hardly meant" (line 39), but it has nevertheless "come to be / Their final blazon…" (lines 39-40) or heraldric pose. The "endless altered people" (line 30) who come to see their monument thus get an "Untruth" (line 38), a stone memorial to a devotion that did not exist.

59. The "almost-instinct" (line 41) to which the speaker alludes is the human desire to **(D) sustain love**.

    The speaker's repetition of the word "almost" in "to prove / Our almost-instinct almost true" (lines 40-41) hints at the fallibility and frailty of humans. We would like to commit to people forever, but statistics show we fail at doing so more than fifty percent of the time. The monument ironically celebrates a fidelity in stone that our real, flesh and blood lives cannot maintain. Even so, that is the human aspiration, even if the attempt falls short more often than not. This is the logic behind the selection of choice C.

60. Which of the following phrases exemplifies the literary technique known as synecdoche? **(C) "succeeding eyes" (line 23)**.

    This is pretty much a straight definition. Synecdoche, a subset of metonymy, substitutes the part for the whole. In this case, the word "eyes" actually means "people."

Question One

(Suggested time—40 minutes. This question counts as one-third of the total essay section score.)

In the following poem a lover invites his beloved Chlora—and the reader—on a figurative "tour" of a gallery devoted to artistic renderings of her image. Read the following poem carefully. Then, in a well-organized essay, discuss what the sequence of images and the manner in which they are described reveal about the complexity of the speaker's relationship with Chlora. In your essay you may wish to consider such things as imagery, choice of detail and figurative language.

The Gallery

CHLORA, come view my soul, and tell
Whether I have contrived it well:
Now all its several lodgings lie,
Composed into one gallery.
(5) And the great arras-hangings,[1] made
Of various facings, by are laid,
That, for all furniture, you'll find
Only your picture in my mind.

Here art thou painted in the dress
(10) Of an inhuman murderess;
Examining upon our hearts,
(Thy fertile shop of cruel arts,)
Engines more keen than ever yet
Adorned tyrant's cabinet,
(15) Of which the most tormenting are,
Black eyes, red lips, and curled hair.

But, on the other side, thou'rt drawn,
Like to Aurora[2] in the dawn;
When in the east she slumbering lies,
(20) And stretches out her milky thighs,
While all the morning quire does sing,
And manna falls and roses spring,
And, at thy feet, the wooing doves
Sit perfecting their harmless loves.

(25) Like an enchantress here thou show'st,
Vexing thy restless lover's ghost;
And, by a light obscure, dost rave
Over his entrails, in the cave,
Divining thence, with horrid care,
(30) How long thou shalt continue fair;
And (when informed) them throw'st away
To be the greedy vulture's prey.

But against that, thou sitt'st afloat,
Like VENUS[3] in her pearly boat;
(35) The halcyons, calming all that's nigh,
Betwixt the air and water fly;
Or, if some rolling wave appears,
A mass of ambergris[4] it bears,
Nor blows more wind than what may well
(40) Convoy the perfume to the smell.

These pictures, and a thousand more,
Of thee, my gallery doth store,
In all the forms thou canst invent,
Either to please me, or torment;
(45) For thou alone, to people me,
Art grown a numerous colony,
And a collection choicer far
Than or Whitehall's, or Mantua's[5] were.

But of these pictures, and the rest,
(50) That at the entrance likes me best,
Where the same posture and the look
Remains with which I first was took;
A tender shepherdess, whose hair
Hangs loosely playing in the air,
(55) Transplanting flowers from the green hill,
To crown her head and bosom fill.

—Andrew Marvell

---

[1] draperies

[2] Roman goddess of the dawn

[3] Roman goddess traditionally associated with love, beauty and fertility

[4] a waxy substance of pleasant fragrance

[5] highly decorative palatial residences

Précis and Explication of Free-Response Question One: Andrew Marvell's "The Gallery"

The work of the 17th century metaphysical poet Andrew Marvell, "The Gallery" features the use of an elaborate conceit such as characterized the poetry of the time. Though the title calls to mind the traditional gallery of a museum, the gallery in the poem is an internal one, a series of chambers in the speaker's soul that have been devoted to various depictions of his beloved, Chlora, whom he invites to tour the gallery in the poem's opening line. As he proceeds to guide his beloved on this gallery tour, he draws back the "great arras-hangings" (line 5) that hide each masterpiece, pointing out to her that "for all furniture, [she'll] find / Only [her] picture in [his] mind" (lines 7-8). Thus, the gallery becomes a symbol of his perpetual and singular devotion to Chlora and his guided tour an attempt to impress her.

In the second through fifth stanzas the speaker begins to reveal the various portraits in the gallery. In the first his beloved Chlora is adorned in the guise of an "inhuman murderess" (line 10) whose "Engines" (the weapons of physical—and sensual—beauty: eyes, lips, hair) are "more keen than ever" (line 13) and employed in torturing her admirers' hearts. Directly across from this representation, however, she appears as Aurora, goddess of the dawn, sprawling innocently among symbols of love ("wooing doves") and spring ("roses") that are set about her "milky thighs" (line 20) while the "morning quire" (line 21) of songbirds serenades her beauteous presence. The diction in this stanza—"quire" (line 21), "manna" (line 22), and "doves" (line 23)—connotes spirituality, suggesting an Edenic heavenly bliss despite its classical allusion. The emphasis on whiteness, evident in "milky thighs," "manna" and "doves," also connotes virginity. In yet another representation Chlora is depicted as an "enchantress… / Vexing [her] lover's restless ghost" (lines 25-26) through some secret ritual over his entrails in a Sibyl-like cave. Said to be "Divining thence, with horrid care, / How long [she will] continue fair" (lines 29-30), she comes across as a mad prophetess who peers into his entrails like the wicked step-mother in *Snow White* peering into her mirror. This and the fact that she tosses his entrails away to the "greedy vulture" (line 32) depicts her as self-centered and callous, the least appealing image yet. Yet, contrary to this, she is depicted across the gallery as Venus, the goddess of love, afloat in a "pearly boat" (line 34) and bringing a fragrant tranquility to all creatures in the sea or in the air. These portraits number four, yet the speaker claims in lines 41-48 of the sixth stanza that he has

> These pictures, and a thousand more,
> In all the forms thou canst invent,
> Either to please me or torment;
> For thou alone, to people me,
> Art grown a numerous colony,
> And a collection choicer far
> Than or Whitehall's, or Mantua's were.

This seems intended to suggest that he has been smitten so powerfully by Chlora that he has created a "colony" of her impressions whose excellence supersedes the fabled art collections in palaces in London and in Mantua, a city in Northern Italy.

In the seventh and final stanza the speaker reveals that of all the portraits in the gallery, he fancies the one at the entrance best because "…the same posture and the look / Remains with which [he] first was took" (lines 51-52). Seen in this depiction as "A tender shepherdess, whose hair / Hangs loosely playing in the air, / Transplanting flowers from the green hill, / To crown her head and bosom fill" (lines 53-56), Chlora is endowed with the simplicity and innocence of nature. This natural association seems to imply that the Chlora the speaker prefers is "natural," neither adorned by lipstick and other embellishments, nor assuming the role of the harsh or indifferent mistress. This image, naturally adorned with grass and flowers, is the one which captured the speaker's heart and the one which his "soul" treasures the most.

Though the soul can undoubtedly have spiritual connotations (see Marvell's own "A Dialogue between the Soul and Body"), it can have more common meanings as well. For example, in Emily Dickinson's "The Soul Selects Her Own Society," it can mean the individual (pun on "sole") as well as the spiritual essence of a person. In "The Gallery," the soul seems to stand for the speaker's being, the interior self he has so devoted to her worship. His request to Chlora to "come view [his] soul" is, on the metaphorical level, a tour of the gallery, but on a literal one, a request for her to appreciate the extent to which he adores her being. And though she at times seems part-*femme fatale*, part-virgin, part-sorceress and part-unapproachable goddess, the image of her that is most true to his core is the least adorned and most natural one.

Scoring Guide for Free-Response Question One: Andrew Marvell's "The Gallery"

8-9 Well-conceived, well-developed, and well-organized, these papers are marked by frequent and accurate references to the text, by an admirable ability to synthesize thought, and by a mature control over the elements of composition. Though not perfect, they clearly indicate the students' ability to discuss what the sequence of images and the manner in which he describes them reveal about the complexity of the speaker's relationship with Chlora, as well as how such things as imagery, choice of detail and figurative language help convey that complexity.

6-7 These essays exhibit a solid understanding of what the sequence of images and the manner in which they are described reveal about the speaker's relationship with Chlora, but are less adept at articulating the complexity of the relationship. This may be due to inconsistencies in textual understanding, or to a lesser facility with identifying and discussing imagery, choice of detail and figurative language. Though these essays reflect their writers' abilities to convey their points clearly, they feature less fluency, less development and less cogency than 8-9 papers.

5 These papers respond to the question about the complexity of the speaker's relationship with Chlora and how the aforementioned literary elements help convey that complexity in superficial, formulaic, inconsistent, or insufficiently supported ways. They may rely primarily on paraphrase, but may still convey an implicit understanding of the passage and the task. The papers are generally written in a satisfactory manner, with occasional errors in composition or mechanics that do not impede the reader's understanding. Nevertheless, these essays lack the organization, persuasiveness and development of upper-half papers.

3-4 These lower-half essays generally suggest an incomplete or overly simplistic understanding of the passage or of the task, an inability to recognize the complexity of the speaker's relationship to his beloved Chlora, or an inability to recognize or comment upon the literary elements in the passage. Their arguments are often characterized by a misreading of the text, a failure to provide adequate support, or insufficient control over the elements of composition. In some instances they may consist entirely of paraphrase and/or feature acute problems in organization, clarity, fluency or development.

1-2 These essays compound the shortcomings of 3-4 papers. They often contain many serious and distracting errors in grammar or mechanics that preclude any successful response to the prompt. Though these essays may attempt to say something about the speaker's relationship to Chlora, they are severely limited by deficiencies in organization, clarity, fluency or development.

0 Papers scored a zero make no more than a passing reference to the task.

— Papers given this score offer a blank or totally off-topic response.

Sample Student Essay One

Though many men have been tormented by women's seemingly two-faced nature throughout history, very few can stock a whole gallery with their woman's many faces. In his poem, "The Gallery," Marvell relays the complexity of the speaker's relationship with his lover, Chlora. Marvell presents various chiaroscuro renderings of Chlora's character along with contrasting images of purity and corruption in order to illustrate her love/hate relationship with the speaker.

The speaker presents his relationship with Chlora through the ultimate contrast, love versus hate, and uses various other contradictions throughout the poem to complement this prominent theme. He first depicts Chlora as an "inhuman murderess" (10), as he laments on how she broke his heart as one of her "cruel arts" (12). His later association of Chlora with "Aurora in the dawn" (18), however, contradicts this previous association with death, as dawn is viewed as a universal symbol for birth and innocence. The speaker also presents contrasting images through color. The reader first sees a darker Chlora with her "black eyes, red lips, and curled hair" (16); later, however, the speaker highlights her "milky thighs" (20) and "hair [which] hangs loosely playing in the air" (53-54). He also contrasts the natural with the supernatural, following descriptions of "light obscure" and divinity (25-29) with ones of "air and water" and "rolling waves" (36-37). In a sense, the reader is not getting a clear physical description of Chlora, but rather the many facets of her inner personality and actions through the eyes of her bewildered lover.

While the speaker recognizes that his lover is a complex creature, it is evident that he is still mystified by Chlora's behaviors and qualities. He paints her as various goddesses, and even as an enchantress, "vexing [her] restless lover's ghost" (26), and in this he transforms Chlora into a supernatural being. Though, at first glance, the poem seems like an agonized lover's exasperated outburst in trying to understand his multifaceted woman, upon closer look the reader is able to see the speaker's unfaltering wonder at Chlora's intricacy. By presenting the different sides of her personality in the form of an art gallery, he encourages the reader to give his awe-inspiring lover the recognition and praise which she deserves. The final stanza exists as the speaker's humble acceptance of Chlora's complexity; despite her fluctuating affections, he prefers to view her in a more simple, natural light, which he conveys through the images of green hills and flowers. In this, he applies his theme of starkly-contrasting images to the poem's structure itself; the poem speaks of Chlora's complexity until the last stanza, which ultimately admits that she has a simple side as well.

Though "The Gallery" speaks specifically of Chlora, it may depict some of Marvell's own frustrations with women as well. By having the speaker claim "that at the entrance likes me best," referring to the simpler image of his lover, Marvell could be making a claim to women's nature on a grander scale. Though the speaker is speaking of the "entrance" to his gallery, perhaps Marvell uses the word to represent the lover's first impression of Chlora. In this, Marvell notes that, while women seem very natural and simple at face value, they can be quite intricate, varying and subtly dark creatures.

Sample Student Essay Two

This foray into the mind of a romantic uses the fickle imagery of an imagined art gallery to convey the turbulence of his relationship with Chlora, the object of his love. The images alternate between those causing him heartbreak and those that return him to the original purity of his love. Likewise, their depictions of Chlora alternate between the malicious (a murderess, an enchantress), and the heavenly (Aurora, Venus). The speaker admits these inconsistencies when he confesses some of these images are "to please me," while others serve to "torment." The speaker's love, it seems, is unrequited. As an explanation for the contrasts of the poem, he is alternately cynical and hopeful of his courtship of Chlora.

The second and fourth stanzas depict Chlora maliciously. First, she is an "inhuman murderess," and significantly, the speaker tells of her victims' hearts, describing them as "Thy fertile shop of cruel arts." Here the speaker makes Chlora come off as manipulative of men with the means of her powers of seduction. The speaker is yet another victim for whom Chlora, he would have us believe, carelessly seduced and then threw away. The end of the stanza confirms that what is most "tormenting," the speaker is her appearance: "Black eyes, red lips, and curled hair." This is not the look of a proper lady, but instead, a whore. Or, to borrow from the literary archetypes that have dominated male-written works about women, Chlora, here, would be labeled as an Eve, the original fallen woman, who brought down Adam from righteousness into sin.

Chlora's depiction in this archetype is continued in the fourth stanza where she is an "enchantress," certainly a sinful role. This stanza conjures images of her huddled in a cave, casting spells over the innards of a dead lover. And when she is done with them, the speaker says, she throws them away, "To be the greedy vulture's prey." Here the speaker reveals his fear that lovers are dispensable to Chlora, that when she no longer has use for them she can throw them away. There is none of the emotional attachment that a romantic like our speaker would desire.

The alternating stanzas, however, portray a very different image of Chlora. Here she is seen as the opposite of the Eve archetype. Instead of the fallen woman, she is portrayed like the Virgin Mary. The imagery of these stanzas conjures innocence. In the first she is compared to the Roman goddess of the dawn and the diction describing her is that of nourishment: the speaker describes her "milky thighs," and "manna falls." All of the imagery is pastoral: in addition to milk and manna, the speaker mentions the singing of the morning quire, and wooing doves approaching her. Appropriately, this ends with the mentioning of "harmless loves," in stark contrast with the dangerous seductions of both the preceding and proceeding stanzas. Meanwhile, the fifth stanza leaves us with a similar image, though gotten from different imagery. This time Chlora is compared to Venus, goddess of love. The diction is all ethereal here: she sits in a pearly boat amidst peaceful times. The waves are gentle, bringing perfume, and the only winds blow just hard enough to carry the scent.

The speaker lets on to this in the final stanza when he says that the image that he still likes best is his first impression of her, likely the most accurate image the reader gets. The pastoral imagery comes back, but it is far more down to earth: no longer is she a goddess at whose feet doves gather, but "a tender shepherdess picking flowers for her hair. With such contrasts, it is probably fair to say that none of the prior depictions, neither the malicious ones nor the glorifying ones, are accurate ones, but that is perhaps too much to ask of the speaker, whose objectivity cannot be counted on as he is both in love and terribly frustrated. The stark disparities between his portrayals of her are manifestations of his turbulent emotions, and like the Eve and Mary archetypes, neither are likely accurate. Just as no one can be pigeon-holed into either being a sinful whore or a virtuous Madonna, likewise Chlora is likely neither a witch nor goddess but merely human, although the speaker's star-crossed eyes leave him blind to this.

Sample Student Essay Three

Andrew Marvell's poem "The Gallery" describes the relationship between the speaker and a woman named Chlora. Although the speaker is clearly taken with Chlora, he acknowledges that she is a complex person with a multifaceted personality. Marvell's use of diction, imagery, and figurative language emphasize the contrasting nature of the speaker's relationship with Chlora: sometimes painful but ultimately tender.

Marvell's choice of words give the reader a sense of the speaker's range of feelings for Chlora, as well as the different aspects of her personality. In the stanzas that describe Chlora's vicious side, Marvell uses phrases such as "inhuman," "tormenting," and "black eyes." Words such as these have an intensity that gives the reader an immediate sense of Chlora's personality and of her negative effect on the speaker. The phrase "...the most tormenting are/Black eyes, red lips, and curled hair" describes how Chlora's beauty disturbs the speaker. In the stanzas devoted to Chlora's tender side, Marvell chooses words of equal intensity; however, they emphasize Chlora's peacefulness and gentleness. Phrases like "slumbering," "milky thighs," "roses spring," and "pearly boat" convey that Chlora can have a calming and blissful effect on the speaker. The contrasting diction effectively expresses the complexity of the relationship between the speaker and Chlora.

The diction in the poem also helps to create detailed images of Chlora. Marvell uses intricate language to help the reader visualize an evil Chlora in frightening settings as well as an ethereal Chlora in beautiful places. For example, in the fourth stanza, Chlora is depicted as a mysterious and sadistic woman who behaves like an enchantress with her lovers. Marvell places this version of Chlora in a cave with "light obscure" where she cruelly tosses away her lovers. However, in the fifth stanza, Marvell portrays Chlora as a goddess in a "pearly boat" in a peaceful and fragrant ocean. The range of images included in the poem helps the reader understand that Chlora is not wholly good nor wholly evil. The final stanza depicts Chlora as a "tender shepherdess" in a green meadow, showing that despite her violent side, she is ultimately loved by the speaker.

Marvell's use of diction and imagery combine to effectively compare Chlora to various types of women. In the first stanza, Chlora is "painted in the dress / Of an inhuman murderess," and in the fourth stanza, she is said to be "like an enchantress." These comparisons to evil and conniving characters expose Chlora's negative side and her detrimental effect on the speaker. In opposition to such comparisons, Chlora is compared to goddesses in the third and fifth stanzas. Marvell alludes to the Aurora, a goddess of the dawn, as well as Venus, the goddess of love, and uses simile to compare Chlora to these divine figures. The poem's setting in a figurative gallery also shows the complicated nature of Chlora's personality, where an image of Chlora behaving violently is juxtaposed with an image of Chlora as a benevolent figure. The variety of comparisons is indicative of the range of feelings that the speaker has for Chlora.

Andrew Marvell effectively combines diction, imagery, and figurative language to give the reader a complete understanding of the speaker's complicated relationship with Chlora. Chlora is not a simple character; her behavior ranges from kind to cruel and thus her relationship with the speaker is complex. She is portrayed as both good and evil and simultaneously pleases and disturbs the speaker, yet ultimately, the speaker loves her and holds in his mind the images of her as a beautiful and gentle woman.

Assessment of Student Responses to Free-Response Question One:
Andrew Marvell's "The Gallery"

Sample Student Essay One:

A. Assessment of Reader One

This essay has a few mistakes, but it deftly constructs how the different paintings of the speaker's soul construct the relationship between the speaker and his lover. The "love/hate" idea is a bit simplistic, but when combined with the presentation of the progress of the imaginary pictures and then the significance of how they portray the relationship, it is first-rate. There is also insight into the poem and into the reason why the speaker shows both sides of his love. This very strong paper would fall in the 8/9 range.

B. Assessment of Reader Two

This is a superb response and the type of essay that regularly makes it into the range-finders as an exemplar of a high upper-half paper. I would score it a 9 primarily because it melds deep insight with a fluent writing style, its sole blemish being a slightly muddled conclusion. The student does a wonderful job with antithetical diction and antithetical characterizations which captures the complexity of both Chlora and his relationship with her. For a forty-minute response, this was impressive.

Sample Student Essay Two:

A. Assessment of Reader One

This writer has decent ideas, but the awkward sentence structure and misuse of vocabulary is a bit "off-putting". The conclusion that the goddess images are like the Virgin Mary is too far-fetched. In addition, the relationship of the speaker to the lover is underdeveloped. This is an upper-half paper that I see as a 6.

B. Assessment of Reader Two

I rate this paper as slightly higher, as a strong 7. I agree that the comparison to the Virgin Mary is wrong-headed, but I do believe that the idea of virginity, supported by all the white images of "milky thighs," "manna" and "cooing doves" is valid. I think that the student sees many of the same contrasts as the writer of Sample Essay One, but I think the writing is not as fluid. I particularly liked the comments about lovers being "dispensable" to Chlora.

<u>Sample Student Essay Three</u>:

A. Assessment of Reader One

This essay jumps around a bit—there are many repetitive phrases and ideas, and a good deal of paraphrase and plot summary—but it writes itself into an upper-half essay. It shows a good understanding of the relationship and how the portraits combine to make it clear. I would score this a 7.

B. Assessment of Reader Two

Depending upon what surrounded this in my grading folder, I might be tempted to go higher with this than a 7. It is, I feel, solidly in the 7/8 range and does many good things with diction and imagery. I particularly liked the contrast of the "evil" and "ethereal" Chloras, but I do concede that a good portion of this is more plot summary than analysis. So in the end I concur with Reader One that this best exemplifies a solid 7.

Question Two

(Suggested time—40 minutes. This question counts as one-third of the total essay section score.)

The following two poems express reactions to the premature death of young athletes. Read each poem carefully. Then, in a well-organized essay, compare and contrast the diction, figurative language and tone of each poem and explain how these elements abet each poem's purpose.

To An Athlete Dying Young

The time you won your town the race
We chaired you through the market-place;
Man and boy stood cheering by,
And home we brought you shoulder-high.

(5) To-day, the road all runners come,
Shoulder-high, we bring you home,
And set you at your threshold down,
Townsman of a stiller town.

Smart lad, to slip betimes away
(10) From fields where glory does not stay
And early though the laurel grows
It withers quicker than the rose.

Eyes the shady night has shut
Cannot see the record cut,
(15) And silence sounds no worse than cheers
After earth has stopped the ears:

Now you will not swell the rout
Of lads that wore their honors out,
Runners whom renown outran
(20) And the name died before the man.

So set, before its echoes fade,
The fleet foot on the sill of shade,
And hold to the low lintel up
The still defended challenge-cup.

(25) And round that early-laureled head
Will flock to gaze the strengthless dead,
And find unwithered on its curls
The garland briefer than a girl's.

—A.E. Housman

On the Death of the Evansville University Basketball Team in a Plane Crash, December 13, 1977

And now we know
why coaches rage,
kick benches,
curse rivals and referees.

(5) Here, on this corpse-strewn hill
where grief smothers hope
with an obscene fog,
finality the only prize,
the orphaned heart knows
(10) that every contest is do or die,
that all opponents are Death
masquerading in school colors,
that each previous season is
mere preliminary for encounter
(15) with this last, bitter cup.

Yet we would not have it so,
it must not be so:
man is not made for death.
Cry foul. Shriek protest.
(20) Claim a violation.
Even in losing, dying,
herald the perfect play.

So scream, all-knowing coaches,
Admonishing priests, scream.
(25) Swear, chew asses, make us work.
Never quit.
What else sustains
in nights when dreams
plummet downward in darkness
(30) to question the betraying earth?

—Robert Hamblin

With permission from the author.

Précis and Explication of Free-Response Question Two: A.E. Housman's "To An Athlete Dying Young" and Robert Hamblin's "On the Death of the Evansville University Basketball Team in a Plane Crash, December 13, 1977."

While A.E. Housman's "To An Athlete Dying Young" is an oft-anthologized elegy which seems to be cited on virtually every occasion of the premature death of a young athlete, Robert Hamblin's tribute to the Evansville University basketball team that was killed in a horrific plane crash in 1977 will be unknown to most. The author, a long-tenured professor at Southeast Missouri State University and esteemed expert on William Faulkner, has been a friend of mine since we first met in 1985 when I was accepted to his NEH Seminar on Faulkner. I have long admired his poetry and perhaps like this one the best, maybe because I am a teacher who over my career has seen too many lives cut short by an array of tragedy too long to mention, maybe because as an English teacher/basketball coach I more intimately understand the poem's metaphor.

Housman's poem, written in the ballad form that marks so much of his work, simply and eloquently pays tribute to a young runner cut down in the prime of life. No details as to the cause of his death are provided; the poem merely begins with a nostalgic recollection of the moment of his greatest triumph when, after winning a race, the runner was "chaired" (line 2) through the market-place and brought home by the ecstatic townspeople "shoulder-high" (line 4) in the traditional ritual of honoring a champion. Though the winner was "chaired" (note the near-homonym, "cheered") victoriously home that day, he is again brought home on the shoulders of others, this time in a casket, and set down at the "threshold" (line 7) of a gravesite, soon to become "Townsman of a stiller town" (line 8), the necropolis. Though he has traversed "the road all runners come" (life), he has done so prematurely, though the speaker surprisingly calls him a "Smart lad" (line 9) for dying while he is still a youth. This seemingly ironic, even distasteful comment is quickly explained by the three stanzas that follow, which point out that he was wise "to slip betimes away / From fields where glory does not stay / And early though the laurel grows / It withers quicker than the rose" (lines 9-12). The speaker's allusion to short-lived flowers—in particular, the laurel which is the floral crown placed on the head of marathon winners—suggests that glory is transient and usually vanishes before one dies. Now the deceased runner, his eyes shut and ears stopped, "Cannot see the record cut" (line 14) or hear the fading of his cheers. He will not be among the rout of "Runners whom renown outran" (line 19), but will leave with his moment of glory forever intact. Because of this, the speaker urges him to "…set, before its echoes fade, / The fleet foot on the sill of shade" (lines 21-22), holding high his victory cup in proud defiance of a death which has been cheated of a complete victory. The final image—of the runner surrounded by the "strengthless dead" (line 26) of the after-life—mirrors the celebratory scene in the opening stanza, and the unwithered garland that he wears on his head affirms the line from First Corinthians, "Oh, death, where is thy victory?"

In contrast to the romantic victory over death enjoyed by Housman's runner, Hamblin's account of the death of the Evansville University basketball team in a plane crash is a much more somber one. The opening four lines, "And now we know / why coaches rage, / kick benches, / curse rivals and referees," state a dark, declarative fact: death wins. Scanning a macabre scene of a "corpse-strewn hill / where grief smothers hope / with an obscene fog" (lines 5-7), the speaker presents a grim and unalterable reality in which the "orphaned heart" (line 9) of family member, friend, teacher and reader can only come to the realization

> that every contest is do or die,
> that all opponents are Death,
> masquerading in school colors,
> that each previous season is
> mere preliminary for encounter
> with this last, bitter cup (lines 10-15).

Here Housman's central metaphor of the "road all runners come" is replaced by a sports' contest in which the outcome and winner are always the same. And though we may, like Jesus in the Garden of Gesthemane, wish to pass on drinking from this "last, bitter cup," it is impossible to do so.

Yet, whereas the speaker in Housman's poem advocates embracing premature death because it enables one to preserve glory—somewhat in line with the sentiment contained in Keats' "Ode on a Grecian Urn," and the Greeks in the Homeric Age who believed that the only way to gain immortality was through being commemorated in song or poetry as Achilles was for his deeds at Troy—the speaker in Hamblin's poem is more akin to the one in Dylan Thomas' "Do Not Go Gentle into that Good Night." He acknowledges the human defiance of death—"Yet we would not have it so, / it must not be so; / man is not made for death" (lines 16-18)—urging people to "Cry foul. Shriek protest. / Claim a violation" (lines 19-20). Though death indeed may have its dominion, one can "Even in losing, dying, / herald the perfect play" (lines 21-22). This emotional defiance of death, intensified by the imperatives, suggests not that one should embrace death passively but that one should fight it to the final buzzer. The final stanza of the poem returns to the image of angry, swearing coaches that was introduced in the first stanza, encouraging them to instill such combativeness in the players whom they coach. The haunting climactic question—"What else sustains / in nights when dreams / plummet downward in darkness / to question the betraying earth?" (lines 27-30)—presents a harrowing image of the plummeting plane, but also suggests that it is only this defiance, this fiery desire to overcome, that enables one to endure a battle in which one is sure to be worsted.

Taken together, both A.E. Housman's "To An Athlete Dying Young" and Robert Hamblin's "On the Death of the Evansville University Basketball Team in a Plane Crash, December 13, 1977," both present responses to premature death. While the first presents a romantic portrait of premature dying in a rhymed, four-line ballad form that uses a central metaphor of a road-race and floral images/symbols to convey its message—that fame is immortalized by premature death—the second presents a bleak, realistic picture of a human tragedy, utilizing free verse, a central metaphor of a sports' contest, and a defiant tone to convey its message that though death ultimately overwhelms, one must do everything in one's power to deter its triumph.

Scoring Guide for Free-Response Question Two: A.E. Housman's "To An Athlete Dying Young" and Robert Hamblin's "On the Death of the Evansville University Basketball Team in a Plane Crash, December 13, 1977."

8-9   Well-conceived, well-developed, and well-organized, these papers are marked by frequent and accurate references to the text, by an admirable ability to synthesize thought, and by a mature control over the elements of composition. Though not perfect, they clearly indicate the students' ability to identify the diverse reactions of the speaker in each poem to the premature death of a young athlete or athletes and to illustrate how the diction, figurative language, and tone of each poem abet each poem's purpose.

6-7   These essays exhibit a solid understanding of the reactions of the speaker in each poem to the premature death of an athlete or athletes, but are less adept at responding to the question. This may be due to inconsistencies in textual understanding, or to a lesser ability to illustrate how the diction, figurative language, and tone of each poem abet each poem's purpose. Though these essays reflect their writers' abilities to convey their points clearly, they feature less fluency, less development and less cogency than 8-9 papers.

5   These papers respond to the question on the reactions of the speakers in two different poems to the death of a young athlete or athletes—and the manner in which the diction, figurative language, and tone of each poem abet each poem's purpose—in superficial, formulaic, inconsistent, or insufficiently supported ways. They may rely primarily on paraphrase, but may still convey an implicit understanding of the passage and the task. The papers are generally written in a satisfactory manner, with occasional errors in composition or mechanics that do not impede the reader's understanding. Nevertheless, these essays lack the organization, persuasiveness and development of upper-half papers.

3-4   These lower-half essays generally suggest an incomplete or overly simplistic understanding of the passages or of the task, an inability to identify the disparity between the speakers' reaction to the premature death of an athlete or athletes, or an inability to show how the aforementioned literary elements abet each poem's purpose. Their arguments are often characterized by a misreading of the text(s), a failure to provide adequate support, or insufficient control over the elements of composition. In some instances they may consist entirely of paraphrase and/or feature acute problems in organization, clarity, fluency or development.

1-2   These essays compound the shortcomings of 3-4 papers. They often contain many serious and distracting errors in grammar or mechanics that preclude any successful response to the prompt. Though these essays may attempt to show some understanding of the speakers' response to premature death or make some observation about literary elements, they are severely limited by deficiencies in organization, clarity, fluency or development.

0   Papers scored a zero make no more than a passing reference to the task.

—   Papers given this score offer a blank or totally off-topic response.

Sample Student Essay One

The death of a young athlete is tragic no matter what the situation. The athlete had a successful career to look forward to and a long and full life ahead of them, and when all this is taken away it is extremely unjust. These deaths prompt varied reactions, as demonstrated by the poem "To an Athlete Dying Young" by A. E. Housman and the poem "On the Death of the Evansville University Basketball Team" by Robert Hamblin. Both poems express the unfairness of an athlete dying either in or before his prime, but the attitudes they take could not be more different. Housman's poem conveys a hopeful outlook on death and is more of a celebration of life than Hamblin's poem, which uses figurative language to convey its hopeless message.

"To an Athlete Dying Young" is an ode to a young runner's life, celebrating the accomplishments that he had rather than the ones left unfulfilled. The tone is mournful: "To-day, the road all runners come / Shoulder-high, we bring you home," and at times resigned. The speaker of the poem knows that there is nothing he can to about this athlete's death, so he is trying to draw something positive from the tragedy. "Eyes the shady night has shut cannot see the record cut, / And silence sounds no worse than cheers / After earth has stopped the ears." Some people's glory fades before the athlete, he is saying. They keep on training and competing while they have already been forgotten. In this case, the runner has died while in his prime, so his glory will live on forever. He will not live to see his records broken, and his name will be forever associated with success that was cut short.

At first glance, "To an Athlete Dying Young" appears hopeful; it does not have the same desperation that Hamblin's poem does. However, the diction conveys a sense of resignation and melancholy. The poem is written in somewhat formal language, which contributes to its funereal undertones. "Now you will not swell the rout / Of lads that wore their honors out," he says. The resignation can be seen when he says that the boy must be celebrated "before [his] echoes fade." This ultimately helps the purpose of the poem, which is to show that life and glory are fleeting, and should be celebrated while they last.

"On the Death…" also is trying to show how life and glory are fleeting, but rather than accepting that, the speaker of the poem conveys people's desperate attempts to give their lives meaning before they die and to try and avoid death. While Housman's poem is mournful, Hamblin's is hopeless and despairing. Using very harsh diction, "On the Death…" conveys a sense that all life simply leads to death. From the first stanza, the tone is set. "And now we know / why coaches rage,/ kick benches, / curse rivals and referees." It is angry, and the sense of loss over the team is overwhelming. These athletes worked hard for their whole careers, ultimately to no avail, since they are going to die anyway. Death is personified as the opponent in a tournament "masquerading in school colors." Each game is thought of as an attempt to prolong one's inevitable death and fruitlessly try to fight against it. Unlike Housman's poem, in which the speakers are resigned to the fact that death is inevitable, those in Hamblin's poem are fighting with every bit of their strength to not give in to death. "Never quit. / What else sustains / in nights when dreams / plummet downward in darkness / to question the betraying earth?" His words are hopeless, yet they show how one must make the most of their life while they can, since death eventually comes to all.

Both poems show the tragedy of an early death, especially that of a young athlete who had a successful life or career ahead of him. Each poem has its own distinct tone and view on death, but they do agree on one thing; death eventually comes to everyone, and whether it is before one's glory days or during, life should be lived so that after one dies, it is a life worth celebrating.

Sample Student Essay Two

The poems "To An Athlete Dying Young" by A.E. Housman and "On the Death of the Evansville University Basketball Team in a Plane Crash" by Robert Hamblin both examine the untimely deaths of athletes. They both use stylistic elements such as figurative language, diction, and symbolism to support their contrasting themes. "To An Athlete Dying Young" uses these elements to show that death preserves glory, whereas "On the Death of the Evansville University Basketball Team in a Plane Crash" uses them to illustrate that death steals glory.

"To An Athlete Dying Young" is about the death of a runner. In the first stanza, the reader learns that the runner was a champion who was "chaired through the market-place" and "carried shoulder-high" by the townspeople. The runner's death is described in the second stanza. The poet chooses to tell us that the runner has moved along the "road all runners come," meaning that he has died. Once more, Housman incorporates the phrase "shoulder-high," but in this stanza, unlike the first, it is used to describe the act of carrying a coffin. The diction in this stanza helps to show the poem's romanticized view of death because it includes euphemisms such as "threshold" instead of "grave" and "stiller town" instead of cemetery. Over the next five stanzas, the poem's theme becomes evident. Housman uses a laurel to represent glory. He states that the laurel "withers quicker than the rose," meaning that glory is short-lived, and says that after death, one "cannot see the record cut," which essentially means that glory and victory cannot be taken away after death. According to Housman, those athletes who die early but have their glory preserved are better off than those "whom renown outran".

"On the Death of the Evansville University Basketball Team in a Plane Crash" differs in several ways from "To An Athlete Dying Young." It has a very angry, resentful tone, much unlike the measured, accepting tone of "To An Athlete Dying Young." The words "rage," "kick," and "curse" are used in the first stanza, which immediately gives the poem an irate tone. In the second stanza, Hamblin compares sports games to battles of life and death: "every contest is do or die, / ...all opponents are Death masquerading in school colors." Hamblin urges the living to "never quit" and to instead work hard and put forth a strong effort. The reader is encouraged to ""Cry foul. Shriek protest. / Claim a violation" because "man is not made for death." The blunt, angry language directed towards death shows the theme that death takes glory away from athletes.

Both A.E. Housman and Robert Hamblin use specific stylistic elements to make opposing points about the early deaths of athletes. Hamblin views untimely death as the foe, whereas Housman casts early death as a way to freeze a youthful moment of glory in time. The poets are successful in supporting their respective themes because they choose to use stylistic elements that reflect their points of view.

Sample Student Essay Three

Housman's and Hamblin's poems both present reactions to the early death of young athletes. The similarity of the two works ends here, however, as each poet expresses sharply contrasting perspectives on life cut short in its prime. Using angry diction and a dismayed tone, Hamblin reflects that the tragic death of a university basketball team revealed the futility of life in the face of inevitable death. Housman, on the other hand, interprets death in a more positive light, using figurative language to describe how the premature death of a small-town hero forever preserved his glory.

The first element that the reader detects in Hamblin's poem is its pervasive anger. This dramatic, irate, and bitter tone begins in the first stanza with, "And now we know / why coaches rage, / kick benches, / curse rivals and referees," and continues unabated throughout the work. The poet reacts to the tragic death of a basketball team with the realization that life unavoidably leads to death, a concept that seems obvious, yet is painfully difficult to grasp. Hamblin uses sports imagery to express the inevitability of death, stating that "each previous season is / mere preliminary for encounter / with this last, bitter, cup." Throughout the poem, the author's diction, including phrases like "Cry foul, shriek protest," and "Scream, all-knowing coaches,/ admonishing priests, scream," indicates physical and profound rage. It is a potent portrayal of man's despair in the face of his own mortality.

Housman presents a comparatively positive perspective on a similar situation. He claims that glory and fame are fleeting in life. By dying young, the athlete is preserved as a hero, rather than being slowly forgotten over the course of his life. The boy will be spared the arguably more painful fate of "Runners whom renown outran / And the name died before the man." Several images thread throughout the poem, including the runners mentioned in the lines above, who represent those traveling the passage of life and death, "the road all runners come." Another vital symbol is the laurel, representing the young athlete's fame, which "withers quicker than the rose." In the last stanza, the laurel is found miraculously "unwithered on (his) curls / The garland briefer than a girl's." The laurel, which usually grows early but then dies before the rose, is preserved by the early demise of the young man at the height of his fame.

Hamblin's angry and pessimistic perspective on death contrasts sharply with Housman's melancholy but more optimistic poem. "To An Athlete Dying Young" in a way offers a response to the accompanying poem. Housman claims that one can escape death through memory, so long as the memory does not die before the man.

Assessment of Student Responses to Free-Response Question Two: A.E. Housman's "To an Athlete Dying Young" and Robert Hamblin's "On the Death of the Evansville University Basketball Team in a Plane Crash, December 13, 1977."

Sample Student Essay One:

A. Assessment of Reader One

This response is marred by quite a few surface errors, but it treats both poems equally and sees the purpose of each poem. The fact that the writer sees Housman as "hopeful" but "resigned" is pretty nice. The explication of the Hamblin poem is somewhat plot-driven, but the idea about the poem's purpose is solid. The student addresses the tone of each piece quite well. I would score this essay a 7.

B. Assessment of Reader Two

I would concur with a 7 on this. The paper is strong in its analysis of both theme and tone and does a good job with individual lines. The student never addresses figurative language in specific terms and the analysis of diction is more broad-based than specific. Still, it is a fluent piece with clear direction from start to finish, quite well-developed for a forty-minute response.

Sample Student Essay Two:

A. Assessment of Reader One

This essay cites lots of lines without explication, but gets the basic idea of both poems. The commentary on tone is also good. This would benefit from a more expansive treatment of diction and figurative language. I would score this a 6, but on the low side.

B. Assessment of Reader Two

I found this to be an interesting response in that it did many things specifically and well that the first essay failed to do. It caught the double-image of "shoulder-high" and made an interesting observation about euphemisms. It reflects upper-half thought in both its interpretation and composition though its lack of development limits the success of the former. The tendency to paraphrase without analysis on several occasions keeps this from rising past a 6.

Sample Student Essay Three:

A. Assessment of Reader One

This student's response is well-written and very concise, but both the introduction and conclusion are extremely simplistic. Though an expansion of the ideas in the essay is sorely needed, I would probably bump this up one point for the quality of the writing from a 5 to a 6.

B. Assessment of Reader Two

I actually see this as a solid 6. The writer is fluent, and though he is rather summative in his commentary, the analysis is on point and admirably dense. This paper tried to do something with figurative language, noting both the road and laurel, though errantly labeling the former an image instead of a symbol. The writing is confident and concise and above the superficiality that tends to characterize papers in the 5 range.

Prepping for Prose: How to Achieve Success on the AP Multiple-Choice and Free-Response Prose Questions

When it comes to prose, many of the techniques that have been discussed in the "Prepping for Poetry" section have equal application. Words are the building blocks of prose as well, and close reading maintains a singular importance. There are, however, some differences. Whereas most poems—unless the exam chooses a segment of lines from the *Odyssey* or from William Wordsworth's *Prelude*—offer tidy, self-contained units of meaning, prose passages are generally cuttings from short stories, novels, plays and (much more rarely since the advent of the AP English Language exam) a literary essay. Though great effort is made to select a piece that stands on its own merits apart from the larger purposes of the fiction from which it has been taken, the fact remains that the reader is forced to consider some sixty to eighty lines from a much larger work of fiction. Now unless you recognize the selection as coming from a work you have read in class, you will be unaware of the relation of this piece to the work as a whole. Second, the structures of prose, large and small, differ from the structures of poetry. Whereas poems may be sonnets, odes, ballads, epics, and haikus, prose forms are labeled novels, short stories, essays, articles, speeches and still others. While poems are many times divided into lines and stanzas, the basic divisions of prose are sentences and paragraphs. And while most poems are not narrative, much of prose fiction is. Third, though diction and choice of detail retain their usual prominence, point-of-view and syntax command greater attention. Whereas we tend merely to label the voice we hear in a poem as "the speaker" or "the persona," identifying from what point of view a narrative is being told is more complex, and the mere shift in person affects the relationship between reader and character as well as the reliability of the information being delivered. As for syntax, one can argue, I think, that it may be the single most important contributor to establishing an individual author's style. Readers familiar with syntax could never confuse Hemingway with Faulkner, the terse simple sentences of the former not even vaguely resembling the long, sprawling (some might say rambling) constructions of the latter. The variations of sentence length, the internal order of their wording, parallel structure and repetition are just some of the elements which demand the reader of prose's attention.

Still, to be fair, such distinctions can often blur, making prose very poetic. Some of our best prose writers create wonderful rhythms through the syntax of their sentences; others employ the same figures of speech regularly used by poets. Many of our best speeches mirror the moving cadences of a dramatic monologue, and some experimental fiction even incorporates poetic forms within the prose. Though I don't wish to reduce the differences between poetry and prose to something mundane, it is interesting to consider the definition of two words: "poetic" and "prosaic." Aside from the rather limited definition of "having the quality or characteristics of poetry," the word "poetic" is also said to mean "marked by romantic imagery;" hence, it is associated with creativity and imagination. The word "prosaic," on the other hand, is often defined as "dull; unimaginative." While this may be selling prose a bit short, it is accurate in that prose *is* the language of direct communication, and much of our communication is unadorned and functional. It does not take much imagination to say "Take out the dog" or "Pick me up after basketball practice." As I tell my class, should something spontaneously combust in a classroom closet, I can evacuate the room with a simple word: "Fire." Were I to say, on the other hand, "Rosy red tongues are thrusting out from yonder door," I doubt if it would have the same effect. I often tell my class to consider "poetic" and "prosaic" to be on a sliding scale. When a poem starts abandoning traditional poetic language, it starts moving toward prose—and perhaps the mundane rhyme of a greeting card. On the contrary, when prose starts to become imagistic and rhythmic and to employ figures of speech, it elevates into the realm of the poetic. However, that is not to say prose must be poetic to be good. It all depends upon authorial intent. It is unlikely that your science textbook, for example, aims to be poetic, but if you're going to understand various principles and formulas in chemistry, you need some straightforward instruction. At the same time many of us have experienced the gifted historian who can really make a period or personality come excitingly to life. It all depends upon the intention.

Much as in the "Prepping for Poetry" section, I can give you some brief words of exam advice. If things look familiar, they should. Prose is just another writing construct—more expansive than most poems, but based on the same elemental structure: the word. Look at the bright side: if you can read one well, you can generally read the other. That's one less thing about which to worry.

1. Focus on Close Reading

The advice here is basically the same as in "Prepping for Poetry" in that you want to get down to "word level," to look at the diction, but you must be equally attentive to the way words are functioning in groups whether they be phrases, clauses, even paragraphs. In short, by looking at word arrangement, you are looking at syntax. Over the years I have found that too many students coming into my AP class don't even know the meaning of that word. Oh, some of them know grammar, which is a useful tool, but syntax in effect puts grammar to its highest use: the creation of aurally appealing, even dramatic rhythms. If you are weak in grammar, it would be good to brush up on some basics because syntax employs a diversity of constructions including the following:

> Action verbs
> Imperatives
> Descriptors such as adjectives and adverbs
> A series of nouns, adjectives or adverbs
> Appositives (nouns that qualify another noun: e.g. John, the fireman)
> Prepositional phrases
> Infinitive Phrases
> Participles and participial phrases
> Exclamations
> Conjunctions (coordinating and subordinating) and Conjunctive Adverbs

Each of the items on the aforementioned list can be used to create interesting syntax; however, these are the mere building blocks that are used to create syntax. Syntax itself is the effect they create within individual sentences and paragraphs. Consider the closing line from Tennyson's famous poem "Ulysses," in which the famed hero defiantly proclaims his life philosophy:

> "To strive, to seek, to find, and not to yield."

The first noticeable feature in this line is the **series of infinitives**. The poet creates a certain iambic (unstressed-stressed) rhythm by stringing the first three infinitives together. However, the fourth infinitive in the sequence is a negative one, one that for lack of a better phrase advises the reader *not* to do something. The sentiment, however, is anything but negative since the action being encouraged is essentially to persevere, not to quit. The infinitives are also arranged in what is called **climactic order**, moving from "strive" (try), to "seek" (look for), to "find" (attain). The concluding phrase "not to yield" is an affirmation by Ulysses to continue to do these things.

Now consider this sentence from Edith Wharton's *The Age of Innocence*, in which an aristocratic woman comments upon the soon-to-be gentrification of her as yet undeveloped neighborhood:

> She was sure that presently the hoardings, the quarries, the one-story saloons, the wooden green-houses in ragged gardens, and the rocks from which goats surveyed the scene, would vanish before the advance of residences as stately as her own…" (Wharton 26).

Here we have something rather different: a **list** (or a **catalog**, if you prefer it) of nouns that depict unsightly locales that, given her privileged status, she would prefer be eliminated. Technically, they are compound subjects of a relative clause started by "that," but even being able to say that she is making a list of architectural unpleasantries allows you to talk about, well, syntax. It you wanted to add a dash of diction to your commentary, you might look at the words "vanish" and "advance," the first which reflects her fervent desire to rid the neighborhood of these eyesores, and the second which suggests the relentlessness with which the rich buy up property and displace the poor.

Let's now look at something radically different, a passage from Margaret Atwood's *The Handmaid's Tale*, in which the narrator is trying to escape from a hostile situation with her young daughter:

> I'm running, with her, holding her hand, pulling, dragging her through the bracken, she's only half-awake because of the pill I gave her, so she wouldn't cry or say anything that would give us away, she doesn't even know where she is. The ground is uneven, rocks, dead branches, the smell of dead earth, old leaves, she can't run fast enough, by myself I could run faster, I'm a good runner…. (Atwood 96).

Here the author, to increase the urgency of the moment, does several things. The first is the use of **action verbs** such as "running," "holding," "pulling," and "dragging." Together these verbs suggest the chaos that the speaker is experiencing, the simultaneous need to run as fast as possible without letting go of her daughter who, because she is small, cannot possibly keep up with her mother. The syntax here antithetically combines speed and resistance, the eagerness of a conscious adult and the reluctance of an oblivious child. Again there is a **list**, this time of elements of nature, specifically things on the ground over which they are stumbling in their haste. You also might notice that there are **comma splices**, something your teacher might have marked up in red on one of your essays. Here, however, in a dramatic scene from a novel, they, too, speed the action, adding to an overall tone of desperation and haste. This type of writing is called **stream of consciousness**, in which the character's thought processes are presented in an uninterrupted flow that is often enhanced by the reduction or elimination of traditional punctuation. (In certain instances this is also labeled **interior monologue**). It is also a **flashback**, a technique that, along with its opposite, **foreshadowing**, allows the writer to break the traditional **chronological approach** of most narratives. The passage from *The Handmaid's Tale* is also written from a **first person** point of view. That gives it an emotional immediacy that is further intensified by the fact that it is that of a mother trying to save her daughter.

2. Travel light—yet again.

Again, just as in poetry, you can confound your mind with dozens of rhetorical terms. However, in addition to the grammatical structures listed in the previous section, there are a number of prose terms that are helpful to know. Start with the four basic sentences types— **declarative** (makes a statement), **interrogative** (asks a question), **imperative** (gives an order) and **exclamatory** (expresses surprise or some other emotion)—then expand your knowledge to include the **periodic sentence** (a long, sometimes convoluted sentence in which the main thought does not appear until the end) and the **loose sentence** (a sentence in which the main idea is established first then followed by other syntactical constructions). **Repetition** (or as some of you may know in its original Greek form, **anaphora**) is a common one and one that is self-explanatory. Repetition obviously provides emphasis, sometimes hammering a particular point home. For example, in his *Autobiography* Frederick Douglass remarks how upon entering a free state he was,

> in the midst of plenty, yet suffering the terrible gnawings of hunger,—in the midst of houses, yet having no home,—among fellow-men, yet feeling as if in the midst of wild beasts… (Douglass 112).

Here the choric repetition of "in the midst of" highlights the cruel irony that though he was surrounded by people and plenty, he nevertheless felt isolated and famished. This repetition of a particular construction also exemplifies **parallel structure**, a centerpiece of good writing. In his speech, Douglass merges these seamlessly as in the lines

> without home or friends—without money or credit--wanting shelter, and no one to give it—wanting bread, and no money to buy it…" (Douglass 111).

Yet another is **contrast** (also known as **antithesis**), a commonly used and extremely efficient technique. Here Douglass contrasts his life with that of a free man:

> You are loosed from your moorings, and are free; I am fast in my chains, and am a slave! You move merrily before the gentle gale, and I sadly before the bloody whip! You are freedom's swift-winged angels, that fly round the world; I am confined in bands of iron! (Douglass 76)

Techniques such as **rhetorical questions** (questions which do not demand an answer), **inverted syntax** (when the typical subject-verb-object order is reversed, placing emphasis on a different element of the sentence) and **negation** (when something is defined by what it is not) are additional terms that are useful to know. And though we have previously mentioned **climactic order**, it is good to be aware of **anti-climactic order** (when the order of importance goes from greatest to least). And, of course, don't forget **figurative language**. Prose writers use this, too.

Point of view, is yet another important narrative device and one that any competent reader of prose must master. To refresh your memory a little, here are the various points-of-view one may encounter in literature:

> **First person**: The narrator is directly involved in the action and is informing the reader what is going on from an insider's perspective. Often the narrator is the protagonist, but he can also be someone who is intimately familiar with the protagonist's thoughts.

Second Person: The narrator speaks to you even more intimately, using the second person, as if you were a confidante.

Third Person Omniscient: A god-like presence, this narrator knows all that is going on and remains outside the action.

Third Person Limited: Such narration is "limited" to the point of view of one character in the story though this character might range from the protagonist to a minor character. When the narrator conveys the thoughts of more than one character, this is called **Third Person Subjective**.

Third Person Objective: In this type of narration the narrator remains outside individual characters' thoughts and presents them without bias.

Unreliable Narrator: This term is often used to represent the type of narration in which the narrative voice cannot be trusted to convey the truth. Often it reflects that of a narrator who is psychologically unstable; thus, the reader cannot always tell when he is speaking truth or falsehood.

Of course, one must not forget the four basic types of writing: **descriptive**, **expository**, **narrative**, and **persuasive**, though some of these will be more apropos to the AP English Language Exam. Unfortunately, there are numerous syntactical variations and narrative techniques, too many for which to supply examples. Thus, you must take each passage on its own merits and explore words, phrases, sentences and paragraphs, looking for interesting constructs. It may be that your teacher desires you to learn some additional terms that are applicable to prose. There are a multiplicity of other terms, many of them of importance. I do not want to suggest these are all—but they are all you need to say something significant about prose writing.

Now let's try putting some of these close reading skills together Read these lines, taken from the James Joyce short story "A Painful Case," in which the speaker is reacting to news of the unexpected suicide of a woman he had been seeing. Then adhere to the instructions that follow it:

> ….The threadbare phrases, the inane expressions of sympathy, the cautious words of a reporter won over to conceal the details of a commonplace vulgar death attacked his stomach. Not merely had she degraded herself; she had degraded him. He saw the squalid tract of her vice, miserable and malodorous. His soul's companion! He thought of the hobbling wretches he had seen carrying cans and bottles to be filled by the barman. Just God, what an end! Evidently she had been unfit to live, without any strength of purpose, an easy prey to habits, one of the wrecks on which civilization has been reared. But that she could have sunk so low! Was it possible that he had deceived himself so utterly about her?... (Joyce 115).

A. **Diction**: Make a list of the interesting words in the passage. Then, look at them: *really* look at them. Can you detect any connection between them? Any pattern?

_____

_____

_____

_____

_____

_____

B. **Syntax**: Is anything interesting happening with word sequences? With specific types of sentences? List these as well.

_____

_____

_____

_____

_____

_____

C. **Tone**: How would you characterize the overall mood of the passage? What words would you choose to reflect it?

_____

_____

_____

_____

_____

_____

D. **Authorial intent**: What do you think the author is trying to get across to you through this particular combination of diction, syntax and tone?

_____

_____

_____

_____

_____

_____

Let's compare notes:

A. **Diction**: I selected these words: "threadbare." "inane," "cautious," "commonplace," "vulgar," "degraded," "squalid," "miserable," "malodorous" and "hobbling".

Now it's time to sort them. From what I can determine, these adjectives describe three discrete things:

- Comments in the obituary: "threadbare," "inane," "cautious"
- The speaker's feelings about the suicide: "commonplace," "vulgar," "degraded" "squalid," "miserable," "malodorous"
- The beggars he saw in the street: "hobbling"

Now common sense says we can eliminate the last category since it has little bearing on the core impression for which we are looking. The adjectives describing the account in the paper suggest a number of things: that the details provided were deliberately sketchy (understandable, given the gruesome nature of the event) but also that the speaker's reaction is rather harsh in dismissing it as "inane." The other adjectives all reveal how he feels about the suicide, suggesting first his belief that she squandered her life, but second, and more importantly, that his response is decidedly self-centered, cold and uncharitable.

B. **Syntax**: Though the shortness of this excerpt may limit our commentary a bit, there are still some interesting things to notice. The opening sentence, with its compound subjects ("phrases," "expressions," "words"), has admirable parallelism and balance, but it also establishes his distaste for reading the account of the woman's death, as if these details drone on without meaning. The exclamation, "His soul's companion!," reeks with disdain, as if he could never associate himself with someone who could do such a gruesome and rash deed, while "Just God, what an end!" and "But that she could have sunk so low!" both suggest a sense of horror. The concluding rhetorical question, "Was it possible that he had deceived himself so utterly about her?....," suggests both his potential misjudgment of her character and his conviction that he played no role in her demise.

C. **Tone**: The overall tone here seems to me somewhat defensive, as if the character is looking for ways to disassociate himself both from the suicide and from any possibility of his having contributed to it. All of the words imply disgust, condescension. This suggests he perceives her as beneath him, unworthy of his respect or regard.

D. **Authorial Intent**: If one puts these three things together, one can see that the narrator is subtly influencing us against the main character whose callous, matter-of-fact and self-centered reaction, evident in his tone, diction and syntax, shifts the sympathy away from him and totally toward the woman. Of course, we are looking at this out of context, but if you read the story, you'll find our conclusions justified.

3. **For essays—you guessed it: Respond to the Entire Question and Frame a Thesis
    and a Rough Outline.**

Once again, the same basics you learned in the Poetry section apply. You want to read the question carefully so as to determine how many things you are being asked to do. Circling or underlining the core parts of the prompt is encouraged since an essay that does not address a specific part of the question will injure its chances of scoring high on the rubric. One other observation: the prose passages, because they are packed into tight paragraphs, are visually denser than the poems you encounter. Oftentimes there is minimal space in the margins and even less between individual lines. Here I recommend an old SAT tactic: namely, making yourself a code, some kind of short-hand you can recognize. You can use things as simple as underlining or circles to designate interesting diction or instances of syntax, but you may also want to use abbreviations such as S for Simile, P for personification, M for metaphor in the margins and draw an arrow to indicate where it is. I also like to annotate as I go along—nothing dramatic—just a word or two like DETAILS or IRONY or RHETORICAL QUESTIONS in the margins to help me quickly to see what I have found. Remember: there is no time to re-read the passage, so collecting as much information as you can on first-read is essential.

4. **The Last Word**

Reading for pleasure and reading on an exam are clearly very different activities. However, reading challenging selections in both poetry and prose in your AP syllabus and practicing on the exercises in this book will make you a better, faster and more accurate reader. Not every student is at the same skill level when an AP course begins, but with a little perseverance and hard work you can improve your skills and enjoy success on the exam.

A Primer for Prose: A Selection from Robert Penn Warren's *All the King's Men*

The first prose passage featured in this edition is from Robert Penn Warren's 1946 novel *All the King's Men* whose main character, Willie Stark, is thought to have been modeled upon Louisiana's real-life populist demagogue, Huey Long. The charismatic Long served as governor of Louisiana from 1928-1932 and as a United States Senator from 1932-1935. As governor, Long sponsored an ambitious public works' project that was responsible for the construction of badly needed infrastructure such as schools, roads and hospitals and garnered the support of the rural poor via the fervent and romantic slogan "Every man a king, but no one wears a crown." Though he was responsible for much civic improvement in the state of Louisiana, the passage of legislation supporting these incentives was many times allegedly achieved through patronage and graft. As Senator, Long advocated, through his "Share the Wealth" platform, a radical distribution of the country's wealth, necessary, he felt, to lift the country out of the economic death throes of the Great Depression. Thus, Long achieved a somewhat antithetical status as both an advocate of (and hero to) the poor and a powerful autocrat who frequently used actions and rhetoric to strong-arm legislation that he favored. However, the student who is unfamiliar with this supposed historical model for Willie Stark comes to the passage without this 'biography' and must take the character and the passage on its own merits.

....He was a lawyer now. He could hang the overalls on a nail and let them stiffen with the last sweat he had put into them. He could rent himself a room over the dry-goods store in
(5)   Mason City and call it his office, and wait for somebody to come up the stairs where it was so dark you had to feel your way and where it smelled like the inside of an old trunk that's been in the attic twenty years. He was a lawyer
(10)   now and it had taken him a long time. It had taken him a long time because he had had to be a lawyer on his own terms and in his own way. But that was over. But maybe it had taken him too long. If something takes too long,
(15)   something happens to you. You become all and only the thing you want and nothing else, for you have paid too much for it, too much in wanting and too much in waiting and too much in getting. In the end they just ask you those
(20)   crappy little questions.

But the wanting and the waiting were over now, and Willie had a haircut and a new hat and a new brief case with the copy of his speech in it (which he had written out in
(25)   longhand and had said to Lucy with gestures, as though he were getting ready for the high school oratorical contest), and a lot of new friends with drooping jowls and sharp pale noses, who slapped him on the back, and a
(30)   campaign manager, Tiny Duffy, who would introduce him to you and say with a tin-glittering hardiness, "Meet Willie Stark, the next governor of this state!" And Willie would

put out his hand to you with the gravity of a
(35)   bishop. For he never tumbled to a thing.

I used to wonder how he got that way. If he had been running for something back in Mason County he never in God's world would have been that way. He would have taken a
(40)   perfectly realistic view of things and counted up his chances. Or if he had got into the gubernatorial primary on his own hook, he would have taken a realistic view. But this was different. He had been called. He had been
(45)   touched. He had been summoned. And he was a little bit awestruck by the fact. It seems incredible that he hadn't taken one look at Tiny Duffy and his friends and realized that things might not be absolutely on the level. But
(50)   actually, as I figured it, it wasn't incredible. For the voice of Tiny Duffy summoning him was nothing but the echo of a certainty and a blind compulsion within him, the thing that had made him sit up in his room, night after
(55)   night, rubbing the sleep out of his eyes, to write the fine phrases and the fine ideas in the big ledger or to bend with a violent, almost physical intensity over the yellow page of an old law book. For him to deny the voice of
(60)   Tiny Duffy would have been as difficult as for a saint to deny the voice that calls in the night.

He wasn't really in touch with the world. He was not only bemused by the voice he had heard. He was bemused by the very grandeur
(65)   of the position to which he aspired. The blaze of light hitting him in the eyes blinded him. After all, he had just come out of the dark....

Now read the first paragraph, even the first sentence, "…He was a lawyer now" (line 1). What does this statement connote? Look closely at the sentences that follow it. Note details such as the nature of Willie's overalls and the quality of his room. What do they reveal about Willie's character? See if you can determine why achieving the bar took Willy so long.

The subsequent paragraphs provide a brief insight into the changes that Willie experiences after becoming a lawyer. How are these changes manifested? How would you characterize Tiny Duffy and his friends? What effect do they have upon Willie and how does the language of the passage—lines such as "He had been called. He had been touched. He had been summoned" (lines 44-45)—reveal both the nature of that effect and Willie's response to it? How does the image of Willie studying long into the night coalesce with the innuendo that surrounds Tiny Duffy? What does the concluding image/symbol/allusion reveal about Willie's character? His aspirations? What do you believe the author is trying to say/show about Willie Stark?

As you might have already guessed, good readers actively ask questions, underline or mark important points or interesting language, and annotate the passage as they read it. In so doing, they often anticipate the types of questions an examination may pose. This helps in several ways—by reassuring the reader that he/she has read the passage well; by making it easier to locate the lines that reveal the most profound thought or the most interesting diction, syntax and/or figurative language; and by helping to crystallize for the reader an overall impression of what the author is trying to convey. Remember: most of these selections are excerpts from longer works and function more as vignettes than as bearers of the entire work's message.

Now it's time to revisit this passage. Let's see how well you have anticipated the questions that follow it.

Questions 1-9. Refer to the following passage.

....He was a lawyer now. He could hang the overalls on a nail and let them stiffen with the last sweat he had put into them. He could rent himself a room over the dry-goods store in
(5) Mason City and call it his office, and wait for somebody to come up the stairs where it was so dark you had to feel your way and where it smelled like the inside of an old trunk that's been in the attic twenty years. He was a lawyer
(10) now and it had taken him a long time. It had taken him a long time because he had had to be a lawyer on his own terms and in his own way. But that was over. But maybe it had taken him too long. If something takes too long,
(15) something happens to you. You become all and only the thing you want and nothing else, for you have paid too much for it, too much in wanting and too much in waiting and too much in getting. In the end they just ask you those
(20) crappy little questions.

But the wanting and the waiting were over now, and Willie had a haircut and a new hat and a new brief case with the copy of his speech in it (which he had written out in
(25) longhand and had said to Lucy with gestures, as though he were getting ready for the high school oratorical contest), and a lot of new friends with drooping jowls and sharp pale noses, who slapped him on the back, and a
(30) campaign manager, Tiny Duffy, who would introduce him to you and say with a tin-glittering hardiness, "Meet Willie Stark, the next governor of this state!" And Willie would put out his hand to you with the gravity of a
(35) bishop. For he never tumbled to a thing.

I used to wonder how he got that way. If he had been running for something back in Mason County he never in God's world would have been that way. He would have taken a
(40) perfectly realistic view of things and counted up his chances. Or if he had got into the gubernatorial primary on his own hook, he would have taken a realistic view. But this was different. He had been called. He had been
(45) touched. He had been summoned. And he was a little bit awestruck by the fact. It seems incredible that he hadn't taken one look at Tiny Duffy and his friends and realized that things might not be absolutely on the level. But
(50) actually, as I figured it, it wasn't incredible. For the voice of Tiny Duffy summoning him was nothing but the echo of a certainty and a blind compulsion within him, the thing that had made him sit up in his room, night after

(55) night, rubbing the sleep out of his eyes, to write the fine phrases and the fine ideas in the big ledger or to bend with a violent, almost physical intensity over the yellow page of an old law book. For him to deny the voice of
(60) Tiny Duffy would have been as difficult as for a saint to deny the voice that calls in the night.

He wasn't really in touch with the world. He was not only bemused by the voice he had heard. He was bemused by the very grandeur
(65) of the position to which he aspired. The blaze of light hitting him in the eyes blinded him. After all, he had just come out of the dark....

1. In the passage the speaker seems MOST interested in exploring the

   (A) arduous road Willie took from obscurity to prominence
   (B) uncharacteristic materialism that Willie experiences upon becoming a lawyer
   (C) negative effect Willie's new political acquaintances might have upon him
   (D) hidden aspirations that fueled Willie's pursuit of power
   (E) sweeping changes Willie might effect if he became governor

2. In documenting Willie's rise to prominence, the speaker uses contrasting images of

   (A) innocence and sin
   (B) darkness and illumination
   (C) youth and age
   (D) sleep and awakening
   (E) silence and sound

3. All of the following are used to show that Willie has moved on to a new aspect of his existence EXCEPT

   (A) his overalls
   (B) his office over the dry-goods store
   (C) his haircut
   (D) his hat and briefcase
   (E) his penmanship

4. The speaker repeats the phrase "He was a lawyer now" (line 1, lines 9-10) to convey Willie's sense of

(A) relief
(B) accomplishment
(C) superiority
(D) dejection
(E) responsibility

5. Ultimately, the speaker's implication that Willy "paid too much for" his success—"too much in wanting and too much in waiting and too much in getting…" (lines 17-19)—likely alludes to

(A) physical stress
(B) marital woes
(C) moral compromises
(D) financial expenses
(E) dilapidated accommodations

6. In the phrase "on his own hook" (line 42), the "hook" represents Willy's

(A) initiative
(B) money
(C) merits
(D) words
(E) personality

7. The three declarative sentences in lines 44-45— "He had been called. He had been touched. He had been summoned"—describe Willie in terms usually associated with a(n)

(A) seer
(B) underling
(C) sycophant
(D) meddler
(E) messiah

8. The details and diction of lines 51-59, "For the voice…of an old law book," depict Willie as

(A) troubled and insomniac
(B) determined and driven
(C) scholarly and reclusive
(D) dutiful and obedient
(E) anti-social and ascetic

9. Lines 65-67, "The blaze of light hitting him in the eyes blinded him. After all, he had just come out of the dark….," are BEST seen as a(n)

(A) visual image of brainstorming
(B) personification of light
(C) metonymy for celebrity
(D) implied metaphor of childbirth
(E) hyperbolizing of his new-found grandeur

Précis and Explication of the Passage from Robert Penn Warren's *All the King's Men*

The passage from Robert Penn Warren's thinly disguised fictional account of the rise and fall of Huey Long and political corruption in Louisiana marks a pivotal moment in the career of the Long-like figure, Willie Stark, who takes the first formal step in his ascension by becoming a lawyer. Though limited to the narrator's reflections on the importance of this achievement in Stark's life, the passage provides a brief but insightful glimpse into the character traits that drove him to it, as well as a figurative description of the possibilities that his becoming a lawyer portend, painting Willie as a messianic figure who has responded to both an external and an internal call.

The declarative statement, "He was a lawyer now" (line 1), that opens the passage is delivered in a tone of accomplishment, and the speaker's subsequent claim that Willie "could hang the overalls on a nail and let them stiffen with the last sweat he had put into them" (lines 1-3) suggests a trading of attire and places, the overalls representing the blue-collar, lower-class, agrarian roots from which he sprang through hard work and a compelling ambition. Now having achieved a professional degree (and the status that goes with one), he could open a practice even if for the moment it was in a ramshackle, Stygian, malodorous locale "where it was so dark you had to feel your way and where it smelled like the inside of an old trunk that's been in the attic twenty years" (lines 6-9). The speaker's observation that "It had taken him a long time because he had had to be a lawyer on his own terms and in his own way" (lines 10-12) conveys a sense of the stubbornness and self-reliance that emerge as important factors in Willie's rise to prominence. Nevertheless, the speaker also sounds an admonitory note, saying "If something takes too long, something happens to you. You become all and only the thing you want and nothing else, for you have paid too much for it, too much in wanting and too much in waiting and too much in getting" (lines 14-19). This implies that success for Willie had become almost an obsession, a compulsion so strong that he would sacrifice almost anything to secure it.

Still, the Willie depicted in the second paragraph seems a man poised on the edge of new and exciting opportunities. With his new hat, new briefcase, and handwritten speech which he had prepared "as though he were getting ready for the high school oratorical contest" (lines 26-27), he seems an innocent, youthful figure, one blissfully unaware of the cadre of suspect-looking political supporters, the "lot of new friends with drooping jowls and sharp pale noses, who slapped him on the back, and a campaign manager, Tiny Duffy, who would introduce him to you and say with a tin-glittering hardiness, 'Meet Willie Stark, the next governor of this state!'" (lines 27-33). In contrast, his seriousness is compared to that of a bishop (lines 34-35), implying a mien and morality that is in sharp opposition to the cronyism with which Tiny Duffy and these others resonate.

In the third and fourth paragraphs the speaker returns once more to commentary on Willie and "how he got that way" (line 36), a line that suggests a change in manner, belief, or both. Referencing Mason County, which seems to be the environment from whence Willie came, the speaker observes that Willie "never in God's world would have been that way" (lines 38-39), once again alluding to the elliptical and undefined "that way" and reinforcing Willie's transformation. In four simple declarative sentences—"But this was different. He had been called. He had been touched. He had been summoned" (lines 43-45)—the narrator paints Willy's ascendance in almost messianic terms, as if Willie had been chosen to do something extraordinary in an equally extraordinary moment. And yet at the same time he suggests that "the voice of Tiny Duffy summoning him was nothing but the echo of a certainty and a blind compulsion within him, the thing that had made him sit up in his room, night after night, rubbing the sleep out of his eyes, to write the fine phrases and the fine ideas in the big ledger or to bend with a violent, almost physical intensity over the yellow page of an old law book" (lines 51-59).

Comprising the longest sentence in the passage, these words imply that the external political machinations (symbolized by the voice of Tiny Duffy) were matched by an equally persuasive internal Siren, whose seductive call drove Willie to labor long into the night with a passion that was almost physically visible. Lines 59-61, "For him to deny the voice of Tiny Duffy would have been as difficult as for a saint to deny the voice that calls in the night," suggest that the fervency of Willie's vision and desire was tantamount to any external stimulus, and his summons to public service an almost spiritual one. Indeed, the final eight lines of the passage almost paint Willie as a mystic or a seer, someone not "really in touch with the world" (line 62). The concluding image of the passage—a comparison to a child's emergence from the darkness of the womb into the brilliance of human existence—provides a appropriate climactic metaphor that figuratively depicts the movement from ignorance to knowledge, from innocence to experience, and from rural obscurity to political prominence that characterized the career of Willie Stark.

1. In the passage the speaker seems MOST interested in exploring the **(D) hidden aspirations that fueled Willie's pursuit of power**.

Though the first two paragraphs focus foremost upon Willie's achievement of becoming a lawyer and the way it affects his attire, his appearance and his status, the speaker does begin to explore Willie's motivations when he talks about how long it took him to achieve this and how he "had to be a lawyer on his own terms and in his own way" (lines 11-12). While this initially seems to be a compliment of his perseverance and his self-reliance, later comments seem to suggest more suspect motives. For example, the speaker observes "It seems incredible that he hadn't taken one look at Tiny Duffy and his friends and realized that things might not be absolutely on the level" (lines 46-49), implying that Willie either had to be totally naïve or conscious of the corrupt political arena he was entering. He adds later that "the voice of Tiny Duffy summoning him was nothing but the echo of a certainty and a blind compulsion within him, the thing that had made him sit up in his room, night after night, rubbing the sleep out of his eyes, to write the fine phrases and the fine ideas in the big ledger or to bend with a violent, almost physical intensity over the yellow page of an old law book" (lines 51-59). The choice of the word "echo" suggests that Tiny's "summons" was a mere reflection of Willie's own secret thought and desire. Moreover, the image of Willie poring over the yellowed pages of a law book deep into the night testifies to his determination to succeed regardless of the sacrifice that he must make to do so. Choice D captures this best.

2. In documenting Willie's rise to prominence, the speaker uses contrasting images of **(B) darkness and illumination**.

This is evidenced by both the image of Willy laboring night after night over the yellow pages of an old law book and the implied metaphor of childbirth in the final paragraph: "The blaze of light hitting him in the eyes blinded him. After all, he had just come out of the dark…" (lines 65-67). As was indicated in the overall explication of the passage, this image of entering the world of light from the world of darkness symbolizes Willie's movement from ignorance to knowledge, innocence to experience, and obscurity to prominence.

3. All of the following are used to show that Willie has moved on to a new aspect of his existence EXCEPT **(E) his penmanship**.

That Willy is able to dispense with his overalls, attire more appropriate for a farmer than a lawyer; that he is able to get his hair cut and purchase a new briefcase; that he is able to rent a space over the dry-goods store and open a law office—all suggest a shift in his status. However, Willy writes out his speech in longhand in the exact same manner as he took notes while studying the law at night. This is the reasoning behind the selection of choice E as the answer.

4. The speaker repeats the phrase "He was a lawyer now" (line 1, lines 9-10) to convey Willie's sense of **(B) accomplishment**.

This is largely determined by tone. The word "now" suggests that Willie has reached a goal, the culmination of all those long nights of study. The fact that he can swap his sweaty overalls for nicer attire, rent a space and open a legal practice, afford a haircut and a new briefcase, and appeal enough to the local political bigwigs to have Tiny Duffy start introducing him as the state's next governor suggests that he has achieved a position of stature, of accomplishment; hence, the selection of B as the best answer.

5. Ultimately, the speaker's implication that Willy "paid too much for" his success—"too much in wanting and too much in waiting and too much in getting…" (lines 17-19)—likely alludes to **(C) moral compromises**.

Though this could possibly refer to the amount of work he put into his studies, these lines have an almost Faustian feel to them, as if Willie has struck some sort of dark bargain. The gerunds "wanting," "waiting," and "getting" are in turn suggestive of strong desire, long patience, and triumphant acquisition, and the speaker later refers to "a certainty and a blind compulsion" (lines 52-53) within Willie that confirm these characteristics. Moreover, the speaker's remark that "It seems incredible that he hadn't taken one look at Tiny Duffy and his friends and realized that things might not be absolutely on the level" (lines 46-49) seems to cast doubts upon Willy's naïveté and to suggest that in climbing this ladder he knew all along where he was headed and what he had to do to get there. Choice C suggests this best.

6. In the phrase "on his own hook" (line 42), the "hook" represents Willy's **(A) initiative**.

The "hook," it may be presumed, is what pulled him into the political arena, which would be his campaign manager, Tiny Jones, who is already introducing him as the "next governor of this state" (line 33). If it were to have been his own hook, that would logically mean his desire or initiative (A).

7. The three declarative sentences in lines 44-45— "He had been called. He had been touched. He had been summoned"—describe Willie in terms usually associated with a(n) **(E) messiah**.

These three lines suggest that Willie is the "anointed one," someone who has been elected to serve the people. The verbs in these sentences make Willie seem singular and special, and they are the type of words one traditionally sees applied to messianic figures. This is further supported by references to Tiny Duffy's "summoning" him and the comparison of Willie to a saint ("For him to deny the voice of Tiny Duffy would have been as difficult as for a saint to deny the voice that calls in the night," lines 59-61). The fact that Tiny sees him as the next governor is also compelling.

8. The details and diction of lines 51-59, "For the voice…of an old law book," depict Willie as **(B) determined and driven**.

The details in these lines show Willie laboring deep into the night, "rubbing the sleep out of his eyes" in order to stay awake and pursue his studies. A phrase such as "violent, almost physical intensity" captures the intensity with which he works. Choice B best reflects this.

9. Lines 65-67, "The blaze of light hitting him in the eyes blinded him. After all, he had just come out of the dark….," are BEST seen as a(n) **(D) implied metaphor of childbirth**.

The emergence from a dark world into a world of blinding light mirrors the movement from the womb into the world and metaphorically parallels Willie's emergence from humble agrarian roots into the world of power and politics. This is expressed by choice D.

Questions 10-18. Refer to the following passage.

Away with Systems! Away with a corrupt World! Let us breathe the air of the Enchanted Island.

(5) Golden lie the meadows: golden run the streams; red-gold is on the pine-stems. The sun is coming down to earth, and walks the fields and the waters.

The sun is coming down to earth, and the fields and the waters shout to him golden

(10) shouts. He comes, and his heralds run before him, and touch the leaves of oaks and planes and beeches lucid-green, and the pine-stems redder gold; leaving brightest footprints upon thickly-weeded banks, where the fox-glove's[1]

(15) last upper-bells incline, and bramble-shoots wander amid moist herbiage. The plumes of the woodland are alight; and beyond them, over the open, 'tis a race with the long-thrown shadows; a race across the heaths and up the

(20) hills, till, at the farthest bourne of mounted eastern cloud, the heralds of the sun lay rosy fingers and rest.

Sweet are the shy recesses of the woodland. The ray treads softly there. A film

(25) athwart the pathway quivers many-hued against purple shade fragrant with warm pines, deep moss-beds, feathery ferns. The little brown squirrel drops tail, and leaps; the inmost bird is startled to a chance tuneless note. From

(30) silence into silence things move.

Peeps of the revelling splendor above and around enliven the conscious full heart within. The flaming West, the crimson heights, shower their glories through voluminous leafage. But

(35) these are bowers where deep bliss dwells, imperial joy, that owes no fealty to yonder glories, in which the young lamb gambols and the spirits of men are glad. Descend, great radiance! Embrace creation with beneficent

(40) fire, and pass from us! You and the vice-regal light that succeeds to you, and all heavenly pageants, are the ministers and the slaves of the throbbing content within.

For this is the home of the enchantment.

(45) Here, secluded from vexed shores, the prince and princess of the island meet: here like darkling nightingales they sit, and into eyes and ears and hands pour endless ever-fresh treasures to their souls.

(50) Roll on, grinding wheels of the world: cries of ships going down in a calm, groans of a System which will not know its rightful hour

of exultation, complain to the universe. You are not heard here.

(55) He calls her by her name, Lucy: and she, blushing at her great boldness, has called him by his, Richard. Those two names are the keynotes of the wonderful harmonies the angels sing aloft.

(60) 'Lucy! my beloved!'

'O Richard!'

Out in the world there, on the skirts of the woodland, a sheep-boy pipes to meditative eve on a penny whistle.

(65) Love's musical instrument is as old, and as poor; it has but two stops; and yet, you see, the cunning musician does thus much with it!

10. Which of the following are implied by the diction and syntax of the opening paragraph?

   I. A need to discard the material and the traditional.
   II. A need to escape from a suffocating confinement to an airy freedom.
   III. A metamorphosis from the mundane to the mysterious.

   (A) I only
   (B) III only
   (C) I and II
   (D) II and III
   (E) I, II and III

11. In his elaborate depiction of the sunset in lines 4-43, the speaker employs all of the following literary devices EXCEPT

   (A) personification
   (B) inverted syntax
   (C) sensory images
   (D) metaphors
   (E) paradox

---

[1] A flowering plant

12. The "heralds" (line 10) that precede the descending sun are most likely

(A) mists
(B) rays of light
(C) tree-limbs
(D) streams
(E) shadows

13. The speaker implies which of the following about the effects of the "flaming West, the crimson heights [that] shower their glories through voluminous leafage" (lines 33-34) upon the "bowers where deep bliss dwells" (line 35)?

(A) That the sun destroys the natural tranquility of the forest.
(B) That the sun illuminates an otherwise dark and foreboding environment.
(C) That the sun makes lush vegetation withered and sere.
(D) That the sun is inferior and subservient to the enchanted beauty of the woods.
(E) That the sun rouses the dormant wildlife in the forest.

14. The phrase "Descend, great radiance!" (lines 38-39) BEST exemplifies which of the following literary techniques?

(A) apostrophe
(B) hyperbole
(C) irony
(D) simile
(E) synecdoche

15. Which of the following adjectives would NOT be an appropriate descriptor for the "home of the enchantment" as it is depicted in lines 44-67?

(A) idyllic
(B) bucolic
(C) secluded
(D) anachronistic
(E) tranquil

16. The speaker's exhortation, "Roll on, grinding wheels of the world....You are not heard here" (lines 50-54), does all of the following EXCEPT

(A) recall the speaker's opening declaration
(B) deride the dehumanization wreaked by industry
(C) suggest the imperviousness of the enchanted island to the disease of progress
(D) contrast the dissonance of the machine with the lines describing the "keynotes" of Richard and Lucy
(E) delight in the sinking of ships that threaten the serenity of this enchanted spot

17. That "Love's musical instrument" (line 65), like the penny whistle played by the shepherd boy, "has but two stops" (line 66) suggests that the speaker is referring to the

(A) "inmost bird" of the forest (lines 28-29)
(B) chorus of angels
(C) human voice
(D) "grinding wheels of the world" (line 50)
(E) human heartbeat

18. The images and contrast of environments that mark the passage seem MOST identified with which of the following literary periods?

(A) Metaphysical
(B) Elizabethan
(C) Romantic
(D) Victorian
(E) Modern

Précis and Explication of the Passage From George Meredith's *The Ordeal of Richard Feverel*

The passage from chapter nineteen of George Meredith's novel *The Ordeal of Richard Feverel* stands quite well on its own though its opening lines and closing romance allude to the central dilemma of the story. At the novel's core is the conflict between Richard's father, Sir Austin Feverel, and the authoritarian manner (called "the System") in which he self-educates his son. Seeing relationships with girls as an unnecessary distraction, Richard's father essentially prohibits him from contact with them, setting up the predictable clash of mores when Richard falls in love with Lucy, the daughter of a farmer. Since both the relationship itself and the agrarian class to which Lucy belongs make her anathema to Sir Austin, he predictably prohibits Richard from seeing her, but the love between them is so strong that they secretly marry in defiance of Sir Austin's ban. This passage thus depicts the archetypal nature of Richard's and Lucy's relationship as well as the Edenic environment in which their love for each other is affirmed.

The passage opens with somewhat of a 'declaration of independence,' though more of a personal one than a political one: "Away with Systems! Away with a corrupt World! Let us breathe the air of the Enchanted Island" (lines 1-3). The prepositional phrases in the first two lines emphasize the "Away" while the understood imperative and the climactic exclamations establish a tone of urgency. While the "Systems" may well refer to the one in with Richard has been educated, the word assumes a more generic connotation, suggesting any rigid set of beliefs that determines human behavior. The invitation here is for everyone who is so restrained by his or her shackles to exchange the stagnant atmosphere of the "corrupt World" for the free air of the "Enchanted Isle." Employing inversion, the speaker notes how "Golden lie the meadows: golden run the streams; red-gold is on the pine-stems" (lines 4-5), his syntax emphasizing the brilliant glow of the setting sun which emblazons all of nature as it descends. The repeated refrain "The sun is coming down to earth" (lines 5-6; 8) not only personifies the sun, but gives it a god-like feel as if Helios or Apollo himself were alighting. The sun's descent affects other aspects of nature as "the fields and the waters shout to him golden shouts" (lines 8-10) while the "long-thrown shadows" engage him in "a race across the heaths and up the hills, till, at the farthest bourne of mounted eastern cloud, the heralds of the sun lay rosy fingers and rest" (lines 18-22). In fact, the third and fourth paragraphs are replete with sensory images: a colorful diversity of trees and other flora, weed-bestrewn river-banks, and "purple shade" (line 26) in which bird and squirrel conduct their business. By the fifth paragraph the flood of crimson light "shower[s] [its] glories through voluminous leafage" (lines 33-34), blessing the natural landscape with "beneficent fire" (lines 39-40). Still, though the description of the descending sun is spectacular, the speaker remarks that this enchanted woodland "owes no fealty to [the setting sun's] glories" (lines 36-37), but rather that such "heavenly pageants, are the ministers and the slaves of the throbbing content within" (lines 41-43).

Like the forest of Arden in Shakespeare's *A Midsummer Night's Dream*, "this is the home of the enchantment" (line 44), a romantic setting in which the prince and princess (Lucy and Richard) meet and "like darkling nightingales…sit, and into eyes and ears and hands pour endless ever-fresh treasures to their souls" (lines 46-49). Here the speaker, recalling his opening declarations, again interjects the exhortation

> Roll on, grinding wheels of the world: cries of ships going down in a calm, groans of a System which will not know its rightful hour of exultation, complain to the universe. You are not heard here (lines 50-54).

Again delivering what seems an indictment of the dehumanizing qualities of industrialization, he instructs these entities to "complain to the universe," suggesting that their cries "are not heard here" in this secluded and idyllic environment.

The concluding lines of the passage introduce the characters of Richard and Lucy, who like their archetypal models Adam and Eve, address each other in this Eden-like setting with timid but loving words—their names—names which the speaker says are the "keynotes of the wonderful harmonies the angels sing aloft" (lines 58-59). These allusions to music help create an idyllic country scene in which "on the skirts of the woodland, a sheep-boy pipes to meditative eve on a penny whistle" (lines 62-64). Building upon the literal penny whistle, the speaker concludes with a musical metaphor, saying "Love's musical instrument is as old, and as poor; it has but two stops; and yet, you see, the cunning musician does thus much with it!" (lines 65-67). Here the musical instrument of love has to be the mouth, and its "two stops" its capacity for sound and silence. However, like the sheep-boy who coaxes out of these two notes a pleasant melody, so the "cunning musician" (either of the two lovers) is able to court his/her beloved with "endless ever-fresh treasures" (lines 48-49).

The multiple instances of sensory (and sensual) images, the archetypal characters and setting, and the concluding musical conceit present opportunities for the emerging AP English Literature student to sharpen his or her skills in a variety of areas as a precursor to the sample exams that appear later in this book.

10. Which of the following are implied by the diction and syntax of the opening paragraph?

    I. A need to discard the material and the traditional.
    II. A need to escape from a suffocating confinement to an airy freedom.
    III. A metamorphosis from the mundane to the mysterious.

(E) I, II and III

Lines 1-3, "Away with Systems! Away with a corrupt World! Let us breathe the air of the Enchanted Island," suggest via the word "Away" that both "Systems" and the "Corrupt World" should be tossed out or disregarded. Inasmuch as the first word connotes an orderly process and the second materialism, I is a valid answer. Moreover, the inverted syntax of the first two sentences, which accents the word "Away," implies a flight or retreat from these types of environments. This lends credence to II. III draws its support from the final sentence of the paragraph, in which the speaker advocates relinquishing the traditional life for a life of enchantment. When taken together, this information determines E to be the best answer.

11. In his elaborate depiction of the sunset in lines 4-43, the speaker employs all of the following literary devices EXCEPT **(E) paradox**.

Personification (A) is evident in the description of the sun which comes down to earth and "walks the fields, and the waters" (lines 6-7), leaving "brightest footprints upon thickly-weeded banks" (lines 13-14). Right before it sets, the sun is said to "lay rosy fingers and rest" (lines 21-22). The waters are also said to "shout to him golden shouts" (lines 9-10). Inverted syntax (B) is evident in lines 4-5, "Golden lie the meadows: golden run the streams; red-gold is on the pine-stems," while sensory images (C) abound, from the golden, red, lucid-green and purple colors, to the fragrance of the pines, to the "tuneless note" (line 29) sounded by the "inmost bird" (lines 28-29). Metaphor (D) is evidenced in the "race" the sun has with the growing shadows (lines 19-20), the references to "fealty" (line 36), the "vice-regal light" (lines 40-41), and "the ministers and the slaves" (line 42), as well as in the comparison of the light to a "pageant" (line 42). There are no examples of paradox (E) in this description.

12. The "heralds" (line 10) that precede the descending sun are most likely **(B) rays of light**.

Inasmuch as "heralds" are literally messengers who come before and that these particular heralds "touch the leaves of oaks and planes and beeches lucid-green, and the pine-stems redder gold" (lines 11-13), B is the most logical choice here.

13. The speaker implies which of the following about the effects of the "flaming West, the crimson heights [that] shower their glories through voluminous leafage" (lines 33-34) upon the "bowers where deep bliss dwells" (line 35)? **(D) That the sun is inferior and subservient to the enchanted beauty of the woods**.

The speaker tells the "great radiance" (lines 38-39), or the sun,"You and the vice-regal light that succeeds to you, and all heavenly pageants, are the ministers and the slaves of the throbbing content within" (lines 40-43). Since the "throbbing content within" refers to the inner sanctum of the forest, D is the appropriate choice.

14. The phrase "Descend, great radiance!" (lines 38-39) BEST exemplifies which of the following literary techniques? **(A) apostrophe**.

The speaker is addressing an inanimate object, the sun. This type of direct address of something natural is known as apostrophe (A).

15. Which of the following adjectives would NOT be an appropriate descriptor for the "home of the enchantment" as it is depicted in lines 44-67? **(D) anachronistic**.

Since the setting consists of flora and fauna and is described as "bowers where deep bliss dwells" (line 35), choices A and B are logical. The fact that this is labeled by the speaker the "Enchanted Island" (lines 2-3) and later described as a place "secluded from vexed shores" (line 45) in which the "grinding wheels of the world" cannot intrude (lines 50-54), lends support to choice C. Moreover, lines and phrases such as "treads softly" (line 24), "From silence into silence things move" (lines 29-30) and "You are not heard here" (lines 53-54) suggest that choice E has validity. Choice D, on the other hand, is not an appropriate choice because the word means "out of its time period."

16. The speaker's exhortation, "Roll on, grinding wheels of the world....You are not heard here" (lines 50-54), does all of the following EXCEPT **(E) delight in the sinking of ships that threaten the serenity of this enchanted spot**.

The reference to the "grinding wheels of the world" (line 50) recalls the speaker's censure of the "corrupt World" in lines 1-2, confirming A as present. The word "grinding," which alludes both to the nature of the machine and to the toll it takes on human beings, supports B while lines 53-54, "You are not heard here," defend C. The near onomatopoeic harshness of the word "grinding," on the other hand, contrasts the keynotes of Richard and Lucy, which are said to mirror the harmonies of heavenly angels. This confirms D. Though the speaker mentions the "cries of ships going down in a calm" (line 51), he does not "delight" in their tragedy, making E the exception.

17. That "Love's musical instrument" (line 65), like the penny whistle played by the shepherd boy, "has but two stops" (line 66) suggests that the speaker is referring to the **(C) human voice**.

This is determined by the loving exchanges of Lucy and Richard which the speaker says are the "keynotes of the wonderful harmonies the angels sing aloft" (lines 58-59). Each of the lovers speaks in turn: "He calls her by her name, Lucy; and she, blushing at her great boldness, [calls] him by his, Richard" (lines 55-57). The speaker uses a simile to compare the two-note melody played on a penny whistle by a shepherd-boy to that of "Love's musical instrument," suggesting that it, too, has "two stops" (line 66). He goes on to say that despite this limitation, "the cunning musician does thus much with it!" (lines 66-67). This extended metaphor of music thus compares the simple melody produced by the shepherd-boy to the simple exchange of devotion between Lucy and Richard. Each, in turn, is the "cunning musician" because, as the speaker relates in lines 46-49, "here like darkling nightingales they sit, and into the eyes and ears and hands pour endless ever-fresh treasures to their souls." Just as the opening and closing of the two holes on the penny whistle generate sound, the opening and closing of the mouth produce either sound or silence; thus, the selection of C as the best answer.

18. The images and contrast of environments that mark the passage seem MOST identified with which of the following literary periods? **(C) Romantic**.

The emphasis on the secluded and tranquil natural setting, one that is apart from what the speaker labels "Systems" (line 1), the "corrupt World" (lines 1-2) and the "grinding wheels of the world" (line 50), has most in common with the sentiments of the Romantic period. The retreat away from industrialization and the "fever of the world" to the tranquil solace of nature is reminiscent of poems written by William Wordsworth such as "The World is Too Much With Us" and "Tintern Abbey." Through its solitude and beauty, the "Enchanted Island" (lines 2-3) provides both an escape from and a spiritual panacea for these evils.

Questions 19-31. Refer to the following passage.

In the following passage a downtrodden, unemployed worker hears a speech that affects him deeply.

It was like coming suddenly upon some wild sight of nature—a mountain forest lashed by a tempest, a ship tossed about upon a stormy sea. Jurgis had an unpleasant sensation,
(5) a sense of confusion, of disorder, of wild and meaningless uproar. The man was tall and gaunt, as haggard as his auditor¹ himself; a thin black beard covered half of his face, and one could see only two black hollows where the
(10) eyes were. He was speaking rapidly, in great excitement; he used many gestures—as he spoke he moved here and there upon the stage, reaching with his long arms as if to seize each person in his audience. His voice was deep,
(15) like an organ....trembling, vibrant with emotion, with pain and longing, with a burden of things unutterable, not to be compassed by words. To hear it was to be suddenly arrested, to be gripped, transfixed.
(20) "You listen to these things," the man was saying, "and you say, 'Yes, they are true, but they have been that way always.' Or you say, 'Maybe it will come, but not in my time—It will not help me.' And so you return to your
(25) daily round of toil, you go back to be ground up for profits in the world-wide mill of economic might! To toil long hours for another's advantage, to live in mean and squalid homes, to work in dangerous and
(30) unhealthy places; to wrestle with the specters of hunger and privation, to take your chances of accident, disease and death. And each day the struggle becomes fiercer, the pace more cruel; each day you have to toil a little harder,
(35) and feel the iron hand of circumstance close upon you a little tighter. Months pass, years maybe—and then you come again; and again I am here to plead with you, to know if want and misery have yet done their work with you, if
(40) injustice and oppression have yet opened your eyes! I shall still be waiting—there is nothing else that I can do. There is no wilderness where I can hide from these things, there is no haven where I can escape them; though I travel to the
(45) ends of the earth, I find the same accursed system—I find that all the fair and noble impulses of humanity, the dreams of poets and

the agonies of martyrs, are shackled and bound in the service of predatory Greed! And
(50) therefore I cannot rest, I cannot be silent....For I speak with the voice of the millions who are voiceless! Of them that are oppressed and have no comforter! Of the disinherited of life, for whom there is no respite and no deliverance, to
(55) whom the world is a prison, a dungeon of torture, a tomb! With the voice of a little child who toils tonight in a Southern cotton mill, staggering with exhaustion, numb with agony, and knowing no hope but the grave! Of the
(60) mother who sews by candlelight in her tenement garret, weary and weeping, smitten with the mortal hunger of her babes! Of the man who lies upon a bed of rags, wrestling in his last sickness and leaving his loved ones to
(65) perish! Of the young girl who, somewhere at this moment, is walking the streets of this horrible city, beaten and starving, and making her choice between the brothel and the lake! With the voice of those, whoever they may be,
(70) who are caught beneath the wheels of the Juggernaut of Greed! With the voice of humanity, calling for deliverance! Of the everlasting soul of Man, arising from the dust; breaking its way out of its prison—rending the
(75) bands of oppression and ignorance—groping its way to the light!"
The speaker paused. There was an instant of silence, while men caught their breaths, and then like a single sound there came a cry from
(80) a thousand people. Through it all Jurgis sat still, motionless and rigid, his eyes fixed upon the speaker....

19. Of the following, which BEST characterizes the transformation undergone by Jurgis in the passage?

(A) boredom to interest
(B) cynicism to certainty
(C) agitation to calm
(D) bewilderment to mesmerism
(E) indifference to engagement

---

¹ listener (in this case, Jurgis)

20. The phrase, "two black hollows where the eyes were" (lines 9-10), implies which of the following about the orator?

    I. That he has been blinded by violence.
    II. That his face has been made skeletal by similar deprivations as those experienced by his audience.
    III. That his eyes are piercing and passionate in nature.

    (A) I only
    (B) II only
    (C) I and III
    (D) II and III
    (E) I, II and III

21. The BEST substitution for the word "things" in line 20 would be

    (A) words of incrimination
    (B) promises of change
    (C) conditions of living
    (D) expressions of empathy
    (E) threats of violence

22. In his attempts to persuade the gathering, the orator relies upon all of the following EXCEPT

    (A) gesticulation and dynamic movement
    (B) repetition of syntax to dramatize injustice
    (C) images of adversity that are recognizable to his audience
    (D) passionate exclamations and exhortations
    (E) an *ad hominem* attack upon those responsible for such suffering

23. The orator's initial words, "'You listen to these things....it will not help me'" (lines 20-24), suggest that his audience has become

    (A) jaded by his previous promises of reform
    (B) resigned to a lifetime of deprivation and suffering
    (C) disillusioned by political promises
    (D) selfish in their desire for individual, not collective, relief
    (E) tired of rehashing the particulars of their suffering

24. The orator uses the metaphor of the mill in lines 26-27 to convey the

    (A) industry's view of the workers as disposable
    (B) workers' invaluable contribution to the economy
    (C) workers' admirable sense of responsibility
    (D) workers' appreciation of steady work
    (E) industry's global accomplishments

25. The figurative phrase, "'the iron hand of circumstance'" (line 35), may be said to convey which of the following?

    I. The stranglehold of deprivation on the working class.
    II. The brute power of the industrial machine.
    III. The insensitivity of industry towards the plight of the labor force and their families.
    IV. The randomness of human suffering.

    (A) I only
    (B) III only
    (C) I, III and IV
    (D) I, II and III
    (E) I, II, III and IV

26. Which of the following BEST paraphrases the thought inherent in the phrase "'want and misery have yet done their work with you'" (lines 38-39)?

    (A) Want and misery have been overcome by individual perseverance and hard work.
    (B) Want and misery have been eradicated by the collective efforts of the workers.
    (C) Want and misery have persuaded the workers to heed the rhetoric of the speaker.
    (D) Want and misery have forced the workers to seek better paying jobs.
    (E) Want and misery have disabled, even killed, the workers.

27. Lines 42-44, "'There is no wilderness where I can hide from these things, there is no haven where I can escape them,'" imply the orator's

    (A) consciousness of the ubiquity of such oppressive conditions
    (B) reluctance to articulate these deprivations and sufferings
    (C) fear of reprisal by industry or by the law
    (D) visceral response to the conditions he sees
    (E) flight from the scruples of his own conscience

28. In referencing the "'millions who are voiceless'" for whom he says he is speaking (lines 51-52), the orator employs which of the following?

    (A) hyperbole
    (B) allusion
    (C) paradox
    (D) apostrophe
    (E) onomatopoeia

29. Throughout the course of his speech (lines 20-76), the orator figuratively associates materialism, industry and the greed which drives these economic pursuits with all of the following EXCEPT

    (A) a machine for grinding grain
    (B) slavery
    (C) a train or carriage
    (D) incarceration
    (E) a pestilence

30. Which of the following is NOT characteristic of the orator's comments in lines 20-76?

    (A) the use of climactic order to suggest the increasingly hopeless progression from suffering to death
    (B) imperatives that ceaselessly demand a redress of injustice by the captains of industry
    (C) a chorus of prepositional phrases that graphically depicts the litany of suffering endured by the poor
    (D) a fatalistic tone: individuals seemingly abandoned to a cruel and undeserving fate
    (E) a bitterly ironic religious allusion to the Resurrection of Jesus

31. Ultimately, the "unpleasant sensation, a sense of confusion, of disorder, of wild and meaningless uproar" (lines 4-6) that Jurgis experiences at the beginning of the passage may be said to foreshadow a(n)

    (A) physical illness
    (B) emotional breakdown
    (C) financial progress
    (D) intellectual epiphany
    (E) spiritual rebirth

Précis and Explication of the Passage from Upton Sinclair's *The Jungle*

This passage from Sinclair's muckraking novel occurs extremely late in the book, long after Jurgis' struggles in Packingtown and subsequent to his three separate turns in prison. By this time Jurgis has seen his family fall apart and his American dream disintegrate under the crushing weight of poverty, the deaths of loved ones, and his own battles with injury, alcoholism and despair. Having reached the nadir of his existence, Jurgis wanders into a political rally where he hears a speech delivered by a socialist orator that eloquently articulates the litany of abuses that Jurgis and others like him suffer at the hands of unscrupulous industry and union bosses. This impassioned call to arms penetrates deep into the consciousness of Jurgis, who gazes fixedly at the orator as if trying to determine his sincerity while still knowing he has experienced all of which the orator speaks.

The passage begins with two scenes of natural turbulence—"a mountain forest lashed by a tempest, a ship tossed about upon a stormy sea" (lines 2-4)—intended to capture the restlessness of the rally into which Jurgis has walked. Jurgis, who seems disoriented and discomfited by the commotion, observes in the orator a virtual mirror of himself, a man "tall and gaunt...[with] a thin black beard cover[ing] half his face, and...only two black hollows where the eyes were" (lines 6-10). The physical description of the man's face is skeletal with the added dimension of the preternatural that frequently characterizes the literary archetype of the seer. Speaking rapidly and charismatically, the man crosses the stage in excited forays, "reaching with his long arms as if to seize each person in his audience" (lines 13-14) and uttering with a voice "trembling, vibrant with emotion... a burden of things unutterable, not to be compassed by words" (lines 15-18).

Mesmerized by the histrionics and passion of the orator, Jurgis listens as he catalogs the many sufferings and privations which afflict the under-class of which Jurgis is a part. The diatribe is highly figurative with the orator metaphorically depicting industry as a "'mill'" which grinds up the poor for profit (lines 25-27), using personification/synecdoche to describe industry's vise-like grip on the poor as "'the iron hand of circumstance'" (line 35), utilizing diction to relate the deplorable conditions of industry to slavery (lines 48-49), and both personifying Greed as a predator and metaphorically presenting it as a "'Juggernaut'" that resembles the 'iron horse' of the railway (lines 70-71). The speech is replete with wonderfully rhythmic syntax, from parallel infinitive phrases ("'To toil long hours...to take your chances of accident, disease and death,'" lines 27-32), parallel inversions ("'There is no wilderness...there is no haven where I can escape them,'" lines 42-44), a dramatic trio of predicate nominatives ("'...a prison, a dungeon of torture, a tomb!,'" lines 55-56), and a long series of parallel prepositional phrases ("'Of them that are oppressed and have no comforter!....Of the everlasting soul of Man, arising from the dust; breaking its way out of its prison—rending the bands of oppression and ignorance—groping its way to the light!,'" lines 52-76). These arresting rhythms and the catalog of horrors which they recount stun Jurgis into silence, and he sits "motionless and rigid, his eyes fixed upon the speaker," perhaps foreshadowing a burgeoning intellectual epiphany (lines 81-82).

Though the passage ends with Jurgis in this frozen position, it is clear that the words have affected him deeply, that he has heard the Baptist-like voice of the orator crying in the wilderness and endeavoring desperately to awaken the slumbering, disillusioned giant that his audience represents. This is a particularly good passage to approach through a Socialist lens since, in the vein of works by Charles Dickens, Jack London and others, it explores the sordid effects of materialism and capitalism upon the working class poor who, like helpless victims, are "'caught beneath the wheels of the Juggernaut of Greed!'" (lines 70-71).

19. Of the following, which BEST characterizes the transformation undergone by Jurgis in the passage? **(D) bewilderment to mesmerism.**

Aside from the opening simile and its accompanying appositive clauses that depict turbulent scenes in the natural world, the speaker articulates the confusion Jurgis feels upon first entering the political rally: "[He] had an unpleasant sensation, a sense of confusion, of disorder, of wild and meaningless uproar" (lines 4-6). However, while listening to the gaunt, haggard orator, a virtual mirror of his impoverished and frustrated self, he becomes entranced by his passionate words, gesticulations, and movements. As the speaker observes, "To hear it was to be suddenly arrested, to be gripped, transfixed" (lines 18-19). Jurgis listens to him rail against the deprivations and abuses he has himself known firsthand in the slaughterhouses of Packingtown, in the crooked dealings of realtors, in the death, dispossession and disgrace that have plagued his family, and, by speech's end, he is frozen in silence, "motionless and rigid, his eyes fixed upon the speaker…" (lines 81-82). This is captured by choice D.

20. The phrase, "two black hollows where the eyes were" (lines 9-10), implies which of the following about the orator?

   I. That he has been blinded by violence.
   II. That his face has been made skeletal by similar deprivations as those experienced by his audience.
   III. That his eyes are piercing and passionate in nature.

(D) II and III.

The black sunken eyes of the orator (as well as his gaunt and haggard face) make him look skeletal, cadaverous, like a "dead man walking." This and his intimate familiarity with the sufferings experienced by his audience point to the validity of II. III, on the other hand, is a natural implication both of the depth of his eyes and of the arresting effect he has upon Jurgis and the rest of the audience. There is no support for I anywhere in the passage.

21. The BEST substitution for the word "things" in line 20 would be **(C) conditions of living**.

The selection of C derives from a subsequent part of that sentence, "'and you say, 'Yes, they are true, but they have been that way always'" (lines 21-22). Though an elliptical line with no direct clarification of its two third-person-plural pronouns, logic suggests that the orator is referring to something that is both unpleasant and seemingly permanent. The subsequent line, also elliptical, suggests that "'Maybe it will come, but not in my time—It will not help me'" (lines 23-24). Again, though neither "it" has a clear antecedent, logic suggests they allude to change or deliverance from suffering, things that he alludes to later in the oration. This is further supported by his subsequent observation, "'And so you return to your daily round of toil, you go back to be ground up for profits in the world-wide mill of economic might! To toil long hours for another's advantage, to live in mean and squalid homes, to work in dangerous and unhealthy places; to wrestle with the specters of hunger and privation, to take your chances of accident, disease and death'" (lines 24-32), which implies that the people in his audience continue to accept these conditions of life because there is no sign of redress on the horizon.

22. In his attempts to persuade the gathering, the orator relies upon all of the following EXCEPT **(E) an *ad hominem* attack upon those responsible for such suffering**.

Lines 10-14 state, "He was speaking rapidly, in great excitement; he used many gestures—as he spoke he moved here and there upon the stage, reaching with his long arms as if to seize each person in his audience," validating A. Passages such as this one in lines 27-32, "'To toil long hours for another's advantage, to live in mean and squalid homes, to work in dangerous and unhealthy places; to wrestle with the specters of hunger and privation, to take your chances of accident, disease and death,'" support B. The images of the child laborer, the tenement mother, the dying beggar, and the young girl torn between becoming a prostitute and committing suicide (lines 56-68) defend C while the description of the orator's voice as "deep, like an organ….trembling, vibrant with emotion, with pain and longing" (lines 14-16) and the numerous exclamation points support D. Inasmuch as the orator never names the sweatshop owners or others who may be responsible but instead indicts a personified "Greed," choice E can have no validity.

23. The orator's initial words, "'You listen to these things….it will not help me'" (lines 20-24), suggest that his audience has become **(B) resigned to a lifetime of deprivation and suffering**.

The fact that the people in the audience believe that deliverance and redress cannot help them or will not come in their lifetimes suggests they have resigned themselves to suffering. This is why the orator remarks "'And so you return to your daily round of toil, you go back to be ground up for profits in the world-wide mill of economic might! To toil long hours for another's advantage, to live in mean and squalid homes, to work in dangerous and unhealthy places; to wrestle with the specters of hunger and privation, to take your chances of accident, disease and death'" (lines 24-32). No one who saw the potential for change would accept these intolerable conditions, but these people have sadly accepted that their lot will never change. Both A and C imply that they have either grown tired of or disillusioned by previous reformers and politicians, something the text does not provide any evidence to support, and D and E are also baseless; thus, the selection of B as the best answer.

24. The orator uses the metaphor of the mill in lines 26-27 to convey the **(A) industry's view of the workers as disposable**.

The selection of choice A comes directly out of the diction which suggests that these people will be "'ground up for profits'" by the "'world-wide mill of economic might!'" The mill, traditionally a machine for grinding corn or a similar agrarian product, here disposes of people in a similarly crushing way. The metaphor also suggests that this is a universal dilemma and that Packingtown is just the Chicago version of this oppressive system.

25. The figurative phrase, "'the iron hand of circumstance'" (line 35), may be said to convey which of the following?

    I. The stranglehold of deprivation on the working class.
    II. The brute power of the industrial machine.
    III. The insensitivity of industry towards the plight of the labor force and their families.
    IV. The randomness of human suffering.

   (D) I, II and III.

   I is supported by the image of asphyxiation inherent in the hand closing on the people tighter and tighter with each passing day. II is supported by the phrase "'ground up,'" which has been sufficiently elaborated upon in the explanation of the previous question, and by the "'iron'" nature of the hand, which calls to mind something industrial or mechanical. Similarly, III also draws upon the word "'iron,'" but in this case as something incapable of feeling, something man-made and 'unnatural,' not flesh and blood. IV is eliminated by the fact that such suffering is being experienced by all and not by some random individuals.

26. Which of the following BEST paraphrases the thought inherent in the phrase "'want and misery have yet done their work with you'" (lines 38-39)? **(E) Want and misery have disabled, even killed the workers**.

   The phrase "'done with you'" suggests a completion, a 'using up' so to speak. Since the orator has earlier suggested that these people are to be "'ground up for profits in the world-wide mill of economic might!'" (lines 25-27) or returned to their intolerable working conditions "'to take [their] chances of accident, disease and death'" (lines 31-32), E is a logical selection here.

27. Lines 42-44, "'There is no wilderness where I can hide from these things, there is no haven where I can escape them,'" imply the orator's **(A) consciousness of the ubiquity of such oppressive conditions**.

   Since the socialist orator is clearly an advocate for these suffering individuals, and since he spends his entire speech documenting these sufferings in graphic and poignant fashion, B, C, D and E are not credible. What he is saying is that were he to wish to turn his back on these miseries, there is no place in the world where he could go to avoid them, the sufferings brought on by "'predatory Greed'" being so pervasive. Choice A captures this most accurately.

28. In referencing the "'millions who are voiceless'" for whom he says he is speaking (lines 51-52), the orator employs which of the following? **(C) paradox**.

   Paradox, defined as an "apparent contradiction," is manifest in the orator's claim that he "'speak[s] with the voice of the millions who are voiceless!'" (lines 51-52). Though the claim seems self-contradictory, the reader understands that the orator sees himself as the articulator of the sufferings of the downtrodden, those who cannot speak for themselves.

29. Throughout the course of his speech (lines 20-76), the orator figuratively associates materialism, industry and the greed which drives these economic pursuits with all of the following EXCEPT **(E) a pestilence**.

The reference to the "'mill'" in lines 25-27 confirms A while the diction in lines 48-49, "'shackled and bound in the service of predatory Greed!'" confirms B. Lines 70-71, "'caught beneath the wheels of the Juggernaut of Greed!'" validate C while lines 55-56, "'a prison, a dungeon of torture,'" as well as line 74, "'breaking its way out of its prison,'" support D. Choice E draws no support from anywhere in the passage.

30. Which of the following is NOT characteristic of the orator's comments in lines 20-76? **(B) imperatives that ceaselessly demand a redress of injustice by the captains of industry**.

Phrases such as "'accident, disease and death'" (line 32) and "'a prison, a dungeon of torture, a tomb!'" (lines 55-56) confirm A while the sequence of six prepositional phrases starting with "Of" in lines 52-76 validates C. The overall tone of the piece—derived from such diction as "'mean and squalid'" (lines 28-29), "'dangerous and unhealthy'" (lines 29-30), "'accident, disease and death'" (line 32), "'the disinherited of life, for whom there is no respite and no deliverance'" (lines 53-54), "'knowing no hope but the grave'" (line 59) and many others—is clearly a fatalistic one (D) while lines 72-76, "'Of the everlasting soul of Man, arising from the dust; breaking its way out of its prison—rending the bands of oppression and ignorance—groping its way to the light!,'" seem to allude to the Resurrection of Jesus. The bitter irony evolves from the fact that in Christian mythology Jesus rises from the dead after three days; however, the allusion here suggests that only the "'soul of Man'" (line 73) enjoys this freedom, that his physical life is spend in bondage to this "'accursed system'" (lines 45-46) of materialism. Only B draws no support from the passage.

31. Ultimately, the "unpleasant sensation, a sense of confusion, of disorder, of wild and meaningless uproar" (lines 4-6) that Jurgis experiences at the beginning of the passage may be said to foreshadow a(n) **(D) intellectual epiphany**.

The final image of Jurgis, sitting "motionless and rigid, his eyes fixed upon the speaker..." (lines 81-82) is somewhat reminiscent of Rodin's famous statue, "The Thinker." These lines reflect back to the speaker's observation in lines 18-19 that "To hear it was to be suddenly arrested, to be gripped, transfixed." Like the Wedding Guest who is stopped by Coleridge's Mariner, Jurgis has heard the 'Word' and finally understands the "'accursed system'" (lines 45-46) that has so ruined his life and the lives of others like him. As a result, choice D seems most appropriate.

Questions 32-44. Refer to the following passage.

In the following passage from Mary Shelley's *Frankenstein, Victor Frankenstein, who has* *created the creature, comes face-to-face with* *his progeny.*

As I said this, I suddenly beheld the figure of a man, at some distance, advancing toward me with superhuman speed. He bounded over the crevices in the ice, among which I had
(5) walked with caution; his stature, also, as he approached, seemed to exceed that of man....I perceived as the shape came nearer (sight tremendous and abhorred!) that it was the wretch whom I had created....
(10) "Devil," I exclaimed, "do you dare approach me? And do not you fear the fierce vengeance of my arm wreaked on your miserable head? Begone, vile insect! Or rather, stay, that I may trample you to dust! And, oh!
(15) That I could, with the extinction of your miserable existence, restore those victims whom you have diabolically murdered!"
"I expected this reception," said the demon. "All men hate the wretched; how, then,
(20) must I be hated, whom am miserable beyond all living things! Yet you, my creator, detest and spurn me, thy creature, to whom thou are bound by ties only dissoluble by the annihilation of one of us. You purpose to kill
(25) me. How dare you sport thus with life? Do your duty towards me, and I will do mine towards you and the rest of mankind. If you will comply with my conditions, I will leave them and you at peace; but if you refuse, I will
(30) glut the maw of death, until it be satiated with the blood of your remaining friends."
"Abhorred monster! Fiend that thou art! The tortures of hell are too mild a vengeance for your crimes. Wretched devil! You reproach
(35) me with your creation; come on, then, that I may extinguish the spark which I so negligently bestowed."
My rage was without bounds; I sprang on him, impelled by all the feelings which can
(40) arm one being against the existence of another.
He easily eluded me and said, "Be calm! I entreat you to hear me before you give vent to your hatred on my devoted head. Have I not suffered enough that you seek to increase my
(45) misery?...I am thy creature, and I will be even mild and docile to my natural lord and king if thou wilt also perform thy part, the which thou owest me. Oh, Frankenstein, be not equitable to every other and trample upon me alone, to

(50) whom thy justice, and even thy clemency and affection, is most due. Remember that I am thy creature; I ought to be thy Adam, but I am rather the fallen angel, whom thou drivest from joy for no misdeed. Everywhere I see bliss
(55) from which I alone am irrevocably excluded....".
"Begone! I will not hear you. There can be no community between you and me; we are enemies. Begone, or let us try our strength in a
(60) fight, in which one must fall."
"How can I move thee? Will no entreaties cause thee to turn a favourable eye upon thy creature, who implores thy goodness and compassion? Believe me, Frankenstein: I was
(65) benevolent; my soul glowed with love and humanity: but am I not alone, miserably alone? You, my creator, abhor me; what hope can I gather from your fellow-creatures, who owe me nothing? They spurn and hate me. The
(70) desert mountains and dreary glaciers are my refuge....These bleak skies I hail, for they are kinder to me than your fellow-beings. If the multitude of mankind knew of my existence, they would do as you do, and arm themselves
(75) for my destruction. Shall I not then hate them who abhor me?....The guilty are allowed, by human laws, bloody as they are, to speak in their own defence before they are condemned. Listen to me, Frankenstein. You accuse me of
(80) murder; and yet you would, with a satisfied conscience, destroy your own creature. Oh, praise the eternal justice of man! Yet I ask you not to spare me: listen to me; and then, if you can, and if you will, destroy the work of your
(85) hands....".

32. The passage implies that the MOST important difference between the speaker, Victor Frankenstein, and the being he has created involves which of the following?

(A) size and strength
(B) speed and agility
(C) misery and suffering
(D) love and responsibility
(E) guilt and innocence

33. Of the following, which BEST captures the respective tones of Victor and the being he has created as revealed by their dialogue?

    (A) remorseful and accusatory
    (B) derisive and appealing
    (C) apologetic and understanding
    (D) indifferent and desperate
    (E) rational and irrational

34. The author stylistically establishes Victor's antipathy for his creation through all of the following EXCEPT

    (A) diction that paints him as miserable and vile
    (B) metaphors that associate him with the diabolical
    (C) imperatives that exhort him immediately to depart
    (D) action verbs that threaten him with violence and destruction
    (E) rhetorical questions which suggest his regret for his action

35. The irony of the initial comments made by Victor to the creature in lines 10-17 involves the

    (A) sheer disbelief he feels at the audacity of the creature's approach
    (B) unexpected vacillation he displays in ordering the creature to go and to remain
    (C) menacing boasts he makes to such a physically superior foe
    (D) bootless wish he makes that he might restore its victims by killing his creation
    (E) ignorant belief that a devil could respond to reason

36. The creature's question to Victor, "'How dare you sport thus with life?'" (line 25), alludes to which of the following?

    I. Victor's initial experiment with procreation.
    II. Victor's callous refusal to acknowledge and embrace him as his own progeny.
    III. Victor's cavalier lack of concern for the welfare of his remaining friends.

    (A) I only
    (B) II only
    (C) I and III
    (D) II and III
    (E) I, II and III

37. In lines 35-37, "'...come on, then, that I may extinguish the spark which I so negligently bestowed,'" Victor does all of the following EXCEPT

    (A) challenge the creature to combat
    (B) allude to the genesis of his illicit creation
    (C) admit to the immorality of his creative action
    (D) rue the calm rationality with which the creature is imbued
    (E) restate his earlier desire to annihilate the creature

38. The creature's mild remonstrance of Victor in lines 41-56 is likely intended to

    (A) flaunt the erudition that he has acquired since his creation
    (B) show the disparity between his deserved recognition and his outcast existence
    (C) indict his creator, Victor, of scientific incompetence
    (D) account for the incongruity between his benign nature and his malicious actions
    (E) confirm Victor's perceptions of him as a demon and devil

39. In lines 51-56, "'Remember that I am....irrevocably excluded,'" the creature attempts to convey the disparity between how he should be treated and how he is being treated through which of the following?

    (A) metaphor
    (B) allusion
    (C) paradox
    (D) apostrophe
    (E) synecdoche

40. That the creature perceives the "'bleak skies'" (line 71) as displaying more kindness than is shown him by humanity BEST exemplifies which of the following?

    (A) hyperbole
    (B) pathetic fallacy
    (C) irony
    (D) apostrophe
    (E) personification

41. The urgency of the creature's appeal in the final paragraph is heightened by which of the following?

    I. A series of questions that reflects the creature's search for empathy and understanding.
    II. Declarations of his innocence of the crimes with which he is charged.
    III. Desperate imperatives by which the creature pleads for Victor's attention.
    IV. Imagery that depicts his status as a social pariah.

    (A) I only
    (B) III only
    (C) I, II and III
    (D) I, III and IV
    (E) I, II, III and IV

42. In light of the context in which it appears, the creature's comment in lines 81-82, "'Oh, praise the eternal justice of man!,'" is likely uttered with

    (A) sardonic bitterness
    (B) sincere gratitude
    (C) speechless wonder
    (D) righteous indignation
    (E) resigned despair

43. Which of the following words or phrases is LEAST effective in establishing the creature's expectation of reciprocal devotion from Victor?

    (A) "'bound by ties'" (line 23)
    (B) "'duty'" (line 26)
    (C) "'thy part'" (line 47)
    (D) "'owest'" (line 48)
    (E) "'satisfied conscience'" (lines 80-81)

44. According to the comments he makes in lines 18-31 and again in lines 41-56, the creature's misery derives MOST from the

    (A) general maltreatment of the wretched by other humans
    (B) equitability that Victor shows to others
    (C) rejection and abandonment of Victor, his creator
    (D) refusal by Victor to accept his "'conditions'" (line 28)
    (E) exclusion from the bliss that is enjoyed by other beings

Précis and Explication of the Passage from Mary Shelley's *Frankenstein*

Throughout Mary Shelley's great Gothic novel *Frankenstein*, the creature that Victor Frankenstein has pieced together from body parts gleaned from cemeteries and charnel houses and animated by a scientific method gleaned from natural philosophy and alchemy tries desperately to find and contact his maker, a maker who, horrified by his creation, has fled his laboratory and disowned the being he has engendered. This passage, taken from Chapter 10, precedes the shift in narration from Victor's perspective to that of the creature itself. Though in the subsequent six chapters the creature recalls both the discoveries he makes in the brave new world about him and the travails he suffers when people confront his ghastly frame, this is the first exchange of dialogue between the creature and Victor, the scientist who created him.

The encounter occurs in Chapter 10 when Victor, having returned to Switzerland to help his family cope with the abhorrent murder of his younger sibling, William—ostensibly by his revered caretaker Justine—elects to take a respite in the Alpine mountains, climbing the dizzying heights of Montanvert and seeking solace in nature. He is engaged in this pursuit when in the distance he beholds "the figure of a man…advancing toward [him] with superhuman speed" (lines 1-3), a figure he knows too well is that of his nefarious creation. Though the pair is almost mirror-like in their opposition, the Creature bounds over crevasses that Victor had negotiated with caution and dwarfs his ordinary proportions with his eight-foot size. These contrasts, however, soon cede the field to the greater contrast—the wide gap between Victor's antipathy and the Creature's sensitivity. Immediately Victor admonishes the Creature for his approach, threatening him with physical violence: "'Begone, vile insect! Or rather, stay, that I may trample you to dust!'" (lines 13-14). Moreover, his subsequent wish, "'And, oh! That I could, with the extinction of your miserable existence, restore those victims whom you have diabolically murdered!'" (lines 14-17), implies more his vindictive bent than any true mourning for the deceased. The diction employed by Victor—words such as "'Devil,'" "'vile,'" "'insect'" and "'miserable'"—paints the creature as infernal and sub-human and, as such, unworthy of compassion. In contrast, the Creature responds placidly and rationally, acknowledging how "'All men hate the wretched'" (line 19) and admitting that he who is "'miserable beyond all living things!'" (lines 20-21) must provoke an enormity of hate. At the same time he seems puzzled by Victor's animosity, the fact that his creator "'detest[s] and spurns[s]'" a creation to which he is "'bound by ties only dissoluble by the annihilation of one of [them]'" (lines 21-24). He admonishes Victor, telling him "'How dare you sport thus with life?'" (line 25) and demands that he "'Do [his] duty'" (lines 25-26) towards him as his creator. Rational though his request may be, his foreboding boast that he will "'glut the maw of death, until it be satiated with the blood of [Victor's] remaining friends'" (lines 30-31) suggests the vindictive carnage of which the monster is capable.

Victor's position, however, remains unchanged. Continuing to describe his creation in vicious or infernal terms—"'monster,'" "'Fiend,'" "'Wretched devil!'" (lines 32-34)—he says to the creature, "'You reproach me with your creation; come on, then, that I may extinguish the spark which I so negligently bestowed'" (lines 34-37). This line is particularly curious in that it both alludes to the lightning bolt that first piqued his scientific curiosity in an earlier chapter of the novel and intimates at least some consciousness of the reckless immorality of his experiment. Criticism of Mary Shelley's novel that views it in light of the Romantic period in which it was created sees *Frankenstein* as a retort to the previous age of Enlightenment, one that perceived the universe as rational and orderly and which firmly believed that leadership founded on an enlightened rationality could best insure progress in all aspects of society. According to William Walling, "the novel stands foremost among Romantic works that warn of the danger of the light privileged by the concept of the Enlightenment—including, not least of all, the active light in lightning and the scientific promise of electricity" (109). As an enraged Victor attempts to throttle his creation, the creature easily evades him and continues to plead his case in eloquent and poignant terms:

> 'Be calm! I entreat you to hear me before you give vent to your hatred on my devoted head. Have I not suffered enough that you seek to increase my misery?...I am thy creature, and I will be even mild and docile to my natural lord and king if thou wilt also perform thy part, the which thou owest me. Oh, Frankenstein, be not equitable to every other and trample upon me alone, to whom thy justice, and even thy clemency and affection, is most due. Remember that I am thy creature; I ought to be thy Adam, but I am rather the fallen angel, whom thou drivest from joy for no misdeed. Everywhere I see bliss from which I alone am irrevocably excluded....' (lines 41-56).

The creature's plea once again reinforces the antithetical nature of their beings: Victor faithless, hateful and quick to reject; the creature devoted, adoring and eager to embrace. In fact, the creature sees their relationship almost as one of fealty, the feudal compact between lord and vassal in which loyalty and service are exchanged for protection and provision. He believes he should have been Victor's Adam, the paragon of all creation; however, finding himself spurned and despised by his creator, he realizes he is closer to Lucifer, the angel driven out of heaven, and bemoans his similarly exiled state.

Despite the creature's entreaties, Victor will not budge. He tells the creature, "'Begone! I will not hear you. There can be no community between you and me; we are enemies. Begone, or let us try our strength in a fight, in which one must fall'" (lines 57-60). Again, he offers neither empathy nor affection, eager either to drive the creature off or to abort his existence. And again, the creature pleads for, if not love, at least justice. He begs Victor to "'turn a favorable eye upon [him]'" (lines 62-63), claiming how his "'soul [once] glowed with love and humanity'" (lines 65-66) though now he is miserable and alone. Conscious of the hatred spawned by his physical appearance, the creature poignantly observes "'These bleak skies I hail, for they are kinder to me than your fellow-beings'" (lines 71-72). Couched in this pathos is an equivalent measure of logos. Aware that the general populace would upon sighting him "'arm themselves for [his] destruction'" (lines 74-75), he asks reasonably, "'Shall I not then hate them who abhor me?....'" (lines 75-76). Noting the paradox of Victor's threats of violence, he posits "'You accuse me of murder; and yet you would, with a satisfied conscience, destroy your own creature'" (lines 79-81). Citing the prisoner's rights in the justice system, how "'The guilty are allowed, by human laws, bloody as they are, to speak in their own defence before they are condemned'" (lines 76-78), he begs Victor to listen to him and then, if it be his desire, to destroy the work of his hands.

This selection from Mary Shelley's *Frankenstein* provides in microcosm a poignant characterization of the creature that is behind the enduring appeal of the novel. It captures the ironic inversion of roles which permits the reader to perceive that despite the violent crimes he commits against humanity, the creature only yearns for love, acceptance and community, and that it is Victor, through his callous degradation and rejection of his creation, who is the true monster.

Walling, William. "*Frankenstein* in the Context of English Romanticism." Approaches to Teaching Shelley's *Frankenstein*. Stephen Behrendt, ed. New York: Modern Language Association, 1990: 105-111.

32. The passage implies that the MOST important difference between the speaker, Victor Frankenstein, and the being he has created involves which of the following? **(D) love and responsibility**.

Though the monster's eight-foot height dwarfs that of its creator (A); though he bounds over dangerous crevices that Victor must negotiate with extreme care (B); and though (at least initially) he is as innocent as a newly-formed Adam (E), none of these three supersedes D in importance. The creature looks upon Victor with adoration and devotion, believing rightfully that Victor owes him love and care as his creator. He tells Victor "'I am thy creature, and I will be even mild and docile to my natural lord and king if thou wilt also perform thy part, the which thou owest me. Oh, Frankenstein, be not equitable to every other and trample upon me alone, to whom thy justice, and even thy clemency and affection, is most due'" (lines 45-51). Victor, however, continually addresses him in derogatory terms, calling him a "'Devil'" (line 10), a "'vile insect'" (line 13), an "'Abhorred monster'" (line 32) and a "'Wretched devil'" (line 34) while more than once expressing his desire to kill him. This makes D the best choice here. Choice C may be eliminated by the simple fact that both Victor and his creation suffer, the former from the guilt of his scientific transgression, the latter from the social rejection and exclusion which he experiences.

33. Of the following, which BEST captures the respective tones of Victor and the being he has created as revealed by their dialogue? **(B) derisive and appealing**.

As was indicated in the explanation of the previous question, Victor addresses his creation in terms that associate him with infernal, wretched and base things. He repeats the command "'Begone'" (lines 13, 57, 59) reflecting his desire to spurn the being he has created, and he expresses the wish to "'trample [him] to dust'" (line 14) or to "'extinguish the spark which [he] so negligently bestowed'" (lines 36-37). The tone of every one of his comments to the creature drips with malice. The creature, on the other hand, asks Victor to do "'[his] duty'" (line 26) towards him. He approaches him with rational, appealing words, saying "'I entreaty you to hear me before you give vent to your hatred on my devoted head'" (lines 41-43), asking Victor to "'be not equitable to every other and trample upon me alone, to whom thy justice, and even thy clemency and affection, is most due'" (lines 48-51). He responds to Victor's malice by exploring new ways in which to reach him: "'How can I move thee? Will no entreaties cause thee to turn a favourable eye upon thy creature, who implores thy goodness and compassion?'" (lines 61-64), appealing to his empathy, his reason, his sense of equity and justice. In lines 82-85, "'Yet I ask you not to spare me: listen to me; and then, if you can, and if you will, destroy the work of your hands….,'" he even agrees to the terms of his own destruction if Victor will only cease his malicious diatribe long enough to hear his tale. Choice B reflects this most accurately.

34. The author stylistically establishes Victor's antipathy for his creation through all of the following EXCEPT **(E) rhetorical questions which suggest his regret for his action**.

Victor labels his creation a "'vile insect'" (line 13) and a "'Wretched devil'" (line 34), labeling his life a "'miserable existence'" (line 16). He calls him a "'Devil'" (line 10), an "'Abhorred monster'" (line 32), a "'Fiend'" (line 32) and a "'Wretched devil'" (line 34). He three times repeats the imperative "'Begone'" (lines 13, 57, 59) and says he wishes to "'trample [him] to dust'" (line 14) and "'extinguish the spark which [he] so negligently bestowed'" (lines 36-37). In addition, he questions the creature "'And do not you fear the fierce vengeance of my arm wreaked on your miserable head?'" (lines 11-13). This information supports the presence of choices A, B, C and D respectively. The questions which Victor asks are not self-directed but rather reflect his amazement that a being who has committed such abominable murders can return to face him; thus, the elimination of E as a plausible answer.

35. The irony of the initial comments made by Victor to the creature in lines 10-17 involves the **(C) menacing boasts he makes to such a physically superior foe**.

That the creature's stature "seem[s] to exceed that of man" (line 6) and that he approaches Victor with "superhuman speed" (line 3), bounding over the dangerous crevices with apparent ease suggests that the threats made by Victor in lines 10-17 are threats in word alone; that the creature is capable of destroying Victor, as he has destroyed previous victims, much more readily than Victor can destroy him.

36. The creature's question to Victor, "'How dare you sport thus with life?'" (line 25), alludes to which of the following?

    I. Victor's initial experiment with procreation.
   II. Victor's callous refusal to acknowledge and embrace him as his own progeny.
  III. Victor's cavalier lack of concern for the welfare of his remaining friends.

(E) I, II and III.

Victor Frankenstein, as we know, has already "'sport[ed] with life'" (line 25) in his decision to fashion this creature out of body parts and animate him via some scientific or near-scientific process. However, this question is directed at Victor's decision to "'detest and spurn'" (lines 21-22) his creation, abdicating his responsibility as creator. The creature demands of Victor, "'Do your duty towards me, and I will do mine towards you and the rest of mankind'" (lines 25-27), but Victor threateningly responds "'You reproach me with your creation; come on, then, that I may extinguish the spark which I so negligently bestowed'" (lines 34-37), paying no heed to the creature's threat to "'glut the maw of death, until it be satiated with the blood of [his] remaining friends'" (lines 30-31). These details confirm the accuracy of I, II and III, making E the best choice.

37. In lines 35-37, "'…come on, then, that I may extinguish the spark which I so negligently bestowed,'" Victor does all of the following EXCEPT **(D) rue the calm rationality with which the creature is imbued**.

The phrase "'come on, then'" is an invitation to combat while the phrase "'extinguish the spark'" restates Victor's earlier wish to "'trample [the creature] to dust'" (line 14). This confirms choices A and E. The word "'spark'" alludes to the lightning that Victor witnesses earlier in the novel, a phenomenon that "sparks" his desire to create while the phrase "'negligently bestowed'" suggests that Victor is at least partially conscious of his wrongdoing. This confirms choices B and C. While the creature certainly displays a calm rationality in his conversation with Victor, this line does not suggest that Victor rues it in any way. This makes D the exception.

38. The creature's mild remonstrance of Victor in lines 41-56 is likely intended to **(B) show the disparity between his deserved recognition and his outcast existence**.

The creature tells Victor to "'Be calm!'" (line 41), begging him not to add further misery to that which he is already experiencing. He reminds Victor that he is his creature and Victor his "'natural lord and king'" (line 46) to whom he will be "'mild and docile'" (line 46) as long as Victor lives up to his obligations to him. He rebukes Victor, saying "'Oh, Frankenstein, be not equitable to every other and trample upon me alone, to whom thy justice, and even thy clemency and affection, is most due'" (lines 48-51). He reminds him in lines 51-56, "'Remember that I am thy creature; I ought to be thy Adam, but I am rather the fallen angel, whom thou drivest from joy for no misdeed. Everywhere I see bliss from which I alone am irrevocably excluded….'." These lines, which allude both to the Book of Genesis and to Milton's *Paradise Lost*, imply that due to Victor's abdication of responsibility for his creation, the creature is less Adam than Lucifer, less the lord of all creation and more the defrocked angel sent plummeting out of heaven into the infernal regions of Hell. The creature's use of the righteous "'ought to be'" suggests that he has been cheated of a deserved position and excluded from a bliss that is deservedly his. Choice B captures this best.

39. In lines 51-56, "'Remember that I am….irrevocably excluded,'" the creature attempts to convey the disparity between how he should be treated and how he is being treated through which of the following? **(B) allusion**.

The references here to Adam, the paragon of all creation, and "'the fallen angel,'" an obvious reference to Lucifer, the rebellious angel cast out of Heaven, are clear Biblical allusions which, taken in tandem, show the disparity between how the monster feels he should be treated and Victor's callous rejection of him.

40. That the creature perceives the "'bleak skies'" (line 71) as displaying more kindness than is shown him by humanity BEST exemplifies which of the following? **(C) irony**.

Though the fact that the "'bleak skies'" show "'kindness'" reflects both personification (E) and pathetic fallacy (B), the best answer here is irony primarily because these are human emotions that virtually none of the humans in the novel display toward the creature. Rather, as the creature himself notes in lines 19-21, "'All men hate the wretched; how, then, must I be hated, whom am miserable beyond all living things!'" He expresses similar sentiments in lines 54-56 ("'Everywhere I see bliss from which I alone am irrevocably excluded....'") and in lines 67-69 ("'what hope can I gather from your fellow-creatures, who owe me nothing? They spurn and hate me'").

41. The urgency of the creature's appeal in the final paragraph is heightened by which of the following?

   I. A series of questions that reflects the creature's search for empathy and understanding.
   II. Declarations of his innocence of the crimes with which he is charged.
   III. Desperate imperatives by which the creature pleads for Victor's attention.
   IV. Imagery that depicts his status as a social pariah.

(D) I, III and IV.

The creature asks questions such as "'How can I move thee? Will no entreaties cause thee to turn a favourable eye upon thy creature, who implores thy goodness and compassion?'" (lines 61-64) and "'what hope can I gather from your fellow-creatures, who owe me nothing?'" (lines 67-69) in an attempt to make Victor empathize with his position (I). He says "'Believe me, Frankenstein'" (line 64) and "'Listen to me, Frankenstein'" (line 79), imperatives that plead for his creator's attention (III). And he uses the desolate images of "'desert mountains and dreary glaciers'" (line 70) and "'bleak skies'" (line 71) to depict the isolation into which he has been driven (IV). However, though he does in lines 64-66 lay claim to an initial goodness ("'I was benevolent; my soul glowed with love and humanity'"), he never suggests that he is innocent of any crimes versus humanity. In fact, part of his appeal to Victor is that "'The guilty are allowed, by human laws, bloody as they are, to speak in their own defence before they are condemned'" (lines 76-78). This acknowledgment of culpability removes II from consideration.

42. In light of the context in which it appears, the creature's comment in lines 81-82, "'Oh, praise the eternal justice of man!,'" is likely uttered with **(A) sardonic bitterness**.

The positioning of this comment largely determines the selection of A as the correct answer. Coming right on the heels of the creature's wry observation that Victor would "'accuse [him] of murder; and yet...would, with a satisfied conscience, destroy [his] own creature'" (lines 79-81), the comment highlights the injustice that the creature has experienced from all humanity, including his maker; how though he approached human beings with benevolence and good motives, he was met with revulsion, rejection and violence; how though he conceives of Victor as his lord and king, a being to whom he owes life, love and fealty, he is met with a denial, detestation, and a desire to extinguish his existence.

43. Which of the following words or phrases is LEAST effective in establishing the creature's expectation of reciprocal devotion from Victor? **(E) "'satisfied conscience'" (lines 80-81)**.

Choice A, "'bound by ties'" (line 23), suggests the closeness of creature and created both figuratively and literally in its recall of the umbilical cord that links mother and infant. Similarly, choices B, C and D all contain words that connote some measure of responsibility. The phrase "'satisfied conscience'" (lines 80-81), on the other hand, refers not to any debt Victor owes the creature as his creator, but to the sense of moral righteousness Victor displays in wanting to destroy his creation. This feeling is manifest in lines such as "'And, oh! That I could, with the extinction of your miserable existence, restore those victims whom you have diabolically murdered!'" (lines 14-17) and "'...come on, then, that I may extinguish the spark which I so negligently bestowed'" (lines 35-37). This makes E, "'satisfied conscience,'" the exception.

44. According to his comments in lines 18-31 and again in lines 41-56, the creature's misery derives MOST from the **(C) rejection and abandonment of Victor, his creator**.

In the first sequence of lines the creature speculates how much he must be hated given the human tendency to hate the miserable and the wretched. However, he specifically laments Victor's rejection and abandonment, saying "'Yet you, my creator, detest and spurn me, thy creature, to whom thou are bound by ties only dissoluble by the annihilation of one of us'" (lines 21-24). The creature feels it is Victor's duty as his creator to embrace, not spurn, him, telling him "'I am thy creature, and I will be even mild and docile to my natural lord and king if thou wilt also perform thy part, the which thou owest me'" (lines 45-48). In calling Victor his lord and king, the creature alludes to the feudal bond of fealty, figuratively linking this mutual commitment to the bond between creature and creator. He pleads with Victor, saying "'Oh, Frankenstein, be not equitable to every other and trample upon me alone, to whom thy justice, and even thy clemency and affection, is most due. Remember that I am thy creature; I ought to be thy Adam, but I am rather the fallen angel, whom thou drivest from joy for no misdeed'" (lines 48-54). Though all of the other choices have a degree of accuracy, it is choice C that has the greatest cumulative merit.

Questions 45-58. Refer to the following passage.

A girl came out of lawyer Royall's house, at the end of the one street of North Dormer, and stood on the doorstep.

It was the beginning of a June afternoon.
(5) The springlike transparent sky shed a rain of silver sunshine on the roofs of the village, and on the pastures and larchwoods surrounding it. A little wind moved among the round white clouds on the shoulders of the hills, driving
(10) their shadows across the fields and down the grassy road that takes the name of street when it passes through North Dormer. The place lies high and in the open, and lacks the lavish shade of the more protected New England
(15) villages....

The little June wind, frisking down the street, shook the doleful fringes of the Hatchard spruces, caught the straw hat of a young man just passing under them, and spun
(20) it clean across the road into the duck-pond.

As he ran to fish it out the girl on lawyer Royall's doorstep noticed that he was a stranger, that he wore city clothes, and that he was laughing with all his teeth, as the young
(25) and careless laugh at such mishaps.

Her heart contracted a little, and the shrinking that sometimes came over her when she saw people with holiday faces made her draw back into the house and pretend to look
(30) for the key that she knew she had already put into her pocket. A narrow greenish mirror with a gilt eagle over it hung on the passage wall, and she looked critically at her reflection, wished for the thousandth time that she had
(35) blue eyes like Annabel Balch, the girl who sometimes came from Springfield to spend a week with old Miss Hatchard....

"How I hate everything!" she murmured.
(40) The young man had passed through the Hatchard gate, and she had the street to herself. North Dormer is at all times an empty place, and at three o'clock on a June afternoon its few able-bodied men are off in the fields or woods,
(45) and the women indoors, engaged in languid household drudgery.

The girl walked along, swinging her key on a finger, and looking about her with the heightened attention produced by the presence
(50) of a stranger in a familiar place. What, she wondered, did North Dormer look like to people from other parts of the world? She herself had lived there since the age of five,

and had long supposed it to be a place of some
(55) importance. But about a year before, Mr. Miles, the new Episcopal clergyman at Hepburn, who drove over every other Sunday—when the roads were not ploughed up by hauling—to hold a service in the North Dormer
(60) church, had proposed, in a fit of missionary zeal, to take the young people down to Nettleton to hear an illustrated lecture on the Holy Land; and the dozen girls and boys who represented the future of North Dormer had
(65) been piled into a farm-wagon, driven over the hills to Hepburn, put into a way-train and carried to Nettleton.

In the course of that incredible day Charity Royall had, for the first and only time,
(70) experienced railway-travel, looked into shops with plate-glass fronts, tasted cocoanut pie, sat in a theatre, and listened to a gentleman saying unintelligible things before pictures that she would have enjoyed looking at if his
(75) explanations had not prevented her from understanding them. This initiation had shown her that North Dormer was a small place, and developed in her a thirst for information that her position as custodian of the village library
(80) had previously failed to excite. For a month or two she dipped feverishly and disconnectedly into the dusty volumes of the Hatchard Memorial Library; then the impression of Nettleton began to fade, and she found it easier
(85) to take North Dormer as the norm of the universe than to go on reading....

45. The speaker's description of the North Dormer village suggests that it is all of the following EXCEPT

(A) remote
(B) idyllic
(C) dormant
(D) vulnerable
(E) populous

46. In light of the context in which it appears, the word "frisking" (line 16) suggests which of the following?

    (A) whimsy
    (B) haste
    (C) intrusion
    (D) discordance
    (E) chill

47. Charity Royall's reaction to the stranger who loses his hat is BEST labeled

    (A) condescending and derisive
    (B) self-conscious and reticent
    (C) jaded and disinterested
    (D) prudish and proud
    (E) bemused and curious

48. The author conveys Charity's initial impressions of the stranger in lines 21-25 through which of the following?

    (A) noun clauses
    (B) participial phrases
    (C) inverted syntax
    (D) active verbs
    (E) implied metaphor

49. The diction in lines 26-31 that describes Charity's initial response to the young man possibly suggests that she

    (A) is embarrassed by her appearance
    (B) has an irrational fear of strangers
    (C) detests holiday spirit
    (D) is chary of romance
    (E) lacks compassion

50. Charity's self-consciousness is manifested by all of the following EXCEPT

    (A) her retreat into the house
    (B) her pretense regarding the key
    (C) her survey of herself in the hall mirror
    (D) her envy of Annabel Balch's eyes
    (E) her notice of the stranger who enters the Hatchard gate

51. Charity's comment in line 38, "'How I hate everything!,'" is BEST labeled a(n)

    (A) philosophical speculation
    (B) categorical condemnation
    (C) emotional outburst
    (D) ironical understatement
    (E) interior monologue

52. In proposing the school-children's trip to Nettleton, Mr. Miles likely desires to

    (A) further their religious instruction
    (B) create an opportunity for socialization
    (C) expand their intellectual horizons
    (D) relieve the tedium of North Dormer
    (E) inspire them to pursue missionary work

53. The nature of the verbs in the series of phrases, "piled into a farm-wagon, driven over the hills to Hepburn, put into a way-train and carried to Nettleton" (lines 65-67), suggests which of the following?

    I. The physical distance between North Dormer and their destination.
    II. The solicitous manner with which Mr. Miles cares for the North Dormer students.
    III. The ambitious nature of Mr. Miles' endeavor.

    (A) I only
    (B) III only
    (C) I and II
    (D) II and III
    (E) I, II and III

54. The list of experiences in lines 68-76 suggests that for Charity and her fellow-students their North Dormer existence has been

    (A) parochial
    (B) arduous
    (C) serene
    (D) vulgar
    (E) ascetic

55. That Charity finds the art lecturer's comments "unintelligible" (line 73) is most likely due to her lack of

    (A) aptitude
    (B) interest
    (C) erudition
    (D) focus
    (E) social refinement

56. The likely thematic intent of the anecdote about the trip to Nettleton is to

    (A) laud Mr. Miles' concern for the students of the North Dormer school
    (B) challenge Charity's assumption of North Dormer's being "a place of some importance" (lines 54-55)
    (C) foreshadow Charity's becoming custodian of the North Dormer library
    (D) deride the cultural vacuity of North Dormer society
    (E) intimate the possibility of escape from the confines of North Dormer life

57. The BEST equivalent for the adverb "disconnectedly" (line 81), used to describe Charity's later pursuit of culture, would be

    (A) tediously
    (B) half-heartedly
    (C) urgently
    (D) haphazardly
    (E) objectively

58. The concluding sentence of the passage (lines 80-86) implies that the epiphany experienced by Charity at Nettleton was

    (A) life-altering
    (B) unsubstantial
    (C) spiritual
    (D) baffling
    (E) ephemeral

Précis and Explication of the Passage from Edith Wharton's *Summer*

The passage from Edith Wharton's novella *Summer* is taken from the opening of the story and is primarily concerned with introducing the character of Charity Royall, daughter of the town lawyer. In fact, the opening sentence of the passage literally marks her debut when she steps out of the door of her father's house on a brilliant June afternoon.

The day is gorgeous with a "springlike transparent sky" that sheds an anomalous "rain of silver sunshine on the roofs of the village, and on the pastures and larchwoods surrounding it" (lines 5-7). North Dormer, the village in which she resides, seems an idyllic place, nestled among hills whose elevation makes it both remote and unprotected, "high and in the open, lack[ing] the lavish shade of the more protected New England villages…." (lines 13-15). Indeed, its name smacks of sleepiness, conjuring the French verb for sleep, *dormir*. It also calls to mind the dormer to a house, a place for an extra bedroom. The "North" dormer would be high and isolated, receiving the least sun and further isolating its resident's experiences. The idea that the town is like a North-facing sleeping room adds to its somnolent character. Upon her emergence from her father's house in town, Charity notices a young man, a stranger to the town, whose straw hat has been blown off his head by the "frisking" wind and spun "clean across the road into the duckpond" (line 20). Though her study of him is brief, Charity notices "that he [is] a stranger, that he [wears] city clothes, and that he [is] laughing with all his teeth, as the young and careless laugh at such mishaps" (lines 22-25). Though no further mention is made of the gentleman, the speaker notes that Charity's "heart contracted a little, and the shrinking that sometimes came over her when she saw people with holiday faces made her draw back into the house and pretend to look for the key that she knew she had already put into her pocket" (lines 26-31). The diction here—words such as "contracted" and "shrinking"—suggests that Charity is wary of contact with members of the opposite sex. As the speaker later notes, the "few able-bodied men [were] off in the fields or woods" (lines 43-44), implying the scarcity of youthful males. Her pretense of looking for a key that she knows is in her pocket, her self-deprecating look in the mirror, and her wish "for the thousandth time that she had blue eyes like Annabel Balch, the girl who sometimes came from Springfield to spend a week with old Miss Hatchard…." (lines 34-37) smack of someone who is trying to avoid encountering a man while her murmured "'How I hate everything!'" (line 38) seems a stereotypical defense of her behavior. Only after noting the young man's passing through the Hatchard gate does Charity emerge into the village street. At the same time her actions may be viewed from a totally antithetical perspective: that of a young girl being amorously stirred for the first time, a young girl who is understandably self-conscious of her physical appearance which, she may feel. is insufficiently appealing to the opposite sex.

In the latter half of the passage the speaker begins to examine Charity's nature, using a rhetorical question—"What, she wondered, did North Dormer look like to people from other parts of the world?" (lines 50-52)—to delve deeper into her character. Though a North Dormer resident since the age of five, Charity has begun to wonder about its relative importance. What initiates this questioning is her recollection of a school excursion arranged by a former teacher, Mr. Miles, who "proposed, in a fit of missionary zeal, to take the young people down to Nettleton to hear an illustrated lecture on the Holy Land…" (lines 60-63). Taking the most promising members of the class, Mr. Miles had "piled [them] into a farm-wagon, driven [them] over the hills to Hepburn, put [them] into a way-train and carried [them] to Nettleton" (lines 65-67), ostensibly to expose them to a cultural experience they were most unlikely to experience in their own village. During this excursion Charity had for the first and only time, experienced railway-travel, looked into shops with plate-glass fronts, tasted cocoanut pie, sat in a theatre, and listened to a gentleman saying unintelligible things before pictures that she would have enjoyed looking at if his explanations had not prevented her from understanding them (lines 69-76),

undergoing a very small intellectual epiphany that made her question, to a degree, her previous perceptions of her native village. The speaker suggests that this trip to Nettleton had "developed in her a thirst for information that her position as custodian of the village library had previously failed to excite" (lines 78-80). However, though she later "dip[s] feverishly and disconnectedly into the dusty volumes of the Hatchard Memorial Library" (lines 81-83), her epiphany is short-lasting, and she soon "[finds] it easier to take North Dormer as the norm of the universe than to go on reading...." (lines 84-86).

The passage describes a girl on the verge of discovery—discovery (perhaps) of love, discovery of learning, discovery of self—and though in this passage the culmination of these discoveries is unresolved and incomplete, the overall tone of the passage is one of expectation and promise and just a bit of disturbance and naïveté.

45. The speaker's description of the North Dormer village suggests that it is all of the following EXCEPT **(E) populous**.

The speaker suggests that North Dormer "lies high and in the open" (lines 12-13); this confirms choices A and D. Lines 42-46, "North Dormer is at all times an empty place, and at three o'clock on a June afternoon its few able-bodied men are off in the fields or woods, and the women indoors, engaged in languid household drudgery," along with a name that connotes sleep (from the French *dormir*), confirm C. Choice B is derived from a combination of this remoteness and the rustic beauty of the pastures, larchwoods, grassy roads, and overall peacefulness of the landscape. The fact that the streets are empty at midday and there are only a "few able-bodied men" (lines 43-44) working in the fields and a "dozen girls and boys" (line 63) who represent the future of North Dormer leads to the selection of E as the exception.

46. In light of the context in which it appears, the word "frisking" (line 16) suggests which of the following? **(A) whimsy**.

The word "frisk" generally means to "search someone's person as for a concealed weapon," but it also means to "skip" or "gambol". In this instance the June wind is personified as "frisking down the street," lifting the hat off the head of a young man who is a stranger to the town, then depositing it in the duck-pond across the way. The wind's actions appear playful, and the man's laughter at this minor "mishap" confirms this. Choice A captures this best.

47. Charity Royall's reaction to the stranger who loses his hat is BEST labeled **(B) self-conscious and reticent**.

Upon first seeing the young man, Charity sizes him up, observing "that he was a stranger, that he wore city clothes, and that he was laughing with all his teeth, as the young and careless laugh at such mishaps" (lines 22-25). The diction in the paragraph that follows suggests that her "heart contract[s] a little" and she "shrinks" and "draws back into the house," pretending to look for a key which she has already placed in her pocket (lines 26-31). These actions suggest someone who is eschewing social contact, and the fact that it is her "heart" that contracts implies that she may be both attracted to and made uncomfortable by members of the opposite sex. Upon retreating into the foyer, she regards her appearance in the "greenish mirror with a gilt eagle over it…look[ing] critically at her reflection, wish[ing] for the thousandth time that she had blue eyes like Annabel Balch, the girl who sometimes came from Springfield to spend a week with old Miss Hatchard…." (lines 31-37). This suggests a young girl who is embarrassed by her own appearance and jealous of another's, perhaps because she does not feel herself sufficiently attractive or worthy of attention. Choice B reflects this most effectively.

48. The author conveys Charity's initial impressions of the stranger in lines 21-25 through which of the following? **(A) noun clauses**.

Lines 22-25, "that he was a stranger, that he wore city clothes, and that he was laughing with all his teeth, as the young and careless laugh at such mishaps," are all noun clauses functioning as the direct object of the verb "noticed."

49. The diction in lines 26-31 that describes Charity's initial response to the young man possibly suggests that she **(D) is chary of romance**.

The choice of D as the best answer is pretty much consistent with part of the explanation of question #47. The fact that it is Charity's "heart" that contracts and forces her to retreat into the hall of her father's house possibly implies that she is discreet and restrained and does not want to show visible emotional interest in the young man who has caught her attention. She also seems unsophisticated and inexperienced, wishing she had the blue eyes of Annabel Balch to attract him since she has no faith in the appeal of her own.

50. Charity's self-consciousness is manifested by all of the following EXCEPT **(E) her notice of the stranger who enters the Hatchard gate**.

This has also been adequately explained both in the overall explication of the passage and by the answer to question #47. Clearly, Charity had planned to walk out into the street, and her retreat into the house (A) is a defense against a potential close encounter with the young man she has observed chasing his hat. Her pretense of the misplaced key (B) is a similar artifice, an excuse for turning around and pretending that she has forgotten something to avoid possible contact with the stranger. Similarly, her gaze into the mirror (C) is not a Cinderella-like "who's the fairest of them all?" one, but a self-critical evaluation of her shortcomings, and her yearning for the eyes of a peer (D) implies a dissatisfaction with her own. Choice E is less a manifestation of her self-consciousness than it is the event which triggers it.

51. Charity's comment in line 38, "'How I hate everything!,'" is BEST labeled a(n) **(B) categorical condemnation**.

The word "hate" suggests "condemnation," the word "everything" is "categorical," a blanket abhorrence of all aspects of her existence. Though C has a measure of validity, it is not the BEST term for her comment among the choices provided.

52. In proposing the school-children's trip to Nettleton, Mr. Miles likely desires to **(C) expand their intellectual horizons**.

The fact that Mr. Miles' proposal to take the school-children to Nettleton is carried out in "a fit of missionary zeal" (lines 60-61) implies that it is devotional but somewhat impulsive, a spontaneous attempt to improve their educational lot. Though the lecture to which he takes them has a spiritual focus, the trip exposes Charity and her classmates to railway travel and colorful shops, to cocoanut pie and pictures of antiquity to which they might never have otherwise been exposed. Though choice A must be weighed carefully, the trip seems more geared toward intellectual edification than toward increasing their moral righteousness. And though it likely serves the ancillary purpose of achieving both B and D, these are not its primary intent.

53. The nature of the verbs in the series of phrases, "piled into a farm-wagon, driven over the hills to Hepburn, put into a way-train and carried to Nettleton" (lines 65-67), suggests which of the following?

    I. The physical distance between North Dormer and their destination.
    II. The solicitous manner with which Mr. Miles cares for the North Dormer students.
    III. The ambitious nature of Mr. Miles' endeavor.

(E) I, II and III.

The fact that Nettleton must be reached by two forms of transportation confirms both I and III since, if Charity is used as an example, it is unlikely that any of these children have been on a train, let alone gone to Nettleton. Moreover, the series of passive verbs suggests the care and solicitousness with which Mr. Miles secures his precious cargo as he shepherds the group from one destination to another; thus, the selection of E as the answer.

54. The list of experiences in lines 68-76 suggests that for Charity and her fellow-students their North Dormer existence has been **(A) parochial**.

The word "parochial" means "provincial" or "limited by experience." The remote nature of the North Dormer village makes it highly probable that this is the first trip to any place significant for the dozen boys and girls who attend the lecture in Nettleton. In fact, Charity calls it an "incredible day," saying that it was the "first and only time" she had "experienced railway-travel, looked into shops with plate-glass fronts, tasted cocoanut pie, sat in a theatre, and listened to a gentleman saying unintelligible things before pictures that she would have enjoyed looking at if his explanations had not prevented her from understanding them" (lines 68-76). These are the determining factors behind the choice of A as the best answer. Choice E, "ascetic," suggests that they have been bound to a North Dormer existence without any chance of seeing these things by a choice of austere lifestyle. This simply is too strong.

55. That Charity finds the art lecturer's comments "unintelligible" (line 73) is most likely due to her lack of **(C) erudition**.

The choice of C as the best answer is determined by the overall sense that a North Dormer existence does not expose one to the world. The trip Charity takes with Mr. Miles is by her admission the "first and only time" she has taken a train, sat in a theater, or eaten a delicacy, and the fact that Mr. Miles organizes the outing suggests that he recognizes the limitations of their North Dormer education. As a visiting clergyman and a man of spiritual erudition, he clearly realizes that these children cannot conceive of the locales of the Bible, having never been beyond the streets of their sleepy hamlet. Charity indicates she would have enjoyed the pictures more if the lecturer's explanations "had not prevented her from understanding them" (lines 75-76). This suggests that the intellectual content of the lecture is "over her head." Even later, when fired by a "thirst for information" (line 78) she pores over the dusty tomes of the Hatchard Memorial Library, this intellectual curiosity soon begins to fade, and she "[finds] it easier to take North Dormer as the norm of the universe than to go on reading…." (lines 84-86). These concluding lines imply that intellectual development is defeated by the parochial nature of North Dormer and that it is easy for Charity to succumb to these limitations.

56. The likely thematic intent of the anecdote about the trip to Nettleton is to **(B) challenge Charity's assumption of North Dormer's being "a place of some importance" (lines 54-55).**

When Charity first notices the strange young man, she poses a rhetorical question: "What, she wondered, did North Dormer look like to people from other parts of the world?" (lines 50-52). She confesses that "She herself had lived there since the age of five, and had long supposed it to be a place of some importance" (lines 52-55). However, the trip to Nettleton exposes her to a somewhat larger world, a world of railways and fancy shops and cocoanut pie. As a result, she admits that "This initiation had shown her that North Dormer was a small place…" (lines 76-77). Choice B reflects this change of perspective best.

57. The BEST equivalent for the adverb "disconnectedly" (line 81), used to describe Charity's later pursuit of culture, would be **(D) haphazardly.**

In the context in which it appears, the adverb "disconnectedly" means "randomly" or "haphazardly." Despite her "thirst for information" (line 78), Charity lacks direction in her studies and merely flips cursorily through dusty volumes, not really knowing upon what she should focus. Mr. Miles had provided Charity with such direction, but left to her own devices she finds that "the impression of Nettleton began to fade, and [that it was] easier to take North Dormer as the norm of the universe than to go on reading…." (lines 83-86).

58. The concluding sentence of the passage (lines 80-86) implies that the epiphany experienced by Charity at Nettleton was **(E) ephemeral.**

This is consistent with the explanation of question #57 in that if the impact of Nettleton upon Charity soon "began to fade" (line 84), it was "short-lived" or "ephemeral."

Question One

(Suggested time—40 minutes. This question counts as one-third of the total essay section score.)

In the following excerpt from Charles Dickens' *Our Mutual Friend* (1864-65), a young lady spurns a marriage proposal from Mr. Headstone, her brother Charley's best friend. Read the passage carefully. Then, in a well-organized essay, discuss the various approaches Charley employs while trying to persuade his sister to retract her decision and show how the author's language abets Charley's attempts to change her mind. In responding to the question, you may wish to consider such things as diction, syntax, choice of detail, and tone.

"Charley Hexam I am going home. I must walk home by myself to-night and get shut up in my room without being spoken to. Give me half an hour's start, and let me be, till you find me at work in the morning. I shall be at my work in the morning as usual."

(5)   Clasping his hands, he uttered a short unearthly broken cry, and went his way. The brother and sister were left looking at one another near a lamp in the solitary churchyard, and the boy's face clouded and darkened as he said in a rough tone: "What is the meaning of this? What have you done to my best friend? Out with the truth!"

"Charley!" said his sister. "Speak a little more considerately!"

"I am not in the humour for consideration, or for nonsense of any sort," replied the boy. "What have

(10)   you been doing? Why has Mr. Headstone gone from us in that way?"

"He asked me—you know he asked me—to be his wife, Charley."

"Well," said the boy, impatiently.

"And I was obliged to tell him I could not be his wife."

"You were obliged to tell him," repeated the boy angrily, between his teeth, and rudely pushing her

(15)   away. "You were obliged to tell him! Do you know that he is worth fifty of you?"

"It may easily be so, Charley, but I cannot marry him."

"You mean that you are conscious that you can't appreciate him, and don't deserve him, I suppose?"

"I mean that I do not like him, Charley, and that I will never marry him."

"Upon my soul," exclaimed the boy, "you are a nice picture of a sister! Upon my soul, you are a

(20)   pretty piece of disinterestedness! And so all my endeavours to cancel the past and to raise myself in the world, and to raise you with me, are to be beaten down by your low whims, are they?"

"I will not reproach you, Charley."

""Hear her!" exclaimed the boy, looking round at the darkness. "She won't reproach me! She does her best to destroy my fortunes and her own, and she won't reproach me! Why, you'll tell me next, that

(25)   you won't reproach Mr. Headstone for coming out of the sphere to which he is an ornament, and putting himself at your feet, to be rejected by you!"

"No, Charley; I will only tell you, as I told himself, that I thank him for doing so, that I'm sorry he did so, and that I hope he will do much better, and be happy."

Some touch of compunction smote the boy's hardening heart as he looked upon her, his patient little

(30)   nurse in infancy, his patient friend, adviser, and reclaimer in boyhood, the self-forgetting sister who had done everything for him. His tone relented, and he drew her arm through his.

"Now, come Liz; don't let us quarrel: let us be reasonable and talk this over like brother and sister. Will you listen to me?"….

"Yes, Charley."

(35)   "Well said! Now, you see….As Mr. Headstone's wife you would be occupying a most respectable station, and you would be holding a far better place in society than you hold now, and you would at length get quit of the river-side and the old disagreeables belonging to it, and you would be rid for good of dolls' dressmakers and their drunken fathers….Now, you see, Liz, on all three accounts—on Mr. Headstone's, on mine, on yours—nothing could be better or more desirable."

(40)   They were walking slowly as the boy spoke, and here he stood still, to see what effect he had made. His sister's eyes were fixed upon him; but as they showed no yielding, and as she remained silent, he walked her on again….

Précis and Explication of Free-Response Question One:
From Charles Dickens' *Our Mutual Friend*

Part of the challenge of this selection from Charles Dickens' *Our Mutual Friend* stems from its *in media res* beginning. The opening declaration in lines 1-3, spoken by a character to whom we have not yet been introduced and who petulantly and peremptorily departs the scene, may initially disorient the reader who must struggle for a number of lines to sort the characters out. Upon reaching lines 11-13, however, the passage's central conflict—Liz's rejection of the marriage proposal of Mr. Headstone, her brother Charley's best friend—becomes clear. Mr. Headstone, who announces that he must "walk home by [him]self to-night and get shut up in [his] room without being spoken to" (lines 1-2), seems to have suffered an injured pride, as if this rejection took him by surprise. The fact that he reassures Charley that he will be at work the next day hints at an attempt at stoicism, the putting up of a brave front in the face of rejection, although the "short unearthly broken cry" (line 4) he utters upon departing certainly suggests he has been emotionally wounded. The greater part of the passage, however, is devoted to Charley's attempts to persuade his sister to retract her decision through a variety of means.

Charley's first reaction is brusque, interrogatory and almost cruel. His face clouds and darkens, and he shouts at his sister in a "rough tone" (line 6), "'What is the meaning of this? What have you done to my best friend? Out with the truth!'" (lines 6-7). Here Charley both admonishes and accuses, painting his sister as the wrong-doer before she can utter a word in her own defense. When she implores him to speak "'more considerately'" (line 8), he dismisses her appeal as "'nonsense'" (line 9) and continues his interrogation, asking "'What have you been doing? Why has Mr. Headstone gone from us in that way?'" (lines 9-10). When Liz responds by telling her brother that Mr. Headstone asked her to be his wife—and she was obliged to refuse—he responds sarcastically and derisively, implying that she is in no position to deny Mr. Headstone's request, cruelly reminding her that he is "'worthy fifty of you'" (line 15), and physically pushing her away. The anger her brother displays seems to imply that he has a stake in his sister's marrying Mr. Headstone and that he regards her happiness as secondary to his own financial advance. When Liz humbly acknowledges her social inferiority to her suitor but again restates the impossibility of her marrying the man, Charley takes a different tack, asking in line 17, "'You mean that you are conscious that you can't appreciate him, and don't deserve him, I suppose?'" Though this suggests an attempt to understand his sister's rationale, it again puts her down, implying she is not worthy. Still, Liz maintains her equanimity, stating clearly and concisely that she does not like the man and will never marry him.

Faced with this roadblock, Charley tries a different approach. Using repetition of a mild oath ("'Upon my soul'") and mild sarcasm ("'you are a nice picture of a sister'"), he lays a guilt trip upon her, accusing her of limiting his opportunities by her selfishness: "'And so all my endeavours to cancel the past and to raise myself in the world, and to raise you with me, are to be beaten down by your low whims, are they?'" (lines 20-21). He then employs apostrophe, shouting "'Hear her'" (line 23) to an absent audience and feigning amazement as he mimics her line by saying repeatedly "'she won't reproach me!'" (lines 23, 24). His mockery reaches its crescendo when he says to his sister, "'Why, you'll tell me next, that you won't reproach Mr. Headstone for coming out of the sphere to which he is an ornament, and putting himself at your feet, to be rejected by you!'" (lines 24-26).

Though clearly stung by her brother's comments, Liz maintains an admirable grace, a grace which eventually softens the anger and frustration that to this point have throttled her brother. As the speaker relates,

> Some touch of compunction smote the boy's hardening heart as he looked upon her, his patient little nurse in infancy, his patient friend, adviser, and reclaimer in boyhood, the self-forgetting sister who had done everything for him. His tone relented, and he drew her arm through his (lines 29-31).

The diction here is particularly interesting. First, "compunction," or feelings of guilt, are said to "smote the boy's hardening heart," implying that his ire weakens. Second, the series of appositives that comprises the middle of this passage—"his patient little nurse in infancy, his patient friend, adviser, and reclaimer in boyhood, the self-forgetting sister who had done everything for him"—reminds him of the diverse formative roles she has played in his life, from infancy to adolescence to the precipice of adulthood. As a result, his tone relents, and he passes his arm affectionately through hers, saying fraternally "'Now, come Liz; don't let us quarrel: let us be reasonable and talk this over like brother and sister. Will you listen to me?'".... (lines 32-33). At this point the reader almost expects a total reconciliation—the understanding brother regretting his selfishness, apologizing for his boorishness, and winning her and the reader back with his admirable empathy. Not so. Rather, employing a contrast between her present life of drudgery and a potentially blissful future, he makes the identical appeal though here masked by a saccharine and insidious reasoning:

> 'Now, you see….As Mr. Headstone's wife you would be occupying a most respectable station, and you would be holding a far better place in society than you hold now, and you would at length get quit of the river-side and the old disagreeables belonging to it, and you would be rid for good of dolls' dressmakers and their drunken fathers….Now, you see, Liz, on all three accounts—on Mr. Headstone's, on mine, on yours—nothing could be better or more desirable' (lines 35-39).

Charley's choice of detail (the "old disagreeables" of toil, drunkenness and social immobility) and his neat logic that such a marriage would benefit all three parties (providing Headstone with a fetching bride, Charley with financial promotion, and Liz with an elevation in society) attack his sister's greatest vulnerability: her love for her brother. Though Charley pauses "to see what effect he had made" (line 40), his sister Liz is seen staring intently at him as if to measure his sincerity or bore through his deception. Yet she "show[s] no yielding" (line 41) and maintains an air of silence. The fact that Charley walks her on again, however, implies that he is not yet willing to quit but will continue to attempt to change his sister's mind for his own purpose.

Scoring Guide for Free-Response Question One: From Charles Dickens' *Our Mutual Friend*

8-9   Well-conceived, well-developed, and well-organized, these papers are marked by frequent and accurate references to the text, by an admirable ability to synthesize thought, and by a mature control over the elements of composition. Though not perfect, they clearly indicate the students' ability to recognize the diverse ways that Charley's discourse attempts to persuade his sister, as well as to show how Dickens' language—things such as tone, choice of detail, syntax and diction—abets these attempts.

6-7   These essays exhibit a solid understanding of the diverse ways in which Charley attempts to persuade his sister, but are less adept at responding to the question. This may be due to inconsistencies in textual understanding, or to a lesser ability to recognize how Dickens' language enhances these attempts. Though these essays reflect their writers' abilities to convey their points clearly, they feature less fluency, less development and less cogency than 8-9 papers.

5   These papers respond to the question on the diverse ways in which Charley attempts to persuade his sister in superficial, formulaic, inconsistent, or insufficiently supported ways. They may rely primarily on paraphrase, but may still convey an implicit understanding of the passage and the task. The papers are generally written in a satisfactory manner, with occasional errors in composition or mechanics that do not impede the reader's understanding. Nevertheless, these essays lack the organization, persuasiveness and development of upper-half papers.

3-4   These lower-half essays generally suggest an incomplete or overly simplistic understanding of the passage or of the task, an inability to perceive the nuances of Charley's approaches, or an inability to illustrate how Dickens' language abets these approaches. Their arguments are often characterized by a misreading of the text, a failure to provide adequate support, or insufficient control over the elements of composition. In some instances they may consist entirely of paraphrase and/or feature acute problems in organization, clarity, fluency or development.

1-2   These essays compound the shortcomings of 3-4 papers. They often contain many serious and distracting errors in grammar or mechanics that preclude any successful response to the prompt. Though these essays may attempt to show the different ways in which Charley attempts to persuade his sister, they are severely limited by deficiencies in organization, clarity, fluency or development.

0   Papers scored a zero make no more than a passing reference to the task.

—   Papers given this score offer a blank or totally off-topic response.

Sample Student Essay One

In this passage, Charley reacts to his sister Liz's rejection of a marriage proposal by his friend, Mr. Headstone. The overall mood is suggested in the opening paragraph of the passage, where Mr. Headstone leaves the scene embarrassed and upset (his name alone conjures funereal imagery that could be representative of what marriage to him would be for the independent-minded Liz). What follows is the dialogue between Charley and Liz discussing the spurned proposal. Charley first reacts with intense anger, then appears sympathetic and understanding, but throughout, his motives are the same: to change his sister's mind. Underlying all these is a conflict between devotion to family and devotion to autonomy.

Charley at first reacts with his raw emotions. When he learns of the situation, he is angry, something evident from his tone and his sister's insistence that he calm down and treat her with greater respect. He is resentful, unable to see his sister's point of view. "Do you know that he is worth fifty of you?" he rhetorically asks. To him, there was always only one valid answer to the proposal. He cannot empathize with arguments of love as he only seems to understand those of social position. Indeed, that is his motivation in pushing the marriage. Charley tries to rationalize it, saying, "You mean that you are conscious that you can't appreciate him and don't deserve him?" he asks, unable to understand that some motivations lie beyond social or monetary gain. He plainly states that it was to raise him—and her—into higher social strata. "You are a nice picture of a sister!" he sarcastically exclaims, continuing: "Upon my soul, you are a pretty piece of disinterestedness!" He essentially accuses her of selfishness in that her rejection apparently undid all his hard work, and he accuses her of selfishness. Of course, she has equal footing in making accusations of selfishness: it is her life, after all, that he demands on using for his gain. (Both their gain, he is careful to remind.)

Yet so far both have been unmoving in their deeply felt positions, so Charley tries a shrewder approach. Rather than attacking as he has unproductively, he becomes coaxing, sentimental and seemingly sensitive, hoping subtler means of persuasion will prove more fruitful. "His tone relented," the narrator states, "and he drew her arm through his." "Don't let us quarrel," Charley pleads. He then enumerates the advantages not he but Liz would gain in marrying Mr. Headstone. Again, he focuses entirely on the social aspect: she would move up in society no longer have to undergo the burdens of a less-privileged life. Yet Liz remains steadfast. Charley's partisans would call her stubborn; Liz's would say resolute. Again, depending on one's point of view those labels could be reversed.

When the passage ends, neither has budged from their original positions. Liz's eyes "showed no yielding," and Charley "walked her on again." Taking sides in this battle requires an assessment of priorities: of class and financial security, but also love and happiness, and these two siblings are separated by these two different camps. This conflict is likely to end in stalemate. The dialogue of this passage has revealed that whatever the tactics, Charley and Liz are equally skilled sparring partners (they do share DNA, after all), and each is firmly—or stubbornly—dedicated to their own motivations.

Sample Student Essay Two

In this passage, a young man tries to convince his sister, Liz, to marry his best friend, Mr. Headstone. Liz has refused Mr. Headstone's proposal of marriage despite her brother's wishes, and in this passage Charley and Liz discuss her decision. Charley's persuasive techniques range from the use of insults to kind reasoning, and the author's use of straightforward dialogue and descriptive language help the reader see how Charley's feelings change throughout the passage.

Charley uses a variety of methods in his attempt to convince his sister to accept the marriage proposal. Upon hearing of her decision, he immediately feels angry and insults Liz, hoping that his emotional attacks will change her mind. He "rudely [pushes] her away" and tells his sister that his best friend is "worth fifty of [her]". Liz, however, stands her ground and calmly tells Charley that she will not change her decision. Charley then uses a different approach: he questions Liz's motives, trying to understand why she rejected his friend. This attempt fails as well, and she continues to coolly defend her decision. Charley's next technique is to make Liz feel guilty, and he tells her that by rejecting Mr. Headstone, she has insulted Charley and his efforts to help her. He also tries to make her feel ashamed of her decision, saying that the shy Mr. Headstone has "[put] himself at your feet, to be rejected by you!". After Liz's next rebuttal, it becomes clear that Charley cannot scare or shame her into accepting Mr. Headstone's proposal. Liz's words somehow touch Charley and remind him of how much he cares for his sister. He tries to speak to her more kindly and says "don't let us quarrel: let us be reasonable and talk this over like brother and sister". He then recites a number of practical reasons why Liz should marry Mr. Headstone, mentioning that as Mr. Headstone's wife, she would be socially respected, wealthier, and free from lower-class people. However, Charley's thoughtful tone continues to have no effect on Liz: her face "[shows] no yielding".

The author's language is crucial in clarifying Charley's attempts to change Liz's mind. The dialogue is revealing and fairly straightforward, giving the reader an immediate sense of the speaker's motives. The author's words give the reader insight into the progression of Charley's emotions. Charley's initial heated dialogue features repetition ("You were obliged to tell him!") that conveys his anger at Liz. The author's descriptive language adds to this dialogue's effectiveness. Surrounding the dialogue are phrases that describe Charley's physical appearance; for example, Charley is described as speaking "in a rough tone" and saying an angry phrase "between his teeth". The author also italicizes certain words to further emphasize Charley's anger and attempts to belittle his sister. At one point, the author has Charley refer to Liz in the third person, a ploy that further demeans her. We see Charley's feelings towards Liz change from anger to care in a single sentence in which Charley remembers how his "self-forgetting sister [has] done everything for him", and his tone becomes kinder and more reasonable after that point.

The dialogue and descriptive language in this passage make Charley's emotions accessible to the reader. We can see the different tactics Charlie employs in trying to change Liz's decision: he insults her, shames her, and eventually tries to reason with her. Although Charley has not convinced his sister to change her decision by the end of the passage, the author has effectively shown Charley's feelings and the nature of his attempts to change Liz's mind.

Sample Student Essay Three

It is often expected that a brother would support his sister in her decisions, especially when it comes to marriage. However, in the case of this passage, Charley Hexam cannot support his sister's decision to turn down a marriage proposal because the one proposing is his closest friend. Charley is obviously very close with Mr. Headstone and is hurt that Elizabeth would reject his love. Throughout the passage, he tries several different approaches to persuade Elizabeth to change her mind, but never does he waver is his belief that she should have said yes. He is at times harsh, condescending, selfish, and tender, but his words appear to have no effect on Elizabeth. The author's use of dialogue and descriptions of Charley's body language demonstrate his attempts to change his sister's mind.

Right after Mr. Headstone storms away, Charley becomes extremely harsh and angry with Elizabeth. "His face clouded and darkened," and he asks her quite rudely what she has done. He is upset that she has hurt his best friend and is extremely impatient with her. When he learns that she has refused to marry him, Charley becomes even angrier, pushing her and speaking "between his teeth." This description portrays someone who is trying to control his anger, to little avail. He can't help himself from turning physical, but is trying to hold back from yelling at his sister. It can also be seen from his reaction that he is acting very selfishly, and does not really care about her feelings. However, Charley immediately sees that his sister is unyielding in her decision, so he needs to switch tactics.

"You were obliged to tell him! Do you know that he is worth fifty of you?" Charley Hexam asks Elizabeth. His words drip with sarcasm, and he is being very condescending towards his older sister. His body language, speaking to the air around him as if to an audience, shows his disbelief at his sister. His new tactic is to make her feel guilty. If he beats her down and tells her that she is worth nothing compared to Mr. Headstone, and that by refusing his proposal not only is she breaking his heart but her brother's as well, perhaps she will relent. Elizabeth's reaction is not seen, but from her words it is clear that she does not care what her brother thinks. She has an iron will, and no amount of condescension will make her change her mind.

When Elizabeth tells Charley that she feels bad for rejecting Mr. Headstone, he melts a little bit: "Some note of compunction smote the boy's hardening heart as he looked upon her...the self-forgetting sister who had done everything for him. His tone relented, and he drew her arm through his." This simple action shows their close bond as siblings, and he realizes that he should not make her feel guilty after all she has done for him. Perhaps if he were kinder she might relent, so his dialogue becomes much gentler as he tries to tell her that marrying Mr. Headstone would be better for everyone involved. He finally addresses her by name, saying "Now, come Liz; don't let us quarrel," and she appears to be more receptive. It seems that he is trying to appeal to her side of the argument by telling her how much better life would be and how she wouldn't have to work in her uncomfortable job any longer. However, the final paragraph shows Charley looking into her eyes for a sign that she has been moved, and yet he finds nothing.

This passage is told primarily through dialogue between Charley and Elizabeth, and also through descriptions of Charley's actions and body language. All of Elizabeth's actions are seen through Charley's eyes, which is very important in demonstrating his attempts to persuade his sister to accept the marriage proposal. This way, he can judge what kind of effect he thinks she is making, and what different methods of persuasion he should employ. Despite the fact that he goes through the spectrum from harsh and almost violent to loving and thoughtful, the final sentence of the passage "and as she remained silent, he walked her on again..." shows his failure to succeed.

Assessment of Student Responses to Free-Response Question One: From Charles Dickens' *Our Mutual Friend*

<u>Sample Student Essay One:</u>

A. Assessment of Reader One

This essay shows some great insight—the comment about Mr. Headstone's name, for example—which initially makes one think it might earn a little higher score. This student certainly recognizes that Charley is the one to benefit most from the marriage, not his sister—and the essay also comments on the irony. The essay provides lines for support, but begins to fall short on the understanding of the techniques involved. The student explains the broader elements of the argument, but fails to dissect the language. The end of the third paragraph "bird walks" a bit, saying what others would think and say about the situation and the characters. I would score this a 7.

B. Assessment of Reader Two

This essay is certainly no less than a 7, but I might nudge it to an 8 simply because I think it does a meritorious job of perceiving the serpentine ways in which Charley tries to shift his sister's adamant stance on the marriage. I like the comment that Charley cannot understand arguments of love, only arguments of social position, as well as the clever DNA comment at the end. True, it does not specifically articulate techniques in any formal terms, but I think the understanding of them is implicit in the discussion.

<u>Sample Student Essay Two:</u>

A. Assessment of Reader One

A "workman-like" essay that covers all its bases. From the straightforward, yet clear opening to the exploration and rhetoric of Charley's argument, this essay accomplishes the points of the 8-9 essay. Many examples are included to discuss tone, diction and point of view. This writer also understands how some things like a shift in point of view and the inclusion of dialogue can create a demeaning tone. One place where the essay falters a bit is in the third paragraph which makes a sort of laundry list of techniques used without appropriate examples for support. The essay begins to explore Charley's physical appearance in this paragraph to no apparent purpose, but, all in all, this student understands the irony and satire of Charley's position and the fact that he cares more for his own advancement than for his sister's happiness. I would score this an 8

B. Assessment of Reader Two

Essays receiving the same score can have diverse features. This is an extremely thorough and accurate response which is better than the first sample essay in terms of applying specific labels to Charley's techniques. On the other hand, the sentences in the first paragraph were marked by rather dull ("He then, etc.") syntax and were very mechanical in their presentation. Very good paper with a different style of approach. I give this an 8 as well.

Sample Student Essay Three:

A. Assessment of Reader One

This student understands the argumentative techniques that Charley uses to persuade his sister to accept the proposal, but gives Charley far too much credit throughout. The essay discusses the techniques of the argument as well as minimally noticing tone, but misses the fact that Charley cares more for his own situation than he cares for his sister's happiness. Good on the idea of dialogue and character development but thin on techniques like language and tone. I would score this essay a 6

B. Assessment of Reader Two

I also would score this essay a 6. There are some questions (this being one of them) which are reasonably accessible to most readers; hence, many see that Charley is trying different approaches. This student, like the two before him, recognizes that Charley continuously changes his tack as he becomes more frustrated by his sister's adamancy in rejecting Mr. Headstone. However, unlike the previous responses, this paper does not see anything behind these attempts to get Elizabeth to change her mind, what personal motivations Charley might have for pursuing this. The writing is certainly upper-half, but the insight and the articulation of how the author uses language are not as persuasive as that contained in the two that preceded it.

<u>Question Two</u>

(Suggested time—40 minutes. This question counts as one-third of the total essay-section score.)

In the following excerpt from Joseph Heller's war satire *Catch-22*, a superior officer is plagued by the outrageous, authority-defying exploits of a singularly zany bomber pilot named Yossarian. Read the passage carefully. Then, in a well-organized essay, analyze how the author uses language to convey Yossarian's effect upon Colonel Cathcart.

Colonel Cathcart was not thinking anything at all about the chaplain, but was tangled up in a brand-new, menacing problem of his own: *Yossarian!*

Yossarian! The mere sound of that execrable, ugly name made his blood run cold and his breath come in labored gasps. The chaplain's first mention of the name *Yossarian!* had tolled deep in his
(5) memory like a portentous gong. As soon as the latch of the door had clicked shut, the whole humiliating recollection of the naked man in formation came cascading down upon him in a mortifying, choking flood of stinging details. He began to perspire and tremble. There was a sinister and unlikely coincidence exposed that was too diabolical in implication to be anything less than the most hideous of omens. The name of the man who had stood naked in ranks that day to receive his Distinguished Flying Cross from
(10) General Dreedle had also been— *Yossarian!* And now it was a man named Yossarian who was threatening to make trouble over the sixty missions he had just ordered the men in his group to fly. Colonel Cathcart wondered gloomily if it was the same Yossarian.

He climbed to his feet with an air of intolerable woe and began moving about his office. He felt himself in the presence of the mysterious. The naked man in formation, he conceded cheerlessly, had
(15) been a real black eye for him. So had the tampering with the bomb line before the mission to Bologna and the seven-day delay in destroying the bridge at Ferrara, even though destroying the bridge at Ferrara, finally he remembered with glee, had been a real feather in his cap, although losing a plane there the second time around, he recalled in dejection, had been another black eye, even though he had won another real feather in his cap by getting his medal approved for the bombardier who had gotten him the
(20) real black eye in the first place by going around over the target twice. That bombardier's name, he remembered suddenly with another stupefying shock, had also been *Yossarian!* Now there were *three!* His viscous eyes bulged with astonishment and he whipped himself around in alarm to see what was taking place behind him. A moment ago there had been no Yossarians in his life; now they were multiplying like hobgoblins. He tried to make himself grow calm. Yossarian was not a common name;
(25) perhaps there were not really three Yossarians but only two Yossarians, or maybe even only one Yossarian—*but that really made no difference!* The colonel was still in grave peril. Intuition warned him that he was drawing close to some immense and inscrutable cosmic climax, and his broad, meaty, towering frame tingled from head to toe at the thought that Yossarian, whoever he would eventually turn out to be, was destined to serve as his nemesis…

Précis and Explication of Free-Response Question Two: From Joseph Heller's *Catch-22*

As anyone who has read Joseph Heller's *Catch-22* knows, the novel provides ample opportunity to examine satire, and this passage exemplifies one of them in Colonel Cathcart's alternately perplexed, perturbed and paranoid response to the unorthodox behavior of the zany bomber pilot known as Yossarian. The language used by Heller in describing the impact of Yossarian upon Colonel Cathcart reveals just how disturbing non-conformist actions can be for someone who has been a career conformist.

The impression made by Yossarian upon the Colonel is so provocative that when he thinks of him, his name requires both italicization and an exclamation point, and he is immediately designated as a "menacing problem" (line 2). In fact, the thought of Yossarian has an adverse physical effect upon the colonel since "The mere sound of that execrable, ugly name made his blood run cold and his breath come in labored gasps" (lines 3-4). Alluding to the first time Colonel Cathcart heard Yossarian's unusual name, the speaker recalls how it "tolled deep in his memory like a portentous gong" (lines 4-5). This simile, which first establishes the stolid nature of the Colonel, is further enhanced by the adjective "portentous" which attaches a sinister and ominous resonance to the bomber pilot's name. Making the connection between this appellation and that of a man who had brazenly appeared naked during a troop inspection shatters Cathcart's composure as the disturbing recollection comes "cascading down upon him in a mortifying, choking flood of stinging details" (lines 6-7). Here the diction ("cascading;" "flood") describes via an implied metaphor the overwhelming nature of this unpleasant memory for the Colonel. Again the mention of the name Yossarian triggers a visceral reaction in the Colonel who begins to "perspire and tremble" (line 7). However, Heller's satire of the Colonel's dim-wittedness cuts particularly sharp with his inability firmly to deduce that this Yossarian "who was threatening to make trouble over the sixty missions he had just ordered the men in his group to fly" (lines 10-11) is the same Yossarian who earlier had "stood naked in ranks that day to receive his Distinguished Flying Cross from General Dreedle…" (lines 9-10).

Heller's diction—words and phrases such as "gloomily" (line 12), "intolerable woe" (line 13) and "cheerlessly" (line 14)—augment the sense of dejection that Yossarian's name has caused in the Colonel, though the Colonel seems torn between being depressed by Yossarian's insubordinate antics (which have been a source of humiliation for him) and being ironically grateful to him for his military actions (which have brought him credit). In the long sentence that spans lines 15-20, Colonel Catchcart is seen recounting Yossarian's insubordinate and heroic actions and using antithetical phrases such as "a real black eye" and "a real feather in his cap" to convey the human contradiction that is Yossarian. In recalling the destruction of the bridge at Ferrara, he undergoes yet another epiphany:

> That bombardier's name, he remembered suddenly with another stupefying shock, had also been *Yossarian*! Now there were *three*! His viscous eyes bulged with astonishment and he whipped himself around in alarm to see what was taking place behind him. A moment ago there had been no Yossarians in his life; now they were multiplying like hobgoblins. (lines 20-24).

Heller's satire of Colonel Cathcart is relentless and unmerciful, painting him as an officer who literally cannot add 1 + 1 + 1 and arrive at, in this case, a very logical 1. Instead, he sees Yossarians "multiplying like hobgoblins," bogeymen bent on furthering his dread and apprehension.

So potent is the psychological impact of Yossarian upon Colonel Cathcart that even attempts to reassure himself—"Yossarian was not a common name; perhaps there were not really three Yossarians but only two Yossarians, or maybe even only one Yossarian" (lines 24-26)—prove futile, and he perceives himself to be in "grave peril" (line 26), to be "drawing close to some immense and inscrutable cosmic climax..." (line 27). The diction here is intentionally hyperbolic, further magnifying the discomfiting sensation caused even by Yossarian's name. The passage's concluding sentence is rife with irony in that Colonel Cathcart, who is described as having a "broad, meaty, towering frame" (lines 27-28), is reduced to a nervous wreck, whose body "tingle[s] from head to toe" (line 28) at the mere mention of a man's name, a man whom he foresees is "destined to serve as his nemesis...." (line 29).

Scoring Guide for Free-Response Question Two: From Joseph Heller's *Catch-22*

8-9   Well-conceived, well-developed, and well-organized, these papers are marked by frequent and accurate references to the text, by an admirable ability to synthesize thought, and by a mature control over the elements of composition. Though not perfect, they clearly indicate the students' ability to discuss the traumatic effect the mere name of Yossarian has upon Colonel Cathcart and to show how the author's language conveys this effect.

6-7   These essays exhibit a solid understanding of the traumatic effect the mere name of Yossarian has upon Colonel Cathcart, but are less adept at responding to the question. This may be due to inconsistencies in textual understanding or to less proficiency at recognizing how Heller's language conveys Yossarian's impact upon the Colonel. Though these essays reflect their writers' abilities to convey their points clearly, they feature less fluency, less development and less cogency than 8-9 papers.

5   These papers respond to the question on Yossarian's impact upon the Colonel and how Heller's language conveys this in superficial, formulaic, inconsistent, or insufficiently supported ways. They may rely primarily on paraphrase, but may still convey an implicit understanding of the passage and the task. The papers are generally written in a satisfactory manner, with occasional errors in composition or mechanics that do not impede the reader's understanding. Nevertheless, these essays lack the organization, persuasiveness and development of upper-half papers.

3-4   These lower-half essays generally suggest an incomplete or overly simplistic understanding of the passage or of the task, an inability to demonstrate Yossarian's impact upon Colonel Cathcart, or an inability to articulate how Heller's language conveys it. Their arguments are often characterized by a misreading of the text, a failure to provide adequate support, or insufficient control over the elements of composition. In some instances they may consist entirely of paraphrase and/or feature acute problems in organization, clarity, fluency or development.

1-2   These essays compound the shortcomings of 3-4 papers. They often contain many serious and distracting errors in grammar or mechanics that preclude any successful response to the prompt. Though these essays may attempt to show Yossarian's impact upon Colonel Cathcart or say something about Heller's language, they are severely limited by deficiencies in organization, clarity, fluency or development.

0   Papers scored a zero make no more than a passing reference to the task.

—   Papers given this score offer a blank or totally off-topic response.

Sample Student Essay One

Joseph Heller's Catch-22 *is a war satire whose protagonist, Yossarian, is given to creating problems for superior officers. In this excerpt, the reader learns of Colonel Cathcart's dealings with Yossarian, who strongly affects Cathcart's emotional security. Heller uses diction and tone to describe Cathcart's feelings of embarrassment, fright, and shock.*

Colonel Cathcart is clearly troubled by Yossarian's actions, as they humiliate him and make him feel powerless. It is revealed that Yossarian stood naked during a ceremony honoring Cathcart, who is quite upset by this. Cathcart recalls the incident in a "mortifying, choking flood of stinging details." Diction such as this allows the reader to get a sense of the scale of Cathcart's embarrassment. Yossarian has shamed Cathcart at other times, although Cathcart does not know this at the beginning of the passage. Cathcart realizes that Yossarian was the cause of many "real black [eyes]" for him. The repetition of this phrase makes the reader understand that Cathcart is overwhelmed by the problems Yossarian has caused him.

Cathcart's feelings of shame change into fear as he realizes that each man who has caused him trouble has been named Yossarian. Heller uses diction to alert the reader to Cathcart's sudden rush of panic. By using words such as "menacing" and "sinister", Heller introduces Cathcart's dread to the reader. Such strong language effectively expresses Cathcart's view of the situation as dire. Heller uses the words "perspire", "tremble", and "labored gasps" to describe Cathcart's physical reaction to Yossarian's actions. These phrases allow the reader to understand the progression of Cathcart's fear, as well as to see its intensity.

Heller's use of tone also helps the reader understand Cathcart's feelings of shock. Heller painstakingly describes each of Cathcart's thoughts, allowing the reader to experience Cathcart's mental connection of Yossarian's actions as Cathcart does. Cathcart's distress is emphasized through contrast, as Cathcart's recollections of various incidents are followed by strong sentences: "That bombardier's name, he remembered suddenly with another stupefying shock, had also been Yossarian! Now there were three!" Heller also uses diction to describe Cathcart's shock. He uses straightforward words such as "astonishment" and "alarm" that immediately alert the reader to Cathcart's feelings. This allows the reader to feel shocked just when Cathcart does. Heller then reminds the reader of the implications of Cathcart's realizations by once again describing Cathcart's notion that he "[is] still in grave peril...drawing close to some immense and inscrutable cosmic climax."

Colonel Cathcart's feelings of fear and shock at Yossarian's actions are emphasized through diction and careful tone. These elements give the reader insight into Cathcart's thought process, making the passage humorous as well as accessible. Heller's writing effectively introduces the relationship between the two characters.

Sample Student Essay Two

In the passage from Joseph Heller's Catch-22, *Colonel Cathcart comes to the realization that the antics of a bombardier named Yossarian have permeated his military life, causing him much grief. Heller expresses the effects that the one soldier has on his superior through frantic syntax, biting diction, emphasizing repetition and graphic simile. Through the employment of these rhetorical devices, Heller conveys the negative effects that Yossarian has on the life of Colonel Cathcart.*

"Yossarian!" (Heller, Line 2), an exclamation that appears elsewhere in the text, emphasizes the exasperation the Colonel has with this soldier. The repetition of the name at instances throughout the passage where Cathcart realizes that more and more of his woes were caused by this single man allows us to make the realizations with him, as well as understand the severity with which this affects the Colonel.

From the passage's first sentence onward, we find examples of syntax building to a cumulative point. Many of the sentences in the passage are long and flow spastically, similarly to the way a person in anger thinks without a filter. Heller uses many adjectives for emphasis and uses commas to continue thoughts to their conclusion: "As soon as the latch of the door had clicked shut, the whole humiliating recollection of the naked man in formation came cascading down upon him in a mortifying, choking flood of stinging details." This sentence functions in the same way it describes what is happening to Cathcart: it cascades with a flood of stinging details. As such, it functions much like a mind in anger.

Heller's diction masterfully conveys the agony Yossarian causes Cathcart. Harshly negative words like "execrable", "gloomy," "hideous," and "diabolical" appear throughout, working to express the wholly damaging effect Yossarian has upon the Colonel's life. Alliteration also stresses the destructive nature of the relationship between Yossarian and Cathcart. Cathcart "concede[s] cheerlessly" (Line 14), Yossarian "threaten[s] to make trouble", and when Cathcart comes to the final conclusion that Yossarian will be his nemesis, he arrives at an "immense and inscrutable cosmic climax" (Line 27). The use of alliteration drives home the point being made through repetitious sound, drilling the intensity behind the words into the mind of the reader. Additionally, phrases with a singsong lilt appear throughout the passage, perhaps indicating that Cathcart feels teased or evaded by his nemesis. "Multiplying like hobgoblins" exemplifies this rhythm.

Heller uses simile to express the dastardly effect Yossarian has on his superior, likening him to a "black eye" and recalling the first time Cathcart thought of the name Yossarian as tolling like a "portentous gong" (4). These comparisons further develop the severity of Cathcart's reaction to this bomber, giving the reader sensory comparisons like the annoyance and pain of a black eye or the ominous echoes of a gong. In addition to simile, Heller uses opposites and drastic comparisons to convey the extremes of the emotions felt in this passage. Cathcart "remembers with glee" his military successes, yet Yossarian has the singular effect of turning that glee into "recalling with dejection."

Using this battery of literary devices, Heller conveys the inescapable annoyance that develops to the "cosmic climax" of the birth of a nemesis. With meticulously chosen and highly effective diction, fluid yet frantic syntax, and alliterative repetition and more, the reader can imagine Cathcart's skin crawling at the mention of a single name: "Yossarian!"

Sample Student Essay Three

In Joseph Heller's satiric novel <u>Catch-22</u>, Colonel Cathcart has an unusually pervasive contempt for Yossarian, the novel's protagonist. In the passage given, Heller illustrates just how much Yossarian irritates the Colonel by using an array of literary techniques. The most important of these is the structure of his prose, which is made to be repetitive to allow the writer to hammer in his idea. Also, the tone, which makes use of such things as punctuation and exaggeration, is made to feel like it is pulsing with Colonel Cathcart's rage. Finally, the passage is written with language that is sensory in nature, so that you can almost hear the voice of the narrator, and the descriptions are all detailed and feel up-close, while appealing to sound as well as sight, so that the reader imagines a whole array of things that emphasize the narrator's point.

The passage is built around the name "Yossarian," which is italicized and followed by an exclamation point when Colonel Cathcart arrives at the sudden and shocking realization that Yossarian had some part in something that happened in the Colonel's memory. "The first mention of the name" at one point "had tolled deep in his memory like a portentous gong." Whenever he remembers the name ("that execrable, ugly name"), he embarks on a rant that is always primarily about the name itself, rather than the person. The only time that he goes off-topic (thinking about battles that he has experienced) he remembers "suddenly with another stupefying shock" that a certain bombardier's name "had also been Yossarian!"

The tone of Heller's prose makes it feel like each time Colonel Cathcart remembers that someone in his memory was Yossarian, it is like he has been struck over the head. He finds it extremely irritating, and makes it sound like he has allergic reactions to its sound. The last time he remembers it he becomes frantic, thinking, "Now there were three [Yossarians]!" and begins to grow desperate. The narrator exaggerates at this point, intending to give the reader a sense of how crazed Colonel Cathcart is: after the Colonel realizes that there is really only one Yossarian, he thinks that he is "still in grave peril" and reasons that "whoever [Yossarian] would eventually turn out to be, [he] was destined to serve as his nemesis."

The sensory language used in the passage is meant to conjure things that are almost tangible. Of course, the name itself is an auditive device, since it is treated as a sound. But when Colonel Cathcart first recalls an event involving Yossarian, the narrator says that "the whole humiliating recollection. . . came cascading down upon him in a mortifying, choking flood of stinging details." The Colonel begins to "perspire and tremble." These verbs and adjectives might seem to be excessive and out-of-place, but they underline the narrator's point. The last time the Colonel remembered about Yossarian, "his viscous eyes bulged with astonishment and he whipped himself around in alarm to see what was talking place behind him." This improbable and comical image serves to illustrate how crazed Colonel Cathcart is. The passage ends with his "broad, meaty frame [tingling] from head to toe."

Joseph Heller writes to be amusing and simple, but also to emphasize his points. With a simple structure, a funny and exaggerated tone, and sensory language, the passage makes it clear that Colonel Cathcart loathes Yossarian, hates the very idea of Yossarian, and is plagued by the very name "Yossarian."

**Assessment of Student Responses to Free-Response Question Two:
From Joseph Heller's *Catch-22***

Sample Student Essay One:

A. Assessment of Reader One

This student describes the effect of Yossarian on the Colonel as being one of fear and shock—without explaining the significance of the effect. The essay does not sufficiently help the reader to see the character of the colonel as a bit of an imbecile. It does, however, do a nice job on diction. I would score this essay a 6.

B. Assessment of Reader Two

I concur with Reader A that this is a prototypical 6. The student does a pretty solid job with diction, citing words that display the impact of Yossarian upon Colonel Cathcart. The treatment of tone is largely ineffectual with the student summarizing it as a "careful tone." Moreover, the student fails to pick up on the satire of the colonel who is portrayed as being so daft that he does not immediately realize that all these Yossarians are one and the same.

Sample Student Essay Two:

A. Assessment of Reader One

This paper does a very thorough job of describing Yossarian's effect upon Colonel Cathcart, but it still doesn't take the reader very far. The paragraph on syntax is a nice try that doesn't quite work. Even so, this is a better written paper than essay one. I would score this a 7.

B. Assessment of Reader Two

For awhile I thought this paper was headed toward an 8, but I think it ultimately comes in as a solid 7. The student does a very good summative job with diction and is particularly insightful in his/her remarks about how the syntax mirrors the Colonel's frenzied response to Yossarian. There is a solid if not fully effective thesis that steers the paper from start to finish. Perhaps a bit too much is made of the powers of alliteration. Still, this essay recognized some of the satire of Colonel Cathcart and featured greater development than essay one.

Sample Student Essay Three:

A. Assessment of Reader One

This essay does seem to try to deal with the effect of Yossarian upon Colonel Cathcart and the significance of it (the Colonel is described as being "crazed"). However, the sheer amount of plot and restatement of the prompt keeps this from going higher. I would score this essay an upper-end 7.

B. Assessment of Reader Two

I did not like this essay as much as my colleague and would have scored it a 6 (though we both agree that it belongs somewhere in the 6/7 category on the scoring guide). I felt that it paraphrased more than it analyzed, and though I can close my eyes to the peccadillo of "auditive language," I was not sold on the presence of "sensory language." I liked the use of the word "nemesis" by the writer, but I felt this was inferior to the second essay.

Prepping for Literature: How to Achieve Success on the AP Free-Response Literature Question

Prepping for the free-response question on literature is a much simpler task than prepping for the questions on poetry or prose. There are no multiple-choice questions to worry about, and there is not much you can do to ready yourself for it other than to do the assigned reading in your AP English class and to try to remember what you have learned in class about it. That said, this section will be significantly shorter than the previous two simply because your teacher plays a more important role in getting you ready for this question than any textbook can ever play.

Though there is no way to predict the direction in which the literature question will go from year to year, there are some basics you can do to prepare yourself for the final question on the exam. The first of these is to relax. The real burden of the test is over in that once you reach this question, you will have successfully navigated the timed readings in poetry and prose that you likely had never seen before. The Literature question is always the highest scoring question on the exam, with a mean slightly above 5. It is also the question to which students tend to write the longest responses because they feel a greater sense of ownership in responding with a book of their own choice. If your AP class has a challenging syllabus that has exposed you to profound ideas and elements of structure and style, you will likely be prepared to answer this question with success. Even so, here are a couple of pointers:

1. **Find the heart of the question.**

   Literature question prompts can sometimes sprawl. On occasion there may be a paragraph preceding the question that contains a citation that is *related to* the question but not the *real* question. Practice finding the "heart" of the question, making sure that you get all parts of it if it should ask you to consider multiple things. A perfect example would be questions that ask you to do something with meaning and elements of language, or questions that ask you to connect your response to the meaning of the work as a whole. Many times we read student papers that address one part very well, but fail to address two others. However, the highest scoring papers will usually be very complete in this regard.

2. **Don't be a slave to the list of titles.**

   The list of titles that is provided generally represents the collective brainstorming of the question-makers who asked themselves "What would be a good book with which to answer this question?" Though many will undoubtedly be titles you recognize, and some titles you might have even read or studied, the list is really a security blanket, there to help you out in case you draw a complete blank. Though you can be assured that a title that appears on the list will be effective in answering the question, it would not be wise to choose a book you read two years ago which you might have somewhat forgotten just because you see it listed. Rather, survey what you have read in your AP class and assess if any of the titles would be effective in answering the question. Make your selection, do a rough thesis and outline, and begin to write.

3. Pre-exam preparation

To be perfectly honest, I do very little with my class to prepare for this particular question. Though we will write multiple timed responses to poetry and prose prompts during the course of a year, we only write one or two responses on the literature question. One reason for this is that it takes a while for them to accumulate some AP titles with which to respond to this question, so we never respond to any Question Three literature prompts before the final quarter. A second is that students in my AP English class are writing on literature *all year*. I am interested in getting ideas firmly imbedded in their heads so when they get to the exam they have something they can recall and draw upon. And finally, I am a firm believer of going into an exam such as this uncluttered. You cannot anticipate the question, and if it is something out of your comfort zone, you're going to have to adapt to it anyway. So trust in the fact that you've learned something and practice on some sample questions using the works that your class has studied.

Still, there are some minor things that I do to prepare my students for this question that I think work well. The first is to play a literature version of "speed chess," in which I read aloud a random Question Three prompt, then ask them to select a book they think will work well in answering it and to frame a rough thesis that will respond to the question. I usually give them seven to ten minutes. We then go round the room, sharing our choices and discussing the merits or shortcomings of each. This helps students to develop the ability to crystallize their thoughts under pressure and forces them not to rely on the list of titles. On most days we can do two or three of these in a class period, and we usually do this for two or three days.

Since students in my class maintain a portfolio of their writing responses, we never really study for this question. During that two-week period in May, many of my students are taking multiple AP exams, several of which are much more content-driven than the AP English Literature exam. As I mentioned earlier, I don't like my students' minds to be 'cluttered,' so I merely encourage them to revisit papers they have previously written on the major novels and plays that we've studied. I do give them a binder of *Masterplots*, but mainly for works that they've read during the previous year or over the summer that may be apropos to the question. However, this is solely to refresh their memories of character names and key developments in the plot. I trust that my colleagues in the department have taught these works well, but I also know that being a year or more removed from a book can make students forgetful. It is also important to understand that this is not the time to pick something you read and liked but *did not* study in class. The question insists that students use a work of recognized literary merit. You have just taken an Advanced Placement, or college-level, English class, one whose syllabus had to be approved by the College Board. It is unwise to be using *Twilight* or something from Harry Potter.

Of course, Question Three remains the only question for which you can specifically prepare, which is the main reason why it is often the highest scoring question on the examination. Although you will not know the specific direction or focus of the question, you can do some specific preparation. One highly respected colleague of mine has her students survey what they have read over the past two years and select three to five novels or plays that can unquestionably be seen as having literary merit. She then has them fill out a 5 x 7 index card with such items as the title, author's name, major characters, significant plot events, the setting, point of view or perspective, major theme(s), even a few great lines. Her students use these to review prior to taking the test. Thus, they know a few works really well and are able to write about them easily. Sounds like a good practice to me.

Other than that, I encourage them all to get a good night's sleep. Rested minds are clear-thinking minds, and if I've done my job, they will do theirs. Over the last thirteen years (or when I started keeping records of such things), 93% of the students in my AP class have scored a 3 or better and almost 65% either a 4 or a 5. As a teacher of English, I don't often deal with numbers, but these numbers tell me that what we do between the first day of class and the examination works.

4. The Last Word

As I said at the beginning, there is not much I can do besides this to prepare you for the Literature question. The primary front for increasing your performance on the AP English Literature Examination is improving your close reading skills in poetry and prose in your own AP English class. This book can abet, but not replace, AP instruction, and the quickest way to improve your score is to learn to love literature, to read often and widely, and to develop your ability to write clearly, cogently, and fluently about what you have read. In the following pages you will be given two literature prompts to consider, in addition to sample student essays on each. Read over the student responses and the comments of the two seasoned AP graders who have assessed them and discuss them with your teacher and your classmates. Then try responding with a work of your own. Hopefully, these will help prepare you not only for the other Question Three prompts in this textbook, but also for the one you will encounter on the exam itself.

Question One

(Suggested time—40 minutes. This question counts as one-third of the total essay section score.)

In many works of literature a character seems bent upon recovering something that has been lost. This loss—which may involve a romantic interest, reputation or status, wealth, property, or even something less tangible such as a dream or freedom—provides an important focal point for the work as a whole in respect to the success or failure of the character's attempt to recover it.

Choose a novel or play in which a character is intent upon recovering something that has been lost. Then, in a well-organized essay, assess the extent to which the character succeeds in this quest and show how his success or failure impacts the meaning of the work as a whole.

You may choose a novel or play from the works listed below or use a work of comparable literary merit.

As I Lay Dying	*Lord Jim*
The Awakening	*A Lesson Before Dying*
Beloved	*Medea*
Brave New World	*The Merchant of Venice*
The Catcher in the Rye	*The Namesake*
Cold Mountain	*The Odyssey*
The Dead	*One Flew Over the Cuckoo's Nest*
Death of a Salesman	*Our Town*
Going After Cacciato	*Richard II*
The Grapes of Wrath	*A Separate Peace*
Great Expectations	*Snow Falling on Cedars*
The Great Gatsby	*A Streetcar Named Desire*
The Handmaid's Tale	*The Sun Also Rises*
Invisible Man	*That Championship Season*
King Lear	*Wuthering Heights*

Précis and Explication of Free-Response Question One: "Recovering Something Lost"

Free-Response Question One required students to choose a novel or play of recognized literary merit in which a character tries to recover something he has lost, be this something material such as wealth or status, or something more intangible such as reputation or a dream. Students were asked to "assess the extent to which the character succeeds in this quest and show how his success or failure impacts the meaning of the work as a whole." To illustrate what a successful response to the prompt might look like, I have chosen a title that I anticipate a number of students might also choose: F. Scott Fitzgerald's *The Great Gatsby*.

In preparing to frame a thesis for this paper, the first logical question to ask yourself is "What does Jay Gatsby lose?" The most immediate response is Daisy, the girl with whom he falls in love. However, to score high on the rubric for this question your essay needs to be more complex, and you need to think about this further. In doing so, you might very well decide that he loses his innocence or his virtue since, in his quest to become wealthy enough to thrust himself into Daisy's "old money" society, he must involve himself in a number of illegal activities and camouflage his identity with a series of fantastic lies. Finally, you might go so far as to say that in pursuing Daisy, he is pursuing something more intangible: lost opportunity, lost youth, a loss of self even. Ultimately, in trying to recover Daisy, he loses something else: his life. Thus, the first part of a really developed thesis might claim that "In *The Great Gatsby*, the mysterious protagonist Jay Gatsby sets out to recover more than the girl that he loved who married another, wealthier man, but the time of youth, innocence and opportunity that she represents."

This, however, is still incomplete because we have yet to address the second half of the question. This has two parts: the extent to which he fails or succeeds, and the connection to the meaning of the work as a whole. Well, we know he does get the girl—at least for a number of afternoons at his mansion—but we also know that the tragic turn of events with Myrtle Wilson effectively ends any possible chance at long-term happiness. So it is a "Pyrrhic victory" of sorts: as the cliché goes, he wins the battle but loses the war. The rest of our thesis should reflect this dichotomy. As to the meaning of the work as a whole, students may express this in a variety of ways. However, most of them will lead back to Gatsby's incredulous response to Nick's suggestion that you can't repeat the past: "Can't repeat the past?...Why, of course, you can." The events of the novel at least prove this exceedingly romantic claim false. So let's add to our thesis: "In *The Great Gatsby*, the mysterious protagonist Jay Gatsby sets out to recover more than the girl that he loved who married another, wealthier man, but the time of youth, innocence and opportunity that she represents; however, though he temporarily succeeds in winning back her affection, ironic events and Daisy's own weak character conspire to prevent this reunion from achieving any permanence, disproving Gatsby's romantic belief that you can repeat the past. Though the final symbol of the novel, 'boats against the current,' shows just how strong the temptation to do so can be, the events of the novel prove that attempts of this nature are fruitless, even fatal."

Now enough of my own students have said this for me to anticipate what some of you may be thinking: "Isn't that a little long? Doesn't a thesis have to be one sentence?" The respective answers are yes—and no. This is a complex prompt that really asked you to do four things: find a novel or play in which a character seeks to recover something he'd lost; identify what that lost something is; show the extent to which the attempt to recover this was successful; and connect the character's action to the meaning of the work as a whole. A *simple* thesis—the kind of one sentence one you were taught as freshmen—simply can't accomplish this. Rather, you need a *complex* thesis, one that may develop over a series of sentences working in concert to convey your full point. In fact, if you tack the thesis sentence that closes the previous paragraph onto a sentence or two that introduces *The Great Gatsby*, you pretty much have your entire introduction. Still, on many of the simpler prompts, a well-developed one sentence thesis will serve as well.

I have taken the time to illustrate this so you might appreciate both the importance of "fully thinking the question out" and the importance of "framing a good, strong thesis" that will direct your paper and the focus of the AP reader. To be fair, I have been doing this as a high school English teacher and a writer for over thirty-five years, so it naturally comes more easily for me. Still, the thought process that I use is exactly the same one I expect students in my AP class to master. Papers that pave the road clearly for the AP reader permit him to relax and actually enjoy reading the essay. There is no struggle at trying to figure out where this paper is going; he is now just looking to see if your evidence from *The Great Gatsby* supports your claim. Remember: a good thesis should be *concise*, but also *precise*—not in the sense that you are providing details of the plot in your introduction, but in a way that makes your claim cogent and clear to the reader. Because of the complexity of this prompt, the thesis for this essay will be more complex as well, but it addresses every aspect of the question and makes several definitive claims.

At seventeen or eighteen years of age, you may feel you are not be capable of creating such a thorough thesis, especially under the constraints of time; however, with practice you can learn to do so and to do so well. It may reassure you that all AP readers are reminded each and every day of two things: to consider each paper as a "rough draft," and to "reward students for what they do well." The closer you come to crafting a fully developed thesis, the easier it will be to organize your essay, maintain good clarity, and line up your supporting details. And, you will find, you are able to write much faster. Consider the difference between driving to someone's house the very first time, when you don't know the directions, and driving there after you've gone there twenty-five times. Having been there before, you make no wrong turns, you do not fumble for directions. You get there with ease. That's what on-demand writing must become.

In that many, many students are intimately familiar with this novel, I am not going to spend a great deal of time rehashing the plot. Let it suffice that the body of a good essay probably needs to articulate some combination of the following:

- Prior to the novel's opening, the circumstances involving when Gatsby first meets Daisy and why he "loses" her (Important details here would be Gatsby's going to serve in the war, and Daisy's being swept off her feet by Tom Buchanan's suave nature and his enormous wealth: think of the ostentatious nature of the wedding and the elaborate wedding present he gives her).

- How Gatsby sets out to "recover" her (You need not spend an enormous amount of time on this—maybe just a few sentences describing the young Gatsby, how he makes his fortune through bootlegging and other clandestine—and most likely criminal—activities, how he purchases the house across the bay because he can't buy into the "old money" section, and how he hosts these outrageous parties as the bait to lure her back to him. After all, he is in the house when the novel begins).

- How his success in doing so is only temporary (You might use the confrontation scene in which Tom forces Daisy to choose between his financial security and status, and Gatsby's romantic love and dangerous new money, and how the best she can say to Gatsby is "I loved you too. Isn't that enough?"—which it clearly isn't).

- How Daisy's fatal and ironic run-down of Myrtle Wilson, Tom's mistress, effectively ends any chance of her relationship with Gatsby (Here you would like to stress how she immediately relies on Tom because, despite his sleazy character, he has the money and clout to get her out of this mess).

Of course, one must always be careful not to fall prey to mere plot summary. Rather, you must use details from the novel to buttress the points you've made in your thesis, points which should be the cornerstones of the body of your essay.

In your conclusion, you might put a nice bow on the package by returning to one or both of the two famous lines from the novel. Gatsby's claim that you can repeat the past, and the "boats against the current" line work together in that the latter suggests we *all* fall prey to this temptation during our lives. I like to point out to students how people, as they begin to age, become conscious of dyeing their hair, putting on make-up, getting into the gym, etc. because everyone secretly fancies himself as being able to recapture the dashing persona that he or she once was—until the unforgiving mirror or the morning backache painfully reminds that those days are long gone. This is the time for a nice universal statement because, as the book clearly states, "And so *we* beat on," suggesting that this is not merely true of Jay Gatsby but of all individuals. This satisfies how the character's attempt to recover something he lost connects to the book as a whole.

Well, there you have it. Obviously the student who picks a different novel will write an essay with different details, but the structure of the thesis should be roughly the same. As was explained in the explication of the previous free-response question, the student essays which follow the Scoring Guide represent attempts by students of mine (as well as those of a helpful colleague) to respond to the question. Read them over and see how well you think they did in answering the question. Discuss this with your teacher, and then see what I and another long-standing AP exam reader had to say about them. When you are done, try answering the question with another novel or play of your own. Remember: you can't really 'prepare' for the question since it changes from year to year; however, you can certainly prepare for the type of brainstorming, thesis-framing, and scaffolding activities that are essential to answering questions of this type. And, by doing so, you can get better at writing them.

The preparatory section of this book is almost over. Good luck on the four Sample Examinations that follow and, more importantly, good luck on the AP English Literature Examination in May.

Scoring Guide for Free-Response Question One: "Recovering Something Lost"

8-9   Well-conceived, well-developed, and well-organized, these papers are marked by frequent and accurate references to the text, by an admirable ability to synthesize thought, and by a mature control over the elements of composition. Though not perfect, they clearly indicate the students' ability to select a novel or play in which a character seems bent upon recovering something lost. They also persuasively illustrate the nature of what has been lost, the degree of success the character enjoys in his attempt to recover it, and how his success or failure impacts the meaning of the work as a whole.

6-7   These essays select a novel or play in which a character seems bent upon recovering something lost, but are less adept at responding to the question. This may be due to inconsistencies in textual understanding, or to a lesser proficiency in illustrating either the nature of what has been lost, the degree of success the character enjoys in his attempt to recover it, or how his success or failure impacts the meaning of the work as a whole. Though these essays reflect their writers' abilities to convey their points clearly, they feature less fluency, less development and less cogency than 8-9 papers.

5   These papers respond to the question on a character being bent upon recovering something lost in superficial, formulaic, inconsistent, or insufficiently supported ways. They may rely primarily on paraphrase, but may still convey an implicit understanding of the passage and of the task. The papers are generally written in a satisfactory manner, with occasional errors in composition or mechanics that do not impede the reader's understanding. Nevertheless, these essays lack the organization, persuasiveness and development of upper-half papers.

3-4   These lower-half essays generally suggest an incomplete or overly simplistic understanding of the task, an inability to identify a character who seems bent upon recovering something lost, or an inability to illustrate either the nature of what has been lost, the degree of success the character enjoys in his attempt to recover it, and/or how his success or failure impacts the meaning of the work as a whole. Their arguments are often characterized by a failure to provide adequate support and/or insufficient control over the elements of composition. In some instances they may consist entirely of paraphrase and/or feature acute problems in organization, clarity, fluency or development.

1-2   These essays compound the shortcomings of 3-4 papers. They often contain many serious and distracting errors in grammar or mechanics that preclude any successful response to the prompt. Though these essays may attempt to show a character who is bent upon recovering something lost, they are severely limited by deficiencies in organization, clarity, fluency or development.

0   Papers scored a zero make no more than a passing reference to the task.

—   This indicates a blank or completely off-topic response.

Sample Student Essay One

Harry "Rabbit" Angstrom, the protagonist of John Updike's Rabbit, Run, *is perpetually running away from reality. At first glance, it seems that he is just running to avoid the harsh reality of his life. However, when he reminisces about his successful athletic career in high school, the reader sees that he is actually trying to escape the confines of society and recover the freedom and success that he used to have. This need to find freedom haunts Rabbit for the entire novel, and as each attempt fails one can see how tight the societal restraints of the 1950's really are.*

The very first scene in the novel shows Rabbit avoiding his adult life in an attempt to recreate his high school success. He stumbles upon a pickup basketball game on his way home from work, and joins in, showing off his basketball skills. He does not know these teens, nor does he introduce himself to them. His action is somewhat inappropriate, as societal norms generally keep children and adults existing in their own separate circles. He does not want to face the reality that he is too old for this kind of play and that he has a job and a family at home to take care of. Ultimately, however, Rabbit snaps back to reality and runs home to where he is needed. He has temporarily resurrected his high school glory,

Rabbit feels terribly confined by his role as a father. His son's whining bothers him, his wife Janice's questions irritate him, and finally he snaps. When Janice sends him out on an errand he just keeps driving, out of the town that he has lived in for his entire life and until he reaches West Virginia. This drive seems like a mindless overreaction to his claustrophobia in Mt. Judge, but it is his natural instinct to run, the instinct that makes his nickname "Rabbit" so fitting, that is the incentive behind his long drive and hunt for freedom. He wants to liberate himself from his responsibilities as a parent. As a teenager, he did not have these responsibilities to worry about, and now he has two other people that look to him for support. This frightens him and confines him. Rabbit knows that he cannot just do whatever he wants as a parent but he feels so stuck in his life that he just wants to break away and leave it all behind, which is what he is trying to do when he essentially runs away from home. Ultimately, Rabbit does not find freedom during his night-long drive. This is small-town America in the 1950's, where everything looks the same, so the town in West Virginia that he ends up in feels as small and confining as Mt. Judge, so he turns around and goes home. His failure to find the freedom he so desperately desires even on the open road helps to demonstrate how the time he lives in is really what is confining him.

As a teenager, Rabbit had an ambition and drive to succeed, which can be seen through his flashbacks to the basketball court. As an adult, he still wants to succeed, he still wants to make something of himself, but he gets lazy. The 1950's were a decade of optimism, but they were also a decade of inaction. It is too easy for Rabbit to get comfortable with whoever he is with, whether it is Janice, Marty Tothero, or Ruth. It is also too easy for him to simply run away when the going gets rough, which contributes to his lack of success as an adult. This contributes to the power of the novel–he is spending his life searching for freedom and the success he has known earlier in life, but is too caught up in the laziness of the time period to really do something about it. Ultimately, Rabbit's failure to find freedom puts the time period in a new light. For many people, behind all the optimism of the 1950's there was an overwhelming sense of hopelessness and entrapment.

Sample Student Essay Two

Loss pervades every aspect of Cormac McCarthy's The Road. *The novel is set in post-apocalyptic America, a ruined landscape void of color, warmth, and life, ravaged by some unknown disaster of a global scale. In this harsh landscape, most survivors quickly abandon all morality and learn to do whatever is needed for survival, preying on the weak and practicing widespread cannibalism. To the narrator and his young son, this deterioration of humanity is the most potent loss of all. They spend the novel moving south, searching for any remnant of the world that they fear is hopelessly lost.*

A central theme of The Road *is the search for and preservation of human morality. The young boy, who the man has devoted his existence to protecting, acts as a symbol for the moral conscience of man. Although he was born after the apocalypse and raised in an extremely harsh and unsympathetic environment, he is highly sensitive. He often begs to offer help and food to other people they encounter, even though contact with others is extremely dangerous and he is often on the verge of starvation himself. When they do find food, the boy requires constant reassurance that the original owners of the food are gone and no longer need it. This acute sense of conscience contrasts sharply with the depravity of the boy's surroundings, highlighting what has been lost and what they long to recover.*

The theme of morality can also be seen in the flame symbol. Both the boy and his father often mention that they are carrying the flame. The father occasionally reassures the boy that there are other "good guys" who carry the flame as well. Although the meaning of the flame is never directly explained by the characters, it obviously represents the sense of humanity that the boy and his father retain, but that has died out in many others. The pair treasures the remnants of morality they carry and maintain hope that somewhere, humanity may still be intact.

In many post-apocalyptic stories, the narrative concludes with the protagonist finally stumbling upon a community of survivors, who heroically begin to rebuild society. This hopeful conclusion is noticeably absent in The Road, *which ends with the death of the father and the adoption of the boy by another small family of survivors. While the ending is not altogether tragic, the reader is left with the suspicion that humanity, vastly overwhelmed by depravity, will eventually die out.* The Road *provides uncomfortable insight into the fragility of our peaceful existence, and shows us what man can become in the face of desperation.*

Sample Student Essay Three

F. Scott Fitzgerald's defining—and indicting—novel of the Roaring Twenties, The Great Gatsby, is centered on Jay Gatsby's mythic, but ultimately tragic, quest to win back the love of Daisy. He courted her many years ago out west in Louisville before he went to war and she married. His single-minded focus drives the plot of the novel, and his ultimate failure makes us empathize with this millionaire and grow frustrated with the materialistic corruption of the American Dream.

At the novel's opening, Daisy has married the wealthy Tom Buchanan and they live together in East Egg. Gatsby follows them, boasting of his new and immense riches in a gaudily decorated mansion of tremendous proportions across the bay in West Egg. He accumulated great wealth with an undoubtedly relentless work ethic and dubious business dealings, and he spends it lavishly, demonstrating the height of ostentation. Gatsby's singular purpose is to attract Daisy's attention. Her love would soon follow, he hopes. For that same reason, he throws such lavish parties that they are talked about all over New York, but he does not care for the parties, only Daisy. From his backyard on the shore, he can see across the bay to the green light at the end of Tom and Daisy's dock, which becomes a symbol of his yearning. Yet the division between Gatsby and Daisy is greater than just the distance across the bay. It is the recurring dichotomy of east and west, where the east belongs to the established wealth while everyone else—in West Egg, the noveaux riches—populates the west.

Gatsby finally begins to see all his work begin to pay off. Nick Carraway, the narrator of the novel and Gatsby's neighbor, is Daisy's cousin and thus Gatsby's connection, and Gatsby and Daisy reunite through him. When Gatsby gives her a tour of his mansion, and Daisy sees a pile of Gatsby's imported silk shirts, she sobs into them. Gatsby believes it is because she has missed him, and at the time, the reader is inclined to agree, although later, it seems more likely that the beauty of the wealth moves her, rather than the reunion with a lost love. So begins an affair in which Gatsby has recaptured the object of all his efforts, and both he and Daisy find happiness, although in secret.

This happiness is disrupted when Daisy's jealous husband Tom suspects the affair, and though an adulterer himself, initiates an uncomfortable confrontation among all the involved characters, at the Plaza Hotel. Gatsby's immense self-confidence—that self-confidence that makes him "great"—assures him that Daisy will choose him and leave Tom. Tom, meanwhile, is equally confident, and rightfully so since Daisy, when forced to choose, ultimately stays with Tom. Gatsby has lost his love once again, and this time, without any hope for the future. In the many years they had been apart, Gatsby romanticized Daisy. He invented a notion of her that was beautiful but false. Maybe she loved Gatsby, maybe not. Gatsby sincerely believed that he could earn Daisy's love with his money. But for Daisy, no amount of either money or love could ever exceed the value of East Egg status, a reality that leaves the once-Great Gatsby deflated and devastated. Towards the novel's end, Gatsby is murdered, but one gets the sense that already he was apathetic to living.

Nick, the first-person narrator of The Great Gatsby, is little more than a passive observer throughout the tumultuous events of the novel, but his comment in the final paragraphs is perhaps the most profound. From the time Dutch explorers first laid eyes on the on the verdant, virgin shores of the New World to the time Gatsby built his flamboyant mansion across the bay from Daisy's green light, the American Dream had been adulterated. It was no longer about happiness but materialism. Gatsby learned this the hard way. He surrounded himself with wealth and lavishness, yet still he died lonely and apathetically, having been rejected by Daisy, the sole motivation for all his wealth and lavishness. Nick is so disgusted by his adopted home in the east that he returns home to the west where, just maybe, the American Dream is still pure.

Assessment of Student Responses to Free-Response Question One:
"Recovering Something Lost"

Sample Student Essay One:

A. Assessment of Reader One

This paper had a good opening. Its thesis covered all aspects of the prompt: one, what was lost (freedom); two, the measure of success in regaining it (failure after failure); three, the connection to the work as a whole (1950's repressive society). The support included the basketball game and the time he ran away from home. The support is plot driven, but there is some good insight as to why he runs. The basketball game should be expanded to provide better support for the thesis. The conclusion is there, but the societal piece needs connection to the novel. The student's comments on the connection to the work as a whole fail; he needs to connect 1950's repression to Updike's theme or driving force. I would give this a 6.

B. Assessment of Reader Two

The student clearly knows this work well and picks a novel that should yield a solid response to the question. The shortcoming of this response is that it does not focus sufficiently on what has been lost, but spends most of its time talking about Rabbit's unhappy present. This has good development (though the writer does towards the end mention a number of characters, he does not introduce or discuss), and it should be a higher scoring essay. However, it needs to place greater emphasis on what has been lost and connect Rabbit's attempts to escape, through sport or flight, to this desire to recover something. This is a solid 6 with a potential to go higher that was unrealized.

Sample Student Essay Two:

A. Assessment of Reader One

This essay's thesis and opening are good. The first two parts of the prompt are well-covered: one, what was lost (humanity and human decency); two, the success at recovering it (seems like they fail, but not fully clear). The connection to the work as a whole, however, is not established. The idea of the young boy as a symbol of what was lost works well. This novel choice is difficult. If a student can write well about it, it can increase the score. The conclusion is confusing. The writer has made the mistake of telling the reader what "is not in the novel" instead of what is. Writing is adequate, but many awkward sentences create the need to reread. I would rate this a low 7.

B. Assessment of Reader Two

Though the writing of this paper falls definitely in the upper-half of the scoring guide, this essay suffers from a similar problem as Sample Student Essay One: a failure to establish explicitly what has been lost. To be fair, a good deal of this is conveyed implicitly, but the reader often has to struggle with digging it out. For example, the writer notes that the flame "obviously represents the sense of humanity that the boy and his father retain, but that has died out in others." One can conclude from "died out" that a "sense of humanity" is one thing that has been lost, yet another sentence alludes to "what has been lost and what they long to recover" without clarifying either directly. I would place this in the 6 range.

Sample Student Essay Three:

A. Assessment of Reader One

The opening and thesis of this essay are okay. The thesis covers it all: what was lost (Daisy); whether Gatsby enjoys success or failure in recovering her (failure); and how this attempt to recover her connects to the work as a whole (materialistic corruption). The background paragraph covers it all and begins to establish the gap in status. The insight regarding East Egg and West Egg is quite good. The description of the failure is complete, but the mention of Gatsby's death with no tie-in or explanation lowers the persuasiveness. Still, despite its flaws, the final paragraph soars. This essay nails the seemingly futile quest for materialism. I would give this a 9.

B. Assessment of Reader Two

This is an extremely thorough response which does everything that the prompt demands. Though it is likely that there would be more eloquently written papers, and though at times this essay drifts a little close to plot summary, the good points of the essay—and there are many—place it at the top of the scoring rubric. Most impressive is its treatment of the connection of Gatsby's quest for what he has lost to the meaning of the work as a whole. I would certainly score this an 8 and probably a 9.

Question Two

(Suggested time—40 minutes. This question counts as one-third of the total essay section score.)

In many works of literature the idea of atonement—of making up for a self-serving, even iniquitous action, or redeeming a cowardly, indifferent inaction—contributes significantly to the author's thematic purpose.

Choose a novel or play in which a character endeavors to atone for something he has done or perhaps failed to do. Then, in a well-organized essay, illustrate the method or nature of that atonement, the degree to which it succeeds in redressing the character's action or inaction, and the measure of closure it brings to the character's conscience. In responding be sure to show how this atonement relates to the meaning of the work as a whole.

You may choose a title from the list below or use another novel or play of recognized literary merit.

Alias Grace	*King Lear*
All My Sons	*The Kite Runner*
All the King's Men	*A Lesson Before Dying*
Antigone	*Mrs. Dalloway*
Arcadia	*The Merchant of Venice*
Atonement	*Oedipus Rex*
The Adventures of Huckleberry Finn	*The Poisonwood Bible*
Crime and Punishment	*The Power and the Glory*
East of Eden	*A Prayer for Owen Meany*
Frankenstein	*The Scarlet Letter*
The Glass Menagerie	*The Sound and the Fury*
Hamlet	*The Things They Carried*
Heart of Darkness	*A Thousand Acres*
Hedda Gabler	*Wise Blood*

Précis and Explication of Free-Response Question Two: "The Idea of Atonement..."

Free-Response Question Two required students taking the examination to complete three distinct tasks. Prior to being given the question, students were asked to consider the following statement: "In many works of literature the idea of atonement—of making up for a self-serving, even iniquitous action, or redeeming a cowardly, indifferent inaction—contributes significantly to the author's thematic purpose." To respond to this question with success, students first had to select a novel or play of acknowledged literary merit in which a character is guilty either of committing a morally questionable deed, or of failing to take action in a circumstance that demanded he do so. Next students needed to "illustrate the method or nature of that atonement, the degree to which it succeeds in redressing the character's action or inaction, and the measure of closure it brings to the character's conscience." Finally students were asked to "show how this atonement relates to the meaning of the work as a whole."

Though a complex question in terms of the steps students must complete in order to answer the question fully, Free-Response Question Two lends itself to many works of literature. To illustrate how a successful essayist might approach this question, let us consider Fyodor Dostoevsky's *Crime and Punishment*. There is little question that Dostoevsky's protagonist, Raskolnikov, commits a iniquitous action in his brutal murder of the pawnbroker and her innocent sister, Lizaveta, with an axe, but it might be said that he turns against his inherently good nature in doing so and almost immediately shows signs of seeking to absolve himself of this unspeakable crime. Prior to the actual murder, he is intent upon liberating himself from the stifling poverty that has forced him to abandon his studies at the university and to pawn his sole item of value, his father's watch, to the old woman. Raskolnikov sees the pawnbroker, an avaricious and usurious crone, as vermin, a creature unfit to live, and through his theory of ordinary and extraordinary men, sees himself as a righteous instrument to strike her from the world. Though he is obsessed with the thought of killing the pawnbroker and has devised a meticulous plan with which to do so, at heart he knows the action he intends to carry out is wrong. Prior to the murder he has a vivid dream in which, as a child walking with his father, he sees a man violently beating an old cart horse, trying to get it to pull a cartload of his friends. Though the age of the horse and the weight of the wagon conspire against movement, the man beats the horse mercilessly with a whip and, later, with a wooden beam, swearing he will kill the animal if it doesn't move forward. Like most dreams, this is filled with flotsam and jetsam, but insights into Raskolnikov are nevertheless apparent. For one, the child wishes to prevent the violence against the horse, an indication of his moral consciousness. At the same time Raskolnikov *is* the horse, and the animal's struggle to pull the cart is his own struggle to overcome scruple and commit the murder.

After Raskolnikov kills the pawnbroker—and Lizaveta who unfortuitously walks in on the murder—he immediately displays signs of wanting to rid himself of his guilt. He hides what little booty he takes not somewhere accessible, but under a large rock, a symbol of his desire to rid himself of these ill-gotten gains. Subsequently he falls physically ill, plagued by a raging fever during which, like MacBeth, he worries about blood on his clothing. He publicly discusses the case with a government clerk, boasting about what he would do if he were the murderer with the reckless audacity of a man who wishes to be caught, then rashly gives away his last kopecks to pay for the funeral feast of a fellow dissolute, Marmeladov, whose drunkenness has led to his being fatally run down by a carriage. He asks the deceased's youngest daughter, Polenka, to pray for him and later asks his eldest daughter, Sonia, to read to him the New Testament account of Lazarus, a dead man who is brought back to life by Jesus. Raskolnikov sees in Lazarus a mirror of himself, the sole difference being that he is spiritually dead. Eventually, he confesses his heinous deed to Sonia who, being a prostitute, has like him morally fallen.

Sonia persuades Raskolnikov to "throw himself down at the crossroads" and beg forgiveness for his terrible crime. Shortly afterwards, Raskolnikov turns himself in to Porfiry, the detective investigating the case, and confesses to the murder. His sentence—to a labor camp in frigid Siberia—formally completes his journey toward atonement in that, after serving his time, he can begin to pick up the pieces of his life with the help of Sonia, who faithfully awaits him.

Raskolnikov's atonement contributes to a unifying theme in Dostoevsky's novel in which several characters—the pawnbroker (avarice); Marmeladov (alcoholism; family neglect), Katerina Ivanovna and Pyotr Luzhin (hubris); and Svidrigailov (spousal abuse; pedophilia)—commit crimes and are punished for them. Unlike the other characters, who are either killed by accident, disease or murder, severely humbled, or commit suicide, Raskolnikov is the only one who seeks spiritual absolution. Thus, he is the only character permitted to continue living because not only has he suffered, but he has also returned to the path of righteousness.

The student essays which follow the Scoring Guide represent attempts by students of mine (as well as those of a helpful colleague) to respond to the question. Read them over and see how well you think they did in answering the question. Discuss this with your teacher, and then see what I and another long-standing AP exam reader had to say about them. Then try answering the question with another novel or play of your own. Remember: you can't really 'prepare' for the question since it changes from year to year; however, you can certainly prepare for the type of brainstorming, thesis-framing, and scaffolding activities that are essential to answering questions of this type. And, by doing so, you can get better at writing them.

Scoring Guide for Free-Response Question Two: "The Idea of Atonement..."

8-9 Well-conceived, well-developed, and well-organized, these papers are marked by frequent and accurate references to the text, by an admirable ability to synthesize thought, and by a mature control over the elements of composition. Though not perfect, they clearly indicate the students' ability to select a novel or play in which a character is guilty either of committing a morally questionable deed or of failing to take action in a circumstance that demanded he do so. They also persuasively illustrate the method or nature of the atonement, the degree to which it succeeds in redressing the character's action or inaction, and the measure of closure it brings to the character's conscience.

6-7 These essays select a novel or play in which a character is guilty either of committing a morally questionable deed or of failing to take action in a circumstance that demanded he do so, but are less adept at responding to the question. This may be due to inconsistencies in textual understanding, or to a lesser proficiency in illustrating either the method or nature of the atonement, the degree to which it succeeds in redressing the character's action or inaction, or the measure of closure it brings to the character's conscience. Though these essays reflect their writers' abilities to convey their points clearly, they feature less fluency, less development and less cogency than 8-9 papers.

5 These papers respond to the question on the idea of atonement—of making up for a self-serving, even iniquitous action, or redeeming a cowardly, indifferent inaction—in superficial, formulaic, inconsistent, or insufficiently supported ways. They may rely primarily on paraphrase, but may still convey an implicit understanding of the passage and the task. The papers are generally written in a satisfactory manner, with occasional errors in composition or mechanics that do not impede the reader's understanding. Nevertheless, these essays lack the organization, persuasiveness and development of upper-half papers.

3-4 These lower-half essays generally suggest an incomplete or overly simplistic understanding of the task, an inability to identify a character who feels a need to make up for a self-serving, even iniquitous action or to redeem a cowardly, indifferent inaction, or an inability either to illustrate the method or nature of the atonement, the degree to which it succeeds in redressing the character's action or inaction, and/or the measure of closure it brings to the character's conscience. Their arguments are often characterized by a failure to provide adequate support and/or insufficient control over the elements of composition. In some instances they may consist entirely of paraphrase and/or feature acute problems in organization, clarity, fluency or development.

1-2 These essays compound the shortcomings of 3-4 papers. They often contain many serious and distracting errors in grammar or mechanics that preclude any successful response to the prompt. Though these essays may attempt to show a character's attempt to make up for an action or an inaction, they are severely limited by deficiencies in organization, clarity, fluency or development.

0 Papers scored a zero make no more than a passing reference to the task.

— This indicates a blank or completely off-topic response.

Sample Student Essay One

The Scarlet Letter is a story of atonement in different forms, and of the consequences of each type of retribution. Hester Prynne, a young married woman whose adultery was revealed after she became pregnant, is publicly scorned by her harsh puritanical community. Although this public atonement for her sin is difficult to bear, Hester is able to maintain pride and dignity as she gracefully accepts the consequences of her actions. Dimmesdale, the father of the illegitimate child, is never exposed as an adulterer, and he remains a greatly respected member of the community. The bitter secret he carries, however, ultimately destroys him. The Scarlet Letter contrasts the effects of public and introverted atonement.

The opening scene is one of the most memorable passages from The Scarlet Letter, and it embodies the character of Hester Prynne. Hester stands in a public square with the bright red "A" on her chest, scorned by the multitude of people who have gathered around her. The author, however, describes Hester as beautiful, strong, and proud, despite the overwhelming atmosphere of judgment and hate. Hester maintains this attitude throughout the novel, and her atonement ironically does more to reveal the hypocritical and excessively strict nature of the community than highlight her own flaws.

Dimmesdale's atonement contrasts sharply with Hester's. Because his crime remains unknown, he suffers no public retribution. The internal shame and guilt that plagues Dimmesdale, however, ultimately does far greater damage than Hester's punishment. To make matters worse, Dimmesdale is the village priest, and he is greatly respected and admired by the community. This hypocrisy of his situation wreaks havoc on Dimmesdale's sensitive conscience and manifests itself as physical illness. In the end, Dimmesdale is destroyed by the overwhelming pressure of his internal conflict.

Hester is able to achieve closure through her public atonement. She lives her life as an outcast, but has the satisfaction of complete honesty, which at times even makes her seem superior to other members of the community. Dimmesdale, on the other hand, is left alone to bear the torment of his guilty conscience, a burden that he proves unable to bear.

Sample Student Essay Two

Khaled Hosseini's novel The Kite Runner, *which is mostly set in Afghanistan, tells the story of Amir, who does something immoral as a boy and does his best to atone for it as a man. Amir watched his friend Hassan get raped, doing nothing. The reasons for this are not entirely clear, but cowardice certainly played a part. The guilt plagues Amir for years, all the way into manhood. In fact, the embarassment causes Amir to commit even more immoral acts. But, many years after he failed to help his friend, Amir tries to find atonement by helping Hassan's son, and this apparently makes up for Amir's sin by a fairly significant amount, though the ending of the novel still leaves him with problems.*

Hassan was Amir's servant when they were boys. They were about the same age, and they were almost always together. As they aged, however, it became increasingly clear that they belonged to different classes. Amir was the son of a powerful man; he went to school and soon had many other friends that Hassan never saw. Meanwhile, Hassan was a Hazara (there is an element of racism in the novel) and his only friend was Amir, to whom he was totally loyal. One day, Hassan was ambushed by a bully and pervert named Assef and his two thuggish friends. Though the other two were unwilling, Assef decided it would be amusing to sodomize Hassan. Amir, watching unseen from a nearby alleyway, did nothing as his best friend was raped.

For many years, Amir did not atone for what he did. In fact, he ostracized Hassan and had him kicked out of the household because he could not bear to face him or speak with him. But, twenty-five years later, as a married writer living in America, he got a phone call. He found out that Hassan was dead. He had been married too, and he and his wife had been shot by the Taliban, but they had left behind a young son. So Amir found a way to atone for his sin, which had been plaguing him since his youth. He set out to return to his homeland to find and help the boy, whose name was Sohrab, so that he would perhaps find closure from what he had done.

His mission was anything but easy. It turned out that Sohrab had been kept at an orphanage which regularly gave out certain children to be molested, so as to provide for the others. Amir ultimately found that Assef, the very same person that had raped Hassan, was now keeping Sohrab as a slave. Amir and Assef faced of in a ferocious fight. After being brutally beaten and losing many of his teeth, Amir got away with Sohrab after Sohrab blinded Assef with a slingshot. (At one point earlier in the book, Hassan had threatened to do the same with a slingshot he was very skilled with.)

It is hard to think that Amir got away from his guilt by rescuing Sohrab, though he adopted the boy and promised to always take care of him. Sohrab was not a happy child, and he attempted to commit suicide while in Amir's care. This added to Amir's guilt. On the other hand, it is evident that Amir did what he could. He cannot be considered a bad person after having made such sacrifices. The fact that Sohrab blinded Assef in the same fashion that his father had threatened to do must symbolize that the two are tied together morally. In other words, helping Sohrab was the same as helping Hassan. At the end of the novel, Amir still feels like a bad person, but the reader feels differently.

The Kite Runner *tells the story of how a boy that did something deeply wrong became a man responsible enough to risk his life for others. Amir was mostly successful in helping Sohrab, and though he certainly didn't find closure, he did do a good thing which redresses his sin, if only to a point.*

Sample Student Essay Three

Fyodor Dostoevsky wrote an entire novel on the theme of atoning for one's sins, entitled <u>Crime and Punishment</u>. *This work is particularly effective because of the way Dostoevsky introduced parallel characters and plotlines, each of which buttresses the overall theme of the novel and compliments the action of Raskolnikov, the main character. One such parallel character, Marmeladov, is particularly interesting because his crime is so acute and his atonement so complete.*

Marmeladov's crime is one of indulgence. He is a raging alcoholic, and his weakness for vice costs him his job, his status, and even his clothing. Ultimately, he steals from his already impoverished family to fund his habit. He forces his wife into consumption as she must work night and day to compensate for his absence. He forces his daughter into prostitution so that she can support the family. He is not callous to his family's needs, however, but burdened with intense guilt. Marmeladov enters willingly into forms of atonement for his terribly self-serving sin. He subjects himself to verbal and physical abuse at the hands of his wife, claiming to Raskolnikov, "It's a consolation to me!" He even helps his wife inflict punishment; Raskolnikov relates how Marmeladov crawled along on his knees toward his wife as she beat him. Marmeladov's almost earnest compliance with his wife's rage strongly suggests that his eventual death beneath the wheels of a carriage was suicidal, a final act of atonement and an attempt to terminate his parasitic presence within his family.

Though his eagerness to be beaten did not actually help the family, his death beneath the carriage tangibly benefited them and therefore partially redressed his wrongdoings. Capable of acquiring a job but not of holding it, Marmeladov drained the family's resources far more than he ever contributed to them. Simply by dying, he removed a significant financial burden on their lives and prevented much misfortune-to-be. The family's income, though still minimal, was far more secure after his death than before. He did not, however, effectively make up for all the hardships he had caused them while alive. To do this, he needed to acquire a steady job and treat his family better, a task for which his resolve was too weak.

Marmeladov led a tortured existence, so his punishment and death brought as much closure to his conscience as they could. Though too weak in character to change his ways, Marmeladov despised himself for treating his family so poorly. He challenged Raskolnikov: "Assert that I am not a pig!" Raskolnikov noticed as well that he had a deep, genuine love for his family, though it was not enough to reform him. The resulting guilt is precisely why he was so grateful and eager for punishment as it somewhat unburdened his conscience. His death, of course, brought ultimate closure as he ceased to exist to hurt his beloved family.

In keeping with his self-indulgent ways, Marmeladov's atonement did more to benefit his own conscience than it did to redress his past sins. It did, however, prevent future crimes and unshackle the family financially. Dostoevsky's sub-plot about Marmeladov greatly enhanced the novel thematically as it underscored Raskolnikov's own need to atone for his sins. Additionally, it showed that sins such as vice, though less directly detrimental to others' well-being than Raskolnikov's murder, can cause great misery and require appropriate penance.

Assessment of Student Responses to Free-Response Question Two: "The Idea of Atonement…"

Sample Student Essay One:

A. Assessment of Reader One

This essay opens with the idea of retribution, not redemption. The opening paragraph contains a fairly good thesis covering the four points of the prompt. The problem is that this student tries to deal with two characters, both of whom are dealing with the idea of atonement, yet the essay would be better served if the writer stayed with one character and developed that idea fully. For example, the paragraph on Hester covers plot but nevers deals with the "nature" of her atonement throughout the novel. The paragraph on Dimmesdale is better in that there is more specific evidence, but the question of whether or not Dimmesdale tries to atone is not covered; the essay discusses his hidden sin only. The final paragraph does not include how the atonement(s) influence the work as a whole. However, the writing is sophisticated and there are occasional insights (Dimmesdale's "bitter secret," for example). I would rate this a 5.

B. Assessment of Reader Two

This paper really epitomizes the 5 category as well as any sample could. The student has picked a very appropriate novel, in that Hester's and Dimmesdale's adultery has endowed them with a mutual culpability. Though the student draws a fine distinction between "public and introverted atonement," she fails to develop either character's atonement to a degree that would elevate this essay into the upper half. Though Dimmesdale's "illness" is mentioned, nothing is made of his secret self-scourging, nor does the writer provide specific details of Hester's atonement or, perhaps, her moral defiance in the form of the elaborately woven A. Like a classic 5, this is nicely written but superficial.

Sample Student Essay Two:

A. Assessment of Reader One

This paper falls into the "plot trap." The opening is "clunky;" it rambles a bit with clichés and verb tense problems. The thesis does describe the supposed "deed"—the fact that the main character watches the rape of his friend and does nothing—but that is not what causes the need for atonement. The thesis also states that the atonement is to help the friend's son—sparse but okay. The thesis is not complete. In paragraph three, the writer continues to insist that the cowardice of the main character is the deed. The writer mentions the subsequent actions of the character but does not connect them to the need for atonement. The atonement itself (paragraph four), describes the "rescue"—very plot driven—no description of the "nature" of the atonement. Writing lacks sophistication with verb tense and pronoun usage problems. Nowhere is the work as a whole addressed. I would score this a 5, but a very different one than the previous paper.

B. Assessment of Reader Two

In general, I found this to be a much more successful paper than Sample Essay One. Though it drifts quite a bit into plot summary, part of this is understandable in light of the sprawling chronological plot of the novel. The choice of novel is apropos to the question, and the student does a good job showing how Amir tries to atone for his shameful inaction by later rescuing and raising his dead friend's son. The student also discusses the degree to which these later actions bring Amir closure. What the student does not explicitly do is connect this atonement to the meaning of the work as a whole. This and the rather spotty nature of the writing would make me award this a low 6.

Sample Student Essay Three:

A. Assessment of Reader One

Students who can write well about a complex novel such as *Crime and Punishment* certainly have a "head-start." This writer chooses to deal with a minor character, Marmeladov, but is able to discuss the character's situation clearly. The opening is skillfully written, but does not contain a strong thesis. Paragraph two describes the deed and beautifully explains the nature of the atonement. Paragraph three is a bit simplistic, but does explain why the "retribution" of Marmeladov's suicide gave him some redemption. In the final paragraph the significance to the work as a whole is covered. This paper has "moments of brilliance," but the general opening and quick "wrap-up" at the conclusion keep it from the 8/9 range. I would score this a 7.

B. Assessment of Reader Two

I found this paper to be similar to, but better than, the previous one on *The Kite Runner*. The student picked an appropriate text and chose, a little surprisingly, to use a minor character whose death removes him from the book rather quickly. Even so, the writer cogently shows the destructive effects of his alcoholism on the family and his feeble attempt at atonement through enduring his wife's verbal and physical abuse. He connects it briefly to the novel's overall motif and abets it with a pair of short citations. There is one minor error (Marmeladov doesn't *order* his daughter into prostitution though his failure to provide for the family certainly impels this) and the writing is solid but not on the level of the highest-scoring papers. As a result, I would score this a strong 7.

Sample Examination I

Section I

Questions 1-14. Refer to the following poem.

The Writer

In her room at the prow of the house
Where light breaks, and the windows are tossed with linden,
My daughter is writing a story.

I pause in the stairwell, hearing
(5) From her shut door a commotion of typewriter-keys
Like a chain hauled over a gunwale.

Young as she is, the stuff
Of her life is a great cargo, and some of it heavy:
I wish her a lucky passage.

(10) But now it is she who pauses,
As if to reject my thought and its easy figure.
A stillness greatens, in which

The whole house seems to be thinking,
And then she is at it again with a bunched clamor
(15) Of strokes, and again is silent.

I remember the dazed starling
Which was trapped in that very room, two years ago;
How we stole in, lifted a sash

And retreated, not to affright it;
(20) And how for a helpless hour, through the crack of the door,
We watched the sleek, wild, dark

And iridescent creature
Batter against the brilliance, drop like a glove
To the hard floor, or the desk-top,

(25) And wait then, humped and bloody,
For the wits to try it again; and how our spirits
Rose when, suddenly sure,

It lifted off from a chair-back,
Beating a smooth course for the right window
(30) And clearing the sill of the world.

It is always a matter, my darling,
Of life or death, as I had forgotten. I wish
What I wished you before, but harder.

—Richard Wilbur

---

[1] type of deciduous (seasonal leaf-shedding) tree with heart-shaped leaves

1. The first three stanzas of the poem feature diction that is derived from

   (A) nature
   (B) architecture
   (C) publishing
   (D) seafaring
   (E) adolescence

2. The father's thoughts primarily depict him as

   (A) intrusive
   (B) empathetic
   (C) solicitous
   (D) nostalgic
   (E) doting

3. The author's use of the "linden" in line 2 seems intended to reinforce the

   (A) daughter's passion for writing
   (B) daughter's youthfulness
   (C) daughter's fragile feelings
   (D) father's love for his daughter
   (E) father's remoteness from his daughter

4. Which of the following BEST articulates the difference between the father's pause in line 4 and the daughter's pause in line 10?

   (A) The former pauses in admiration, the latter in contemplation.
   (B) The former pauses in annoyance, the latter out of guilt.
   (C) The former pauses in curiosity, the latter to maintain secrecy.
   (D) The former pauses in confusion, the latter due to fatigue.
   (E) The former pauses in preoccupation, the latter in reflection.

5. By which of the following does the speaker BEST capture his daughter's intense focus?

   (A) the image of the windows "tossed with linden" (line 2)
   (B) the simile of the "chain hauled over a gunwale" (line 6)
   (C) the metaphor of the "great cargo" (line 8)
   (D) the metaphor of the "passage" (line 9)
   (E) the personification of the "thinking" house (line 13)

6. The speaker is likely reminded of the starling by which aspect of his daughter?

   (A) her youthful innocence
   (B) her delicate beauty
   (C) her mellifluous voice
   (D) her dogged perseverance
   (E) her seated position

7. The speaker likely links his daughter with the starling for all of the following reasons EXCEPT

   (A) her physical confinement
   (B) her struggle versus an obstacle
   (C) his ardent wish for her to succeed
   (D) his pained awareness of his inability to assist
   (E) the hour at which the episode takes place

8. The simile used to describe the starling in line 23 emphasizes its

   (A) brilliant color
   (B) feathered softness
   (C) tenacious claws
   (D) lithesome flight
   (E) fragile anatomy

9. The figurative phrase, "the sill of the world" (line 30), BEST exemplifies which of the following?

   (A) hyperbole
   (B) metonymy
   (C) personification
   (D) allusion
   (E) paradox

10. The shift from complete, often periodic sentences in the first half of the poem to loose sentences characterized by enjambment in the second half is likely done to enhance which of the following contrasts?

    (A) frustration and triumph
    (B) youth and maturity
    (C) constraint and autonomy
    (D) ignorance and knowledge
    (E) home and world

11. Ultimately, the father's MOST sincere wish for his daughter involves her

    (A) finishing her story
    (B) moving out of the house
    (C) maintaining her psychological well-being
    (D) learning to respect her elders
    (E) navigating life's obstacles successfully

12. The major structural transition in the poem involves the

    (A) father's entry into the house
    (B) daughter's pause in typing
    (C) father's recollection of the trapped starling
    (D) starling's assault on the windowpane
    (E) father's concluding wish for his daughter

13. Which of the following words or phrases BEST unites the speaker's hopes for both girl and starling?

    (A) "shut door" (line 5) and "helpless hour" (line 20)
    (B) "lucky passage" (line 9) and "smooth course" (line 29)
    (C) "bunched clamor" (line 14) and "Batter against the brilliance" (line 23)
    (D) "easy figure" (line 11) and "iridescent creature" (line 22)
    (E) "stillness greatens" (line 12) and "spirits / Rose" (lines 26-27)

14. In the poem, the pronoun "it," used in lines 8, 10, 14, 19, 26, 28 and 31, does NOT refer to which of the following?

    (A) the act of writing
    (B) the speaker's daughter
    (C) the clamor of the typewriter
    (D) the starling's attempt to find an exit
    (E) the concerns of adolescence

Questions 15-26. Refer to the following passage.

Little Chandler sat in the room off the hall, holding a child in his arms. To save money they kept no servant but Annie's young sister Monica came for an hour or so in the morning
(5) and an hour or so in the evening to help. But Monica had gone home long ago. It was a quarter to nine. Little Chandler had come home late for tea and, moreover, he had forgotten to bring Annie home the parcel of coffee from
(10) Bewley's. Of course she was in a bad humour and gave him short answers. She said she would do without any tea but when it came near the time at which the shop at the corner closed she decided to go out herself for a
(15) quarter of a pound of tea and two pounds of sugar. She put the sleeping child deftly in his arms and said: "Here. Don't waken him."

A little lamp with a white china shade stood upon the table and its light fell over a
(20) photograph which was enclosed in a frame of crumpled horn. It was Annie's photograph. Little Chandler looked at it, pausing at the thin tight lips. She wore the pale blue summer blouse which he had brought her home as a
(25) present one Saturday....When he brought the blouse home Annie kissed him and said it was very pretty and stylish; but when she heard the price she threw the blouse on the table and said it was a regular swindle to charge ten and
(30) elevenpence for it....

He looked coldly into the eyes of the photograph and they answered coldly. Certainly they were pretty and the face itself was pretty. But he found something mean in it.
(35) Why was it so unconscious and ladylike? The composure of the eyes irritated him. They repelled him and defied him: there was no passion in them, no rapture.... Why had he married the eyes in the photograph?....
(40) He caught himself up at the question and glanced nervously round the room. He found something mean in the pretty furniture which he had bought for his house on the hire system. Annie had chosen it herself and it reminded
(45) him of her. It too was prim and pretty. A dull resentment against his life awoke within him. Could he not escape from his little house? Was it too late for him to try to live bravely...Could he go to London? There was the furniture still
(50) to be paid for. If he could only write a book and get it published, that might open the way for him.

A volume of Byron's poems lay before him on the table. He opened it cautiously with his
(55) left hand lest he should waken the child and began to read the first poem in the book:

> Hushed are the winds and still the
>   evening gloom,
> Not e'en a Zephyr wanders through
(60)   the grove,
> Whilst I return to view my
>   Margaret's tomb
> And scatter flowers on the dust I love.

He paused. He felt the rhythm of the verse
(65) about him in the room. How melancholy it was! Could he, too, write like that, express the melancholy of his soul in verse? There were so many things he wanted to describe....

The child awoke and began to cry. He
(70) turned from the page and tried to hush it: but it would not be hushed. He began to rock it to and fro in his arms but its wailing cry grew keener. He rocked it faster while his eyes began to read the second stanza:

(75)
> Within this narrow cell reclines her clay,
> That clay where once...

It was useless. He couldn't read. He couldn't do anything. The wailing of the child pierced the drum of his ear. It was useless,
(80) useless! He was a prisoner for life....

"A Little Cloud", from DUBLINERS by James Joyce, copyright 1916 by B.W. Heubsch. Definitive text Copyright (c) 1967 by the Estate of James Joyce. Used by permission of Viking Penguin, a division of Penguin Group (USA) Inc.

15. The passage is primarily concerned with the

(A) monetary struggles of a family
(B) doting thoughtfulness of a husband
(C) dwindling passion in a marriage
(D) hapless frustration of artistic potential
(E) incessant needs of infants

16. The protagonist's name does which of the following?

     I. It matches the meager nature of his residence.
    II. It links him to the feeble helplessness of the infant.
    III. It comments wryly on the grandiose nature of his ambitions.

    (A) I only
    (B) III only
    (C) I and II
    (D) II and III
    (E) I, II and III

17. All of the following are used by the author to convey the underlying specter of financial constraint EXCEPT

    (A) the nature of the family's domestic assistance
    (B) the meager purchase Little Chandler was to make at Bewley's
    (C) the lamp with the white china shade
    (D) Annie's belief that the charge for the blouse was a "swindle"
    (E) the installment plan through which they secured their furnishings

18. The speaker likely includes the incident of the forgotten coffee (lines 7-16) to establish which of the following?

    (A) Little Chandler's negligence
    (B) Little Chandler's forgetfulness
    (C) Little Chandler's profligacy
    (D) Annie's self-reliance
    (E) Annie's self-centeredness

19. The second paragraph anecdote about the blouse (lines 23-30) introduces which of the following aspects of Annie?

    (A) her control over Little Chandler
    (B) her desire to be pampered
    (C) her absence of gratitude
    (D) her necessary frugality
    (E) her volatile temperament

20. Which BEST expresses the primary function of the photograph in the passage?

    (A) It reminds Little Chandler of his failure to bring home the coffee.
    (B) It reaffirms why Little Chandler married Annie.
    (C) It provides a visual reminder of a nostalgic moment in Little Chandler's married life.
    (D) It triggers a dissatisfaction that makes Little Chandler regret his marriage.
    (E) It makes Little Chandler long for Annie's rapid return from the shop.

21. All of the following help to exacerbate Little Chandler's discontentedness EXCEPT

    (A) the ten and elevenpence he had wasted on Annie's blouse
    (B) the countenance of his wife in the photograph
    (C) the furniture in the room and the manner of its purchase
    (D) the romantic verses he reads in the volume of Byron
    (E) the uncontrollable wailing of the child

22. In the passage, the infant functions primarily as a(n)

    (A) poignant symbol of the impoverishment of the family
    (B) cherished object of Little Chandler's affection
    (C) audible reminder of Little Chandler's inescapable lot
    (D) precious embodiment of Annie's and Little Chandler's enduring love
    (E) ironic counterpoint to the symbols of death in the poem

23. Little Chandler's attempts to silence the crying infant (lines 69-74) are BEST labeled

    (A) desperate
    (B) befuddled
    (C) uninformed
    (D) punitive
    (E) admonitory

24. The final portrait of Little Chandler in lines 77-80 is

    (A) blissful and idyllic
    (B) despairing and pathetic
    (C) resigned and indifferent
    (D) nostalgic and sentimental
    (E) venomous and misanthropic

25. Upon completing the story, the reader perceives the opening sentence of the passage as

    (A) celebrating the intimacy between father and child
    (B) presenting a poignant moment of domestic bliss
    (C) parodying the traditional image of maternity
    (D) honoring the lonely offices of parenthood
    (E) forshadowing the later departure of the mother

26. In light of Little Chandler's feelings about his marriage, a psychological reading of the passage might focus on which aspect of the poem by Byron?

    (A) the total absence of a relieving breeze
    (B) the idyllic setting of the grove
    (C) the deceased state of Margaret
    (D) the devotion shown by the speaker in the poem for the deceased
    (E) the flowers left by the speaker in the poem at the gravesite

Questions 27–39. Refer to the following poem.

XXXIV

Why art thou silent! Is thy love a plant
Of such weak fibre that the treacherous air
Of absence withers what was once so fair?
Is there no debt to pay, no boon to grant?
(5)   Yet have my thoughts for thee been vigilant—
Bound to thy service with unceasing care,
Thy mind's least generous wish a mendicant
For nought but what thy happiness could spare.
Speak—though this soft, warm heart, once free to hold
(10) A thousand tender pleasures, thine and mine,
Be left more desolate, more dreary cold
Than a forsaken bird's-nest filled with snow
"Mid its own bush of leafless eglantine—
Speak, that my torturing doubts their end may know!

—William Wordsworth

27. Which of the following BEST articulates the primary concern of the speaker in the sonnet?

(A) lamenting his outcast state
(B) discovering his personal shortcomings
(C) indicting his beloved of infidelity
(D) confirming the status of his relationship
(E) redressing an injury or affront

28. In the course of the poem, the speaker displays each of the following emotions EXCEPT

(A) frustration
(B) jealousy
(C) uncertainty
(D) impatience
(E) defensiveness

29. Initially, the speaker accuses his beloved of

(A) lacking hardiness
(B) becoming repulsive
(C) acting unjustly
(D) spending prodigally
(E) forfeiting virginity

30. The exclamatory "Why art thou silent!" (line 1) and the imperative "Speak" (lines 9 and 14) do all of the following EXCEPT

(A) reveal the speaker's frustration at his beloved's discomfiting silence
(B) intimate the beloved's displeasure with the speaker
(C) demand the identity of the beloved's paramour
(D) convey the speaker's desire for a resolution
(E) mirror a popular sonnet theme: unrequited love

31. The phrase "the treacherous air / Of absence" (lines 2-3) may be said to imply which of the following?

I. That physical separation from his beloved has prompted this display of displeasure.
II. That trust in a relationship may be as ephemeral as a flower in cold weather.
III. That the beloved suspects the speaker of some sort of infidelity.

(A) I only
(B) III only
(C) I and III
(D) II and III
(E) I, II and III

32. The question, "Is there no debt to pay" (line 4), which the speaker directs to his beloved likely alludes to

    (A) his earlier manifestations of his love for her
    (B) a dowry promised by her father
    (C) contrition for his absence
    (D) a sum of money he had previously lent her
    (E) gifts he had previously given her

33. The diction of the second quatrain (lines 5-8) primarily paints the speaker as

    (A) stalking and obsessive
    (B) servile and embittered
    (C) devoted and doting
    (D) impoverished and unworthy
    (E) penitent and remorseful

34. With the phrase "Bound to thy service" (line 6), the speaker compares his thoughts about his beloved to the duty of a

    (A) serf
    (B) knight
    (C) prisoner
    (D) husband
    (E) lackey

35. The most notable change in the sestet—the final six lines of the poem—is the speaker's

    (A) urgency in his appeal to his beloved
    (B) increased sense of resignation
    (C) affirmation of his passion
    (D) use of natural images to describe their relationship
    (E) ability to elicit an answer

36. Which of the following literary devices is NOT used to convey the speaker's angst over the loss of his beloved's favor?

    (A) an apostrophe to the beloved who had earlier forsaken him
    (B) comparative adjectives that attempt to measure his somber isolation
    (C) images of cold and barrenness
    (D) the metonymy of the "forsaken bird's-nest"
    (E) alliteration and assonance that aurally mirror his disconsolate state

37. Which of the following lines contains a hyperbole?

    (A) Line 2
    (B) Line 4
    (C) Line 5
    (D) Line 10
    (E) Line 14

38. In light of the context in which it appears, which of the following words offers two rich veins of interpretation?

    (A) "boon" (line 4)
    (B) "Bound" (line 6)
    (C) "spare" (line 8)
    (D) "tender" (line 10)
    (E) "end" (line 14)

39. The overall tone of the speaker's comments is

    (A) groveling and obsequious
    (B) accusatory and admonitory
    (C) ingratiating and imploring
    (D) rational and reflective
    (E) rueful and embittered

Questions 40-52. Refer to the following passage.

On the starboard side of the *Indomitable's* upper gun deck, behold Billy Budd under sentry, lying prone in irons, in one of the bays formed by the regular spacing of the guns
(5) comprising the batteries on either side….Guns and carriages, together with the long rammers and shorter lintstocks[1] lodged in loops overhead—all these, as customary, were painted black; and the heavy hempen breechens,[2]
(10) tarred to the same tint, wore the like livery of the undertakers. In contrast with the funereal hue of these surroundings the prone sailor's exterior apparel, white jumper and white duck trousers, each more or less soiled, dimly
(15) glimmered in the obscure light of the bay like a patch of discolored snow in early April lingering at some upland cave's black mouth. In effect he is already in his shroud or the garments that shall serve him in lieu of one.
(20) Over him, but scarce illuminating him, two battle-lanterns swing from two massive beams of the deck above…..Other lanterns at intervals serve but to bring out somewhat the obscurer bays which, like small confessionals or side-
(25) chapels in a cathedral, branch from the long dim-vistaed broad aisle between the two batteries of that covered tier.

Such was the deck where now lay the Handsome Sailor. Through the rose-tan of his
(30) complexion, no pallor could have shown. It would have taken days of sequestration from the winds and the sun to have brought about the effacement of that. But the skeleton in the cheekbone at the point of its angle was just
(35) beginning delicately to be defined under the warm-tinted skin. In fervid hearts self-contained, some brief experiences devour our human tissue as secret fire in a ship's hold consumes cotton in the bale.
(40) But now lying between the two guns, as nipped in the vice of fate, Billy's agony, mainly proceeding from a generous young heart's virgin experience of the diabolical incarnate and effective in some men—the
(45) tension of that agony was over now…Without movement, he lay as in a trance. That adolescent expression previously noted as his, taking on something akin to the look of a slumbering child in the cradle when the warm
(50) hearth-glow of the still chamber at night plays on the dimples that at whiles mysteriously form in the cheek, silently coming and going there. For now and then in the gyved[3] one's trance a serene happy light born of some
(55) wandering reminiscence or dream would diffuse itself over his face, and then wane away only anew to return.

The Chaplain coming to see him and finding him thus, and perceiving no sign that
(60) he was conscious of his presence, attentively regarded him for a space, then slipping aside, withdrew for the time, peradventure feeling that even he the minister of Christ, tho' receiving his stipend from Mars, had no
(65) consolation to proffer which could result in a peace transcending that which he beheld. But in the small hours he came again. And the prisoner, now awake to his surroundings, noticed his approach, and civilly, all but
(70) cheerfully, welcomed him. But it was to little purpose that in the interview following the good man sought to bring Billy Budd to some godly understanding that he must die, and at dawn. True, Billy himself freely referred to his
(75) death as a thing close at hand; but it was something in the way that children will refer to death in general, who yet among their other sports will play a funeral with hearse and mourners….

40. The opening paragraph of the passage establishes which of the following antitheses?

(A) war and peace
(B) liberty and imprisonment
(C) black and white
(D) spring and winter
(E) innocence and guilt

---

[1] a forked-stock used to light a cannon

[2] the ropes used to secure a gun to the side of a ship and protect the crew from its recoil

[3] shackled or chained

41. Which of the following may NOT be said about the purpose of the opening paragraph?

    (A) It determines the nautical, wartime setting.
    (B) It features a distinctly moribund tone.
    (C) It establishes the unfortunate plight of the protagonist.
    (D) It identifies the narrator as a shipmate of Billy's aboard the *Indomitable*.
    (E) It contains figurative language that seems spiritual.

42. In the opening paragraph the layout of the ship is likened to that of a

    (A) church
    (B) labyrinth
    (C) tenement
    (D) cemetery
    (E) factory

43. The primary purpose of the figurative language in lines 15-17 —"like a patch of discolored snow in early April lingering at some upland cave's black mouth"—is to

    (A) establish the time of the *Indomitable's* military deployment
    (B) contrast the sullied nature of Billy's attire with the admirable nattiness of the sentries
    (C) censure Billy's lack of shipboard discipline in failing to maintain his uniform properly
    (D) symbolize and foreshadow the youthful protagonist's premature death
    (E) mirror the contrast of shadow and light created by the battle lanterns

44. The lines cited in the previous question exemplify all of the following EXCEPT

    (A) simile
    (B) paradox
    (C) metonymy
    (D) personification
    (E) imagery

45. The "small confessionals" to which the gun bays are compared in line 24 anticipate which of the following?

    I. The internal turmoil that is devouring Billy's outward serenity (lines 33-39).
    II. The "diabolical incarnate," or natural depravity, that corrupts some men (lines 40-44).
    III. The intentions of the Chaplain in coming to see Billy (lines 58-74).

    (A) I only
    (B) III only
    (C) I and III
    (D) II and III
    (E) I, II and III

46. Lines 33-36, "But the skeleton in the cheekbone at the point of its angle was just beginning delicately to be defined under the warm-tinted skin," likely imply a(n)

    (A) gradual fading of his ruddy tan
    (B) unsightly emaciation caused by his imprisonment
    (C) premature aging triggered by emotional duress
    (D) physical cadaverousness that anticipates his fate
    (E) inner resolve that manifests itself in his face

47. In the context in which it appears, the word "delicately" (line 35) is BEST interpreted as

    (A) barely
    (B) imperceptibly
    (C) gingerly
    (D) prominently
    (E) feebly

48. The simile in lines 38-39, "as secret fire in a ship's hold consumes cotton in a bale," likely refers to the

    (A) bitter animosity over the events that have led to Billy's being jailed
    (B) righteous indignation at the manner in which Billy has been treated by the sentries
    (C) total chagrin at the ignominy which has accompanied Billy's arrest
    (D) emotional anxiety over Billy's upcoming arraignment
    (E) inner turmoil that is devouring Billy

49. The simile, "as nipped in the vice of fate" (lines 40-41), is possibly intended to link Billy's fate to his

    (A) rank
    (B) name
    (C) apparel
    (D) complexion
    (E) repose

50. The analogy and diction in lines 45-57 that focus intensely on Billy's infant-like slumber in the cannon bay seem MOST intended to bring out which of the following?

    (A) his unfortunate naïveté as to the terms of his punishment
    (B) his blissful ignorance of the wickedness of others that has effected his demise
    (C) his puerile inability to recognize the seriousness of his circumstance
    (D) his calm acceptance of the fate that awaits him
    (E) his overwhelming fatigue from the strain of the ordeal

51. The Chaplain's initial withdrawal is prompted by

    (A) his belief that Billy is unrepentant
    (B) a self-consciousness of his hypocrisy as both a minister of God and an accomplice to war
    (C) his unwillingness to disturb Billy's sublime sense of tranquility
    (D) Billy's stalwart rejection of any spiritual consolation
    (E) Billy's profound and irreconcilable despair

52. Billy's response to his imminent death at the end of the passage is BEST labeled

    (A) defiant
    (B) carefree
    (C) resigned
    (D) dismissive
    (E) guileless

Section II

Question One

(Suggested time–40 minutes. This question counts as one-third of the total essay section score.)

In the following passage from Kenneth Grahame's *The Wind in the Willows*, the Water-Rat listens to a tale of the sea told by a Seafarer. Read the passage carefully. Then, in a well-organized essay, explain how Grahame uses language to enhance the compelling impact of the Seafarer's story. In your essay, you may wish to consider such devices as diction, imagery, figurative language, syntax and tone.

By this time their meal was over, and the Seafarer, refreshed and strengthened, his voice more vibrant, his eye lit with a brightness that seemed caught from some far-away sea-
(5) beacon, filled his glass with the red and glowing vintage of the South, and, leaning towards the Water-Rat, compelled his gaze and held him, body and soul, while he talked. Those eyes were of the changing foam-
(10) streaked grey-green of leaping Northern seas; in the glass shone a hot ruby that seemed the very heart of the South, beating for him who had courage to respond to its pulsation. The twin lights, the shifting grey and the steadfast
(15) red, mastered the Water-Rat and held him bound, fascinated, powerless. The quiet world outside their rays receded far away and ceased to be. And the talk, the wonderful talk, flowed on—or was it speech entirely, or did it pass at
(20) times into song—chanty of the sailors weighing[1] the dripping anchor, sonorous hum of the shrouds in a tearing North-Easter, ballad of the fisherman hauling his nets at sundown against an apricot sky, chords of guitar or
(25) mandolin from gondola or caique?[2] Did it change into the cry of the wind, plaintive at first, angrily shrill as it freshened, rising to a tearing whistle, sinking to a musical trickle of air from the leech of the bellying sail? All
(30) these sounds the spellbound listener seemed to hear, and with them the hungry complaint of the gulls and the sea-mews, the soft thunder of the breaking wave, the cry of the protesting shingle. Back into speech again it passed, and
(35) with beating heart he was following the adventures of a dozen seaports, the fights, the escapes, the rallies, the comradeships, the gallant undertakings; or he searched islands for treasure, fished in still lagoons or dozed day-
(40) long on warm white sand. Of deep-sea fishings he heard tell, and mighty silver gatherings of the mile-long net; of sudden perils, noise of breakers on a moonless night, or the tall bows of the great liner taking shape overhead
(45) through the fog; of the merry homecoming, the headland rounded, the harbor lights opened out; the groups seen dimly on the quay,[3] the cheery hail, the splash of the hawser;[4] the trudge up the steep little street towards the
(50) comforting glow of red-curtained windows....

---

[1] lifting out of the water

[2] both variations of skiffs or rowboats

[3] dock

[4] a cable or rope used to secure a ship to land

Question Two

(Suggested time–40 minutes. This question counts as one-third of the total essay section score.)

In the following dramatic monologue from Edmund Rostand's 1897 masterpiece *Cyrano de Bergerac* (Hooker translation), Cyrano, the main character, responds to a friend's suggestion that he would enjoy more success if he conducted himself in a less flamboyant and less independent fashion. Read Cyrano's response and, in a well-organized essay, analyze his reaction—and the reasons for it—and show how Rostand's language eloquently conveys it.

Cyrano:

What would you have me do?
Seek for the patronage of some great man,
And like a creeping vine on a tall tree
Crawl upward, where I cannot stand alone?
(5) No thank you! Dedicate, as others do,
Poems to pawnbrokers? Be a buffoon
In the vile hope of teasing out a smile
On some cold face? No thank you! Eat a toad
For breakfast every morning? Make my knees
(10) Callous, and cultivate a supple spine,—
Wear out my belly groveling in the dust?
No thank you! Scratch the back of any swine
That roots up gold for me? Tickle the horns
Of Mammon[1] with my left hand, while my right
(15) Takes in the fee? No thank you! Use the fire
God gave me to burn incense all day long
Under the nose of wood and stone? No thank
       you!
Shall I go leaping into ladies' laps
And licking fingers?—or—to change the
       form—
(20) Navigating with madrigals[2] for oars,
My sails full of the sighs of dowagers?
No thank you! Publish verses at my own
Expense? No thank you! Be the patron saint
Of a small group of literary souls
(25) Who dine together every Tuesday? No
I thank you! Shall I labor night and day
To build a reputation on one song,

And never write another? Shall I find
True genius only among Geniuses,
(30) Palpitate over little paragraphs,
And struggle to insinuate my name
Into the columns of the *Mercury*?[3]
No thank you! Calculate, scheme, be afraid,
Love more to make a visit than a poem,
(35) Seek introductions, favors, influences?—
No thank you! No, I thank you! And again
I thank you!—But . . .
       To sing, to laugh, to dream,
To walk in my own way and be alone,
(40) Free, with an eye to see things as they are,
A voice that means manhood—to cock my hat
Where I choose—At a word, a Yes, a No,
To fight—or write. To travel any road
Under the sun, under the stars, nor doubt
(45) If fame or fortune lie beyond the bourne—
Never to make a line I have not heard
In my own heart; yet, with all modesty
To say: "My soul be satisfied with flowers,
With fruit, with weeds even; but gather them
(50) In the one garden you may call your own."
So, when I win some triumph, by some chance,
Render no share to Caesar—in a word,
I am too proud to be a parasite,
And if my nature wants the germ that grows
(55) Towering to heaven like the mountain pine,
Or like the oak, sheltering multitudes—
I stand, not high it may be—but alone!

---

[1] avarice or greed; often personified as a deity that represents greed.

[2] 16th-17th century secular songs, often with themes of love

[3] a tabloid

<u>Question Three</u>

(Suggested time—40 minutes. This essay counts as one-third of the total essay section score.)

Many works of literature are focused around a dream or aspiration, a powerful motivating force that compels and determines the central character's action. Though this force can be a driving aspiration that spurs and elevates the character to prosperity and prominence, it can just as readily be a seductive illusion that consumes and destroys the character, reducing him to degradation and ruin, or even an artificial world in which the character may escape from reality.

Select a novel or play in which a character's actions are focused around such a dream or aspiration. Then, in a well-organized essay, discuss the effect this ambition has upon the fortunes of the character and the people around him and show how the pursuit of this dream impacts the meaning of the work as a whole.

You may choose from the titles below or use a novel or play of comparable literary merit.

All the King's Men	*Hedda Gabler*
An American Tragedy	*Jude the Obscure*
Beloved	*The Jungle*
Crime and Punishment	*Long Day's Journey Into Night*
Death of a Salesman	*MacBeth*
Don Quixote	*Moby Dick*
Equus	*The Piano Lesson*
Frankenstein	*A Prayer for Owen Meany*
The Glass Menagerie	*The Sound & the Fury*
The Grapes of Wrath	*A Streetcar Named Desire*
Great Expectations	*Things Fall Apart*
The Great Gatsby	*Tom Jones*
Heart of Darkness	*Wuthering Heights*

Sample Examination II

Questions 1-14. Refer to the following passage.

….Gwendolyn, clad in riding dress, with her hat laid aside, clad also in the repute of having been chosen by Mr. Grandcourt, was naturally a centre of observation….

(5) She had not been at Diplow before except to dine; and since certain points of view from the windows and the garden were worth showing, Lady Flora Hollis proposed after luncheon, when some of the guests had
(10) dispersed, and the sun was sloping towards four o'clock, that the remaining party should make a little exploration. Here came frequent opportunities when Grandcourt might have retained Gwendolyn apart, and have spoken to
(15) her unheard. But no! He indeed spoke to no one else, but what he said was nothing more eager or intimate than it had been in their first interview….

The path was too narrow for him to offer
(20) his arm, and they walked up in silence. When they were on the bit of platform at the summit, Grandcourt said—

"There is nothing to be seen here; the thing was not worth climbing."

(25) How was it that Gwendolyn did not laugh? She was perfectly silent, holding up the folds of her robe like a statue, and giving a harder grasp to the handle of her whip, which she had snatched up automatically with her hat when
(30) they had first set off.

"What sort of place do you like?" said Grandcourt.

"Different places are agreeable in their way. On the whole, I think, I prefer places that
(35) are open and cheerful. I am not fond of anything somber."

"Your place at Offendene is too somber."

"It is, rather."

"You will not remain there long, I hope."

(40) "Oh yes, I think so. Mamma likes to be near her sister."

Silence for a short space.

"It is not supposed that you will always live there, though Mrs. Davilow may."

(45) "I don't know. We women can't go in search of adventures—to find out the North-west Passage or the source of the Nile, or to hunt tigers in the East. We must stay where we grow, or where the gardeners like to transplant
(50) us. We are brought up like flowers, to look as pretty as we can, and be dull without complaining….".

"But a woman can be married."

"Some women can."

(55) "You certainly, unless you are obstinately cruel."

"I am not sure that I am not both cruel and obstinate." Here Gwendolyn suddenly turned her head and looked full at Grandcourt, whose
(60) eyes she had felt to be upon her throughout their conversation. She was wondering what the effect of looking at him would be on herself rather than on him….

"Ha! My whip!" said Gwendolyn, in a
(65) little scream of distress. She had let it go—what could be more natural in a slight agitation?—but this seemed less natural in a golden-handled whip which had been left altogether to itself—it had gone with some
(70) force over the immediate shrubs, and had lodged itself in the branches of an azalea halfway down the knoll. She could run down now, laughing prettily, and Grandcourt was obliged to follow; but she was beforehand with
(75) him in rescuing the whip, and continued on her way to the level ground, when she paused and looked at Grandcourt with an exasperating brightness in her glance and a heightened colour, as if she had carried a triumph….

(80) "It is all coquetting," thought Grandcourt; "The next time I beckon, she will come down…".

168

1. The opening paragraph helps to establish which of the following contrasts?

   (A) Gwendolyn's cavalier attitude and Grandcourt's sober demeanor
   (B) Gwendolyn's innate athleticism and Grandcourt's physical ineptitude
   (C) Gwendolyn's bashful reticence and Grandcourt's ostentatious personality
   (D) Gwendolyn's independent spirit and Grandcourt's social entitlement
   (E) Gwendolyn's inappropriate attire and Grandcourt's formal wear

2. The author of the passage mirrors the oscillating position of control enjoyed in turn by Grandcourt and Gwendolyn via all of the following EXCEPT

   (A) mildly contentious dialogue
   (B) changes in their physical positions in the landscape
   (C) intervals of discomfiting silence
   (D) facial expressions and interior ponderings
   (E) similes that contrast their gender-determined lots

3. The central irony in the second paragraph involves

   (A) Lady Hollis' belief that her property is worth showcasing
   (B) Grandcourt's failure to engage other guests in conversation before they departed
   (C) Grandcourt's reluctance to speak more intimately to Gwendolyn in an otherwise private setting
   (D) Gwendolyn's coincidental appearance at Diplow
   (E) Gwendolyn's indifference to the wealthy Grandcourt

4. The primary authorial intent of the phrase "first interview" in lines 17-18 is to

   (A) emphasize the newness of Gwendolyn's and Grandcourt's relationship
   (B) imply the passionate nature of Gwendolyn's and Grandcourt's initial rendezvous
   (C) accent the formality with which Grandcourt views a potential union with Gwendolyn
   (D) clarify the intent of Lady Hollis' "little exploration" (line 12)
   (E) suggest the social scrutiny of Lady Hollis

5. In response to Grandcourt's observation to Gwendolyn that "It is not supposed that you will live there, though Mrs. Davilow may" (lines 43-44), Gwendolyn does all of the following EXCEPT

   (A) align herself with the plight of the 'weaker sex'
   (B) feign a helplessness that is inconsistent with her self-reliant spirit
   (C) deride the double-standard that lets men embark on exciting adventures while women remain domestic and conservative
   (D) employ figures of speech that capture the delicacy with which women are viewed and treated
   (E) confirm definitively that she will indeed remain living at Offendene

6. The gardening metaphor that is introduced in lines 48-52 suggests that women in this time period are largely

   (A) ignorant and unimaginative
   (B) subservient and ornamental
   (C) timorous and reserved
   (D) home-bound and contented
   (E) delicate and prissy

7. Gwendolyn's looking "full" at Mr. Grandcourt in lines 58-61 may be perceived as which of the following?

    I. A visual retort to his prolonged scrutiny.
    II. A meditative measuring of her own interest in the gentleman.
    III. An angry glare designed to thwart further conversation.

    (A) II only
    (B) III only
    (C) I and II
    (D) II and III
    (E) I, II and III

8. Which of the following BEST articulates the figurative function of the whip in the passage?

    (A) It symbolizes Gwendolyn's desire to retain autonomy and self-control.
    (B) It foreshadows how Gwendolyn would dominate a potential marriage.
    (C) It represents Gwendolyn's envy of the adventurous life-path afforded men.
    (D) It reveals the innate carelessness of Gwendolyn's character.
    (E) It serves as a prop to make Grandcourt attempt to wait upon Gwendolyn.

9. Which of the following LEAST clarifies the true meaning behind Gwendolyn's loss of the whip?

    (A) the mock concern—"Ha! My whip!"—she displays upon dropping it
    (B) the expensive nature of its golden handle
    (C) the "force" with which it is propelled into the shrubbery
    (D) the haste with which Gwendolyn retrieves it
    (E) the reversal of power that results from her dropping it

10. The exchange between Gwendolyn and Grandcourt and the former's dropping of the whip suggest that the rhetorical question, "what could be more natural in a slight agitation?" (lines 65-67), be seen as

    (A) explanatory
    (B) tongue-in-cheek
    (C) acrimonious
    (D) rueful
    (E) foreboding

11. The physical description of Gwendolyn's face—the "exasperating brightness in her glance and a heightened colour..." (lines 77-79) —suggests a(n)

    (A) satisfaction at successfully thwarting Grandcourt
    (B) mortification at her inept fumbling of the whip
    (C) flush brought on by the physical exertion of retrieving the whip
    (D) embarrassment at their earlier conversation about marriage
    (E) coquettishness designed to increase Grandcourt's desire

12. The final lines of the passage—"It is all coquetting," thought Grandcourt; "The next time I beckon, she will come down" (lines 80-82) —seem intended to reveal

    (A) Grandcourt's admirable doggedness
    (B) Grandcourt's intolerable egocentricity
    (C) Grandcourt's intractable possessiveness
    (D) Gwendolyn's demure flirtatiousness
    (E) Gwendolyn's marital desperation

13. In which of the following responses to Grandcourt does Gwendolyn most directly articulate her singularly (for her time) independent spirit?

    (A) "I am not fond of anything somber." (lines 35-36)
    (B) "Oh yes, I think so. Mama likes to be near her sister." (lines 40-41)
    (C) "We must stay where we grow, or where the gardeners like to transplant us." (lines 48-50)
    (D) "Some women can." (line 54)
    (E) "Ha! My whip!" (line 64)

14. The passage is likely taken from a(n)

    (A) autobiography
    (B) travelogue
    (C) coming of age story
    (D) comedy of manners
    (E) historical fiction

Questions 15-27. Refer to the following poem.

From the Dark Tower

We shall not always plant while others reap
The golden increment of bursting fruit,
Not always countenance, abject and mute,
That lesser men should hold their brothers cheap;
(5) Not everlastingly while others sleep
Shall we beguile their limbs with mellow flute;
Not always bend to some more subtle brute;
We were not made eternally to weep.

The night whose sable breast relieves the stark,
(10) White stars is no less lovely being dark,
And there are buds that cannot bloom at all
In light, but crumple, piteous, and fall;
So in the dark we hide the heart that bleeds,
And wait, and tend our agonizing seeds.

—Countee Cullen

Reprinted with permission from the Amistad Research Center.

15. In the poem the speaker is primarily concerned with which of the following?

(A) delineating the hardships and abuses of slavery
(B) conveying a warning that the subjugation of African-Americans will be met with militant and deadly action
(C) reassuring his people that the tenure of their suffering is not everlasting
(D) reasserting the inherent value of the downtrodden and demeaned slaves
(E) bemoaning the failure of their meager crop

16. The opening stanza of the poem conveys the speaker's sense of

(A) impatience and threat
(B) reassurance and hope
(C) envy and bitterness
(D) resignation and surrender
(E) admonition and defiance

17. The BEST equivalent for the verb "countenance" (line 3) would be

(A) blindly ignore
(B) blissfully accept
(C) passively tolerate
(D) vociferously reject
(E) actively abet

18. Which of the following offers the BEST explanation for the unusual word "beguile" that is used in line 6?

(A) It serves as a contrast to the abject and mute demeanor maintained in the fields by slaves.
(B) It represents the efforts of slaves to relieve their own physical exhaustion brought on by arduous labor in the fields.
(C) It conveys the deep but underappreciated affection held by most slaves for their masters.
(D) It masks the fermenting anger of the plantation slaves who are planning to throw off their shackles and assert their humanity.
(E) It derides the sleeping plantation owners by sardonically suggesting that their fatigue is a product of their own hard labor.

19. The phrase "Not always bend to some more subtle brute" (line 7) reflects all of the following EXCEPT

    (A) the speaker's abhorrence of the back-breaking field labor
    (B) the speaker's growing resistance to constant submission
    (C) the speaker's resentment of the people who have devised such brutal and inequitable exploitation
    (D) the speaker's lack of self-worth
    (E) the speaker's belief that the true 'brutes' are the slave-owners

20. The final line of the octet (lines 1-8) differs from the preceding seven in its

    (A) sudden abandonment of diction associated with time
    (B) weary concession to despondency
    (C) adamant negation of their sorrowful lot
    (D) romantic denial of an unfortunate reality
    (E) rancorous indictment of God the Creator

21. The natural image of "The night whose sable breast relieves the stark, / White stars…" (lines 9-10) resembles MOST closely which of the following?

    (A) the reaping of the "golden increment of bursting fruit" (line 2)
    (B) the "abject and mute" faces of the field workers (line 3)
    (C) the mellow evening flutes played by slaves to "beguile" their masters' limbs (lines 5-6)
    (D) the eternity of mournful weeping that epitomizes the slaves' experience (line 8)
    (E) the slaves' concealment of their bleeding hearts (line 13)

22. Overall, the most subtle implication of the octet (lines 1-8) involves the

    (A) enormous profitability of slavery
    (B) plantation owners' exploitation of slave labor
    (C) slaves' tacit acceptance of their abject lot
    (D) slaves providing musical entertainment for their oppressors
    (E) foreshadowing of a day of emancipation or judgment

23. All of the following can be said about the "buds that cannot bloom at all / In light" (lines 11-12) EXCEPT

    (A) They contrast the fecundity of the "golden increment of bursting fruit" (line 2).
    (B) They fail to thrive because they are never given opportunity to be "planted."
    (C) They "crumple, piteous, and fall" (line 12) due to the slaves' own negligence.
    (D) They symbolize the stymied potential of slave children.
    (E) They account for the nocturnal nurturing of "agonizing seeds" (line 14).

24. Perhaps the most poignant aspect of Cullen's sonnet is the

    (A) pervasive pessimism as to the slaves ever improving their lot
    (B) tantalizing profit that the slaves are prohibited from sharing
    (C) tawdry manner in which the plantation owners "hold their brothers cheap" (line 4)
    (D) simple comfort provided by the "sable breast" (line 9) of nightfall
    (E) persistent nocturnal nurturing by slaves of their "agonizing seeds" (line 14)

25. Of the following, which BEST parallels the rhetoric and theme of the poem?

    (A) "But the brave king departed from the place, / With smiles of gladness sparkling in his face: / Nor could contain, but, as he took his way, / Impatient longs to make the first essay. / Down from a lowly branch a twig he drew, / The twig strait glitter'd with a golden hue…" (from Ovid's *Metamorphosis*)

    (B) "Blessed are the meek / For they shall possess the earth. Blessed are they who hunger and thirst for justice / for they shall be satisfied." (from the Gospel of Matthew 5:5-6)

    (C) "A man saw a ball of gold in the sky; / He climbed for it, / And eventually he achieved it— / It was clay." (from Stephen Crane's "A Man Saw a Ball of Gold")

    (D) "The woods are lovely, dark and deep. / But I have promises to keep, / And miles to go before I sleep, / And miles to go before I sleep." (from Robert Frost's "Stopping By Woods on a Snowy Evening")

    (E) "OH! Lift me as a wave, a leaf, a cloud! / I fall upon the thorns of life! I bleed!" (from Percy Bysshe Shelley's "Ode to the West Wind")

26. Which of the following would NOT be an accurate observation about Cullen's poem?

    (A) It imitates the English (Shakespearean) sonnet form.
    (B) It utilizes a repetition of time words to help convey its theme.
    (C) It uses metaphor and understatement to disguise its contentious content.
    (D) It utilizes the editorial "We" to connect the plight of speaker and subject.
    (E) It is predominantly written in iambic pentameter.

27. The title of the poem, "From the Dark Tower," suggests which of the following?

    I. An inversion of the roles of plantation owner and slave.
    II. A visionary, even prophetic, perspective of the future.
    III. An image of confinement and imprisonment.

    (A) I only
    (B) III only
    (C) I and II
    (D) II and III
    (E) I, II and III

Question 28-40. Refer to the following passage.

    At seven twenty-eight Mr. Frederick Jack awoke and began to come alive with all his might. He sat up and yawned strongly, stretching his arms and at the same time
(5) bending his slumber-swollen face into the plump muscle-hammock of his right shoulder, a movement coy and cuddlesome. "Eee-a-a-a-ach!" He stretched deliciously out of a thick, rubbery sleep, and for a moment he sat upright
(10) rubbing at his eyes with the clenched backs of his fingers. Then he flung off the covers with one determined motion and swung to the floor....padded noiselessly across the carpet to the window and stood, yawning and stretching
(15) again....
    Below Mr. Frederick Jack the cross street was a narrow bluish lane between sheer cliffs of solid masonry, but to the west the morning sunlight, golden, young, immensely strong and
(20) delicate, cut with sculptured sharpness at the walls of towering buildings. It shone with an unearthly rose-golden glow upon the upper tiers and summits of soaring structures whose lower depths were still sunk in shadow. It
(25) rested without violence or heat upon retreating pyramids of steel and stone, fumed at their peaks with fading wisps of smoke. It was reflected with dazzling brilliance from the panes of innumerable lofty windows....
(30) Among the man-made peaks that stood silhouetted against the sky in this early sun were great hotels and clubs and office buildings bare of life. Mr. Jack could look straight into high office suites ready for their
(35) work....The offices stood silent, empty, sterile, but they also seemed to have a kind of lonely expectation of the life that would soon swell up swiftly from the streets to fill and use them. In that eerie light, with the cross street still bare
(40) of traffic and the office buildings empty, suddenly it seemed to Mr. Jack as if all life had been driven or extinguished from the city and as if those soaring obelisks were all that remained of a civilization that had been famous
(45) and legendary.
    With a shrug of impatience he shook off the moment's aberration and peered down into the street again....It was empty as before, but already along Park Avenue the bright-hued
(50) cabs were drilling past the intersection like beetles in flight. Most of them headed downtown in the direction of Grand Central Station. And everywhere, through that shining, living light, he could sense the slow-mounting
(55) roar of another furious day beginning. He stood there by his window, a man-mite poised high in the air upon a shelf of masonry, the miracle of God, a plump atom of triumphant man's flesh, founded upon a rock of luxury....
(60) for he had bought the privileges of space, silence, light and steel-walled security out of chaos with the ransom of an emperor. And he exulted in the price he paid for them....
    Another man, looking out upon the city in
(65) its early-morning nakedness, might have thought its forms inhuman, monstrous, and Assyrian in their insolence. But not Mr. Frederick Jack. Indeed, if all these towers had been the monuments of his own special
(70) triumph, his pride and confidence and sense of ownership could hardly have been greater than they were. "My city," he thought. "Mine." It filled his heart with certitude and joy because he had learned, like many other men, to see, to
(75) marvel, to accept, and not to ask disturbing questions. In that arrogant boast of steel and stone he saw a permanence surviving every danger, an answer, crushing and conclusive, to every doubt....

28. The diction in the opening paragraph suggests that Mr. Frederick Jack is

    (A) paranoid and insomnolent
    (B) comfortable and contented
    (C) indolent and stolid
    (D) slothful and sensitive
    (E) precise and sequential

29. In conveying the arrogance and self-absorption of Mr. Jack, the speaker largely depends upon

    (A) a detailed description of the early rising of Mr. Jack
    (B) a pervasive repetition of first-person pronouns that stresses the intolerable vanity that characterizes such men
    (C) the physical perspective from which Mr. Jack surveys the city buildings before him
    (D) diction that emphasizes his regal and pharaoh-like qualities
    (E) the taxicabs and other mundane examples of local color

30. The second paragraph establishes an important contrast between

    (A) the man-made and the natural
    (B) heat and cold
    (C) illumination and darkness
    (D) openness and confinement
    (E) industry and relaxation

31. Which of the following is NOT used by the speaker to emphasize the striking grandeur of the city in which Mr. Jack resides?

    (A) diction that emphasizes the height and durability of its edifices
    (B) imagery that conveys its ethereal beauty in the light of the sunrise
    (C) allusions to enduring monuments of lost civilizations
    (D) a metaphor comparing the skyscrapers to a range of tall mountains
    (E) a personification of the skyscrapers as sentinels of the still-sleeping city

32. The description of the as yet empty office suites that Mr. Jack observes from the vantage point of his apartment (lines 35-38) figuratively compares them to

    (A) ghost towns
    (B) arid deserts
    (C) bleak prisons
    (D) immaculate hospitals
    (E) womb-like cubicles

33. The BEST equivalent for the word "aberration" in line 47 would be

    (A) blunder
    (B) miscalculation
    (C) delusion
    (D) reverie
    (E) amnesia

34. Lines 55-59—"He stood there by his window, a man-mite poised high in the air upon a shelf of masonry, the miracle of God, a plump atom of triumphant man's flesh, founded upon a rock of luxury...."—contain all of the following EXCEPT

    (A) a hyphenated phrase that ironically understates the powerful position of Mr. Jack
    (B) a homonym that relates Mr. Jack to the first being created
    (C) a metaphor that juxtaposes precariousness and insecurity with prominence and power
    (D) a comparison of Mr. Jack's achievements to those of modern architects
    (E) a series of appositives that satirize the secular foundation of Mr. Jack's prominent position

35. The fragment, "But not Mr. Frederick Jack," that occurs in lines 67-68 does which of the following?

    I. It separates Mr. Jack's self-perceptions from those of more ordinary individuals.
    II. It sets up Mr. Jack's later exultation at being an individual of wealth and power.
    III. It tonally reinforces the smugness that defines Mr. Jack's character.

    (A) I only
    (B) II only
    (C) I and III
    (D) II and III
    (E) I, II and III

36. In light of the context in which it appears, the "disturbing questions" mentioned in lines 75-76 could possibly be seen as satirizing all of the following EXCEPT

    (A) the means by which the wealth and power of Mr. Jack and his brethren have been acquired
    (B) the "insolence" (line 67) of erecting such vainglorious structures
    (C) the legality of Mr. Jack's claim, "My city…Mine." (line 72)
    (D) the exorbitant cost of purchasing these "privileges of space, silence, light and steel-walled security…" (lines 60-61)
    (E) the ignored but disturbing consciousness of future loss and mortality

37. Which aspect of Mr. Jack do the final two paragraphs of the passage seem intent upon emphasizing?

    (A) his overwhelming fatigue
    (B) his diminutive stature
    (C) his limited patience
    (D) his narcissistic affluence
    (E) his pensive reflection

38. The final portrait of Mr. Frederick Jack depicts him as

    (A) rueing the emperor's ransom it had cost him to achieve such security
    (B) chortling internally with a sense of self-accomplishment and possession
    (C) fretting over threats to his economic welfare
    (D) displaying chagrin over the ostentatious excess of the towering edifices
    (E) comparing his accomplishments to those of the Assyrian architects of the past

39. The repeated references to elevation (lines 17, 21, 29, and 43) and the characterization of the cityscape as an "arrogant boast of steel and stone" (lines 76-77) perhaps imply an allusion to which of the following?

    (A) the flight of Icarus
    (B) the theft of fire by Prometheus
    (C) the erection of the Biblical Tower of Babel
    (D) the greed and betrayal of Judas
    (E) the sinful forging by the Israelites of the golden calf

40. The multiple references to light that pervade the passage ultimately serve to

    (A) connect the early hour at which Mr. Jack habitually rises with his impressive financial success
    (B) imply that Mr. Jack is having a profound epiphany about the ephemeral nature of his prominence
    (C) associate the inception of Mr. Jack's day with the dawn of creation
    (D) foreshadow the increased frenzy of people and traffic on the streets below
    (E) suggest that Mr. Jack is blinded by vanity

Questions 41-54. Refer to the following monologue.

In the following excerpt from William Shakespeare's *The Life and Death of King John*, Philip, an envoy from the King, has just completed an audience with the French cardinal, who has told him that the French will not lay down their arms. In the following lines he responds:

>   …Now hear our English king:
> For thus his royalty doth speak in me.
> He is prepared, and reason too he should.
> This apish and unmannerly approach,
> *(5)* This harnessed masque and unadvised revel,
> This unhaired sauciness and boyish troops,
> The King doth smile at, and is well prepared
> To whip this dwarfish war, these pigmy arms,
> From out the circle of his territories.
> *(10)* That hand which had the strength, even at your door,
> To cudgel you and make you take the hatch,
> To dive like buckets in concealed wells,
> To crouch in litter of your stable planks,
> To lie like pawns locked up in chests and trunks,
> *(15)* To hug with swine, to seek sweet safety out
> In vaults and prisons, and to thrill and shake
> Even at the crying of your nation's crow,
> Thinking his voice an armed Englishman;
> Shall that victorious hand be feebled here
> *(20)* That in your chambers gave you chastisement?
> No. Know the gallant monarch is in arms
> And like an eagle o'er his aery towers
> To souse annoyance that comes near his nest.
> And you degenerate, you ingrate revolts,
> *(25)* You bloody Neroes, ripping up the womb
> Of your dear mother England, blush for shame.
> For your own ladies and pale-visaged maids,
> Like Amazons, come tripping after drums,
> Their thimbles into armed gauntlets change,
> *(30)* Their needles to lances, and their gentle hearts
> To fierce and bloody inclination…

---

[1] a dramatic performance
[2] seize upon like a predatory bird
[3] rebels
[4] According to Tacitus, Nero ordered the murder of his mother, Agrippina, who upon being waylaid by assassins, asked them to "Smite her womb," rueing the organ that had given birth to him.

41. Philip's opening sentence, "Now hear our English king" (line 1), is MOST accurately labeled a(n)

(A) apostrophe
(B) proclamation
(C) manifesto
(D) invocation
(E) imploration

42. In light of the nature of his comments, Philip's primary goal seems to be to

(A) negotiate acceptable terms for a truce
(B) offer concessions that might deter battle
(C) defer the inception of battle until the king's forces are ready
(D) convey the foolhardiness of the French incursion
(E) insist upon an unconditional surrender

43. Philip's language in lines 4-9 implies that King John views the French aggression as all of the following EXCEPT

    (A) juvenile and naïve
    (B) flamboyant and theatrical
    (C) feeble and impotent
    (D) menacing and significant
    (E) bemusing and presumptuous

44. In categorizing the increasing terror that the French will feel upon provoking King John's wrath (lines 10-18), Philip primarily relies upon

    (A) personification and metonymy
    (B) climactic order and anaphora
    (C) hyperbole and simile
    (D) onomatopoeia and alliteration
    (E) apostrophe and zeugma

45. The infinitives employed in lines 10-18 establish which of the following contrasts between King John and the French?

    (A) retribution and flight
    (B) mercy and ingratitude
    (C) patience and vexation
    (D) nobility and commonness
    (E) readiness and unpreparedness

46. Lines 10-11 ("That hand, which had the strength...make you take the hatch") and lines 19-20 ("Shall that victorious hand....gave you chastisement") imply which of the following about King John?

    I. That he has had an earlier confrontation with the French.
    II. That he views his French opponent condescendingly.
    III. That he feels impregnable fighting on English soil.

    (A) I only
    (B) II only
    (C) I and III
    (D) II and III
    (E) I, II and III

47. The BEST equivalent for the word "thrill" in line 16 would be

    (A) excite
    (B) tremble
    (C) start
    (D) faint
    (E) flee

48. The transition that Philip employs that darkens the tenor of his comments is effected by which of the following?

    (A) a cessation of figurative language
    (B) an elaborate paean to King John's martial prowess
    (C) a tersely answered rhetorical question
    (D) a caesura
    (E) frequent imperatives

49. The comparison of King John to an eagle (lines 22-23) is intended to reinforce which aspect of the king?

    (A) his royal nature
    (B) his fervent patriotism
    (C) his stalwart vigilance
    (D) his shrewd statesmanship
    (E) his divine being

50. The words "degenerate" and "ingrate" (line 24) that Philip applies to the rebels are likely intended to

    (A) reinforce the earlier depiction of their cravenness
    (B) imply their traitorous disavowal of allegiances they owe to King John
    (C) cast personal aspersions at specific individuals
    (D) hyperbolize the extent of their disloyalty
    (E) question the legitimacy of their births

51. In lines 24-31, Philip accuses the rebels that are abetting the French forces of which of the following?

    I. Ravaging the countryside.
    II. Forcing women to become soldiers.
    III. Perverting through their aggression the naturally pacific and domestic nature of womanhood.

    (A) II only
    (B) III only
    (C) I and II
    (D) I and III
    (E) I, II and III

52. In delivering his comments to the French cardinal, Philip employs all of the following EXCEPT

    (A) an allusion that figuratively accuses the French of matricide
    (B) sanguinary images that forebode the violent end that awaits the French
    (C) action verbs that flout the fear and cowardice of the French
    (D) parallelism and inverted syntax that increase the histrionic nature of the French actions
    (E) a simile that likens King John to a vengeful predator

53. Which of the following exemplifies the literary technique of synecdoche?

    (A) "his royalty" (line 2)
    (B) "unhaired sauciness" (line 6)
    (C) "That hand" (line 10)
    (D) "nation's crow" (line 17)
    (E) "armed gauntlets" (line 29)

54. Which word in Philip's address, in the context in which it is used, may be perceived as having more than one meaning

    (A) "harnessed" (line 5)
    (B) "hatch" (line 11)
    (C) "pawns" (line 14)
    (D) "aery" (line 22)
    (E) "tripping" (line 28)

Section II

Question One

(Suggested time—40 minutes. This question counts as one-third of the total essay section score.)

The following poem, "Appeal to the Grammarians" (2007) by Paul Violi, proposes the creation of a new type of punctuation mark. Read the following poem carefully. Then, in a well-organized essay, explain the reasons behind the speaker's proposal. In developing your response, be sure to show how Violi uses literary devices such as perspective, tone and choice of detail to enhance the poem's message.

Appeal to the Grammarians

We, the naturally hopeful,
Need a simple sign
For the myriad ways we've capsized.
We who love precise language
(5) Need a finer way to convey
Disappointment and perplexity.
For speechlessness and all its inflections,
For up-ended expectations,
For every time we're ambushed
(10) By trivial or stupefying irony.
For pure incredulity, we need
The inverted exclamation point.
For the dropped smile, the limp handshake,
For whoever has just unwrapped a dumb gift
(15) Or taken the first sip of a flat beer,
Or felt love or pond ice,
Give way underfoot, we deserve it.
We need it for the air pocket, the scratch shot,
The child whose ball doesn't bounce back,
(20) The flat tire at journey's outset,
The odyssey that ends up in Weehawken.
But mainly I need it—here and now
As I sit outside the Caffé Reggio
Staring at my espresso and cannoli
(25) After this middle-aged couple
Came strolling by and he suddenly
Veered and sneezed all over my table
And she said to him, "See, that's why
I don't like to eat outside."

—Paul Violi

Reprinted with permission from the GREEN MOUNTAIN REVIEW.

Question Two

(Suggested time: 40 minutes. This question counts as one-third of the total essay section score.)

In the passage below from Jane Austen's novel *Persuasion* (1818), Anne Elliott and Lady Russell, a family friend, discuss the possibility of Anne's marrying her newly widowed cousin, Sir Walter Elliott. Read the passage carefully. Then in a well-organized essay, analyze how Austen's narrative technique illustrates each generation's arguments in support of—or against—the union.

Lady Russell was now perfectly decided in her opinion of Mr. Elliott. She was as much convinced of his meaning to gain Anne in time, as of his deserving her; and was beginning to
(5) calculate the number of weeks which would free him from all the remaining restraints of widowhood, and leave him at liberty to exert his most open powers of pleasing. She would not speak to Anne with half the certainty she
(10) felt on the subject, she would venture on little more than hints of what might be hereafter, of a possible attachment on his side, of the desirableness of the alliance, supposing such attachment to be real, and returned. Anne heard
(15) her and made no violent exclamations. She only smiled, blushed, and gently shook her head.

"I am no match-maker as you well know," said Lady Russell, "being much too well aware
(20) of the uncertainty of all human events and calculations. I only mean that if Mr. Elliott should some time pay his addresses to you, and if you should be disposed to accept him, I think there would be every possibility of your
(25) being happy together. A most suitable connection every body must consider it—but I think it might be a very happy one."

"Mr. Elliott is an exceedingly agreeable man, and in many respects I think highly of
(30) him," said Anne; "but we should not suit."

Lady Russell let this pass, and only said in rejoinder, "I own that to be able to regard you as the future mistress of Kellynch, the future Lady Elliott—to look forward and see you
(35) occupying your dear mother's space, succeeding to all her rights, and all her popularity, as well as to all her virtues, would be the highest possible gratification for me.—You are your mother's self in
(40) countenance and disposition; and if I might be allowed to fancy you such as she was, in situation, and name, and home, presiding and blessing in the same spot, and only superior to her in being more highly valued! My dearest
(45) Anne, it would give me more delight than is often felt at my time of life!"

Anne was obliged to turn away, to rise, to walk to a distant table, and, leaning there in pretended employment, try to subdue the
(50) feelings this picture excited. For a few moments her imagination and her heart were bewitched. The idea of becoming what her mother had been; of having the precious name of "Lady Elliott" first revived in herself; of
(55) being restored to Kellynch, calling it her home again...she could not immediately resist. Lady Russell said not another word, willing to leave the matter to its own operation....The charm of Kellynch and of "Lady Elliott" all faded away.
(60) She never could accept him. And it was not only that her feelings were still adverse to any man save one; her judgment, on a serious consideration of the possibilities of such a case, was against Mr. Elliott.
(65) Though they had now been acquainted a month, she could not be satisfied that she really knew his character. That he was a sensible man, an agreeable man,—that he talked well, professed good opinions, seemed
(70) to judge properly as a man of principle,—this was all clear enough...nor could she fix on any one article of moral duty evidently transgressed; but yet she would have been afraid to answer for his conduct. She distrusted
(75) the past, if not the present. The names which occasionally dropt of former associates, the allusions to former practices and pursuits, suggested suspicions not favourable of what he had been, She saw that there had been bad
(80) habits...a period of his life (and probably not a short one) when he had been, at least, careless on all serious matters; and, though he might now think very differently, who could answer for the true sentiments of a clever, cautious
(85) man, grown old enough to appreciate a fair character....

<u>Question Three</u>

(Suggested time—40 minutes. This essay counts as one-third of the total essay section score.)

Oftentimes in literature a character feels compelled to honor the terms of a vow, a promise, or a contract. However, honoring this commitment, which may be a social, financial, moral or spiritual one, may prove difficult, forcing the character to compromise, even betray the commitment that he feels he must uphold.

Choose a novel or play in which a character is compelled to honor such a vow, promise or contract. Then, in a well-organized essay, identify the nature of the character's commitment, the degree to which the character is able to honor it, and the impact that the character's honoring or reneging on the commitment has upon the work as a whole.

You may choose a novel or play from the works listed below or use a work of comparable literary merit.

The Adventures of Huckleberry Finn   *Jane Eyre*
The Awakening   *Jude the Obscure*
Cat's Eye   *The Kite Runner*
Cold Mountain   *A Lesson Before Dying*
The Color Purple   *A Man for All Seasons*
The Crucible   *The Merchant of Venice*
Death of a Salesman   *Montana 1948*
A Doll's House   *Oedipus Rex*
Ethan Frome   *The Portrait of a Lady*
Faust   *The Power & the Glory*
Frankenstein   *Pride and Prejudice*
The Grapes of Wrath   *Rabbit, Run*
Great Expectations   *The Road*
Hamlet   *The Scarlet Letter*
Heart of Darkness   *A Tale of Two Cities*

Sample Examination III

Questions 1-12. Refer to the following poem.

The Trees Are Down

And he cried with a loud voice:
Hurt not the earth, neither the sea,
nor the trees.

—Revelation 7:3

They are cutting down the great plane-trees at the end of the gardens.
For days there has been the grate of the saw, the swish of the branches
    as they fall,
The crash of trunks, the rustle of trodden leaves,
With the 'Whoops' and the 'Whoas,' the loud common talk, the loud
    common laughs of the men, above it all.

(5)   I remember one evening of a long past Spring
Turning in at a gate, getting out of a cart, and finding a large dead rat
    in the mud of the drive.
I remember thinking: alive or dead, a rat was a god-forsaken thing,
But at least, in May, that even a rat should be alive.

The week's work here is as good as done. There is just one bough
    on the roped bole, in the fine grey rain,
(10)   Green and high
        And lonely against the sky.
            (Down now!—)
        And but for that,
        If an old dead rat
(15)   Did once, for a moment, unmake the Spring, I might never have
    thought of him again.

It is not for a moment the Spring is unmade to-day;
These were great trees, it was in them from root to stem:
When the men with the 'Whoops' and the 'Whoas' have carted the
    whole of the whispering loveliness away
Half the Spring, for me, will have gone with them.
(20)   It is going now, and my heart has been struck with the hearts of the
    planes;
Half my life it has beat with these, in the sun, in the rains,
    in the March wind, the May breeze,
In the great gales that came over to them across the roofs from the
    great seas.
    There was only a quiet rain when they were dying;
    They must have heard the sparrows flying,
(25)   And the small creeping creatures in the earth where they were lying—
    But I, all day, I heard an angel crying:
        'Hurt not the trees.'

—Charlotte Mew

---

[1] the book of the Bible that foretells apocalyptic events

[2] Sequoias, huge expansive trees which live for many years

[3] the trunk of a tree

1. The primary purpose of the epigraph from the Biblical Book of Revelation is to

   (A) foreshadow the destruction of the great plane-trees
   (B) intimate God's sadness upon carrying out punitive action
   (C) imply divine displeasure at the human destruction of the environment
   (D) suggest the futility of divine admonition
   (E) show the restraint of the divine at man's wickedness

2. The declarative sentence that opens the poem does all of the following EXCEPT

   (A) announce an irrevocable fact
   (B) compliment the majesty of the trees
   (C) imply the speaker's indictment of the anonymous transgressors
   (D) confess the speaker's craven reluctance to intervene
   (E) offer an emotional but impotent admonition to her audience

3. The speaker utilizes sound devices in the opening stanza to establish which of the following contrasts?

   (A) the harmony of nature and the encroachment of man
   (B) the transience of nature and the permanence of man
   (C) the indifference of the work crew and the concern of the residents
   (D) the slowness of the job and the haste of the workers
   (E) the loftiness of the trees and the short stature of the men

4. The speaker's repetition of the word "common" in line 4 does which of the following?

   I. It implies the frequency with which men despoil nature.
   II. It highlights the brutish and insensitive rabble that comprises the work crew.
   III. It reemphasizes the regal majesty of the fallen plane-trees.

   (A) I only
   (B) III only
   (C) I and II
   (D) II and III
   (E) I, II and III

5. The speaker clearly views the cutting down of the great plane-trees as a(n)

   (A) untimely inconvenience
   (B) dire necessity
   (C) unnecessary carnage
   (D) civic improvement
   (E) inept undertaking

6. The speaker likely includes the anecdote of the rat (lines 5-8) to

   (A) deplore the infestation of the neighborhood
   (B) contrast the beauty of the plane-trees
   (C) confess her general lack of awareness
   (D) establish her sensitivity to nature
   (E) imply that Spring is a season of life, not of death

7. In the third stanza, the speaker's tone shifts to one of

   (A) nostalgic longing
   (B) dispirited resignation
   (C) defiant optimism
   (D) bitter anguish
   (E) ironic relief

8. Which of the following contributes LEAST to the speaker's callous characterization of the tree-cutters?

   (A) "trodden" (line 3)
   (B) "roped bole" (line 9)
   (C) "(Down now!—)" (line 12)
   (D) "carted" (line 18)
   (E) "sparrows flying" (line 24)

9. That the speaker perceives the felling of the trees to be an 'unnatural' act is conveyed by the

   (A) "Whoops" and "Whoas" of the workmen (line 4, line 18)
   (B) ominous emergence of the dead rat (lines 6-8)
   (C) tether attached to the final tree (line 9)
   (D) contrived words "unmake" (line 15) and "unmade" (line 16)
   (E) turbulence of the "great gales" (line 22)

10. All of the following trouble the speaker about the felling of the great plane trees EXCEPT

   (A) the irreverent laughter of the tree-cutters
   (B) the permanence of their removal
   (C) her perception of them as landmarks of growth and time
   (D) its violation of a spiritual mandate
   (E) their victimization by encroaching industrialization

11. The speaker's observation that "There was only a quiet rain when they were dying" (line 23) is BEST characterized as which of the following?

   I. A pathetic fallacy in which nature deplores the mournful occasion of the tree-felling.
   II. An ironic counterpoint to the trees' survival of the "great gales" (line 22).
   III. A wry understatement that downplays the natural calamity.

   (A) II only
   (B) III only
   (C) I and II
   (D) I and III
   (E) I, II and III

12. Which of the following is NOT a characteristic of the poem?

   (A) an intricate and irregular pattern of rhyme
   (B) onomatopoeic diction
   (C) a flashback to an earlier Spring
   (D) imagery that captures the changing seasons
   (E) a mournful, nostalgic tone that laments the permanent decimation of the majestic trees

Questions 13-25. Refer to the following passage.

…The three women sat talking about various miseries they had had, their cure or abatement, what had helped. Over and over again they returned to Aunt Jimmy's condition.
(5) Repeating its cause, what could have been done to prevent the misery from taking hold…Their voices blended into a threnody of nostalgia about pain. Rising and falling, complex in harmony, uncertain in pitch, but
(10) constant in the recitative of pain. They hugged the memories of illnesses to their bosoms. They licked their lips and clucked their tongues in fond remembrance of pains they had endured—childbirth, rheumatism, croup,
(15) sprains, backache, piles. All of the bruises they had collected from moving about the earth—harvesting, cleaning, hoisting, pitching, stooping, kneeling, picking—always with young ones underfoot.
(20)   But they had been young once. The odor of their armpits and haunches had mingled into a lovely musk; their eyes had been furtive, their lips relaxed, and the delicate turn of their heads on those slim black necks had been like
(25) nothing other than a doe's. Their laughter had been more touch than sound.
    Then they had grown. Edging into life from the back door. Becoming. Everybody in the world was in a position to give them
(30) orders. White women said, "Do this." White children said, "Give me that." White men said, "Come here." Black men said, "Lay down." The only people they need not take orders from were black children and each other. But they
(35) took all of that and re-created it in their own image. They ran the houses of white people, and knew it. When white men beat their men, they cleaned up the blood and went home to receive abuse from the victim. They beat their
(40) children with one hand and stole for them with the other. The hands that felled trees also cut umbilical cords; the hands that wrung the necks of chickens and butchered hogs also nudged African violets into bloom; the arms
(45) that loaded sheaves, bales, and sacks rocked babies into sleep. They patted biscuits into flaky ovals of innocence—and shrouded the dead. They plowed all day and came home to nestle like plums under the limbs of their
(50) men….

Then they were old. Their bodies honed, their odor sour. Squatting in a cane field, stooping in a cotton field, kneeling by a river bank, they had carried a world on their heads.
(55) They had given over the lives of their own children and tendered their grandchildren. With relief they wrapped their heads in rags, and their breasts in flannel; eased their feet into felt. They were through with lust and lactation,
(60) beyond tears and terror. They alone could walk the roads of Mississippi, the lanes of Georgia, the fields of Alabama unmolested. They were old enough to be irritable when and where they chose, tired enough to look forward to death,
(65) disinterested enough to accept the idea of pain while ignoring the presence of pain. They were, in fact and at last, free. And the lives of these old black women were synthesized in their eyes—a purée of tragedy and humor,
(70) wickedness and serenity, truth and fantasy….

13. The passage is MOST accurately labeled a

(A) memoir of individual hardship
(B) history of plantation labor
(C) diatribe against female oppression
(D) panegyric to the endurance of black women
(E) satire of social rituals

14. In describing the conversation of the three women about Aunt Jimmy's illness, the author's diction and syntax imply a metaphor drawn from

(A) medicine
(B) folklore
(C) music
(D) agriculture
(E) language

From THE BLUEST EYE by Toni Morrison, copyright ©1970 and renewed 1998 by Toni Morrison. Used by permission of Alfred A. Knopf, a division of Random House, Inc.

15. The women's recollections of their legacy of hard work and suffering are enhanced by all of the following EXCEPT

    (A) a metaphor that compares their illnesses to cherished offspring
    (B) a series of gerunds that catalogs the diversity of their labor
    (C) participles that convey the volume and inflection of their voices
    (D) a tone of embitterment fostered by the arduousness of their existence
    (E) a series of nouns cataloging the maladies that they had endured

16. In describing the women's youth in lines 20-26, the speaker primarily focuses upon a description of their

    (A) physical features
    (B) youthful activities
    (C) comparisons to animals
    (D) pleasant memories
    (E) displays of emotion

17. Which of the following may be said about the structure of the final three paragraphs?

    I. It parallels the chronological aging of the three women and of women like them.
    II. The relative brevity/length of the paragraphs reflects the duration of youth and happiness, or of aging and suffering.
    III. It mirrors the gradual movement from enslavement in the South to liberty in the North.

    (A) I only
    (B) III only
    (C) I and II
    (D) I and III
    (E) I, II and III

18. The phrase, "Edging into life from the back door" (lines 27-28) suggests that black women have traditionally been

    (A) timid
    (B) marginalized
    (C) assertive
    (D) deceitful
    (E) indolent

19. In lines 30-32 the author employs which of the following to depict the expected subservience of black women?

    (A) participles
    (B) contrast
    (C) imperatives
    (D) anaphora
    (E) climactic order

20. Lines 34-36, "But they took all of that and re-created it in their own image," imply what about black women and their social position?

    (A) That they willingly embraced their subservient roles.
    (B) That they resisted being ordered about by whites and blacks alike.
    (C) That they pretended that things were not as intolerable as they seemed.
    (D) That they made accommodations to their lot that made it more bearable.
    (E) That they plotted eventual rebellion or escape.

21. Lines 36-50 are marked by all of the following contrasts EXCEPT

    (A) nurture and discipline
    (B) indoor chores and outdoor chores
    (C) birth and death
    (D) ruthlessness and tenderness
    (E) hope and despondency

22. Lines 52-54—"Squatting in a cane field, stooping in a cotton field, kneeling by a river bank, they had carried a world on their heads"—do which of the following?

    I. They utilize participial phrases to portray the various physical tasks performed by Southern black women.
    II. They capture the experience of Southern black women in a variety of locales.
    III. They equate the physical exertions of Southern black women with the feats of a mythological character.

    (A) I only
    (B) III only
    (C) I and III
    (D) II and III
    (E) I, II and III

23. The freedom alluded to in line 67 likely refers to

    (A) liberty granted by the Emancipation Proclamation
    (B) a cessation of duty and labor
    (C) separation from their abusive menfolk
    (D) voting rights achieved during the 1960s
    (E) physical death

24. The speaker likely refers to the three women as a "purée" (line 69) because they have become a(n)

    (A) grey-haired monument to a backward and bygone age
    (B) feeble symbol of a people that has been worn down by toil
    (C) enduring amalgam of the experiences of Southern black women
    (D) important resource for history and local color
    (E) taxing burden on the young

25. Which of the following does NOT depict an irony in the experiences of the black women that are described in the passage?

    (A) "They hugged the memories of illnesses to their bosoms" (lines 10-11).
    (B) "They ran the houses of white people..." (line 36).
    (C) "When white men beat their men, they cleaned up the blood and went home to receive abuse from the victim" (lines 37-39).
    (D) "the hands that wrung the necks of chickens and butchered hogs also nudged African violets into bloom..." (lines 42-44).
    (E) "They were old enough... to accept the idea of pain while ignoring the presence of pain" (lines 62-66).

Questions 26-40. Refer to the following poem.

FOR THE COMMANDER OF THE 'ELIZA'

...the others, with emaciated faces and prominent,
staring eyeballs, were evidently in an advanced state
of starvation. The officer reported to Sir James
Dombrain . . . and Sir James, 'very inconvienently,'
wrote Routh, 'interfered'.

— Cecil Woodham-Smith: *The Great Hunger*.[1]

Routine patrol off West Mayo; sighting
A rowboat heading unusually far
Beyond the creek, I tacked[2] and hailed the crew
In Gaelic. Their stroke had clearly weakened
(5)   As they pulled to, from guilt or bashfulness
I was conjecturing when, O my sweet Christ,
We saw piled in the bottom of their craft
Six grown men with gaping mouths and eyes
Bursting the sockets like spring onions in drills.[3]
(10)   Six wrecks of bone and pallid, tautened skin.
'Bia, bia
Bia.'[4] In whines and snarls their desperation
Rose and fell like a flock of starving gulls.
We'd known about the shortage but on board
(15)   They always kept us right with flour and beef
So understand my feelings, and the men's,
Who had no mandate to relieve distress
Since relief was then available in Westport—
Though clearly these poor brutes would never make it.
(20)   I had to refuse food: they cursed and howled
Like dogs that had been kicked hard in the privates.
When they drove at me with their starboard oar
(Risking capsize themselves) I saw they were
Violent and without hope. I hoisted
(25)   And cleared off. Less incidents the better.

Next day, like six bad smells, those living skulls
Drifted through the dark of bunks and hatches
And once in port I exorcised my ship
Reporting all to the Inspector General.
(30)   Sir James, I understand, urged free relief
For famine victims in the Westport Sector
And earned tart reprimand from good Whitehall.[5]
Let natives prosper by their own exertions;
Who could not swim might go ahead and sink.
(35)   'The Coast Guard with their zeal and activity
Are too lavish' were the words, I think.

— Seamus Heaney

---

[1] The epigraph, taken from Cecil Woodham-Smith's *The Great Hunger*, an account of the Irish potato famine of the 1840s, recounts a merciful action
taken by the Inspector General of the Coast Guard, Sir James Dombrain, in response to an English captain's report of his ship's having been approached
by a boatful of starving men. The Routh referred to in the epigraph was the English general in charge of the Relief Commission in Dublin. (The poem
itself refers to action taken by the commander of another vessel, the *Eliza*, in a similar encounter.)

[2] turn into the wind

[3] shallow trenches

[4] food (Gaelic)

[5] street in London readily associated with the seat of English political power

26. The speaker in the poem is

    (A) a member of the watch
    (B) the ship's captain
    (C) one of the starving boatmen
    (D) the Inspector General
    (E) an outside narrator

27. In light of the poem which follows it, the epigraph from Cecil Woodman-Smith's *The Great Hunger* is primarily intended to

    (A) provide a larger historical context
    (B) relate an incidence of insubordination
    (C) laud a samaritan action
    (D) establish an important contrast in behavior
    (E) appeal to the pathos of the reader

28. Of the following, which BEST articulates the conflict which the speaker of the poem experiences?

    (A) idealism vs. reality
    (B) duty vs. conscience
    (C) courage vs. fear
    (D) altruism vs. self-preservation
    (E) salvation vs. damnation

29. Which of the following are accurate observations about the fragment, "Routine patrol off West Mayo" (line 1), that opens the poem?

    I. It intentionally mimics the terse, official style of a shipboard log.
    II. It identifies a specific location in Ireland that is suffering from terrible famine.
    III. It intensifies, through understatement, the impact of the subsequent encounter.

    (A) I only
    (B) III only
    (C) I and III
    (D) II and III
    (E) I, II and III

30. The phrase, "O my sweet Christ" (line 6), that the speaker utters to himself is BEST labeled a(n)

    (A) allusion
    (B) intercession
    (C) imprecation
    (D) euphemism
    (E) apostrophe

31. Which of the following contributes LEAST to the graphic description of the rowboat crew's suffering in lines 7-13?

    (A) participles
    (B) similes
    (C) choric repetition
    (D) color imagery
    (E) onomatopoeic diction

32. The poet employs similes to convey each of the following aspects of the famished men EXCEPT

    (A) their physically distorted features
    (B) their dire pleas for sustenance
    (C) their anguish at being spurned
    (D) their violent attempt to board the vessel
    (E) their lingering effect upon the speaker's conscience

33. The word "right" in the phrase "kept us right" (line 15) is MOST accurately interpreted as

    (A) provisioned
    (B) trim
    (C) docile
    (D) disciplined
    (E) spoiled

34. Which of the following does NOT impact the speaker's conviction that he "had to refuse food" (line 20)?

    (A) his knowledge that famine relief had been established at another locale
    (B) his reluctance to set further precedent by assisting the civilian population
    (C) his lack of a direct mandate to redress such desperation
    (D) his lack of empathy for the starving men
    (E) his recognition that the men were volatile and desperate

35. Both the diction and the figurative language in lines 26-29 suggest that the men to whom the captain of the *Eliza* refuses aid become

    (A) rotting corpses
    (B) distant memories
    (C) rancorous loiterers
    (D) heroic survivors
    (E) troubling specters

36. The thought in lines 33-34, "Let natives prosper by their own exertions; / Who could not swim might go ahead and sink," reflects the mindset of all of the following EXCEPT

    (A) the speaker
    (B) the English government
    (C) the other seaman aboard the *Eliza*
    (D) the Inspector General, Sir James
    (E) Routh

37. At the conclusion of the episode the speaker primarily feels

    (A) appalled
    (B) cowed
    (C) remorseful
    (D) vindicated
    (E) elated

38. The final two words of the poem, "I think" (line 36), are likely intended to make the reader

    (A) question the veracity of the speaker's memory
    (B) wonder if the speaker disagrees with the official government position on not aiding the hungry
    (C) question the wisdom of Whitehall's reprimand of Sir James
    (D) speculate as to what was really said to Sir James
    (E) deplore the ease with which the speaker puts the incident behind him

39. Which of the following words or pair of words is NOT used metaphorically in the poem?

    (A) "wrecks" (line 10)
    (B) "whines and snarls" (line 12)
    (C) "hoisted" (line 24)
    (D) "exorcised" (line 28)
    (E) "swim" and "sink" (line 34)

40. Ultimately, Routh's comment in the epigraph—that Sir James "*very inconvienently… interfered*"—does which of the following?

    I. Highlights the extent to which Sir James tried to ameliorate the desperate situation of the Irish.
    II. Implies Routh's displeasure at having been drawn into the crisis by Sir James' compassionate action.
    III. Portrays Routh and the captain of the *Eliza* as men whose pragmatism surmounts their charity.

    (A) I only
    (B) II only
    (C) I and III
    (D) II and III
    (E) I, II and III

Questions 41-53. Refer to the following passage.

And now Carrie had attained that which in the beginning seemed life's object, or, at least, such fraction of it as human beings ever attain of their original desires. She could look about
(5)   on her gowns and carriage, her furniture and bank account. Friends there were, as the world takes it—those who would bow and smile in acknowledgment of her success. For these she had once craved. Applause there was, and
(10)   publicity—once far off, essential things, but now grown trivial and indifferent. Beauty also—her type of loveliness—and yet she was lonely. In her rocking-chair she sat, when not otherwise engaged—singing and dreaming....
(15)   Man has not yet comprehended the dreamer any more than he has the ideal. For him the laws and morals of the world are unduly severe. Ever hearkening to the sound of beauty, straining for the flash of its distant
(20)   wings, he watches to follow, wearying his feet in traveling. So watched Carrie, so followed, rocking and singing.
    And it must be remembered that reason had little part in this. Chicago dawning, she
(25)   saw the city offering more of loveliness than she had ever known...In fine raiment and elegant surroundings, men seemed to be contented. Hence, she drew near these things. Chicago, New York; Drouet, Hurstwood; the
(30)   world of fashion and the world of stage—these were but incidents. Not them, but that which they represented, she longed for. Time proved the representation false.
    Oh, the tangle of human life! How dimly
(35)   as yet we see. Here was Carrie, in the beginning poor, unsophisticated, emotional; responding with desire to everything most lovely in life, yet finding herself turned as by a wall. Laws to say: "Be allured, if you will, by
(40)   everything lovely, but draw not nigh unless by righteousness." Convention to say: "You shall not better your situation except by honest labour." If honest labour be unremunerative and difficult to endure; if it be the long, long
(45)   road which never reaches beauty, but wearies the feet and the heart; if the drag to follow beauty be such that one abandons the admired way, taking rather the despised path leading to her dreams quickly, who shall cast the first
(50)   stone? Not evil, but longing for that which is better, more often directs the steps of the erring. Not evil, but goodness more often allures the feeling mind unused to reason.

    Amid the tinsel and shine of her state
(55)   walked Carrie, unhappy. As when Drouet took her, she had thought: "Now I am lifted into that which is best;" as when Hurstwood seemingly offered her the better way: "Now I am happy." But since the world goes its way past all who
(60)   will not partake of its folly, she now found herself alone....
    Sitting alone, she was now an illustration of the devious ways by which one who feels, rather than reasons, may be led in the pursuit
(65)   of beauty. Though often disillusioned, she was still waiting for that halcyon day when she should be led forth among dreams become real...It was forever to be the pursuit of that radiance of delight which tints the distant
(70)   hilltops of the world.
    Oh, Carrie, Carrie! Oh, blind strivings of the human heart! Onward, onward, it saith, and where beauty leads, there it follows. Whether it be the tinkle of a lone sheep bell o'er some
(75)   quiet landscape, or the glimmer of beauty in sylvan places, or the show of soul in some passing eye, the heart knows and makes answer, following. It is when the feet weary and hope seems vain that the heartaches and
(80)   the longings arise. Know, then, that for you is neither surfeit nor content. In your rocking-chair, by your window dreaming, shall you long, alone. In your rocking-chair, by your window, shall you dream such happiness as
(85)   you may never feel.

41. The overriding tone of the passage is BEST labeled

   (A) moralizing
   (B) cynical
   (C) disparaging
   (D) elegiac
   (E) fault-finding

42. The diction and syntax of the opening sentence seem intended to

    (A) celebrate Carrie's remarkable accomplishment of her life's object
    (B) acknowledge Carrie's dogged perseverance in pursuing her life's dream
    (C) imply Carrie's utter dislike of constantly being in the public eye
    (D) foreshadow Carrie's disturbing incompleteness despite attaining her desires
    (E) indict Carrie's growing complacency upon achieving popular status

43. The depiction of Carrie's career by the speaker suggests that it is marked by all of the following EXCEPT

    (A) monetary gain
    (B) public acclaim
    (C) romantic attention
    (D) inner contentment
    (E) opulent possessions

44. The speaker likely claims that for the dreamer "the laws and morals of the world are unduly severe" (lines 17-18) for which of the following reasons?

    (A) Laws and morals impede the ready attainment of desires.
    (B) Laws and morals favor the rich and powerful.
    (C) Laws and morals promise spiritual rewards rather than temporal ones.
    (D) Laws and morals confound individuals with their complexities.
    (E) Laws and morals differ from municipality to municipality.

45. The speaker uses the cities, names, and realms in lines 29-30—"Chicago, New York; Drouet, Hurstwood; the world of fashion and the world of the stage"—as which of the following?

    (A) ironies
    (B) metonymies
    (C) personifications
    (D) hyperboles
    (E) allusions

46. Lines 39-41, "Laws to say: 'Be allured, if you will, by everything lovely, but draw not nigh unless by righteousness,'" do all of the following EXCEPT

    (A) provide one example of the "wall" referred to in line 39
    (B) mirror, via their syntax and tone, the social obstacles that deter Carrie
    (C) allude to the story of temptation: Eve and the forbidden Tree of Knowledge
    (D) echo in its admonitory tone the warning of a deity
    (E) imply that Carrie cannot thrive because she is morally tainted

47. The three conditional "if" clauses (lines 43-49) that precede the rhetorical question, "who shall cast the first stone?" (lines 49-50), present

    (A) examples of "honest labour"
    (B) excuses for Carrie's indolence
    (C) expressions of Carrie's frustration
    (D) exonerations of Carrie's expediency
    (E) explanations for a loss of faith

48. The syntax of the sentences in lines 50-53—"Not evil, but longing for that which is better, more often directs the steps of the erring. Not evil, but goodness more often allures the feeling mind unused to reason"—does which of the following?

    (A) It absolves the protagonist via the prominent positioning of "Not evil" at the start of each sentence.
    (B) It mirrors in its length the "long, long road which never reaches beauty" (lines 44-45).
    (C) It defends the righteousness of the laws and conventions.
    (D) It uses antithesis to suggest the eternal triumph of goodness over evil.
    (E) It indicts humanity for its inability to see what leads individuals astray.

49. The images of the "radiance of delight" (line 69) and the "tinkle of a lone sheep bell" (line 74) suggest that for Carrie genuine happiness is

(A) elusive
(B) incomprehensible
(C) ephemeral
(D) uplifting
(E) delusionary

50. The speaker's final pronouncements—"Know, then, that for you is neither surfeit nor content" (lines 80-81), and "In your rocking-chair, by your window, shall you dream such happiness as you may never feel" (lines 83-85)—suggest that in later years Carrie will be

(A) immobile and dependent
(B) placid and contented
(C) restive and longing
(D) rueful and embittered
(E) aged and forgetful

51. Which of the following does NOT contribute to the impression that Carrie was either deluded by her ambition or by the limited success she had already achieved?

(A) "Friends there were, as the world takes it—those who would bow and smile in acknowledgment of her success" (lines 6-8).
(B) "In fine raiment and elegant surroundings, men seemed to be contented. Hence, she drew near these things" (lines 26-28).
(C) "Here was Carrie, in the beginning poor, unsophisticated, emotional… yet finding herself turned as by a wall" (lines 35-39).
(D) "Amid the tinsel and shine of her state walked Carrie, unhappy" (lines 54-55).
(E) "…she was still waiting for that halcyon day when she should be led forth among dreams become real…" (lines 65-68).

52. In the passage the rocking-chair functions as a symbol of which of the following?

I. The prosperity and ease that Carrie's theatrical success has brought her.
II. The physical aging that such a tenuous career can wreak on an individual.
III. An ironic symbol of the contentment which Carrie can never experience.

(A) I only
(B) II only
(C) I and III
(D) II and III
(E) I, II and III

53. Which of the following aphorisms BEST captures the situation presented in the final paragraph of the passage?

(A) "Illusory joy is often worth more than genuine sorrow." – Samuel Johnson
(B) "The search for happiness is one of the chief sources of unhappiness." – Eric Hoffer
(C) "When one door closes, another door opens; but we often look so long and so regretfully upon the closed door that we do not see the ones which open for us." – Alexander Graham Bell
(D) "What makes old age so sad is not that our joys but our hopes cease." – Jean Paul Richter
(E) "The years teach much which the days never knew" – Ralph Waldo Emerson

Section II

Question One

(Suggested time–40 minutes. This question counts as one-third of the total essay section score.)

In the following excerpt from a Paule Marshall short story, the speaker recalls a childhood visit to her maternal grandmother Da-duh in Barbados. Read the passage carefully. Then, in a well-organized essay, discuss how the young girl's stories of New York impact her grandmother and show how the author uses literary devices such as contrast and dialogue to make a point about naïveté and knowledge.

....From then on, whenever I wasn't taken to visit relatives, I accompanied Da-duh out into the ground, and alone with her amid the canes or down in the gully I told her about New

(5) York. It always began with some slighting remark on her part: "I know they don't have anything this nice where you come from," or "Tell me, I hear those foolish people in New York does do such and such...". But as I

(10) answered, recreating my towering world of steel and concrete and machines for her, building the city out of words, I would feel her give way. I came to know the signs of her surrender: the total stillness that would come

(15) over her hard dry form, the probing gaze that like a surgeon's knife sought to cut through my skull to get at the images there, to see if I were lying; above all, her fear, a fear nameless and profound....

(20)   Over the weeks I told her about refrigerators, radios, gas stoves, elevators, trolley cars, wringer washing machines, movies, airplanes, the cyclone at Coney Island, subways, toasters, electric lights: "At night,

(25) see, all you have to do is flip this little switch on the wall and all the lights in the house go on. Just like that. Like magic. It's like turning on the sun at night"....

      "But tell me," she said to me once with a

(30) faint mocking smile, "do the white people have all these things too or it's only the people looking like us?"

      I laughed. "What d'ya mean," I said. "The white people have even better....".

(35)   One morning toward the end of our stay, Da-duh led me into a part of the gully that we had never visited before, an area darker and more thickly overgrown than the rest, almost impenetrable. There in a small clearing amid

(40) the dense bush, she stopped before an incredibly tall royal palm which rose cleanly out of the ground, and drawing the eye up with it, soared high above the trees around it up into the sky. It appeared to be touching the blue

(45) dome of sky, to be flaunting its dark crown of fronds right in the blinding white face of the late morning sun.

      Da-duh watched me a long time before she spoke, and then she said very quietly, "All

(50) right, now, tell me if you've got anything this tall in that place you're from."

      I almost wished, seeing her face, that I could have said no. "Yes," I said. "We've got buildings hundreds of times this tall in New

(55) York. There's one called the Empire State Building that's the tallest in the world. My class visited it last year and I went all the way to the top. It's got over a hundred floors. I can't describe how tall it is. Wait a minute.

(60) What's the name of that hill I went to visit the other day, where they have the police station?

      "You mean Bissex?"

      "Yes, Bissex. Well, the Empire State Building is way taller than that."

(65)   "You're lying now!" she shouted, trembling with rage. Her hand lifted to strike me.

      "No, I'm not," I said. "It really is, if you don't believe me I'll send you a picture postcard of it soon as I get back home so you

(70) can see for yourself. But it's way taller than Bissex."

      All the fight went out of her at that. The hand poised to strike me fell limp at her side, seeing not me but the building that was taller

(75) than the highest hill she knew, the small stubborn light in her eyes (it was the same amber as the flame in the kerosene lamp she lit at dark) began to fail. Finally, with a vague gesture that even in the midst of her defeat still

(80) tried to dismiss me and my world, she turned and started back through the gully, walking slowly, her steps groping and uncertain, as if she were suddenly unsure of the way, while I followed triumphant yet strangely saddened

(85) behind....

"To Da-Duh, In Memoriam", was originally published by The Feminist Press of the City of New York, © Paule Marshall 1983, and is used here with the permission of the Author through the Faith Childs Literary Agency, Inc.

Question Two

(Suggested time—40 minutes. This question counts as one-third of the total essay section score.)

The speaker in each of the following two poems declares his intent to terminate a relationship. Read each poem carefully. Then, in a well-organized essay discuss how the poets use language to reveal the commitment of each speaker to his vow. In responding to the prompt, you may wish to consider such things as diction, figurative language, syntax and tone.

A Renouncing of Love

Farewell, love, and all thy laws for ever,
Thy baited hooks shall tangle me no more;
Senec and Plato[1] call me from thy lore
To perfect wealth, my wit for to endeavor;
(5)   In blind error when I did persever,
Thy sharp repulse that pricketh aye so sore,
Hath taught me to set in trifles no store,
And scape forth since liberty is lever.[2]
Therefore, farewell, go trouble younger hearts,
(10)   And in me claim no more authority;
With idle youth go use thy property,
And thereon spend thy many brittle darts.
For hitherto though I have lost all my time,
Me lusteth[3] no longer rotten boughs to climb.

—Thomas Wyatt

[1]classical philosophers

[2]more precious

[3]lust or yearn for

Since There's No Help

Since there's no help, come let us kiss and part;
Nay, I have done, you get no more of me.
And I am glad, yea glad with all my heart
That thus so cleanly I myself can free;
(5)   Shake hands forever, cancel all our vows,
And when we meet at any time again,
Be it not seen in either of our brows
That we one jot of former love retain.
Now at the last gasp of love's latest breath,
(10)   When, his pulse failing, passion speechless lies,
When faith is kneeling by his bed of death,
And innocence is closing up his eyes,
Now if thou wouldst, when all have given him over,
From death to life thou mightst him yet recover.

—Michael Drayton

<u>Question Three</u>

(Suggested time-40 minutes. This question counts as one-third of the total essay section score.)

"It was the best of times, it was the worst of times, it was the age of wisdom, it was the epoch of belief, it was the season of Light, it was the season of Darkness...": so Charles Dickens opens his novel, *A Tale of Two Cities*, its most dramatic action taking place within the historical setting of the French Revolution. Like Dickens' *A Tale of Two Cities*, novels and plays are often set during a carefully selected historical epoch or inspired by an actual historical event.

Select a novel or play that takes place in an historically significant setting or has been influenced by an historical event. In a well-organized essay, discuss the importance of the setting to the central conflict in the play or novel and show how the author uses this setting to comment upon the age in which it takes place. You may choose a work from the list below or another novel or play of recognized literary merit. Avoid plot summary.

The Adventures of Huckleberry Finn	*The Grapes of Wrath*
The Age of Innocence	*The Great Gatsby*
All My Sons	*Heart of Darkness*
All Quiet on the Western Front	*Henry IV, Part I*
All the King's Men	*Julius Caesar*
Atonement	*The Jungle*
Becket	*Main Street*
Beloved	*My Antonia*
Billy Budd	*Les Miserables*
The Book of Daniel	*The Poisonwood Bible*
Cold Mountain	*The Power and the Glory*
The Crucible	*The Scarlet Letter*
Cry, the Beloved Country	*Snow Falling on Cedars*
Falling Man	*Things Fall Apart*
A Farewell to Arms	*The Things They Carried*
The French Lieutenant's Woman	*The Trojan Women*

Sample Examination IV

Section I

Questions 1-6. Refer to the following poem.

The Apparition

When by thy scorn, O murd'ress, I am dead,
And that thou thinkst thee free
From all solicitation from me,
Then shall my ghost come to thy bed,
(5)   And thee, feign'd vestal, in worse arms shall see:
Then thy sick taper will begin to wink,
And he, whose thou art then, being tired before,
Will, if thou stir, or pinch to wake him, think
        Thou call'st for more,
(10)   And, in false sleep, will from thee shrink:

And then, poor aspen wretch, neglected thou
Bathed in a cold quicksilver sweat wilt lie,
        A verier ghost than I.
What I will say, I will not tell thee now,
(15)   Lest that preserve thee; and since my love is spent,
I'd rather thou shouldst painfully repent,
Than by my threatening rest still innocent.

—John Donne

---

[1] Priestesses of the Roman goddess Vesta, traditionally associated with
chastity

[2] Quivering; from the poplar tree whose leaves flutter in the lightest
breeze

[3] (archaic) truer; more genuine

1. Which of the following MOST accurately identifies the cause of the speaker's 'death' in the poem?

   (A) murder by a rival suitor
   (B) a plague-like contagion
   (C) an accident triggered by his acute insomnia
   (D) his beloved's rejection of his affection
   (E) suicide triggered by his despondency

2. The phrase "worse arms" (line 5) is BEST labeled a(n)

   (A) synecdoche
   (B) personification
   (C) allusion
   (D) hyperbole
   (E) paradox

3. Of the following pairs of adjectives, which BEST describes the attitude of the speaker?

   (A) fawning and solicitous
   (B) remorseful and apologetic
   (C) stoic and impassive
   (D) bitter and vindictive
   (E) maudlin and disconsolate

4. With which of the following words/phrases does the speaker mock the woman's integrity?

   (A) "Oh, murd'ress" (line 1)
   (B) "feign'd vestal" (line 5)
   (C) "sick taper" (line 6)
   (D) "poor aspen wretch" (line 11)
   (E) "verier ghost" (line 13)

5. All of the following contribute to the 'Gothic' ambience of the poem EXCEPT

   (A) the poem's title
   (B) the nightmarish nocturnal setting
   (C) the flickering candle
   (D) the voyeuristic actions of the speaker
   (E) the threats uttered by the speaker

6. An ironically humorous element of the poem involves

   (A) the speaker's nocturnal haunting of his beloved
   (B) the speaker's refusal to reveal what he will say to her
   (C) the speaker's belief that his love has been "spent"
   (D) the beloved's panicked perspiration
   (E) his rival's ruse to avoid the beloved's amorous intentions

Questions 7-18. Refer to the following passage.

In the following excerpt from an eighteenth century novel, a parson, imprisoned by a vindictive landlord for an inability to pay his rent, delivers a sermon to his fellow prisoners.

"My friends, my children, and fellow-sufferers, when I reflect on the distribution of good and evil here below, I find that much has been given man to enjoy, yet still more to
(5)   suffer…. In this life, then, it appears we cannot be entirely blest, but yet we may be completely miserable.

"Why man should thus feel pain; why our wretchedness should be requisite in the
(10) formation of universal felicity…. these are questions that can never be explained, and might be useless if known. On this subject Providence has thought fit to elude our curiosity, satisfied with granting us motives
(15) for consolation.

"In this situation man has called in the friendly assistance of philosophy; and Heaven, seeing the incapacity of that to console him, has given him the aid of religion. The
(20) consolations of philosophy are very amusing, but often fallacious; it tells us that life is filled with comforts, if we will but enjoy them; and, on the other hand, that though we unavoidably have miseries here, life is short, and they will
(25) soon be over. Thus do these consolations destroy each other….Thus philosophy is weak: but religion comforts in a higher strain. Man is here, it tells us, fitting up his mind, and preparing it for another abode. When the good
(30) man leaves the body, and is all a glorious mind, he will find he has been making himself a heaven of happiness here; while the wretch that has been maimed and contaminated by his vices, shrinks from his body with terror, and
(35) finds that he has anticipated the vengeance of heaven. To religion, then, we must hold in every circumstance of life, for our truest comfort….

"But though religion is very kind to all
(40) men, it has promised peculiar rewards to the unhappy; the sick, the naked, the houseless, the heavy-laden, and the prisoner have ever the most sacred promises in our sacred law….The unthinking have censured this as partiality, as a
(45) preference without merit to deserve it….

"But Providence is in another respect kinder to the poor than to the rich, for as it thus makes the life after death more desirable, so it smoothes the passage there. The wretched have
(50) had a long familiarity with every face of terror. The man of sorrows lays himself quietly down, without possessions to regret, and but few ties to stop his departure: he feels only nature's pang in the final separation, and this is no way
(55) greater than he has often fainted under before; for, after a certain degree of pain, every new breach that death opens in the constitution nature kindly covers with insensibility….

"To us then, my friends, the promises of
(60) happiness in heaven should be peculiarly dear; for if our reward be in this life alone, we are then, indeed, of all men the most miserable. When I look round these gloomy walls, made to terrify as well as to confine us; this light,
(65) that only serves to show the horrors of the place; those shackles, that tyranny has imposed, or crime made necessary; when I survey these emaciated looks, and hear those groans—oh, my friends, what a glorious
(70) exchange would heaven be for these! To fly through regions unconfined as air—to bask in the sunshine of eternal bliss—to carol over endless hymns of praise—to have no master to threaten or insult us, but the form of Goodness
(75) himself for ever in our eyes!—when I think of these things, his sharpest arrow becomes the staff of my support; when I think of these things, what is there in life worth having? when I think of these things, what is there that
(80) should not be spurned away? Kings in their palaces should groan for such advantages; but we, humbled as we are, should yearn for them….".

7. The speaker's purpose seems to be to

   (A) explain suffering
   (B) inspire fear
   (C) offer commiseration
   (D) lament inequity
   (E) instill hope

8. In the course of the passage, the speaker's attitude changes from

   (A) a disdain for philosophy to an acceptance of its necessity
   (B) a belief in man as innately good to a conviction that he is naturally depraved
   (C) a confidence in salvation to a crisis of faith
   (D) a resignation to suffering to an appreciation of its purpose
   (E) a hatred of royalty to an envy of their privileged lot

9. In the opening two paragraphs (lines 1-15), the speaker does all of the following EXCEPT

   (A) relate to the plight of his audience
   (B) lament an unfortunate disparity
   (C) accept the mystery of human suffering
   (D) rail at the arbitrary nature of the divine
   (E) establish a tone of resignation

10. In lines 16-26 philosophy is depicted as which of the following?

    (A) deceptive and ineffectual
    (B) profound and revelatory
    (C) arcane and confusing
    (D) enlightening and consolatory
    (E) trivial and aphoristic

11. According to the speaker, religion, as opposed to philosophy, teaches which of the following?

    I. That the bliss of heaven far surpasses temporal happiness.
    II. That divine retribution will indeed be carried out.
    III. That the end of man is to prepare himself for the afterlife.

    (A) I only
    (B) III only
    (C) I and II
    (D) I and III
    (E) I, II and III

12. In the context in which it appears, the word "anticipated" (line 35) is BEST interpreted as

    (A) awaited
    (B) misconstrued
    (C) foreseen
    (D) interrupted
    (E) misjudged

13. Which of the following does the speaker NOT suggest about the poor in lines 39-58?

    (A) That they have long been the objects of persecution and suffering.
    (B) That they have been inured to death by their previous suffering.
    (C) That they are unburdened by material concerns.
    (D) That they will be better off in death than they were in life.
    (E) That their final moments are agonizing and unbearable.

14. The "few ties" alluded to in line 52 likely refer to

    (A) close relationships
    (B) material possessions
    (C) business commitments
    (D) unresolved debts
    (E) resuscitation efforts

15. Which of the following is the primary characteristic of the speaker's rhetoric in lines 63-70?

    (A) a first-person perspective that flaunts the speaker's ability to tolerate such wretched conditions
    (B) hyperbolic diction that exaggerates the conditions of their confinement
    (C) an optimistic tone that bravely masks the despondency he has begun to feel
    (D) parallel subordinate clauses that catalog the miseries of their incarceration
    (E) pervasive onomatopoeia that aurally captures the mournful sounds of the oppressed

16. In addition to referencing the prison in which they are currently held captive, the "'gloomy walls'" (line 63) may be figuratively seen as the

    (A) dark womb in which life is conceived
    (B) deep depression which can, on occasion, paralyze
    (C) temporal existence that precedes death
    (D) dim prospects of their imminent release
    (E) indefinite nature of their salvation

17. The diction within the series of infinitive phrases in lines 70-75 suggests all of the following EXCEPT

    (A) spiritual absolution
    (B) boundless freedom
    (C) perpetual exultation
    (D) restful succor
    (E) protective asylum

18. Lines 75-77—"'when I think of these things, his sharpest arrow becomes the staff of my support?'"— exemplify which of the following?

    (A) personification
    (B) irony
    (C) synecdoche
    (D) allusion
    (E) syllogism

Questions 19-30. Refer to the following poem.

The Pact

We played dolls in that house where Father staggered with the
Thanksgiving knife, where Mother wept at
noon into her one ounce of
cottage cheese, praying for the strength not to
(5) kill herself. We kneeled over the
rubber bodies, gave them baths
carefully, scrubbed their little
orange hands, wrapped them up tight,
said goodnight, never spoke of the
(10) woman like a gaping wound
weeping on the stairs, the man like a stuck
buffalo, baffled, stunned, dragging
arrows in his hide. As if we had made a
pact of silence and safety, we kneeled and
(15) dressed those tiny torsos with their elegant
belly-buttons and miniscule holes
high on the buttock to pee through, and all that
darkness in their open mouths, so that I
have not been able to forgive you for giving your
(20) daughter away, letting her go at
eight as if you took Molly Ann or
Tiny Tears and held her head
under the water in the bathinette
until no bubbles rose, or threw her
(25) dark rosy body on the fire that
burned in that house where you and I
barely survived, sister, where we
swore to be protectors.

—Sharon Olds

---

[1] a portable bathtub for babies, usually made of rubberized cloth

19. The title of the poem, "The Pact," likely alludes to the

(A) marriage vow taken by the speaker's parents
(B) sisters' decision not to talk about their parents' dysfunctional marriage
(C) sisters' commitment never to discard their childhood playthings
(D) mutual vow the sisters made to look after each other
(E) speaker's determination never to forgive her sibling

20. Which of the following contributes LEAST to establishing the domestic unrest in the household?

(A) action verbs that convey the father's instability and the mother's sadness
(B) a series of participles that depicts the wounded nature of each parent
(C) similes that convey the psychological damage the parents have inflicted on one another
(D) diction that connotes the sisters' need for mutual protection
(E) the rueful, repeated phrase "that house" (lines 1 and 26)

21. The word "staggered" (line 1) is likely intended to imply the Father's

    (A) ineptitude at carving a turkey
    (B) fatigue from his arduous labors
    (C) response to his wife's rebuke
    (D) problems with alcohol
    (E) potential for spousal violence

22. The poem implies that the mother and father are both

    (A) naturally affectionate
    (B) physically battered
    (C) ruefully apologetic
    (D) visibly frustrated
    (E) psychologically abusive

23. Which of the following would be the LEAST plausible explanation for the mother's "praying for the strength not to / kill herself" (lines 4-5)?

    (A) a gnawing guilt spawned by her own weak character
    (B) a innate love of her two daughters
    (C) a severe depression caused by her perpetually troubled marriage
    (D) a dire need to shield her daughters from the peril of their father
    (E) an acute consciousness of her natural role of provider

24. In the poem the dolls function as all of the following EXCEPT

    (A) a means to keep the children out of their parents' hair
    (B) symbols of childhood innocence
    (C) reflections of the sisters themselves
    (D) objects of maternal care that offer a temporary haven from the external conflict
    (E) a metaphor for the rift caused by the elder sister's abandonment

25. The actions of the sisters toward the dolls (lines 5-9, 14-18) may plausibly be interpreted as which of the following?

    I.   An attempt to escape a nightmarish reality.
    II. A subconscious compensation for the lack of maternal care that they themselves have experienced.
    III. A refusal to grow up and accept domestic responsibilities.

    (A) I only
    (B) III only
    (C) I and II
    (D) I and III
    (E) I, II and III

26. The posture that the girls assume while carrying out their imaginary duties symbolically calls to mind

    (A) terror
    (B) subservience
    (C) supplication
    (D) adoration
    (E) mortification

27. Which of the following is inherent in the "pact of silence and safety" (line 14) that the sisters make with one another?

    (A) a tacit agreement to protect their mother from domestic violence
    (B) a mutual expectation to look after each other's well-being
    (C) a vow to protect the dolls from being damaged or discarded
    (D) an intention to pray for the reform of their father
    (E) a commitment to run away

28. The long sentence (lines 13-28) that completes the poem suggests that the speaker views her sister as a(n)

    (A) confidante
    (B) accomplice
    (C) defender
    (D) betrayer
    (E) role model

29. The rift between the two sisters is dramatized MOST by the speaker's

    (A) obvious and stubborn refusal to talk to her sibling
    (B) abandonment of their mutual play at motherhood
    (C) reference to herself as her sister's "daughter" (line 20)
    (D) comparison of her sister's abandonment to infanticidal actions
    (E) noisy tantrum upon the desertion of her older sibling

30. The speaker's tone in the closing three lines, "where you and I / barely survived, sister, where we / swore to be protectors," is BEST labeled

    (A) remonstrative
    (B) wistful
    (C) relieved
    (D) stony
    (E) grateful

Questions 31-42. Refer to the following passage.

It was a blue room—walls of dark wet morose blue, furniture made of walnut, including the bed on which the event was taking place. Fronting the fireplace was a huge (5) lid of a chocolate box with the representation of a saucy-looking lady. The tassel of the blind kept bobbing against the frosted windowpane. There was a washstand, a basin and ewer of off-white with big roses splashed throughout (10) the china itself, and a huge lumbering beast of a wardrobe. The midwife recalled once going to a house up the mountain, and finding the child smothered by the time she arrived; the fatherless child had been stuffed in a drawer. (15) The moans filled that room and went beyond the distempered walls out into the cold hall outside, where the black felt doggie with the amber eyes stood sentinel on a tall varnished whatnot. At intervals the woman apologized to (20) the midwife for the untoward commotion, said sorry in a gasping whisper, and then was seized again by a pain, that at different times she described as being a knife, a dagger, a hell on earth. It was her fourth labor. The previous (25) child had died two days after being born. An earlier child, also a daughter, had died of whooping cough. Her womb was sick unto death.[1] Why be a woman. Oh cruel life, oh merciless fate, oh heartless man, she sobbed. (30) Gripping the coverlet and remembering that between those self-same much-patched sheets, she had been pried apart, again and again, with not a word to her, not a little endearment, only rammed through and told to open up.

(35) When she married she had escaped the life of a serving girl, the possible experience of living in some grim institution but as time went on and the trousseau drawer was emptied of its gifts, she saw that she was made to serve in an (40) altogether other way. When she wasn't screaming she was grinding her head into the pillow, and praying for it to be all over. She dreaded the bloodshed long before they saw any. The midwife made her ease up as she put (45) an old sheet under her and over that a bit of oilcloth. The midwife said it was no joke and repeated the hypothesis that if men had to give birth there would not be a child born in the whole wide world.

(50) The husband was downstairs getting paralytic. Earlier, when his wife had announced that she would have to go upstairs because of her labour, he said, looking for the slightest pretext for a celebration, that if there was any (55) homemade wine or altar wine stacked away, to get it out, to produce it, and also the cut glasses. She said there was none and well he knew it since they could hardly afford tea and sugar. He started to root and to rummage, to (60) empty cupboards of their contents of rags, garments and provisions, even to put his hand inside the bolster case, to delve into pillows; on he went, rampaging until he found a bottle in the wardrobe, in the very room into which (65) she delivered her moans and exhortations. She begged of him not to, but all he did was to wield the amber-coloured bottle in her direction, and then put it to his head so that the spirit started to go glug-glug. It was (70) intoxicating stuff. By a wicked coincidence a crony of his had come to sell them another stove, most likely another crock, a thing that would have to be coaxed alight with constant attention and puffing, to create a draught. The (75) other child was with a neighbor, the dead ones in a graveyard six or seven miles away, among strangers and distant relatives, without their names being carved on the crooked rain-soaked tomb.

(80) "Oh Jesus," she cried out as he came back to ask for the knitting needle to skewer out the bit of broken cork.

"Blazes," he said to her as she coiled into a knot and felt the big urgent ball—that would be (85) the head—as it pressed on the base of her bowels, and battered at her insides....

---

[1] From Isaiah 38:1—according to the philosopher Kierkegaard, the state of being in despair but not being able to die

31. The author's primary purpose in the passage seems to be to

    (A) depict the agony of childbirth
    (B) document the high incidence of infant mortality in impoverished households
    (C) recount the privations caused by dire poverty
    (D) lament the unfortunate lot of women in earlier time periods
    (E) laud the crucial role of midwives in delivering infants prior to modern times

32. The author develops the contrast between the husband and wife in the passage by using all of the following EXCEPT

    (A) where they are positioned in the house
    (B) what they focus on as the event nears
    (C) how they feel about the birth of a fourth child
    (D) what gender child they prefer: a girl or a boy
    (E) what they utter at the episode's end

33. It may be inferred from the context in which it appears that a "what-not" (line 19) is most likely a(n)

    (A) object d'art
    (B) curio cabinet
    (C) area rug
    (D) grandfather clock
    (E) staircase

34. In light of the context in which it appears, the BEST equivalent for the adjective "untoward" (line 20) would be

    (A) embarrassing
    (B) untimely
    (C) ceaseless
    (D) loud
    (E) uncharacteristic

35. The woman's description of her pain alternately being "a knife, a dagger, a hell on earth" (lines 23-24) exemplifies which of the following?

    (A) purple prose
    (B) allusion
    (C) hyperbole
    (D) analogy
    (E) climactic order

36. Of the following, which provides the most logical explanation for the lengthy gap between the woman's reference to her first child (lines 24-27) and her mention of her last (lines 74-75)?

    (A) labor pains that distract the woman's thought
    (B) a subconscious desire not to experience the death of another infant
    (C) concerns that future children may be sent to a "grim institution" such as the workhouse
    (D) a distraction caused by the midwife's commentary on childbirth
    (E) the annoying distraction of her drink-seeking husband

37. The phrase, "looking for the slightest pretext for a celebration" (lines 53-54) primarily implies that the husband in the passage is

    (A) delighted by the imminent delivery of the child
    (B) apprehensive about yet another mouth to feed
    (C) eager for an opportunity to get drunk
    (D) defiant in face of their meager economic circumstances
    (E) maudlin about the deaths of earlier children

38. Lines 59-65 convey all of the following about the husband in the passage EXCEPT

    (A) the incorrigible nature of his addiction
    (B) his consciousness of his wife's deception
    (C) the doggedness of his pursuit of spirits
    (D) his exact knowledge of where the liquor is hidden
    (E) his disdain for the sanctity and intimacy of the childbirth

39. The husband's gesture in lines 66-68 is BEST regarded as

    (A) threatening
    (B) dismissive
    (C) acquiescent
    (D) taunting
    (E) apologetic

40. The "Oh, Jesus" (line 80) that the woman in labor utters may plausibly be interpreted as which of the following?

    I. A response to the severity of the birth pangs.
    II. An expression of her incredulity at her husband's shameless effrontery.
    III. A futile appeal for divine intercession.

    (A) I only
    (B) III only
    (C) I and II
    (D) II and III
    (E) I, II and III

41. Which of the following contributes LEAST to the author's depiction of the grim lot of women such as the one depicted in the passage?

    (A) the absence of a question mark in "Why be a woman" (line 28)
    (B) the parallel interjections "Oh cruel life, oh merciless fate, oh heartless man…" (lines 28-29)
    (C) physical verbs such as "pried" (line 32), "rammed" (line 34) and "battered" (line 86)
    (D) her understated epiphany that "…she was made to serve in an altogether other way" (lines 39-40)
    (E) the newly bought stove that would have to be "coaxed alight with constant attention and puffing…" (lines 73-74)

42. Ultimately, the passage suggests that the only viable alternative to the woman's unhappy marriage and her equally unhappy labor would have been

    (A) entering a religious order
    (B) marrying another suitor
    (C) enduring a lifetime of servitude
    (D) divorcing her husband
    (E) committing suicide

Questions 43-54. Refer to the following poem.

MEMORIAL VERSES
April 1850

Goethe[1] in Weimar[2] sleeps, and Greece,
Long since saw Byron's[3] struggle cease.
But one such death remain'd to come;
The last poetic voice is dumb—
(5)   We stand to-day by Wordsworth's tomb.

When Byron's eyes were shut in death,
We bow'd our head and held our breath.
He taught us little; but our soul
Had *felt* him like the thunder's roll.
(10)   With shivering heart the strife we saw
Of passion with eternal law;
And yet with reverential awe
We watch'd the fount of fiery life
Which served for that Titanic[4] strife.

(15)   When Goethe's death was told, we said:
Sunk, then, is Europe's sagest head.
Physician of the iron age,
Goethe has done his pilgrimage.
He took the suffering human race,
(20)   He read each wound, each weakness clear;
And struck his finger on the place,
And said: *Thou ailest here, and here!*
He look'd on Europe's dying hour
Of fitful dream and feverish power;
(25)   His eye plunged down the weltering strife,
The turmoil of expiring life—
He said: *The end is everywhere,*
Art still has truth, take refuge there!
And he was happy, if to know
(30)   Causes of things, and far below
His feet to see the lurid flow
Of terror, and insane distress,
And headlong fate, be happiness.

And Wordsworth![5]—Ah, pale ghosts, rejoice!
(35)   For never has such soothing voice
Been to your shadowy world convey'd,
Since erst, at morn, some wandering shade
Heard the clear song of Orpheus come
Through Hades, and the mournful gloom.
(40)   Wordsworth has gone from us—and ye,

Ah may ye feel his voice as we!
He too upon a wintry clime
Had fallen—on this iron time
Of doubts, disputes, distractions, fears.
(45)   He found us when the age had bound
Our souls in its benumbing round;
He spoke, and loosed our heart in tears.
He laid us as we lay at birth
On the cool flowery lap of earth,
(50)   Smiles broke from us and we had ease;
The hills were round us and the breeze
Went o'er the sunlit fields again;
Our foreheads felt the wind and rain.
Our youth return'd; for there was shed
(55)   Our spirits that had long been dead,
Spirits dried up and closely furl'd,
The freshness of the early world.

Ah! Since dark days still bring to light
Man's prudence and man's fiery might,
(60)   Time may restore us in his course
Goethe's sage mind and Byron's force;
But where will Europe's latter hour
Again find Wordsworth's healing power?
Others will teach us how to dare,
(65)   And against fear our breast to steel;
Others will strengthen us to bear—
But who, ah! who, will make us feel?
The cloud of mortal destiny,
Others will front it fearlessly—
(70)   But who, like him, will put it by?

Keep fresh the grass upon his grave
O Rotha,[6] with thy living wave!
Sing him thy best! For few or none
Hears thy voice right, now he is gone.

---

[1] Germany's greatest man of letters (1749-1832) whose interests included literature, philosophy, theology and science.

[2] city in Germany

[3] charismatic and controversial English Romantic poet (1788-1824)

[4] early Greek mythological deities who were overthrown by the Olympians

[5] English Romantic poet (1770-1850)

[6] a river

43. According to the speaker, Byron's greatest poetic gift was his

    (A) reverence for nature
    (B) evocation of emotion
    (C) didactic eloquence
    (D) devotion to form
    (E) vibrant delivery

44. The diction in lines 25-26 ("His eye . . . life") and lines 30-33 ("and far . . .fate") suggests that the speaker sees Goethe as a(n)

    (A) observer of world events who refused appeals for assistance
    (B) prophetic seer who foresaw impending calamity
    (C) sage witness who was too craven to intervene in a time of crisis
    (D) god-like presence standing above and apart from the fray
    (E) sadistic voyeur who reveled in the suffering of others

45. The speaker suggests Goethe differed from Byron and Wordsworth because of his tendency to be more

    (A) passionate and confrontational
    (B) comforting and revitalizing
    (C) disillusioned and morose
    (D) fiery and inspirational
    (E) probing and reflective

46. The speaker exalts Wordsworth over the other two writers by doing all of the following EXCEPT

    (A) alluding to his prolific catalog of literary accomplishments
    (B) comparing him to Orpheus, the famed musician of mythology
    (C) crediting him with the capacity to restore lost innocence
    (D) personifying a river and asking it to maintain his burial site
    (E) devoting to him the largest number of lines

47. According to lines 42-46, the state of the world in Wordsworth's time impacted the speaker and his compatriots in which of the following ways?

    (A) It stultified them.
    (B) It bewildered them.
    (C) It corrupted them.
    (D) It emboldened them.
    (E) It infuriated them.

48. Which of the following may be said about the imagery in lines 48-57?

    I. It alludes both to Eden and the archetypal earth-mother.
    II. It implies that nature can be physically and emotionally restorative.
    III. It validates Goethe's earlier exhortation that "*Art still has truth, take refuge there!*" (line 28).

    (A) II only
    (B) III only
    (C) I and II
    (D) I and III
    (E) I, II and III

49. Which of the following phrases does NOT allude to the turmoil and anxieties of the times in which these writers lived?

    (A) "dying hour" (line 23)
    (B) "weltering strife" (line 25)
    (C) "insane distress" (line 32)
    (D) "mournful gloom" (line 39)
    (E) "iron time" (line 43)

50. The speaker ultimately avers that difficult "iron" times, such as those alluded to in lines 23-33 and lines 43-46, do which of the following?

    (A) perpetually silence the great voices of the age
    (B) temporarily cripple institutions of business and finance
    (C) ironically spur sage and fervent efforts to combat them
    (D) completely vitiate any vestige of human innocence
    (E) effectively thwart any potential for human salvation

51. The speaker links the three great writers—Byron, Goethe and Wordsworth— through which of the following?

   I. Euphemistic diction that depicts each man's decease.
  II. References to the individual gifts each man possessed.
  III. Allusions to the social problems of the age in which each man lived.

   (A) I only
   (B) III only
   (C) I and II
   (D) II and III
   (E) I, II and III

52. Which of the following words is intended to conjure a homonym?

   (A) "told" (line 15)
   (B) "read" (line 20)
   (C) "morn" (line 37)
   (D) "clime" (line 42)
   (E) "bear" (line 66)

53. All of the following are stylistic traits of the poem EXCEPT

   (A) contrasting images of conflict and bliss
   (B) predominantly iambic tetrameter
   (C) rhyming couplets
   (D) pathetic fallacy
   (E) classical and Biblical allusions

54. The tone of the poem is MOST accurately labeled

   (A) pessimistic
   (B) scholarly
   (C) jingoistic
   (D) elegiac
   (E) resigned

Section II

<u>Question One</u>

(Suggested time: 40 minutes. This question counts as one-third of the total essay section score.)

In the following lines from Shakespeare's *Henry the Fifth*, Henry reflects upon the quality of his life as king as compared to the quality of a common man's existence. Read the passage carefully. Then, in a well-organized essay, discuss how Shakespeare uses language to reveal the king's thoughts and the conclusion he ultimately reaches about whose lot is better. In responding to the question, you may wish to consider such literary devices as diction, choice of detail, figurative language and tone.

> ....Upon the King! Let us our lives, our souls,
> Our debts, our careful wives,
> Our children, and our sins lay on the King!
> We must bear all. Oh, hard condition,
> (5) Twin-born with greatness, subject to the breath
> Of every fool, whose sense no more can feel
> But his own wringing![1] What infinite heartsease
> Must kings neglect that private men enjoy!
> And what have kings that privates have not too,
> (10) Save ceremony,[2] save general ceremony?
> What kind of God art thou, that suffer'st more
> Of mortal griefs than do thy worshippers?
> What are thy rents?[3] What are thy comings-in?
> O Ceremony, show me but thy worth!
> (15) What is the soul of adoration?
> Art thou aught else but place, degree and form,
> Creating awe and fear in other men?
> Wherein thou art less happy being feared
> Than they in fearing.
> (20) What drinkst thou oft, instead of homage sweet,
> But poisoned flattery? Oh, be sick, great
>   greatness,
> And bid thy ceremony give thee cure!
> Thinkst thou the fiery fever will go out
> With titles blown from adulation?

> (25) Will it give place to flexure[4] and low bending?
> Canst thou, when thou command'st the beggar's
>   knee,
> Command the health of it? No, thou proud
>   dream,
> That play'st so subtly with a king's repose,
> I am a king that find thee, and I know
> (30) 'Tis not the balm, the scepter and the ball,[5]
> The sword, the mace, the crown imperial,
> The intertissued[6] robe of gold and pearl,
> The farcèd title running 'fore the king,
> The throne he sits on, nor the tide of pomp
> (35) That beats upon the high shore of this
>   world—
> No, not all these, thrice-gorgeous ceremony,
> Not all these, laid in bed majestical,
> Can sleep so soundly as the wretched slave
> Who with a body filled and a vacant mind,
> (40) Gets him to rest crammed with distressful
>   bread,
> Never sees horrid night, the child of Hell,
> But, like a lackey, from the rise to set
> Sweats in the eye of Phoebus[7] and all night
> Sleeps in Elysium[8]....

---

[1] suffering; hardship

[2] pomp and splendor

[3] here used figuratively to mean benefits, profits

---

[4] bending at the knee

[5] a symbol of office

[6] interwoven

[7] in Greek mythology, Helios or the sun

[8] in Greek mythology, the section of the Underworld reserved for heroes

Question Two

(Suggested time—40 minutes. This question counts as one-third of the total essay section score.)

In the following passage from Garrison Keillor's *Lake Wobegon Days* (1985), the narrator and his classmates struggle over how best to donate money their graduating class has saved as a "class gift." Read the passage carefully. Then, in a carefully organized essay, show how the author uses language to achieve a comic effect in the passage. In planning your response, you may wish to consider such things as choice of detail, imagery, figurative language and characterization.

...It was only September, we had eight months left, and yet nostalgia lay heavy on our hearts and the premonition that in real life we would cease to be special. In this quiet little pond,
(5) encouraged by doting teachers, we felt successful and shining in some way, but once graduated we would disappear into the crowd of faceless adults and be like everyone else, old, a little tired, disappointed, and things not
(10) work out. College would be too hard and flunk us; the Army would unmask us as cowards; marriage would turn sour and love would die. One way or another, we would find disgrace, as others had. A man who had quarterbacked
(15) the Leonards in 1951 when the team was 10-0 and went to Grand Forks and won the Potato Bowl: he was in St. Cloud Reformatory for stealing $219 from a blind person. A good student and a member of the Student Council,
(20) now doing time behind bars. There were others like him. When Donna Bunsen said, "I want our class gift to be something special, that we can all be proud of," she was right, and she didn't have to add: "This may be one of the
(25) last things we'll ever do right"—we all knew that.

Previous class gifts didn't say much for them. The portrait of Henry Ford from the Class of 1920 honored a man nobody cared
(30) about; 1928's trophy case was an embarrassment (half-empty), and the marble water fountain, compliments of 1931, was a big waste of money. The gold auditorium curtain from 1951 was ugly, and the globe in
(35) the library was all but useless. The gift of the class of 1917, it was a world that no longer existed. A plaster bust of Shakespeare was the legacy of 1947, a nice idea, but succeeding generations had gone to work on it with

(40) crayons and made the Bard look like an old cocktail waitress.

After we voted down the less fortunate, President Tollefson opened the floor for nominations and got (1) a stained-glass
(45) window, (2) a piano, (3) sending Clara the cook to cooking school (ha ha), (4) a clock, (5) a student-citizenship trophy, and each had a few supporters and the rest of us groaned. That wasn't what we wanted at all!
(50) When Marjorie stood up, I thought she was going to nominate a gift to the missionaries, she was that sort of person. She focused her big watery green eyes on us and said, "I think we should do something to recognize teachers.
(55) We owe so much to them, and someday we'll think back and remember, so I think the money should be spent on a tribute to teachers." I couldn't see Miss Falconer, our adviser, sitting in back, but she was probably beaming at
(60) Marjorie like a lighthouse. "I nominate an oil painting of a teacher who has been very important to us, and I nominate Miss Falconer as the teacher"....

....This was some kind of joke. We all had
(65) Miss Falconer, we knew who she was. She had it in for boys. In choir, every day she looked around to see who hadn't learned his part—she could smell fear like an animal—and made him stand up and die for a few minutes. To think
(70) that we would perpetuate her in a work of art was something we could look back on in later years and get sick all over again. Miss Falconer was the last person I'd want to see in a painting: oil, finger, or any other kind. She
(75) had, all by herself, cured me of a longstanding fascination with choirs. She had almost cured me of music.

Question Three

(Suggested time-40 minutes. This question counts as one-third of the total essay section score.)

Oftentimes in literature a character faces a crisis of belief, a moment in which his faith in personal or institutional values is sorely threatened. This critical moment may result in a character's overcoming these doubts and reaffirming beliefs, or succumbing to these qualms and abandoning them.

Choose a novel or play in which a character experiences such a crisis. In a well-organized essay illustrate how this critical moment either strengthens or dissolves the character's faith in a personal or institutional values, and show how his reaction to this crisis contributes to the meaning of the work as a whole. You may choose a work from the list below or another novel or play of recognized literary merit.

The Adventures of Huckleberry Finn	*J.B.*
Antigone	*Jude the Obscure*
The Awakening	*Julius Caesar*
Becket	*A Lesson Before Dying*
Billy Budd	*Montana 1948*
Catch-22	*Native Son*
The Crucible	*1984*
A Doll's House	*The Piano Lesson*
Farenheit 451	*Portrait of a Lady*
Frankenstein	*A Portrait of the Artist as a Young Man*
The Grapes of Wrath	*The Power and the Glory*
Hamlet	*Pride and Prejudice*
Heart of Darkness	*The Scarlet Letter*
Invisible Man	*The Things They Carried*

CANADA

P. T. BABIE AND CHARLES J. RUSSO

THE
WORLD
TODAY
SERIES®
2023-2024

38TH EDITION

Making its debut as Canada 1985, and annually revised, this book is published by

Rowman & Littlefield
An imprint of The Rowman & Littlefield Publishing Group, Inc.
4501 Forbes Blvd., Suite 200, Lanham, MD 20706
www.rowman.com

Library of Congress Control Number Available

ISBN 978-1-5381-7606-1 (pbk. : alk. paper)
ISBN 978-1-5381-7607-8 (electronic)

Cover design by Sarah Marizan

Cartographer: William L. Nelson

Typography by Barton Matheson Willse & Worthington
Baltimore, MD 21244

The World Today Series has thousands of subscribers across the U.S. and Canada. A sample list of users who annually rely on this most up-to-date material includes:

Public library systems
Universities and colleges
High schools
Federal and state agencies
All branches of the armed forces and war colleges
National Geographic Society
National Democratic Institute
Agricultural Education Foundation
ExxonMobil Corporation
Chevron Corporation
CNN

P. T. Babie

Dr. Babie is Bonython Chair and Professor of Law in The University of Adelaide, Australia. He joined the Adelaide Law School in 1999, was promoted to a personal chair in law in 2015, and was named the holder of the Bonython Chair in Law in 2021. He is currently associate dean of law (International) and director of the research unit for the Study of Society, Ethics, and Law, and has previously been associate dean of law (research) and associate dean of law (learning and teaching). He was elected a fellow of the Australian Academy of Law in 2017 and a fellow of the Royal Society of Arts in 2021. He received the 2021 Australian Legal Education Awards (ALEA) Excellence in Research Supervision Award, a 2011 Executive Dean's Prize for Excellence in Undergraduate Teaching, the 2007 Adelaide Law School Excellence in Teaching Prize, 2015 and 2016 Executive Dean's Awards for Excellence in Research, and 2014 and 2017 Executive Dean's Commendations for Excellence in Research.

He holds a BA in sociology and political science from the University of Calgary, a BThSt from Flinders University, a LLB from the University of Alberta, a LLM from the University of Melbourne, writing a thesis on the transferability of water entitlements, and a DPhil in law from St Catherine's College, the University of Oxford, completing a thesis on the nature of the Crown (state) interest in Australian land. At Oxford, he was a Viscount Bennett, a Canadian Centennial, and a Landau Scholar.

Following law school, he was an associate with Howard, Mackie (now Borden Ladner Gervais (BLG) in Calgary, Canada, specializing in securities and natural resources law. Prior to his appointment to the Adelaide Law School, he was lecturer in Law at St Catherine's and Balliol Colleges, University of Oxford, and the Melbourne Law School, The University of Melbourne. He is a barrister and solicitor (inactive) of the Court of Queen's Bench of Alberta (Canada), and an associate member of the Law Society of South Australia (of which he is a member of the Property Law Committee). He is frequently consulted on issues relating to real property law and law and religion (especially in relation to the Australian Constitution).

His research, throughout his career, has involved asking what property is and how, if at all, it can be justified. He has explored those questions from legal theoretical and from theological perspectives. He is assistant editor of the *Australian Property Law Journal*, was editor in chief and South Australia editor of the *Property Law Review*, and is an editorial board member of the *Journal of Law and Religion*, the Routledge Research Series in Law and Religion, the Springer Research Series in Law and Religion, and of the Forum on Religion & Ecology (FORE) @ Australia (affiliated with FORE, Yale University (USA).

He teaches property law, property theory, law and religion, and Roman law.

Dr. Charles J. Russo

Charles J. Russo, M. Div., J.D., Ed. D., is the Joseph Panzer Chair in Education in the School of Education and Health Sciences, director of its Ph.D. Program, and Research Professor of Law in the School of Law at the University of Dayton. The 1998-99 President of the Education Law Association, 2002 recipient of its McGhehey (Achievement) Award, and 2021 recipient of the Distinguished Scholar Award from the Religion and Education Special Interest Group of the American Educational Research Association, he authored or co-authored almost 350 articles in peer-reviewed journals; authored, co-authored, edited, or co-edited 78 books as of this volume, and has more than 1,200 publications. Dr. Russo also speaks extensively on issues in Education Law in the United States and other nations. In addition, he edits two journals and serves on more than a dozen editorial boards.

Along with having spoken in thirty-four states and thirty nations outside of the United States on all six inhabited continents, Russo taught summer courses in England, Spain, and Thailand. He has served as a visiting professor at Queensland University of Technology in Brisbane, and the University of Newcastle, Australia; the University of Sarajevo, Bosnia and Herzegovina; South East European University, Macedonia; the Potchefstroom and Mafeking Campuses of Northwest University, Potchefstroom, South Africa; the University of Malaya in Kuala Lumpur, Malaysia; the University of Sao Paulo, Brazil; Yeditepe University, Istanbul Turkey; Inner Mongolia University for the Nationalities, Tongliao, Inner Mongolia; and Peking University and Capital Normal University in Beijing. He is presently a visiting professor at the University of Notre Dame of Australia, Faculty of Law, in Sydney, and the College of Education at Capital Normal University in Beijing.

Before joining the faculty at the University of Dayton as professor and chair of the Department of Educational Administration in July 1996, Dr. Russo taught at the University of Kentucky in Lexington, Kentucky, from August 1992 to July 1996 and at Fordham University in his native New York City from September 1989 to July 1992. He taught high school for eight and one half-years, both prior to and after graduation from law school. He received a Bachelor of Arts degree in Classical Civilization (1972), Juris Doctor Degree (1983), and Doctor of Education degrees in Educational Administration and Supervision (1989) from St, John's University in New York City. He received a Master of Divinity degree from the Seminary of the Immaculate Conception in Huntington, New York (1978). He received a Ph.D. Honoris Causa from Potchefstroom University, now the Potchefstroom Campus of Northwest University, in Potchefstroom, South Africa, in May 2004, for his contributions to the field of Education Law.

ACKNOWLEDGMENTS

It is with great gratitude that we thank Dr. Wayne C. Thompson, former editor of this volume for his stellar work in the preparation of the text. We have relied heavily on his good work. We have also depended on the various official federal and provincial websites as well as major Canadian media sources to update this book.

We also thank Ms. Rhiannon Jones at the University of Calgary for her assistance in the preparation of the previous edition of this volume.

Charlie Russo would like to offer his deepest love, now, always, and forever, as well as his thanks, to his wife and best friend, Debbie, for her loving support over the years.

Courtesy of iStock.com/Orchidpoet

CONTENTS

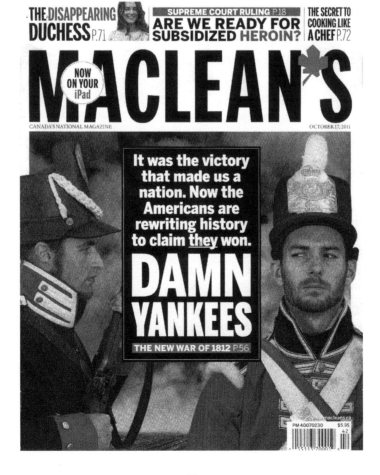

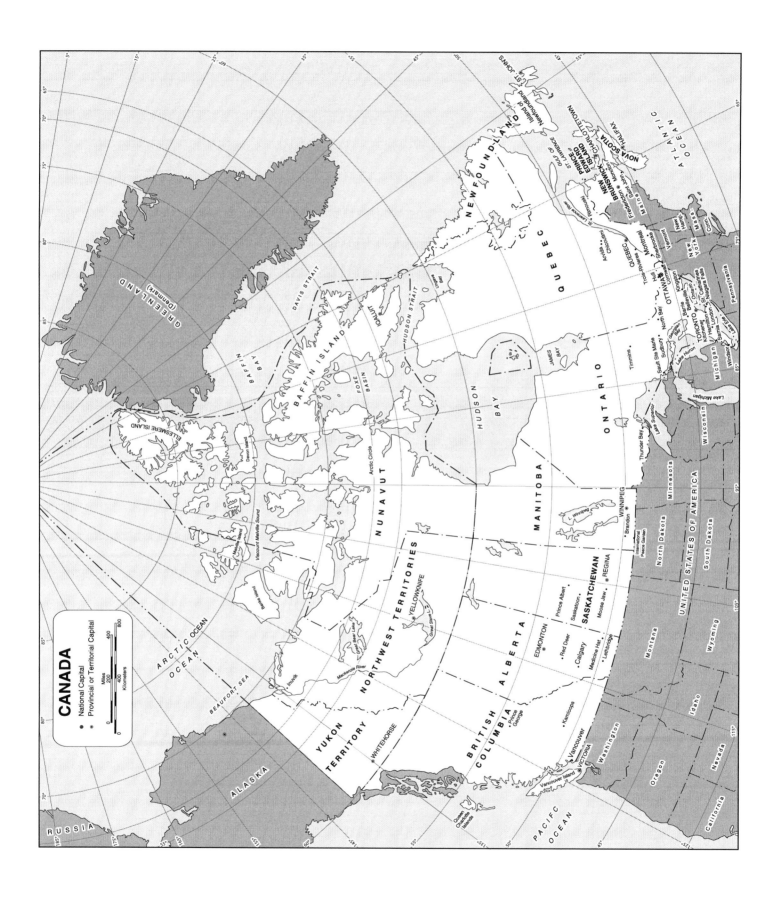

CANADA

King Charles and Queen Camilla

Photo credit: Hugo Burnand/Buckingham Palace

**The Rt. Hon. Justin Trudeau
Prime Minister of Canada**

**Her Excellency the Right Honourable
Mary Simon, C.C., C.M.M., C.O.M., O.Q.,
C.D., Governor General and Commander-in-
Chief of Canada**

Photo credit: Sgt Johanie Maheu, Rideau Hall © OSGG-BSGG, 202

Aerial view of Parliament

Canadian Prime Ministers since Confederation

Rt. Hon. Sir John A. Macdonald	(C)	July 1867–Nov. 1873
Hon. Alexander Mackenzie	(L)	Nov. 1873–Oct. 1878
Rt. Hon. Sir John A. Macdonald	(C)	Oct. 1878–June 1891
Hon. Sir John J. C. Abbott	(C)	June 1891–Nov. 1892
Rt. Hon. Sir John S. D. Thompson	(C)	Dec. 1892–Dec. 1894
Rt. Hon. Sir Mackenzie Bowell	(C)	Dec. 1894–Apr. 1896
Rt. Hon. Sir Charles Tupper	(C)	May 1896–July 1896
Rt. Hon. Sir Wilfrid Laurier	(L)	July 1896–Oct. 1911
Rt. Hon. Sir Robert L. Borden	(C)	Oct. 1911–Oct. 1917
Rt. Hon. Sir Robert L. Borden	(U)	Oct. 1917–July 1920
Rt. Hon. Arthur Meighen	(U–L & C)	July 1920–Dec. 1921
Rt. Hon. Wm. Lyon Mackenzie King	(L)	Dec. 1921–June 1926
Rt. Hon. Arthur Meighen	(C)	June 1926–Sept. 1926
Rt. Hon. Wm. Lyon Mackenzie King	(L)	Sept. 1926–Aug. 1930
Rt. Hon. Robert B. Bennett	(C)	Aug. 1930–Oct. 1935
Rt. Hon. Wm. Lyon Mackenzie King	(L)	Oct. 1935–Nov. 1948
Rt. Hon. Louis Stephen St. Laurent	(L)	Nov. 1948–June 1957
Rt. Hon. John G. Diefenbaker	(C)	June 1957–Apr. 1963
Rt. Hon. Lester B. Pearson	(L)	Apr. 1963–Apr. 1968
Rt. Hon. Pierre Elliott Trudeau	(L)	Apr. 1968–June 1979
Rt. Hon. Charles Joseph Clark	(C)	June 1979–Mar. 1980
Rt. Hon. Pierre Elliott Trudeau	(L)	Mar. 1980–June 1984
Rt. Hon. John Napier Turner	(L)	June 1984–Sept. 1984
Rt. Hon. Martin Brian Mulroney	(PC)	Sept. 1984–June 1993
Rt. Hon. Kim Campbell	(PC)	June 1993–Nov. 1993
Rt. Hon. Jean Chrétien	(L)	Nov. 1993–Dec. 2003
Rt. Hon. Paul Martin	(L)	Dec. 2003–Feb. 2006
Rt. Hon. Stephen Harper	(C)	Feb. 2006–Nov. 2015
Rt. Hon. Justin Trudeau	(L)	Nov. 2015–present

(C) Conservative
(L) Liberal
(U) Unionist
(PC) Progressive Conservative

Note: The number in parentheses immediately following their names reflects the ranking of the prime ministers in 2011 by Canadian experts in history, political science, international relations, economics and other relevant fields. Their criteria were: longevity in office, a broad vision of Canada, ability to shape their age, managing a political party, and impact on Canada's international role, national unity and economy. The survey was conducted and published by *Maclean's*. In its 2016 ranking the top four, in order, were King, Laurier, Macdonald, and Pierre Trudeau. Justin Trudeau ranked above Harper.

Canada Today
Against All Odds

It has often been said that Canada is a "geographic improbability" a huge, sparsely settled country whose diverse people have only two things in common: a map and a preference not to be absorbed by the United States. As poet Al Purdy put it, it is "an opposite nation talked into existence." Because of Canadians' enormous differences in language and cultural heritage, it is difficult to call its people a "nation." Nor is it politically correct, in the opinion of journalist Andrew Coyne: "The very idea that we are a nation . . . has disappeared. The Parliament of Canada may be so bold as to recognize 'the *Québécois*' as a nation, but it would not dare to say the same of Canada. We are a superstructure, a federation, perhaps a country—but never a nation." Indeed, many disagree with what Prime Minister Justin Trudeau said after the 2015 national election: "There is no core identity, no mainstream in Canada,' [but] there are shared values—openness, respect, compassion, willingness to work hard, to be there for each other, to search for equality and justice." He started that Canada was a "post national state."

Whatever the case, Canadians have shaped a democratic, peaceful, and prosperous country seemingly against all odds. Canada was created in the middle of the nineteenth century from the remnants of the British empire in North America which managed to escape the United States' momentous revolution in the 18th century and its exuberant "Manifest Destiny" in the 19th century which harbored dreams of the "Stars and Stripes" flying all over North America. Canada was a country born of patience and compromises, not of violent revolution whose unity has been preserved through the years by forbearance and concessions, not by civil war.

For residents of the United States (U.S.), Canada is no longer a region for expansion or merely for recreation. Rather, they see Canada as a vibrant sovereign, country with a British governmental system and characteristics that should be studied and understood. Canada is a neighbor, a very desirable neighbor at that. Former Prime Minister Brian Mulroney was right when he said not long after his 1984 election victory that "if I were the President of the United States, I'd wake up in the morning and probably look at the events around the world—Americans under attack here, U.S. Embassy attacked there, acts of terrorism and violence—I'd look at all that, and I'd look at Canada and say, 'Thank God I have Canada for a neighbor. Now, what can I do for Canada today?'" Canada and

Population: 36,991,981 in 2021
Capital City: Ottawa (Pop. 1,488,307 in 2021).
Other Principal Cities: Toronto (6,202,225 in 2021), Montreal (4,291,732 in 2021), Vancouver (2,642,825 in 2021), Edmonton (1,418,118 in 2021), Calgary (1,481,806 in 2021), Winnipeg (834,678 in 2021).

Climate: Varying climatic regions from moderate to bitterly cold Arctic, with generally mild summers in the southern areas and long, cold winters.
Neighboring Countries: Canada is bordered by the United States and shares maritime boarders with Russia, Greenland (an autonomous territory of Denmark) and the French Territory of the island St. Pierre and Miquelon. A portion of the United States is also within Canada due to a 1700s error in mapping: the Minnesota Northwest Angle; this land is part of the Northern Lake of the Woods County of Minnesota but is in Canada.
Official Languages: English and French.
Other Tongues: A broad spectrum of languages spoken by immigrants from Europe and Asia with many primary languages and dialects being of First Nations and Inuit Peoples.
Major Religions (2022):

Rank	Percent-Population
1. Roman Catholic	39%
2. Protestant	29%
3. Atheist/Agnostic	24%
4.. Islam	3%
5. Hinduism	2%
6. Sikhism	1%
7. Buddhism	1%
8. Judaism	1%
9. Jndigenous	+/-1%

Note(s): Religion refers to the person's self-identification as having a connection or affiliation with any religious denomination, group, body, sect, cult or other religiously defined community or system of belief. Religion is not limited to formal membership in a religious organization or group. Persons without a religious connection or affiliation can self-identify as atheist, agnostic or humanist, or can provide another applicable response.
Source(s): Statistics Canada, National Household Survey, 2011.

Chief Commercial Products: Canada is a highly industrialized nation producing a wide variety of sophisticated goods; it is also rich in natural resources. Canada's leading exports are natural resources, especially crude petroleum and natural gas, metal ores, diamonds, wheat, lumber, paper and pulp along with automobiles and parts, machinery and equipment, and high technology products.
Major Trading Partners: Below is a list showcasing 15 of Canada's top trading partners, countries that imported the most Canadian shipments by dollar value during 2018. Also

shown is each import country's percentage of total Canadian exports.

United States: US$337.8 billion (75.1% of total Canadian exports)
China: $21.3 billion (4.7%)
United Kingdom: $12.6 billion (2.8%)
Japan: $10 billion (2.2%)
Mexico: $6.3 billion (1.4%)
South Korea: $4.5 billion (1%)
Germany: $3.7 billion (0.8%)
Netherlands: $3.7 billion (0.8%)
India: $3.2 billion (0.7%)
Hong Kong: $3 billion (0.7%)
Belgium: $2.8 billion (0.6%)
France: $2.6 billion (0.6%)
Italy: $2.3 billion (0.5%)
Norway: $1.9 billion (0.4%)
Brazil: $1.7 billion (0.4%)
Over nine-tenths (92.8%) of Canadian exports in 2018 were delivered to the above 15 trade partners.

Currency: Canadian Dollar. Its nickname is the "loonie" or "loon" ("toonie" or "toon" for the two-dollar coin) because of the aquatic bird depicted on it. Notably, in 2019 the Canadian Mint issued a one-dollar Gay coin to celebrate the 50th anniversary of the changes

Retrieved from: https://www.pinknews.co.uk/2019/04/23/canada-equality-coin-decriminalisation/

to the national Criminal Code decriminalizing homosexual acts between consenting adults.
National Holiday: Canada Day (July 1). In Quebec, the main holiday is June 24, the Fête Nationale, formerly called St-Jean Baptiste Day.
Head of State: Her Majesty Queen Elizabeth II of Great Britain (since February 6, 1952).
The Queen's Representative: Her Excellency the Right Honourable Mary May Simon (from July 26, 2021).
Head of Government: The Rt. Hon. Justin Trudeau, Prime Minister (Leader of the Liberal Party), since November 4, 2015.
National Flag: A stylized red maple leaf on a white square flanked by red bars one half the width of the square.

the U.S. conduct the world's largest bilateral trade agreement, are each other's best trading partners and are each other's most preferred country for foreign investments.

Moreover, the two Nations are close allies in the North Atlantic Treaty Organization (NATO) and the North American Aerospace Defense Command (NORAD).

Canada

What other country but Canada would have harbored the six American diplomats for three months after the escaped from their Embassy in Teheran, Iran, on the fateful day in 1979 when scores of their colleagues were taken hostage and held captive for more than a year? At great risk to their own diplomatic personnel, the Canadians and their ambassador, Ken Taylor, worked with the Central Intelligence Agency to devise an escape plan, issued diplomatic passports to the Americans, closed their embassy in the Iranian capital, and escorted the nervous Americans through the checkpoints and controls onto an airplane bound for home.

The United States accurately conveyed the Nation's gratitude for protecting its diplomats when its government ordered that a sign be posted on a giant billboard overlooking the border into Canada reading, "Thank you, Canada!" This daring rescue was partly fictionalized in the Ben Affleck film, *Argo*, which won the Oscar for best movie in 2012. Responding to charges that the film gave Canada and its ambassador too little credit for the escape, actor/director Affleck publicly stated that the "Canadians did absorb the risk."

After the terrorist attacks of September 11, 2001, that claimed the lives of 24 Canadians as well as over 3,000 Americans and persons from other nations, hundreds of flights were diverted to Canada, including 224 over the Atlantic and 90 over the Pacific; 250 more flights had enough fuel to return to Europe). Communities housed and fed the stranded passengers, mostly Americans. Transport Minister David Collenette remembered: "I felt an immense pride in what Canada was doing to help our American friends. . . . No one complained or argued about financial compensation. Canadians were pulling together in a remarkable way. . . . No one held back. . . . Thank God we got it right." The residents of Gander, Newfoundland, who extended their generosity to 6,700 travelers are commemorated in a successful Broadway musical, "Come from Away."

More than 100,000 Canadians gathered on Parliament Hill in Ottawa to raise American and Canadian flags to honor the victims of 9/11, the largest gathering there ever known. The American embassy was deluged with flowers, and charter buses carried thousands to New York for a grand "Canada Loves New York" weekend in December 2001. Vancouver firefighters raised $535,000 for their fallen comrades and a fourth of them traveled to New York at their own expense to pay their respects at funerals.

Only two weeks after the tragedy, more than 60 skilled tradesmen from Ontario and Alberta went to help rebuild the

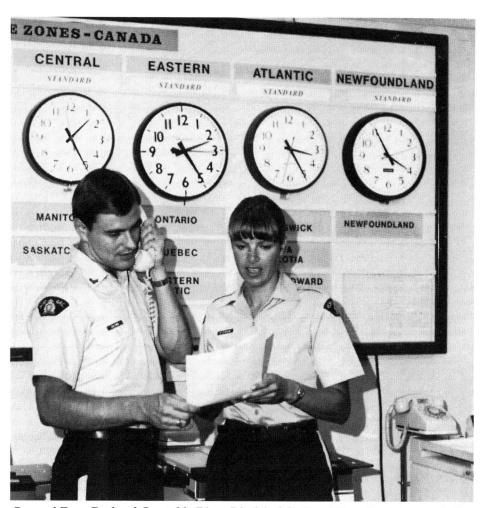

Corporal Doug Ford and Constable Diane Bérubé of the Royal Canadian Mounted Police

stricken city. New Yorkers on the sidewalks stopped to shake their hands with one businessman speaking for an entire nation when he told them: "This has been so hard for us all, but because of people like you, we'll all get through it. You have no idea what this means to us. As your neighbor, I thank you." Then Prime Minister Jean Chrétien received the "Statesman of the Year Award" in New York the following year. In 2013, the US gave to Appleton Peace Park in Newfoundland a piece of steel wreckage from the World Trade Center to recall Canadians' help to stranded Americans on 9/11.

John F. Kennedy said about Canada: "Geography made us neighbors. History made us friends. And economics made us partners." A quarter century later, President Ronald Reagan made no secret about his reasons for meeting with the Canadian prime minister in March 1985, a practice usually repeated twice a year: "No other country in the world is more important to the United States than Canada, and we are blessed to have such a nation on our northern border." In both of his terms in office, Reagan's first foreign trips were to

Canada, as was President Barack Obama's first foreign outing in February 2009.

The first non-citizen of the United States to fly into space with American astronauts was a Canadian, Marc Garneau, later the Liberal party spokesman in the House of Commons. Garneau worked at NASA the rest of the century, flying his third shuttle mission in 1999. Two other Canadians served in the space station: Julie Payette, who made a return visit in May 2009, and Chris Hadfield, who walked in space and commanded the International Space Station.

Canada is the only foreign country that is permitted to locate its embassy on Pennsylvania Avenue. Former Canadian Ambassador Derek Burney had this to say about the modern building, opened in 1989 and situated halfway between the White House and the Capitol: "It conveys the message that I want to convey: Canada counts." Ottawa extended the same privilege to the United States by allowing it to open its new embassy in 1999 on the last vacant lot on Parliament Hill. The site is prominent on Sussex Drive, the ceremonial parade route between Parliament and

the Prime Minister's residence. When the U.S. embassy was opened in Ottawa, it was the first time a sitting president, Bill Clinton, left the U.S. to do so. Alas, the architecture of the bomb-resistant, four-story steel and concrete structure with 3-inch glass, situated near the National Gallery and Chateau Laurier Hotel, was not universally praised by aesthetically minded Canadians.

The United States and Canada are different countries, but perhaps no two other nations in the world need to remind themselves so often of this fact. As of 2021, Canada had a population of more than 38 million as compared to that of the U.S. with a population (332 million) and an economy ten times larger. However, the land mass of the US is 10% smaller than Canada's. The relationship between the two countries is therefore lopsided and sometimes difficult for the smaller of the two. Former Prime Minister Pierre Elliott Trudeau once remarked that sharing a border with the US is like "sleeping with an elephant. No matter how friendly or even-tempered is the beast, if I may call it that, one is affected by every twitch and grunt!"

Nevertheless, Canada is that country with which the U.S. is most successful at settling differences; the frictions existing between the countries are always manageable. The most important reason for these good relations is the common-sense and good will they are inclined to show toward

the other. In fact, Americans and Canadians have been well practiced at "splitting the difference" yet with the end of the North American Free Trade Agreement (NAFTA) and of the U.S.-Mexico-Canada Agreement (USMCA), some discord has occurred. Enacting only minor changes, however, the USMCA took effect and replaced the NAFTA on July 1, 2020.

CULTURE

Canadians tend to focus on the differences between them and persons from the US even though, as Pierre Berton admitted, they are often "tongue-tied" when asked to define these distinctions. "We know we're not the same but we can't express it succinctly." Americans are inclined to emphasize the similarities. Canadians do not appreciate it when their neighbors to the south view them as "just like us," not considering Canada a foreign country. Still, there is, to be sure, an extraordinary degree of military and economic interdependence between the two countries.

According to a 2005 SES Research poll, Canadians and Americans still find their countries to be defined more by their similarities than by their differences. Asked which country in the world is most like Canada in terms of human rights, Canadians chose the U.S. more than any (43%), while 51% of Americans chose Canada. Two thirds of Canadians (67%) had a generally positive attitude toward the U.S. The sincere and constant references to Canada as the U.S.' "partner" and "good neighbor" help erase in Americans' minds the sharp line that usually appears between "us and them." In fact, U.S. residents traveling in Canada see people who dress almost exactly as they do. Canadians wear baseball caps, jeans, jogging shoes, sweatshirts, and T-shirts with writing on them—basically the same things that are in style in the United States.

People from the U.S. also meets people who, by and large, speak English as they do except those 22% who speak French as a mother tongue and who therefore might speak English with a French accent. The English that Canadians speak much more closely resembles that spoken in the United States than in the United Kingdom. This is understandable in an age of radio and television, quick travel and strong trade ties. A few British usages do linger on in Canada, though. Most say "aluminium," with the accent on the third syllable, "controversy" with the accent on the second syllable, and "schedule," as if there were no "c" in the word. "Been" is pronounced like "bean," and "again" like "a-gane." A "lieutenant" is addressed as "leftenant." Also, the "i" in the last

syllable of words ending in "-ile" is likely to be pronounced distinctly, rather than to be swallowed, as most Americans do. "Out" and "house" are spoken more like "ute" or "whuse."

Perhaps the most distinctive sign that a Canadian is speaking is the "eh?," pronounced as a long "a," which is frequently tacked onto the end of sentences. There is a rough French equivalent in Quebec: *hein*. In addition, writing in Canada is slightly different: not all Canadians have dropped the "u" when writing such words as "labour" or "colour." "Centre," "cheque," "theatre" and "connexion" are not American spellings, and "defense" is still spelled with a "c," as is the custom in Britain.

French-speakers, called "francophones" in Canada, in contrast to "Anglophones," English-speakers, have opened the gates to let in hundreds of English words, such as le *fun, dialer* ("to dial"), la *potate* ("potato"), le *smoked beef, le hamburger, les king pins, le brake drum, un party,* or *une shop*. An example of this usage can be seen in an advertisement for an *Atelier Mecanique-Machine Shop Crankshaft* which once appeared in the yellow pages of the Montreal telephone book: *Moteur nettoyé et testé. Moteur grindé all surfaces. Crankshaft nettoyé et testé with sonoflux process. Crankshaft grindé with micro finish.*

The mixture of the two languages to form what is often derisively referred to as "Franglais" or "Frenglish" has perhaps reached its height among Acadians in New Brunswick. One francophone from Moncton provided *Maclean's* with an example of the "chiac" dialect: *J'ai drivé mon friend à l'airport, but la plane a také off à dix minutes de quatre. Too bad que j'avais pas findé ça out avant.* The French spoken elsewhere in New Brunswick sounds little different from that in Poitou and Brittany, France, from whence their ancestors hailed. Yet, the pronunciation and slang of the French spoken on the streets of Quebec and Acadia are intriguingly different from Parisian French.

In recent years, there has been a tremendous improvement in the quality of French spoken in Quebec due to the

Totem poles at Museum of Anthropology, University of British Columbia
Credit: Province of British Columbia

Canada

provincial legislation on the use of French on Radio Canada; TV is also a good example of international French. Nevertheless, Candice Bergen's French-language Sprint ads were taken off the air in 1995 because her French was "too Parisian."

Americans also find that most Canadians know far more about the United States than Americans know about Canada. For instance, a 1995 Louis Harris poll revealed that a mere 1% of residents of the U.S. knew that Jean Chrétien was prime minister. Conversely, only 11% of American university students surveyed in 1989 knew which city Canada's capital is; only 1% knew the name of the premier of Quebec, a province much larger than Texas, bordering three New England states, and the United States' sixth-largest trading partner in the world.

Further the results of a 2011 survey published in Canada's *National Post* revealed "that fewer than half of all Americans can name Canada's capital and that close to two-thirds of our neighbours to the south admit they learned nothing about this country's history in school."

In another example of how little residents of the U.S. knew about their neighbor to the north, almost twenty years ago, entertainer Rick Mercer became famous by producing TV specials such as *Talking to Americans* that brought howls of laughter to Canadians. He asked people on the streets of America, including Congressmen and Harvard professors, ludicrous questions highlighting just how little they knew about their northern neighbor.

Canadians watch more American television than Canadian, and what Canadian news programs they watch bring incomparably more news about the United States than American newscasts bring about Canada, despite the penetration into the American broadcasting elite of such Canadians as ABC's former anchorman Peter Jennings, Kevin Newman (formerly of ABC's Nightline), and CBS's Morley Safer. Controversial talk-show hostess Jenny Jones hails from Canada, as does Robert (AKA Robin) MacNeil of the earlier MacNeil-Lehrer Report. McNeil, who has had a summer home in his native Halifax, the setting of the first of his novels, *Burden of Desire*, confesses to "a sense of sentimental curiosity" about Canada, but admits: "The Canada I grew up in was white bread, dominated by Anglo-Scots and Quebec. Now Canada is a wondrously multi-coloured, multilingual country. It's fascinating, but it's not the Canada I grew up in." This is why he became an American, as he described in *Looking for my Country. Finding Myself in America.*

Canadians often read such newsmagazines from the U.S. as *Time*, while few Americans have ever even held a Canadian magazine, such as *Maclean's*, in their hands, let alone read one. Insofar as 88% of all residents in the U.S. live farther than 100 miles from the Canadian border and cannot see or hear Canadian programs by simply switching on their dial, Americans must make a more concerted effort to become informed about Canada, and few do.

The imbalance as to what U.S. residents know about Canada is slowly changing. Major American newsmagazines and newspapers carry much more news about Canada. In the past, few American institutions offered Canadian studies courses; now, this is a popular field of study for undergraduates, especially those attending colleges and universities in proximity of the Canadian-U.S. border. Moreover, as of 2022, the Association for Canadian Studies in the United States (ACSUS) has more than 500 individual and institutional members from the United States, Canada, and other countries. The *Toronto Star* even complained: "Curse those Americans. They are taking away one of our great Canadian preoccupations. They are not ignoring us anymore." In any case, visitors from the U.S. can still chat with Canadians about a wide variety of subjects ranging from the president's difficulties with Congress and midwestern farmers' financial problems to the World Series, Super Bowl, and Academy or Grammy Award nominations, forgetting in the process that he is talking to a foreigner.

The popular culture on both sides of the border is strikingly similar. One hears rock, country-western and gospel music, in rock or traditional form. either blaring out from car radios or softly channeled into homes by radio. Hank Snow, Gordon Lightfoot, Neil Young, Anne Murray,

Bryan Adams, Michelle Wright, Buffy Sainte-Marie, a native North American who wrote the Oscar-winning theme song for the film, "An Officer and a Gentleman," Sarah McLachlan (who has starred both as rock singer and women's rights advocate), rhythm and blues diva Deborah Cox, jazz pianist and singer Diana Krall from Nanaimo, British Columbia (BC), the rock groups Crash Test Dummies, Barenaked Ladies (a fun-loving male quintet), Drake, Bublé and Nickelback are all Canadians who have been popular on both sides of the border.

In 1997 Ottawa rocker, Alanis Morissette, who won the favorite album and female artist awards at the American Music Awards along with Justin Bieber are Canadian artists who have done well in the U.S. Ontario native, Shania Twain,

Nia Vardalos in *My Big Fat Greek Wedding*

4

was named best female country artist. Her "The Woman in Me" surpassed "Patsy Cline's Greatest Hits" as the best-selling female country album ever. By 1999, she had become history's top-selling country singer and was named the entertainer of the year at the 2000 Academy of Country Music Awards. Quebec superstar, Céline Dion, who is the top-selling singer of all time in France, won top album and best pop album at the Grammys in 1997. By 2007, she had sold 200 million records, and her Las Vegas show, "A New Day," had grossed more than US$400 million during its four-year run. Because Morissette, Dion, and Twain each won two Grammy awards in 1999 and Joni Mitchell of Saskatchewan received the U.S. National Academy of Recording Arts and Sciences lifetime achievement award in 2001, few persons disputed *Maclean's* claim that "Canadian divas virtually rule the world of female pop."

Canadians laugh at the same comedians, such as Dan Aykroyd, Bob and Doug McKenzie, Jim Carrey, and "Wayne's World" star Mike Myers, all Canadians. One of the biggest box office hit in the history of screen comedy, *Ghostbusters*, was a product of Canadian filmmaker Ivan Reitman. His Montreal-born son, Jason Reitman, directed one of 2008's hottest movies, *Juno*, which was filmed in Vancouver and starred two Canadians—Ellen Page and Michael Cera. Two years later, his football film, *The Blind Side*, was a blockbuster; its female lead, Sandra Bullock, won the best actress Oscar. Even Warner Brothers was founded by Canadians.

Quebec's cinema is thriving, and Quebecers produce excellent French-language films which are of a different style than those viewed by Americans. An example is *Maria Chapdelaine*, based on Louis Hemon's classic 1914 novel, a moving portrait of the restricted life led by Quebec women in the frontier.

While residents of the U.S. anglophone Canadians usually go to the same movies, Canadians watch more Hollywood films than films produced in Canada, and English Canadian filmmakers must search hard for audiences. In fact, only 2% of box office revenues are derived from Canadian films. Canadians have far less money to spend. Additionally, Canadian producers have trouble getting some of their films shown on Canadian screens because U.S. companies largely control distribution of movies in Canada. In order to stimulate the industry, an annual Whistler Film Festival awards prizes for promising Canadian feature films.

Some films to which Americans flock are Canadian, often unbeknownst to Americans. Winnipeg's Nia Vardalos took the cinema world by storm in 2002 with

her award-winning film, *My Big Fat Greek Wedding*, which was filmed in Toronto and was the year's fifth-highest grossing movie. Norman Jewison, one of the world's most successful directors as a result of such blockbusters as *Fiddler on the Roof* and *Moonstruck*, much of which was filmed in Toronto, is Canadian. In 1999, Jewison, who received a special Academy Award for lifetime achievement, founded the Canadian Film Centre in north Toronto, an elite institution for ten highly selected filmmakers annually and the only film school in the world that produces its own features.

James Cameron, born in Kapuskasing, Ontario, and raised near Niagara Falls, studied physics at Fullerton College, specializes in gargantuan high-tech films of mass destruction, such as *The Terminator*, *Judgment Day*, *Aliens*, *The Abyss*, *True Lies*, and *Titanic*. In 2010, his three-dimensional *Avatar* broke all records for box office receipts to date. In the words of Fox's president, Cameron "has taken Hollywood by the throat and they do what he says."

The 1997 Academy Award for best film was given to *The English Patient*, based on the best-selling novel by Canadian author Michael Ondaatje. Assisted in his research by a grant from the Canada Council, in 1992 Ondaatje shared the Booker Prize, the world's most prominent English-language literary award. His *Anil's Ghost* won him both the Governor-General's Award and the Prix Médicis, France's highest prize for a foreign novel, in 2000. Later, in 2007 Ondaatje's *Divisadero* won him his fifth Governor General's Literary Award for English-language fiction, tying the record of the late Hugh MacLennan.

In 2004, Canadian director Denys Arcand made history when his film, *The Barbarian Invasions*, became the first Canadian movie to win an Oscar for best foreign-language film. In 2007, Indian-born Canadian director, Deepa Mahta, won a best foreign-language Oscar nomination for her extraordinarily successful Hindi-language film, *Water*. This was the first non-French-Canadian film to receive such an honor. In the same year, Mahta's *Partition* opened, depicting the tragic carnage following the division of India in 1947.

Many American films and TV shows are filmed in Canada. With the average cost of film-making in the U.S. having soared to $76.9 million by 2000, and close to double that today, it is small wonder that producers are attracted to Canada with its generous provincial and federal tax breaks to foreign and domestic film companies and its film crews. To lure more American filmmakers back to Ontario in the wake of a rising value of the Canadian dollar, which has scared off some Hollywood

productions, the province offered even greater tax inducements.

Toronto has become the third-largest film-producing center in North America after Los Angeles and New York City. Two of the 2006 Oscar nominations were filmed in the Canadian West: *Brokeback Mountain* near Calgary and *Capote* in Winnipeg, Manitoba. U.S. TV networks, including ABC and CBS, buy Canadian police serials like "Rookie Blue" and "Flashpoint" at the discount rate of $350,000 per episode, far cheaper than the typical license fee of well above $1 million an episode.

Vancouver and Montreal also attract more and more American moviemakers. British Columbia boasts of $1 billion annual revenues from film production, two-thirds of which comes from the U.S. This can also cause problems for Canadian filmmakers because high-cost American productions inflate the prices that Canadian film crews charge. However, the "runaway productions" are an unmistakable boon for Canadian film people. Yet, some union actors in the U.S. call Canada a scab country for aggressively courting American film, television and advertisement production with tax rebates and other incentives. Films of the past have featured Canadians such as Genevieve Bujold, Margot Kidder, Christopher Plummer, William Shatner, Raymond Massey, Michael J. Fox (the "all-American boy"), Keanu Reeves, and Donald Southerland.

Canadians and U.S. residents read much of the same literature, by such authors as Jack Kerouac, Will Durant, Saul Bellow, Arthur Hailey, Robertson Davies, Mordecai Richler, Brian Moore, Morley Callaghan and Alice Munro. All are Canadians. Both countries also sometimes forbid the same books. In 2005, Nova Scotia's

Canada

education department banned Harper Lee's *To Kill a Mockingbird*.

Alice Munro, who hails from southern Ontario, is one of the greatest short-story writers of all time. With her stories focusing on Canadians and their peculiarities, Munro is praised for her exploration of large themes in small-town settings of Ontario. Having won her second Giller Prize for her collection of eight stories entitled *Runaway*, which appeared on the *New York Times'* bestseller list as well as on Canada's, in 2009 she became the first short-story writer to win the Man Booker international prize. The judges called Munro's body of work "practically perfect." In 2012, at age 81, Munro published her fourteenth volume, *Dear Life* and a year later she became the first Canada-based author to win the Nobel Prize in Literature, being cited as the "master of the contemporary short story."

Other authors focus on their native Canada and are read and admired in both countries. Perhaps the best-known Canadian author is Lucy Maud Montgomery, whose precocious, pert, and lovable book about *Anne of Green Gables* has delighted children and adults from scores of nations since its publication in 2008.

Hugh MacLennan's *Two Solitudes* is the classic study of the separate worlds in which the *Québécois* and anglophone Canadians live. In 2001, Alistair MacLeod became the first Canadian to win the world's richest literary prize, the International IMPAC Dublin Literary Award, for his debut novel, *No Great Mischief*, a work later translated into 14 languages. Pierre Berton was perhaps Canada's most prolific writer, producing best-selling books on the country's history and people almost on an annual basis. When he died in 2004, writer June Callwood said of him: "It's as if the biggest tree has fallen down."

Margaret Atwood writes about the lives and challenges of modern women. In her view, "survival" is the "single unifying and informing symbol . . . which holds the country [Canada] together and helps the people in it for common ends." Atwood also points to the search for identity: "Canadians are forever taking the national pulse like doctors at a sickbed; the aim is not to see whether the patient will live well but simply whether he will live at all. . ." Atwood's ninth novel, *Alias Grace*, a murder mystery, was a global sensation in 1996, winner of the Giller Prize that was made into a TV miniseries. A televised adaptation of her novel, *The Handmaid's Tale*, won the 2018 Golden Globe for best TV drama.

Many of Attwood's books had been translated into other languages and in 2000 she became only the second Canadian to win Britain's highly competitive Booker Prize for *The Blind Assassin*, an epic tale about a once-wealthy family in Ontario. Attwood's sly, operatic and feminist retelling of *The Odyssey* from the perspective of the dutiful wife of Homer's hero in her 2005 *The Penelopiad: The Myth of Penelope and Odysseus*, was an instant success. Attwood's 2003 novel, *Oryx and Crake*, followed in 2009 by *Year of the Flood*, a story of a totalitarian dystopia, led in 2013 to the last book in a trilogy, MaddAddam.

By 2006, Attwood's popularity was such that that she began using an electronic pen to activate a remote robotic arm that replicated her autograph for fans thousands of miles away. In 2016, Atwood moved to a different genre, co-authoring a superhero comic book series Angel Catbird, with illustrator Johnnie Christmas. The central character in these graphic novels, scientist Strig Feleedus, is victim of an accidental mutation that left him with the body parts and powers of both a cat and a bird.

In 2002, Saskatoon novelist Yann Martel beat out two other Canadians on the short list, Rohinton Mistry and the late Carol Shields, to win the Booker Prize with his novel, *Life of Pi*, a magical fable of a young man ship-wrecked with a Bengal tiger. In 2012, it was made into a movie and captured multiple Oscars, including best director. Clearly Canada's book business is thriving.

Stephen Leacock was one of the most famous Canadians of his time and in his heyday from 1910 to 1925 was the world's best-selling English-language humorist. His stories bring alive the early Ontario of his childhood. Rudy Wiebe's writings, including The Temptations of Big Bear and *The Scorched-Wood People*, describe with great vision and understanding the lives of Indians, Métis and white settlers in the Canadian West. Northrop Frye, who hailed from Ontario and taught his entire career at the University of Toronto, is widely acclaimed as perhaps the greatest literary critic of our time. American-born Carol Shields, who moved to Canada in 1957 and died in 2003, won the 1995 Pulitzer Prize for her novel about sexual and family values, *The Stone Diaries*. In 2013, the Ontario-born and New Zealand-based Eleanor Catton was presented the ManBooker Prize for The Luminaries; at 28 she was the youngest writer ever to win this award.

Quebec also boasts authors of international renown. Anne Hebert, who died in 2000, became famous in 1970 through her great novel, *Kamouraska*, which was later made into a film in Quebec. Gabriele Roy wrote Quebec's first urban, socially aware novel, *Bonheur d'Occasion*, known to anglophones as *The Tin Flute*, just after the Second World War. This novel, like *Maria Chapdelaine*, deals with survival and a young girl's rejection of a glamorous lover who could have taken her out of the narrow French Canadian world in which she lived. Also, like *Maria Chapdelaine, The Tin Flute* was made into a movie in Quebec in 1983.

Roch Carrier has written perceptively and humorously about the gulf between the *Québécois* and anglophone Canadians. In *La Guerre, Yes Sir* he describes Quebecers' negative attitudes about fighting in the two world wars. In a short story, "The Hockey Sweater," the mother of a young boy in rural Quebec orders a Montreal Canadiens hockey shirt from a Montreal department store, which in error sends a Toronto Maple Leafs jersey instead. The boy is panic-stricken. But with no other hockey shirt to wear, he goes out to play with his friends, only to be shunned with the parish priest ordering him from the ice. The boy is devastated and goes to the parish church and prays that moths will descend from heaven and consume the shirt so that his mother will buy him another. In an interview with *Maclean's*, Carrier implied that the wall which once separated Quebec from anglophone Canada has become much more porous: "When my books were first translated, everybody felt it was a kind of treason, giving my books to the rest of the country. But today everybody wants to be on the other side of the frontier."

Translation into English can today be indispensable for a French-language novel, as Gil Courtemanche discovered. His first novel, *A Sunday at the Pool in Kigali*, was a modest success in Quebec when it was published in French in 2000. But after Knopf Publishers had it translated into English in 2003, it quickly won him international fame and was translated into 13 more languages. How many more nuggets might there be in the Quebec literary scene?

If residents of the United States do not want to go to films, read books or listen to music, they can simply sit at home and immerse themselves in Americana by playing "Trivial Pursuit," a game invented by two Canadians, Chris Haney and Scott Abbott. Or they can pick up a telephone, invented by Canadian Alexander Graham Bell in Canada before moving to the U.S. If they are hungry, they can go to McDonalds, founded by Canadians. One gradually begins to wonder whether what is sometimes called the "Americanization" of Canadian culture might, in some cases, be better called the "Canadianization" of American culture.

American films, television and radio broadcasting, reading material, music, slang and styles do continue to pour northward across the border because these are attractive to most Canadians.

Canadians are usually the first to admit that American culture is produced primarily for domestic consumption and that no American can ever force it on Canadians. Nevertheless, Canadians worry about the massive influx of American customs and usages. It is therefore Canadian policy to encourage and to subsidize Canadian cultural products in order to avoid being engulfed by American culture and to make it possible for talented Canadians to work in Canada rather than seeking their fame and fortune in the United States. The government wishes to help offer the population an alternative.

As of 2022, the federal budget devotes $500 million for the recovery of the arts, culture, heritage, and sports sectors as well as to support community-level festivals and other in-person cultural events, a, sums lower than in most western European countries. These cuts come at a time of intense upheaval in many spheres of the arts. A communications minister in the federal cabinet disperses money through a variety of institutions which enjoy a high degree of autonomy from the federal government and which have become powerful lobbying groups when their freedom or budgets are trampled on as the National Film Board and Telefilm financially support Canadian cinema. Provincial governments also help finance the production of films, and their censorship can prevent "X-rated" movies from being shown in Canadian theaters.

The Canadian film industry had created an Academy Awards ceremony of its own called the "Genie Awards" that were given out between 1980 and 2012. In 2012, the Genie Awards combined with the Gemini Awards, the equivalent of the Emmy Award in the U.S., creating the Canadian Screen Awards. These new awards are conferred annually by the Academy of Canadian Cinema & Television to recognize excellence in Canadian film, English-language television, and digital media productions.

The National Arts Centre in Ottawa, which began operating in 1969, contains stages of various sizes entertaining audiences of all ages. The semi-independent Canada Council dispenses grants to a wide array of professional artists and organizations including writers, publishers, translators, musicians and composers, dancers, painters, sculptors, photographers and film makers. Government money was instrumental in building and maintaining the National Ballet Company in Toronto, le Theatre du Nouveau Monde and les Grands Ballets Canadiens in Montreal, the Canadian Opera Company, the Stratford Shakespearean Festival in Ontario, and more than 160 theater groups across the country. Cirque du Soleil, founded in 1984,

Typical road sign in English and French

and based in Montreal received initial funding from the government; the largest theatrical producer in the world, it offers shows on all six inhabited continents.

Canadians, most of whom live along the U.S. border, listen freely to American radio and watch much American television. The most heavily cabled country in the world, Canadians are among the most generous donors to American public television stations along the U.S. border. The Canadian federal and provincial governments do nothing to prevent their citizens from tuning in to U.S. stations, but do go to great expense and effort to provide Canadian alternatives and to reinforce a sense of Canadian community by making it possible for Canadians everywhere in the country to learn about each other.

Canada's first television stations, CBLT in Toronto and CBFT in Montreal, began operations in 1952, under the banner of the leadership of the government-created Canadian Broadcasting Corporation or CBC, called *Radio Canada* in Quebec. The CBC operates radio and television networks in French and English, as well as in many native languages, throughout the country. CBC sponsors a 24-hour all-news channel in English—*Newsworld*—while *Radio Canada* does the same in French through RDI. To strengthen its bottom line, CBC carries advertising on its TV networks and two it its four radio networks.

There are two rapidly proliferating, privately-operated networks: Canadian Television (CTV) in anglophone Canada and *Reseau de Television* (*TVA*) in francophone Canada. Since 1998, TVA, Quebec's most popular French-language TV network must be included in the mandatory cable-TV selection across Canada. In 1997, CTV launched Canada's first round-the-clock headline news service—CTV News 1. Demonstrating its reach, CTV outbid CBC for the 2010 and 2012 Olympic Games. There are many private radio stations and a proliferation of specialty channels on cable. A variety of Canadian channels beam into American homes through DirecTV, setting a trend to bring more Canadian programming to viewers in the U.S.

Public money enables the CBC to offer more elevated and experimental programming. However, the CBC is not freed from the constant battle over ratings as the country entered a 500-channel universe. The beleaguered service has tried to compete with private broadcasters by imitating their programming in some ways, but this has weakened the public's willingness to continue to support it. It seems that only the lucrative *Hockey Night in Canada* keeps them alive; CBC and Radio-Canada face a continual identity crisis: do they offer a service or a product?

In order to ensure that Canadian networks, private or public, do not simply buy cheaper American programs, the Canadian Radio-Television and Telecommunications Commission establishes "Canadian Content" guidelines. "Canadian Content" is defined by means of a complicated formula involving whether the cast, singers, songwriters or production team are Canadian citizens. This applies even to pornography films. The exact quotas change according to the political winds. Radio stations must devote 30% of their airtime to Canadian music, even though only 13% of music purchased in record stores is Canadian. Further ownership of TV and radio stations, newspapers and magazines is restricted to Canadians or Canadian companies.

The government's efforts notwithstanding, Canadian television programs claimed only a fraction of the audience share when compared with programming from the U.S. This has led many Canadians to wonder whether the nation has a national culture distinct from the culture of the U.S. While Canada does have a culture of its own, many find it difficult to preserve insofar as such a culturally magnetic country as the U.S. is so close. Of course, it is difficult for Canadian culture to remain distinct in light of the facts that about 80% of magazines on newsstands, more than 60% of books, 90% of recordings, 64% of TV programs, and 94% of films are foreign, overwhelmingly from the U.S.

In order to "have the means to communicate with our own people," in the words of ex-Prime Minister Chrétien, Canada insists on exempting cultural industries from its two free-trade agreements with the U.S. Such Canadian governmental decisions as slapping an 80% excise tax on *Sports Illustrated Canada* and other "split-run" magazines (which have Canadian editions and advertising, but mostly American editorial content) and withdrawing Country Music Television's broadcasting license and awarding it to a Canadian-owned country channel, are bound to antagonize Americans. In 1997, the U.S. sought and won a ruling from

Canada

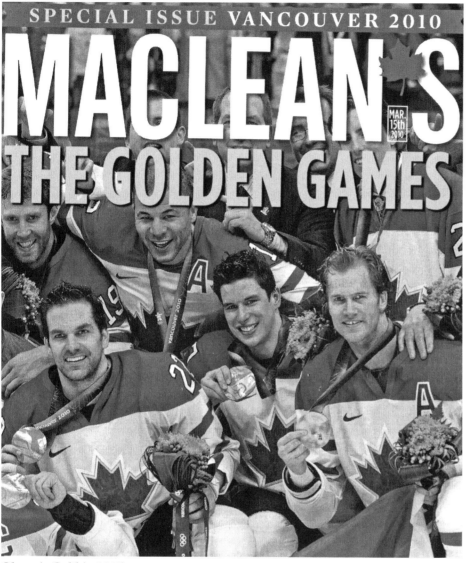
SPECIAL ISSUE VANCOUVER 2010
MACLEAN'S MAR. 15th 2010
THE GOLDEN GAMES

Olympic Gold in 2010!

the World Trade Organization: Canadian punitive taxes on split-run magazines, as well as postal subsidies to Canadian magazines, violate international trade rules. The dispute was resolved in 1999.

Canada's next moves were to convene a summit meeting of 20 culture ministers (excluding Americans) to discuss international misgivings about the "onslaught" of U.S. films, TV and music. Then, in 1999. Parliament passed legislation prohibiting Canadians from advertising in split-run magazines; negotiations between Ottawa and Washington were commenced to head off a conflict, and the dispute was resolved. For the first time, the U.S. accepted the principle that countries can take steps to limit imports in order to protect the viability of local culture. The Canadians agreed to allow American publishers to produce special Canadian editions as long as less than 18% of its advertising pages are from

Canadian advertisers aimed at Canadian readers. The Canadian government would provide annual operating subsidies to the Canadian magazine industry. In cultural terms, the border is not undefended. In 2005, Canada approved in UNESCO the first international treaty designed to protect music, movies and other cultural treasures from foreign competition; the U.S. found itself in a minority of two.

The American sports fan notices a few unfamiliar sports in Canada, such as curling, but most are strikingly similar. Ice hockey, reportedly invented at Kingston's Tete du Pont Barracks on a Christmas day in 1855 by a group of bored soldiers, who tied blades to their boots and used field hockey sticks and an old lacrosse ball, is a Canadian export to the world. As of 2018, Canada leads the world with 3,000 indoor and 5,000 outdoor rinks, compared with 584 and 2665

in Russia, respectively, and 1,535 and 500 respectively in the United States.

The National Hockey League (NHL) is, in fact, *international*, with more professional teams in the U.S. than in Canada. Six Canadian teams faced serious financial difficulties and threatened to relocate in the U.S. The Winnipeg Jets left in 1995, and the Quebec Nordiques went to Denver a year later. In 2001, 80% of the fabled Montreal Canadiens, once known as *Les Glorieux*, and all of the Molson Centre where they play were bought by a Colorado businessman, George Gillett. The Canadiens remain in Montreal, and Gillett respects the Canadiens' spirit, which he calls "truly a religion and a passion." In 2003 the Ottawa Senators filed for bankruptcy protection, and fears were openly expressed that half the Canadian teams might not exist a year later.

Canada produced the first woman in the NHL, Mamon Rhéaume, backup goalie for the Nashville Knights. One had to admire a 122-lb Québécoise wearing size 5 skates and children's-sized equipment who shared the ice with players almost twice her size. Along with other female stars, she helped inspire thousands of Canadian girls to take up ice hockey. In the 2002–03 season, a record 61,000 females registered for teams across Canada, 7,000 more than the previous season and five times more than a decade earlier. In rural areas ,some former boys-only squads are filling their rosters with girls. The payoff came in the 2006 Olympic Games in Turin, where the Canadian women took gold; they repeated this feat in the 2010 Vancouver Games.

American teams are well-stocked with Canadian players; in fact, 45% (down from 96.7% in 1967) of the NHL players are Canadian. Priceless hockey property such as Wayne Gretzky, the "Great One" who retired in 1999 and later coached the Phoenix Coyotes, and widely considered to be the greatest to ever play the game (and ranking among the pantheon of Canadian hockey greats: Maurice "The Rocket" Richard, Gordie Howe, and Mario Lemiuex), is known and admired almost as much in the United States as in Canada and helped make professional hockey so popular in the U.S. One mystery remains unexplained in this cross-border sport: most Canadian players (including Gretzky) shoot left-handed, while most Americans shoot right-handed.

The 2010 and 2014 Winter Olympics in Vancouver and Sochi brought Canada glorious victories over the Americans in both men's and women's hockey, a sport many Canadians think they own. After all, what other country in the world puts the sport on its currency? The five-dollar bill shows kids playing hockey on a pond with a quotation from Roch Carrier's beloved short story, "The Hockey Sweater: "The winters of my childhood were long, long seasons. We lived in three places—the school, the church and the skating rink—but our real life was on the skating rink." Canadian writer Adam Gopnik asserted: "the way that you show yourself to be authentically Canadian is by engaging with hockey." In what other country would a sitting prime minister write a detailed history of the sport, as Stephen Harper did: *A Great Game: The Forgotten Leafs and the Rise of Professional Hockey.*

Even Canadian troops in Afghanistan put down their weapons to view their teams' triumphs. They were joined by 85% of Canadians at home who reportedly watched their men's hockey team defeat the American players 3–2 in a sudden-death overtime thriller in the last event of the games. Sidney Crosby, captain of the NHL's Pittsburgh Penguins and the youngest captain ever to lift the Stanley Cup in victory, fired the magic shot. This was Canada's eighth Olympic men's hockey gold medal since 1920, and it ignited an outburst of Canadian patriotism few people could have ever imagined in this divided country. There were red maple leaves all over, on flags, signs and clothing, and *O Canada* could be heard everywhere. Even many normally modest Canadians were taken aback by their

own public outpouring of pride in their athletes, who in 2010 won the most gold medals any country had ever won in any Winter Olympic Games—fourteen—capturing medals in nine different sports.

The success of the national team was the result of a program to finance the Olympic athletes' preparation to the tune of $117 million. The motto was controversial: "Own the Podium." Some found this too arrogant, too boastful, yes, too American. But it worked. The Vancouver Games were a smashing success from beginning to end. Three billion persons watched the opening ceremonies, and 3.5 billion tuned in to the Games at some point during the

17 days to see what a winter sport superpower Canada had become.

Canadians' winning ways continued at the Sochi Olympics in 2014, where they captured 24 medals, including 9 golds. The first gold and silver medals were won by two sisters from Quebec in mogul skiing: Justine and Chloé Dufour-Lapointe, with big sister Maxime finishing 12th. Only Russia, the U.S. and Norway earned more. Their men's and women's hockey teams captured gold at Sochi. The men became the first team to win back-to-back titles since 1980. The women won a barn burner against their American rivals 3-2.

Canadian women take Olympic hockey gold in 2006 and again in 2010 and 2014.

Source: *Maclean's*

Canada

A troubling aspect of professional hockey in Canada came to light in 1997. To claw their way into the NHL, many adolescent Canadian boys enter an intense and regimented system, which has deep roots in Canada. It culminates in 49 "major junior" teams divided into three leagues and lumped together under an umbrella organization called the Canadian Hockey League (CHL). Talented players as young as ten are drawn into the system and beginning at age 14 top prospects hire agents and are aggressively pursued by the top clubs. At age 16 or 17 players often move away from home and are billeted with families paid by the clubs. Attending unfamiliar high schools where they do not play on school teams, they become so dependent on their all-powerful coaches that they are easy prey for abuse, sexual and otherwise. The NCAA, to which only Simon Fraser among Canadian universities belongs, considers CHL teams to be professional, so its players are barred from college athletics on both sides of the border.

Fifty-two percent of NHL players come through the CHL system, and over the years it has produced more professional hockey players than any other organization in the world. Only 10% come from college or high school teams although 30% of NHL players went to college. But since only 6% of players coming out of major junior or college teams ever play in the NHL, more and more young players weigh their options between the CHL and intercollegiate hockey that results in a college education.

Players who do not survive the CHL are unable to continue playing on American or Canadian university teams. With this in mind, Dave Dupuis turned his back on the CHL and became the first Inuit to play NCAA hockey. His coach at Skidmore asked: "How many kids who go to a private liberal arts college can say they've hunted a wolf, a walrus, tracked a polar bear or set up a fishing net on a fall salmon run to help feed his community?" Unlike their American counterparts, Canadian universities do not offer athletic scholarships.

It is no wonder that enrollment in the CHL system is declining steeply. Even the number of young Canadians playing hockey is going down as more now play soccer than hockey. It is a problem that the high costs of maintaining ice rinks have caused a distressing number of them to close. One way to deal with this is the introduction at some rinks of artificial ice made with a plastic polymer. Nobody is happy with this alternative since it makes stopping and turning harder, and experts admit it is only "80% like a real ice surface." One small aboriginal community in northern Alberta, Fort Chipewyan, opened the first such rink.

Although two-thirds of Canadians say that hockey is important for the country, according to a 1999 poll, 60% think the player development system needs change; 85% believe the sport needs to be overhauled. One player put it this way: "There's too much emphasis on size and hitting, and not enough on finesse and skill." A March 6, 2000, *Maclean's* cover story was entitled "Blood Sport," and the magazine reported in 2003 that a third of the 33,000 referees in minor-league hockey quits every year because of abuse from parents, players and coaches. Its message: "Relax, it's just a game."

One would not have known that in 2004 when the NHL's Todd Bertuzzi brutally attacked Steve Moore from behind and broke his neck in an internationally televised game. Bertuzzi was banned for the rest of the season. Nevertheless, the NHL cannot bring itself to ban fighting even though a 2011 poll showed that 60% of Canadians favored banning it and another 9.5% were "torn" over the issue. Nor can it draft tougher rules on violence; regrettably, fighting seems to sell tickets. It is said only half in jest that the only time Canadians' politeness ends is when they strap on skates. Rules are selectively enforced as frontier justice of revenge and retribution is encouraged, not just tolerated.

That "rink rage" is a continuing problem was demonstrated in 2006 when a father, who was furious that his son had been benched, choked the coach until the latter lost consciousness. Another dad slammed a referee's head against a metal door, while a mother threw coffee in the face of a player who had cross-checked her son from behind. Forgiving judges gave them all light fines and temporary bans from rinks.

One observer noted: "Outside the rink, hockey adults can be the nicest people. It's almost like they check their brains at the door." In Vancouver fan rage ran out of control after the Stanley Cup playoffs in June 2011. The defeat of the Vancouver Canucks ignited one of Canada's worst ever experiences of rioting. Mobs went on a four-hour rampage through the heart of the city leaving much property damage and many terrified citizens in their wake.

On January 2, 2009, the inevitable happened: York University student Donald Sanderson was killed when his head slammed against the ice after his helmet came off during the fight. It takes a long time to change the rules in a sport that Canadians have long claimed teaches values like respect, discipline and grace under pressure. Polls in 2011 revealed that 30% still believed that fighting is an integral part" of the sport; 60% thought pro hockey had become more violent in the past five years, and four out of five (79%) believed the NHL had not done enough to protect its players from head injuries. But only a minority (41%) thought that hockey would be better off if fighting were banned. One exasperated Canadian said: "I can see a time when hockey will be like a Roman circus: no referees and lots of body bags."

It remains to be seen if automatic ejections, escalating fines and suspensions, and prohibitions on removing helmets and gloves become a part of Canadian hockey. A small but welcome step was taken in 2010 to ban blindside hits to the head in order to curb the many concussions in the NHL. Also head injuries are no longer treated on the bench with mere smelling salts, but any player suspected of having a concussion will be removed from the game and evaluated by a doctor. Putting pressure on the NHL clubs to do

O Canada

O Canada!
  Our home and native land!
True patriot love
  in all thy sons command.
With glowing hearts
  we see thee rise,
The True North
  strong and free!
From Far and wide,
  O Canada,
We stand on guard
  for thee.
God keep our land
  glorious and free!
O Canada,
  we stand on guard for thee.
O Canada,
  we stand on guard for thee.

Ô Canada

Ô Canada!
  Terre de nos aïeux,
Ton front est ceint
  de fleurons glorieux!
Car ton bras
  sait porter l'épée,
Il sait porter
  la croix!
Ton histoire
  est une épopée
Des plus
  brillants exploits.
Et ta valeur,
  de foi trempée,
Protegera nos foyers
  et nos droits,
Protégera nos foyers
  et nos droits.

The Canadian National Anthem

more to protect its players are some powerful corporate sponsors, such as Air Canada, which threatened to end its sponsorship arrangements. Governor General David Johnston, a former two-time hockey All-American at Harvard, worries about a culture of violence: "we're teaching our children things that are contrary to the Canadian character."

By 2015 violence on ice had declined by a third since 2000. The thirst for victory is increasingly trumping the desire to see blood. All feeder programs for the NHL are taking steps to eliminate fighting and it is hoped that it will disappear from the sport.

Asked in 1996 what professional sports they preferred, 60% of Canadian respondents said hockey, 16% baseball, and only 6% basketball. Ten years later that had changed remarkably: 19% preferred Canadian football and only 13% favored hockey, 13% baseball and 7% basketball. Three years later, though, a 2019 report, in the World Atlas, without percentages, listed hockey, followed by lacrosse, football and baseball as the most popular sport in Canada. Nevertheless, the unique contribution that hockey makes to national identity is that it bridges English- and French-speakers, native and non-natives, eastern and western Canadians.

With the highest paid stars commanding $14 million pay packages, the NHL teams are in some economic trouble despite a US$50.3 million team salary cap. Overall their profit margin is a razor-thin 4%. But by 2011, because sponsorship revenues were up by a third, the NHL signed seven-year deal for $400 million with Molson Coors making it the "official beer" on both sides of the border.

Canadians also play basketball, although as a winter sport it must always take the back seat to hockey. One NBA team remains in Canada, the Toronto Raptors, after the Vancouver Grizzlies moved to Memphis. Americans can thank a Canadian, Dr. James Naismith, who devised this game in a Springfield, Massachusetts, YMCA in 1891 as a more interesting indoor alternative to calisthenics. Canada reached its basketball pinnacle in 2006 when Steve Nash, a dazzling point guard who came from Victoria, BC, and starred at Santa Clara before joining the Phoenix Suns and then the Los Angeles Lakers, won the NBA's most-valuable player award two consecutive years. This put him in the company of such greats as Michael Jordan, Magic Johnson, Larry Bird, Wilt Chamberlain, and Bill Russell. He is said to be the greatest pick-and-roll point guard of his generation.

Football was also first played in Canada and brought to the United States about a century ago when a group of McGill University students came down to Harvard to teach a few of its people the new game. With team names like, the "Winnipeg Blue Bombers," the "Ottawa Rough Riders," the "Calgary Stampeders" or the "B.C. Lions," and with Americans composing 45% of the professional players on the nine Canadian teams, American football fans feel right at home in Canada (at least until they count 24 players on the field, notice scores on the board like "four to one," and see teams punting on third down from the fifty-three yard line!) Even the cheering sections chant familiar yells, such as "Give me a "B," an "l," a "u," an "e," "what do you have?! . . ."

Canadians were asked in a 1999 poll which icons and institutions helped most to define Canada. The Canadian Football League placed third behind the Order of Canada and the beaver and just ahead of health care, maple syrup, and beer. Polls in 2006 indicated that more Canadians (19%) preferred their professional football than their pro hockey (13%).

Due to insurmountable financial difficulties, the American teams in the Canadian Football League (CFL) disappeared. Some Canadian teams in the league teeter on the brink of bankruptcy. Despite average annual salaries of only $89,000 and team salary caps, American players still play in the cash-strapped CFL. With no mandatory drug testing, the CFL attracts American players who have the talent to play in the NFL.

Baseball and softball are played everywhere in Canada. Even the legendary Babe Ruth hit his first home run in organized baseball in Toronto's Hanlan's Point Stadium on September 5, 1914 and blasted his longest homer (600 feet) at Montreal's Guybourg Grounds in a 1926 exhibition game. His first wife (Helen Woodford) was from Halifax, and his favorite hunting and fishing destinations were New Brunswick and Nova Scotia. Jacky Robinson first broke the sport's race barrier in Montreal's de Lorimier Grounds with the Royals in 1946.

Although the Expos packed their bags in 2005 for a move to Washington D.C., with a new name—The Nationals, major league teams still play "America's favorite pastime" against the Blue Jays in Toronto. Canadian professional teams in all sports face daunting financial problems which drive more and more of them south. They are usually located in smaller towns that are not as willing as American cities to subsidize stadiums and arenas or to reduce property taxes. The popular resentment against millionaire players discourages governments from assisting clubs.

Fans at Blue Jays home games are treated with the usual major league fare: hot dogs, peanuts, cokes and beer, organ music and comic figures both on huge electronic boards and in costume running around the sidelines and into the crowd. Games are begun, though, by playing two national anthems, not just one. In 1985, New York Yankees fans booed when O Canada was heard in Yankee Stadium prior to a game against the Toronto Blue Jays. That incident was so embarrassing that the American ambassador in Ottawa formally apologized to the Canadians. During the 1992 World Series, the president of the United States himself had to do the same after a Marine honor guard unfurled Canada's flag upside down in a pre-game ceremony. Within days T-shirts could be seen all over Canada bearing the inverted Stars and Stripes and the words, "Sorry, eh?"

A similar international incident occurred before a key playoff hockey game between the Edmonton Oilers and the San Jose Sharks on May 14, 2006, when San Jose fans loudly booed the singing of the Canadian national anthem. During the next game, played in Edmonton, the singer of the national anthem held up the microphone to allow the crowd to loudly sing part of the anthem; this is a tradition that continues to this day in Canadian arenas.

Horrified Canadians had sweet revenge when the Blue Jays captured the series in a six-game thriller. To rub salt in the wounds, the Blue Jays won again in 1993. In 1997, Larry Walker of the Colorado Rockies became the first Canadian to win the National League's most valuable player award. The next year he led the league in batting and won the Lionel Conacher Prize. In 2003, the Blue Jays ace, Roy Halladay, was the American League's Cy Young winner, while Montreal's Eric Gagné won the National League's Cy Young Award for best pitcher. The National League's Most Valuable Player in 2010 was Toronto-born first baseman for the Cincinnati Reds, Joey Votto. He was the third Canadian to win an MVP award in "America's favorite pastime."

In the first decade of the 21st century, more than a dozen Canadian players filled All-Star roster spots. In the 2011 season, 20 Canadians played in the major leagues, double the number only a decade and a half earlier. Over 70 were in the minor leagues, and another 600 played American college baseball. Every year about 30 young Canadians are drafted by big league clubs.

The American fan was confronted with intriguing language differences when attending a home game of the Montreal Expos. In Montreal, O Canada had to be sung in two languages. Announcers used both languages, and the American experienced such play-by-play accounts as this: "The

Canada

RCMP mourning death of four comrades

Source: *Maclean's*

situation is tense for the Expos; there are already two *retraits* (outs). The *frappeur* (batter) steps up the plate. The *lanceur* (pitcher) receives the signal from the *receveur* (catcher) and uncorks a mighty pitch. The *frappeur* is undaunted, though. He swings and, hurray, slams a *circuit* (home-run)!" This vocabulary is no longer needed in Washington, D.C.

The American motorist also notices few differences, except that road signs show distances in kilometers, are in French in Quebec and are often in both French and English outside of the French-speaking regions. The chances are that he will not notice that he is paying more for gasoline (though not as much as if he were driving in most other foreign countries), since it is measured in liters (spelled "litres" in Canada), not in American gallons. Even when a Canadian speaks in terms of "gallons," he means an imperial gallon, which contains a fifth more than an American one. Canada has already adopted the metric system, although many Canadians still talk in terms of inches, feet, miles, pints, quarts, pounds and tons. It cannot be denied that a system of measurement which makes a mile equal the distance a Roman legion could march in 1,000 double steps, a yard equal to the distance from Henry I's nose to his fingertips and an inch as equal to the width of three barleycorns laid side-by-side, is not as logical as the metric system.

Canadian roads are good, unless, of course, he wants to drive deeply into the far northern parts of the country. He sees American-looking cars and pickup trucks everywhere. In 1995, the young racing sensation, Jacques Villeneuve, became the first Canadian to win the Indianapolis 500, snatching victory in the final laps from another Canadian, Scott Goodyear. In 1997, he became the first Canadian to clinch

the world Formula One championship. In 2011, another Canadian race driver, Alex Tagliani, won the pole position at the Indianapolis 500.

What the American may not know is that all major North American automotive producers have plants in Canada and that completely free trade in automotive vehicles and parts exists between the two countries. In 2004, for the first time, Ontario produced more vehicles than Michigan. The American tourist may, in fact, be driving a Canadian car, rather than an American one.

Most cities have a North American look, with the full rundown of fast-food chains, gasoline stations and convenience stores. There are some charming exceptions, such as Quebec City and Victoria, BC. There are far fewer slums and less litter and graffiti; concern grows over the noticeable increase of homeless Canadians in its chilly cities. But the cores of cities remain vital and have been largely spared the kind of urban deterioration that afflicted some American cities.

Canadian cities are still somewhat safer than their American counterparts. In a 2003 World Health Organization report, five Canadian cities were listed as among the safest in the world—Sault Ste. Marie, Brockville and Rainy River in Ontario, as well as Calgary and Fort McMurray in Alberta. A 2019 *Maclean's* report stated that 29 out of the 50 sleepiest crime spots are in Ontario, and the other eight are in Quebec. The chances of being murdered are four times lower than in a U.S. city. An Internet definition of a Canadian is not far off the mark: "An unarmed American with health insurance."

There has been a decline in violent crime in Canada from the mid-1990s, and the overall crime rate by 2015 had fallen to its lowest level since the 1970s.

Nevertheless, nearly as many Canadians reported encountering violent crime as did Americans (21% to 26% in 2007). Fear of street violence is widespread: a third (36%) of Canadians (and half the women) said in 2006 that they "would not walk alone at night within one kilometer of my own home." The percentage is down from 40% in 1975 and about the same for American respondents.

Since the mid-1990s, there has been a threefold growth in gang-related killings. It is not only rising, but it is overwhelming authorities. One out of five persons killed in Canada is the victim of a gang hit, and there are few arrests and very few convictions. Vancouver has the spotlight, but Saskatoon, Winnipeg and Regina are the cities most plagued by violent crime. It is often connected to the drug trade. This is not only in organic drugs, such as cocaine and heroin, but increasingly also in synthetic drugs, such as methamphetamine and ecstasy. It has become North America's leading producer and exporter of these synthetic substances.

Quebec experienced one of the longest and bloodiest gang wars in North American history as the Hell's Angels showed shocking brutality in seeking to gain control of the province's drug trade. More than 160 had died by 2003. In May 2009, a long overdue OperationSharQc, planned for four years and involving more than 1,200 police officers from 20 different forces, arrested 111 Hell's Angels and their hangers-on in Quebec. This ended the infamous biker club's stranglehold on Quebec's drug trade. Admitted illegal drug use in Canada is high, according to the UN's "World Drug Report 2007": it has the highest percentage of marijuana users among developed countries (16.8% in 2004 vs. 6.1% in the Netherlands), and 2.3% use cocaine. The attitude toward marijuana use hardened with the Conservative victory in 2006. One of Prime Minister Stephen Harper's first acts was to terminate the laws liberalizing the use of marijuana.

The omnipresence of potential violence was seen in tragic killing rampages in schools since 1999. In that year, a ninth-grade dropout terrorized a rural high school in Taber, Alberta, killing one student and seriously wounding another with a 22-caliber rifle. A year later three teenage boys were shot and wounded by a fellow student at a Toronto high school, Emery Collegiate Institute. Some argued that Canada's tighter gun control measures made these senseless attacks less deadly: instead of accumulating an arsenal of guns and explosives, as in Columbine, Colorado, the Taber boy could only get his hands on his father's rifle. But in 2006 a young man was able to arm himself with a Baretta semi-automatic rifle, a Glock .45 pistol, a shotgun and a tote bag with 1,000 rounds of ammunition. He walked into Montreal's Dawson College, the province's biggest junior college, and proceeded to kill one student and wound 19 others before turning his gun on himself. Only a brilliant police response prevented the carnage from being much worse.

Guns are increasingly used in such violence; they were involved in two-thirds of Toronto murders in 2005, twice the rate from previous years. Police gun seizures in British Columbia rose by 50% from 2002 to 2005. Controls on the sale of handguns are stricter than in the U.S., but they are not banned. There is a 28-day waiting period to buy a handgun, and one must have the support of two people vouching for him. According to the world population review, in 2020 the number of guns per 100 people was 34.7 in Canada and 125 in the U.S. The overall murder rate per 100,000 persons was 1.6 in Canada and 5.3 in America, and gun murders per 100,000 was 0.61 in Canada and 4.46 in the U.S. In the two decades to 2013, two people died in five shootings inside a Canadian elementary or secondary school. During the same period in the U.S., more than 230 died in 70 school shootings.

Many of the guns used in the kind of violent incidents that are now alarming Canadians are smuggled in from the U.S. Canadian crime experts claim that half come from south of the border, a figure that American authorities dispute although nobody denies that many guns find their way north into Canada. Canadian border agents seized 5,400 firearms from the U.S. in the five years since 2000, and that is only a fraction of the true number. Canadian gun orders reached

such a high volume in 2000 that the U.S. federal government suspended the export of handguns, rifles and ammunition to Canada. Canada had been at the center of one of the largest firearms-smuggling operations in North American history. In 2000, nearly 23,000 vintage U.S. military guns, which are legal in Canada but not in the United States, were seized in Toronto and Montreal gun shops before they could be shipped south of the border.

High-powered hunting guns, including semiautomatics, are widely available. A fourth of all households possess firearms. In 1995, the Liberal government enacted a stricter gun law, banning some small handguns and requiring registration of firearms. In 2000, it tightened the law by requiring registration of all guns by 2003. There was a powerful lobby against gun registration, including by six provinces and two territories that contend that this is an unconstitutional intrusion into their authority. The federal auditor-general criticized its large cost, and the four Western provinces and Newfoundland opted out of administering the program. But the Supreme Court of Canada ruled in June 2000 that both laws had been "passed in the spirit of protecting the public" and were therefore valid.

At the same time that gun- and gang-related crime is dangerously increasing, there are worries that the legendary Royal Canadian Mounted Police (RCMP) is no longer up to the job of maintaining peace and order. The RCMP is a federal force that is contracted by 200 cities and every province and territory but Quebec and Ontario (which have their own provincial police forces) to help enforce the law. It also patrols the Great Lakes and St. Lawrence River. Thus it is caught between the need to meet the growing demand for sophisticated federal policing services, such as immigration, weapons enforcement, counter-terrorism and commercial and white-collar crime, and the "contract policing" at the provincial and local level, which requires that well-trained officers patrol the streets of small towns and answer citizens' calls. It is not performing either duty as effectively as it could.

The force is struggling to cope with the challenge of replacing many baby-boom officers while fewer young Canadians are interested in law-enforcement careers. There are only 183 policemen per 100,000 people, compared with 238 in the U.S. and 211 in Britain. The RCMP began recruiting women in 1974; ; they now constitute 21.7% of its 30,092 officers.

The eight provinces and three territories that use the Mounties' services have little interest in creating their own police forces since Ottawa pays up to 30% of the policing tab, 10% for municipalities. By and large, Canadians still trust the RCMP

so much that its occasional use of phone buggings, wire-tappings, break-ins, use of general search warrants, forgery of income-tax forms, mail tampering, planting of incriminating evidence on innocent persons and harassing left-wing political groups—actions that would seldom be tolerated by American courts or the public if they were known—are generally accepted by Canadians. However, the public's tolerance has its limits. This was shown in 2007 when four RCMP officers at Vancouver International Airport killed an innocent, unarmed, and distressed Polish traveler who spoke no English by shooting him with a taser stun gun when he did not understand and respond to their orders. This lamentable incident was captured on video. Two years later a 200-page report concluded that such use of the electronic weapon was both premature and inappropriate.

Canadians go about their daily lives in a way similar to Americans, with a few minor differences. As in the U.S., schools are run by local school boards under the overall authority of the individual provinces. Their aim is now mass education in comprehensive schools, not academically tracked education in separate schools, as in most European countries. Depending on the province, children begin school at age six or seven, generally attending elementary school for six years, junior high school for three and senior high school for three. In Quebec, pupils enter a two- to three-year *college d'enseignement general et professionnel* (college of general and professional instruction) to prepare either for the university or a specific occupation.

Canadian pupils score very well in international comparisons. On the darker side, there is an alarmingly high dropout rate for black high school pupils: at 40% it is almost double the rate for the student population as a whole.

Dinnertime at the Royal Military College of Canada

Canada

Alberta's lake and mountain landscape.

A lower percentage of Americans age 25-34 (43%, including community colleges) have a college education than in Canada (54.0%); the percentage is much higher for Asian students (ca. 70%) but lower for Caribbean (12%). Canadian universities have strictly meritocratic admission policies, and Canadian-born and foreign Asian students have the reputation for studying the hardest and having the most success. The immigration process attracts highly educated parents, who pass on their high aspirations to their children. Immigrants are an answer to the country's slowing birthrate and aging population; they constitute three-fourths of the annual net growth in the work force.

More students are being admitted, and over the decade before 2003 university enrollment increased by 20%. Following a trend also noticeable in the U.S., 60% of undergraduates in Canadian universities are women, and this can be as high as 79% at such institutions as Mount Saint Vincent University in Halifax. This is especially pronounced in medicine: the majority of students at 13 of Canada's 17 medical schools are women, and at the Université Laval the percentage rises to 70%. No wonder 52% of doctors under age 35 are women.

Those who wish to study have a wide variety of universities from which to choose. There are elite research universities, such as McGill, University of Toronto, University of British Columbia, University of Alberta, and Université de Montréal. These five

institutions alone enroll 22% of undergraduates and produce 45% of doctorates. They receive 46% of all the public monies distributed for research and innovation. In the global Shanghai rankings of the top 100 universities, four Canadian institutions and 54 American ones are included. There are also fine primarily undergraduate institutions, such as Mount Allison, Acadia, Brandon, Lethbridge, Mount Saint Vincent, St. Thomas, Moncton, Bishop's, St. Francis Xavier, Wilfrid Laurier and the Royal Military College of Canada (RMC).

These universities and colleges, all public with a few exceptions in Ontario and BC, are not as expensive as equivalent American institutions. Tuition in 2020-2021 ranged from $7,938 in Ontario, $7,829 in New Brunswick, $8,757 in Nova Scotia, and $3,036 in Newfoundland, to $3,500 in Quebec. Tuition is much higher for international students. Canadian institutions are severely cash-strapped and overcrowded because the federal government reduced its transfer payments to the provinces. In 1999, Canadian universities spent 60% per pupil of what large public universities do in the U.S. In the final five years of the century, state allocations to U.S. universities increased by 28% (50% in California) while they dropped by 6% in Canada.

In a 2010 survey, two-thirds of parents said they could not afford the four-year average cost of $60,000 to send their children to university. Three-fifths of all

students have to take loans to finance their studies, and the average debt on graduation stood at $26,680 in 2015, roughly the same as the average college debt in the U.S. Many wonder if college is worth the price. In the U.S., a college education enables men to earn $365,000 more in a lifetime; in Canada only $169,000. A third of those with doctorates have employment that does not require a PhD. The tough job market goes a long way to explaining why 42% of Canadians between age 20 and 29 live with their parents.

Canadian universities are learning how to raise private funds, but it will be years until they catch up with their American counterparts. For example, the university with the largest endowment is Toronto, with only $1.3 billion, less than one-twentieth of that of Harvard and Yale.

In 2017, nearly 27,000 Canadians went to the U.S. for their post–secondary education, a decrease in approximately 1,000 since 2005. They constitute the largest group of foreigners at Harvard (150 or 2.3%) being 787 (2018). This educational migration is particularly true of Ph.D. students. The word that many would-be professors hear in Canada is that an American Ph.D. may give one an edge. American-trained professors are in the majority in many departments, especially at leading Canadian research universities. Canada confers fewer than 10% as many doctorates as does the much larger U.S. Nevertheless, Canadians still earn five times as many Ph.D. degrees in Canada as they do in America.

Approximately 10,000 (2018) Americans attend Canadian universities. This may well be due to the much lower cost of attending a Canadian university due to the difference in the Canadian and American currencies' values notwithstanding a higher tuition paid by non-Canadians attending Canadian universities. In fact, when considering currency differences and cost of living in Canadian university cities other than in British Columbia, the cost is approximately 50% less than that paid at an American college. At the same time, some Canadian universities are aggressively recruiting American high school students, promising gun-free schools, good ski possibilities and quality education for less tuition. Also popular are branch campuses of American universities in Canada, primarily for teachers and other professionals. By 1990, seven U.S. universities (including Niagara and Central Michigan) offered extension programs for about 500 students in Ontario alone, and such operations are expanding in Alberta and British Columbia. Despite the higher tuition costs, these programs offer study opportunities at night and on weekends.

Five provinces provide state support for religiously affiliated schools. Also, the federal government is directly responsible for educating Indians and Inuit children and indirectly involved in education through financial support for higher education and bilingual teaching throughout Canada. Canadian public schools, which 95% of children attend, are suffering under the strain of funding cuts, labor strife and the needs of an increasingly diverse student body. Since 1995 the percentage of provincial wealth spent on education has declined dramatically.

Canadian-American Images

Americans are quick to recognize Canadians as a friendly, open and pragmatic people. Canadians are a bit more reserved than Americans. As Pierre Berton noted, "we are not a back-slapping race" and Canadians themselves admit to being somewhat embarrassed by public displays of emotions. A publication of the Royal Bank once encapsulated how many Canadians react to their more ebullient neighbors: "Americans prefer first to second names, and, in conversation, they seem to use yours in every sentence or two . . . They belong to clubs and lodges named after animals. They talk to strangers on street corners and at lunch counters.

As they themselves would put it, they're friendly as hell."

Polls consistently reveal that Americans have a positive impression of Canadians: friendly (29%), peaceful, polite, helpful. Canadian's viewed Americans as more "dangerous" than "compassionate." Americans use the words "tolerant," "compassionate" and "funny" to describe Canadians. Only 1% of Canadians thought Americans are "funny" or "humorous."

A *Maclean's* poll asked Americans what country they liked after their own, and they said Canada, favored by 90%, followed by Britain. Only 3% had a negative view of Canada. A quarter of Canadians and Americans indicated that they would accept citizenship in the other country, and a third of *Québécois* said they would accept an offer to become U.S. citizens. A resounding 91% of Americans agreed in 2007 that they would have a better quality of life if they moved to Canada.

Many people argue that there is no such thing as Canadian patriotism because there is no such thing as a Canadian nation. Although Canadians are patriotic, they feel uncomfortable when they display it too much in public. In his 1988 book, Peter C. Newman wrote that "becoming a Canadian never required conversion to a burning faith or even a salute, since we had no distinctive flag during the first 98 years of our existence."

The two countries' standing in the world is very different. Reflecting on the differences between his Canadian and American students, Northrop Frye said: "American students have been conditioned from infancy to think of themselves as citizens of one of the world's great powers. Canadians are conditioned from infancy to think of themselves as citizens of a country of uncertain identity, a confusing past and a hazardous future." That seems to resonate as Prime Minister Justin Trudeau has called Canada the first post-national state. Toronto academic Former *New York Times* bureau chief in Toronto, Andrew H. Malcolm, reported an example of the differing manifestation of patriotism. At the start of a stock car race in Calgary, the announcer asked the crowd to stand for the national anthem. A few seconds after a record of "O Canada" had begun to play, he stopped the music with a wrenching scratch and said, "You all know the rest," as the racecars' engines began to roar. Such an incident would be unthinkable in the United States.

Asked at the end of the century about factors that are important parts of what makes them Canadian, 80% named the flag (60% in Quebec) and only 41% named the British Queen (20% in Quebec). Nevertheless, rather than pledging allegiance to the flag, most Canadian pupils

make their pledge to the Queen. In May, they are released from school for a day in order to celebrate Victoria Day, in honor of Queen Victoria, despite the fact that she never visited Canada during her long reign. The birthday of Canada's "founding father," Sir John A. Macdonald, is not a federal holiday, but school children observe Martin Luther King Jr. Day in January. Thanksgiving comes the second Monday in October, almost six weeks earlier than in the United States. There is certainly no Fourth of July celebration in a country which remained loyal to Britain during the American Revolution and which was a haven for Loyalists who either left or were driven out of the Thirteen Colonies. Canadian school children still learn about such heroic men of principle as *Benedict Arnold*, who demonstrated their devotion to order and the English sovereign. Canadians' national holiday is July First, the day on which both the country's constitutions were enacted in 1867 and 1982.

Canada has its own history, has been shaped by more challenging geographical conditions, has different cultures and languages, and has a different political heritage. Its political system is British by origin, even though it has been powerfully influenced by political practices in the United States. And Canadians have tended to place a greater emphasis on order than have Americans, who tend to treasure liberty above all else. Canadian-born sociologist, Seymour Lipsit, gave an example: "Canadians were told to go metric and they did. Americans were told to go metric and they didn't."

Courtesy of iStock.com/onepony

Canada

Canada's first constitution, the British North America Act (BNA) of 1867, set up the objectives of "peace, order, and good government" rather than "life, liberty and the pursuit of happiness." Canada never had a "Wild West" because, unlike in America, organized society in the form of the mounted policeman, the railway agent, the bank manager, the missionary and agents of the Hudson's Bay Company usually arrived before or along with the settlers. Therefore, there has always been less violence and greater respect for authority in Canada than in the United States. What other country in the world uses a policeman (the Mountie) as a national symbol?

Canadians know that their emphasis on order makes them seem boring to the rest of the world. In a "boring headline" contest held in 1986 by the U.S. magazine, *The New Republic*, the winner was: "Worthwhile Canadian Initiative." In an interview with *The Economist* in 2003, one Canadian compared Canada to a "boring party where the guests are too polite to leave." The book titles of two earlier bestsellers were: *Canada on the World Stage: Is Anyone Listening* and *The Future of Canada: Does Nationalism Even Matter?* Some Australians call Canadians "frozen Yanks." Nevertheless, when asked in which country they would rather live other than their own, Australia was Canadians' first choice (18%), followed by the U.S. (14%).

In a 1992 editorial, "Boring, and proud," *The Globe and Mail* countered: "The reason Canada is considered boring is because nothing apocalyptic ever happens here— no civil wars, no nuclear disasters, no famine. On a global scale, Canada just can't cut it when it comes to violence and tragedy. We discuss our possible national break-up over lunch beside a lake. Blame our Canadian forefathers for the cruel hand we've been dealt. Didn't they realize that when they founded this country on the principles of Peace, Order, and Good Government that it would never make CNN?"

Although they are changing, Canadians have tended to be less assertive of their rights than have Americans. Peter Newman put it this way: "In dramatic contrast to the individualism of the United States, the idea was to be careful, to be plainly dressed, quiet-spoken and, above all, close with one's money and emotions . . . You could immediately spot a Canadian at any gathering: he or she was the one who automatically chose the most uncomfortable chair."

The *Maclean's*/CBC end-of-century poll provided ample evidence that Canadians believe they have a unique identity, separate and distinct from all other countries, as 90% of respondents indicated. Fully 77% believe it is based on a strong sense of their own history and appreciation of what they have accomplished as a nation, rather than simply a desire not to be American; 81% hold the view that they can thrive in the twenty-first century by keeping their own values and not trying to become more like Americans. A subsequent *Maclean's* poll published on July 1, 2006, concluded that the endless and mostly futile search for a single national identity and vision had been replaced by a growing sense that Canada's greatest asset is its diversity of lifestyles, beliefs and opinions. Former Prime Minister Jean Chrétien expressed this confidence: "We are North Americans but not Americans. We are different because of history and geography, but basically we have built a different society." Further, a 2016 study by Angus Reid revealed that almost eight in ten Canadians (79%) say they are either "very proud" (52%) or "proud" to be Canadian, though this sentiment is lower in Quebec.

Events from the 1960s on tended to sharpen Americans' and Canadians' awareness of the differences between their countries and objectives. The United States' seemingly endless involvement in the Vietnam War became unpopular in Canada, where an estimated 50,000 or more Americans fled to avoid military service; all but 20,000 returned to the U.S. after a 1977 amnesty. Those who stayed include several judges, scores of university professors, a popular radio host, a music promoter, a well-known film critic and numerous politicians. Less known is the fact that as many as 40,000 Canadians fought in that war, and more than a hundred Canadians' names are etched on the Vietnam Memorial in Washington, D.C.

In 2004 four American soldiers deserted their Iraq-bound units and fled to Canada, where they requested refugee status. But unlike in 1969, when Prime Minister Pierre Elliot Trudeau declared his country to be "a refuge from militarism," the Canadian government, backed by a board that hears refugee cases, opposed their applications, arguing that they were not persecuted and that the war was not illegal. Canada is no longer an open-armed sanctuary despite the fact that three in five Canadians thought American deserters should be granted permanent residency. Parliament approved nonbinding resolutions in 2008 and 2009 to stop the deportation of deserters, but the government refused to do so. In July 2008, the first American soldier was deported, and more followed. There are still more Canadians serving in the U.S. military forces than any foreign nationality.

From 1968 to 1984, Trudeau felt freer to criticize American foreign policy in public, and many Canadians agreed with him. Also, racial violence in America and the disillusionment stimulated by the Watergate scandal sullied the image of America in Canadian eyes. Further, Canadians began to feel a surge of nationalism and sought to lessen their country's economic dependence on the United States in ways

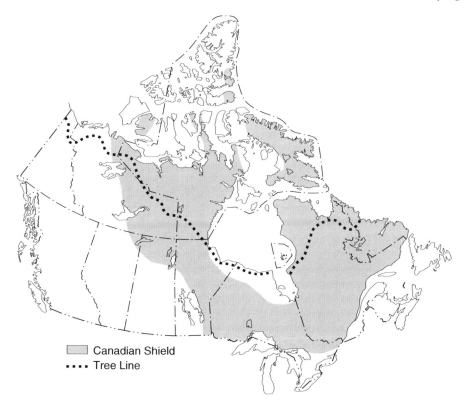

Canadian Shield
•••• Tree Line

that greatly irritated American businessmen and their government.

More and more Americans began to take notice of the fact that Canada is a sovereign country that defines its own interests. As Americanized as Canadians might have become, they seem determined to be a different kind of society, which tries to avoid the kinds of problems the United States faces. One young Canadian, Neil Bishop, noted, "It's not that U.S. civilization is bad; on the contrary, it is truly great. But one U.S.A. is surely enough."

GEOGRAPHY

Canada is the second-largest country in the world; only Russia is larger. Covering almost four million square miles, it is 10% larger than the United States (including Alaska) and 40 times bigger than Great Britain; it is roughly the same size as the entire European continent and occupies 46.6% of North America. It is bracketed by huge islands, such as Newfoundland, Vancouver and Baffin, the world's fourth largest island, with 16,000 miles of crinkled coastline.

Canada stretches 4,545 miles east to west and almost 3,000 miles north to south, and it spans one fourth of the world's time zones. Its three coasts, when combined, are the world's longest coastline, with an enormous store of offshore riches. Inland Canada has more than a million rivers, streams and lakes, containing over a fifth of the world's fresh water supply. Manitoba alone has one lake for every 10 inhabitants. It also shares the world's largest body of fresh water, the Great Lakes, with the U.S. Canada possesses a fourth of the world's wetlands and 15% of its forests. Even though it occupies the "winter half" of North America, it has a wide range of climates, and there are regions in Canada that experience one-hundred degree drops of temperature in the wintertime.

Almost one-half of Canada is located on a massive shield of ancient Precambrian rocks hewed and scraped by a gigantic prehistoric glacier. It covers the bulk of six provinces and most of the Northwest Territories. It is a sparsely-populated physical environment of forests, wilderness, lakes and rocks jutting from the earth. This landscape differs remarkably from the lowlands south of it and keeps Canadians hemmed in close to the U.S. border, where most of them live. This Shield has always been a formidable barrier to settlement, to the building of roads and railways and to the movement of Canadians from east to west or from south to north.

Because so much of it is practically uninhabitable, Canada cannot be compared to the United States. A thousand miles of

Former Governor General visiting Parliament in Ottawa

rocks, eroded mountain chain and bogs placed a wall between the Prairie provinces (the West) and the settled portion of Ontario, which belongs to Canada's East, even though Toronto is closer to such Midwestern cities as Cleveland, Detroit and Chicago, than to New York and Boston. It has always threatened to cut off the Canadian West from the East and has contributed to a greater feeling of separation from each other on the part of westerners and easterners than is felt in the United States.

It has helped to create and perpetuate a western dependence on eastern financial power that has always been resented in the West. Finally, it has strengthened Canadians' reliance upon government and has helped shape the Canadian character. As Pierre Berton wrote, "if we are a solemn people, it is partly because the Shield and the wilderness bear down upon us, a crushing weight, squeezing us like toothpaste along the borders of your country."

Nevertheless, the rugged Shield also contains treasures that help make Canada a natural resource powerhouse. It was an ideal habitat for beavers, which had almost single-handedly attracted European attention to Canada three centuries ago and provided the first important economic stimulus to Canadian settlement. Beaver fur was so popular that the animal faced extinction in the 19th century. One result is that Canada is the only country in the world with a rodent for its national animal: the beaver. Its image was on the first Canadian postal stamp in 1851 and is on today's nickel; in 1971 the government made it the official emblem. No wonder there was such a furious outcry in 2011

when Senator Nicole Eaton dared propose that the polar bear replace the beaver as the national animal. Calling the beaver, a "dentally defective rat," she argued that the white beast is "the world's largest terrestrial carnivore and Canada's most majestic and splendid animal."

The beaver is an amazing creature, which can cut down 216 trees a year with its bare teeth. But it suffered a horrible indignity in 2010. In 1920, the Hudson Bay Company had founded a journal of popular history called *The Beaver*. On its ninetieth birthday, the editors felt compelled to change its name to the dull *Canada's History* because the iconic animal's name had become a slang carnal term referring to a certain location on a woman's body. The death knell was rung by the internet. If spam filters did not bury it, users of its website were often disappointed to discover that the content was history rather than something else, and they clicked out on average after only eight seconds. Editors hope the publication's new name will expand its 50,000 circulation.

Today, much of the Shield remains richly endowed with nickel, cobalt, zinc, copper, gold and silver; it is the source of 40% of Canada's mineral production. It contains the trees that make Canada one of the two major pulp and paper producers in the world, the uranium mines in northern Saskatchewan and the huge Ungava iron ore deposits. It is a major source of waterpower, which supplies Canada with 70% of its electricity and enables it to export hydroelectricity to the United States, especially to the Northeast.

The Shield's rugged landscapes, scenery and wildlife, particularly multitudes

Canada

of birds including millions, even billions, of ducks and geese, have inspired some of Canadians' best painting, especially since the 1920s, when seven talented Canadian artists (known as the "Group of Seven") captured its majestic beauty on their canvases. It also attracts vacationers from all over North America and helps to perpetuate that erroneous image which some Americans have of modern Canadians: as lumberjacks or rugged frontiersmen who carve a precarious living out of a beautiful, but hostile, land. As can be seen, Canadians are predominately city-dwellers who have learned to exploit the riches of the Shield in order to create and maintain a comfortable standard of living similar to that enjoyed by most Americans.

Canada is a very sparsely settled land, with an overall population density of only 3.7 people per square kilometer, compared with 36 in the United States. Even Saudi Arabia has a higher population density than Canada. The most densely populated provinces are in the Maritimes: New Brunswick, Nova Scotia, and Prince Edward Island: pointedly Newfoundland/Labrador is not part of the Maritimes. The Maritimes climate and geography have powerfully influenced settlement patterns. The Shield and climate compressed Canadians to close proximity to the U.S. border. There were further incentives to settle in the extreme south. Many settlers to Canada came from the United States and wanted to remain close to that country. Many Canadian manufacturing facilities were owned by Americans or were intentionally located close to the American market, which is the world's largest and the target for 75% of Canadian exports. Also, in the level plains between the southern rim of the Shield and the U.S. border are fertile farmlands and a fortuitous string of lakes and rivers connected in places by canals that provide inexpensive transportation and water power.

The result of these forces is that three-fourths of all Canadians live within 100 miles of the U.S. border, and 90% live within 200 miles. In fact, three-fourths of all Canadians live *south* of the northernmost point of the 48 contiguous United States. By contrast, most Americans live far away from Canada, and only 12% of them live within 100 miles of the Canadian border. This percentage is decreasing as more and more Americans move south within the U.S.

If one regards only population distribution, Canada more closely resembles the snake-shaped country of Chile, rather than the well-proportioned geographic configuration that Canada is. It could be seen as a country 4,545 miles wide and a hundred miles tall, albeit with a hinterland which

stretches straight to the permafrost, the ice pack and the North Pole. Even within this thin band of settlement, Canadians are not dispersed evenly. Four out of five Canadians live in cities; 31% live in the three largest—Toronto, Montreal, and Vancouver—and half of new immigrants settle in these three cities. One-third of Canadians live in communities with fewer than 10,000 inhabitants. Political pollsters detect an urban-rural split on such issues as gun control and gay rights, and the economic disparity is growing. Differing lifestyles are also reflected in the facts that rural Canadians are more likely to smoke, drink underage, and be obese.

Urban concentrations are strung out from east to west, "an archipelago of population islands walled off from each other by the terrifying obstacles of Precambrian rock, muskeg (bogs), mountain barriers, storm-tossed waters," to quote Pierre Berton. The bulk of Newfoundland's people have to cross the Gulf of St. Lawrence to get to the Canadian mainland. French-speaking Acadia and Quebec separate anglophones in the east from those in Ontario. Distance and the southern extremity of the Shield, which juts through western Ontario, separate most inhabitants of Ontario, the most populous Canadian province, from the prairie prov-

inces of Manitoba, Saskatchewan, and Alberta. Finally, the Rocky Mountains provide a majestic separation of the prairie region from British Columbia.

These sharply divided regions are, in many ways, northward thrusts of the North American continent. Indeed, a serious challenge to Canada has always been that only man-made barriers separate Canadian from American regions, whereas daunting natural barriers divide most of Canada's regions from each other. This has made the forging of unnatural east–west links and the overcoming of the natural north–south ties absolutely essential if Canada were to become and to remain a unified country. A closer look at these distinct regions will demonstrate

why this has always been difficult and why author Arthur Malcolm described Canada as a "puzzling collection of frequently feuding fiefdoms."

THE ATLANTIC PROVINCES: In the East are the Atlantic Provinces, composed of the three Maritime provinces of Nova Scotia, Prince Edward Island (Canada's smallest province although twice the size of Rhode Island) and New Brunswick (40% of whose population is French-speaking Acadian) plus Newfoundland and Labrador, Britain's first overseas colony. Officially renamed Newfoundland and Labrador in 2001, this is Canada's most recent province. It had Dominion status equal to Canada's from 1907 to 1933, when it lost its self-rule. Not until 1949 did it join Canada, after a very close (52%) vote by its people. It still remains remote from the rest of the country and even has its own time zone 30 minutes ahead of the Maritime provinces. Less urbanized than Ontario and Quebec, this region is covered by forested hills and low mountains. Water is everywhere. These provinces are largely encircled by rocky coastlines, coves, isolated fishing villages and port cities, such as St. Johns and Halifax.

With about 2.3 million inhabitants, 7% of the country's population, Atlantic Canada is the most ethnically homogeneous region of Canada. Acadians, remnants of those ten thousand hardy pacifist folks brutally rooted out and resettled by the British in 1755 for trying to stay neutral in the war between England and France, are immortalized in Longfellow's moving poem "Evangeline." No longer discriminated against because of their French language, they now live along New Brunswick's northern border and eastern shore and are sprinkled around in other parts of the region, especially in the southwest corner of Prince Edward Island and on Cape Breton in Nova Scotia. On August 15, 2005, thousands of them assembled at the site of their ancient village of St. Pré in the heart of their lost homeland to celebrate their survival of that deportation 250 years earlier, now referred to as *le grand dérangement* (the Big Inconvenience).

About 80% of the Atlantic Provinces inhabitants are of British descent (higher in Newfoundland), especially Scottish, by whom Nova Scotia, meaning "New Scotland," was named. Perhaps the most famous Scotsman to grow up and live here was Alexander Graham Bell, who invented the telephone. It is reported that more people speak Gaelic in Nova Scotia today than in Scotland itself. One still hears a distinctive Scottish burr when many Nova Scotians speak English, especially in Cape Breton, which is experiencing a revival of Gaelic cultures and language.

This predominantly British population has long valued its transatlantic ties with Great Britain, and it has always maintained thriving trading relations with the northeastern seaboard cities south of the border. Because of its window to the Atlantic, it has always been strategically important. During the two world wars its ports were assembly points for convoys of ships carrying troops and supplies from North America to Europe. It is no surprise that Canada's small navy is headquartered in this part of the country. In fact, Halifax, the capital of Nova Scotia, is the home of Canada's largest defense establishment, which provides employment for almost a fourth of the city's work force.

Despite their strategic location, the Atlantic Provinces have always been the poorest of Canada's provinces. They have been excessively reliant upon fishing and timbering. A greater percentage of their jobs are dependent upon the extraction of primary resources and increasingly upon tourism, and this has resulted in a large number of single-industry towns. They have too little arable land, population and industry to have a more balanced economy and be prosperous on their own. They are just now finding reliable alternatives to their former economic mainstays of fishing, lumber and military bases. Average wages were until recently only two-thirds of the national figure, but they are now rising. Their population is aging rapidly, and unemployment is well above the national average. Numerous attempts to form a Maritime union to combat these problems more effectively have failed.

Their present economic hopes and success stem from discoveries of natural gas and oil off the coasts of Nova Scotia and Newfoundland and Labrador. These capital-intensive industries do not generate many jobs directly, nor do they spread cash around as cod fishing once did. But they boost government resources and trickle down to others. The importance of these discoveries explains the history of bitter struggles with Ottawa over the question of who owns or controls these valuable resources: Canada or the individual provinces. The people in these provinces are proud of their more relaxed, less urbanized life, but they have also tended to resent the economic and political domination of Canadian life by provinces to the west. In 2000, the region's four premiers formed a joint council to lobby in Ottawa. By 2009, Newfoundland had become a "have" province, sending more financial assistance to other provinces than it receives from them.

Although the region lacks a very large urban center, Halifax is an important and interesting city. With a population of around 280,000, it is a showcase of 19th century architecture with the leisurely air of a small, tree-lined community. Its significance as Atlantic Canada's most important port city suffered with the opening of the St. Lawrence Seaway, which enabled ships to bypass Halifax and churn their way directly into the Great Lakes.

ST. LAWRENCE LOWLANDS: The two provinces of Quebec and Ontario form the heartland of the Canadian Confederation. They were formerly two separate colonies, called Lower Canada (Quebec) and Upper Canada (Ontario). Their merger in 1840 signaled the imperfect wedding of Canada's "two founding peoples" in one country. Although very large portions of these two provinces are covered by the Canadian Shield, they share in the south the St. Lawrence Lowlands, which form the most heavily populated, most industrialized and, therefore, traditionally the richest part of Canada. It contains 60% of Canada's entire population. It has more cities of over 100,000 inhabitants than any other region, and it includes Canada's two largest cities, Toronto and Montreal, as well as the federal capital, Ottawa.

About three-fourths of the total value of Canada's manufactured goods are produced in this region. Its moderate climate and excellent agricultural lands attracted many settlers in the 18th and 19th centuries, and farms here still help feed the country's most densely populated region. A further blessing for this region is the waterway formed by the St. Lawrence River, the Great Lakes and connecting canals and locks, the last of which were completed in 1959. The economic importance of the Great Lakes cannot be underestimated: the eight American states and Ontario that share the lakes account for 30% of North America's employment and output and 36% of manufacturing jobs.

This entire waterway is ice-free about nine months a year and gives this inland area enviable access to the Atlantic Ocean and from there to the rest of the world. For example, although located 1,000 miles from the sea, the port of Toronto receives ocean-going ships and is the same shipping distance from Britain as is New York City. Also, many vessels can travel almost 2,000 miles from the Atlantic Ocean all the way westward to Thunder Bay, the railhead for products and grain from the West and located on the northern shore of Lake Superior, and then return to the high seas.

QUEBEC: While the St. Lawrence Seaway binds the eastern half of Canada, it could never erase the crucially important cultural differences of the people who live close to its banks. This Canadian heartland is sharply divided into francophones in Quebec and anglophones in Ontario. With a land area three times larger than France, Quebec is Canada's largest province and is as wide at its widest point as the distance between Dallas and Washington, D.C.

Home to about 22.5% of Canada's population, it is a French-speaking island in the midst of an anglophone sea in which francophones are outnumbered by fifty to one. About 87% of Quebec's 8.1 million people speak French as a mother tongue, 7% speak English at home, 6% speak another native language, and 16% of the total population is fluent in a third language. A relatively small percentage (20.6%) of the

Railway magnate William Van Horne points westward, Banff, Alberta

Canada

francophones speak only French, especially those living outside the larger cities of Montreal and Quebec City. In Montreal, two-thirds speak both French and English. A 2013 poll revealed that 85% of Quebecers think it is important to be bilingual. The *Québécois*, as they are now called most of the time even outside of francophone Canada, have a distinctive language, culture, and heritage.

In the past they tended to consider themselves more as *Québécois*, than as Canadians. In the 1994 *Maclean's*/CTV poll, only 45% of Quebec respondents identified themselves as "Canadian." By 2001 that figure had risen to 75%, and in *Maclean's* 2003 year-end poll an unprecedented 69% claimed they were "proud to be Canadian." That percentage continues to go up: *La Presse* published a poll in 2007 showing that 85% were proud to be Canadian, a 20-year high. Due largely to a serious Liberal Party scandal in Quebec, the number of *Québécois* who considered themselves "very proud to be Canadian" fell from 65% in 1985 to only 32% in 2006 (in Anglophone Canada the percentage fell from 80% to 61%). Nevertheless, a former separatist (PQ) premier, Bernard Landry, said in 2007 that "being Canadian isn't dishonorable." That was high praise from a man who once called the Canadian flag "a piece of red rag." In the wake of Canada's superb Olympic performance in 2010, fewer than one-third of *Québécois* supported the notion of having their own Olympic team.

Québécois still regard themselves as a nation, even though they are linked politically with the rest of Canada. For the first time the Canadian parliament gave this formal expression by declaring in November 2006 that *Québécois* are "a nation within a united Canada." Constituting almost a fourth of all Canadians, they have always doggedly resisted assimilation with the English-speaking world around them. They have successfully asserted their right to manage most of their own affairs and largely to determine their own destiny. They have their own national day on June 24, a week earlier than Canada Day on July 1. The Quebec government officially renamed it the Fête Nationale, but *Québécois* still refer to it as Fête de la St-Jean-Baptiste, or "La St-Jean."

A dramatic change had taken place by 2004. *Québécois* seem to accept Canada more than they used to. Only 2% of them considered national unity a major issue. As the most socially liberal Canadians, *Québécois* like the social experimentalism they see in Canada, such as gay marriage, abortion and legalization of marijuana: 69% endorsed the statement that they are proud of what Canada is becoming "because it shows what a socially progressive

and diverse country we live in." The figure in the rest of Canada was 54%.

The *Québécois* also now share anglophone Canadians' views on the nation's place in the world. *Québécois* were more critical of the 2003 war in Iraq; 90% opposed it, and some of the world's largest anti-war rallies had been held in Montreal. Thus, from being the most pro-American Canadians, *Québécois* have become perhaps the most skeptical of the foreign and social policies pursued by the United States—60% said their attitude toward the U.S. had become more negative in recent years, compared with just under half of Canadians as a whole. A broad dislike for President George W. Bush and the war in Iraq had much to do with this. A final reason for this unprecedented *Québécois* embrace of common Canadian values is the confidence *Québécois* now have that their language and culture are more firmly entrenched than ever before.

A third of all *Québécois* live in metropolitan Montreal, a city of about 4.2 million people and the world's third-largest French-speaking city after Paris and Kinshasa, Congo. This city dominates the economic and cultural life of Quebec. Quebec's major newspapers are published here: the one with the largest circulation is the unabashedly sensational tabloid, *Le Journal de Montreal*. *Le Devoir* is the influential French-language daily. *La Presse* occupies the middle ground between those two dailies and is the voice for Canadian unity. The *Montreal Gazette* is the major English-language daily. The newsmagazine, *L'Actualité*, the French-language sister of *Maclean's*, is published in Montreal. All major Quebec political parties have their headquarters in the city, even though the provincial political capital is Quebec City.

At one time Montreal was the cultural and economic heart of Canada. Its population doubled from 1941 to 1971. Most of that growth came from the migration of unilingual Quebecers from the solidly-French countryside into this city, which offered hope for advancement and a better standard of living. Urbanization greatly changed the culture and outlook of the Quebecois and brought about a "Quiet Revolution" in the 1960s and 1970s. The influx also greatly altered the city of Montreal by bringing unilingual Quebecers to live side by side with anglophones, who dominated the city's economy. Nowhere else in the province was there such contact. Montreal became more and more French and again became the focus of Canada's most divisive debates, as it had been during the conscription controversies in both world wars.

It has experienced terrorism, so rare in Canadian history, and serious political

tension resulting from the vigorous assertion of French-language rights. An increasing number of anglophones and major corporate headquarters abandoned the city, and investments in the city dwindled. During the 1970s its economy and population declined, as Toronto overtook it as Canada's major city. Although that economic and population decline was halted in the mid-1980s, Montreal's position as Canada's primary city was lost perhaps forever. Today it is corruption and organized crime that drive the citizens of Montreal into the suburbs and head offices elsewhere. In the six years to 2008, more than 20,000 city residents left for the suburbs.

In the 21st century, Montreal has become a leading high-tech center. A 2000 Price Waterhouse Coopers study of large North American metropolitan areas ranked the city fourth in concentration of high-tech jobs on a per-capita basis. *Wired* magazine also singled it out as the only Canadian city on a list of 46 global high-tech hubs to watch. Bombardier Aerospace, which built the high-speed train for the Washington-Boston run in 2000 and produces rail engines and cars for the European market, is in Montreal.

ONTARIO: In the middle of the 19th century, Queen Victoria located the federal capital of Ottawa on the banks of the Ottawa River, presumably because it was a safe distance from the United States insofar as the War of 1812 was still a fresh memory and because it was on the boundary separating English and French Canada. Ottawa remains Canada's most determinedly bilingual city. It is a pretty, comfortable city of 1,407,928 (2021) inhabitants, making Ottawa Canada's fourth largest metropolitan area. Ottawa is distinguished by its scenic drives, the Rideau Canal, its colorful downtown market district, and, of course, its stately gothic architecture which houses Parliament, the Supreme Court and other government institutions. This capital city is resplendent with pomp and pageantry, with scarlet-coated Mounties guarding

Parliament Hill on horseback and Canada's Guards wearing bearskin hats, red coats and black trousers performing rituals before Parliament and the residence of the governor general.

Bruce Phillips, a television correspondent and former aide to the prime minister, remarked: "most people who live outside Ottawa see it as a place peopled with fat-cat civil servants with bullet-proof jobs." Some Canadians look down on Ottawa as a boring, bureaucrats' city with little nightlife (other than that which takes place in the bars and nightspots in Gatineau, across the river in Quebec, after Ottawa's citizens have gone to bed). A typical crack at the town was made by one of Trudeau's ministers, who contended, "the best thing about Ottawa is the train to Montreal." Some people also complain that the cultural life is not what one would expect in a federal capital. That is now changing, and, to quote Phillips again, "the city is sprouting a few cultural wings." In 2008 a *Maclean's* cover story named Ottawa Canada's "smartest city" and the fourth "most cultured" after Calgary, Victoria and Gatineau, Quebec.

Ottawa has long had a National Arts Centre near parliament, which houses a chamber orchestra, theaters and facilities for touring opera companies and shows. In 1988, a dramatic neo-Gothic glass and granite palace for the National Gallery, with a panoramic view of the city and Ottawa River, was opened. Designed by the Israeli-born Montreal architect Moshe Safdie, this gigantic magnificent edifice, which is a third larger than the National Gallery in Washington, finally relieves a major embarrassment of having a national collection of art, established in 1880, with no permanent home for it. In 1988, a new structure for the Canadian Museum of Aviation was also completed.

In 1989, a Museum of History (previously named Museum of Man and Museum of Civilization) across the river in Gatineau, Quebec (known until 2002 as Hull), connected to the Ottawa side and the National Gallery by a footbridge. The construction of two connecting museums in English and French Canada symbolizes the strengthening of fragile bonds that tie together Canada's two founding nations. In 2005, on the 60th anniversary of VE Day, a remarkable War Museum opened on the LeBreton Flats, a short distance from Parliament. Its primary architect, Raymond Moriyama, is a Japanese-Canadian who was interned in Canada during the Second World War. A National Holocaust Monument was opened in Ottawa in 2017.

The economic and cultural power of Toronto reflects the weight of Ontario within Canada. This province alone is

Flatiron Building and CN Tower, Toronto, Ontario Courtesy: Tourism Canada

three times as large as Japan. It occupies the entire northern shores of the Great Lakes, while eight American states are washed by their southern shores. No American state has such a commanding position within the American republic as does Ontario within the Confederation. Its predominance would be even greater if Quebec were ever to separate from Canada; Ontario would then become half of Canada, and it is uncertain whether any federal state could bear this. Because of the leading rank that Ontario has traditionally enjoyed, it tends to be most satisfied with the status quo. Just as some Americans once believed that "what is good for General Motors is good for America," people in Ontario tend to believe that "what is good for Ontario is good for Canada."

With almost 15 million inhabitants, Ontario is not only the most populous province, but it is ethnically the most diverse. About 5% of its population, concentrated basically in the eastern part of the province, speaks French as a mother tongue, and in 1989 Bill 8 improved government services to Ontario's half million francophones. Non-British immigrant groups from a variety of European and Asian countries have settled here.

Greater Toronto has 6.4 million inhabitants and lively ethnic neighborhoods, restaurants, and small businesses that are reminiscent of New York or Chicago a half century ago. The idea of neighborhood is strong, and in 1996 *Forbes* magazine rated Toronto as the best place in the world to balance work and family. Of its residents, half are immigrants, and Toronto is the favorite urban destination for newcomers to Canada. A fourth of the country's immigrants live there. A fifth of its people arrived in Canada after 1981 and a tenth after 1991. By 2007, 49% of its population had been born outside the country, the second highest figure in the world after Miami. Almost half (43%) of the overall population belongs to a visible minority. In fact, Toronto at the turn of the century was home to 42% of Canada's non-whites. Since 1967 the largest Caribbean festival in North America, Caribana, takes place in Toronto. A tenth of the population is either Chinese or Filipino by ethnic origin. The airwaves are filled with a Babel of foreign languages; one radio station beams programs in 30 languages, while one television station shows films in many different languages.

The city government prints official notices in six languages, including Portuguese, Italian, Greek and Chinese. Drivers' tests are given in 12 languages. Half the children in state schools speak a native language other than English. Nevertheless, Ontario has maintained a fundamentally British air and sentiment. Its provincial flag still has a Union Jack prominently in the upper left-hand corner, and the word "Loyalist" has wholly positive connotations here.

Along with Alberta and British Columbia in the West, Ontario is one of Canada's high growth areas. Indeed, that cluster of cities around the western end of Lake Ontario extending from Niagara Falls and St. Catharines (north of Buffalo, New York) westward through Hamilton and Oshawa (the center of Canada's automotive industry) to Windsor (Detroit's twin-city) is called Canada's "golden horseshoe." While Canada's population between the 1996 and 2001 census takings grew by 4%, the population of the "golden horseshoe" had increased by 9.2%; 59% of Ontario's people and 22% of Canada's live there. Here is the center of gravity for Canadian industry, and its heart is Toronto, the country's capital of finance, culture, publishing and fashion. It is home to one out of seven Canadians. Almost 10 million people live within 75 kilometers (50 miles) of Toronto. The city has not only been spared the mountains of litter, the hundreds of square miles of graffiti and a high crime rate, but it has remained freer of the racial tensions

Canada

Vancouver, B.C.

which have plagued some American, British, and Canadian cities.

There has been a long-simmering feud with Michigan over the trucking of Toronto's trash to dump sites south of the border. Even presidential candidate John Kerry, fishing for votes in that important swing state, declared in 2004: "It's time to end the Canadian trash-dumping in Michigan!" He was supported by the Canadian-born ex-governor of Michigan, Jennifer M. Granholm. The U.S. Supreme Court has repeatedly ruled that garbage is a commodity that is as subject to free trade as any other product. It also travels on a two-way street. An American company, Clean Harbors Environmental Services, operates a hazardous-waste landfill incinerator in Ontario that treats the contaminated remains primarily from U.S. auto plants around the Great Lakes. In fact, the trucks pass each other at the border.

Toronto did not have the European sophistication of Montreal or the natural beauty of Vancouver, and for a long time it was called "Hogtown." That has all changed. Profiting from the shift of wealth from Montreal and fighting off the challenge of Calgary in the West, Toronto remains the financial heart of Canada. Its Bay Street is the equivalent of Wall Street in America, even though the Toronto Stock Exchange and most brokers and investment houses have moved to more spacious, modern quarters on other streets. Toronto is the home of the University of Toronto (Canada's largest and arguably most renown). The headquarters of ten of the 20 leading corporations are domiciled there. The next in order are Calgary (6), Vancouver and Montreal. It is the center for hundreds of suburbs and satellite towns involved in a broad range of economic activities and which economically nourish and are nourished by Toronto.

Asked in a 1989 Gallup poll "which province has the greatest future?" half of

Canadian respondents said Ontario. That changed as economic and political influence moved westward, especially toward oil-rich Alberta. A 2010 poll revealed how uncertain Ontarians have become: half responded that Ontario's influence in national affairs is declining and that the province is not treated with the respect it deserves.

Most of Canada's leading English-language publications are produced in Toronto. According to the *New York Times*, the *Toronto Star* is the largest newspaper in Canada by circulation as of 2021. It also introduced a weekly section of articles from the *New York Times*, as well as a reduced version of the *Times Book Review*. The *Globe and Mail* (ca. 291,571 daily [2013]) is owned by Canada's richest man, Ken Thomson and is one of Canada's most influential dailies. In 2010, it introduced a slightly smaller size and became the first major daily Canadian newspaper to print high-quality color on every page.

To compete with it, in 1998, Conrad Black, a peer of the British House of Lords and, in 2007 convicted in an American court on criminal charges related to company matters, founded the somewhat rebellious *National Post* (ca. 186,000 daily in 2015), which is willing to sneer at some of Canada's traditional values. The *National Post* still survives despite the determined efforts of the *Globe and Mail* to crush it. The *Post* is deeply in debt and has never made a profit. It filed for bankruptcy in 2010, but it emerged from it and competes in the market. The *Financial Post* is the equivalent of the *Wall Street Journal* in the U.S. Other dailies in Canada are regional newspapers, with the exception of the *Ottawa Citizen*. Unlike their counterparts in the U.S., Canadian papers have largely avoided precipitous financial decline and have not been quite as overwhelmed by digital competitors.

By century's end Black already controlled more than half of Canada's dailies from his corporate headquarters in Toronto, and he was the world's third-largest newspaper publisher. But he sold most of them, including his 50% stake in the *National Post*. That left most major English-language newspapers in the hands of five TV or telecom giants. CanWest, owned by Canada's most powerful media mogul, Izzy Asper, bought the *National Post* and 135 other daily newspapers from Black for $2.2 billion. This was the largest media deal in Canadian history. University of Toronto journalism professor, Vince Carlin, asserted, "This is not a healthy situation. There is competition in the United States. There is no competition here." Nevertheless, a 2002 study by Reporters Without Borders found that Canada ranked fifth in the world in terms of press freedom; the U.S. placed seventeenth.

Canada's second oldest magazine and most-read news magazine with three million readers, *Maclean's*, is produced in Toronto. It emphasizes Canadian news, but it gives some coverage to events in the U.S. as well. Reacting to slumping sales, it overhauled its management in 2005 and became livelier and more provocative. It seeks to avoid the criticism often leveled at the Canadian press and broadcasters that they are bland and politically correct. Financially strapped, it is largely online; its hard copies are reduced to one issue per month. Its French-language sister version is *l'Actualité*. Also published in Toronto is *Saturday Night*, a monthly that covers a multitude of subjects and is perceptive and well informed. It closely resembles *Harper's* and *Atlantic* in the United States. Finally, the women's monthly, *Chatelaine*, whose English- and French-language editions sell about 1.3 million copies, is produced in Toronto.

Toronto is filled with art galleries, museums, opera houses and more than 40 independent theater companies. It is a frequent location for first-run openings, and the Toronto Film Festival is a major event in North America. Its major league baseball team, the Blue Jays, and other athletic

teams play in the SkyDome, renamed in 2005 the Rogers Centre, a 60,000-seat indoor-outdoor stadium with a unique retractable roof. By century's end, it was insolvent, but for a while it symbolized a new era of urban dynamism, as did the CN Tower, which is twice as high as the Eiffel Tower. Torontonians no longer have to say that the best thing about their town is that it is close to New York City.

PRAIRIE PROVINCES: Manitoba, Saskatchewan and Alberta could generally be described with the words "flat, prairie, wheat and petroleum." They form a region of new economic opportunity and wealth. The West is the fastest growing part of Canada. The discovery of oil and natural gas primarily in Alberta in 1947 greatly helped to diversify the prairie economy. This region

always was and still is Canada's "breadbasket." Half of its area is covered by forest, but much of the other half is occupied by large farms, which are responsible for making Canada the world's second largest exporter of grain, behind the U.S.

The Prairie provinces have a very diverse ethnic mix. A resilient knot of francophones, some of them descendants of the Métis (a mixed race of French and Indian), have survived in Manitoba. Although they constitute only 6% of that province's population, they have been very successful in reasserting their rights to be schooled and to be spoken to in French. In this region, a quarter of the population is made up of non-Anglo-Saxon immigrants from Germany, Eastern Europe, Ukraine, and Russia. Entire villages or sections of towns are inhabited by persons whose every-day language is other than English, and one sees almost as many onion-shaped domes of Russian and Greek Orthodox churches in this region as grain elevators.

This region was never a frontier area, as was the American West, because of the different ways in which the two Wests were won. The American West was won by "six-shooters" and by settlers advancing before the American flag and the forces of "law and order." The Canadian West was largely organized by Mounted Police. Settlers attracted by governmental policies and land-grants traveled to their new homesteads on transcontinental railways, rather than in covered wagons.

Canada's Westerners are an independent-minded people with a strong sense of regional identity. They long felt that Ottawa's policies favored central Canada, whether that favoritism be expressed in

dictated freight rates on the railways, high interest rates set by banks headquartered in Montreal or Toronto, the high price tags on goods manufactured in the East which result from protective tariffs and federal subsidies, or attempts to force bilingualism on a people who, despite the many different languages they speak at home, wish to see English remain as Canada's only official language.

These Westerners have been confidently assertive in federal-provincial relations during the past decades. In 1979, for the first time, a westerner (Joe Clark, leader of the Conservative Party) became prime minister although he remained in office less than a year. They have been inclined to form protest parties, such as the New Democratic Party (NDP), the Social Credit Party, or the Reform Party (renamed in 2000 the Canadian Alliance and in 2004 the Conservative Party, whose leader, Stephen Harper, became prime minister in February 2006). All have played very important roles in both regional and federal politics. Thus, one sees in the Prairie provinces a bastion of both conservative politics and of Canada's brand of socialism.

Since cities in the prairies were settled mainly in the 20th century, they have a slightly different appearance than those in the East. They have fewer old buildings and narrow winding streets, but newer construction and broad thoroughfares. They also are very spread out, as are many cities in the American West. Winnipeg, the capital of Manitoba, resembles Denver. Here is Canada's commodity exchange, where buyers and sellers determine the price of grains. One can hear French spoken in the streets, especially in the suburb of St. Boniface. Also, one can visit the monument to and home of Louis Riel, the leader of the French-speaking Métis. He led a rebellion against Ottawa in 1885 but now receives a hero's homage because he fought for the rights of francophones in the West. Moreover, on May 24, 2019, Prime Minister Justin Trudeau apologized and provided an exoneration of the First Nations Chief, Poundmaker, of his 1885 convictions for "treason-felony" for his allegedly instigating violence in the 1885 Northwest Rebellion. Canada has no difficulty owning up to past injustices—although it seems to take many years to do so.

Another major metropolis in the prairies is Calgary. Perhaps no city in Canadian history ever experienced such a boom as this city. In 1947, large reserves of oil were discovered. The Leduc oilfield was North America's largest at the time. The world energy crisis beginning in 1973 made Alberta's oil extraordinarily precious, and the entire province's economy felt the immediate benefit of swollen oil revenues.

Baffin Island, Nunavut, with stone marker ("Inukshuk") at left built by the Inuit
Courtesy: Michael J. Hewitt

Canada

Almost overnight, Calgary became Canada's second-largest head office city, and easterners moved westward in one of the country's most massive migrations.

At one point, Calgary was growing at the astonishing rate of 2,500 newcomers a month. Americans joined this massive influx and now constitute a fifth of the city's population. Practically no new construction was necessary to accommodate the 1988 Winter Olympics in Calgary. With the recovery of Alberta's oil industry in the 1990s, prosperity returned to the city. However, with the fall of oil prices and the inability to build oil pipelines to the east and west of Canada and south to the United States a recession has overtaken Alberta. Yet, it remains a magnet for high tech companies and corporate head offices.

Alberta has displaced Montreal and Vancouver as Canada's biggest business and financial center after Toronto. Indeed Alberta, with a population of 4.3 (2018) million, is a magnet for residents of other provinces. Some speak of "an internal brain drain to Alberta," and the vice president of the Business Council of British Columbia noted: "It's almost as if we are creating a small version of the United States built right here into Canada."

The Calgary-Edmonton corridor has become the fasting growing economic region in Canada, boasting a per-capita GDP 40% higher than the national average.

The Prairie provinces and BC have replaced Ontario as the engine of Canada's economic growth. The West's combined GDP surpassed that of Ontario for the first time in 2008. Taken together, Alberta and British Columbia now have a higher population (ca. 7.5 million) than Quebec. Statistics Canada projects that the West will have almost a third of Canada's total population by 2031. The West is younger, has more babies, attracts more migrants, is more open to change, displays a higher degree of egalitarianism and shows less deference to authority.

With the election of Albertan Stephen Harper as prime minister in 2006, the

country's political and commercial centers of gravity shifted westward. However,

Alberta is vulnerable to the ups and downs of oil prices. The plunge below $30 per barrel in 2015 cast the province into recession. The price of oil has increased since then but Alberta has not yet recovered from the downturn and due to the lack of support from British Columbia and Quebec, as well as the blockage of the pipeline to the USA. The current (2019) Bill 12 in the Canadian parliament promises to land lock Alberta's oil again causing great concern in that province.

BRITISH COLUMBIA: This is Canada's window to the Pacific and the Far East, with which Canada maintains a growing volume of trade. Vancouver, Canada's largest port, is 350 miles closer to Tokyo than to Halifax. British Columbia (or "BC," as it is called) is a third larger than Texas. It is cut off from the rest of Canada by the Rocky Mountains, whose various ranges cover most of the province, forcing three-fourths of the province's people into the southwest corner around Vancouver. Because of its isolation and great distance from the rest of Canada, BC has an even more pronounced sense of regional pride than do the Prairie provinces. It shares the Canadian West's traditional distrust and hostility toward the East. It also has traditionally felt a certain kinship with the northwestern states in America, which it considered joining in the 19th century and with which it does a large volume of trade. The unnaturalness of east-west ties is felt more strongly in BC than in any other Canadian province. A cross-border alliance, called "Cascadia," encompasses an array of cooperative links between BC and the states of Washington and Oregon.

BC, with a population of 3.8 million, is a relatively prosperous province within the Canadian Confederation. It has very little arable land, but it possesses a panoply of mineral resources, almost unlimited hydroelectric power and huge forests, which provide its major product: timber. Its waters also produce a rich harvest of fish, including salmon. However, one does not see the countless quaint fishing villages along its coast, as one does in the Maritimes. The introduction of modern, long-range fishing vessels, and the existence of a few major processing and canning plants along a few rivers, especially the Fraser and the Skeena, have enabled the province's fishing industry to become centralized. BC's broad resource base has enabled the province to have considerable industrial growth and diversified production.

Victoria, the capital of BC, located on Vancouver Island. It is a city with a distinctive British air, complete with red double-decker buses and statues of the great 19th century queen for whom it was named. In 2010, *Maclean's* placed it on top

Population Density

☐ Less than 6 people per square mile
▨ 6-45 people per square mile
■ Over 45 people per square mile

of its ranking of Canada's "smartest" and most cultured cities. With only 78,000 inhabitants, it has two universities and two smaller colleges, its citizens are well-read, half its residents visit local museums, and it sustains a symphony, two ballets, an opera and a philharmonic choir.

The most important city in this province is Vancouver, with a population estimated to cross 2.4 million by the end of 2022 (up from its current 2.26 million), making it Canada's third largest city. It has a very mild climate by Canadian standards, and is, without question, one of the world's most beautiful cities. It boasts a magnificent physical setting of mountains and sea, and it has a dazzling city center and Canada's first domed stadium. In 2019, Mercer's Quality of Living Survey ranked Vancouver third in the world (after Vienna and Zurich) in terms of quality of life. No U.S. city was in the top 25, but Toronto, Ottawa, Montreal and Calgary joined Vancouver in that category. A 2009 examination by *Maclean's* named Vancouver the best-run city in Canada, and the Economist Intelligence Unit's business travel index placed it first in the world as a desirable business meeting location, followed by Toronto. Its image is being tarnished by rising brutal gang violence and drug and gun trade.

Vancouver is truly a world city. One fifth of its residents work for American companies. It has an ethnically diverse population, 30% of whom are immigrants and 40% of whom are of Asian origin. Half of the Asians are Chinese, giving rise to one of the city's controversial nicknames: Hongcouver. With only about 13% of Canada's population (2016), BC absorbs almost a fourth of all immigrants; 80% of those are Asian. Non-Whites comprised more than 40% of the city's population by 2005. It is one of the world's most integrated cities with 13% of young couples being inter-racial.

Its school system must struggle with the problem of teaching 55,900 pupils, 61% of whom speak a first language other than English. Almost half the school children in 1997 required English as a Second Language (ESL) courses. Such ESL instruction demands a growing share of shrinking education budgets. Pupils in Vancouver's Richmond School District represent 75 distinct languages and cultures. In Lord Strathcona Elementary School, 90% of the children are of Asian descent, and Chinese Cantonese interpreters must be present at PTA and parent-pupil meetings. In Grandview/Uuqinak'uuh Elementary School, 52% of the students are First Nations (Indians), and 30% are recent immigrants or refugees.

With the Chinese community comprising a fifth of the population, Vancouver

has Canada's most vibrant Chinatown, covering eight square blocks. This concentration has made the Chinese-language media—four newspapers, three radio stations and two TV stations—influential players in provincial and national politics. In the past, the predominant dialect in the city was Cantonese. But newcomers and visiting dignitaries now largely speak Mandarin.

All eyes were on Vancouver in February 2010 when it hosted the Winter Olympic Games. Canada emerged with more gold medals than any other country. These Games were a grand success by any definition.

THE NORTH: The Yukon, Northwest Territories, and Nunavut are vast, covering about 40% of Canada's land area. They are wild, cold, isolated, ruggedly beautiful and almost entirely uninhabited. Its few residents have to adjust to long, dark winters and short summers. The northern parts are Arctic regions of packed ice, frozen fjords, icebergs, countless islands and glaciers, 70% of which are melting. Living there is a hardy people, whom Americans call "Eskimo," meaning "meat-eaters," but who prefer to be called "Inuit," meaning "the people." About 51,000 of the world's Inuit live in Canada. They represent less than half the Arctic's aboriginal people, who in turn account for only 10% of the region's population. Their communities tend to be located on bays, river mouths, inlets or fjords; this reflects the fact that their lives were always tied to hunting, fishing and gathering.

During the past quarter century, the isolation of the Inuit has been decreasing, and mainstream Canadian life-styles have penetrated their communities. Traditional hunting and fishing activities are not as important for their economy as they once were. The Inuit have grown dependent on the comforts and conveniences of Canadian life: kayaks and dog sleds have by and large been replaced by canoes, motorized toboggans, snowmobiles, trucks and airplanes as their major means of transportation. Electricity, oil stoves and furnaces, schools, hospitals, films, television and

Chinese-Canadians in Vancouver

radio (which beam some programs in their language—Inuktitut, for which there is no uniform alphabet or spelling, and which has more than 40 words for "snow") have greatly changed life in the extreme North. Unfortunately, some of these changes have so disturbed or destroyed traditional roles and ties within the communities that alcoholism, drug abuse and suicide have become frighteningly commonplace among the Inuit.

South of this Arctic area is a vast region of tundra and permafrost, covered by forests, filled with wild animals, and inhabited mainly by Indians, called aboriginals or "First Nations" in Canada, who value their traditional identity. There are few roads and railways running northward into these areas, and the few cities there, such as Whitehorse, Yellowknife and Iqaluit, are small frontier towns, whose residents must become accustomed to paying high prices and having all but air links severed during much of the bitter winter.

As a whole, the Canadian North contains important natural resources. These are not distributed evenly over the entire area. The extremely high costs of extraction and transportation, as well as the impact of mining and drilling on native cultures, greatly limits the extent to which they can be exploited.

That this vast, sparsely populated northern expanse had to be defended necessitated close defense links with the United States. American defense planners were well aware that Canada lies directly between the U.S. and Russia. They were therefore more than willing to cooperate with the Canadians in creating NORAD

Canada

and in maintaining a costly Distant Early Warning (DEW) line of radars in the Canadian North in order to be able to detect any hostile penetration of North American airspace. The shortest distance between U.S.-based missiles and the strategic cities of the former Soviet Union—and vice-versa—was via Canada over the North Pole. This route is only 3,600 miles versus 8,000–10,000 miles parallel to the Equator.

To ensure that Arctic concerns are given a higher priority, the Chrétien government appointed the first aboriginal ambassador of Circumpolar Affairs, Mary May Simon, a longtime Inuit activist, to spearhead federal efforts to protect Arctic ecology. In 1996, an eight-nation Arctic Council was created, consisting of Canada, the United States, Russia, Denmark (Greenland), Finland, Iceland, Norway and Sweden; it has a permanent secretariat at Tromso in northern Norway. In addition, non-voting membership in the council with the same status of sovereign states has been granted to six indigenous Arctic peoples and the Inuit Circumpolar Conference (ICC), a non-governmental group that draws together Inuit representatives from Alaska, Greenland, Canada and Russia every three years to develop common policies. In 1989, it agreed to develop a standardized script. In April 2009, the ICC declared "sovereignty" over the Arctic's natural resources.

The ICC has become a vigorous lobby and has resisted efforts by the U.S., Russia and environmental groups to declare the polar bear an endangered species. It argues that this would hurt the local economies by, among other things, deterring American hunters from paying millions of dollars a year for the right to shoot them. The killing continues in Greenland and Canada under quotas set by territorial governments. Two-thirds of the world's estimated 25,000 polar bears roam the Canadian Arctic.

The Arctic Council also includes the Sami Council (representing Scandinavian aboriginals), the Association of Indigenous Peoples of the North of Russia, and the Aleuts on the islands between Alaska and Russia. The first foreign ministers' meeting of the members was held in Nunavut's capital, Iqaluit, in 1998. Canada is implementing its goal of a "Northern dimension" to Canadian foreign policy that strives to gain input from the peoples of the North rather than imposing "southern" values on them. Simon noted, "Northerners are really the pioneers of circumpolar cooperation."

PEOPLE

Unlike the United States, Canada is often described as a "mosaic," rather than a

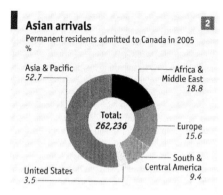

Asdian arrivals 2
Permanent residents admitted to Canada in 2005 %

Asia & Pacific 52.7

Africa & Middle East 18.8

Total: 262,236

Europe 15.6

South & Central America 9.4

United States 3.5

Source: *The Economist*

"melting pot." In many ways, this is accurate. In Canada, there are many population groups that speak different languages, or that are ethnically distinct from one another. Many vigorously resist assimilation with other Canadians; they are less inclined to lose their former identity in a larger "Canadianism," than have been most ethnic groups in the United States. The Canadian government recognizes this diversity by having an official policy of multiculturalism administered by a minister of state with cabinet rank.

Given the specific conditions of the country, this is an enlightened approach. It should be recognized, though, that this policy makes a virtue out of a necessity. Few British Canadians in the 18th and early 19th centuries foresaw that French Canadians would struggle so successfully against assimilation and that, one day, ambitious anglophone children would be flocking to French-immersion schools in order to get a leg up on those who cannot speak French. Multiculturalism in Canada grew out of the need to conciliate francophones and has been broadened to include other ethnic groups as well. Many francophones were uneasy about such broadening because it seemed to undercut their view of Canada as a union of *two* peoples, rather than as a collection of ethnic minorities in which francophones are merely one of many. Yet it was Quebec nationalism that necessitated the official policy of multiculturalism, which is of such benefit to other minorities as well.

Some Canadians need reminders that Canada is multicultural and multilingual whether they like it or not. When in 1983 the unilingual John Crosbie challenged the completely bilingual Brian Mulroney and Joe Clark for leadership of the Conservative Party, he declared that Canada's 3.7 million bilingual Canadians should not regard themselves as "some sort of aristocracy" from which the country's prime ministers would be drawn. The fact is, though, that no unilingual Canadian does have the chance to become prime minister any more. Crosbie's unfortunate

utterance completely destroyed his bid for leadership; Canada never was, is not and will not become a homogeneous, wholly English-speaking country.

Of course, terms like "mosaic" and "melting-pot" are over-simplifications in the case of both neighbors, even though they are not "myths," as some persons claim. Some suggest that Canada is really a "mosaic of mosaics." The goal has never been to transform Canada into a land of isolated communities, but to accommodate cultural differences in a way that newcomers can be integrated into a shared civic space.

Since the 1960s many countries have experienced ethnic revivals, including the United States. The number of black, brown and yellow faces, "hyphenated Americans," bilingual schools and Spanish-language documents and signs reveal the limits of cultural and ethnic assimilation in the United States. American blacks have successfully demanded *group* rights for people of their race, as opposed to the traditional American emphasis on *individual* rights, which has been an American creed since the country's founding. Thus, the United States has also moved in the direction of a "mosaic" society.

Any implication that each "stone" in the Canadian "mosaic" shares equally in the overall product is misleading. To use Orwellian language, some Canadians "are more equal than others." A Canadian's race, language and/or ethnic background are still socially relevant. For instance, only slightly over 3% of all Canadian marriages and common-law unions are mixed race, and most of them are likely to be between Asian-Canadians and Caucasians. Political, economic and social power is still held by people of European heritage. For example, of the 200 top corporate chief executives surveyed by the *Financial Post* in 1997, only seven were non-white, and they were all Asian.

Nevertheless, there is something remarkable about the way the parts stick together. Former Saskatchewan Premier Roy Romanow described it this way: "Each province, territory and region, plus our many cultures and different stories, can be likened to individual pearls making up a beautiful necklace, connected to each other by the strand of shared destiny. That strand, however, is fragile and requires constant attention."

Population Groups

The largest "stone" in the "mosaic" is the British one. By the mid-1980s, Canadians of British ancestry made up a little more than 40% of the total population, a proportion which has steadily decreased over the years, even though 76% of all Canadians claimed in the 1981 census

Canada

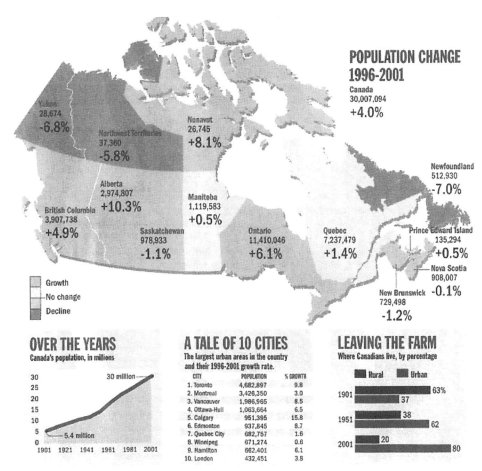

POPULATION CHANGE 1996-2001

Canada
30,007,094
+4.0%

Yukon 28,674 **-6.8%**

Northwest Territories 37,360 **-5.8%**

Nunavut 26,745 **+8.1%**

Newfoundland 512,930 **-7.0%**

Alberta 2,974,807 **+10.3%**

Manitoba 1,119,583 **+0.5%**

British Columbia 3,907,738 **+4.9%**

Saskatchewan 978,933 **-1.1%**

Ontario 11,410,046 **+6.1%**

Quebec 7,237,479 **+1.4%**

Prince Edward Island 135,294 **+0.5%**

Nova Scotia 908,007

New Brunswick 729,498 **-0.1%**

-1.2%

- Growth
- No change
- Decline

OVER THE YEARS
Canada's population, in millions

30 million

5.4 million

1901 1921 1941 1961 1981 2001

A TALE OF 10 CITIES
The largest urban areas in the country and their 1996-2001 growth rate.

CITY	POPULATION	% GROWTH
1. Toronto	4,682,897	9.8
2. Montreal	3,426,350	3.0
3. Vancouver	1,986,965	8.5
4. Ottawa-Hull	1,063,664	6.5
5. Calgary	951,395	15.8
6. Edmonton	937,845	8.7
7. Quebec City	682,757	1.6
8. Winnipeg	671,274	0.6
9. Hamilton	662,401	6.1
10. London	432,451	3.8

LEAVING THE FARM
Where Canadians live, by percentage

- Rural
- Urban

	Rural	Urban
1901	63%	37
1951	38	62
2001	20	80

Source: *Maclean's*

to have at least one British ancestor. By 1997, the UK had fallen to tenth place as a source country for Canadian immigrants. Of course, this grouping is not as homogeneous as it might seem at first glance: it includes Scots and Welsh, who are not English, and it encompasses Irish Protestants from Ulster and Catholics from the rest of Ireland, groups which are by no means interchangeable.

The second largest "stone" is the French one, which makes up 22.9% of the total population (2001) and is declining. The French were the first Canadians, and they now constitute the overwhelming majority of Quebec's population, about 40% of New Brunswick's, 5% of Ontario's, and 6% of Manitoba's. Because of Quebec nationalism since the 1960s and the federal government's response to it, francophones' opportunities within the entire Canadian Confederation have been markedly improved. Its oil-based economy attracts immigrants from all over Canada. Therefore, Alberta is experiencing the country's greatest growth in francophone population—12.6% each year. It is the only province since 1996 to experience an increase in francophone children under age 5. The country as a whole is experiencing an uptick in the number of French moving to Canada.

The third largest group of Canadians is of German ancestry, constituting 3.3% of the total. This group is perhaps the most fully assimilated minority in all of Canada, although there is a notable exception to this generalization: the Hutterites in the Prairie provinces, who came to Canada from South Dakota during the First World War because of their refusal to serve in the armed forces. They are a religious sect similar to the Amish and Mennonites, except that they believe in the communal ownership of property and rearing of children. They shun contact with the outside world as much as possible. On grounds of faith, they object to being photographed for their driver's licenses. Then come Italians, who make up 2.8% of the population and whose numbers have grown enormously since the Second World War. One Canadian citizen, Gino Bucchino, even won a seat in the Italian parliament in 2006.

In fifth place are Ukrainians, who make up 1.5% of all Canadians. Canada has the world's third-largest Ukrainian population after Ukraine itself and Russia. During the First World War about 5,000 Ukrainian Canadians were interned in a fit of ethnic fear, their property was confiscated, and many were forced to perform hard labor. Former Prime Minister Paul Martin

acknowledged that this was "a dark day in Canadian history" and offered both a formal apology and $25 million to Ukrainians and other groups for educational exhibits and memorials. Roy Romanow, whose father left Ukraine in the 1920s, remembered growing up in Saskatoon: "Our family's universe was comprised of the Ukrainian hall, St. George's Ukrainian Greek Catholic Cathedral, our schools, and the shopping area of 20th Street just a few blocks away. We could go to church, visit friends and neighbours and buy our necessities without using either one of Canada's two official languages." Ukrainian communities in Canada were deeply concerned for, and acted to support those still living there in light of the horrendous destruction caused by the Russian invasion in early 2022.

The same was true of many other immigrants, including Icelanders, whose descendants in Canada outnumber the population of Iceland itself. The largest congregation of Finns outside of Scandinavia lives in Canada, especially in Thunder Bay, Ontario.

Canada was always a land of immigration. Today there are over 200 immigrant groups there, and more than a fifth of Canadians were born outside the country; the figure is 12.2% in the U.S. and 4.8% in the United Kingdom. Forty members of the 2006 parliament were born outside Canada. The 2016 census confirmed that Canada now has the highest proportion of foreign-born persons since 1931. In 2016, the foreign-born population represents 21.9% of the total population, the highest proportion of G8 countries. When the data of the 2021 census are updated, these percentages may change.

Immigrants, only 44% of whom come with the ability to speak English or French, were responsible for the 4% growth of the Canadian population between 1996 and 2002. In 2016, however, 93.2% could conduct a conversation in French of English. Nevertheless, Canada's population is aging: 37% are over 45, increasing to 43% in 2011.

An important demographic trend in Canada is the decreasing percentage of citizens of European heritage, from 79.7% in 1971 to only 66.9% in 1981, and 13.7% in 2011 and 11.6% in 2016. The reason for this is a decreasing birth rate (1.66 children per woman in 2011) and a change in the composition of immigrants to Canada. In the 1960s, the Canadian Parliament liberalized the country's immigration policy, opening the door to Asians, Africans, Caribbean islanders, Latin Americans and other groups from the third world, which make up more than three-fourths of all immigration to Canada. Their percentages of Canada's total population changed

Canada

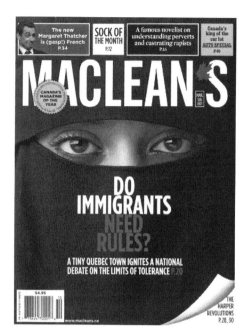

noticeably from 1971 to 1981: Asians grew from 4.2% to 14%. In 2006, Asia accounted for 52.7% of new arrivals, while 15.6% were from Europe, 18.8% from Africa and the Middle East, 9.4% from Latin America and the Caribbean, and only 3.5% from the U.S. Those coming from the Caribbean have fallen sharply.

The top countries of origin for immigrants during the past five years (2011-2016) are Asians (including those from the Middle East), who made up 61.8% of newcomers, which is slightly higher than the 2006 census. Immigration from Africa, Caribbean, and Central and South America increased slightly. Asian countries accounted for seven out of ten of the immigrant countries which included: the Philippines, India, China, Iran, Pakistan, Syria, and South Korea. They bring with them much university education and potential for high-paid occupations.

By 1996, the number of European immigrants had for the first time fallen below 50% of the total immigrant population. As of 2016, only 27.7% of immigrants were from Europe. The vast majority of the foreign-born population live in four provinces: Ontario, Quebec, British Colombia and Alberta (2016). Seven out of ten lived in the largest census metropolitan areas: Toronto, Montreal and Vancouver (2016). The magnets are Toronto (46% of immigrant in 2016), Vancouver (40.8%) and Montreal (23.4%), making these three metropolitan areas increasingly distinct from the rest of Canada. Only 6% of newcomers chose to live outside major urban areas, and Canada's immigration policy seeks to attract young, large foreign families to rural Canada. Toronto is now home to 62 different ethnic groups numbering

more than 10,000 people and 15 groups with more than 100,000. Geography professor Larry S. Bourne of the University of Toronto admits: "We just don't know how a Toronto of the future, which is 60 percent nonwhite with 110 different ethnic groups and languages, is going to relate to the rest of Canada."

The first Chinese came to Canada in 1858 to work as laborers in the gold mines that had begun to be opened during the Fraser River gold rush. From 1881 to 1884, they were used as laborers to construct the Canadian Pacific Railway. Many died doing their dangerous work, and from 1923 to 1947 they were banned from entry altogether. By 2004, they constituted 16% of Canada's immigrants and more than 3% of the total population (1.1 million). The Philippines is now Canada's largest source of immigrants, followed by China. Chinese wield considerable political and economic influence, and they form a crucial link in the country's growing trade with China. Acceding to a long-standing demand in 2006, the Canadian government offered both an apology and compensation for their past mistreatment.

During World War II, as in the U.S., thousands of Japanese who immigrated were suspected of disloyalty and received the same undignified treatment as Japanese-Americans: the 22,000 Japanese-Canadians, 17,000 of whom had Canadian citizenship, were forced to resettle in internment camps deep in the interior of the country, "to safeguard the defences of the Pacific coast of Canada." Their property was disposed in an attempt to prevent them from returning.

Most Canadians today regret that action, which Brian Mulroney called "one of the greatest blots on civil liberties ever inflicted on citizens of this country," and in 1988 the government agreed to pay about $291 million in compensation. From 1933 to 1945 Canada accepted only 5,000 Jewish refugees from Nazi Germany, compared with 200,000 by the U.S. and 15,000 by Bolivia.

Asians poured in from war-torn Indochina, including thousands of "boat-people" from Vietnam. At the end of the 1990s an organized attempt to smuggle Chinese into the country sparked angry demands for tighter controls. Chinese-based gangs receive down payments of up to $60,000 to drop Chinese onto Canada's shores. They are moved through an underground network to eastern Canada or the United States, where they are forced to work off their debts through low-paying jobs or prostitution. Canada's large Chinese community denounces these illegal Chinese as queue-jumpers.

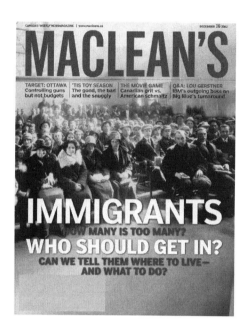

In the past, Canadians have viewed each successive wave of immigration with suspicion; however, the fact that most newcomers are now non-white makes their reception even frostier. Pollster Allan Gregg noted, "you do not have to scratch too deep to find racist views." Despite Canadians' growing uneasiness about the goal of a "cultural mosaic," Ottawa passed a multiculturalism act in 1988 making Canada "in essence a microcosm of the world." Officials talk about Canada as a "community of communities," and the government provides more money to ethnic societies than it spends to encourage immigrants to become Canadians. Nevertheless, anglophone Canadians regard multiculturalism as central to their national identity. According to a 2014 poll, they rank it below universal health care and the Canadian flag, but above ice hockey, the Mounties and the Queen.

Polls in 1994 indicated that 72% of Canadian respondents believed at that time that the multicultural mosaic was not working and should be replaced by an American-style cultural melting pot, which insists that immigrants put their ethnic differences aside and embrace American values and customs. Some Canadians fear that the waves of newcomers will alter their way of life.

An example of this attitudinal change was the outcry against the decision to permit male Sikhs, who are required to wear turbans, to continue wearing them after becoming Mounties, as Sikhs were already allowed to do in the Canadian armed forces, unless safety is an issue. In 2006, the Supreme Court of Canada struck down the Montreal school board's ban on Sikh ceremonial daggers (kirpans), citing freedom of religion. It did allow the boards to restrict

An Eastern Orthodox church, Thunder Bay, Ontario

Now constituting roughly a fifth of the population (about twice that in the U.S.), the numbers of immigrants allowed to enter Canada each year had risen from 84,000 in 1985 to over 300,000 in 2019, including 44,610 Syrian refugees. Those with job offers are favored. More than half are skilled workers and their dependents picked for their potential contribution to the economy. Half have college degrees (only 27% in the U.S.). Family reunification accounts for 28% of immigrants (compared with almost two-thirds in the U.S.). Canada now takes in .85% of its population in new immigrants every year (compared to .6% for Australia and .3% for the U.S.), and most of them head for the three largest cities: Toronto, Vancouver and Montreal. Most learn a good deal about Canadian history, politics, culture and geography. This was tested in 2009 by the Dominion Institute: given a mock examination that mirrored the citizenship test, 70% of immigrants passed it, but only 40% of Canadians were able to do so. Asked what Canada's defining symbols were, both immigrants and Canadians ranked the maple leaf and hockey at the top.

A majority of immigrants now admitted are members of visible minorities, particularly South Asians, Arabs and Blacks. They join the 11.47% of Canada's population that, according to the 2011 census, were visible minorities. This varied from 25.9% in BC, 19.1% in Ontario (where some communities, such as Markham, had as many as 53%) and 18.4% in Alberta to only 11% in Quebec, .9% in PEI and .8% in Newfoundland. Prime Minister Justin Trudeau named a refugee, Ahmed Hussen, as "immigration czar."

the size of such daggers and require that they be sheathed and out of sight. Sikhs make up 2% of Canada's population. Justin Trudeau's cabinet has four Sikh members including the defense minister. The leader of the opposition New Democratic Party, Jagmeet Singh, is also Sikh.

In 2007, a debate broke out in Quebec over how specific Canadians are willing to give advice and set rules and guidelines concerning how immigrants should live. Some Canadians argued that one should be able to expect "reasonable accommodation" of newcomers, especially Muslims, who constitute only 3% of Canada's population (6% by 2050), in adapting to the language, attitudes and lifestyles of the majority population. A 2018 government online survey conducted by the Privy Council Office found that Canadians feel that they are being asked to change and adapt too much and 59% believed many immigrants don't adopt "Canadian values." Further, a 2017 Angus Reid Survey poll found that 53% of Canadians thought the country did too much to accommodate religious diversity. For example, Muslim parents in Toronto requested that their children be exempted from mandatory music classes, citing Islam's ban on listening to or playing musical instruments.

There were geographic differences: 77% of Quebecers thought that immigrants should fully adapt, compared with 49% in Ontario. These results were confirmed two years later, in 2009, when 62% of Canadians believed that laws and norms should not be modified to accommodate minorities (74% in Quebec). In 2017, Quebec banned women from wearing face coverings when providing or receiving public services. In rare cases, hatred can get the upper hand. In Ste-Foy in 2017, a Québécois student entered Quebec City's largest mosque and murdered six Muslims.

The Quebec government sponsored a long series of sometimes inflammatory public hearings on the subject and concluded that conflicts between lifelong *Québécois* and immigrants are rare, even if highly publicized in the media. Nevertheless, in 2010 the Quebec government passed legislation requiring woman to take off their veils and show their faces when receiving government services. Bill 94 was the first legislation in North America to ban face coverings in any government building, including schools and universities. A poll revealed that 95% of Quebecois and three-fourths of non-Quebecers approved of the law. Support for accommodation was highest in the Atlantic provinces, the Prairies and Alberta. In 2012, Canada's immigration minister, Jason Kenney, banned face veils worn by immigrants taking the citizenship oath. However, the Supreme Court of Canada ruled later that year that female witnesses could under some circumstances cover their faces for religious reasons when testifying in court.

There are some doubts as to whether the traditional pattern of assimilation works any more. In the past, immigrants tended to congregate in enclaves, and then their children and grandchildren mastered English or French, moved out and integrated with Canadians. That does not always work these days. Incomes and employment rates are lower for immigrant families, and offspring of visible minorities reportedly tend to feel less Canadian and experience more racism than their parents.

Miss Universe Natalie Glebova

Canada

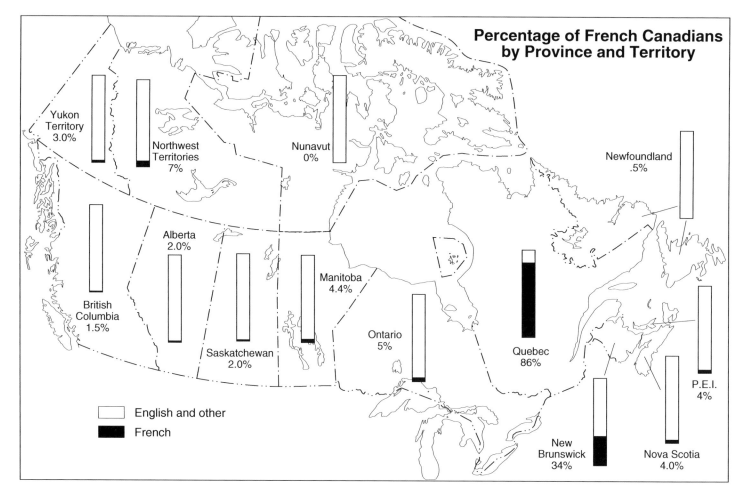

Percentage of French Canadians by Province and Territory

Yukon Territory 3.0%

Northwest Territories 7%

Nunavut 0%

Newfoundland .5%

British Columbia 1.5%

Alberta 2.0%

Manitoba 4.4%

Ontario 5%

Quebec 86%

Saskatchewan 2.0%

New Brunswick 34%

Nova Scotia 4.0%

P.E.I. 4%

English and other

French

The government ordered that greater priority be given to immigrants with high job skills and competence in English or French than to those joining families. In 2002, a point system was introduced that assigned points for such things as years in school, numbers of university degrees, age, working experience and language skills; it favors higher-skilled and higher earning persons. This created problems since foreigners with trade skills needed in the labor market often do not qualify. This made certain labor shortages even worse and sparked discussion on how to make immigration reflect the country's new economic and demographic needs. Also some who get in through the point system have difficulties applying their education due to discrimination, language handicaps or the problem of having their credentials recognized. By 2007, four-fifths of skilled immigrants to Canada had a university degree, but their earnings lagged behind those of native Canadians. By contrast, immigrants to the U.S. with college degrees earn more than their American counterparts. Nevertheless, immigrants to Canada managed in 2012 to send an estimated $23.4 billion in remittances back to their families overseas. In 2017, fearing

deportation from the U.S., a storm of Italians illegally crossed unguarded border areas in upstate New York seeking asylum. Authorities had to create temporary tent encampments and open the Montreal Olympic Stadium to house them. Half the applicants were rejected.

A stunning and successful immigrant is Natalie Glebova. A shy 12-year old who stepped off a plane from Russia in 1994 speaking only a few words of English, Glebova's family settled in Toronto and she graduated in IT from Ryerson University. In 2005, she was crowned Miss Universe, the second Canadian to wear the crown after Karen Baldwin in 1982. In 2012, Jenna Talackova, who had undergone a sex change at age 19, failed to win the Miss Universe crown, but the Canadian beauty captured the title of Miss Congeniality. Canada's Miss World candidate in 2016, Chinese–Canadian Amastasia Lin, infuriated China by publicly criticizing its human rights abuses.

The July 2006 war in Lebanon prompted a lively discussion over what it means to be a citizen and what responsibilities Canada has toward its dual citizens living abroad; 15,000 Canadian passport holders were evacuated from that war-torn

country to safety at a cost to the Canadian taxpayer of almost $100 million. How is it that 50,000 "Canadians" lived in Lebanon? They constitute about 1.3% of the total population and more citizens than the U.S., Britain, and Germany combined have living there.

Canada permits dual citizenship since 1977. Among the best known dual citizens is former Governor General Michaëlle Jean (Haitian). All that is required to get a Canadian passport is three-years of residency. Many then leave the country and become what critics call "Canadians of convenience," with no ties to the country except an additional passport. Indeed, 40% of the Chinese who went to Canada in their working years during the late 1990s left the country for higher-paying jobs in Hong Kong or the U.S. Many Indo-Canadians also moved on. As many as half the Canadians who move to the U.S. are born outside of Canada.

They can vote in overseas elections, as well as in Canadian. Unlike American citizens, Canadians are not required to pay Canadian taxes no matter where they live. Therefore, Ottawa has no idea how many dual citizens live abroad, or even inside of Canada. The Asia Pacific Foundation of

Canada calculates that there are 2.7 million overseas passport holders, roughly 9% of the population. That would represent proportionally the world's fourth-largest Diaspora, and it includes some of Asia's wealthiest people. An estimated quarter of a million reside in Hong Kong alone. Close to a million live in the U.S.

Canada faces a tormenting dilemma about what kind of help it can offer to the world's 21.5 million political refugees and who precisely is a "political refugee." For example, after 2007 the number of claimants from former communist countries in Europe shot up. The top source were Roma (Gypsies) from Hungary, who maintain that they face life-threatening discrimination at home. Only 2% were accepted in 2010. The backlog of individual applicants for visas, the increase in the number of refugees around the globe, and the tighter immigration controls in other nations all contribute to an illegal stampede to Canada—not unlike what the U.S. is experiencing at its southern border.

Every year about 25,000 persons claim refugee status in Canada. Once the claim is made, the newcomers are entitled to all the legal rights and benefits of Canadian citizens. They are allowed to work for at least four years and receive free medical care and social assistance for years while their cases are processed and appealed. As in the U.S., more than half of refugee claims are approved, compared with only about 15% in most countries. Even if they are ultimately rejected, they have a good prospect of never being removed. In 2007, there was a backlog of about 50,000 unexecuted deportation orders. All Canadians agree that they need an orderly and selective infusion of immigrants in order to keep their country strong and healthy. But critics are divided over whether too many or too few illegal newcomers are being permitted to stay. Many Canadians think that the country's present immigration system is unable to handle the problem.

Attitudes hardened after the September 11, 2001, terrorist attacks in New York and Washington. They destroyed the prior assumption that all newcomers to Canada shared its fundamental values. Ottawa expanded police powers and the use of preventive arrests to deal with immigrants or refugees who might be involved in terrorist activities. These measures especially worry Canada's diverse population of more than 600,000 Muslims (about 3% of the population) from dozens of nationalities, upwards to 44 different ethnicities, and many different languages, cultures, economic and political backgrounds. Roughly half were born in Canada. Of those born abroad, about a third is Arab-Muslim, and another third is from Pakistan and India. More than 148,000 speak Arabic as their mother tongue.

One third of Canada's Muslims said in 2004 that their lives had changed for the worse after September 11, while 22% thought their lives had changed for the better because they now have the opportunity for greater dialogue and debate. An opinion survey in 2009 revealed that 45% of Canadians believed that mainstream Islam encourages violence. In a 2017 poll, 62% of respondence agreed that Islamaphobia is a problem. At the same time, B'nai Brith Canada reported that an unfortunate consequence of the post-September 11 tension was an increase in anti-Semitic violence usually involving young Arab and Muslim men.

In 2011 voters in Calgary elected Naheed Nenshi, a visible-minority Muslim academic as the first Muslim mayor of a major Canadian city. The son of immigrants, he won a scholarship to do graduate study at Harvard after graduating from the University of Calgary. This city's dynamic economy and cosmopolitan character have attracted more immigrants per capita than Montreal; one out of four inhabitants is a visible minority.

Hate crimes are also rising against Muslims, even at universities. Sometimes compromises would lessen tensions. An example was the request by Muslim art students at the University of Western Ontario to be given an alternate assignment instead of having to sketch nude models. The university rejected this. At the same time, more than 80% of respondents in a 2007 CBC poll of the Muslim community said they are broadly satisfied with their lives in Canada; 73% were "very proud" to be Canadian, and only 17% sensed that Canadians were hostile to Islam. In another poll, a mere 6% of Canadians claimed to be uneasy about the idea of a Muslim living next door. Rapid change is often most difficult to absorb. From 1991 to 2001 Canada's Muslim population doubled. This makes Islam the country's fifth largest religion and the second largest in every big city except Vancouver. This will rise even more with the influx of at least 25,000 Syrians fleeing violence in their country.

One immigrant group that is shrinking in Canada is Americans; from 1971 to 1981 their percentage of the Canadian population dropped from 9.3% to 8.06%. Canada's immigration laws make it more difficult to enter. In the 1980s, two times more Canadians moved to the U.S. than *vice versa*. Nevertheless, Canada remains the favorite destination for American expatriates, followed by Mexico and Britain. In 2019, the number of Americans settling in Canada—10,800—was more than double the number in 2000 (5,800) and a 30-year high. The most common reason was the labor market. Their challenges in adjusting were such that the first American ex-pat support group was formed in Vancouver. The 60 or so regular members not only socialize with each other but discuss Canadian pet peeves, such as Americans' habits of talking loudly and neglecting to take off their shoes when entering a Canadian's house.

A visible portion of those former Americans is black. While it is true that the Underground Railway before the American Civil War extended all the way into Canada and that abolitionism was strong in Canada during the first half of the 19th century, slavery did exist there for more than 200 years. It had been introduced in New France in 1628 and was not abolished until the British Emancipation Act of 1833.

Even after emancipation, blacks in Canada continued to suffer discrimination and tended to be confined to all-black ghettos in the larger cities. Further black immigration from the United States was never officially barred, but blacks were normally prevented from crossing the border on all kinds of specious grounds, such as disease or inability to withstand Canada's harsh climate. Reports reveal that black children suffered violence and abuse in a Halifax orphanage. Discrimination has declined now, but it still exists in employment and housing, and racial prejudice has not been purged from Canadian social life. Festering racial tension in Montreal, Halifax and Toronto confirm that. Of course, not all Canadian blacks, who make up 4% of the population, are from the United States. Many have poured in from Africa, the U.K., and the Caribbean.

Ex-National Chief Shawn Atleo
Assembly of First Nations

Canada

Some, such as Haitians, do not speak English, and those who settled in Montreal have had difficulties in becoming equal citizens in Quebec society. Such diversity has meant that blacks remain the least cohesive of Canada's minority groups; they form distinct communities whose members arrived at different times.

Individuals can rise to prominence. A notable example was Ontario's former lieutenant general, Lincoln Alexander, who passed away in 2012. Born in Toronto, he was the son of Caribbean immigrants. He became Canada's first black member of parliament, first black cabinet minister (of labor), and first black lieutenant governor. Ex-Governor General Michaëlle Jean, who subsequently became secretary-general of La Francophone, was born and raised in Haiti. The stunning world record in the 100-yard dash set by Ben Johnson in 1987 focused attention on Canadian blacks. An immigrant from Jamaica, he especially did Canadians' hearts good by beating the brash, flag waving American, Carl Lewis, whose cocky manner epitomized that which irks many Canadians about Americans. However, Olympic gold turned to dust when a urine test following his 1988 victory revealed that the now-disgraced Johnson had used performance-enhancing steroids. The 1996 Olympic Games produced a new hero: Donovan Bailey, who won the 100-meter sprint without the aid of drugs. He did manage to ignite a national furor when he said to a *Sports Illustrated* interviewer that Canada is as racist as the U.S.

Aboriginal Peoples

One minority of particular importance to Canadians and their governments is the native Inuit, Métis and Indian population, which constitute only 1.4 million (about 4.3%; in BC 17%) of all Canadians. It is growing six times the rate of the general Canadian population. In fact, the Aboriginal population increased 42.5% from 2006 to 2016. No one questions the fact that they were the first humans to settle what is now Canada, having migrated at least 12,000 years ago over the Bering Strait, a narrow stretch of water, about 50 miles wide, separating Siberia from Alaska. The Inuit remained in the Arctic North, while other tribes moved southward to the more temperate climate. Anthropologists still do not agree upon exactly when they came and how they crossed the Bering Strait, nor can they find any lingual connection between the 58 Indian languages and dialects spoken in Canada and languages spoken in Asia today.

When the first Europeans began to settle Canada in the 16th century, there were already an estimated 200,000 Indians and a few thousand Inuit living rather evenly distributed there. Culturally none had advanced beyond the stone-age. Most sustained themselves by hunting and fishing, but a few tribes, such as the Iroquois, had begun to establish semi-permanent settlements and had begun to derive a part of their livelihood from agriculture. They were indispensable to the first Europeans, teaching them how to survive in the rugged and cold North American setting.

There are about 553,000 "Status Indians" (also called "First Nations people") registered under the Indian Act of Canada. They belong to 633 different bands (tribes, averaging 650 persons, with the largest numbering 18,600—the Six Nations of the Grand River in Ontario), and about 326,000 of them live on 2,300 reservations, which are largely self-governing. Ontario has the largest native population, and BC has the greatest number of bands—197. There are also about 405,000 "Non-Status Indians," who do not enjoy special benefits. Many women married non-Indians, and other Indians gave up their status as Indians. Of registered Indians living off reservations who have children, 70% have their kids with non-status partners thereby relinquishing their registration entitlements.

The Canadian government's policy since 1970 of encouraging Indians to assimilate with Canadian society has led to no dramatic changes. Since the birth rate on reservations is about the same as Indians who leave, the reservations' populations are remaining stable. Forty-four percent of natives live in cities. Because of their high birth rate (twice the national average), aboriginals are Canada's youngest and fastest-growing ethnic group. About two-thirds are younger than 35, and half are under 25.

The federal government runs schools on Indian reserves. By 2004, one in four schoolchildren in Manitoba and Saskatchewan were aboriginal. The infant mortality rate is double the Canadian average, and half the children live in poverty. The high school graduation rate for aboriginals in 2013 was 36%, about half that of non-natives. A depressing statistic is that a First Nation boy is more likely to go to jail than graduate from high school. Compared with the national average in 2004, aboriginals on reservations have only half the national average income, a lower life expectancy (68 years vs. 80 for men, 75 vs. 84.2 for women), and greater dependence upon social assistance; 40% are on welfare. Canada as a whole is always ranked toward the top of the UN's annual Human Development Index, but its aboriginals alone would rank only 63rd.

Nevertheless, comparisons of the 1981 and 2001 census figures show that there has been some improvement in the social conditions of urbanized aboriginals. From a half to two-thirds of aboriginal youths age 15 to 24 attended school in 2001, as opposed to only a third to a half two

Stanley Park, Vancouver, BC   Credit: Province of British Columbia

decades earlier. The high school dropout rate in 2011 for urbanized aboriginals was 43% versus 60% for Inuit and reservation aboriginals and only 10% for other Canadians. More attend and graduate from institutions of higher learning although only 9% of Métis, 7% of First Nations and 4% of Inuit have university degrees, compared with one-quarter of non-aboriginal Canadians. More of those in urban areas are employed, and fewer depend on welfare assistance.

Not only do Indians occupy huge tracts of Canadian territory, but they have a wide variety of special relations, both by treaty and by legislation, with the rest of Canada. About half the registered Indians, mainly those living in the three Prairie provinces and Ontario, receive treaty payments as a result of prior agreements with the British Crown. Those rights were incorporated in the 1982 constitution. Still, the Canadian government continues to face difficult challenges from Indian and Métis (French-Indian) groups stemming from unsettled claims, the problems of defining who should be considered as a registered Indian, and what precisely the natives' rights should be. So controversial are some of these questions that Canadians were not yet prepared in 1982 to spell out native rights in their new constitution.

Native frustration exploded in 1990, only weeks after the rancorous Meech Lake debate designating Quebec as a "distinct society" had already laid bare the intercommunal fractures in Canadian society. It had failed to be ratified because a Cree Indian representative in Manitoba's legislative assembly, Elijah Harper, had singlehandedly prevented that body from voting for it because it ignored native rights.

In Oka, Quebec, 18 miles west of Montreal, Mohawk Indians from the nearby Kanesatake reserve, joined by warriors from the United States, protested a proposed expansion of a local golf course into what they claimed was their ancestral land. Ottawa agreed to buy the land and turn it over to the Mohawks, but militants seized upon the situation to publicize wider native grievances, including demands for sovereignty. Mulroney categorically stated that "native self-government does not now, and cannot ever, mean sovereign independence."

A fatal clash on July 11, 1990, was tinder for a massive escalation, as the violence moved to Montreal, where Mohawks blocked the Mercier Bridge, one of the main arteries connecting the island of Montreal with the southern shore of the St. Lawrence, creating immense inconveniences for commuters. All over Canada, Indians showed their support by mounting demonstrations and blockades of roads and rail lines. The Quebec police

were unable to control the violence, and the provincial government requested Ottawa to send troops to quell the uprising. After 90 days of skirmishes and negotiations, the Indians surrendered, leaving Canadians perplexed about how to deal with the dilemma of native claims to more than half of Canada's land.

After that standoff, the Quebec police, RCMP and politicians stayed out of the Kanesatake community of 2,000 Mohawks, located at the far edge of northwest Montreal. This left a void that, according to elected Grand Chief James Gabriel, was filled by three dozen or so organized criminals, who traffic in cigarettes, alcohol, drugs, weapons and illegal immigrants. Mohawks do not regard themselves as Canadian. In 2010, they evicted 25 non-natives from their reserve just south of Montreal. First Nations have the right to determine who can live on their reserves.

Natives demand respect in symbolic ways as well. They blocked the naming of a road in Whitehorse, Yukon, after the author Jack London, who had once traveled in the territory. He was charged with having written insulting observations about aboriginals and having advocated white supremacy, charges that some literary experts dispute. In 2006, violence again erupted, this time in Caledonia, 80 km (50 miles) southwest of Toronto. When a new housing development broke ground on land claimed by the Six Nations Iroquois Confederacy, aboriginals occupied the site.

Much more peaceful protests began the end of 2012. Indians blocked roads and railways, performed impromptu dances in shopping malls and chanted outside the office of ex-Prime Minister Harper, whom they accused of neglect. One female Cree chief, Theresa Spence, pitched a tepee near the parliament and went on a partial six-week hunger strike, refusing solid food. Canada spends over $11 billion a year on its aboriginal population.

As a whole, Indians and the estimated 153,000 surviving Métis are among Canada's poorest citizens despite the various forms of state assistance available. They are plagued by unemployment, and many live on welfare. Their alcoholism rate is 13 times that among whites, their life expectancy is eight years less, infant mortality is twice as high, and their suicide rate is three times higher (six times among youth). Aboriginals account for as much as 8% of HIV infection, a higher percentage than any other ethnic group. About a quarter of new cases involve the native population. One reason is the large numbers of young aboriginals who travel from inner cities to rural communities and reservations carrying infections back and forth. They are also disproportionately represented in prisons,

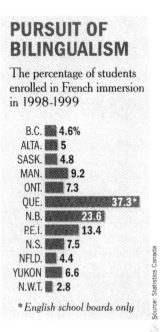

PURSUIT OF BILINGUALISM

The percentage of students enrolled in French immersion in 1998-1999

B.C.	4.6%
ALTA.	5
SASK.	4.8
MAN.	9.2
ONT.	7.3
QUE.	37.3*
N.B.	23.6
P.E.I.	13.4
N.S.	7.5
NFLD.	4.4
YUKON	6.6
N.W.T.	2.8

*English school boards only

Source: Statistics Canada

a known breeding ground for disease. Only half of all Métis reach the ninth grade in school. Métis males are eight times more likely to be jailed than non-Métis; aboriginals as a whole are seven times more likely to be incarcerated. Winnipeg's problem of gang violence stems largely from Métis and native youths.

In 1992, a breakthrough occurred in native (called "aboriginal") standing. Aboriginals were admitted to the negotiating table to work out a new constitution and were granted the "inherent right of self-government." The Canadian government is attempting to settle the hundreds of land claims made by native groups. It spends C$9 billion each year on aboriginal programs. But the problems are mind-boggling. The 553,000 status Indians and 51,000 Inuit have different demands than the half million Métis and non-status Indians, who have no land base and often live in inner-city poverty.

The Assembly of First Nations (AFN), led by Perry Bellegarde, is made up of the chiefs of over 600 reserve communities and is divided between moderates and radicals. They disagree on how to respond to settlement offers. Native groups' land claims often overlap each other. The AFN presses such key issues as resource-revenue sharing and education. Aboriginals can tie resource projects up in legal knots for years. Another organization, the Congress of Aboriginal Peoples (CAP), represents off-reserve natives. In 2017, the government gave these aboriginal organizations the former U.S. embassy building facing parliament.

Self-government is difficult to define, especially before the thorny issue of boundaries is settled. Native leaders

Canada

demand that aboriginals live only under their own laws, but this would create a patchwork of differing legal zones across Canada. Finally, although there are some female chiefs, women in the male-dominated bands might have fewer rights than those guaranteed them by the Charter of Rights and Freedoms.

In 1997, the Supreme Court of Canada ruled that native people can have clear, definable title to their land based on their oral histories and that governments have a moral duty to negotiate with them. This ruling has profound ramifications, especially in British Columbia, where most native groups have never signed land treaties and where more than 230 of them are pursuing land claims that cover the entire province.

On January 7, 1998, the Canadian government apologized to all aboriginal peoples for decades of mistreatment. The "Statement of Reconciliation" dealt with an array of offenses, including the hanging of Métis leader Louis Riel in 1885. Finally, the statement was linked to a federal initiative called "Gathering Strength" to work with the provinces, territories and aboriginal groups to give native peoples more control over their land, government, and economic development. Hundreds of land claims throughout the country are being negotiated. The federal government claimed in 2007 that there were 790 outstanding

claims, but the AFN said the number is 1,100. Around eight are settled every year.

The "Statement of Reconciliation" included earlier policies that had sought to stamp out native culture through "aggressive assimilation" by confining Indian children to government schools. Beginning in 1920 attendance at such schools was mandatory for Indian children between ages 7 and 16. About 150,000 were forced to do so. Half of them were physically or sexually abused, and 6,000 died. Most were closed by the mid-1970s, and the last one shut its doors in 1996. They were secluded from their families and forbidden from speaking their own languages. At that time about 100,000 native children also were separated from their parents to attend a hundred or so residential schools operated by the major Christian churches all over Canada from the 1880s to 1996; 60% were run by Catholic orders. The children were often poorly fed and clothed, compelled to work long hours, whipped if they spoke their native languages, and sometimes subjected to physical or sexual abuse. The former national chief of the Assembly of First Nations, Phil Fontaine, claimed that he had suffered sexual mistreatment.

A royal commission documented these offenses in 1996, and by 2000 more than 6,200 aboriginals had sued the federal government and the churches. The

government has settled out of court and paid a few hundred claims. The churches, which publicly apologized and begged forgiveness, the last one being the Catholic Church during former Pope Benedict's April 2009 visit, fear bankruptcy if they are pressed too far. Native leaders show little sympathy. They blame the traumatic experiences in those schools for much of the alcoholism, sexual abuse, suicide and divorces in their communities. One in seven of the 90,000 former students still alive launched abuse claims against Ottawa and various churches, and new claims continue to pour in.

In 2002, the federal government and the Anglican Church of Canada agreed to divide liability for the increasing number of abuse claims by Indians, capping the Church's liability at $16 million and thereby saving it from insolvency. In 2006, the federal government announced $2 billion in payments to 80,000 natives who were abused in these residential schools. By 2015, twice this amount had been paid. The sum includes about $120 million for a foundation to promote traditional native healing therapies and finance a "truth and reconciliation commission" to hear victims' testimony. The churches involved also agreed to open up their archives.

In June 2008, then Prime Minister Stephen Harper offered a second public apology: "Today we recognize that this policy

Hockey game at the Royal Military College, Annual Classic against West Point.
Begun in 1923, the standing in 2004 was West Point 37, RMC 28.

of assimilation was wrong, has caused great harm and has no place in our country." The apology was combined with an agreement to pay an additional $Can1.9 billion to the surviving students. In a seldom break with tradition, native leaders were permitted to speak from the House of Commons floor, some in their native languages. In 2015, the governments of Manitoba (where Métis' claims include the land on which Winnipeg is located) and Alberta also officially apologized, and a new report was published by the Truth and Reconciliation Commission. In 2021, thousands of unmarked graves were discovered on the former grounds of many residential schools across Canada, compounding the ongoing deep trauma suffered by Canada's First Nations Peoples.

In this era of truth, Canadians are discussing the emotionally charged subject of how to regard the country's founder, John A. MacDonald, who called native peoples "savages" among other racist terms. What should be done about the hundreds of statues, schools, and streets that were named after him?

In 1998, Ottawa, BC and native leaders initialed the Nisga'a land claim. The settlement, approved the following year by Parliament, gave that northern British Columbian tribe self-government, land, resource rights, and $253 million over 15 years. Fifty other BC claims are under negotiation.

In 1999, the Federal Court of Appeal handed the Mi'kmaq of New Brunswick a victory by ruling that the National Energy Board had not satisfactorily dealt with native interests when it granted a private company rights to build the Sable Island natural gas pipeline. There have been numerous cases where the tide is turned by aboriginal insistence that their rights be acknowledged and that there be assurances of job creation, revenue-sharing, and land ownership before industrial development is permitted to proceed. Companies put pressure on governments to reach a deal.

Only a month earlier, the Supreme Court of Canada had decided that a 1760 treaty gave the Mi'kmaq and other Maritime natives year-round fishing rights. The Mi'kmaq thereupon claimed the right to control their own lobster fishing. This sparked conflict and violence with non-native fishermen, who are obligated to observe limitations on their fishing. Shots were fired, boats were rammed, and fishing traps were destroyed in the months of scuffling. Finally, in 2000, the Mi'kmaq agreed to remove a substantial number of their lobster traps from the water, to shorten their fishing season, and to cooperate with federal authorities to maintain peace.

Aboriginals have become increasingly involved in politics as Canada's

Quebec recruits immigrants from Europe

fast economic expansion has pushed forestry, mining and hydroelectric companies deeper into their living area in the resource-rich wilderness. By 2012, there were a record seven aboriginals with seats in Parliament in Ottawa and five in the Saskatchewan legislature. In 2015, 54 aboriginals ran for federal seats. In March 2012, Quebec Cree member Romeo Saganash, who represents a sprawling parliamentary constituency extending over the northern half of Quebec, became the first aboriginal to run for the leadership of a national political party: the NDP.

Demographic Characteristics

The 2021 census and subsequent demographic surveys provide a good snapshot of Canadians today. Canadians are one of the few peoples in the world who are even more mobile than are Americans. Almost one out of three Canadians changed provinces during the 1970s, and many more move either from one city to another or from the city centers to the suburbs or small towns. Canada is heavily urban today, with 80% living in towns of more than 10,000 people (compared with 56% in 1956). In fact, in the 21st century the most visible division in Canada is not between francophones and anglophones, but between five large urban areas that are dynamic, successful and appealing and the rest of Canada that is mainly rural with declining economies, high unemployment and heavy dependence on federal assistance.

The most noticeable regional shift is from the East to the West, a movement that continues in the 21st century. The

Calgary-Edmonton corridor in Alberta has seen its population grow by 12.3% since 1996 and now has more people than the four Atlantic provinces combined. These shifts in population also brought a westward shift in economic and political power. Central Canada has lost some of its economic pre-eminence. Since seats in the House of Commons are distributed according to population, those regions that increased in population grew in political clout. The Atlantic Provinces have slipped significantly, and Ontario, where more than half of immigrants have settled since 1996 (two-thirds of whom in Toronto), has increased. The biggest gains in political power were made in Alberta and British Columbia.

The efficient distribution of medical services and the amenities of life enable Canadians to live longer (80 years for men and 84 for women) and to lower the infant mortality rate to 10.4 per 1,000, compared with 12.5 per 1,000 in the United States. Their family lives have also changed dramatically. Social changes, a decline in religious beliefs and liberalized divorce laws have meant that the proportion of marriages ending in divorce was frighteningly approaching one-half by the mid-1980s. Therefore, more Canadians are living alone than used to be the case.

It can hardly be doubted that the decline in religious belief is one contributor to the growing divorce rate. In a 2006 *Maclean's* Canada Day poll, only 34% of Canadians admitted that they attended a religious service "once a month or more," down from 41% in 1975. It is lowest in Quebec and BC. Two years later, only one

Canada

in five Canadians identified themselves as "regular churchgoers."

Nevertheless, God is not dead in Canada: 81% believe in God, 62% in heaven, 62% in angels, and one third in hell. Two-thirds believe Jesus Christ is God's divine son. A third believes earthlings can communicate with the dead. Three out of ten (28%) say "religion plays an important part in my life" (down from 61% in 1992), compared with 60% in the U.S. (down from 83%). In the 2005 annual *Maclean's* poll, almost a third of Canadians defined themselves as born-again Christians or evangelicals, but two thirds also said that political leaders should never use their religious beliefs to guide their actions. Only 3% claim to be out-and-out atheists (1% in the U.S.).

Sociologist Seymour Martin Lipset noted from diverse polling results, Americans are more inclined to believe in God, attend church regularly or adhere to religious beliefs than are either anglophone or francophone Canadians. They are also more inclined to apply their religious beliefs to politics than are Canadians. Canadians therefore often perceive American political views as too moralistic and uncompromising. This may seem surprising, given the fact that although Canada has officially separated church and state, the state in Canada does provide more support to religious institutions, particularly schools. Such support is understandable in the Canadian context, however; unlike the majority of Americans, most Canadians have belonged to the Roman Catholic or Anglican churches, both of which are hierarchically organized and historically linked with and supportive of the state.

According to the last published census numbers on belief, Catholicism is the biggest denomination, with 43% or 11.2 million members, followed by the United Church of Canada (formed in 1925 by the merger of the Presbyterian, Methodist, and Congregational faiths, 3.8 million), the Anglican Church (2.5 million), and a myriad of conservative Christian denominations (2 million), the largest being the Pentecostal Assemblies of Canada, with a quarter million adherents. In all, Protestants account for 29%. The Eastern Orthodox Church claims 1.5%, most of Ukrainian ancestry, while 1.1% of Canadians are Jewish, a percentage that is growing slowly. Roughly 1% each are Hindus, Sikhs or Buddhists. Muslims make up 2%, while 16% of Canadians claim no religion.

Women are leaving their homes in large numbers to enter the work force. In 1951, 24% of Canadian women worked; in 2004 the figure was 57% (63% of mothers with children under age 3). Although the most blatantly discriminatory laws

have been off the books for years and though Canada's new constitution spells out equality before the law, women in the work force still earned only about 60% as much money as males. This is in part because 28% of working women are part-timers compared with 11% of working men. This wage differential does not exist to any extent, however, in the professions and managerial positions into which women have poured. Since 1971 the number of female lawyers increased six-fold, engineers five-fold and accountants three-fold. Three-fourths of female executives in 2004 believed that commitments to family hinder advancement. Nevertheless, in its gender equality rankings in 2005, the World Economic Forum placed Canada seventh in the world, ahead of the U.S. in 17th place.

Even though the Canadian population had steadily grown to 33.9 million by 2013, the Canadian birth-rate has declined rapidly. In 1971, the average woman who was past childbearing age had statistically given birth to 3.2 children. In 2011, that figure was down to 1.66, well below the 2.1 needed to maintain a constant population (and which the U.S. maintains). These changes in birth-rate differed regionally. In the Atlantic Provinces, it remained high, whereas it was lowest in British Columbia and Quebec.

In Quebec, where families used to be large because of the strength of Catholicism and because of the determination to maintain the Quebec nation in the face of a perceived anglophone threat, the birth-rate plummeted, reaching 1.5 children per woman past childbearing age in 1992, below the country's average and below the 2.1 necessary to maintain Quebec's 6.5 million population in 1990. In an attempt to reverse this downward trend, the Quebec government adopted policies in 1988 and 1989 to create 60,000 more day care spaces and to make tax-free cash payments to parents of $500 for the first child, $1,000 for the second, and $4,500 for each additional child. These measures have helped raise Quebec's birth rate since 2001. Upon taking office in February 2006, Prime Minister Stephen Harper promised parents $1,300 in cash annually to help defray the costs of day care.

Fewer women are marrying in their teens. The average marrying age for a Canadian woman was 28.5 in 2008 (compared with 25.1 in the U.S.). More are waiting to have their first child. The proportion of Canada's population under age 15 has decreased and over age 65 has increased. The result of this drop in births is noticeable in declining school enrollments. More and more parents are not marrying at all: in 2008, 25.6% of children (38.5% in the U.S.) were born out of wedlock. This

figure was higher in Quebec, where 30% of all couples have common-law relationships, compared with 14% in Canada as a whole. More Canadians cohabit (18.4% of all couples) than Americans (7.6%).

The low birth-rate does not help Canada deal with the consequences of the baby-boom of the 1950s and 1960s, described by John Kettle in his book, *The Big Generation*: "Something extraordinary happened in Canada between 1951 and 1966. It has already wreaked havoc in our lives and will go on echoing down the years into the middle of the next century, disrupting and reshaping and rebuilding most of our society and economy in the process." This boom, which poured large numbers of young people into the job market in the early 1980s was more than the Canadian job supply could bear. It is a major factor in Canada's unemployment problem.

Although this swollen younger generation has gradually worked its way through the employment bottleneck, it will ultimately cause a different kind of problem in the 21st century. As a result of the declining birth-rate now, by the year 2030 there will be one pensioner for every two Canadians in the work force. The country's 240,000 immigrants each year help to boost the fertility rate in the short term, but they will not be able to solve the problem in the long run. This future reality cannot help from putting pressure on Canada's pension and social welfare system. To help alleviate this, the federal government eliminated the mandatory retirement age in 2007, but only 6% work past age 65.

Despite the problems with employment, the work ethic remains essentially intact. Canadians want to work, but they are compelled to find jobs in an economy that is changing and modernizing. Fewer and fewer Canadians are working on the land or in factories, and more and more are working in the service sector, including the public service.

Bilingualism

According to the 2016 census, Canada is an increasingly multilingual society, with more than five million inhabitants having a mother tongue other than English or French. Called "allophones," these people now constitute one out of six Canadians, up 12.5% from 1996. More than 100 languages are spoken in Canada. According to the 2016 data, 57% of Canadians speak English while 22% say French is their mother tongue of 22.9%, while 22% speak some other language, with Chinese is the third most common native language

One change since the early 1970s is that more Canadians have become bilingual in both of the languages proclaimed to be equal by the country's Official Languages Act in 1969: French and English. Today 17.7% of the population (9% of anglophones and 43.4% of francophones, according to the 2001 census) have become bilingual in French and English, up from 13.5% in 1971. Traditionally, the great majority of bilingual Canadians were francophones who needed to learn English to get ahead in an anglophone country. Even in the mid-1980s, 60% of bilingual Canadians were francophones. But the remarkable development is the percentage increase of anglophones who had acquired French: 56.7% for English as opposed to 13.4% for French speakers. In other words, anglophones are becoming bilingual at a quicker pace than are francophones. Westerners, who have shown considerable resentment to the conversion of Canada into a country with two official languages, have led the way toward bilingualism.

In Quebec, where most francophones live, the percentage of anglophones has steadily declined since the 1960s and now numbers 750,000 representing less than 10% of the population; 83% and rising are francophones, 11% speak English at home, and 6% speak other languages as their mother tongue (and are referred to as "allophones"). Thee anglophones who remained in Quebec are now far more likely to be able to speak French and therefore feel more comfortable in their surroundings; 61% and rising of Quebec's anglophones now consider themselves to be functionally bilingual (up from 36% in 1971); 32% of Quebec francophones are bilingual (up from 26%).

A minority of anglophones in Quebec has even begun to speak French at home. This means that for the first time in Canada's history, English-speakers are assimilating into the French-speaking world. By 2005, a surge in marriage and coupling outside the communities was underway: 40% of anglophones have non-anglophone partners, and a fourth have paired with a francophone. There are economic incentives as well. Without French, an anglophone in Quebec is twice as likely to be unemployed; if employed he would earn only two-thirds as much as if he were bilingual. Enrollment in English-language schools has declined by 60% since the 1960s, and they are closing or switching to French instruction by the dozens. This has significant implications for Quebec politics since the fortunes of the independence movement were always dependent upon language tensions that are now slowly disappearing.

An "estates general" set up by the Quebec government in 2001 concluded that French is no longer under threat in the province. Although it did not recommend any loosening of the language laws, it saw no need to make them stricter. The problem, it found, was the poor quality of French spoken in Quebec. Perhaps that was embarrassingly demonstrated in 2001 when 20% of 8,055 prospective French-language teachers failed a written French test that is a prerequisite for employment by most francophone school boards.

This assimilation has affected the English which Quebec anglophones speak. So many French words, such as *depanneur* (convenience store) have seeped into their English that some worried observers are warning against "Frenglish." The Montreal *Gazette* decided to test the extent to which this process has gone by printing an article filled with Frenglish: "The work conflict has been a long one and the main revendications of the syndical militants have been for lower cotisations, more subventions for prestation beneficiaries and better social advantages." In standard English, this means: "The strike lasted a long time, and the principal demands by union representatives were for lower dues, more grants for social benefit programs and better working conditions." For better or worse, all readers understood the report perfectly.

Seeking to strengthen its French character, Quebec spends almost twice as much per capita on cultural activities as does Ontario. Despite the outcry against the policies of the Quebec government during the past quarter of a century designed to protect and strengthen the French-speaking character of the province, Quebec remains the only province in Canada that requires the study of a second language in school. Beginning in 2001 francophone pupils started English in Grade 3 instead of Grade 4 in order to improve their skills. Although 98% of *Québécois* children study English, there are no English-immersion schools in Quebec; 37.3% of anglophone children in the province educated under the authority of English school boards were registered in French immersion by the year 2000.

A 1993 study of secondary education in Montreal concluded that anglophone Quebecers are leaving school more or less competent in both languages, while most francophones are not. Even though a majority of *Québécois* still speaks French only, there are a fifth more bilingual francophones in Quebec than there were in 1971. Quebec nationalists encourage individual bilingualism while opposing institutional bilingualism. Indeed, 56% of young Québécois age 19 to 34 were bilingual in 2014. A perfectly bilingual Jacques Parizeau proclaimed in 1992: "By God, I'll boot the rear end of anyone who

can't speak English. A small people like us must speak English."

How have so many Canadians become bilingual so quickly? Some have buckled down and learned French out of necessity. Over a quarter of the federal civil service jobs now require *both* languages, and that percentage slowly rises every year. Thus, government employees have taken advantage of state-financed extra language courses. Also, many of the top jobs in politics, the judiciary and some of the professions, including journalism, public relations and economics, require proficiency in both languages. The federal capital of Ottawa has been proclaimed a bilingual city, so almost *any* job that involves dealing with the public demands facility in both tongues. The result, complained Mark Steyn, is that about 83% of Canadians are ineligible for the country's most prominent jobs. Therefore, night schools and crash language courses have experienced a boom.

Perhaps the most significant innovation in the long run is French-immersion schools for the children of English-speaking parents. They are largely funded by the provinces, which control education. During the 1990s Ottawa reduced its contribution by half, leaving it to the provinces to pick up the slack. In these schools, anglophones learn all or part of their subjects totally in French. The programs vary, but most enrollees study exclusively in French for two to four years and then take about half their courses in French as long as they remain in the program. They enter "early" immersion beginning in kindergarten or "late" immersion, usually starting in the sixth or seventh grade.

This concept swept the country, and the supply of such state-financed schools and qualified teachers cannot keep pace with the demand. Some ambitious parents reportedly wait in line through the night in order to get their children signed up for such programs. One such parent was former PEI premier Joe Ghiz, who himself took French lessons in 1988 to improve his prospects for higher federal office. He and 122 other applicants stood in line all night in 1989 to enroll their children in French language kindergarten. The tired premier grumbled: "There must be a better way to get your child into French immersion." His favor helped young Robert Ghiz's political career; at age 29 he led his father's Liberal Party to victory in the 2003 PEI provincial elections and was later reelected.

These schools hardly existed before the 1970s. By 1979, they had an enrollment of 38,000, a figure that topped the 100,000 mark by 1983 and 342,000 by 2011. It is still rising, thanks in part to the fact that

Canada

Ottawa remains a major booster of the program. Its annual budget for official-language education grew to $219 million in 2000, and it requires provinces to develop a formal action plan for such schooling. By 1989, immersion teaching and conventional French instruction reached roughly half of all anglophone elementary and high school pupils.

The stampede to bilingual schools has tended to drown out the criticism that has been leveled against them. Some purists claim that these schools make pupils "little butchers of French despite the fact that 42% of high school seniors in the program achieve the marks of "advanced or higher." While it is true that many of the graduates of these schools do not speak French perfectly, they understand it and are wholly functional in standard (called "international") French, that form which is spoken and written by educated *Québécois* and Acadians in business, schools, newspapers and on the air. Acadian and Quebec dialects, such as *Joual*, that French spoken in the streets of Montreal and which contracts syllables and drops sounds, remain largely incomprehensible to outsiders, even to visitors from France. In fact, English-language films dubbed in Quebec must be re-dubbed for audiences in France. Other critics claim that these schools contribute to the creation of a "new cultural and economic elite."

The kinds of children who tend to enroll in these schools already come from middle-class or upper-income families, and their acquisition of French language competency in a country which lays so much stress on that enhances even further the social and economic advantages they already had. A survey in 1997 to determine the reasons parents chose early French immersion for their children revealed that the chief motives were "future employment enhancement," "a more stimulating learning environment," and "a better student-teacher ratio," in that order.

To some extent they serve the same purpose as private schools in other countries, such as the U.S. In other words, the social gap between Canadians from upwardly mobile families and those who are not becomes even wider. Statistics bear this point out: bilingual graduates entering the work force, especially the professions, do earn more on average than their unilingual counterparts outside of Quebec, bilingual men earn on average 3.8% more and women 6.6% more. There are problems: there is a shortage of French teachers and the dropout rate is high.. Most Canadians find the value of bilingualism indisputable. In a 2000 poll, 87% of respondents said they believe the ability to speak a second language is important. Employers agree. Some Canadians see bilingualism, not as a cultural fetish, but as the glue for a unified Canada. Nuclear physicist, John Madden, asserted: "If you believe in Canada as an entity, then you speak both of its official languages. It's as simple as that."

It is possible that Quebec's influence in Anglophone Canada will diminish over time. Given the composition of immigration to Canada, each future generation of francophone Canadians living outside of Quebec and Acadia will be half the size of the previous one. Among the fourth of all Canadians outside of Quebec who speak a different mother tongue than English, there are almost as many who speak Chinese as speak French. Soon the Chinese-speakers will surpass the francophones. This is already the case in British Columbia, where they outnumber French-speakers 15 to 1. With francophones shrinking as a minority outside of Quebec and Acadia, their claims for special treatment might become weaker.

Despite intense efforts and expense by the federal government, only 17.7% of Canadians are truly bilingual, and even fewer use both languages on the job. The truth is that few Canadians outside Quebec need French because its use has not spread appreciably. In Ontario, dozens of communities have declared themselves as officially English-only, sending a powerful symbolic message across Canada and reflecting the deep divisions between the country's two language communities.

Nevertheless, one cannot speak of the failure of bilingualism. In fact, support for it reached an all-time high by 2006: 64% of Canadians favor it, while 89% of *Québécois* do. This continues to grow, rising to 49% in British Columbia and 47% in the Prairies. By 2017, the favorable percentage had risen to 78%. Only 12% of Canadians consider the state of English-French relations as a very serious problem. The percentage that thinks Quebec will one day separate from Canada fell to 8% (25% and declining in Quebec).

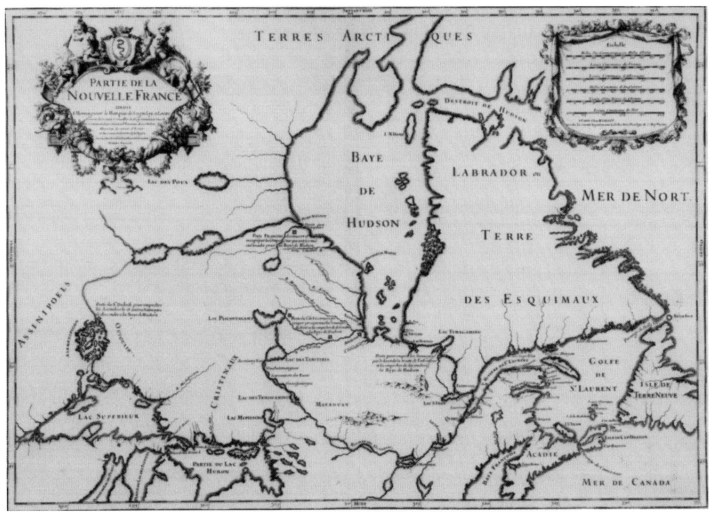

17th century French map of eastern Canada—*New France*
Public Archives Canada/C42132

HISTORY

Identity, Unity, Survival

Canadian history has been decisively influenced by three concerns: identity, unity, and survival. The problem of identity, of defining what it means to be Canadian has never been satisfactorily resolved. Is there such a thing? Right up into the 20th century, anglophone and francophone Canadians tended to regard each other as "racially" different.

Québécois still view themselves as a separate nation, referring to their provincial parliament as the "*National* Assembly." In any case, the concept of nationhood is problematic in a country that makes a virtue out of describing itself as a "mosaic," rather than a "melting pot."

To what extent does being Canadian simply mean not being British? Francophones have always resented the English connection, and for a long time,

anglophones were ambivalent about how much they should share in Britain's institutions and destiny. In past wars, any call by the federal government to Canadians to go to the aid of Britain as the "mother country," inevitably divided Canadians. In 1982 Canadians severed most of their constiutional/legal ties with Britain when they finally revised and repatriated their constitution: the British North America Act, 187—renamed the Constitution Act, 1867 and the Canada Act. The latter acts were passed by the British Parliament. However, the British monarch is still the head of state in Canada and the country's political system continues to resemble that of the United Kingdom .

Canadians on the whole are more inclined than Americans to try to define their own identity as a people. Most Canadians tend to describe themselves in terms contrasting themselves to Americans. When asked what it means to be a Canadian, many preface their answer with such words, "well, unlike Americans, we . . ."

Even Pierre Berton's work, *Why We Act Like Canadians. A personal exploration of our national character,* is written in the form of letters to an American friend named "Sam." The Canadian state took shape in a context of distrust toward the American Revolution and republicanism. As Northrop Frye once said, "historically, a Canadian is an American who rejects the revolution." Looking south, many Canadians saw too much democracy which seemed to create unacceptable instability and violence. While Canadians can all agree that they are not Americans, such a negative definition of their own identity is barely strong enough to withstand the forces of division that often plague Canada. At the same time, though, many Canadians have always been irresistibly attracted to certain aspects of the United States (U.S.) and have come to resemble Americans.

The second concern in Canadian history is unity. Canada has often been accurately described as a "geographic improbability." Distance and rough terrain have

Canada

always made communication and transportation difficult. Canada was occupied by the aboriginal peoples then settled by many different European and other peoples with differing national backgrounds, languages and cultures. Geography aided Canadians in preserving these differences. Regional diversity was always a salient fact in Canadian life with politics always characterized by a tug-of-war between the center being the capital of Canada Ottawa and the provinces which have often regarded themselves almost as separate legal entities – which of course they are in a federalized state.

Third, Canadian history has been shaped by the continual struggle for survival as a unified state. Canadians have viewed the threat as having different sources. For the *Québécois, la survivance* meant the survival of their language and culture which they feared were vulnerable to the ever-growing power of anglophone culture in Canada. The powerful melting pot to the south also potentially threatened to destroy the Quebec nation. Anglophones, who were always a minority in the province of Quebec, have feared that their survival was threatened by the francophone majority, especially since the 1960s.

Anglophone Canadians have usually perceived the primary threat as emanating from the U.S.. At every step in Canadian history, the dynamic, expanding, populous and economically powerful U.S. was a challenge and entered mightily into Canadian deliberations. Canadian governments were always on guard against potential annexation. Moreover, American culture's overwhelming presence has threatened to destroy whatever distinctive characteristics existed in Canadian culture. In the past, Canada's leaders have often been so busy maintaining their country's independence from the U.S. that they had little inclination to count their blessings at having such a democratic, tolerant and basically friendly country with which to share their 5,524-mile border.

Canada's first inhabitants were, of course, the indigenous peoples, First Nations, Inuit and Metis. The white man's presence in the new world permanently changed the lives of Canada's native population. The story of the colonization and the attempt to assimilate indigenous peoples into Canadian society is fraught with shame and crystalized in 2015 with the report of the Truth and Reconciliation Commission of Canada. That report represents a defining moment in Canadian history and its many recommendations have been embraced by both the federal and provincial governments as well as Canadian society as being essential for a true reconciliation with Canada's indigenous peoples. The Truth and Reconciliation Commission of Canada was a truth and reconciliation commission active in Canada from 2008 to 2015, organized by the parties of the Indian Residential Schools Settlement Agreement.

In the 10th and 11th centuries the first Europeans set foot on Canadian shores. Norsemen such as Leif Ericson set out from Iceland and Greenland to explore the uncharted West, and after perilous sailing sighted the Labrador coast. For 30 harsh years off and on, a small winter base-camp of Vikings eked out an existence at L'Anse aux Meadows in what is now Newfoundland. Its main purpose was to supply the larger Viking settlement of about 500 persons in Greenland. The Vikings struck out from L'Anse aux Meadows as far as what is now New Brunswick. This is known because the butternuts they brought back were only to be found there. Based on archeological excavations, these temporary Viking settlers averaged five-feet ten-inches, very tall by the standards of their time. The European average was only five-feet five-inches. The Vikings wore cone-shaped helmets, not the horned models one sees in Hollywood films. Despite their reputation for fighting and pillaging, they mainly survived by raising livestock and cutting hay. The Vikings were also innovative shipbuilders and skilled artists who decorated woodwork and cast-metal ornaments with sophisticated designs.

Champlain trading with the Indians
Public Archives Canada/C103059

Quebec in 1640
Public Archives Canada/06492

Lacking both numbers of potential settlers and fire-arms necessary to subdue the Indians, the Norsemen withdrew from North America. A millennium later, in 2000, a replica of a Viking ship, accompanied by a flotilla of other Viking vessels, sailed from Iceland for a six-week voyage to L'Anse aux Meadows on the northern tip of Newfoundland. There they were greeted by hundreds of onlookers who remain fascinated by the mysterious Nordic mariners.

The New World remained hidden in Norse legend until three Spanish galleons under the command of the Italian mariner Christopher Columbus bumped into a Caribbean island in 1492 while searching for a passage to the riches of China and India. As soon as Columbus reported his discovery to an enthused Europe, a stream of hardy French and English explorers began steering their ships toward Canada. In 1497 the Italian seaman John Cabot (who lived in England) rediscovered Newfoundland.

In a series of three daring voyages in 1534, 1535, and 1541, Jacques Cartier sailed into the Gulf of St. Lawrence and up the St. Lawrence River as far as the present city of Montreal. On one such voyage, he reportedly went ashore to inquire as to his whereabouts. Believing that he was asking about their village, the Indians answered "Kanata," which was the Huron-Iroquois term for "a small fishing village." On returning to France, Cartier used this word to refer to the land he had seen, and the name, "Canada," stuck. In 1610 the Englishman Henry Hudson discovered the

Hudson and James Bays, gigantic waterways that gave the English relatively easy and inexpensive access to the very heart of the vast Canadian half-continent. Between 1609 and 1615 Samuel de Champlain penetrated what is now eastern Ontario and pointed in the direction where the lucrative fur trade would develop.

These explorers were driven by a burning spirit of gain. Even though they did not succeed in finding a direct sea route to China, the fur trade provided fortunes for anyone who could move beaver pelts from the dense North American forests to the chic shops of London and Paris. Following in the wake of these explorers and frontier entrepreneurs came a different brand of Europeans: settlers.

NEW FRANCE

The first permanent European settlers to move to this new land were French and they dominated most of what is now Canada until 1760. In 1604 they established a short-lived settlement on the island of St. Croix, and one year later French pioneers established a community at Port Royal, now Annapolis on Nova Scotia. But the explorer and soldier, Samuel de Champlain concluded that these two early sites were too exposed militarily and too unpromising economically. Therefore, he moved up the Gulf of St. Lawrence to the narrows guarded by the imposing cliffs of Cape Diamond. Here de Champlain founded the city of Quebec and befriended the Algonquin Indians, thereby establishing a secure and well-placed base in the heart of the

continent. Soon thereafter an outpost was established up the river at Trois Rivières.

In 1642 a Catholic mission to the Indians was established at Montreal. This outpost was situated on an island near the points where the Ottawa and Richelieu rivers flow into the St. Lawrence but was subjected to constant Indian attacks. The fiercest assault occurred in 1660 but was stopped by Adam Dollard and a small band of Jesuit followers in a legendary struggle to the death. Once secured, Montreal became the natural control point for the fur trade and for westward expansion. Because of a brief but vigorous French governmental immigration policy initiated in 1666, the number of inhabitants in New France rose to 6,705 by the year 1672 when the French court ceased supporting emigration. The population ultimately climbed to between 60,000 and 70,000 by 1760, when the English conquered the French in North America.

The French settlers' motives were varied. The Reformation in Europe divided Europeans religiously with intolerance that resulted in some of the most bestial and bloody conflicts known to civilized man. Thousands escaped religious persecution by coming to the New World. Others, especially the Jesuit Order, came to North America in order to try to preserve the French Catholic tradition and to convert the Indians to Catholicism. From 1625, when the first Jesuits landed at Quebec, right up until the 1960s, Quebec province was a hostile place for French Protestants. No Huguenots were permitted to emigrate to New France. Thus, not only

Canada

were some of the most industrious and imaginative elements of French society kept out, but the French population in the New World remained religiously homogeneous and conservative.

Settlers were also attracted to Canada by the longing for a new life and for economic gain. The northern half of America possessed all the basic economic resources for settlement: fish, furs, timber and agricultural land. Throughout the 17th and 18th centuries the most important of these resources by far was the fur trade which ultimately provided the financial basis for the government and the church. From their bases in the north and south, the British hemmed in the French fur trade in the 17th century.

In 1670 the British monarch, Charles II, granted to the Hudson's Bay Company not only a trade monopoly but also the privilege of ruling all the land draining into that gigantic bay. The British trading posts, which were established along the edge of the most lucrative fur-producing territory, had the enormous advantage of being supplied by sea and were therefore economical. To the south of New France, the British replaced the Dutch in the Hudson River Valley and had established a powerful base in Albany. Having inherited the Dutch alliance with the Iroquois Indians, the British could challenge the French bid for control of the Ohio Valley fur trade.

The English pincers to the north and south forced the French to push into the interior of the continent in search of the beaver. The French forged into the Great Lakes and into the Saskatchewan and Mississippi Valleys. The Jesuit priest Jacques Marquette and the trader-explorer Louis Jolliet joined efforts in 1673 and paddled from Green Bay on Lake Michigan all the way down the Mississippi to the confluence with the Arkansas River.

In 1682 Robert Cavalier de la Salle pressed on to the mouth of the Mississippi River and in 1699 the French founded a colony on the Gulf of Biloxi, close to what is now the Gulf of Mexico. Bby the dawn of the 18th century, French *voyageurs* had established a far-flung network of trading posts embracing the entire Mississippi Valley and Great Lakes region. *Coureurs de bois*, literally "runners of the woods," gathered furs from the Indians deep in the Ohio Valley, as far north as Hudson Bay, and as far west as the plains.

This huge fur trading network brought great wealth to New France but it also created severe problems. The French had to build a string of forts over a massive area in order to protect their share of the fur trade from the English, a process calling for large expenditures for soldiers with long supply lines into the interior that were both vulnerable and expensive to maintain. Also, the fur trade retarded development in other economic sectors and prevented New France from diversifying its economy. Perhaps worst of all, the fur trade forced the French to make territorial claims which continually brought them into conflict with the British, whose population in the New World soon far exceeded that of New France. From the early 17th century on, the French and English were rivals for control of North America and the undefined borders between their colonies were a constant source of war.

From 1627 New France was governed by private, chartered companies, such as the Company of New France which performed governmental services in return for trade monopolies and control of land. In 1663 the status of New France changed, becoming a royal French province, with all the trappings of French provincial law and government. In typical French fashion, all institutions, from the government and church to the fur trade, were highly centralized.

The government was dominated by three offices: the governor was usually a military man and was appointed by the King to oversee defense and foreign relations. The *intendant*, a lawyer and administrator, was appointed by the King to maintain royal power, regulate the economy, and administer justice. For a while, these persons were assisted by an appointed council, but its influence shrank quickly. New France was unable to develop an effective form of representative government at any level as the British had done.

The third pillar of power was the Catholic Church. Due largely to the personality and force of the first Bishop of Quebec, Francois Laval, no major governmental decisions were made without the influence of the Bishop being involved.

At the communal level, the two top leaders were the *curé* or pastor, who represented the Church, and the *seigneur*, or Lord, a powerful and wealthy figure appointed by the governor. The *seigneur* was not necessarily a nobleman, but he had control over a feudal estate to whom

Montreal in 1720
Public Archives Canada/06497

View of Louisbourg in 1731
Public Archives Canada/C23082

peasants rendered feudal services in the form of rents and work.

The system was not as rigid as in France because of the peasants' possibility of escaping by merely running away into the woods. Also, because the captain of the militia provided military protection, the *seigneur* did not bear the feudal responsibility for protecting the peasants. Nevertheless, this communal order left important legacies for French Canada. The form of land ownership which was granted by the governors under the influence of the Church, and which was *not* bought and sold in a free market, greatly irritated and thereby limited English settlers to Quebec, who desired the kind of freer economic activity to which they had become accustomed in the British colonies. Clearly, politics in Quebec involved from the beginning a close link between Church and state.

Slavery existed for almost two centuries in Canada until it was abolished in the 19th century. During French rule, about 1,500 black slaves were imported and 2,000 more were brought north by loyalists fleeing the American Revolution. Most slaves belonged to urbanized elites.

THE CONQUEST or *LA CONQUÊTE*

While the French established an early permanent presence in what is now Canada, the English first settled in what is now the U.S.. Even so, the line between French and British America was not clearly defined, a factor that caused continuous tension. Because New France was unified, and British North America was divided up into many separate colonies, New France could mobilize its resources more effectively and compete well, even though by 1760 it had only 10% of the British colonial population. Yet, throughout the 18th century Britain whittled away at the French possessions in North America. The origins of the conflicts were

often to be found in momentous events in Europe such that, for instance, the War of the Spanish Succession of 1702–13 brought skirmishes in North America that influenced the Treaty of Utrecht in 1713.

The settlement of the War of Spanish Succession required the French to renounce their claims to the Hudson Bay, Newfoundland, except the French shore, and all of Acadia, except Isle Royale, now known as Cape Breton Island. Acadia had been an area of French settlement that encompassed at that time most of the present-day provinces of Nova Scotia and New Brunswick. The British were also granted the right to trade with the western Indian tribes. Because the scales were thus tipped in favor of the British, only their inability to coordinate an effective attack against Quebec enabled the French to survive in North America for another half century.

Determined to prevent further losses of territory to the British and to try to secure their vital exits from the St. Lawrence, the French built a further series of forts, including the magnificent Louisbourg. This elegant and imposing fortress was constructed on Isle Royale according to plans drawn up by the great French military engineer, Sebastien Vauban, and could accommodate 1,400 regular soldiers, the governor and his retinue, merchants, craftsmen, and fishermen. The British seized the fort in 1745 during the War of Austrian Succession, only to return it reluctantly to the French at the Peace of Aix-la-Chapelle in 1748 in exchange for Madras in far-away India. The French diplomatic victory was a short-lived one, though. The British intended to rid North America of their perennial French rival.

The decisive conflict soon began in the Ohio Valley, which the French regarded as crucial for maintaining communications with their colony in Louisiana and for protecting their fur trade in the west. In 1753 the French sent a force into the Ohio Valley. Virginia responded by sending a

wealthy planter by the name of George Washington to inform the French that they were treading on British territory. Rebuffed, Washington returned with an army in 1754, but his army was defeated at Ft. Necessity. Establishing Fort Duquesne, now Pittsburgh, and successfully conducting guerrilla warfare with their Indian allies, the French were resolved to make good their claim to the Ohio and to prevent the restless Virginians from pressing into the western side of the Allegheny Mountains.

Of four principal attacks on New France in 1755, only one succeeded, the one against French positions in French-speaking Acadia. The 13,000 Acadians had announced their decision to remain neutral in all struggles between the British and French and not to swear loyalty to the British Crown, even though they had fallen under British rule in 1713. Equally disturbing to the British was the fact that a few Acadians helped the French to construct a fort on the isthmus separating Nova Scotia and mainland Acadia, now New Brunswick.

In 1775, a jittery British colonial government in Nova Scotia chose to deal with this looming danger in a brutally effective way, reflecting just how serious the British were at seeking to eliminate their French rival from the New World. The British hunted Acadians down in Nova Scotia, expelled them from their towns and villages, and dispersed 10,000 of them to France as well as among the English-speaking colonies to the south. In his moving poem, "Evangeline" Longfellow immortalized this tragic diaspora, remembered as "*le Grand Dérangement*," The Big Inconvenience; the poem was also the inspiration for Antonine Maillet's play, *La Saguine*.

A few Acadians escaped expulsion and hid in the forests, fled to the French islands of Saint-Pierre and Miquelon, or took refuge in New Brunswick along the Restigouch and Miramichi rivers and along the shores of the Bay of Chaleur.

Canada

Some returned from exile in the late 1700s and joined those Acadians who fled to New Brunswick.

In northern Nova Scotia and northwestern New Brunswick, their offspring and the Quebecers who immigrated to New Brunswick more than a century later continue to form a French-speaking minority distinct from the Quebecers and still noticeably neutral in the present debates between Quebec and the rest of Canada. In its final cabinet meeting in December 2003, the government of former Prime Minister Jean Chrétien approved a proclamation acknowledging the historic wrongs done by the British Crown between 1755 and 1763 when about 10,000 Acadians were expelled from the Maritimes.

Hostilities in the New World broadened rapidly, and both contenders were set on a collision course when in 1756 the Seven Years War erupted in Europe between the two mother countries. Known in North America as the French and Indian War, this grave struggle demonstrated the extent to which the colonial conflict was influenced by events in Europe as much as by concerns of the North Americans themselves. Determined to crush the

Newfoundland

Saint-Pierre & Miquelon
(France)

French in the New World, William Pitt, the British minister of war, sent fresh land and naval reinforcements to America. The French court could send their colony little more than feeble moral support after 1756. One fortress after the other around

the Great Lakes and Lake Champlain and along the Ohio River fell to the British onslaught. The most significant prize was Louisbourg, whose capture in 1758 opened up the St. Lawrence to Britain's formidable naval power.

In the summer of 1759 British ships entered the St. Lawrence and set their sights on the cornerstone of French power in America: the commanding fortress at Quebec City. After a nerve-wracking siege and a prolonged military cat and mouse game around Quebec, the British commander, General James Wolfe, succeeded in landing his army in the darkness of night. The army scaled the cliffs to appear on the Plains of Abraham, just outside the fortress walls in the early morning light of September 13, 1759. The surprised French commander, the Marquis de Montcalm, hastily assembled his army to face the British army outside the security of the fortress.

For the first time during the entire French and Indian War, the French unwisely chose to engage the British according to the European rules of battle rather than employing the irregular manner of guerrilla warfare which had often been so

General Wolfe mortally wounded on the Plains of Abraham, September 1759
Public Archives Canada/C12248

successful. Within ten ferocious minutes of fateful fighting, both armies suffered more than 2,000 casualties, including both the commanding generals. The French army was routed but not captured. Not until it was crushed at Montreal a year later did the final British "conquest," as French Canadians have called it ever since, occur.

The financial cost to Britain of the Seven Years War was so high that Britain had to raise taxes on its American colonies, thereby ultimately precipitating the American revolution 17 years later. Thus, the foundations of both Canada and the U.S. were laid that day on the Plains of Abraham. Further, the terms of surrender drafted by General Wolfe, who died on the battlefield, established the protection of Quebec's unique culture, language, law, and religion that has since become the hallmark of modern Canada's identity.

The memory of the *Conquête* has continued to nourish and invigorate French Canadian nationalism. In 2009 the long-scheduled re-enactment on the occasion of the 250th anniversary of the most important battle ever fought on Canadian soil had to be canceled because Quebec separatist groups, some hinting at violence, claimed such an event would be humiliating and evidence of federal propaganda. Canadian history has been politicized.

In the Treaty of Paris, the French lost to Britain all their North American holdings east of the Mississippi, except the two small islands of Saint-Pierre and Miquelon, which were needed as stations for the French naval and fishing fleets and which remain in French possession to this day. In addition, the French relinquished all of their holdings west of the Mississippi to Spain. In 1801 Napoleon secretly forced Spain to cede these western lands to France. But before he repossessed them, he sold them to the U.S. for $15 million in the Louisiana Purchase of 1803.

BRITISH NORTH AMERICA

By 1763, the British controlled of all land east of the Mississippi, but the magnitude of the problems facing them soon cut short their celebration of this great imperial victory. The British faced the problem of how to rule the newly conquered French citizens in Quebec, which at that time was called "Canada." Some of the leading French political leaders returned to France, but there was no mass French exodus from Quebec. The Catholic clergy remained and, absent the former French political leadership, the Catholic Church retained a leading position in Quebec life that lasted for two centuries. British law and administration, which was newly introduced, forbade Catholics from holding public office. Therefore, those citizens

who clung to that faith were barred from participation in the political life of the province.

The new masters viewed the application of this law as an incentive for the French to give up their language and religion. Hoping that many French would emigrate and that those remaining would be swallowed up by an influx of English-speaking Protestants, the British assumed that the new French minority would be simply digested into British North America. The French viewed this design as a dangerous threat to their culture and identity, and to this day they have never lost their fear of such assimilation. This danger made the French more resistant than ever and continues to harden the backbone of the *Québécois* when facing anglophone Canadians.

By 1774 the British realized that their earlier hopes for a rapidly Anglicized Quebec had been naive and that it would be necessary to deal with a resilient French-speaking community through the leaders who remained: the *seigneurs* and the clergy. The Quebec Act of 1774 reflected this realization by declaring that: French Canadians need not take an anti-Catholic oath; the Church could continue to take tithes; French civil law could be practiced, although criminal law had to be English; the seigniorial land system would be permitted, in contrast to the British free-holding system; Quebec would be governed through an appointed council, as opposed to a representative council, as in other British colonies; and, the boundaries of Quebec would be extended to include much of the old French empire between the Ohio and Mississippi Rivers where Montreal fur traders continued to dominate the economy.

This 1774 Act was good news to most French leaders who saw it as protecting many of their former practices. However, the Act stimulated nervousness or downright anger in the minds of many Americans to the south who saw it as evidence of shaky British commitment to representative government; they also viewed it as an unacceptable limitation on their westward expansion. As a response to that nervousness, two American armies led by Richard Montgomery and Benedict Arnold marched on Canada in 1775, captureing Montreal and besieged Quebec City before withdrawing in 1776. But the year 1776 was only the beginning of the major threat to British North America posed by the American Revolutionary War.

In that struggle few Quebecers took up arms for the British, a refusal which was to be repeated in later conflicts, including the two world wars in the 20th century. Still, few French Canadians supported the American war effort either,

even though France had openly sided with the Americans. The U.S. clearly had its eye on all the British holdings to the north. The Americans convened a Continental Congress, and their Articles of Confederation contained a section that was a door through which other British North American colonies could enter the newly independent country.

In the peace treaty of 1783 Britain retained its holdings north of the Thirteen Colonies while granting the Americans a peace so conciliatory that many Canadians still consider it an "astonishing give-away" which allegedly severely crippled Canada's prospects for future growth. In the peace talks the American negotiator, Benjamin Franklin, asked for Quebec, Nova Scotia, Newfoundland, and the Hudson Bay territory. The British negotiator did not consider this proposal to be unreasonable but was overruled by George III and parliamentary leaders in London, who insisted on maintaining Halifax and Quebec as rampart against the northern expansion of the U.S. as well as a refuge for loyalists from the Thirteen Colonies. Consequently, the northern half of the continent was to remain separate from the southern half.

The British were probably inclined to make a lenient peace with the U.S. in order to woo the Americans away from their alliance with France. The British conceded the entire Ohio country, the great triangle west of the Appalachian Mountains between the Mississippi and Ohio Rivers, even though it was still controlled by the British and it was a traditional dependency of Canada which, when populated, could ultimately changed the power and economy of Canada.

The northern boundary was also generous to the new nation as it followed the St. Lawrence River where it intersects with the 45th parallel, through the Great Lakes to the Lake of the Woods, from which it aimed straight westward to the Mississippi River. This boundary was imprecise at important points and provided a constant source of tension between Britain and the U.S., particularly because Britain decided to maintain its string of forts, such as Michilimackinac, Detroit, Niagara, and Oswego, which were located on territory granted by the treaty to the new nation. Also, some Indian tribes refused to recognize the new boundaries and looked to the British to back up traditional Indian claims. Finally, the Americans were given access to the inshore fisheries of Nova Scotia and Newfoundland.

There were many consequences of the peace settlement of 1783 that helped shape the future development of Canada. First, Canada's contacts with the far West could no longer run through the Great

Canada

Lakes and the shorter and less hostile lands to the south. Instead, they had to be maintained over the rugged terrain of the Precambrian Shield north of Lake Superior. This ultimately necessitated the construction of a coast-to-coast railway in order to weld together the different parts of Canada.

Second, 32,000 loyalists, mainly city-dwellers from the eastern seaboard who sought refuge in New York, Charleston, and Savannah, sailed in British ships from the newly independent U.S. into Nova Scotia, trebling the population there and ultimately prompting the founding of New Brunswick. Many of the 8,000 free blacks who gained their freedom by fleeing their patriot owners for the British promise of emancipation for those who took up arms for the king, settled in Nova Scotia. A smaller number of loyalists, who were to form the nucleus of what would later become Ontario, trekked across the wilderness of northern New York to Niagara and Kingston and across the northern shore of Lake Ontario. Some even penetrated into the valley of the Ottawa River.

As loyalists, these settlers brought with them an aversion to the particular American variety of republican democracy even though they were former Americans who still had emotional and personal links with the U.S.. Like the rebels, they too desired a new relationship between the colonies and the mother country. The settlers later pressed successfully for the expansion of representative assemblies and democratic reforms in what became Canada.

About 8,000 loyalists, chiefly from Pennsylvania and New York, moved into Quebec north of the St. Lawrence, Lake Erie, and Lake Ontario, for the first time creating a sizable English-speaking minority in the province and demanding to live under British political institutions. They received support from London after the French Revolution in 1789. The momentous changes wrought by that first democratic revolution in Europe stiffened British views on the subject of representative democracy.

At the same time, most French-speaking Canadians were critical of the democratic revolution in France which led to a bloody onslaught against the Catholic Church and clergy there. The French Revolution drove a powerful wedge between revolutionary France and conservative Quebec. Not until the 1920s did Quebecers begin to look again toward Paris. A final important consequence of the French Revolution was that it ultimately produced a European war that so loosened the ties which France had to the New World that the U.S. was able to acquire the huge Louisiana territory from Napoleon Bonaparte in 1803.

British General Sir Isaac Brock enters Queenston, 1812
Public Archives Canada/C46958

This ultimately greatly enlarged and strengthened the energetic and ambitious southern neighbor.

With a mixed population in British North America, in 1791 London saw a need to divide Quebec into two separate provinces: Upper Canada, later Ontario, and Lower Canada, present-day Quebec, then called lower because it was closest to the point where the St. Lawrence met the Atlantic Ocean. English common law and freehold land tenure were established in Upper Canada. In that new province, then, considerable tension arose between small freeholders and an elite around the governor.

On the other hand, Quebec was permitted to retain French civil law, a decision which infuriated the largely English-speaking merchants in Montreal who nevertheless continued to control the economic life of the province and who forged close links with the senior clergy and wealthy seigneurs. This "Chateau Clique," which included some anglophones, stimulated French nationalist opposition from the bulk of ordinary Quebecers. As such,, the Canada Act of 1791 left both new provinces with simmering social and political tensions and left to the north of the U.S. a variety of British colonies with no links to each other. Separated by geographical barriers, language, and customs, each had its own governor or lieutenant governor, an appointed council, and an elected legislative assembly with limited powers.

THE WAR OF 1812

The British masters of these loosely connected colonies continued to have tense relations with the young and restless U.S. The flashpoints were many: the British possession of such forts as Niagara and Detroit on

Bytown in 1830, later renamed Ottawa
Public Archives Canada/C607

American territory continued to be a bone of contention until the British finally relinquished the western posts in Jay's Treaty of 1794–5. Continuous Indian wars in Indiana and Ohio kept alive American suspicions that the British were actually encouraging and supporting the Indians.

The American defeat of some western tribes in 1795 enabled the state of Ohio to be founded in 1803. The Americans, led by future president William Henry Harrison defeated at Tippecanoe in 1811 an alliance of Indian tribes forged by the prodigious Shawnee orator, warrior and chief, Tecumseh, and his brother, the Prophet, Americans living in the West continued to be convinced that there were many Canadian traders and British officials who were prepared to stir up and arm the Indians for profits and politics. Finally, Americans strongly objected to British violations of neutral rights on the high seas involving the boarding of American ships and the conscription of sailors on the grounds that they were still British subjects.

For a while these disputes could be settled peacefully, but that possibility diminished as time passed. Any armed struggle between the U.S. and Britain could only be fought on Canadian or American soil with Canada vulnerable. Canada had only a fraction of the American population; by 1812 there were a half million persons living in British North America, compared to 7.5 million in the U.S. Also, many loyalists had emigrated from the U.S. after the Revolutionary War, and subsequently many more Americans had emigrated to Canada, especially to what is now Ontario, for economic, not political, reasons. Therefore, it could not be known at that time how enthusiastically many Canadians would fight for Britain. Further,

British hands were tied by the struggle in Europe against Napoleon, and they could spare few troops and material for a war in North America. The 5,000 British troops in North America would have to be used primarily to defend Quebec and Montreal, while the areas to the west seemed to lie wide open to attack.

By 1812 many Americans in the western part of the country saw the British colonies as ripe pieces of fruit waiting to be picked. They prevailed on President James Madison and a majority in Congress to declare war on Britain even though the latter offered to rescind its hated practice of intercepting American shipping to enforce its blockade against Napoleon. A confident Henry Clay declared that "I verily believe that the militia of Kentucky are alone competent to place Montreal and Upper Canada at your feet." The American war effort was, indeed, mainly a Kentucky affair, and two-thirds of the American casualties were from that state as Clay soon learned how badly mistaken he had been. The U.S. was poorly prepared for the War of 1812, and from the beginning there was little enthusiasm for actually conducting the fighting.

Most state militiamen refused to fight outside the borders of their own states with the New England states refusing to participate in the war as they kept their ports open to British shipping throughout the conflict and regularly traded with the enemy. In this way, the British did not even have to mount a defense for a large portion of the frontier separating the U.S. and their colonies to the north and could therefore concentrate on American attacks in the west.

The American campaigns into Canada in 1812, 1813 and 1814 were dispersed,

and ineptly conducted. American hopes that French-speakers and settlers from the U.S. would side with them were in vain. The American forces were composed largely of Indian fighters and backwoodsmen, who did not fight according to the "rules of the game." Instead of standing shoulder-to-shoulder and advancing politely and openly toward the enemy, the American forces ran through the woods with their squirrel rifles and hid behind rocks and trees. Frustrated British regulars screamed, "Show us our enemy!" This was a different kind of American than the easy-going farmers who had immigrated earlier into Canada, and they helped change Canadians' image of Americans.

The well-trained British regulars, supported by Indians, blunted all American attempts to seize and hold territory. The charismatic and energetic General Sir Isaak Brock, who had a mere 1,200 troops under his command, supported sporadically by natives and settlers, won three stunning victories in the first months of the conflict. Brock captured the U.S. Fort Mackinac before the garrison was even aware that war had been declared. He then bluffed the nervous American General William Hull into surrendering his whole army in Detroit without firing a shot. Brock died on the battlefield at Queenston Heights, near Niagara Falls, after repelling another U.S. force. American forces did gain control of the Great Lakes, and they captured and burned to the ground the capital at York, now (Toronto.

Both sides plundered and murdered civilians, engaging in brutal guerilla combat and tit-for-tat retaliatory strikes on both sides of the border. The governor of Michigan Territory ordered Brigadier-General Duncan McArthur to create "a desert

Canada

between us and them." The burning of York prompted the British in 1814 to seize the American capital of Washington and to burn much of it in retaliation. Only the specter in Europe of a Napoleonic resurgence in 1814 saved the Americans at the eleventh hour as it inclined the British to accept a quick peace settlement with the U.S.. The Treaty of Ghent confirmed the 1783 boundaries between British North America and the U.S. but did not mention maritime law, the original reason for the war. Even so, Britain never again interfered with American ships.

The War of 1812 was the last American attempt to expand northward into Canada east of the Rocky Mountains, but it was also significant for the two countries' relationship in other ways. The war stimulated among most Canadians a sense of distinctiveness and separateness from the American nation and created the beginnings of a definite, though still weak, Canadian identity. Unlike General Wolfe's victory against the French at Quebec City in 1759, which divided Canadians, the outcome of the War of 1812, in which British and French Canadians fought together, helps to unite them. The war also ultimately helped Americans and Canadians develop a tolerance for each other.

To make sure that there would always be an alternative route between Toronto and Montreal in case the Americans ever seized control of the St. Lawrence, Canadians dug by hand the 123-mile Rideau Canal with 47 locks between Kingston and what is now Ottawa. By 1832 it was completed, after only six years of work. This canal is one of the first examples of the state-sponsored mega-projects that have helped to build and to bind Canada together. Fortunately, the canal never had to be used for military purposes and today is a beautiful placid waterway flowing right through the middle of Ottawa.

The memory of the War of 1812 ultimately led in 1858 to Queen Victoria's decision to establish the Canadian national capital in Ottawa, a tiny backwoods lumber town called Bytown, which grew into the "city of saws and laws." Located on the Ottawa River, which now separates the provinces of Ontario and Quebec, Ottawa was therefore a symbolic cord linking Canada's two founding peoples. More important, though, it was safely located out of reach of possible American attacks. The war stimulated on both sides a desire for more peaceful relations. One of the first steps in that direction was the Rush-Bagot convention of 1817, which limited naval armament in the Great Lakes to police vessels. This was an important beginning for the establishment of what until September 11, 2001, was the longest undefended border in the world.

Leaders also established diplomatic machinery to facilitate the peaceful settlement of disputes among the neighbors. This machinery has functioned ever since. An 1818 convention established the northwestern boundary along the 49th parallel all the way to the Rockies. Unfortunately, this convention was unable to settle conflicting claims on the Pacific Coast and provided for joint occupation of that area for the time being. Tempers were again to flare over this territory a quarter of a century later, with some Americans defiantly screaming "Fifty-four forty or fight!", meaning that the U.S. should have all the land west of the Rockies up to the fifty-four forty parallel.

After 1814 these neighbors were never to fight again over disputes, and the boundary was firmly established in 1846 along the 49th parallel, with only a minor southward dip to the Strait of Juan de Fuca so that Vancouver Island would remain entirely within British North America. After the northern border had been agreed nn, the U.S. could concentrate on its western destiny, and Canada could turn its attention to creating a unified nation in the less hospitable northern part of the American continent.

THE ROAD TO INDEPENDENCE

The period from 1815 to the rebellions of 1837 was one of adjustment to rising demands for more democracy and for responsible government, a government responsible not to a monarch or his governors, but to a popularly elected legislature. The revolutions in America and France had contradictory effects on many Canadians. These convulsions caused some Canadians to fear instability resulting from too much democracy. Canadians tended to see British institutions as the best bulwark against such instability and saw American democracy as offering too little order, an impression later greatly strengthened by the American Civil War. At the same time, the revolutions fanned the desire for more representative self-government in British North America.

During those years the immigration patterns changed so that the make-up of the Canadian population also changed. Following the War of 1812 the British showed less tolerance toward American immigration into their Canadian colonies. Therefore, the influx of Americans practically stopped until the end of the century. At the same time, economic and social distress in the British Isles led to a flood of emigration to the New World. Most went to the U.S., but between 1815 and 1850 approximately 800,000 went to Canada. About 100,000 settled in the Maritime

Provinces, strengthening the British character of that area with most moving into the uncleared portions of what is now Ontario, whose population by 1850 had practically reached a million.

These settlers left a motherland which was experiencing significant reform movements; some brought British progressive ideas with them and enthusiastically supported democratic reform in Upper and Lower Canada such as William Lyon Mackenzie and Louis-Joseph Papineau. While both admirered British institutions, they opposed aristocratic rule and favored the popular election of executive officers, as had long been practiced in the U.S..

In 1837 followers of both men rebelled in Toronto and Montreal, but their uprisings were promptly crushed. Both leaders were forced to make hair-raising escapes to the U.S.. where they hoped to gain the support of the American government for their causes. However, American leaders were not willing to risk conflict with Britain by granting assistance. Even though Canadians have never experienced as much domestic violence as their American neighbors, the rebellions of 1837 were among the few incidents of political violence there. While they failed in the short term, these uprisings did succeed in prompting the British to sit up and take notice of political conditions in Canada as they launched an investigation that ultimately led in 1867 to a largely independent Canada.

The British remembered the futility of attempting to erect dams against the democratic tide in the U.S. six decades earlier. In 1838 they dispatched John Lambton, the first Earl of Durham, to Canada to serve as Governor General of all the provinces and to investigate the grievances of the rebels. Because of his hand in the passage of the Great Reform Bill in Britain in 1832, Durham earned the nickname of "Radical Jack." Soon after his debarkation at Quebec City, Durhm became embroiled in quarrels with his government at home. He returned to England only five months

later and submitted his now famous Durham Report early in 1839. While the report dealt with a wide range of North American problems, Durham's most important recommendations were the establishment of responsible government, the union of Upper and Lower Canada, ultimately aiming toward the union of all British North American provinces, and the practice of permitting the provincial governments to make most decisions, reserving only a few important matters, such as defense and foreign policy, for the imperial government.

Ultimately all of Lord Durham's proposals were enacted and it became a major milestone in the transformation of the British Empire into a Commonwealth of self-ruling nations and in the evolution of democratic government in Canada. In 1841 the provinces of Upper and Lower Canada were united as the first step toward a unified Canada. A single legislature was created with each former colony having equal representation, even though initially only English could be spoken in the debates. By the end of the decade responsible government had been established.

Durham noted the gulf that divided anglophones from francophones: "I found two nations warring within the bosom of a single state; I found a struggle, not of principles, but of races." He had developed a low opinion of French Canadians, believing them to be "an utterly uneducated and singularly inert population . . . destitute of all that can invigorate and elevate a people." Durham therefore believed it to be a "vain endeavor to preserve a French-Canadian nationality in the midst of Anglo-American colonies and states." He mistakenly believed that unity would ultimately anglicize the French. Such remarks understandably stung French Canadians who openly opposed the Durham Report. Further, these remarks and attitudes also hardened their determination to resist assimilation at all costs and to survive as a cultural entity as they were convinced to demonstrate that Canada could not be ruled without French cooperation. Tthrough toleraance, solidarity, and constructive parliamentary work, the French showed in the years that followed that Canada could be ruled with their collaboration.

The political union of the two provinces proved to be cumbersome, resulting in frequent elections and changes of government. By the 1850s it was clear to many that a new and different kind of political framework, still linked with Britain, would ultimately be necessary in order to enable Canada to face the challenges posed by economic development and the ever-present dynamism of the U.S. The need to compete with the U.S. for business investments and immigrants, as well as to ward off the powerful American force

Letter dated October 3, 1840, in the hand of the Governor of Nova Scotia, Viscount Lucius Bentinck Cary Falkland (1840–46), to a London merchant requesting lamps plus sherry and claret glasses, ending the hasty request with "I am, gentlemen, your obed[ient] servant, FALKLAND."

of manifest destiny, stimulated Canadian determination to develop the West, to improve transportation within the colonies, and to steer toward national unity.

The growing pressures for self-government also pointed toward greater unity. While the American political experience helped to whet many Canadians' own appetite for self-rule, the actual political modelin the U.S. had considerably less appeal. In Canadian eyes, the American Civil War of 1861–1865 revealed serious weaknesses in the decentralized regime with excessively powerful states and no mature mother country to act as a stabilizer. Nevertheless, 40,000 Canadian fought in the Civil War, participating in every major battle, and 29 were awarded the Congressional Medal of Honor. In fact, a Canadian led the troops who captured Lincoln's assassin, John Wilkes Booth.

More and more Canadians wanted self-rule, but few wanted complete independence from Britain. What the reformers who were ultimately successful wanted was a large measure of self-rule under the British constitution and within the British Empire. The American Civil War further stimulated some talk in America of acquiring Canada. For years some Americans were angry about the fact that Canada was the last station of the "Underground Railway" for 30,000 runaway slaves. To this end, Harriet Beecher Stowe based *Uncle Tom's Cabin* on an escaped slave residing in Canada. Canada had abolished slavery in 1833.

Others were irritated by the fact that Britain tolerated Confederate raids on the northern states launched from Canadian soil during the Civil War. President Lincoln's Secretary of State, William H. Seward, was reported to have been an interested listener to talk about taking possession of Canada, but Lincoln turned a deaf ear to it.

Canada

The Charlottetown Conference, September 1, 1864
Public Archives Canada/C733

CONFEDERATION

By 1864 the forces supporting Canadian unity really began to gain momentum. Legislative deadlock had been created over such explosive issues as "representation by population," or "Rep by Pop" for short, which would have awarded legislative seats according to the size of population, thereby discriminating against Quebec. The reformist governing coalition since 1854 led by John A. Macdonald, who came to dominate Canadian politics until his death in 1891, and by the *Québécois*, George-Etienne Cartier, could no longer rule. In 1864 these two helped form a broader coalition which initiated discussions among the colonies and London aiming toward some form of confederation.

It is characteristic of Canadian politics that this coalition rejected all forms of coercion to muscle unwilling provinces into a new confederation or to maneuver a province into a situation where it could simply be outvoted by the majority. Canada is very much a compact among powerful provinces so that even today politicians address many important issues in semi-annual "summit conferences" involving the prime minister and the ten provincial premiers.

The "Fathers of Confederation," as they later came to be known, found the greatest resistance to union in Quebec and the Maritimes. In September 1864 representatives of the Maritime provinces assembled in Charlottetown, Prince Edward Island, to discuss the possibility of uniting the four Atlantic provinces. This Charlottetown Conference is reverently regarded in Canada as the first step toward Canadian unity.

The Charlottetown Conference was only a first step because the astute John A. Macdonald mobilized a delegation to attend and to persuade the Maritimers to consider a larger vision of Canadian unity. The latter agreed to postpone their decision and to attend a conference of all provincial leaders in Quebec City in October where they met behind closed doors for two weeks. The delegations thoroughly discussed the ever-explosive Canadian question of the relationship between provincial and central authority as they sought a way to create a central government sufficiently strong to hold the confederation together and to block possible American northward expansion without being so strong that it could crush the important cultural differences in the individual provinces.

In the end, the delegates could agree on the general shape of confederation, and the "72 Quebec Resolutions" were a detailed outline of the structure of government and the division of powers and financial responsibilities which became the basis for Canada's first constitution in 1867. Obtaining the approval of all the provincial legislatures proved to be considerably more difficult. There was relatively little opposition in what is now Ontario, the most populous part of Canada and well poised to benefit economically from westward expansion that was sure to follow unification.

Francophone Canadians were much more skeptical, fearing that union would make them an even smaller minority and therefore threaten their survival as a distinct cultural entity. Cartier was able to persuade a slim majority of *Québécois* that they would face a greater danger of extinction by remaining outside, rather than inside, the new union. He pointed out that a solitary Quebec would risk annexation by the U.S. There the force of the "melting pot" would surely destroy French Canadian culture, as was actually demonstrated in the case of most French-Canadian emigrants to the U.S. Cartier stressed that confederation would leave the provinces authority over educational and religious matters, that French civil law would remain in Quebec, and that French would be one of two official languages in both the federal parliament and the province. Most importantly, Cartier maintained that confederation would recreate the separation of Lower from Upper Canada and create a province of Quebec in which there would again be a French-speaking majority.

The greatest resistance was found in the Atlantic provinces which always had closer ties with Britain and New England than with the provinces farther west. The Atlantic provinces viewed the new constitutional scheme as favoring the more populous and economically powerful central Canada. Prince Edward Island and Newfoundland rejected union, with the latter not reconsidering its action until 1949, when its people chose in a close referendum to become a part of Canada. Because Britain wanted a united Canada and put great pressure on Nova Scotia and New Brunswick. While both chose to join, Nova Scotia almost backed out of the union nine years later.

The next step took place in London in 1867, where a delegation of Canadians met British leaders to draw up the British North America Act (BNA). This act differed little from the Quebec Resolutions except that it contained some compromises sought by the Maritimes. The British Parliament accepted the BNA without serious opposition and it served as Canada's constitution until 1982. The differences in the way Canada and the U.S. adopted their first constitutions is revealing. Because there was no constitutional convention in Canada, there was much less haggling over details.

ANNO TRICESIMO

VICTORIÆ REGINÆ.

****

C A P. III.

An Act for the Union of *Canada, Nova Scotia*, and *New Brunswick*, and the Government thereof; and for Purposes connected therewith.

WHEREAS the Provinces of *Canada, Nova Scotia*, and *New Brunswick* have expressed their Desire to be federally united into One Dominion under the Crown of the United Kingdom of *Great Britain* and *Ireland*, with a Constitution similar in Principle to that of the United Kingdom:

And whereas such a Union would conduce to the Welfare of the Provinces and promote the Interests of the *British* Empire:

And whereas on the Establishment of the Union by Authority of Parliament it is expedient, not only that the Constitution of the Legislative Authority in the Dominion be provided for, but also that the Nature of the Executive Government therein be declared:

And whereas it is expedient that Provision be made for the eventual Admission into the Union of other Parts of *British North America*:

Be it therefore enacted and declared by the Queen's most Excellent Majesty, by and with the Advice and Consent of the Lords Spiritual and

The British North America Act, July 1, 1867
Public Archives Canada/C104073

Some of the constitution's terms or concepts were stated in general terms, and, in good British style, some important political practices were left entirely unwritten. The document explicitly provided that Canada should have "a constitution similar in principle to that of the United Kingdom" but it also revealed an awareness of the special difficulties of ruling a vast federation with sharp racial, cultural, and regional differences. The constitution left much room for the Canadian political system to evolve and to adapt to such a diverse and far-flung country.

On July 1, 1867, the Dominion of Canada, composed of Ontario, Quebec, Nova Scotia, and New Brunswick, came into existence. This date remains Canada's main national holiday. To soothe *Québécois* feelings after the 1960s, the federal government officially renamed the holiday "Canada Day," but some Canadians still call it "Dominion Day."

Canadians did not regard themselves as being independent of Great Britain, but only as being self-governing in their own domestic affairs. Indeed, as Pierre Berton noted, "we did not separate violently from Europe but cut our ties cautiously in the Canadian manner—so cautiously, so imperceptibly that none of us is quite sure when we actually achieved our independence." The tie with Britain, insofar as foreign and defense policy were concerned, was still considered to be of great importance in assisting this loose collection of provinces in defending their interests against the more powerful and self-confident American republic, which, Canadians feared, still had territorial ambitions north of their border. They saw evidence of this only four months before the Confederation was founded in 1867 when the U.S. purchased Alaska from Russia.

A transcontinental Canadian confederation was visibly taking shape, despite formidable obstacles. One of the first hurdles cleared was the Canadian government's 1869 purchase of the Hudson's Bay Company's charter and trade monopoly in the West and Northwest. The company had, in a sense, held the Canadian West in trust until Canada became ready to develop it. The company relinquished a huge expanse of land with a settled population of only about 7,000 persons, concentrated mainly around Fort Garry, now Winnipeg, in the Red River Colony,(now Manitoba.

The Canadian acquisition of the Hudson's Bay charter was not good news to most of the inhabitants of the Red River Colony. Most residents were Métis, a racial mixture of Indians and French and British fur traders who spoke both French and English. The Métis had few contacts with or interest in Eastern Canada, and over the years developed a strong sense of their own identity. They feared that their traditional way of life would be destroyed leading to clashes with the new government in Ottawa. Uunder the leadership of the legendary Louis Riel, the Métis formed a provisional government and prepared to resist Ottawa's authority.

The Canadian government was torn over how to respond. In Ontario there was outrage at Riel's order to execute a Canadian official who had been sent to the colony. On the other hand, Quebecers sympathized with the French-speaking Métis. Faced with such differences, the infant Canadian government developed a two-pronged strategy: it sent troops to Fort Garry, forcing Riel to flee to Montana, where he became a poverty-stricken school teacher for the next 15 years; it also received a delegation from the Red River Colony in Ottawa to discuss terms for entry into the Canadian federation.

Ottawa conceded all the essential rights which Riel sought, especially demands for religious schools and the equality of French and English as official languages. The Colony entered the federation as the province of Manitoba in 1870, but the problems of ensuring the French language rights that were granted in 1869 continue to plague Manitoba and Ottawa today.

Canada

The next step in building Canada was to induce the colony of British Columbia to join the federation. Heavily attracted to the U.S., not until 1869 did the sentiment to join Canada outweigh the inclination to enter the American union. Finally, in 1871 Ottawa struck a deal with British Columbia. As a price for the colony's entering Canada, Ottawa promised to assume its accumulated debt and to build a railway all the way to the Pacific. This latter promise proved an exceedingly difficult one to keep.

In 1871 British Columbia entered Canada. Also in 1871, the new country entered into difficult negotiations with the U.S. in which many specific disputes were settled. The major significance of this Treaty of Washington was that the U.S. officially recognized the facts that the American continent north of Mexico was forever to be divided between the two countries and that Canada was a federation extending from coast to coast. In 1873 Prince Edward Island, which saw union as the only solution to its desperate financial problems, joined Canada.

Leaders in Ottawa skillfully hammered together a unified Canada by enticing wavering colonies into the federation through promises of economic benefit. This tool was particularly important and effective because of a severe world-wide economic downturn which began in 1873 and lasted until the mid-1890s. This seemingly endless economic depression was the longest and worst the modern world has ever known. It greatly hampered the construction of a northern transcontinental railway which the Canadian government had promised the new provinces in the East and West. The crucial importance of the railway, which would staple together all the far-flung provinces of Canada and attract investments and immigrants from Europe, was revealed in a letter which Prime Minister Macdonald wrote to London: "Until this great work is completed, our Dominion is little better than a geographical expression."

TIGHTENING THE EAST–WEST LINK

Short railways had begun to be built in the 1840s and 1850s to link trading terminals and to connect with the rail networks which were being constructed in the U.S. Macdonald knew that in order to prosper, though, Canada had to establish an East–West transportation and trade axis to counteract the more natural North–South trade axis. Voted back into power in 1878, Macdonald proclaimed a "national policy," which called for raising the protective tariff to shelter Canadian companies from excessive competition by bigger and financially stronger American firms. Such protectionist economic measures were vigorously debated at that time.

One of the ironies of such a lasting protectionist policy is that American companies circumvented it by establishing their own subsidiaries in Canada. They thereby created what many observers and critics would later call the "Americanization" of the Canadian economy. Indeed, the large degree of foreign, especially American, ownership of the economy remains an unsolved and perhaps insoluble dilemma.

Macdonald's policy also called for the fulfillment of the Dominion's promise to British Columbia to complete the railway to the Pacific. He was also determined that this railway be constructed entirely within Canada, rather than to extend partly through the less foreboding American landscape. This was a daunting task. In light of Canada's immense size, formidable terrain, extremely variable climate and sparse population, economic development depended far more on gigantic projects and close cooperation between the government and business leaders than was ever considered necessary or desirable in the U.S.. This pattern of a large governmental hand in the nation's economy continues to this day.

In order to persuade British and Canadian businessmen to take the great risks of building a transcontinental railway, the government offered an assortment of cash subsidies, special privileges, and huge land grants in the unsettled areas through which the rail lines would run; much of this land is still owned by the Canadian Pacific Railway Company (CPR). The opposition Liberal Party strongly criticized the generosity of the contract offered to the CPR. Every dollar the CPR could lay its hands on was needed to build the railway

Rt. Hon. John A. Macdonald
Public Archives Canada/C5327

through the twisted, rocky countryside of western Ontario, across the Prairies and though the treacherous Kicking Horse Pass in the Rocky Mountains. On November 7, 1885, Macdonald received a telegram informing him that the railway was finally completed.

The central government in Ottawa moved energetically to secure order and to enlarge its powers throughout Canada. The Royal Canadian Mounted Police (RCMP) controlled the western settlements more tightly than their counterparts did in the U.S., so the shooting iron and the violence that characterized much of life in the early American West were largely absent. Hollywood helped to create a myth about the Royal Canadian Mounted Policeman that is misleading. Pierre Berton noted in his book, *Hollywood's Canada,* that Hollywood made 575 movies about Canada between 1907 and 1975, and in 256 of them the "Mountie" always "got his man," a name and a slogan the RCMP dislikes today.

Although the Mountie's guns blazed in the movies, he, in fact, seldom drew his weapon. He did enforce the law, but also dispensed social services, helped persons get to far-away hospitals, tried to secure food for the settlers and Indians in his area in time of need, and sometimes even sorted and delivered the mail. His patient, tactful paternalism helped to prepare Canadians' receptivity to the idea of the state as the generous dispenser of social services like family allowances and universal medical treatment. This is a notion less firmly implanted in the minds of most Americans.

Trying to avoid the bloody Indian wars the American settlers had experienced, the Canadian government negotiated what it thought at the time were fair treaties with the Indians, with some allowing themselves to be relocated on reservations. Indeed, there were fewer Indian wars and massacres of natives in Western Canada than in the U.S.. However, in the late-20th century Indians began to challenge many of those treaties as well as their status as second-class citizens in modern Canadian society.

The last two decades of the 19th century were not a golden age of harmony for the young dominion. Most of the provinces resented the growth of Ottawa's power, resulting in one crisis after the other. Western farmers resented both the high freight prices caused by the CPR's monopoly and the high price of goods manufactured in the East which resulted from the country's high tariff policy.

In the territory that is now Alberta and Saskatchewan, the mainly Indian and Métis inhabitants resented the intrusion of government agents into their lives. They

Lord Strathcona drives in the last spike completing the Canadian Pacific Railway, November 1885
Public Archives Canada/C3693

feared a radical disruption of their traditional way of life. The great Cree Indian chief, Big Bear, was attempting to unify the Indians to renegotiate the treaties with the white men. Also, the Métis in the Saskatchewan River Valley were pressing for surveys of their land claims in order not to be dispossessed of their farms again, as they had been in Manitoba after the government had allegedly broken its promises to them. In short, the region was ripe for a rebellion.

Because the Macdonald government showed little interest in these concerns, in 1884 the Métis asked Louis Riel to return from his American exile in order to lead them in their resistance to Ottawa. He proclaimed the provisional government of

Saskatchewan on March 19, 1885. Aided by his able adjutant general, Gabriele Dumont, he led an ill-fated uprising, known as the Northwest Rebellion of 1885, which pitted a guerrilla force of 600 Métis and Plains Indians against a poorly trained Canadian army of 8,000 men. The war opened with a Métis victory at Duck Lake, with Riel, a self-proclaimed "Prophet of the New World," riding unarmed within range of the Canadians waving a crucifix and yelling, "Fire! In the name of the Son and the Holy Ghost! Fire!"

The brave natives ultimately lost to the railway which carried thousands of green Canadian troops to the West in 10 days. After 51 days of fighting, including an indecisive battle at Fish Creek and a stinging

loss at Batoche, the uprising was crushed. The last human barriers to white settlement of the West were thereby eliminated.

Dumont escaped and fled to the U.S. where he later joined Buffalo Bill's Wild West Show as a sharpshooter on horseback and the "hero of the half-breed revolution." Riel was captured, and despite vigorous protests by Quebecers, who regarded him as a staunch defender of French and Catholic rights, he was hanged on November 16, 1885, in the Mounted Police barracks at Regina, Saskatchewan.

Macdonald, who said that "Riel shall hang, though every dog in Quebec bark in his favor" and his Conservative Party suffered greatly from Riel's execution one of the most significant events in Canadian history. English Protestants at the time viewed Riel as a common criminal, but francophones saw him differently. His execution reignited French Canadian nationalism and exacerbated the animosities between anglophones and francophones.

The debate over Riel was the first time since Confederation that anglophones and francophones were diametrically opposed, paving the way for the Liberal Party's acquisition of national power in 1895, five years after Macdonald's death. In addition, it was the beginning of the Conservative Party's almost complete political exclusion from Quebec which continues to the present. Quebec has consistently reacted to any perceived attack on the rights of French speakers anywhere in Canada in the same way as it did to Riel's execution.

In 1985, the centennial of the Northwest Rebellion, many Canadians were still uncertain that a war had to be fought in

Louis Riel in front of Manitoba's legislature

Canada

order to deal with the Métis' and Indians' grievances. The fight seems to symbolize the basic tensions that still exist in Canadian life: the struggle for minority rights and for regional autonomy. With the resurgence in the 1970s of various forms of nationalism in Canada, many Western Canadians came to regard Riel as a defender of Western interests, socialists see him as a staunch opponent of imperialism, and francophones still view him as the champion of French language rights. Riel's home and grave in Winnipeg are maintained as befitting a hero, not a rebel to be despised.

In 1992 the House of Commons, which was desperately trying to keep Quebec in Canada and placate the West, officially recognized Riel's "unique and historic role as a founder of Manitoba." This act was, in former Prime Minister Joe Clark's words, "an indication that we have matured as a nation." In 1998 the Canadian government apologized to all aboriginal peoples for past mistreatment and offenses, including the hanging of Riel. Nevertheless, the Métis National Council regretted that the apology fell short of an official pardon. The fact that most Canadians want Riel exonerated was revealed in a 1999 poll that showed Riel as the most popular Canadian politician; his "approval rating" was 75%, the same percentage of respondents who believe it was wrong to hang him as a traitor.

In 1999 the first overt political act of Governor General Adrienne Clarkson was to attend a ceremony honoring Riel, calling him "the founder of Manitoba" who "played a key, vital role in opening up Canada's West." On the occasion of Canada's 150th anniversary in 2017, the Canadian Opera Company again staged the opera "Louis Riel." The opera explores in musical form Canada's mistreatment of its indigenous people and its efforts to take away their rights and land.

Within months of leading his party to electoral victory 1891, John A. Macdonald died. He had made the role of prime minister a powerful centralizing force. Without him Canada would have become a different country. Five years later the era of Conservative Party dominance in Canada came to an end. In the three decades of that era, Canada had survived the initial challenges of self-government. Canada had expanded its borders from coast to coast.

As a young country with only four million citizens in 1885, it had tied the country from East to West with a railway; the U.S. had completed its first transcontinental railway a quarter of a century earlier, but America's population and market were ten times larger than Canada's at that time, and its terrain is much more amenable to railroad construction than is

Louis Riel addresses the jury before his conviction, Regina, Saskatchewan, 1885
Public Archives Canada/C1879

that of its neighbor to the north. Canada had survived the effects of the worldwide recession which had begun in 1873 and which had seemed interminable. Moreover, Canada had worked out a national economic policy, which had foreseen not only the expansion of the railways, but also increased immigration and the erection of a tariff barrier to encourage the growth of Canadian manufacturing.

In 1896 Sir Wilfrid Laurier led the Liberal Party to victory in the federal elections and launched practically a century of almost continuous Liberal Party rule in Canada. Laurier was a handsome, urbane, superbly educated man, who was equally articulate and elegant in both his native French and in English, which he spoke with an appealing French touch. Laurier was regarded as a master of rationality and compromise whose skill at finding the middle ground enabled him to govern as prime minister for 15 years.

Laurier helped to unify both French and English concerns, calling on all his countrymen to remember that "your duty is simply and above all to be Canadians." He gave his party something of a basic philosophy. Because Laurier believed that his party was heir to British, not continental European liberalism, he thought that cultural toleration should be a guiding rule in which anti-clericalism, the view that organized churches have no place in political affair,) should have no part. Laurier did expect the Catholic Church to restrain itself, though.

By the time Laurier became prime minister, Canada had already begun to pull out of the economic crisis. In fact; for decades the Liberal Party benefited from this fortunate coincidence of gaining power at the threshold of a long

period of prosperity and development. The Conservative Party would not be so lucky as it would have to bear much of the blame for the suffering that World War I and the Great Depression of the 1930s would inflict on Canadians.

Canada was beginning to take full advantage of the world-wide rise in grain prices. Canadian wheat began to represent in the economy what fur had once been in the French-Canadian economy: it played the dominant role until well into the 1930s. Gold was discovered in the Yukon in 1898. The headlines unleashed a stampede north, but only a few became wealthy. This was followed by rich mining strikes elsewhere in Canada.

This was also a time of robust industrial development; the net value of manufacturing production grew by more than two and one-half times from 1901 to 1911. A new mood of optimism, which began to attract hundreds of thousands of immigrants from the United Kingdom, continental Europe, and the U.S., emerged. Most came to the Canadian West where there was still free land to be had. By the 1890s most of the free land in the U.S. had already been claimed. With the practical closing of the American frontier, Canada had become the place for landless people with dreams. In 1896, almost 17,000 immigrants came, but by 1913 this inflow became a flood-tide of a half million annually. From 1896 to 1911 over two million persons poured into Canada. From 1897 to 1930 almost a million and a half American farmers from Minnesota, the Dakotas and other border states crossed the line into the Prairie provinces.

Such an explosive migration into Canada was an important boon to the young country. Even so, the boon did bring social, political and economic changes that would trouble Canada. A multitude of new, relatively short, railroads were constructed west of Winnipeg to provide transport for the produce of new farms which were opening up. The financing of these lines, obtained in Canada, New York, and London from private sources, was a high risk, as the investors would find out within a few decades. Because almost none of the immigrants came from France, despite the higher birth-rate in Quebec, the percentage of French in the overall Canadian population continued to decline.

This decline was aggravated by the steady stream of French Canadians who left Quebec and the Maritimes for New England during the second half of the 19th century. From the late 1800s to the early 1900s, almost a million French Canadians poured across the border to work in textile and shoe mills. In 1881, one Massachusetts official called them "the Chinese of the eastern states." Even more English Canadians moved south, with peaks in the 1880s and 1920s and ending with the Great Depression.

By 1900 the number of Canadians residing in the U.S. equaled 22% of Canada's entire population. Today at least two million of their descendants live in Maine, New Hampshire, Vermont, and Massachusetts. These population trends and patterns disturbed Quebec's leaders, who were angrily watching French language rights being whittled away not only in Manitoba but also in Saskatchewan and Alberta, which had become provinces in 1905. Despite legal assurances to francophones in 1875, separate French Catholic schools and the status of French as an official language alongside English were largely abolished. French Canadians have often shown that they have long memories, and the recollection of these actions at the end of the 19th century would in the 1970s and 1980s again spark bitter conflict over French language rights in Manitoba.

More than a fourth of the newcomers came from Central Europe and the Ukraine. Settling in the prairies, they faced ethnic and cultural condescension and resentment from settlers of British descent. These Central European and Ukrainian people had, and still hav,e an important cultural influence in the West, but they were forced to earn the respect they now enjoy. Distressing to the Quebecers was the fact that when these non-British immigrant groups finally became integrated, they integrated into English, not French language and culture, whether they settled in Quebec or not. With this phenomenon in mind during the 1970s, the Quebec government required by law that immigrant children in Quebec province be schooled in French, not English.

Almost none of the immigrants stayed in the Maritime Provinces, and the economic boom of this era touched these provinces less than elsewhere, thereby helping to deepen the economic distress that still exists there. Further, the journey of some of the less fortunate immigrants stopped in the urban slums of major cities in Quebec and Ontario with their restlessness for social and economic improvement bringing ferment into urban politics and labor union activity.

LOOSENING THE APRON STRINGS

The 1898 Yukon gold rush in the Klondike fields sparked another of many border disputes with the U.S. This one involved the eastern border of the Alaska Panhandle, through which supplies to the Klondike had to pass. Russia had obtained Alaska from Britain in 1825 and had sold it to the U.S. in 1867. The U.S. insisted on the border that was recognized in 1867. Insofar as the British government wanted time to defuse disputes with the U.S., it agreed to have the question adjudicated in 1903 by a commission composed of three Americans, two Canadians and one Englishman. When the Englishman sided with the three Americans in accepting the American claim, Canadians were incensed against both the U.S. and Britain.

This 1903 incident was a helpful reminder to Canadians that their interests were by no means identical to those of the U.S. and that Britain could no longer be relied on energetically to back up Canadian demands in the face of American opposition. Of course, this realization had not come suddenly. Macdonald believed that Canada's independence in the face of "American Manifest Destiny" depended on its ties with Britain; he also was convinced that the colonial apron strings must gradually had to be cut if Canada were to fully mature as a nation.

Macdonald began sending ambassadors to London after 1880. Despite a strident Quebec nationalist stance early in his career, because Laurier was a great admirer of many things British he accepted a knighthood. Nevertheless, he, like many of his countrymen, feared a more active British imperial policy in the world, and he had staunchly opposed the creation of a permanent Imperial Council which could have imposed tariffs and military measures on all of the colonies.

This controversy, and the entire series of negotiations since 1867 with the Americans on a wide variety of issues ranging from commerce, fishing, waterways, and boundary lines persuaded both neighbors that an International Joint Commission (IJC), composed of three representatives each from the U.S. and Canada would be a useful permanent body to settle bilateral disputes, particularly ones dealing with waterways. This commission has worked effectively since its creation in 1909. That same year the Canadians also decided that because it had to look out for its own interests, leaders should create a Department of External Affairs through which a Canadian foreign policy could be conducted. This began as little more than an archive and it would be more than a decade before Canada could truly handle its own foreign affairs.

Foreign policy disputes created a strong anti-American sentiment in Canada, which boiled to the surface in the federal elections of 1911 when voters rejected the aging Laurier because he dared to negotiate tariff reductions with Washington.

Panning for gold in the Yukon, 1898
Public Archives Canada/C16459

Canada

Anti-British feeling had also become a greater force to be reckoned with, as Canada's leaders were to make the painful discovery at the time of the outbreak of the World War I in 1914.

WORLD WAR I

When Britain entered the war in September 1914, many Canadians and most Britons considered Canada automatically to be at war also. Yet, many Canadians, particularly francophones, who saw this matter differently. An early warning of francophones' reaction to a British war effort had already been given 15 years earlier when the Boer War had broken out in South Africa. In 1899, while the Laurier government faced emotional demands from English-speaking Canadians to stand by Britain during this conflict, francophones made it equally clear that their sons should not be called on to die for Britain in far-away wars unrelated to the defense of Canada. Laurier's compromise, that volunteers could be sent to fight for Britain, prompted his brightest follower in Quebec, Henri Bourassa, to break with him.

Bourassa became a rallying point for dissident francophones. In 1907 he declared: "There is Ontario patriotism, Quebec patriotism or western patriotism, but there is no Canadian patriotism." Bourassa laid the groundwork in Quebec for the bitter resistance to Canada's participation in World War I.

As a member of the British Empire, Canada found itself legally at war in 1914. Canada was sparsely peopled, overwhelmingly rural, mired in an economic recession, and divided by language, faith and region. A majority of Canadians favored national involvement but not all shared a willingness to sacrifice blood and resources for a European dispute. This split was evident in the makeup of the First Canadian Contingent that was raised and sent overseas within two months of the war's outbreak. Of its 36,267 volunteers, only 1,245 were francophones, only 10,880 had been born in Canada, and over 23,000 were British-born with close ties to the old country.

Many anglophones felt retained loyalty to Britain. However, *Québécois*, who represented three of the eight million Canadians at the time, neither shared that loyalty nor had a sentimental attachment to France, where the bloodiest battles of the war were fought. The France of the 20th century was no longer the France to which the *Québécois* ancestors belonged. The French Revolution had beheaded the king and his family, proclaimed a republic, decapitated 25,000 persons, and brutally attacked the Catholic Church. The Jacobin regime even went so far as to proclaim, for a brief time, a worship of reason, instead of God, renaming the Cathedral of Notre Dame the "Temple of Reason."

During the entire 19th century the controversy over the role of the Church in French society had been a dominant issue in French politics. This was shocking to a people like the *Québécois*, who until the 1960s were a deeply Catholic people and who accepted the Church's active hand in politics. Also, French society had become socially experimental in ways that shocked many Quebecers, who until the 1960s, were socially conservative. As McGill historian Pierre Boulle noted: "The name of Quebec as a special, protected entity—very different from nasty revolutionary France—essentially existed until the 'Quiet Revolution' in the 1960s." In short, *Québécois* did not regard Frenchmen in 1914 as brothers in distress who should be saved.

The turmoil that followed entry into the "Great War" in 1914 revealed the lack of unanimity concerning how much Canada should be integrated in the British Empire and how much the nation should have contributed to the war effort. The uneasiness about the war increased as casualties piled up and as Canadians began to realize that this war was going to be much longer than they had initially thought. The Canadians' first major engagement was the Second Battle of Ypres in April 1915, where gas was first used as a weapon. This bloody battle inspired Canadian doctor John McCrae to write the war's most famous poem: "In Flanders Fields."

On Easter morning, April 9, 1917, the Canadian Corps fought together under their own commanders for the first time. It was also the first time that all four divisions of the Canadian Army came together. In a fierce battle lasting four bloody days, they defeated the Germans at Vimy Ridge, near Arras, France, after suffering terrible casualties: 3,598 killed and 7,004 wounded. Of the 15,000 Canadians who "went over the top," one-third were killed or wounded.

Many argue that the Canadian nation was born on that day. The victory also made the Canadians the sharp point of the Allied spear. Joined by the Australians, they broke through the German lines at Amiens on August 8, 1918 and helped set off the drive that would win the war three months later. This ugly four-year conflict would claim 66,000 Canadian lives (12,000 more than the U.S.). One out of ten Canadian soldiers died in the conflict. The nation called 619,636 Canadians to arms, all but 75,000 of whom for overseas duty.

Canadian troops performed extremely well, showing themselves and the world that their country was capable of things undreamed of before 1914. The last Canadian veteran of this "Great War," John Babcock, died in February 2010 at age 109. Then Prime Minister Stephen Harper called him "the last living link" to a conflict "which in so many ways marked our coming of age as a nation."

After the war bogged down in the trenches, unimaginative mass suicidal assaults against the well-entrenched enemy claimed more and more lives. The demands on Canadian manpower became so great that leaders reached politically explosive crossroads. Recruiting declined dramatically in 1916, endangering the Canadian commitment to maintain four divisions on the Western front. Therefore, in 1917 the Canadian government felt compelled to present legislation to introduce conscription, just as the Americans did on entering the conflict in April of that year. This decision ushered in the greatest threat to Canada's internal harmony since confederation almost a half century earlier.

The most prominent French-Canadian politician, Sir Wilfrid Laurier, vigorously opposed the draft, although he continued to support the war effort. Other Quebec leaders had greater difficulty understanding why the Canadian government justified its calling for greater sacrifices. After all, a considerable number of *Québécois* had volunteered for military service, and with a few exceptions, they had served in English-speaking units. A notable exception was the highly decorated Twenty-Second Regiment of Quebec called the "Vandoos." In the midst of the struggle, an affront that deepened the antagonism was the elimination of bilingual schools in Manitoba and severe restrictions on French-language instruction in Ontario.

The actual introduction of conscription in June 1917 ignited intense emotions in Quebec as many Quebecers openly protested the measure or went into hiding to avoid the recruiters. In March and April 1918 serious riots protesting Canada's war policy took place in Quebec City.

The conscription issue split the Liberal Party. Quebec Liberal membership was solidly opposed the draft. In a bitter and virulently racist federal electoral campaign in December 1917 over the issue of conscription and the formation of a united government, one which would include all the country's major parties, the Liberal Party won all but three seats in Quebec but captured only 20 seats outside of Quebec. The Conservative Party, under Prime Minister Robert Borden, won the hard-fought contest. Borden's majority Unionist government introduced measures that would have been unthinkable a few years earlier: the vote for women, railway nationalization, the income tax, and prohibition. Yet, this election decisively altered party alignment and effectively banished the Tory Party to English Canada for

Rt. Hon. William Lyon Mackenzie King
Public Archives Canada/C86772

decades. Not until the federal elections of 1984 were there signs that the Liberal Party lock on Québécois' votes in federal politics had broken.

Borden and his Conservatives, which had been in office throughout the war, paid a high price for willingly aiding the victorious allies. The war widened the gulf between English and French-speaking Canadians. Voters presented the Conservatives with the bill in the first post-war election on December 6, 1921, handing them a stinging defeat as they won only 49 seats, 37 of which were in Ontario. Thus, the Conservative Party, which in 1917 was practically eliminated from Quebec politics, was banished to the wilderness in federal politics as well.

THE INTERWAR YEARS

The World War I sparked a huge expansion of the central government and bureaucracy in Ottawa. Its end saw a problem identical in both Canada and the U.S. Almost all railroads had gone broke. In the U.S., they went into receivership under the Railroad Administration, later to be returned to private ownership. In Canada, all but the Canadian Pacific were bankrupt. The government, which made generous grants of land and money for their construction held the first mortgage, with priority over the private sector investors.

Ultimately the government took permanent control of these lines in 1923, combining them into the Canadian National, which remains its property today; this includes what used to be the venerable Grand Trunk Railroad, running from Portland, Maine, via its subsidiary, the Central of Vermont,

and the Grand Trunk Pacific, with a line to Prince Rupert, British Columbia. A few privately-owned lines remained in operation, but the government was permanently in the railroad business, combining lines it already owned into a massive system stretching from the Maritime Provinces to Vancouver and Prince Rupert.

The 1921 election ushered in a long era of Liberal Party domination in federal politics, first under the leadership of William Lyon Mackenzie King, who governed Canada for most of the rest of his life, until his death in 1950. King, who received a Ph.D. from Harvard and served for years as an industrial relations consultant for the Rockefellers in the U.S., remained a bachelor all his life, and is widely regarded as the strangest, but largely respected, politician in Canadian history.

King who was deeply immersed in spiritualism, had a kind of psychopathic devotion to his deceased mother, and thought he had worked out a way to talk to her. This might sound odd, but a *Maclean's* poll on Canada Day 2006 revealed that about half, or 55%, of Canadians believed in psychic powers, and a third thought that earth-bound human beings can communicate with the dead. Despite all his personal quirks, though, King was responsible for making the Liberal Party an effective and attractive "all-things-to-all-men" grouping which could gather together Canadians of many different persuasions.

In addition to renewed Quebec nationalism and division between anglophones and francophones, the World War I brought other important changes to Canada. The heavy demand for military production stimulated Canadian industry. With Britain's hands tied, Canadians turned to the U.S. for investment capital. New York replaced London as Canada's chief source for outside capital, and during the war American investment in Canada increased more than three-fold. The rate of such investment grew steadily thereafter, until it became a matter of grave concern to Canadians after the World War II. Moreover, the war sparked a renewed wave of immigration from Europe into Canada.

The "Great War" boosted Canadian nationalism and the determination to become an entirely self-ruling country. During the war the Canadian government made an important assertion of independence by insisting that a Canadian, Sir Arthur Currie, not an Englishman, command Canadian troops. The government also demanded that Canada be treated as an ally, not a colony. Accordingly, in 1917 all the prime ministers of the dominions, the British colonies settled primarily by whites, were included in the Imperial War Cabinet.

At the 1919 Versailles Conference, which patched Europe together again, Canada was represented as a separate country, signing the treaty as an independent land. Professor Margaret MacMillan, great-granddaughter of British Prime Minister Lloyd George and former Trinity College provost at the University of Toronto, described the conference in her prize-winning study, *Paris 1919: Six Months that Changed the World*. Asked how she could be so even-handed in her treatment, MacMillan answered: "When you're a Canadian, you're looking at great events from a distance."

Unlike the U.S., Canada joined the League of Nations, which had sprung from the imagination of American President Woodrow Wilson. Like the U.S., though, Canada remained largely aloof from European affairs during the interwar years, and it was not actively supportive of the League.

There was much disagreement within Canada about how quickly the country should move toward autonomy from Britain, but while the debate was going on, the government took concrete steps. In 1922 Prime Minister King notified British leaders that Canada could no longer be committed in advance to military actions on the basis of its association with the British Empire. In 1923 Canada assumed the right to negotiate and sign treaties and to make its own foreign policy. It did promise Britain the courtesy of keeping it informed about what Canada was doing. In 1927 Canada sent its first ambassador to the U.S.

At a large gathering of nations within the British Commonwealth in 1926, leaders of Britain and the dominions proclaimed that they were "equal in status and in no way subordinate one to another." This understanding became law when the British Parliament passed the Statute of Westminster in 1931. This statute formally deprived the British Parliament of the right to legislate for the dominions. There remained a few apron strings, though. In Canada's case, the British Parliament retained the exclusive right to amend Canada's constitution, the British North America Act (BNA), whenever the issue involved the distribution of political powers between the central government and the provinces. Canada would probably have obtained this right also if the various provincial governments in Canada could have agreed on a formula for doing so.

It was not until 1982, though that the parties reached an agreement regarding constitutional amendments on all subjects. Finally, the Judicial Committee of the Privy Council, which is lodged in the British House of Lords, remained the highest court of appeal for Canadians until 1935 for criminal cases and until 1949 for civil cases.

Canada

Even though the decade following the end of the war was relatively prosperous when compared with the 1930s, it was a time of political radicalization. Canadians were confronted with a wave of labor agitation and strikes throughout the land. Canadian labor unions had doubled their membership during the war, but with returning veterans vying for jobs, unemployment grew and union leaders feared that their power and influence would become weakened. Employers were especially resistant to demands for collective bargaining and workers resented what they saw as employers' excessive profiteering and conspicuous consumption. Frustration increased due to high inflation, which was stimulated during the war. Frustration also grew due to the perennial perception on the part of Westerners that the government in Ottawa, supported by industrial and financial powers in Eastern Canada, regulated the economy to the advantage of the East and at the expense of the West. On top of this catalogue of concrete economic grievances, some labor leaders espoused socialist convictions and syndicalism, a radical trade unionism to achieve political objectives.

The unrest came to a dramatic crescendo in the Winnipeg General Strike which lasted from May 15 until June 25, 1919. At first, only workers in the building and metal trades struck to protest their employers' refusal to grant either higher wages or collective bargaining. Yet, weeks later the Winnipeg Trades and Labour Council struck in sympathy, paralyzing the economic life of the city within a few hours. Unionists in Vancouver and other Western cities then joined the strikers.

For a time the strike remained free of violence, but many employers and members of the federal and provincial government were inclined to see it as a deliberate attempt by Bolsheviks to undermine the democratic order in Canada. In the U.S. a similar "Red Scare" was afoot in 1919. The Canadian government had sent 4,400 troops to Russia after the overthrow of the czar in 1917. Although public opinion and the government turned against this deployment, it was not until April 1919 that the last Canadians withdrew from the Soviet Union.

A particularly unfortunate event occurred when Mounties and militia troops in Winnipeg broke up a banned march by strikers. In the confused situation that developed, one person was killed and 30 were injured. This tragic development prompted the government to arrest the leaders of the strike on charges of sedition and to patrol the streets of Winnipeg with soldiers. Finally, on June 25 the strike was called off after the government promised to look into the underlying causes of the

strike. A governmental commission did conclude that the aim of most of the strikers had been to achieve collective bargaining and better working conditions.

The commission's findings notwithstanding, the jailed union leaders were tried, convicted of seditious activities and given jail sentences from six months to two years. This strike created bitterness in Winnipeg and elsewhere that took decades to remove, stimulating the creation of protest sentiments and movements, which, through many twists and turns, continue to survive today.

Canada's social and economic problems became desperate in the aftermath of the New York stock market crash in 1929. Canada was vulnerable to the severe and prolonged worldwide economic depression that set in. The country always depended on foreign capital and on the exportation of raw materials to industrial nation which now could no longer buy the things that Canada had to sell.

By 1933 almost a fourth of Canada's labor force was unemployed and one was confronted everywhere with the same images as in the U.S.: bankruptcies and evictions, farm foreclosures, tent cities, soup-kitchens, and itinerant Canadians desperately looking for work. Government officials spent much of their time and attention on maintaining law and order. The terrible economic situation sparked bitter labor unrest with the government responding by sending in Mounties to disperse demonstrations, infiltrating union meetings with agents, and censoring literature the government perceived to be radical.

Such a charged political atmosphere was an ideal greenhouse for diverse populist protest parties. They were heirs to the defunct Progressive Party which reared up against the dominance of the eastern financial centers, but which lost all its

strength by the early 1930s. Two of these parties, which still have a role in Canadian politics, sprang up in the West. The Social Credit Party, headed by a fiery radio evangelist, William Aberhart, aimed its appeal to ranchers and farmers and excoriated the eastern bankers, who allegedly manipulated credit, freight rates and tariffs for their own selfish interests. This party won the Alberta provincial elections in 1935. Although most of its anti-banking legislation was struck down by the Supreme Court, it managed to establish a foothold in Albertan politics which remained firm for decades. It always rejected socialism and became an increasingly conservative party, which seeks to protect "the little guy" and Western Canadian interests. Today the party rules in British Columbia as it cooperates with the Conservative Party in federal politics.

The second party that was, from its beginning, socialist in nature was the Cooperative Commonwealth Federation (CCF). It set out to organize laborers and farmers in order to "eradicate capitalism and put into operation the full programme of socialized planning which will lead to the establishment in Canada of the Cooperative Commonwealth," as its Regina Manifesto proclaimed in 1933.

As doctrinaire as it program seems to be on first reading, the CCF never sought to abolish private property; it promised the "security of tenure for the farmer on his farm." Also, unlike many radical parties, the CCF strongly favored parliamentary government and reform by legal, nonviolent means, gaining ground among urban intellectuals and trade unionists while becoming a permanent fixture in Canadian politics, although it never established firm roots in Atlantic Canada or Quebec. The CCF's electoral fortresses were always in the West, and in 1944 it became the ruling

Winnipeg General Strike, June 10, 1919
Public Archives Canada/C26782

58

The Great Depression: unemployed men board a train for Ottawa, June 1935
Public Archives Canada/C29461

party in Saskatchewan. The CCF changed its name to the New Democratic Party (NDP) in 1961.

A third party that rose up at this time was the Union Nationale or the UN in Quebec. In 1935, under the leadership of the former Quebec Conservative party leader, Maurice Duplessis, it gathered together the scraps of that province's Conservative and Liberal parties. As in almost all times of adversity, Quebec nationalism flared up again during the depression. No doubt nationalism was aggravated by the fact that almost all of the major employers in the province were anglophones, while an overwhelming majority of unemployed were francophones.

Claiming that the provincial government was ridden with corruption and that reform was needed in Quebec, Duplessis became premier in 1936. Despite repeated charges that he and his ruling clique were as corrupt as the leaders they replaced and that they were not genuine reformers, the UN gained a hold on Quebec politics that would not be broken until 1970 as it pursued a conservative policy and maintained close relations with the Church. In addition, the UN opened the door widely to foreign investment. Until it was finally swept aside by a new breed of Quebec nationalists and reformers who gained momentum in the late 1960s, the UN could always reap a rich harvest of votes by championing Quebec provincial rights in opposition to the government in Ottawa.

Economic depressions often spark energetic governmental intervention in the economy, especially in Canada, where the state's role in the economy was always larger than in the U.S. Amid so much anxiety and human misery, a Conservative Party government was elected. The new prime minister was R.B. Bennett, an energetic and competent lawyer from Calgary, but an authoritarian manager, was was elected by promising social welfare and employment for hard-pressed Canadians.

In January 1935 Bennett introduced a far-reaching "New Deal" to Parliament which proposed no less than "modifications of the capitalist system to enable that system more effectively to serve the people." He advocated state-supported farm credit, unemployment insurance, minimum wages and maximum hours of work. Bennett's program stunned many of his fellow Conservatives as his Liberal opponents charged that the measures were unconstitutional on the grounds that they infringed on provincial powers, a charge which the Supreme Court of Canada largely upheld in an important decision a year later. The prime minister had already become so unpopular that he and his party were thrown out of power by a landslide in October 1935; the Liberal Party won a stunning 171 seats to the Tories' 39, with Mackenzie King again assuming the helm.

The discredited Conservative Party, which had had the misfortune of being in power during the depression, was banished to the political wilderness for most of the next half century. Even so, in the long run, the party did not repudiate the strides Bennett took. Today, the Conservative Party in Canada still advocates a wider social welfare net and a more activist government than do most Americans, Democrat, or Republican. Also, the federal government's intervention in the economy continued, despite the 1936 Supreme Court decision.

In 1934 the Bank of Canada was established, and in 1938 it was fully nationalized. In 1935 the government created the Wheat Board, a body which still exists to stabilize prices. The Canadian Radio Broadcasting Commission was created during this time and renamed the Canadian Broadcasting Corporation (CBC) in 1936. The CBC continues to provide and regulate radio and television broadcasting with a heavy Canadian content. Moreover, the Bennett government began the process of establishing a state-controlled air transport system, which in 1937 became the Trans-Canada Air Lines, a nationalized "Crown" corporation and forerunner to Air-Canada. Clearly, the government's hand was in the economy to stay.

WORLD WAR II

Canadian economic life remained wretched throughout the 1930s. However, in 1939 an event came which not only led Canada out of the depression, but ushered in momentous political, diplomatic, and military challenges and changes for the nation: the outbreak of World War II. Canada had pursued a basically isolationist foreign policy during the 1920s and 1930s.

Until 1939, Canada resisted any efforts to involve itself in any collective security arrangement stemming from its membership either in the League of Nations or the

Canada

British Empire. Further, Canada remained neutral in the Spanish Civil War from 1936–9 although 1,700 Canadians defied the law and formed the Mackenzie-Papineau Battalion to fight on the republican government's side; over 400 were killed.

In 2013 Canada's last veteran of that conflict, Jules Paivio, died at age 96. Because Canada had done little to keep up the size and quality of its armed forces prior to 1939 it was unprepared for war.

Unlike in 1914, when Canada become automatically involved in the war on Britain's entry, in September 1939 the government and Parliament deliberated for a week after fighting commenced before declaring war on Britain's side. Also, the King government felt free to negotiate a defense agreement with the U.S. at Ogdensburg in 1940.

In August 1940 Prime Minister King and President Roosevelt agreed to a Permanent Joint Board on Defense, which could design defense arrangements for the North American continent. In 1941 these two leaders penned the Hyde Park Declaration, which provided for the sharing of defense production and for increased trade in defense equipment. These were measures that deepened the meshing of the two countries' economies while serving as a clear indication that Canadian defense was no longer linked exclusively with that of the British Empire.

World War II created a potentially dangerous domestic political situation for Canadians and threatened to open up the terrible wounds of 1914–18. Parliament adopted the declaration of war almost unanimously, but support from French-speaking Canadians stemmed largely from the King government's promise not to draft Canadians into the armed forces for service abroad. Most Canadians understood that their country's contribution was to be mainly economic. Canada was indeed a crucial source of supplies for Britain in the 27 months before the U.S. entered the war. Throughout the war, Canada's eastern ports continued to be important points of origination for convoys that churned back and forth across the submarine-infested Atlantic bringing indispensable supplies to the Allies.

The government assured Canadians that their fighting forces would be composed exclusively of volunteers. The contribution of these soldiers was considerable during the war: almost a million Canadians served admirably in all theaters of operation. Following the disaster on the Belgian beaches at Dunkirk, Canadian soldiers formed the primary armed forces defending Britain, while that island nation caught its breath and reequipped itself for the onslaught which

lay ahead. In addition, Canadians bore many casualties in the unsuccessful attempts to defend Hong Kong from the Japanese in December 1941.

On August 19, 1942, 5,000 Canadians led an allied force that included 1,000 British to probe the European coastal defenses at Dieppe. It was long believed that the objective was to demonstrate that a fortified port could be seized from the sea. The attack was a disaster: 907 Canadians were killed and 1,154 were wounded while 1,954 were captured. Later research revealed that the main goal was to provide assistance and cover for a top-secret British Royal Marines commando unit to steal highly valuable intelligence material, including Ultra coding secrets, from the German naval headquarters inside the town. Due to faulty planning and preparation, the raid was an epic failure.

Three months after D-Day 1944, the 2nd Canadian Division liberated Dieppe. Canadian divisions were heavily involved in the invasion of Sicily in 1943 and the subsequent liberation of Italy. An elite integrated Canadian-American commando unit, the First Special Service Force (FSSF), fought at the bloody Anzio beachhead. In addition, Canadian soldiers played an important role at the Normandy beaches in June 1944. Numbering 15,000 they dominated the landing at Juno Beach. One can still visit the fortified beaches in northern France which they were assigned to conquer. One out of ten soldiers who went ashore on June 6 was Canadian, as were 350 of the 4,500 Allied dead, of which 2,500 were American, on D-Day. Canadian troops moved inland quickly and were the only ground unit to attain all of its assigned D-Day objectives.

Another 7,600 Canadians were killed liberating the Netherlands in the closing months of the war, something the Dutch have never forgotten. To this day schoolchildren tend the graves of fallen Canadians. By war's end, 42,000 Canadians had lost their lives.

Another Canadian contribution was its development and administration of the British Commonwealth Air Training Plan which provided airfields and training schools on Canadian soil for more than 131,500 airmen and air mechanics from Britain and the Dominions. Canadian pilots flew in Britain's Royal Air Force and in 41 Canadian squadrons which protected the sea lanes and which joined in the air attack against Germany.

It is scarcely surprising that the massive Canadian participation in the world war would put intense pressure on the government's commitment not to draft soldiers into the armed forces. Conscription for duty inside Canada had

Recruitment poster for World War II
Public Archives Canada/C87427

already begun in the summer of 1940. However, by April of 1942 the mounting casualties and the lagging of volunteers from Quebec forced the government to hold a controversial plebiscite asking Canadians whether they would free the government of its pledge not to introduce conscription for overseas duty. The results of the vote revealed clearly how divided the country was over this historically explosive issue. In English Canada 80% of the voters said "yes," but 72% of *Québécois* said "no."

Even though Germany occupied and controlled France, French-speaking Canadians were inclined to perceive the conflict as a "British war." Two *Québécois* who later become prominent in Canadian politics were among the many French-speaking Canadians who avoided military service. Pierre Elliott Trudeau managed to avoid ever putting on a uniform while René Lévesque served as a public information officer in the American army and wore an American uniform.

Because Prime Minister King unmistakably sensed the danger, he resisted sending conscripts to war zones until November 1944, when he finally ordered 16,000 draftees overseas. Angry riots broke out in Quebec province, and some *Québécois* came close to mutiny in some military bases. Victory in Europe in May 1945 fortunately defused this gathering domestic political storm, and a relieved Canada proceeded to demobilize its draftees as quickly as possible.

In 1997 a panel of 25 scholars of Canadian history evaluated and ranked

Canada's 20 prime ministers. They especially valued a leader's coherent vision of the country and well-articulated goals in domestic and foreign policy. In their opinion, William Lyon Mackenzie King was the best. They were impressed by his great political skills, his devotion to unity, his establishment of Canada's international identity, his steps towards establishing the social welfare safety net, and the brilliant way he ran Canada's enormous war effort. On May 8, 2005, the sixtieth anniversary of Victory in Europe (VE) Day, a spectacular new War Museum was opened on LeBreton Flats upriver from Parliament Hill in Ottawa to commemorate the sacrifices of Canadian soldiers.

AFTER 1945

World War II and its aftermath changed the face of Canada and its people. The end of the most destructive war the world has ever known churned up a wave of immigration into Canada, as millions of persons in war-torn Europe sought security and a more promising life in this huge and sparsely populated land. The massive influx helped to more than double the country's population from 11.5 million in 1941 to 25 million in 1985. These modern immigrants tended to settle in cities, joining the masses of native-born Canadians who were leaving the countryside, changing the country almost overnight into one that was, and is, predominantly urbanized. Moreover, because only a third of the newcomers were of British stock, citizens of British heritage no longer constitute a majority of the population, falling to less than 45% in the 1990s.

It is true that the newcomers, who often continued to speak a wide variety of languages in their homes and churches, almost invariably adopted English, not French, as their new language, even if they settled Quebec. This distressed francophones, who already had dramatically lowered their own birth-rate; their percentage among the Canadian population dropped from 31% in 1945 to under 23% today. While these demographic shifts meant that every Canadian had become a member of a minority within Canada, they stimulated an anxiety in francophone Canada that would ultimately find a Quebec nationalist expression.

While the Canadian population underwent significant alteration, four other developments that were set in motion in the 1930s and 1940s were to demand much of the country's attention right into the 1980s. First, the economic depression and the war significantly increased the power of the central government at the expense of the provincial governments. Second, the war demonstrated Canada's almost total

independence from the apron strings of the mother country and had made even more glaring the anachronism of having to request a foreign parliament to amend some important parts of its constitution. It seemed to more and more Canadians that a country that still could not amend its own constitution was not yet entirely sovereign.

Third, Canada accumulated far more wealth than it had expended during the war. It had become even more highly industrialized and had emerged from the war as one of the world's major industrial and trading nations. The war had fostered a more intense interrelationship between the economies of Canada and the U.S., and, as had been the case in 1918, had brought another burst of American capital investment across the border. Canadians did absolutely nothing to stem that flow, and in the 1960s they woke up to find that much of their economy and natural resources were in the hands of a single foreign country, its neighbor to the south. Fourth, despite ugly riots that took place in Quebec in the closing months of the war, Canada had emerged from the armed struggle far more unified as a country than it had in 1918.

All four developments sparked further changes in the post-war era. The provinces energetically reasserted themselves and challenged Ottawa's hold on a wide variety of powers from taxing to the pricing of natural resources extracted within their borders. Moreover, the long and bitter disputes over the shape of the new constitution revealed just how muscular the provinces have become. The result of those prolonged disputes was a new constitution, signed into effect in 1982 by the British Queen and the Canadian prime minister, which left Canadians as the undisputed political masters in their own house. The only symbolic link with the mother country that remains is that the British monarch is still formally the Canadian head of state.

Moving on to the next armed conflict, 20,000 Canadians fought with their allies in the Korean War of 1950–53, with 516 of them killed. An additional 7,000 remained as peacekeepers for two years after the armistice. However, the war in Vietnam (1965–1974) forced Canadians to reexamine their relationship with the U.S. Canada's participation in the International Control Commission in Indochina from 1954 until 1973, along with Poland and India, caused some friction when American leaders sometimes thought that the Canadians, who had been appointed with the expectation that they would be biased toward the American view while Poland was selected to provide the opposite bias, did not show enough sympathy toward the U.S. position. There was evidence that these charges were untrue most

of the time, but the Vietnam War was indeed a landmark in Canadians' appraisal of America's leadership in the world.

As was true of many of the U.S.' other allies, Canadians were uneasy about American policy in Indochina, even though up to 40,000 Canadians served as volunteers in the American armed forces in Southeast Asia. Canadians were more skeptical of containment of communism based on military force and were more inclined to see the roots of third-world instability in poverty and social problems rather than in Soviet or Chinese meddling.

Prime Minister Lester Pearson spoke for most of his countrymen when he delivered a speech at Temple University, in Philadelphia, in 1965 calling for a bombing halt in North Vietnam. President Lyndon B. Johnson was livid. What angered him was not only that Canada departed from its usual quiet diplomatic style to criticize the U.S. publicly in a time of crisis but also that he did so on American soil. Johnson put it unofficially in his typically crude way: Pearson had "pissed on my rug."

Pearson was the best diplomat Canada ever produced. He played a pivotal role in creating NATO and the United Nations and he was elected president of the UN General Assembly in 1952. For his negotiation skills, he was awarded the Nobel Peace Prize in 1957. More than any other, Pearson popularized the image of Canadians as an understated, compassionate and peacemaking people.

Perhaps Pearson was wrong to deliver such a speech in Philadelphia. Perhaps also Canadians do not fully appreciate the difficulties of America's position as a superpower. Even so, the speech and Canadians' general support of its basic message revealed at least two things: Canadians do view the world somewhat differently than do Americans and no Canadian government could support every American policy, regardless of its nature.

Canada thus experienced a birth or rebirth of two forms of nationalism in Canada: first, because Canadians grew nervous about the extent to which foreigners controlled their economy, the nation developed a sense of economic nationalism that was strongest in English Canada. The economic nationalism visible in Quebec was directed as much against English Canada's penetration of the Quebec economy as against that of the U.S. Second, the dramatic assertion of political and cultural nationalism in Quebec from the 1960s on represented the greatest threat to Canadian unity since confederation in 1867. At times, one could not be sure that Canada as a country would survive into the 21st century.

Canada

THE "QUIET REVOLUTION" IN QUEBEC

The "French fact" had, of course, existed in Canadian life for more than two centuries, despite the illusions of many anglophones that the *Québécois* would become absorbed into the Anglo-Saxon mainstream, as had been so many other groups in North America. All too often, *Québécois* were viewed condescendingly "as priest-ridden, traditional-bound, backward, clannish and occasionally sullen or riotous," in the words of sociologist Jane Jacobs.

Francophones resented what they interpreted as an arrogant sense of superiority on the part of anglophones, who indeed did dominate much of Quebec's economy, and, in the opinion of many *Québécois* sought to destroy their culture. In times of crisis, Quebecers repeatedly demonstrated that they could not be expected to react as anglophones thought they should. Quebecers were Canadians, but they were distinct and intended to remain that way. Profound disagreements could always be papered over by compromise. Yet each side often thought that the necessary compromises had been foisted on it by the other, reactions that intensified into festering resentment giving rise to yet other grievances.

Quebecers had always proved to be an extraordinarily resilient people who would never permit their language and culture to die. The French nobleman and politician, Alexis de Tocqueville, had discovered their traditional secret for survival during his trip to North America in 1831–1832, a journey that resulted in a seminal work, *Democracy in America.* The *Québécois*, he noted, "is tenderly attached to the land which saw his birth, to his church tower, and to his family."

Traditionally, Quebecers turned their backs on the cities which threatened their families and society by placing them at the mercy of English employers and customs. For a long time, Quebecers tended to remain in rural areas, where the Catholic Church shielded them from alien influences, provided a firm guiding hand and administered an educational system which shunned commercial and technical subjects, and reinforced traditional values and French language and society.

The Québécois were prodigious procreators, responding to the threats, often described vividly from the pulpit, presented by an almost total absence of immigrants from France, and by a constant emigration to northeastern U.S. of young Quebecers who were unable to find farmland or employment in their own province. Between 1851 and 1931 over 700,000 Quebecers left for the melting pot south of the border. To help stem this tide, the Church sponsored

Rt. Hon. Louis St. Laurent, 1949
Public Archives Canada/C20048

colonization drives to channel Quebecers into the formerly anglophone Ottawa Valley and Eastern Townships or into the Quebec interior around Lac St. Jean and in the Laurentian Mountains. The best defense, though, was the *revanche des berceaux*, "revenge of the cradles." Until the post-1945 era, Quebecers maintained the highest birth-rate in Canada.

Like all Canadians, Quebecers have always been concerned with survival. even so, their worries were a different kind of survival from that of their English-speaking compatriots. For English Canadians, it meant survival of the union

against the hostile forces of geography, climate, internal diversity, and the dynamic southern neighbor, with a population ten times the size of Canada's. It meant coping with these challenges and reconciling the diversities in order to preserve the whole. For the *Québécois, la survivance* meant the preservation of their separate *nation,* against domination or, worse, absorption by anglophones in both English Canada and the U.S.

An important motto in Quebec has been *Exister c'est survivre!*: To exist is to survive!." This nation has always been held together by a common memory of Quebecers' past and a separate language and culture. On every Quebec license plate today are the words, *Je me souviens*, "I remember." They are an allusion to a poem with the bitter line, "I remember that I was born under the *fleur-de-lis* and grew up under the [English] rose." They underscore the importance of Quebec's past for the present values and feeling of community. Survival as Quebecers' goal cannot be denied. The question now is how survival can be guaranteed when the traditional supports of religion, rural isolation and educational and economic backwardness have broken down.

Quebec nationalism was clearly visible during the World War II, but it was prevented from boiling over by the timely end of the war, by the election of Maurice Duplessis, who had been returned to the Quebec premiership in 1944, and by the accession of a French Canadian Liberal, Louis St. Laurent, to the prime ministry of Canada when Mackenzie King retired in in 1948. On the death of King's chief lieutenant, Ernest Lapointe, in 1941, he appointed St. Laurent, a successful bilingual

Flag of the Province of Quebec

lawyer from Quebec City with close connections with the leading Montreal and Toronto businessmen.

As a conservative French Canadian and as King's loyal lieutenant during World War II, St. Laurent earn the gratitude of many anglophones and the criticism of ardent Quebec nationalists who accused him of "selling out" to the English. This well-educated, silver-haired statesman became so well liked in English Canada that he was dubbed "Uncle Louis" by the English-language press. St. Laurent quickly came to symbolize Canada's post-war stability and affluence, thereby gaining respect in both anglophone and francophone Canada. Until his retirement in 1957, St. Laurent provided a psychologically important French presence in Ottawa, even though he was a conservative French Canadian, much in the mold of Sir Wilfrid Laurier.

Another French-Canadian conservative, Maurice Duplessis, remained Quebec's premier until his death in 1959 and his Union Nationale ruled uninterruptedly for the next 16 years as well as for one last term from 1966 to 1970. Duplessis and his party resorted to Quebec nationalist rhetoric at every opportunity. In two important cases Duplessis followed his words with concrete steps: he introduced a provincial income tax to make Quebec somewhat less dependent financially on Ottawa. Additionally, he adopted a new Quebec flag that underscores the province's French character: the *fleur-de-lis* which portrays a white cross on a blue field and a white *fleur-de-lis* in each quadrant. This flag still flies over the National Assembly building in Quebec City and is far more visible throughout the province than the Canadian maple leaf flag which was adopted in the 1960s to placate Quebec sensitivities by purging all traces of the British heritage.

Nevertheless, Duplessis was an older, more conservative form of nationalism. By raising the specter of integration with English Canada, he maintained the support of the Catholic Church in the province, which in return retained its hold over the education of the Catholic French majority. By the 1950s many Quebecers were beginning to call on the government to follow the example of other provinces and become more active in the fields of education, health and welfare, and even to wield the state's power in the economic sector in order to loosen anglophones' grip and to stem the inflow of investment capital and companies from English Canada and the U.S.

Before the "conquest" of 1763, the state in New France always intervened heavily in economic affairs. Yet, for the next 200 years energetic state activity had not

Quebec Premier Jean Lesage, April 1964
Public Archives Canada/PA108147

been a part of the Quebec political tradition. Under British rule, Quebecers were suspicious of the state, even including the province's political system, which had originally been modeled on British governmental practice.

Quebecers considered it to be safer to rely on traditional French-Canadian institutions, especially the Catholic Church, to educate the young and to provide any additional health or welfare assistance that individuals might need. Duplessis respected these traditions as he still clung to the belief that the Quebec nation was and always would remain essentially rural and agrarian.

The Union Nationale merely papered over temporarily the momentous social, economic, and attitudinal changes that were occurring in Quebec. Quebec was already becoming rapidly industrialized and urbanized; by 1945 less than a third of Quebecers lived in rural areas, as opposed to three-quarters in 1900. Also, the bitter Asbestos strike of 1949 revealed how militant some of Quebec's trade unions had become. As René Lévesque, who would later be Quebec's premier, noted, modern *Québécois* had become "city dwellers, wage-earners, tenants. The standards of parish, village, and farm have been splintered." More and more articulate reformers began to criticize the conservative and, they claimed, corrupt Quebec government while calling for fundamental changes in the way the province was ruled. These critics were at first centered at Laval University and the University of Montreal.

Laval was established in 1852 as an outgrowth of the Jesuit seminary of Quebec City, been inspired in part by the desire to have a French-language alternative to McGill, the venerated English-speaking university in Montreal. Later, the University of Montreal was created, first as a French-language branch of Laval and then in 1920 as a university with its own charter.

No critic was more prominent than a young, brilliant, and wealthy law professor at the University of Montreal, Pierre Elliott Trudeau. Born into a prominent Montreal family of a Scottish mother, from whom he learned to speak perfect English, and a *Québécois* father, Trudeau was given a first-rate classical education at the Jesuit-operated College Jean de Brebeuf in Montreal.

Trudeau rounded off his education at the University of Montreal Law School, the Sorbonne, the London School of Economics, and Harvard University. Deftly managing to elude the recruiters during World War II, Trudeau instead, spent an enviable youth reading philosophy and traveling both to Europe and to exotic places such as the Holy Land, China, and Tibet, unreachable at the time to young, or any, people without sizable private means. Always eccentric Trudeau, often wore gaudy and intentionally inappropriate clothing and drove his sports car to the site of the 1949 Asbestos strike to show his support for the strikers. Nevertheless, he always had at his disposal one of the most powerful minds ever produced in Canada.

In his many articles in the journal *Cite Libre*, or,"Free City", for which he was the principal contributor and editor, along with Gerard Pelletier, Trudeau used his powerful logic and language to attack his fellow Quebecers' notions of authority. Trudeau called for the use of political power as a positive instrument of the people's will to bring about social and economic progress. Trudeau advocated a kind of social democracy, free from the Church and centered in the city, rather than in the villages and farms. He and increasingly more Quebec intellectuals wanted a modern, forward-looking Quebec, in step with the times, while retaining its French character.

The year 1960 was a watershed in Quebec history. In 1960 the Quebec Liberal party, under the leadership of Jean Lesage, toppled the conservative Union Nationale government and ushered in a wave of reform that unalterably changed the province and the attitudes of its people. So momentous were the changes that everyone began speaking of a *revolution tranquille* or "quiet revolution." This term was first coined by an English Canadian journalist, but was well suited to the character of the people to whom it applied. René

Canada

Lévesque, one of its most important proponents, explained that the "quiet gives us to understand that Quebec could not change radically. Nonetheless this same old Quebec, where a system of values had broken down, was trying to organize itself to face the modern world."

The change was indeed revolutionary. From the early 1960s on, the most fundamental assumptions and beliefs of Quebecers about politics, religion, economics, and society were being carefully scrutinized and, to a large extent, discarded. Rather than viewing technology, business, industrialization and urbanization as a threat to their unique culture, *Québécois* began to regard them as instruments for elevating and improving their people. Instead of turning to traditional social institutions, such as the Catholic Church, to protect them from the modern world, they became more secular in their outlook and began to take a more positive view of the state as a tool to help Quebec develop itself to catch up with the rest of Canada.

During the "quiet revolution," Quebecers drew a much sharper boundary around their conception of the Quebec "nation" to fit the geographical boundaries of the province. Although they were to remain sensitive to the treatment of francophones in other parts of Canada, Quebecers no longer felt a national link with them; the term "French Canadian" fell into disfavor in Quebec. Most importantly, *Québécois* gained the self-confidence that they could change things if they really wanted to do so, acquiring a mood of optimism that they could be progressive and modern, while still being completely French in outlook, institutions, and language.

At first, anglophones greeted these developments as signs that Quebecers were finally developing a pragmatic Anglo-Saxon outlook which would help bring about a greater unity of Canada's two founding peoples. It was not long, though, until the opposite became obvious. Rather than becoming more attached to Canada, Quebecers were becoming more attached to Quebec. The Quebecers developed the courage, not only fundamentally to challenge Canadian federalism, but perhaps even to question the very existence of Canada as a unified country.

The Liberal Lesage government was determined that Quebec would make more of its own decisions, meaning that the provincial government would have to wield many of the powers which had long been exercised by the federal government in Ottawa. This was a direct challenge to the prevailing distribution of powers between Ottawa and the provinces. It was a matter that no government in the country's capital could ignore because it went to the core of the Canadian political system.

In coming years Ottawa made some important concessions. It agreed to give Quebec, without strings or conditions, funds which the federal government would have used to administer and finance a program in the province. The province could then design and execute the policy in its own way. An example of this so-called "opting-out" possibility was the hard-fought Quebec Pension Plan, which protects Quebecers, while other Canadians are covered by the Canada Pension Plan. By aggressively seeking out political terrain into which exclusive Quebec governmental authority could be extended, the province's political leaders were able to take advantage of numerous such "opting out" opportunities in a variety of areas, including health, education and welfare. By doing this, Quebec secured for itself a *de facto* special status within the Canadian federation.

The Lesage government, which was re-elected in 1962 under the slogan *Maitres chez nous*, "masters in our own house," was able to act decisively in the field of education, which has always been a provincial prerogative. Although it was often a controversial matter, Quebec schools had always been in the hands of the Catholic Church which was regarded as the chief protector of Quebec's values and culture. One of the most dramatic changes during the Quiet Revolution, though, was the weakening of religious sentiments that occurred almost overnight. Quebec author Roch Carrier, who was living in France at the onset of the Quiet Revolution, recalled that what surprised him most when he returned to Quebec in the early 1960s was that so few people seemed to go to church.

Two decades later, during a visit to the province, Saint Pope John Paul II went so far as to call Quebec a "dechristianized society." Polls in 1994 revealed that only 19% of *Québécois* attend religious services at least "once a week or so," the second lowest percentage among Canadian provinces; only 56% said that maintaining Christian values "is very important to me," the lowest percentage in Canada outside British Columbia. It had become secularized, and this fact was bound to affect the schools and almost everything else in Quebec society.

Many changes were introduced in rapid order, perhaps the most important of which was the creation in 1964 of a provincial Ministry of Education and a non-denominational Advisory Committee to replace the separate Catholic and Protestant Committees. The practice of appointing only Catholic clergymen as rectors of Laval and the University of Montreal was eliminated, as both universities completely severed their ties with the Catholic Church.

In 1968 a new University of Quebec, with branches all over the province, was founded with no ties to the Church. Tuition-free state high schools were created to compete with Catholic-operated schools and to break the Church's stranglehold on university admissions. This deemphasis on religion and secularization of the province's schools occurred at all levels of the school system and dramatically affected the preparation and the attitudes of the students who emerged from Quebec schools to become a part in the modernized Quebec society. In 1997 the Quebec National Assembly voted to replace the denominational school boards with French and English ones.

This secularized school system produced a new kind of graduate: one with less knowledge of philosophy, French poets and Catholic scholasticism, but with more technical and business training. This system produced a much larger middle class, with the kinds of technical skills that would enable young *Québécois* to operate in the province's business elite and to enter the civil service. Because a large portion of these graduates was unable to find jobs in the private economy, they became employees of the state, either as teachers, civil servants, or managers in newly nationalized corporations.

During the Quiet Revolution, the public sector swelled, as the Quebec state took on more and more responsibilities. This "state middle class," as it was often called, became the motor and backbone for the continuing Quiet Revolution and, as we shall see, for that separatist party which gained power in 1976: The *Parti Québécois or Quebec Party* (PQ).

The activism of the Quebec state was apparent in the province's economy. The basic rationale was that if Quebecers were to be "masters in their own house," they would have to have more influence within the economy, which was largely controlled by anglophone Canadians and Americans. The Lesage government tackled this objective head-on by creating and expanding state economic enterprises. The most successful of these, Hydro-Quebec, created in 1962, was the project of one of Lesage's cabinet ministers, René Lévesque. This new state-owned enterprise integrated Quebec's many hydro-electric facilities and became the province's largest employer. Its cheap electricity became essential for the industrial rebirth and revival of business confidence in Quebec during the late 1980s and 1990s.

More important for Quebec nationalists was the fact that the working language within Hydro-Quebec was made exclusively French because this insured that the management of the enterprise would be solely in the hands of francophones.

France's President de Gaulle: "Vive le Québec libre!"
Public Archives Canada/C6013

In order to demonstrate further that successful economic undertakings need not be directed by anglophones, French was made the exclusive working language of the Manicougan Dam construction, the largest such structure in the world, even though the capital for this mega-project had to be raised in the U.S. French was also the working language of the later massive hydro-electric project at James Bay in the 1970s. Even though francophone ownership of and management positions within the economy grew by leaps and bounds in the 1960s and 1970s, the goal of wresting control over the province's economy from anglophone hands never succeeded.

In 1966 the *Union Nationale* defeated the Liberal Lesage government and experienced its last chance to hold the reins of Quebec provincial power before disappearing from the political scene. The event most remembered during this four-year period was the Montreal Exposition in 1967. The federal government in Ottawa gave full support for this world fair, which commemorated the centennial of the founding of the Canadian confederation in 1867. This massive event was to underscore the success in creating a unified Canada. But the aftermath of this Expo would reveal and widen the rifts existing in the confederation.

The Expo 67, arguably the most successful of all world fairs, was a source of great pride for Quebecers, one-third of whom live in Montreal. Expo displayed to the world that the Quebecers could successfully manage a large, glittering project the people of many nations could enjoy. The fair attracted the world's attention to the accomplishments and the aspirations of a province that had changed so much in less than a decade while also alerting it to the festering wound right in the heart of Canada.

The unpredictable French president, Charles de Gaulle, traveled to Montreal to visit the Expo in July of 1967. There were signs of trouble when his cruiser, the *Colbert*, picked him up on the French island of Saint Pierre and sailed up the St Laurence, dispensing with the customary naval courtesy of flying the Canadian flag. de Gaulle's enthusiasm was whetted during his 10-hour motor trip to Montreal through 22 communities along the St. Lawrence River. He noted: "I have encountered an atmosphere the same as at the Liberation" (of France in 1944–5). Prime Minister Lester Pearson commented: "Canadians do not need to be liberated." The irony was that during World War II, anglophone Canadians were much more sympathetic to de Gaulle's Free French mission than were francophone Canadians, many of whom were staunch supporters of Marshall Pétain.

The French president went to Montreal intending to make trouble. de Gaulle told his son-in-law before leaving for Quebec, "I will hit hard. Hell will happen, but it has to be done." Further, he told his aide that his visit "will make waves" and that he would "make history." de Gaulle was right as he gave an unforgettable speech from the balcony of Montreal's City Hall in which he repeated the separatist slogan: *Vive le Québec libre*, "Long live free Quebec." This utterance unleashed chants among the thousands of Quebecers who heard it: *Québec libre! Oui, Oui, Oui! De Gaulle l'a dit! Oui, oui!* Or "A free Quebec! Yes, yes, yes! De Gaulle said it! Yes, yes!" The Canadian government immediately and indignantly announced that such support for the separatists on the part of a foreign chief of state was "unacceptable." The proud Frenchman left the country within hours.

Some of de Gaulle cabinet thought he went too far. Foreign Minister Couve de Murville called his speech "bloody stupid." Yet, de Gaulle showed no remorse. In a November 1967 press conference, de Gaulle hailed Quebec as a "sovereign state, master of its national independence." A decade later, René Lévesque admitted, "we owe him enormous recognition for having made us known throughout the world with this fortunate blunder." Yet, Lévesque and other cooler heads were aware that such pronouncements could propel irresponsible forces that become difficult to control and that thereby endanger, rather than facilitate, the achievement of important goals.

It is important to note that it was not until two decades later, in 1987, that a French president again visited Canada. This time the tone of the visit was very different. President François Mitterrand made a point of arriving in Ottawa, not Quebec, and his toast to his Canadian hosts was: *Vive le Canada! Vive la France!*

The political developments and the violence that were taking place in Quebec toughened the will of the political leaders in Ottawa and Quebec to seek solutions that went to the very roots of the problem. The Liberal government in Ottawa intensified its efforts to so change Canada that francophones could not help but recognize Canada as a congenial home for all of them.

Pierre Elliott Trudeau is often incorrectly credited with having ushered in the kinds of changes in Canada that ultimately undercut the separatist movement in Quebec. He was later to lend his prestige and intellect to bridging the huge gulf that had developed between Quebec and the rest of Canada. Even so, Trudeau had not yet joined the Liberal Party in 1963 when the new Liberal government of Lester Pearson appointed a Royal Commission on Bilingualism and Biculturalism to find and document the causes of the crisis and to propose ways of dealing with the serious frictions that existed between "the two founding races."

The Commission's first report in 1965 left no doubt that francophones were severely limited in their efforts to advance economically and to preserve their language and culture. The report documented the fact that these two aspirations were linked. The conclusion was that "Canada, without being fully conscious of the fact, is passing through the greatest crisis of its history." Many of the subsequent reforms were based on this groundbreaking report. Affectionately called "Mike," Pearson also played the leading

Canada

role in introducing universal medicare, the Canada-U.S. Auto Pact, and the Canada Pension Plan. In 1965 he also ordered the new Canadian maple leaf flag to be run up parliament's Peace Tower. By getting rid of the remnants of the British flag on Canada's colors, Pearson eliminated another potential irritant in Quebec's adjustment to Canada.

Pearson found an undeniably competent and effective lieutenant and ultimate successor in Trudeau, who joined the Liberal Party in 1965 and was elected to the House of Commons in the same year. Trudeau wanted to demonstrate that the aspirations of francophone Canada could be furthered in Ottawa as well as in Quebec City. He feared that the kind of Quebec nationalism that was emerging would not only destroy Canada but would drive Quebec into isolation. Trudeau believed that only a tolerant federalism could remedy the situation.

In 1966 Trudeau was appointed as Justice Minister, lending his support to enlarging what was called "cooperative federalism." This meant in practice that all ten provinces would be granted their full powers under the BNA and that Ottawa would return to the provinces all the powers that it had assumed during the 1950s. "Cooperative federalism" also led to periodic meetings and consultations between the governments in Ottawa and the ten provincial capitals, so that provincial concerns could be aired and influence on federal policy strengthened. These meetings are still a part of routine Canadian political practice.

The Liberal Party government decided that it would be appropriate to remove a symbol from the country's flag which many francophones found to be insulting: the Union Jack, a reminder of Canada's imperial heritage. The debate over the design of the new flag was bitter and protracted. One proposal, to combine the Union Jack and the *fleur-de-lis,* was rejected. Finally, the present flag, with a single red maple leaf on a white field, was adopted.

Perhaps the most important measure the Liberal government took to quell the fears of francophones was to create a bilingual Canada, in which francophones would feel equal and at home everywhere. In 1969 the Official Languages Act made Canada officially a bilingual country. The brunt of this new law was felt most immediately in the federal civil service, where more and more jobs were reserved for bilingual Canadians. In coming years this law had a greater and greater impact on many dimensions of Canadian life. The move to transform Canada into a bilingual country was not greeted positively in all quarters of Canadian society. Many anglophones,

particularly in the West, found it to be an unnecessary and unjustified imposition while many Quebecers viewed it as not going far enough in protecting French language rights.

The policies which the Liberal governments of Lester Pearson and Pierre Elliott Trudeau introduced were in the long run were important for the salvation of Canada as a unified country. However, in the 1960s and 1970s they were unable to satisfy the ardor of Quebec nationalism. No Canadian needed a reminder in the 1970s that the country faced dangers which threatened to rip it asunder. It was clear that if a peaceful solution could not be found, then Canada could be buffeted by something rather rare in the Canadian experience: violence.

In the early 1960s a rough separatist group emerged, the *Rassemblement pour l'Independence Nationale,* led by the young socialist firebrand Pierre Bourgault. A few bombing incidents occurred in Montreal in February 1963, and in October 1964 a visit by the British Queen to Quebec City to commemorate the 1864 Confederation Conference ignited frightening riots.

The stakes were raised considerably in the summer and fall of 1970 when an extremist separatist organization, the *Front de Liberation du Québec,* the Front for the Liberation of Quebec, or FLQ perpetrated a series of violent deeds, beginning with bombings and robberies, culminating in the twin kidnapping of Richard Cross, senior British trade commissioner in Montreal, and Pierre Laporte, Quebec's minister of labor and immigration. Because flurry of police and political activity could not defuse the crisis, Premier Bourassa requested Ottawa to send in the army. In a now famous television

Trudeau and Lévesque

confrontation on the steps of Parliament on October 13, Trudeau scornfully noted, "bleeding hearts just don't like to see people with guns and helmets. Go on and bleed. It is more important to keep law and order." When queried about how far he would go to maintain order, he snapped "just watch me!"

On October 16, Canadians held their breath as Prime Minister Trudeau proclaimed the War Measures Act and outlawed the FLQ and any organization promoting the use of force. Extremists wasted no time in responding to Ottawa's sternness; the next day they murdered Pierre Laporte and left his bloodied body in the trunk of an abandoned car.

Political assassinations are rare in Canadian history; only two have occurred since 1867. When they do occur, though , the federal government acts with an energy and determination to which Americans are unaccustomed. For instance, when the political leader, D'Arcy McGee, was assassinated on the steps of his Ottawa

War Measures Act: soldiers at the Palais de Justice (police headquarters), Quebec
Public Archives Canada/PA129838

Lighting the flame at the Summer Olympic Games, Montreal, July 1976
Public Archives Canada/PA115800

boardinghouse in 1868, the government suspended Habeas Corpus, arrested 70 suspects and held them for four months without charging them or permitting them to speak to lawyers.

A century later, Trudeau had the full support of his countrymen to respond to the Laporte murder by whatever means, signaling that he was willing to take full advantage of that support. After a wave of searches and arrests, Cross was located alive and he was freed in return for allowing his kidnapers to fly off to Cuba. This frightening crisis reminded Canadians that they were not free of the scourge of violence that was afflicting other democratic countries at the time. Still, it demonstrated the willingness of Canadian governments to act with great energy and determination against overt threats to undermine the constitutional order in Canada. Between 1963 and 1970, the FLQ ignited over 200 bombs in Montreal, killing at least five and wounding dozens. Terrorism never entrenched itself in the Quebec separatist movement.

From 1970 to 1976 Quebec was again governed by the *Liberal Party* under the leadership of Robert Bourassa. Bourassa and his Liberal government sought to maintain many of the gains that transpired since the Quiet Revolution, but they were leery of the central assumption of the revolution that a continuing expansion of the government's powers and activities was necessary or good for Quebec. The Liberals were concerned that excessive confrontations with anglophones who were well-entrenched in the province's economy would damage the investment climate in the province and thereby hurt Quebecers more than help.

Bourassa was not convinced that much good could flow from Quebec's separation from Canada. Consequently, he by and large supported Canada's federal system. Under his administration there were no major transfers of powers or resources from the federal capital to Quebec City. Critics contended that Bourassa had not pressed Quebec's demands energetically enough.

The Bourassa government did become the first in Quebec to pass comprehensive legislation dealing with the status of French in Quebec. His government did not believe that the federal Official Languages Act of 1969 was strong enough to shore up the French language in Quebec and to satisfy nationalist sentiments. Bill 22 declared that French alone is the province's "official language."

Bill 22 bitterly angered Quebec's anglophones, some of whom went so far as to accuse the government of using "Nazi-like tactics" and committing "cultural genocide." Still, by the standards of language legislation that was to come later, Bill 22 was mild. For instance, it did not require that English-language schools in the province be restricted exclusively to children whose mother tongue was English. Because the majority of immigrant children continued to go to English-language schools, many francophones viewed the bill as a farce that would not really change their status within Quebec.

On the occasion of the second gala event in Montreal within a single decade, the 1976 Olympic Games, the world again had the opportunity to witness the political and economic turmoil in a province so deeply in process of change. The opening of the games was preceded by bitter labor strikes and protests which had strong Quebec nationalist overtones. Many labor union leaders and members had clearly become militant and nationalist. All was

not in order in *la belle province*, and in 1976 important challenges to Canadian unity were again on the horizon.

Both Ottawa and Quebec City had sought in different ways to satisfy francophone desires. The result is a tug-of-war that will dominate Canadian politics for the rest of the century. Many *Québécois* remained frustrated and political forces were emerging within Quebec that steered toward independence. In the 1960s a heterogeneous coalition of Quebecers who wanted to push the Quiet Revolution further sought a fairer relationship between Quebec and the rest of Canada or who wanted a totally separate Quebec took shape. This diversity was never easy to manage, but for at least two decades it was held together by the only Quebecer who possessed the necessary charisma, political skill and patience to be its leader: René Lévesque.

The son of a French-speaking country lawyer in New Carlisle, a predominantly English-speaking town of about a thousand inhabitants surrounded by the French-speaking world of Quebec's Gaspé Peninsula, Lévesque grew up bilingually. Therefore, as an adult who could speak perfect English, he personally suffered neither discrimination for being a francophone nor the trauma of having to learn English as a foreign language. Nevertheless, he remembers the taunts exchanged by bands of French and English Canadians: "They used to call us 'peasoupers'; we called them 'crawfish'."

Lévesque's Quebec nationalism flowered early; while a student in the Jesuit-run Garnier College prep school, he wrote in one of his papers: "Never forget that you are French Canadians, that your own people have been stagnating for generations, and that if they, the people, *your* people do not act, they are lost!" In the early 1940s he abandoned his law studies, or, as he remembers it, "they began to abandon me." Because it was wartime, Lévesque was under the threat of being drafted into the Canadian army. His attitude about this prospect was vintage *Québécois*: "Though I was willing to go overseas, I was not willing to go in the uniform of His Majesty. I therefore went to New York in 1943 and managed to join an information office, and then to be appointed war correspondent in the American Seventh Army. I went to war on a purely intuitive impulse."

Lévesque sailed from Halifax to London early in 1944 on a ship that was not a part of a convoy, a voyage understandably resulting in ten days of "acute anxiety, especially during the night," as he recalls. At the age of 21, Lévesque edited and announced messages to occupied France.

In February 1945 Lévesque was attached to the Sixth Army and moved with this

Canada

unit and the First French Army eastward through France to the Rhineland, Bavaria and Austria. Lévesque was present at the battle of Nuremberg and was among the first to discover the horrors of Dachau concentration camp a few miles outside of Munich and to speak with the liberated French leaders, including Edouard Daladier, Leon Jouraux, Paul Reynaud, and General Weygand, whom the Germans had imprisoned in comfortable confinement in a castle. Lévesque saw Mussolini's mutilated body and he was one of the few journalists to hear Hermann Goering a few minutes after his surrender.

After the war, Lévesque became a political journalist, a job that took him across Canada and the U.S., to Korea and back to Europe. In the mid-1950s he switched from radio journalism to become one of Canada's first TV journalists. Lévesque's half-hour Sunday evening program, *Point de Mire*, "Focal Point," first aired in October 1957 and made him a celebrity as it focused on international issues. Because most Quebecers at that time had little schooling and exposure outside of French Canada, this became their window to the world. Moreover, because Radio-Canada, the Quebec equivalent to the Canadian Broadcasting Corporation, had a TV monopoly in Quebec at that time, he became extremely popular with his ratings sometimes reaching 100%. The show made Lévesque's diminutive figure, his gravelly voice, and his well-informed opinions familiar to millions of Canadians.

Lévesque's program consisted of a study of one event or one problem occupying a central point in the news. This focus enabled him to make the transition from international problems, which had occupied him for more than a decade, to domestic politics. The federal government's rough handling of a 68-day strike at Radio Canada greatly angered Lévesque. "I was scared, even traumatized by that experience, so that sooner or later I felt I would have to enter politics."

In politics, Lévesque served in the Liberal Party cabinet of Jean Lesage for six years as the minister of natural resources and came to incorporate the aspirations of the Quiet Revolution. However, he gradually grew impatient with the Liberal provincial government, which, he believed, did not press vigorously enough for an independent Quebec. Lévesque was unable to persuade the Liberals to adopt a manifesto he had published calling for sovereignty for Quebec within a common market association with Canada. Therefore, Lévesque and a group of moderate, but disgruntled, Liberals left their party in 1967 and formed the *Mouvement Souverainete-Association*, the Movement for Sovereignty-Association or MSA. A year later the *MSA* merged with other smaller separatist parties, the right-wing *Ralliement national or National Rally* (*RN*) and the somewhat demagogic, "grass roots" *Rassemblement pour l'independence nationale* or Rally for National Independence (RIN) to form the *Parti Québécois* (*PQ*). Because the precise objectives of these three parties were never the same, the internal strains would always plague the larger group, weakening and fragmenting it in the 1980s.

The *PQ* became a basket for a diverse collection of Quebecers who wanted to see the Quiet Revolution carried on with greater energy even though they disagreed on how radical the political and economic changes should be and who wished to see some kind of sovereign Quebec even though they could not agree about just how sovereign. Only René Lévesque could hold such a movement together.

Lévesque was a cautious leader who insisted that the party be democratic and respectable. His notion of sovereignty-association was a compromise around which party members could unify. Although Lévesque was always careful not to define this notion too concretely, he said that "we do not want to end, but rather to radically transform, our union with the rest of Canada, so that, in the future, our relations will be based on full and complete equality." Quebec was only a "half-fledged state" in conflict with the rest of Canada; "in order to end once and for all the struggle of wills, the costly dividing up of energies and resources, the system must be replaced."

The finished product Lévesque envisaged was not a francophone nation that would completely turn its back on Canada. For him, sovereignty-association "means a sovereign State of Quebec which will accept, or rather offer in advance, new links of interdependence with Canada, but links which will this time be negotiated between equal peoples, as a function of their geographic and other unquestionable common interest." Thus, although the "obsolete constitutional links" would have to be cut, there would still be links of free trade, free travel without passports between Quebec and Canada, a common currency, a joint administration of the St. Lawrence Seaway and a military alliance with Canada, the U.S., and NATO.

Although Quebecers were not unified insofar as their precise expectations for a new relationship with Canada were concerned, many of them were drawn to the PQ, which appealed to all the diverse values which francophones in Quebec considered important. The reward was 30% of the popular vote in 1973 and a stunning electoral victory for the PQ in the Quebec provincial elections in November 1976. Lévesque's party won only 41% of the vote in Quebec, and as a government without a majority of the inhabitants behind it, he had to move cautiously. However, Lévesque had won an absolute majority of francophones' votes, winning in every region in Quebec except in the anglophone-dominated West Montreal. He drew votes from all classes of *Québécois*, but his showing was particularly strong among the young and the professional and semi-professional middle class, especially teachers.

With the support of a majority of francophones, Lévesque perceived that he had a mandate for change. However, the terms for that mandate were not clear. The PQ voters who wanted sovereignty did not agreement on exactly what form it should take. Many Quebecers voted for the PQ because they wanted "clean government" after Bourassa's administration

Young Quebecers with the provincial flag

was tainted by scandals. Their vote was by no means an endorsement of Quebec sovereignty. What most PQ voters did agree on, though, was that the protections for the French language should be even tighter than those provided in Bill 22.

The result was Bill 101, which required that all public signs, including road signs, and every form of commercial advertising be exclusively in French. Thus, Eaton's and Ogilvy's department stores were compelled to remove the apostrophe from their name. In contrast, McDonald's survived in Quebec with its apostrophe. Yet, a greasy spoon diner in Montreal, "Irv's Light Lunch," had to be renamed "Chez Irv."

Quebec's language officials ruled in 2000 that companies with English-language registered trademark names cannot be forced to use French versions in Quebec. The officials argued that international law protects the use of such names. This did not help Quebec-born race driver Jacques Villeneuve who was reported to the language police in 2001 for naming his new Montreal restaurant "Newtown," the English translation of his last name and his nickname in racing circles. Villeneuve responded to those who complained: "You have to look further than the tip of your nose. It's a big world!"

Another change was that access to English-language schools was restricted to children with at least one parent who was educated in English *in* Quebec. That meant that not only immigrant children, but the offspring of anglophones from other Canadian provinces were required to attend French-language schools. Thanks to a decision by the Supreme Court of Canada, the last provision was softened to permit children with a parent who was educated in English anywhere in Canada to attend English-language schools.

By 2007, 80% of immigrant children learned in French and more than half of those whose mother tongue was neither French nor English could converse in both languages. However, in 2000 a Superior Court in Quebec upheld legislation forbidding francophone children from attending English schools. The judge ruled that Quebec has a responsibility to protect French. The Supreme Court of Canada by a vote of 7–0 reached the same outcome in 2005.

Bill 101 went beyond Bill 22 by requiring that French alone be used for provincial legislation, public administration, the judicial system, most public institutions. It originally required that laws and tribunals would be in French only, but that was later struck down. Ultimately, Bill 101 would have to be used as the working language in all businesses within the province. Employers were obligated to write all communications to their employees

The late Hon. René Lévesque

in French and they could not dismiss or demote employees simply because they spoke no English.

A watch-dog *Office de la langue française*, the Office of the French Language, was set up to settle disputes arising from this law. It could be anticipated that this office would be overly vigilant in protecting the French language. Perhaps the most widely publicized and most regrettable instance of overreaction was the 1983 case of an elderly patient in Montreal's St. Mary's hospital. Officials in this Office determined that a patient was denied her "right to die in French." The investigator maintained that the patient's nurses spoke little or no French in the intensive care ward during 34% of the time she was dying. The official waived off the hospital's objections that services were always available in French, arguing that humane and legal treatment required that all contact and every sound uttered within hearing distance of a francophone patient had to be in French.

Bill 101 understandably antagonized many anglophones in Quebec. The Lévesque government dismissed the demand of anglophones that the language rights of the minority be respected; the government correctly pointed out that the language rights of the French minority in other provinces had never been effectively guaranteed. The law created new opportunities for francophones and forced the anglophone minority, not the francophone majority, to pay the economic price for unilinguallism.

The *PQ* made little headway in bringing more of Quebec's economy under state domination and in wresting control from anglophones in the rest of Canada or the U.S. Some members of Lévesque's party were demanding that the government

break the anglophone capitalists' hold over the province's economy, no matter what the costs. Yet, Lévesque believed that the economic recession that led to growing unemployment in the 1970s made any such moves risky. Instead, he focused in the late 1970s on finding the right moment to fulfill a promise he and his party had made during the 1976 election campaign: to conduct a referendum in order to establish Quebec as a sovereign state. This finally happened in May 1980.

Remembering that the bloodiest war in American history was fought from 1861 to 1865 in order to deny states the right to secede from the Union, an American is likely to be amazed by the fact that a Canadian government would permit the citizens of a province to hold a vote over whether they wished to destroy the country's unity. It is true that the prime minister made a veiled threat that he would resort to force if Quebec tried anything "illegal," but he never clarified what action might be illegal.

During the entire campaign, Lévesque and his party stressed the peaceful and democratic nature of their cause. He had amply demonstrated in the past that he wanted nothing to do with firebrands willing to depart from democratic terrain. In any case, the entire campaign proceeded without violence, and there is absolutely no evidence that any kind of fear of civil war influenced the outcome of the vote. This forbearance and absence of violence indicated how different the political temperaments of Canadians and Americans are.

Lévesque had always been aware of how sensitive the question of Quebec independence had always been. He knew well that while many *Québécois* were dissatisfied with the federal structure as it existed, they were not in favor of complete independence. Lévesque therefore was ambivalent and hesitating as he preferred to proceed toward his goal in stages which he termed *étapisme*, thereby reaping scorn from the separatists who wanted immediate and decisive action.

The wording of the referendum revealed Lévesque's sensitivity for a wavering francophone attitude about independence: "The Government of Quebec has made public its proposal to negotiate a new agreement with the rest of Canada, based on the equality of nations; this agreement would enable Quebec to acquire the exclusive powers to make its laws, levy its taxes and establish relations abroad—in other words, sovereignty—and at the same time, to maintain with Canada an economic association including a common currency; no change in political status resulting from these negotiations will be affected without approval from the people through another referendum;

Canada

on these terms, do you give the Government of Quebec the mandate to negotiate the proposed agreement between Quebec and Canada?"

Clearly, the premier feared a "once and for all" vote to secede and merely asked for the right to talk to Ottawa about a new kind of arrangement. By watering down the gravity of the choice, Lévesque hoped to gather in as large a flock of *Québécois* as possible.

The Trudeau government in Ottawa campaigned enthusiastically against the question, and it no doubt influenced the vote. For one thing, it was difficult for the *PQ* to argue persuasively that Quebecers were an exploited and degraded race within the Canadian federation when the government in Ottawa was led by a prime minister, Trudeau, a finance minister, Marc Lalonde, and a justice minister, Jean Chrétien, all of whom were Quebecers. Also, the long-standing differences in income and opportunity that existed between anglophones and francophones in Quebec had largely disappeared.

As debate continued, the government of Canada and of all other provinces announced they would not negotiate any form of sovereignty-association with Quebec, including an economic common market. Finally, the Trudeau government promised that a *non* vote would result in the BNA's being replaced by a new constitution which could be amended at home and which would bring about a kind of "renewed federalism" which would be satisfactory to all of Canada's ten provinces.

The results of the vote stunned the *PQ:* 59.5% of Quebecers voted against Lévesque's proposal. As anticipated, an overwhelming majority of Quebec's anglophone population voted against the proposition. However, his followers were shocked that a narrow majority of 52% of francophone *Québécois* also voted against the proposition. Quebecers under the age of 40 voted overwhelmingly for the proposition, but their votes could not salvage the battered dreams of Quebec separatism. In provincial parliamentary elections on April 13, 1981 less than a year later, 49% of Quebecers voted for the PQ, giving the party a majority of 80 of 122 seats in the Quebec National Assembly. Nevertheless, the road to a separate, sovereign Quebec had become hopelessly blocked. The 1980 referendum brought a palpable change in Quebecers' political attitudes toward the *PQ* and separatism.

By the end of 1984 it was clear to Lévesque that separatism had reached a dead end and that it would be disastrous for the *PQ* to make this issue the centerpiece of the next provincial election.

Already, polls were indicating that only a fifth to a third of Quebecers would vote for the *PQ*. Since 1981 the *PQ* has suffered a distressing loss of members, down to 113,000 from an all-time high in 1982 of 300,000. Without the belief in Quebec sovereignty, which had united the party's faithful in the past, the PQ had increasingly become a loose coalition of social democrats and conservatives who had little in common.

A deep economic recession in 1982–3, which drove unemployment figures upwards to 15%, prompted a series of severe government austerity measures to roll back the salaries of provincial civil servants and halted labor negotiations in the public sector. These measures, to which Lévesque saw no alternative, eroded the *PQ's* image as a social democratic movement and alienated Quebec's public sector employees, labor union members and young people, who had been among the PQ's staunchest supporters. Also, a series of embarrassing scandals in the highest leadership levels of the PQ rocked the party's image as a party of honesty and clean government; these included the conviction of one leader on charges of sexually molesting young girls and of another for shoplifting in a Montreal department store.

Paradoxically, a major reason why separatism had ebbed temporarily as a mainstream political force was that the nationalist thrust had accomplished so much in the preceding quarter of a century. These successes convinced many Quebecers that they could advance their social and cultural causes within the Canadian Confederation. Because of the Official Languages Act of 1969, the use of French has been expanded throughout Canada, and the number of bilingual Canadians has greatly increased.

Québécois also made gigantic strides that were obvious to almost everyone. In the 1960s only 4% of *Québécois* went to universities, compared with 20% in the 1980s. One in six of these students studies business or economics now, as compared with one in ten in the rest of Canada. Francophones have become more comfortable in the boardrooms of Quebec's businesses. In the 1960s they owned only 20% of the province's economy; by the 1980s that figure had doubled to 40%.

The government in Ottawa did, in fact, produce a new constitution for Canada after tireless discussions with provincial governments. The 1982 constitution spells out provincial rights more accurately than did the BNA, and it contains a bill of rights that can be invoked by those who perceive language discrimination anywhere in Canada.

Feeling that he had been out-maneuvered in the negotiations leading up to the new constitution, Lévesque refused to sign the new document. Instead, he indicated in 1984 that he would not require as a condition for his signature a Quebec veto over future amendments. His willingness to cooperate with Ottawa on this important issue was not only due to the fact that the air had gone out of the separatist balloon. Lévesque was then dealing with a prime minister in Ottawa, Brian Mulroney, a Quebecer himself, and whom Lévesque found much more con genial and sympathetic than Trudeau.

Bill 101 made French the sole official language and greatly expanded its use in all sectors of Quebec society, despite the judicial restrictions that have been placed on it. The bill prompted scores of anglophone firms, such as the Sun Life Assurance Company's huge corporate headquarters, and thousands of English-speaking citizens to leave the province, reducing the percentage of Quebecers who listed English as their mother tongue from 14.7 in 1971 to 12.7 in 1981. In fact, a University of Montreal demographer, Jacques Henripin, even predicted that if anglophones continued to leave the province at the rate that they did during the 1970s, the English community would disappear within 50 years. This result is unlikely.

Just as Quebec City, which was once 40% English, is now almost wholly French, so Quebec province has become more French and will probably continue to do so. The problem remains in Montreal, though, where the percentage of French-speaking residents declined from 64% in 1951 to 60% in 1992. This is partly because 90% of all immigrants in Quebec settle there, and two-thirds of them do not speak French. The anglophone exodus opened new economic opportunities for francophones. Francophone businesses supplied 61.6% of the jobs in 1987, compared with 54.8% in 1978. Many formerly anglophone neighborhoods opened to francophones, a fact which helps break down the "Two Solitudes" which had long characterized these groups' lack of contact with each other.

Quebecers seemed to be tired of language battles but have unmistakably heard the message that Quebec is a French-speaking province, at least on the surface. Yet, numerous appeals to the Supreme Courts of Quebec and Canada progressively weakened the application of Act 101. At the end of 1986, the Quebec Court of Appeal declared that those parts of Act 101 mandating French-only signs violated Quebecer's rights to freedom of expression and were therefore unconstitutional. This decision provoked a storm

Former Prime Minister Chrétien meeting with provincial premiers

Photo: J.M. Carisse

among nationalists just when the new premier, Bourassa, and new mayor, Jean Doré, were trying to put the linguistic wars behind them and revitalize Montreal as an international finance center. Businesses taking advantage of the new ruling faced a rash of bomb threats, window smashing and a fire-bombing. Language tension reentered *"la belle province."*

In the long run, more and more *Québécois* are becoming bilingual. One prominent advocate of English rights noted: "There is linguistic peace. . . . We have evolved from perceiving ourselves as part of the English-Canadian majority to learning to live naturally and willingly as a minority."

Even though polls in 1985 indicated that only four percent of Quebecers favored the complete independence of the province, the dream of such a future died hard. The radical separatist and professor at the University of Quebec at Montreal, Pierre Bourgault, called this development an "end of a dream. End of an era . . . Today it is possible to see that all along Lévesque was on the wrong track with the wrong people. He was still pursuing the Quiet Revolution while his troops wanted something else . . . It all goes back to a big mistake that happened at the beginning: separatists had an idea about Quebec, and it came to fruition in René Lévesque. But he had different ideas at different times. The truth is that Lévesque flirted with separatism because the idea seduced him, but in the end, he lacked the will to promote separatism. And in the end, he betrayed himself. What now?"

Also, the Montreal playwright Michel Tremblay declared: "It took us 200 years to wake up, and now we seem to be going back to sleep. I don't even dare consider the future, things are so bad. We had

promised our children a country, and we haven't delivered."

With an eye to Quebec's history, it would be safe to say that Quebec nationalism never dies; it just dies down temporarily. Nevertheless, Lévesque decided that the time was not ripe for independence. In 1984, at the end of a bitter intra-party debate that raged since 1982, he declared that in the next provincial election "sovereignty must not be at stake, neither wholly nor in parts that are more or less disguised." This pronouncement prompted the resignation of seven of his cabinet members, and further resignations and by-election losses reduced his party's majority in the National Assembly from 80 to 65. But in an extraordinary *PQ* convention held in 1985, a majority of delegates (869 to 453) voted to shelve the issue of Quebec sovereignty. This caused such an uproar within the party that Lévesque himself announced his resignation in mid-1985.

At the end of 1985, the *PQ* handed the reins of power back to the man and the party from whom it had wrested them in 1976, Robert Bourassa and the *Liberal Party*. A freelance journalist, Benoit Aubin, wrote: "Quebecers, for better or for worse, seem to have decided to join the rest of North America." Yet, in 1989 separatism roared back on the political agenda when the *PQ*, led by Jacques Parizeau and running again on an independence platform, won 40% of the votes in the provincial elections.

MEECH LAKE ACCORD

Thus, 1987 appeared to be a good time for the Canadian government to take audacious steps toward securing language harmony and finally winning Quebec endorsement of the 1982 Constitution,

introducing legislation to revise and update the 1969 Official Languages Act. The aim was to bring it in line with the 1982 Charter of Rights and Freedoms by stating that federal services will be provided in both official languages where there is "significant demand." It also reached a ground-breaking "Meech Lake Accord" with the 10 provincial premiers at an isolated Quebec retreat north of Ottawa.

The agreement they struck would have become a part of the Constitution and would have made Quebec "a distinct society." The agreement would have explicitly recognized the coexistence of French and English language groups as "a fundamental characteristic of Canada," and given Parliament and the provincial legislatures the role of preserving—but not promoting—the francophone and anglophone character of Canada. The Prime Minister sought a settlement that, in his words, would reflect "a country organized and governed in a manner that corresponds to the diversity of the Canadian people" and end "Quebec's estrangement from the Canadian constitutional family, on terms that are good for Quebec, good for our other regions and good for Canada." It is no surprise that Quebec was the first province to ratify the accord.

What were good for all provinces were the decentralizing clauses which would permit them to opt out of shared-cost programs as long as their own conformed to "national objectives," had more say on the nomination of senators and Supreme Court justices and determined their own immigration policy. Most importantly, each province would have an absolute veto on future constitutional amendments.

This accord reflected Mulroney's belief in government decentralization, local initiative, and power sharing as well as

Canada

his attachment to cultural and linguistic rights. There were many critics of the accord, the most noted of which was Pierre Elliott Trudeau, who feared a dangerous weakening of Ottawa's power: "Those Canadians who fought for a single Canada, bilingual and multicultural, can say goodbye to their dream." His close associate and later prime minister, Jean Chrétien, shared this view, and women and native peoples found in it no protection of their particular rights.

Constitutional expert Eugene Forsey called it riddled with "ambiguities and obscurities," which could actually limit the rights of linguistic minorities. His warning seemed to be borne out by events in Saskatchewan in the spring of 1988, which threatened to open wide the language wounds in Canada, which seemed to have been healed. The origin of this dispute goes back to 1980, when a francophone priest insisted on using French to enter his plea for a speeding ticket. This demand was based on Section 110 of the North-West Territories Act of 1886, which stipulated that both languages could be used in courts and assemblies and that all statutes had to be in both languages. The Canadian Supreme Court ruled in February 1988 that that statute was still valid in Saskatchewan but that the province was free to repeal Section 110 of the act.

Faced with the same problem in 1985, Manitoba chose to comply by beginning the laborious and expensive process of translating all past and present laws. Still, despite pleas from Prime Minister Mulroney, Saskatchewan's premier, Grant Devine, chose a different route. His government introduced legislation to repeal the bilingual provision of the old law. Devine argued that he had to pay attention to anglophone sentiment and to the budgetary strains that would result from translating thousands of prior laws for only 2.3% of the province's population that is francophone.

Minority language groups throughout all of Canada were incensed, despite Devine's promises to translate some of the more important laws and to provide some French-language services at an undetermined time in the future. Quebec Premier Bourassa supported Devine, but this did not quiet the storm. Coming at a time when the Meech Lake agreement was under growing attack, critics charged that Saskatchewan's actions made the agreement's commitment to "preserve" minority language rights worthless and made it clear that nobody knows exactly what the accord would do for minorities.

In 1989–90 the gulf of understanding between anglophones and francophones was widened in a way which endangered the delicate Accord. English Canadians reacted angrily in 1988 when Bourassa, faced with an intense resurgence of separatist sentiment in Quebec, prohibited the use of English on outdoor commercial signs, an action that seemed to violate the rights of Quebec's anglophones. This struck critics as a foretaste of how Quebec would use the powers implied by the "distinct society" clause in the accord, provoking a backlash and making bilingualism harder to sell in the rest of Canada. Moreover, the political storm increasingly focused on Meech Lake, as momentum against the accord gathered force in English Canada, especially in the West, New Brunswick, and Newfoundland. As the clock turned midnight on June 23, 1990, Meech Lake was dead.

In the Manitoba legislative assembly, the only native member, Elijah Harper, who wanted the accord to fail because it did not address native issues, stalled debate by procedural tricks and prevented a vote from being taken. Newfoundland's premier, Clyde Wells, objected to the "fabricated precipice" which the deadline created, and called off his own legislature's vote. Mulroney's feverish last-minute efforts to find a compromise merely antagonized opponents even more.

The outcome ignited a new wave of Quebec nationalism which. in turn, stirred up even more anti-*Québécois* resentment in anglophone Canada. It helped nurture a new sense of alienation in the West and sparked native assertiveness throughout Canada. In addition, this left a legacy of polarization and volatility and brought to the surface stresses and strains in the very fabric of Canadian society. It put wind in the sails of a new party, the *Bloc Québécois*, and carried the *PQ*, which opposed Meech Lake, to victory in the two succeeding Quebec provincial elections and perhaps more in the new century. A rising Reform Party, renamed the Canadian Alliance in 2000, thrived in the West. Because of Trudeau's and Chrétien's opposition to Meech, the federal *Liberals* became near pariahs in Quebec, but they became more popular in English Canada.

Perhaps most important, this vent left Quebec's signature off the Canadian constitution and thereby rendered Canada vulnerable to calls for Quebec separation, sending Mulroney's approval rating into the cellar at 14%. One pollster noted in 1991 that in terms of popularity, he "is tied with Fidel Castro, but higher than Saddam Hussein." The conflict alienated Mulroney from his old friend, Lucien Bouchard, and from Chrétien, with whom he shared a courteous relationship. A cover story in *Maclean's* commemorating the tenth anniversary of the Meech Lake Accord was entitled, "June 23, 1990: The Day that Changed Canada." Canada was never the same again.

A NEW CONSTITUTION FOR CANADA?

Many Quebecers interpreted the downfall of Meech Lake as their being rejected by the rest of Canada and they acted accordingly. Polls in 1991 revealed that more than two-thirds favored full sovereignty. Premier Bourassa named a "Belanger-Campeau Commission" to conduct four months of public hearings to gather opinions from Quebecers on the province's future. In March 1991, the Commission issued its report, calling for a plebiscite no later than October 26, 1992, to determine its future status, unless the federal government could present an acceptable alternative. Bourassa favored continued links with Canada, but envisaged a country that would leave the federal government with little more responsibilities than protecting the borders, managing the currency, and repaying the federal debt.

Seeing that his countrymen were unnerved, uncertain, and pessimistic, Mulroney asserted, "a sense of hurt over a constitutional failure—however real—is insufficient reason for Quebecers to give up on Canada." He promised that his government would put forward its own proposals for constitutional change to build "a new and stronger Canada. We have every intention of restructuring Canada. We have no intention of dismantling it." Mulroney added: "Let me be clear: Canada is not up for grabs. Either you have a country, or you don't. You can't have it both ways."

Mulroney's problem was to devise constitutional reforms far more comprehensive than the Meech Lake Accord in only 18 months to satisfy Quebec and all the other groups clamoring for greater autonomy from the central government. Remembering how many Canadians resented the secretive way the Meech Lake talks had been conducted behind closed doors and the fact that they had focused on Quebec's demands, the government opened up the debate and negotiations to the public and interest groups and to include something for the anglophone provinces and native peoples as well.

Mulroney's action was a radical shift in constitutional talks which had always been tugs of war between Ottawa and the provinces over who controls. To sound out the wishes of all those groups and to try to understand the deep malaise in Canada, Mulroney created a Citizens' Forum on Canada's Future, led by Keith Spicer. It organized hearings throughout the land to hear the complaints and suggestions of hundreds of thousands of Canadians, and it reported them to the government. Six provincial commissions were simultaneously held traveling hearings.

In 1991 Mulroney turned to former Prime Minister Joe Clark to head a new Ministry for Constitutional Affairs and a cabinet committee which would produce a draft proposal for amending the constitution. The challenge, in Mulroney's words, was to come up with "a new, modern and dynamic Constitution that will be accepted by all the provinces."

A bilingual Westerner, Clark's job was to turn around Westerners' and other anglophones' anti-Quebec sentiment and to get them to accept a constitutional plan that would also be compatible with Quebec's demands for recognition as a "distinct society." He had at the same time to offer Quebecers a palatable alternative to sovereignty. No one envied his task, but his performance gained him almost universal trust and respect. Clark's secret was patience, fairness, and elegant, well-crafted speeches "We can be the first generation of Canadians to pass on to the next less than was passed on to us. There is nothing automatic about this country. Canada was not here at the beginning of the last century. There is no logic that says it must be here at the beginning of the next. We have to work to keep it. We always have. This is a large and diverse country. Keeping it large without destroying its diversity has always been our challenge."

A process was set into motion that would have dramatically reduced the federal government's role in the country's affairs and enlarged the powers and responsibilities of the provinces. This was already taking place, but a constitutional change would have given added authority to the on-going shift in the balance of federal and provincial powers, which is reversing a decades-old trend toward

an ever more powerful central government. The center seemed to no longer be holding and the parts defined the whole. Ontario's premier, Bob Rae, declared "we cannot just turn the federal government into a post office. It leaves out the soul of Canada."

After two years of intense work, the premiers of the nine anglophone provinces, native leaders, and the prime minister agreed to the "Charlottetown Accord" on August 28, 1992. It included:

1. **Senate reform:** The existing appointed body would be replaced by a more powerful one elected by proportional representation at a different time than the House of Commons in which Quebec would be guaranteed one-fourth of the seats. In response to Western demands, each province would have six seats. The territories, aboriginal groups, and women would also be represented.

2. **Aboriginal rights:** The inherent native right to self-government was accepted, subject to the Charter of Rights and Freedoms, with aboriginal governments recognized as one of three orders of government, alongside Ottawa and the provinces.

3. **Division of powers:** Ottawa would recognize the provinces' exclusive power over such areas as tourism, forestry, housing, and culture. Powers would be divided more efficiently.

4. **Social and economic issues:** Commitments to preserve universal health care, the equalization between richer and poorer provinces, and the free flow of goods, capital and services throughout Canada would be enshrined in the constitution.

5. **Quebec:** It would be recognized as a "distinct society," characterized by its language, culture, and civil-law tradition,

and it would choose three Supreme Court justices.

6. **Minorities:** Anglophone communities in Quebec and francophone communities elsewhere would be protected.

Every mainstream political party and institution supported the package except the Reform Party and the *Parti Québécois*. Former Prime Minister Trudeau also opposed it. On October 26, 1992, 54% of the voters, six provinces, and the Yukon Territory said no to the accord. Only Newfoundland, New Brunswick, Prince Edward Island, and, by the closest of margins, Ontario, said yes.

Insofar as the package needed the ratification of every province and the federal government, the rejection could not have been more decisive. One drinker in a Montreal bar reportedly called it "horrendously Canadian: a populist revolt in favor of the status quo." It was a popular vote against Canada's leaders. Westerners thought the accord gave too much to Quebec, and Quebecers thought it did not do enough for them. For Quebec separatists, the Western no-vote confirmed that Canada would never recognize Quebec's special character. Parizeau said, "with Meech they said no to Quebec; this time we said it to each other."

Looking back on his dramatic 1993 election victory, Prime Minister Jean Chrétien declared that the *Tories* had "spent too much time on constitutional affairs and not enough on the economy. So I want to do exactly the reverse." He did not have that luxury. Many Canadians seemed to sense an imminent challenge to their country's unity. Canadians saw the separatist *Bloc Québécois* functioning as the official opposition in the federal parliament and the *PQ* emerging victorious in the 1994 Quebec provincial elections.

PQ leader Jacques Parizeau ordered a referendum on October 30, 1995 to clear the way for an independent Quebec. This time, the separatists came closer to victory than ever before, winning 49.4% of the votes in a huge 94% turnout. This was a gain of 10 percentage points since 1980; 60% of Quebec's francophones voted "*oui*," while nearly all anglophones and immigrants voted *non*.

Subsequent investigation revealed that many "no" ballots had been declared invalid for mysterious and trivial reasons, leading to charges of possible *PQ* election rigging. Nevertheless, Quebecers never displayed such deep dissatisfaction with the status quo. Regarding the outcome as a moral victory, Quebec's new leader, Lucien Bouchard, evoked the memory of Lévesque by proclaiming: "Let us keep the faith. The next time will be the right one. And the next time may come sooner

Quebec's Parliament Building

Canada

than people think." Parizeau, who resigned as premier after the disappointing defeat, was correct in saying that for many Canadians "this Quebec problem is like a never-ending visit to the dentist."

In the midst of the 1997 federal parliamentary elections Parizeau showed that he, himself, was that dentist. After Prime Minister Chrétien called early elections to focus on the country's economic success and challenges, Parizeau published his memoirs, *For a Sovereign Québec*, in which he admitted that he had been prepared to declare Quebec's independence immediately after a yes-vote in 1995, not after negotiations with Ottawa, as his party had proposed during the referendum campaign. The PQ government had also set aside $17 million to buy up provincial bonds it feared nervous investors might dump on the market.

This reminded Canadians that those who support Quebec sovereignty, though divided among themselves on tactics and on the definition of the term, are dead serious about Quebec independence. Quebec Premier Lucien Bouchard promised another referendum by the year 2000, but flagging interest in Quebec for complete separation has caused it to be postponed indefinitely. Polls continue to show that *Québécois* are divided on the question and that a majority continues to oppose independence. The uproar caused by Parizeau brought the issue of unity back into the center of Canadian politics

In 1995 Chrétien promised to reexamine Quebec's constitutional demands. Yet, resistance to that in anglophone Canada and in the *Reform Party,* as well as Premier Bouchard's and the *Bloc Québécois'* rejection of another round of constitutional talks, limited the prime minister to a meaningless resolution in parliament recognizing the distinct nature of Quebec. His then finance minister, Paul Martin, and most of his closest advisers were *Québécois,* and he appointed Montreal political scientist Stéphane Dion as Canada's first minister of intergovernmental affairs.

Dion, who in 2006 became party leader, helped the Liberal government in Ottawa formulate a two-pronged approach to Quebec, known as "Plan A" and "Plan B." Plan A was a national unity strategy of economic growth and job creation that would have benefited Quebec and won support throughout Canada for the notion that Quebec is a "distinct society." Plan B was hardball involving tough talk designed to disabuse *Québécois* of illusions about what life would be like if they voted for independence. Under Plan B, *Québécois* could not expect to continue using Canadian passports or money, to remain in the North American Free Trade Agreement (NAFTA), or even retain all

the territory within Quebec's current borders. In Chrétien's words, "if Canada is divisible, Quebec is divisible."

The message was clear: if anglophones, Indians, or Inuit in Quebec wanted the areas in which they live to remain in Canada, they could do so. At the end of 1997, it was clear that any abrupt move by Quebec to secede, even after a big "Yes" vote to separate, would be illegal. "There will be a negotiation with the federal government . . . no doubt about that." Federal lawyers asked the Supreme Court in 1997 to rule on the legality of a unilateral Quebec secession. Dion emphasized: Plan A was "the plan is reconciliation;" Plan B

involved "the rules of secession." "We are not governing an ordinary country. We are governing a great federation that is in danger of collapse."

On August 20, 1998, the nine Supreme Court justices issued a unanimous ruling: Quebec did not have the right under the constitution to declare independence unilaterally. The Court held that insofar as Quebec was neither a victim of "alien subjugation" nor an "oppressed people," provincial leaders had no automatic right to self-determination under international law. The Court explained that any referendum would have to offer a "clear question," such as Chrétien's proposed "Do

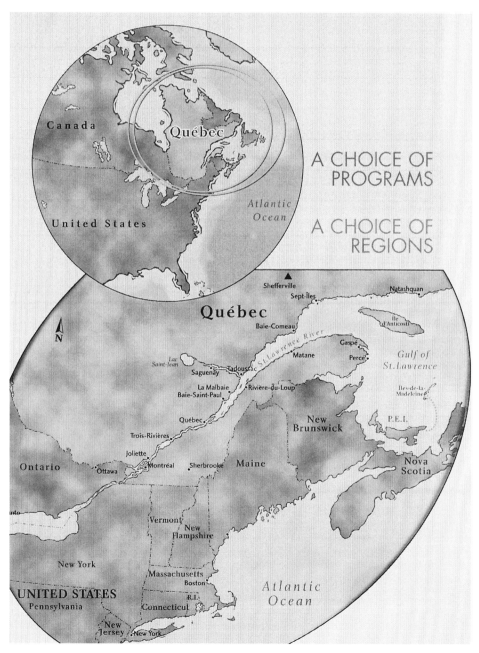

Quebec lures tourists

Quebec City

the *PQ's* intergovernmental affairs minister, "all rules governing the next referendum will be determined by the national assembly of Quebec." This declaration, along with polling results indicating that a third of those who had voted "Yes" in the 1995 referendum had thought Quebec would still be a province of Canada even if the "Yes" side won, prompted the federal government to take the initiative over the secession question for the first time in three decades.

Bill C-20, known as the "clarity bill," was introduced in December 1999. For the first time the legislation legitimizes the right of any province to hold a referendum on secession but it establishes stringent conditions. First, the question would have to be direct and concise and make no mention of future economic or political partnerships with Canada. To ensure that any future question would be sufficiently clear, it would first have to be vetted by the federal parliament and get its approval. Second, a referendum majority itself must be clear. The bill does not clearly spell out what the word "clear" means, but only that the traditional 50%-plus-one would not be sufficient. Not until the House of Commons had determined that "a clear expression of the will of the population" had been given would the federal government enter negotiations about a secession agreement.

According to former Prime Minister Chrétien, "we are forcing them to be honest." It goes without saying that the *PQ* seethed over the clarity bill. However, voters in Quebec supported the concept. In a 1999 poll, seven out of ten believed 60% represents the clear majority required by the court; 93% favored a clear question, and 61% did not think the 1995 question was clear.

you want to separate from Canada?" and that if a "clear majority" voted in favor of independence, then negotiations with the rest of Canada would be "necessary" and a constitutional amendment would be required. Federalists rejoiced at the ruling. The Quebec government unexpectedly joined the celebration.

Seeing much room for interpretation, Bouchard emphasized the requirement that Ottawa negotiate with Quebec after a successful referendum and read the "clear majority" mandate narrowly. Bouchard pointed out that Newfoundland had entered Canada in 1949 with only 52% support in a referendum. In its headline the *Ottawa Citizen* summed up the differing interpretations: "One ruling, two solitudes."

After initially greeting the 1998 Supreme Court decision, the *PQ* let it be known in October 1999 that it no longer felt bound to follow an interpretation of a judiciary whose judges were appointed by Ottawa. In the words of Joseph Facal,

Canada

Constitution Act,
1867

Constitution Act, 1982

Canadian Charter of
Rights and Freedoms (1982)

POLITICAL SYSTEM

For a person interested in comparing different governmental systems, Canada is an extraordinarily intriguing case conceived over concern it might be swallowed up by its southern neighbor and born of compromise. In the 19th century a majority of Canadians wanted to retain ties with Britain and have a parliamentary system of government influenced by the political experiences of the British, French, and American nations but that was adapted to Canada.

In 1867 the British Parliament passed the British North America Act (BNA), granting the Canadian government the authority "to make Laws for Peace, Order and Good Government" which was in stark contrast to the United States (U.S.) constitutional document stating the individual's right to" life, liberty and the pursuit of happiness." Typically Canadian, the BNA was a short, sober, legalistic document, focusing on a pragmatic communitarian view of society not the individualistic liberal view seen in the Declaration

of Independence, penned almost a century earlier by Thomas Jefferson.

The BNA was written exclusively by Canadians at conferences that no British delegates attended. When it was presented to the British government for formal approval, the latter objected to only two minor points: it was nervous about calling the new country "the Kingdom of Canada" as the Canadians wanted because such a name might be offensive to the Americans, who reacted violently to the notion of monarchy 90 years earlier. The Canadians therefore settled on the word "Dominion," taken from the 72nd Psalm, "He shall have dominion also from sea to sea and from the river unto the ends of the earth." To the "Fathers of the Constitution," as Canada's founders were called, this term, which had never been used before to describe a nation, embodied the monarchial principle so subtly that the Americans would not even notice it.

The second minor point on which the British insisted was a provision

for breaking a deadlock between the two houses of parliament. Other than these two points, the BNA was purely a Canadian creation in prescribing "a Constitution similar in principle to that of the United Kingdom." This meant that Canada would have a parliamentary democracy in which the cabinet, called the "Privy Council," would be responsible to the House of Commons, not to the British monarch.

It also meant that custom and tradition, together called "constitutional conventions" would be an unwritten but essential part of the country's constitution. Thus, such fundamental constitutional principles and practices as "responsible government," "collective responsibility," "parliamentary supremacy," the fusion of executive powers and legislative powers as opposed to "separation of powers, "votes of confidence" for the government, with regard to budgetary matters as well as the need for both prime minister (PM) and cabinet, to be appointed by the

Governor General (the Queen's representative to the federal parliament) and although a member of Cabinet may not be a member of parliament – indeed at least one member of the Senate is normally a member of cabinet, the norm is that a cabinet member should have been elected to the House of Commons. These matters are not written into the BNA Act.

The trappings of Canadian politics evoke the strong British heritage: Privy Council, governor general, the House of Commons, the position of prime Minister, Throne Speech, Parliament meeting only on royal summons, and Crown corporations. After they arrest criminals, the Royal Canadian Mounted Police turn them over to Crown prosecutors to charge them. In the United States, criminal charges are stated as the People versus the accused individual, whereas in Canada it is the King or Queen, as the case may be, versus the individual reflecting the difference between a Republic and the Dominion. America has military colleges such West Point or Annapolis, and in Canada, military Officers are educated at the Royal Military College of Canada, in Kingston, Ontario (English) and its French-speaking equivalent, the Royal Military College Saint-Jean, 40 km south of Quebec city. In 2011, after 43 years as the unified "Canadian Forces," the word "Royal" was again added to the Canadian Air Force and to the Canadian Navy; the land forces became the "Canadian Army."

All federal acts begin with the words: "Her Majesty, by and with the advice and consent of the Senate and the House of Commons, enacts as follows." Provincial laws commence with similar wording and all bills need "Royal Assent" to be enacted. Even the Canada Act, 1982 requested "that Her Majesty may graciously be pleased to cause a Bill to be laid before the Parliament of the United Kingdom . . . by and with the advice and consent of the Lords Spiritual and Temporal, and Commons . . ." Immigrants who become citizens pledge their "loyalty and allegiance to Canada and Her Majesty Elizabeth II, queen of Canada."

While the vestiges of the British heritage are still visible, there have been recent reminders that Britain has only a limited hold on the hearts and minds of many Canadians. In 1965 Britannia's stripes were removed from Canada's flag with a simple maple leaf replacing the Union Jack. In 1970 the "E II R" cipher, meaning "Elizabeth II Regina." was removed from Canadian mailboxes. In 1980 the country adopted a new anthem, "O Canada," which can be sung in two languages, to replace "God Save the Queen," which, it need not be said, was only sung in English. Twenty-first-century political correctness objected to the words "all thy sons command" in O Canada which seem to exclude that 50% of the population which is female which caused the anthem to be changed to "in all of us command".

Shortly thereafter, the 12,000-member Monarchist League lost other battles: the country's major holiday, Dominion Day, celebrated July 1st, was rechristened "Canada Day," and even the BNA was renamed the "Constitution Act 1867." One member of the Royal Commonwealth Society rudely referred to each of these changes as a "sop to Quebec." A more accurate explanation is that each of those symbols rubbed salt in the unhealed wound with which Canada was born: the English-French division. Each was a brick in the wall that separated the majority of Canadians from the third of their countrymen who were francophones.

Perhaps no country in the world has been more successful than Canada in reconciling the claims of two founding colonial peoples who are determined to preserve their languages and cultures. It has not been easy, but the English-speaking majority has recognized the "French fact" in Canada. Canadian politics has been significantly influenced by that fact. In Quebec itself, French civil law prevails, and Quebec's anglophones have accepted the necessity of speaking French in their native province. In other provinces, such as New Brunswick, French and English are both used in public life, and everywhere in Canada a francophone can deal with the federal government in French. In Ottawa, French and English are both used on the street and in Parliament. Every PM, governor general, and speaker of the House of Commons, as well as at least three of nine Supreme Court justices, must speak both languages and parliamentary debates are freely conducted in both.

Primarily because of the "French fact," Canada had to be created as a federal state. This means that law-making authority is divided between the central government and the provinces. It was unthinkable that Canada be a unitary state like Britain. Quebec's persistent assertion of provincial rights also benefited other provinces, especially in the West, which wanted to lighten Ottawa's hand on their shoulders. Indeed, in 2019 the premier of Alberta seeks a modus vinendi with Quebec in order to stop federal legislation which threatens to block the creation of resource-based businesses in Canada. Further, Quebec prevented Canada from ever being a "melting pot," like the U.S. where many now prefer the analogy of a "salad bowl" where the ingredients remain as they were originally even as they are part of something larger. Canada has adopted a policy of multiculturalism, overseen by a cabinet minister. In other words, other minority groups in Canada owe the official recognition and legislative protections largely to the existence of the *Québécois*.

The influence of the British and French heritages on Canadian political life is obvious. Even so, another nation has had a powerful influence on Canada, the United States. Much of the Canadian experience was an attempt to survive as a sovereign country and as a unique cultural product in the face of powerful challenges by the American neighbors. In 1812 the Americans were beaten back after a half-hearted attempt to spread their "Manifest Destiny" northward. In 1837 the rebellions in Upper and Lower Canada, which resulted in the Durham Report and ultimate independence, were led by men infected by the idea of rule by the people. These were populist notions that had come alive again during the Jacksonian era of the 1830s. Canadians could learn about them right across the border in the U.S.

Canadians adopted federalism for reasons of their own size and diversity. However, their brand was shaped by their horror of the American Civil War, which seemed to have resulted from the South's concept of states' rights. The "Fathers of Confederation" did create an upper house called a Senate which was supposed to defend regional interests, something that it utterly failed to do. Today, such things as the hoopla of Party conventions where leaders are selected, the increasing observance of four years as a long enough time between national elections, a written bill of rights, and a written constitution, are a but four of many examples of America's impact on Canadian politics.

Even though they heavy borrowed from the other countries' political traditions and practices, it has been Canadians themselves who have shaped their own political system. It is they who have adapted to their unique situation as a huge, regionally and culturally diverse country. The Canadian regime may be a hybrid, but the mix is uniquely Canadian. Its basic outline is as follows: voters elect 338 members of the House of Commons, the lower house of Parliament; the Harper government's 2011 Fair Representation Bill added 30 seats to this total. The leader of the party that wins a majority of seats or can get a majority of votes in the House of Commons on important issues becomes the PM, the most powerful political figure in the land. Queen Elizabeth II, the Queen of Canada, is the head of state, but neither she, nor her representative, the governor general, makes any important political decisions.

The PM selects other ministers who are also usually experienced parliamentary leaders in the Party, to sit in the cabinet. Together, the PM and cabinet are called "the government," which rules

Canada

"collectively." Put another way, all members of the government must publicly support its policies or resign from office. Also, the entire team assumes responsibility for the overall policy. The government rules as long as it maintains a majority in the House of Commons or until it loses a "vote of confidence" on an important bill. The PM must call an election at least five years after the preceding election, but can announce one earlier if that would be to his or her party's advantage.

Unlike in the U.S., where both houses of Congress are equally powerful, the Canadian upper house, the Senate, has far less power than the House of Commons. Moreover, unlike in the U.S., there is no "separation of powers" among the executive, legislative, or judicial branches. Executive and legislative powers are fused, making the PM both the chief executive and chief legislator of the land. Through a tightly disciplined party, the PM controls the House of Commons. Finally, as in the U.S., but unlike in Britain, with the exception of the European courts where the UK has given jurisdiction, laws can be judged unconstitutional by the Supreme Court of Canada. In Canada "parliamentary supremacy" is subject to provincial legislative supremacy in issues reserved in the Constitution Act, 1867 for the provinces and matters touching upon the Canadian Charter of Rights and Freedoms, where such jurisdiction is applicable.

CONSTITUTION

The government in Canada is both democratic, insofar as the people elect the representatives who govern them, and constitutional, in that rules that bind all political actors, limit the exercise of governmental power, impose obligations on the governments, and provide for the judicial enforcement of the rules. In a federal state such as Canada, a constitution has an additional function: it distributes legal power to the central and the provincial legislatures; in the words of Canadian political scientist David Milne, it "forms a master power grid from which all the governmental players get their authority", subject to the federal constitutional power of disallowance.

It should not be surprising that any effort to change the constitution, such as took place in Canada in the early 1980s, would expose the very nerves of government. A change of this nature would inevitably reveal the tensions and power struggles in federal-provincial, inter-provincial, and ethnic group relations.

As to the form of its constitution, Canada stands between the United Kingdom and the U.S.. The British constitution remains unwritten; it is a collection of clearly defined documents, such as the Magna Carta of 1215, the Statute of Westminster of 1931, as well as of important customs and traditions that no government would dare violate. However, any portion of the constitution could be changed by Parliament, which is "supreme." How this interrelates with the power of the courts of Europe is an interesting topic itself and indeed how will be altered with Brexit makes the reversion of all authority to the British Parliament a complex issue.

At the other democratic continuum is the U.S., which has a written constitution to spell out the powers of the institutions of governments, with a few prominent omissions, such as political parties. The American constitution is intentionally difficult to change and has been amended only 27 times in more than 200 years. Congress cannot change the constitution because it rather, than Congress, is "supreme." Unlike Britain and Canada, which had not experienced revolutions, the U.S. fought for its independence. After successful revolutions, winners are far more inclined to put in writing the kind of guarantees and rights their former rulers denied them.

The BNA called for a political system like that of Britain. This included customs and traditions, such as the need for the PM to have the confidence of the House of Commons, or the understanding that the monarch "reigns but does not rule." In typical British fashion, these things were not written down, and most of them are still unwritten but are referred to in law as constitutional conventions.

Canada's founders faced a challenge that could not be met by merely adopting British practices. The founders had to create a form of government that was sufficiently strong to hold such a huge, sparsely populated, country together, while at the same time decentralizing it in a way so as to meet the aspirations of different regions and peoples. In so doing, the founders were able to coax the various strong-willed colonies into the new union by promising them that they could share the responsibility for ruling the country with the central government. The founders even used a misnomer to describe the new governmental structure: a "confederation," a loose alliance of sovereign nations. Actually, the founders created a federation which does not recognize the provinces as sovereign states, but which divides authority between the central and provincial governments.

Since 1867, the written portion of the BNA has been supplemented by other important documents with constitutional standing. In all, 24 documents, called "organic laws," make up the constitution; there are 13 acts of the British Parliament, amendments to the BNA, also called British North America Acts; seven acts of the Canadian Parliament; and four British orders-in-council, government declarations permitted by law. This collection includes such statutes as the acts admitting other provinces to Canada after 1867, provincial constitutions, the Supreme Court Act of 1875, the War Powers Act of 1914, the Statute of Westminster of 1931, the Elections Acts, the House of Commons Act, the Legislative Assembly Acts, the Public Service Acts, the Bill of Rights of 1960, and the Official Languages Act of 1969. With all these acts and the many customs that provided the ground rules for Canadian politics, one might think that all the bases had been touched and that Canadians could settle down and live by their voluminous, complicated constitution. Yet, they could not because some important items were missing.

The 1970s and 1980s were decades of both nationalist and regional resurgence in Canada. Many *Québécois* demanded separation from Canada, or at least a radically different kind of federal structure that would enable them largely to govern themselves. Discontent was also reaching the boiling point in the energy-rich western provinces which believed that their economic development was being seriously threatened by Ottawa's policy toward their natural resources. The western premiers banded together to form the first regional bloc in Canadian history that could seriously threaten the predominance of Ontario and Quebec. The Atlantic provinces always resented Central Canada's dominance, fearing that it would find a way of depriving them of the benefits from the oil and gas discovered off of their shores and which, they hoped, could finally enable them to catch up economically with the rest of Canada.

On top of this regional turmoil, the Trudeau government in Ottawa embarked on a nationalist campaign to increase the Canadian hold over the country's own economy and energy resources. The joints of the Canadian state began to creak under the weight of competing visions of federalism, nationalism and regionalism. Because Canada was in crisis, its political and legal minds set out to find a constitutional solution that could save the country from tearing apart.

The result was the Canada Act 1982, which served as the basis for the Constitution Act. Canada did not adopt an entirely new constitution. Instead it refined many existing arrangements and added important provisions to the existing constitution. It was a compromise, but one that was reached only after an enormous hue and cry and some of the most determined political maneuvering in Canadian history. It was a high-stakes intergovernmental struggle among giants. In David Milne's words, "because the battle concerned the kind of state (or states) Canada was to be, it challenged every Canadian to define his sense of country more sharply than ever before. Predictably there was no consensus among Canadians as a whole."

The struggle involved many twists and turns before it was resolved; it also revealed how many power centers must be dealt with in Canadian politics. The Trudeau government had been voted back into power in February 1980 after a nine-month breather. It fought a successful battle against the *Parti Québécois'* effort to win a provincial referendum in May 1980 that could have paved the way to some form of separatism.

In order to undercut the *PQ's* appeals during the campaign, Trudeau promised a new federal arrangement. In July 1908, intergovernmental negotiations began but reached an impasse by September 13. On October 6, Trudeau placed a unilateral proposal before Parliament to force the provinces back into action. The latter wasted no time by challenging Trudeau's move in court. By November 1980, Britain's Select Committee on Foreign Affairs began to study the UK's role in the constitutional debate and concluded two months later that "Westminster cannot act as a mere rubberstamp on all requests coming from Parliament to Canada."

After months of further debate, deliberation, and challenges in provincial high courts, the Supreme Court of Canada rendered its judgment on September 28, 1981, declaring that Trudeau's resolution in Parliament was legal and that a province did not have a veto over the entire process. This order practically forced the premiers to reenter negotiations with the Canadian government, culminating a substantial agreement among all parties, except Quebec, in 1980. In December 1981 the constitutional resolution cleared both houses of the Canadian Parliament, was signed by the governor general, and delivered to Buckingham Palace in London.

Premier Lévesque, who felt betrayed and outmaneuvered by Trudeau and the other premiers, unsuccessfully appealed to Prime Minister Margaret Thatcher to delay the proceedings until Quebec's veto power could be established by the Quebec Court of Appeal. Also, Canadian Indigenous people appealed unsuccessfully to the British Court of Appeals, claiming that their full rights had not been secured in the new agreement. In March 1982 the Canada Act breezed through both houses of the British Parliament.

On April 17, 1982, while thousands of *Québécois* and Indigenous people publicly protested and mourned, Queen Elizabeth proclaimed the Canada Act in a signing ceremony in front of the Canadian Parliament. This act terminated the British Parliament's power over Canada and transferred the entire Canadian constitution to the Canadians themselves. Bitter about having been deprived of an absolute veto power, the Quebec government never accepted the validity of the act. The Meech Lake Accord sought to resolve this deadlock.

Under the terms of this Canada Act, the national government was able to proclaim the Constitution Act, 1982. This act lumped together and renamed the BNA and all its amendments the "Constitution Acts, 1867–1975." Canada's major holiday, July 1, was renamed "Canada Day."

In adopting a new constitution, Canada had entered a new age. Canadian government was changed in a variety of important ways. Perhaps the most significant change was that Canada could now amend every part of its constitution without having to secure British approval. This is surely a power any truly sovereign country must possess. Because it is so important, Canadians spoke of the patriation or bringing home of their constitution. In 1927 the first attempts had been made to secure this right. However, for more than a half-century all such efforts foundered due to inability of the federal and provincial governments to agree on a method of amendment. This inability should not be surprising if one remembers that the power to amend a constitution is the power to change the political rules of the game. It is therefore a matter of utmost importance.

The American constitution provides for only one feasible amending process other than an untried new constitutional convention, but the Constitution Act, 1982, elaborates four different formulae or processes, depending on the issue. Important changes dealing with such matters as the monarchy, the governor general, the use of the French and English languages in the federal government or the Supreme Court of Canada, require the ultimate approval of the House of Commons and every provincial legislature.

In other matters, a single province would not have a veto; two-thirds of the provinces need to approve. There are two prominent exceptions which reveal the extent to which provincial powers were respected. First, a proposed change impacting one or more provinces, but not such matters as boundary changes or the use of French or English in a particular province, affords the affected provinces the right of veto. Also under this provision, a province can "opt out" of any amendment seeking to take away any of its powers, rights, or privileges. Fourth, and final, an amending formula deals with most changes in Canada's executive, Senate, or House of Commons; in these instances, changes can be made by an ordinary act of Parliament.

A second important change under the Constitution Act, 1982, is that it

Queen Elizabeth II signs the Canadian Constitution, 1982. Prime Minister Trudeau is seated at left. Public Archives Canada/PA/140705 Photo by Bob Cooper

Canada

Rideau Hall, residence of the Governor General

"entrenches" certain parts of the written constitution, making it impossible for Parliament or any provincial legislature to change them by simple legislative acts. This applies to the monarchy, the governor general, the composition of the Supreme Court, or the amending formulae themselves. The existence of such "entrenched" portions of the constitution that are out of Parliament's reach is a conscious departure from the British doctrine of "parliamentary supremacy," which gives Parliament the right to decide anything in the political realm.

Pursuant to the third change, the provinces were granted more control over the taxing and exportation of their own natural resources. The fourth change was that the Constitution Act, 1982, included a Charter of Rights and Freedoms to strengthen the liberty of individual Canadian citizens. This was also a break from the tradition in Britain under which to the extent that individual liberties are protected adequately by common law, they were never written down as they were in the American Bill of Rights in 1791.

The "Charter" also allows the federal or provincial governments to suspend rights, be they freedom of conscience, religion, thought, belief, opinion, expression, freedom of the press, and/ or association as well as other rights under section 33 for five years. This applies to statutes passed with reference to section 33 of the Charter. Quebec, Saskatchewan, and Alberta have used section 33 to override Charter rights.

Without section 33 the provinces would not have agreed to having the Charter become part of the Constitution Act, 1982,

The Constitution Act, 1982, was a carefully constructed compromise between the central and provincial governments containing some significant innovations. Even so, much of it consolidated and refined many existing arrangements in the political system. It left intact the main structure of government, including the division of powers between Ottawa and the provinces, including the federal power of disallowance of any provincial act under the Constitution Act 1867, section 90.

GOVERNMENTAL STRUCTURE

As in the United Kingdom, Canada distinguishes between a "formal executive," who is the head of state, and the PM, who really wields the political power. Americans make no such distinction. Their president must not only be the chief policy maker, but he must also spend many hours meeting visiting heads of state, pinning badges on scouts, congratulating winning athletic teams, posing with and reprieving Thanksgiving turkeys, and smiling at cameras while turning on Christmas tree lights. In Canada, such ceremonial functions are performed by the representatives of the political figure in whom executive authority is still theoretically vested: the Queen of Canada, who spends most of her time being the British monarch.

The Monarch

The Queen and her representatives, the governor general and the lieutenant governors in the 10 provinces, are surrounded by a glittering group of advisers known as the Queen's Privy Council in Canada. This is composed of present and former prime ministers, cabinet members, speakers of both houses of Parliament, chief justices of the Supreme Court, and various other prominent citizens.

This large group of people in Queen's Privy Council in Canada rarely assembles and only at such ceremonial occasions as the accession of a new monarch. The only people among these advisers who actually wield any power are the PM and cabinet, referred to in the constitution as "the Committee of the Privy Council." All cabinet decisions are issued as decisions of the Privy Council. Even though no federal or provincial bill could be enacted without Royal Assent, no monarch would make a decision without being having the PM offer advice bout what to do. Despite the sweeping powers which the constitution seems to give her, the Queen "reigns but does not rule."

If the Queen and her representatives have so little power, a question remains about why Canada retains the monarchy. Monarchs have often served useful functions in countries that have become democracies. In Britain, for example, the Queen symbolizes national as part of a continuous thread through English history, thereby making her the focus of national pride. In Canada, though, the monarch often symbolizes and exacerbates the disunity of the nation. *Québécois* have seldom revered the monarch of a nation that conquered New France in 1760. When Queen Elizabeth II visited Quebec during the Quiet Revolution, her presence sparked serious riots. She and her family seldom set foot in the *"la belle province."*

In 1987, the Queen made her first tour of Quebec in almost a quarter century but was greeted with polite indifference. To most Quebecers, she is no longer a hated symbol of English oppression. As Pierre Bourgault, a former radical who organized the 1964 protests against her visit, noted: "Our problems are with the English in Quebec who still refuse to speak French, not with the Queen. She simply comes for a short visit, speaks French while she's here and then goes back to England." In the tense weeks following the failure of Meech Lake in 1990, nationalists made it clear that she was not welcome in Quebec. When Prince Charles and Camilla visited Montreal in 2009, hundreds of nationalist rowdies turned the affair into a tear-gas spectacle of riot police and protesters.

The spectacularly successful July 2011 visit of Prince William and Kate to Quebec showed how much of an emotional hold the British royals actually have in a province where 74% said at the time that the monarchy was irrelevant. A half a million Queberers tuned in to see the pair's wedding in the wee hours of an April morning. Then, the glamorous pair accepted the invitation of the Quebec and federal governments, taking part in a cooking lesson and dining on their self-cooked Quebec meal. The prince gave a public address entirely in French, praising Quebecers' vigor and vitality. Although he apologized for his language skills, the prince spoke it better than do most anglophone Canadians. Chants of "Kate and Will" drowned out the dozens who were yelling "royals go home."

Many young anglophone Canadians are no longer stirred by the monarch. One 18-year old who joined the crowd to see the Queen and her consort during a visit to Canada in 1984 confessed, "I'm here because she's famous, I guess." Quipped one young lady when Prince Andrew and Princess Sarah visited Canada in 1989, "I don't see why we should have to curtsy to a person who a few years ago was living with a race-car driver!"

In 1982, a CBC TV journalist dared not to curtsy before Her Majesty and continued her work unrepentant and unscathed. If one compares the yawning public response to that act with that toward another CBC interviewer in 1959, one can see just how much monarchical sentiments had weakened in Canada the last quarter of a century: when Joyce Davidson remarked on the air that "like most Canadians, I am indifferent to the Queen's visit," she required police protection from irate viewers and finally was forced to leave the country in order to find further employment.

Today, most Canadians ignore Commonwealth Day, which is commemorated on differing dates in late winter or early spring, when the Queen traditionally gives a broadcast message. Prince Charles experienced the spirit of Canadian equality in 2001 when he was required to wipe his shoes on a special disinfectant mat like every other passenger when stepping off a plane from the UK, which was plagued by hoof and mouth disease.

In a poll after the passage of the Constitution Act, 1982, three-fourths of the Canadian respondents thought that the importance of the monarchy was declining. Asked at the end of the twentieth century to name the symbols that are important for the Canadian nation, the monarchy was at the bottom of the list. Only 41% of respondents cited it, 34% of men and 48% of women; the figure in Quebec was 20%. While some historians argue that the splendid royal visit in 1939, nostalgically reenacted by the Queen Mother in July 1989, helped solidify Canadian support for Britain when Hitler invaded Poland a few weeks later. It is all but unthinkable that British royalty could sway an important Canadian political decision today.

The royal family can still electrify crowds. Many older anglophone Canadians regard the Queen as a regal symbol of Canadian patriotism. As one 60-year old Royal Canadian Air Force veteran in New Brunswick admitted, "Whenever a band plays 'God Save the Queen,' I drop my cigar and stand up straight as wood."

When the Queen Mother died in April 2002, a cry of disgust rang out throughout the country when the most widely read weekly Canadian newsmagazine, *Maclean's*, inadvertently placed the address labels across the photo of her face on the cover. The embarrassed editor had to send a letter of apology to all subscribers assuring them that the magazine meant no disrespect to the deceased monarch.

Warm crowds greeted Queen Elizabeth II wherever she went in Canada, including Nunavut, during her triumphant 12-day Jubilee tour in October 2002. However, the visit elicited a variety of public thoughts about the monarchy. The most prominent was then Deputy PM John Manley, who repeatedly expressed his preference for "an entirely Canadian institution" to replace the monarchy after Elizabeth's reign. Journalist Allan Fotheringham wrote: "She's a magnificent monarch. But she's not ours." Peter Donolo tactfully suggested: "What better gift could we give ourselves on the occasion of this Golden Jubilee year than to give the Queen a hearty handshake, thank her for all her services, wish her the best, and do what any self-respecting nation does: choose our own head of state?" The Queen's nine-day return visit in mid-summer 2010, her 22d official tour of Canada, elicited little such commentary.

Elizabeth herself is well-liked: 84% of Canadians polled in 2005 thought she has done a good job. In 2010, 69% had a "mostly favorable" opinion of the Queen, but in a March 2005 poll taken two months before her visits to the centennials in Alberta and Saskatchewan, 46% supported replacing the monarch as Canada's head of state, while 37% opposed such a move. At the same time, 49% believed Elizabeth should remain the monarch until she dies. Only 6% thought she should abdicate in favor of Prince Charles, and 18% wanted her to cede the throne to Prince William. Perhaps because of the popularity of William and Kate, the monarchy ascends in the polls: 56% in 2017 wanted to keep it, but only 34% of Québécois agreed.

Another poll taken four years later, on the eve of the first visit by Prince Charles and his second wife Camilla as a couple, found that 65% were in favor of cutting ties to the Crown and only 35% wanted her successor to rule Canada. Six in 10 Canadians agree that the Queen and the royal family should not have any formal role in Canadian society, up two points since 2016. According to a 2019 poll, 31% of Canadians believe that Canada should remain a monarchy. The royal couple's unenthusiastic reception during this 10-day visit in November 2009 seemed to back up these polling figures. The constitutional difficulty of abolishing the monarchy ensures that this would not happen quickly or easily.

William's glittering wedding to Kate Middleton on April 29, 2011, sent a current of excitement through Canada. The PM could not attend because he faced an election a few days later. Toronto's venerable King Edward Hotel opened its Sovereign Ballroom at 5 AM to broadcast the wedding live, accompanied by a "royal breakfast" costing $68 a head. When this event sold out, the overflow was invited to afternoon tea to watch a taped rebroadcast of the nuptial event for a fee of $69 per person.

The couple chose Canada for their first official foreign visit in July 2011. The outpouring of affection for them was so overwhelming that *Maclean's* selected them as the "newsmakers of the year." Their appearance on Parliament Hill on Canada Day, July 1, attracted 300,000 well-wishers, many shouting "Will and Kate." Ordinarily about 50,000 show up as Will and Kate set aside much of the usual royal etiquette: the duchess greeted a group of veterans in Ottawa by telling them to "call me Kate." They hugged each other openly, and they ate in public, something that would once have horrified royal watchers. William

Queen Mother, an unintended cover up

Canada

flew a Sea King helicopter on Prince Edward Island, landing it on water, a tricky maneuver known as waterbirding.

In Calgary the couple attended a stampede in cowboy garb. In the Northwest Territories they played street hockey with youngsters and canoed on Blachford Lake. Will ended his speeches there by adding his thanks in the languages of the Dene and Inuit. Before the 9-day visit, two out of three Canadians said they would follow the royal tour; it is almost certain that many more were drawn into the magic.

In 2016, William and Kate took their children on a successful tour of the West. They were politely confronted with misdeeds committed by the British toward the indigenous people. No offense was taken when Prince George rebuffed the Prime Minister's attempt to give him a high-five.

The royal wedding of 2018 between Prince Harry and Meghan Markle delighted Canadians as it reflected an acceptance of a divorced woman of colour, and an American actress, into the Royal family. The addition of the song "Stand by Me' by an American gospel choir showed the modern nature of the British monarchy.

For some Canadians, the monarchy is still an emotional and nostalgic link with their country's and the British Empire's heritage. The Queen's photo adorns the currency and hockey rinks while toasts are offered in her honor. As a democratic country without a revolutionary tradition, Canada has always taken an evolutionary view of the future and has never turned its back abruptly on its past.

It is certain that the British monarch will remain in Canada's constitution, as well as on its currency, well into the 21st century. Even if a constitutional amendment were proposed, passage would require the unanimous consent of the federal government, both houses of parliament and each of the ten provinces. Any sensible politician would prefer to jump off a cliff than to attempt to achieve such a degree of unanimity in a country like Canada.

The same procedure applies to changing the rules of royal succession. Still, none one anticipated difficulties or opposition when the government submitted legislation in February 2013 to permit the eldest born to ascend to the throne regardless of sex. The amendment, which conforms to the change in Britain and the 15 other royal realms, also allows the monarch and his or her heirs to marry a Roman Catholic, although a Catholic is still excluded from becoming sovereign.

The Governor General

Inside Canada the Queen is represented by the governor general. The governor general normally holds office for

Throne Speech 2006

five years, a term that can be extended for up to two years. For about 60 years, the British government decided who would occupy this post, but in 1926 the Canadian government assumed the right to select the person. Consequently, since 1952 the governor general has always been a Canadian. The position alternates between an anglophone and a francophone although by custom all must be bilingual. For example, an anglophone, Edward Schreyer, was succeeded by Madame Jeanne Sauvé. In 1990 she was followed by Ramon Hnatyshyn, who, in a break from the norm, was not fluently bilingual. His successor in 1995 was an Acadian francophone from New Brunswick, Roméo LeBlanc. In October 2010 anglophone David Johnston replaced Michaëlle Jean.

There is an equivalent of the governor general, called a lieutenant governor, in each of the ten provinces. This official is also nominally appointed by the Queen, but, in fact, is selected by the PM after seeking the advice of the appropriate provincial government.

In defining the job of the governor general, one only looks at the written part of the Canadian constitution, one would have the impression that this individual wields enormous power. According to the job description for governor general, this person must approve all legislative acts, appoint the PM, hire and fire cabinet members, dissolve or convoke Parliament, decide when elections are to be held and, since 1947, command Canada's armed forces. Former Governor General Michaëlle Jean provided a reminder of this latter honor in the Remembrance Day ceremony in November 2009. Standing next to Prince Charles, she presided wearing a resplendent uniform, visited Afghanistan twice, and regularly

attended repatriation ceremonies to honor those soldiers killed in combat.

The governor general has almost never exercised any of the powers just delineated; paradoxically, these powers exist only as long as they are never used. This person usually acts on the "advice" of the PM, a nice way of saying that she or he almost always does what she or he is told to do. Never in Canadian history has a governor general rejected a federal bill. When delivering the Throne Speech laying out the government's policy at the beginning of each parliamentary session, the governor general merely reads word for word a speech written by the PM and cabinet and put into his or her hands. There has never

Their Excellencies the Rt. Hon. Adrienne Clarkson, former Governor General of Canada, and her husband, Mr. John Ralston Saul   Photo: Sgt. Michel Roy

Their Excellencies the Rt. Hon. Michaëlle Jean, Governor General of Canada, and her husband, Mr. Jean-Daniel Lafond, and daughter

been a constitutional crisis with Canada's governor generals as occurred in Australia in 1975 when Sir John Kerr dismissed the PM and commissioned the opposition leader to form the government.

At the same time, the governor general does perform a function that some Canadians still consider to be important, possessing a residue of powers called "prerogative power" that could be used in times of crisis. For example, if a group attempt to seize power unconstitutionally, the governor general could serve as a rallying point for Canadians who support the democratic form of government.

The governor general can also be useful in a time when no party leader could get enough support in the House of Commons to form a government, a collective term in Canada to refer to the PM and the cabinet, similar to what Americans mean when they speak of "the administration." In such a situation, the governor general would be charged with finding a person who could gain such support or calling a new election. When there is a government, this person invariably follows its advice; when there is none, the individual is free to act independently. When the Conservative or Tory government lost a vote of confidence in December 1979, Prime Minister Joe Clark went to the governor general to ask that a new election be called. Edward Schreyer discussed the various alternatives with Clark for almost an hour, informing him in a later phone call that he would approve of a new election.

This important role in the formation of government became the topic of intense discussion in 2004 when it became clear that no party would win a parliamentary

majority. Suddenly Canadians realized that then Governor General Adrienne Clarkson's position could be more than mere pomp and ceremony. Clarkson became the one who would decide which party leader would be capable of commanding enough support in the House of Commons to conduct government business and win sufficient parliamentary votes for the longest possible time before new elections would be necessary.

If no party wins a majority of seats, it is normally the incumbent PM's privilege to approach the governor general and explain why he or she would like to continue to rule along with how this could be done. The PM would inform the governor general of the plan and commitments from other parties for support, having the authority to require such commitments be in writing or set conditions and a time limit for such commitments to be acquired.

Acting in a non-partisan manner and stressing loyalty is to Parliament, not to any particular party, a PM could turn to the head of another party with fewer seats if she or he concluded that a different leader would have a better chance of creating a stable government. Finally, a PM can defer or refuse to make last-minute patronage appointments such as ambassadorships or Senate seats that outgoing PMs often make before leaving office.

In December 2008, Governor General Michaëlle Jean had to cut short a foreign visit and return home quickly to deal with one of the biggest and most unexpected political crises in the country's history. Prime Minister Harper's minority government had strengthened its position in early elections in October 2008 only to face a possible vote of confidence on its budget because it contained no stimulus spending and sought to cut public financing for parties that the three opposition parties need more than the Conservatives. By tradition, a lost budget vote invariably leads to new elections. In an attempt to prevent such a vote, the PM sought the governor general's permission to prorogue parliament, meaning to prevent it from acting on bills or other business.

Harper's move was not unprecedented and never in history has a governor general rejected a request to prorogue. However, this was the first time such a measure was used in the midst of a political crisis over the objections of a majority in parliament. While a passionate constitutional debate throughout Canada ensued, Jean decided to allow the PM to do what he wanted. A month later the Liberals supported a revised Tory budget and the crisis subsided.

This happened again on December 30, 2009, when Harper prorogued parliament for two months ostensibly to prepare the budget. Opponents charged that it was

intended to end embarrassing inquiries into charges that Canadian soldiers turned detainees over to Afghan authorities who might have then tortured them. Such a shutdown means that all committees in both houses are disbanded, and government bills die. This was a break with tradition because such proroguing usually occurs only after most of the legislative business has been completed.

A letter signed by over 200 political and constitutional experts alleged that the PM sought to evade democratic accountability." Subsequently, a March 2010 poll revealed that 57% of Canadians thought parliament should limit the prime minister's powers. A further break in tradition was that the PM phoned the governor general to get her permission rather than appearing before her in person. This was interpreted as gravely insulting.

In perform the duties of the office, a governor general has the same right as the British Queen "to be informed, to advise and to warn." As a rule, the PM meets with the governor general least every other week to provide an update on the political situation. Every three months the governor general dutifully sends the Queen a report on the political and economic situation in Canada. The extent to which a governor general could influence a PM would, of course, depend on the rapport they share. Because the governor general was not a member of the same political party as Brian Mulroney, Jeanne Sauvé was said to have had little influence. In one celebrated snub, she was even excluded from the ceremonies surrounding the American president's visit to Quebec City in March 1985. By contrast, because Hnatyshyn was Mulroney's leader in the House of Commons from 1984–86 and his justice minister from 1986–88, when he lost his seat in parliament, he therefore had more influence on the PM.

Canadian governors general are usually leading politicians in their own right who have been appointed because of their political service to the country. Schreyer was one of the *New Democratic Party's* (NDP) most successful politicians and had been the premier of Manitoba. He was the first westerner to be appointed, a symbol of the West's rising importance in Canadian politics. He was also a non-white Anglo-Saxon Protestant such that his appointment was a form of recognition that Canadians of British descent are a minority today.

Jeanne Sauvé was perhaps the most successful female politician in Canadian history whose appointment in 1983 was greeted by all major parties. She was almost too good to be true: born in the francophone community of Prud'homme, Saskatchewan, she was the second westerner in a row to serve. Sauvé rose to

Canada

prominence as a journalist and Liberal Party politician in Quebec, and in the 1970s she had held various portfolios in Trudeau's cabinet; she was only the third female and the first Quebec woman ever to sit in the cabinet. In 1980, Sauvé became the first woman ever to serve as speaker of the House of Commons. Her impartial and competent performance in that trying job marked her as an ideal candidate for the position of governor general. In 1988 she became the first governor general ever to make a state visit to France.

The governor general's most frequent role is a ceremonial one demonstrated by having to entertain important foreign dignitaries, support many worthy causes and events, confer honors and awards Canadians who have distinguished themselves in various walks of life, cut ribbons, and opens new hospitals and museums. For these functions, the governor general is housed in Rideau Hall, an estate on 88 acres, across from the PM's residence at 24 Sussex Drive, a building "guarded" by red-coated soldiers wearing bearskin hats and is surrounded by woods, a park, a skating rink, toboggan slide, cricket field, tennis courts and three greenhouses. A governor general conducts a great deal of business in the main ballroom underneath a 12,000-piece crystal chandelier with two massive paintings on each end of the room: one a portrait of Queen Elizabeth II and the Duke of Edinburgh and the other of the Fathers of Confederation, entitled *Charlottetown Revisited*. The governor general also has a secondary residence inside The Citadel in Quebec City with a staff of about 100 and a budget of about $5,00,000.

A governor general's ceremonial activities are a full-time job and unquestionably take a heavy burden from the shoulders of the PM. For instance, Adrienne Clarkson participated in 908 events during 2003, three times as many as her predecessors, an average of 17 per week. For some Canadians, though, a governor general's most important function is to link Canada with the majesty of its past.

Few people can fail to be impressed with the spectacle of a governor general riding in a brilliant carriage to Parliament who then proceeds with much fanfare to the throne in the ornate Senate chamber; in British tradition, she or he is not permitted to set foot in the House of Commons. A governor general then sends a messenger to the House, instructing it to choose a speaker. Later in the day the governor general invites the Members of Parliament (MPs) to come to the bar of the door to the Senate to hear a speech in both English and French, even though everybody knows that it was written by the PM's staff.

President Obama and Governor General Jean in Ottawa, February 2009

Queen's University historian David Mitchell argues that the job of the governor general is actually harder than it looks because the individual faces two contradictory expectations: if one presents oneself royally, then the governor general appears to be embracing the lofty position too enthusiastically. Conversely, if a governor general fails to read the Throne Speech with verve, then he or she is perceived of demeaning the institution.

At the conclusion of the speech, the governor general leaves and the MPs return to the House of Commons. There, again in accordance with three centuries of British parliamentary tradition, the PM promptly introduces a dummy bill, usually a "Bill Respecting the Administration of the Oaths of Office," which is then forgotten by all. This is done to prove that the House has the right to discuss anything it wishes before turning to the monarch's concerns. The MPs then begin to discuss the points made in the governor general's speech.

A governor general is expected to be absolutely impartial, a frustrating experience for politicians. As a former incumbent, Earl Grey, once said, the essential task is walking "the tightrope of platitudinous generalities." *Maclean's* even wrote about "the governor of generality." Canada's 15th governor general, Lord Tweedsmuir, counted the days when he could again be "a free and independent politician" to "liberate my mind on any subject, anywhere, at any time, at any length I please."

Schreyer had wanted to change this by speaking out on the country's pressing issues, but he found himself in a minefield every time he did so. His press conference in 1981, the first ever for a governor general, was not well received, and the Prime Minister's Office (PMO) insisted on absolute control over any of his formal statements. When he indicated that he would have forced an election if Trudeau had attempted to ram his constitutional changes

through Parliament in the face of provincial opposition, he was criticized by virtually everybody.

The idea that Schreyer might actually use any of his formal powers was unthinkable. Even Quebec Premier René Lévesque, who did not like at all what Trudeau was doing, told Schreyer in 1982 to return to his "normal occupation—sleeping." From every direction, he was consistently criticized for either not saying enough, for saying too much or for saying the wrong thing. As one of Schreyer's aides noted, the job would drive anyone "stark raving mad from boredom."

In a classic text, *The Government of Canada,* Professor R. MacGregor Dawson wrote that the governor general is "the social head of the country and has always been supposed to exercise moral leadership as well." It is difficult to exercise moral leadership when one is not permitted to express opinions. There is another problem in knowing what it means to be the "social head of the country." Canada is a predominantly middle-class country. Many Canadians preferred Schreyer's kind of down-to-earth style which did not restrain children and dogs from charging through the ballroom or which permitted him and his wife to invite ordinary Canadians, friends, and family to Rideau Hall for a party or an overnight stay.

Richard Gwyn, columnist for the *Ottawa Citizen*, spoke for many Canadians when he said of all the regal glitter and dressy tea parties: *c'est magnifique, mais ce n'est pas le Canada!* or "It's magnificent, but it's not Canada!" Others preferred the sophisticated elegance and impeccable propriety the gracious and polished Sauvé brought to Rideau Hall. The only certainty is that no matter what kind of style the governor general sets, it will not be right for all Canadians. After completing his "damned if you do, damned if you don't" job, Schreyer sardonically thanked all those who had given him "free advice" on his shortcomings as in his role and took his leave.

The next governor general, Roméo LeBlanc, was a former journalist, fisheries minister, Senate speaker, and political ally of former Prime Minister Jean Chrétien. One of seven children of subsistence farmers, he was the first Acadian to occupy the position. LeBlanc's appointment was intended to send a clear political message to *Québécois* at a critical juncture in Canadian history: Acadians and their culture have prospered *within* the Canadian Confederation.

In 1999, LeBlanc was succeeded by the very embodiment of the immigrant success story, Adrienne Clarkson. Born in Hong Kong, she escaped with her family in 1942. Clarkson made her mark in Canada as a talented and strong-willed broadcaster, writer, publisher and diplomat. She is the first member of a visible minority to hold the position and only the second woman. In her inauguration, she described a Canada that is a work in progress that was originally built on the French, English and aboriginal cultures, but was expanding to include all colors and religions, with immigrant parents like hers "dreaming their children into being Canadians."

Most agree that Clarkson performed her duties with elegance, intelligence, diligence, and a sense of purpose. She even criticized America in her regal style: "Our cold climate has created our character, that sense of solidarity. America isn't as cold as we are." In describing her performance in office, *Maclean's* called Clarkson "simply the best." At the end of her five-year term in October 2004 Prime Minister Paul Martin secured the Queen's consent and asked the much-loved governor-general to remain in office for an unusual sixth year. He wanted the experienced Clarkson on hand during the experiment with minority government after the June 2004 elections.

Canadians are somewhat ambivalent about the post of governor general; in a 2010 poll, a quarter of them considered the position to be "useless." It is difficult for an incumbent to exercise moral authority and leadership when the public questions the position's legitimacy. This is why outgoing Governor General Adrienne Clarkson proposed that the choice be subject to public review and ratification by Parliament. Clarkson suggested that the PM present a name to a parliamentary committee, which would study the candidate's suitability for the position. Then the committee's recommendation would be put to a vote of the entire Parliament. Without such a reform, there is no consultation or review; a PM simply decides whom to select wants, and the Queen always approves.

In September 2005, a young, charismatic, soft-spoken, multilingual woman who spoke French, Creole, English, Spanish, Portuguese, and Italian, a former TV journalist in Quebec, Michaëlle Jean, became Clarkson's successor. The story of her life is remarkable, coming to Quebec as a young Haitian refugee, working with battered women and supporting causes to improve the lot of the downtrodden.

Jean had some frantic explaining to do when a separatist magazine, *Le Québécois*, claimed that she and her controversial award-winning French filmmaker husband, Jean-Daniel Lafond, had supported Quebec independence. The evidence came from one of his documentaries in 1991, *La Manière Nègre*, showing him and Jean toasting Quebec separatists. He also wrote in a book soon thereafter: "So, a sovereign Quebec? An independent Quebec. Yes, I applaud with both hands." Only after Jean issued a formal statement that she and her husband had "never belonged to a political party or the separatist movement" and were "fully committed to Canada" could majority public opinion accept her, and her appointment could move forward.

In her installation speech to parliament, Jean declared that the earlier "two solitudes" were over a last, and she called for an end to ethnic and linguistic divisions. The *Globe and Mail* applauded her for personifying "the free and open country Canada wants to be." Jean was a good listener, and in office she agreed to pass on to the PM concerns expressed to her by such advocacy groups as those supporting the homeless and subsidized housing in Quebec. Given her reportedly strained relationship with Prime Minister Harper, it is uncertain how this information was received.

Some Canadians questioned whether such activity is compatible with her largely neutral ceremonial role. Queen's University constitutional expert Ned Franks argued that such actions are indeed within the bounds of the governor general's functions. In his words, a governor general has the often ignored role "to represent Canada and Canadians to government." In 2014 Jean was chosen as secretary-general of La Francophonie.

On October 1, 2010, David Johnston was sworn in as governor general at age 69. Born in a small town in northern Ontario, he went on to become a two-time All-American and Hall of Fame hockey player at Harvard. Johnston was also educated at Cambridge and Queen's Universities. The long-time principal, or second in charge, of McGill University in Montreal and then president of another of Canada's best universities, Waterloo, he is regarded as one of Canada's leading advocates of higher education, possessing 13 honorary degrees to prove it. In 1995 Johnston took leave from McGill to head up the "no" campaign during the cliff-hanging Quebec referendum. "I guess I was driven by the sense of this marvelous country breaking up."

Johnston is also a former law professor, making him especially qualified to deal with the kind of tough constitutional issues a governor general must now tackle such as when it is legitimate for a PM to prorogue parliament, at what time can one say a government has lost the confidence of the House of Commons, and whether governor general always follow a PM's advice? His predecessor had to call in expert advice on these questions; Johnson is himself a constitutional expert.

In order to ensure that the new governor general would have unquestioned authority in the office and be independent of party, the Harper government appointed an independent expert committee to vet and recommend the best candidates. Political staffers were kept out of the process. Harper's spokesman made it clear: "This is not about politics." Commenting on the result, a former Liberal Justice Minister, Irwin Cotler, admitted: "I can't think of a better choice." A near majority (49.3%) of respondents agreed that "he's an impeccable choice."

Maclean's described the position in these terms: "The job is, by turns, ceremonial and essential, powerless and unifying. Governors General must assert themselves, but not too much. They can rally us to causes, but they mustn't get involved in the politics of the day. They represent the Crown, but may also speak on behalf of the people. Whoever they were before, they suddenly have medals pinned to their chest and people are compelled to stand when His (or Her) Excellency enters a room. It is an odd job."

On July 26, 2021, Mary Simon became Canada's 30th governor general. Her biography reads (Retrieved from: www.gg.ca/en/governor-general/governor-general-mary-may-simon/biography):

Her Excellency the Right Honourable Mary May Simon was sworn in on July 26, 2021, as Canada's first Indigenous governor general. She is the 30th governor general since Confederation. Mary Simon was born on August 21, 1947, in Kangiqsualujjuaq, Nunavik (Quebec), to Nancy May (Angnatuk-Askew), her Inuk mother, and Bob Mardon May, her father, who moved to the Arctic to work for the Hudson's Bay Company. Ms. Simon gained national and international recognition for her work on Arctic and Indigenous issues and for her efforts in advocating for Inuit rights, youth, education and culture. Ms. Simon began her career as a radio broadcaster with the CBC Northern Service (now CBC North)

Canada

**Her Excellency the Right Honourable
Mary Simon, C.C., C.M.M., C.O.M.,
O.Q., C.D.,
Governor General and Commander-in-
Chief of Canada**

Photo credit: Sgt Johanie Maheu, Rideau Hall
© OSGG-BSGG, 202

in the 1970s. Following this, she held a series of executive positions with the Northern Quebec Inuit Association (now Makivik Corporation) and Inuit Tapiriit Kanatami, which centred on negotiating the first land claims agreement in Canada, the James Bay and Northern Quebec Agreement.

As president of Makivik Corporation, she was directly involved with the implementation of the agreement, along with the protection and promotion of Inuit rights. Along with fellow Indigenous leaders, Ms. Simon was also actively involved in the negotiations leading to the 1982 patriation of the Canadian Constitution, which formally entrenched Aboriginal and treaty rights in the supreme law of Canada.

Ms. Simon later joined the executive council of the Inuit Circumpolar Conference (now the Inuit Circumpolar Council), for which she served two terms as president. In addition, she was commissioner of the Nunavut Implementation Commission and policy co-director of the Royal Commission on Aboriginal Peoples. From 1994 to 2003, Ms. Simon served as ambassador for Circumpolar Affairs, becoming the first Inuk to hold an ambassadorial position.

During this time, Ms. Simon negotiated the creation of the Arctic Council. Concurrently, she served as ambassador of Canada to Denmark from 1999 to 2001. Beginning in 2006, Ms. Simon served two terms as president of Inuit Tapiriit Kanatami. In 2008, in the House of Commons, she delivered a response on behalf of Inuit to the formal apology on residential schools. She is the founder of the Arctic Children and Youth Foundation and,

until 2014, she was the chairperson of the National Committee on Inuit Education.

In 2017, as the Minister's Special Representative, Ms. Simon delivered a report to the Minister of Indigenous and Northern Affairs on A New Shared Arctic Leadership Model, setting the stage for important policy and program development in support of the Arctic and its residents. Among other distinctions, Ms. Simon is an Officer of the Ordre national du Québec. She is also a recipient of the Governor General's Northern Medal, the Gold Order of Greenland, the National Aboriginal Achievement Award, the Gold Medal of the Canadian Geographical Society and the Symons Medal. Upon becoming governor general, Ms. Simon was promoted by Her Majesty The Queen as Companion of the Order of Canada (C.C.), and invested as Commander of the Order of Military Merit (C.M.M.) and Commander of the Order of Merit for Police Forces (C.O.M.). Her Majesty The Queen is the Sovereign of these Orders.

Ms. Simon plays the accordion and loves nature and berry picking. She is anaana (mother) to a daughter and two sons, anaanatsiaq (grandmother) to 12 children and amauq (great-grandmother) to four children. She also has three stepchildren from her marriage in 1994 to Mr. Whit Grant Fraser, former head of the Canadian Polar Commission, former executive director of Inuit Tapiriit Kanatami and a long-time former CBC journalist.

THE POLITICAL EXECUTIVE

On an official visit to Paris in October 2009, Governor General Jean twice referred to herself as Canada's "head of state." The PMO and the Monarchist League of

Canada reminded her immediately that that title belongs to Queen Elizabeth II, not to the governor general. Surprisingly, a December 2008 poll revealed that only 24% of Canadians knew this. Almost twice that percentage thought the PM was head of state, and one-third thought it was the governor general. Almost a year later, 30% of respondents in another poll answered that they could not care less about such ceremonial titles.

There is obviously some confusion in Canada about the precise distinction between a formal executive or head of state, who has a largely ceremonial function, and a political executive or head of government who actually makes policy and wields power. The confusion about these roles stems no doubt from the fact that the PM is the undisputed nerve center of the entire Canadian political system. Within the government, the PM is far more than "first among equals" as he used to be called, the towering political figure. Indeed, in federal elections, many Canadians vote according to whom they want as PM, not for whom they wish to be their local representatives in the House of Commons. Most PM serve a long time in office. Those who can survive the first few months have averaged eight years; four were in power for 15 years or more.

Since 1951, the PM and family are housed in an imposing residence at 24 Sussex Drive on the bluffs overlooking the Ottawa River, built in 1868 by a lumber baron named Joseph Merrill Currier, a member of parliament (MP). Not having been built to house the country's top leader, it is said to oppress those who live there. The building was drafty, its walls were lined with asbestos, lacked fire sprinklers, and was in desperate need of repairs to the tune of $12 million. Prime

24 Sussex Drive, residence of the prime minister Photo: J.M. Carisse

Minister Justin Trudeau's family had to move into another government house, the Rideau Cottage behind Rideau Hall, while waiting for completion of the repairs. Not far away is Stornaway, the official residence of the opposition leader. The PM has an official summer residence at Harington Lake in Gatineau Park, Quebec.

The PM's immense power comes from six sources. First, the PM is the head of his party. Second, the PM's party either has a majority of seats or more seats than any other party in the House of Commons. In the U.S., it is possible for the president to be of one party and for one or both houses of congress to be controlled by the other party, a situation that reduces the ability to enact policy. This is never the case in Canada, where a person is PM by virtue of being the leader of the party with the majority of votes in the lower house. The majority in the House expresses confidence in a PM by voting in favor of bills the PM supports. PMs who lose "a vote of confidence" are replaced or new elections are called, a matter that is resolved within a matter of weeks.

The Canadian leader can control a party for various reasons. At election time the "coat-tails" effect is strong in Canada, and many MPs are elected because of the popularity of their leader. This was especially true in the 2015 elections in which over a hundred Liberals were swept into office by the popularity of Justin Trudeau. Many MPs elected that way depend on the leader's success to advance their own political careers.

The PM, who by tradition must have a seat in the House of Commons or get one within a reasonable time, can also rely on "party discipline" to keep party members in the House of Commons loyal. A government stands or falls depending on whether it retains its majority in the House of Commons. Therefore, it is a serious matter when a MP votes against the party on an important vote. The party could halt an MP's political advancement and deny the member a variety of perks. Therefore, most MPs would never consider voting against their party. Historian Christopher Moore wrote: "The night they are elected you know what an MP is going to do for the next four years: vote how the government tells it, whenever it needs it. They should just fax in their votes if that's all they're going to do."

The third source of the PM's power is the fact that this person is not only the country's chief executive, but its chief legislator as well. The PM and the cabinet draft all the important legislation the two houses of Parliament, the House of Commons and the Senate, consider. Until 2002 the PM could also appoint all committee chairmen. However, in a rare backbench rebellion

against Prime Minister Chrétien, many in his own party supported an opposition motion to give MPs the right to elect committee chairmen of their own choice.

For Americans who value the notion of "separation of powers" as a necessary safeguard against tyranny, the Canadian fusion of executive and legislative powers seems surprising. Still, the benefit of such fusion, inherited from Britain, is a much greater degree of government efficiency. The kind of prolonged deadlocks between the president and congress are unknown in Canada, whose governments are given much power and are expected to get on with their work. For example, if a PM's party could win as many votes as President Barack Obama did in 2008 at 52.5%, the government could command an overwhelming majority of seats in Commons. In 2015, the Liberals won only 39.5% of the votes, but were awarded 184 out 338 seats allowing it to achieve most of its legislative goals.

The fourth source of a PM's authority is the power to appoint all Senators, Supreme Court justices, federal judges, the governor general, the chief of the defense staff, and the RCMP commissioner. The PM has the final approval over the placement of every senior public servant and controls thousands of appointments to public agencies and commissions. In addition, the PM has the exclusive right to deal with the governor general; any member of the government can have access to the formal executive only through the PM.

At the same time, the PM can determine when elections will be held as long as one is held within five years and with the approval of the governor general, which is not necessarily automatic. Unlike in the U.S., where congressmen and Senators are elected for fixed terms, in Canada nobody above the level of mayor is ever elected for a fixed term. In some cases, the cabinet can

help influence a PM on when to call an election, as it did when John Turner announced an early election in 1984. Even so, PMs usually reserves this privilege for themselves; this is a powerful weapon not only for keeping the opposition off guard, but also for securing the loyalty of one's own party members in Parliament, who dread having to go on the hustings too often.

Former Prime Minister Stephen Harper was committed to democratizing governmental institutions. Under Harper's leadership, Supreme Court nominees were supposed to have been subject to review by a parliamentary committee' Further, he proposed filling vacant Senate seats by elections and limiting Senatorial terms to eight years. Yet, he found it expedient to violate these pledges.

Three months after taking office in February 2006, Harper announced bills allowing elections to take place at fixed four-yearly intervals and this became law but because this did not amend the constitution, it could always be changed. The PM could also call an election on losing a vote of confidence. All parties supported this but the Liberals, who accused Harper of trying to make Canada be like the U.S., always a potent charge. A majority of Canadians told pollsters they favored this reform. Three provinces had already adopted fixed election dates. Harper decided on his own, though, to strengthen his mandate by calling new elections a year earlier, on October 14, 2008, and again on May 2, 2011. The 2006 election laws were no obstacle. The October 2015 voting was the first fixed-term election.

The fifth source of power is the fact that the PM is the center of publicity. Especially in the era of television, the PM is always in the limelight; in fact, the enormous growth of the modern PM's awesome political power has coincided with the

Chamber of the House of Commons
Public Archives Canada/PA51823

Canada

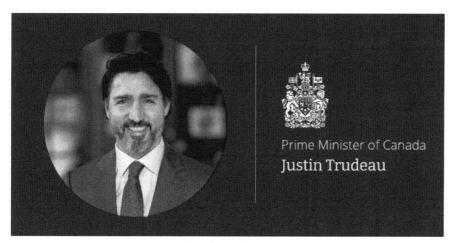

Justin Trudeau

advancement of television. No other political figure can begin to compete with him in terms of media exposure, except during election campaigns, which in Canada normally last only seven or eight weeks. Today, a successful PM must learn to use television effectively and to cultivate his image carefully. Mulroney was reported to be particularly obsessed with and adept at this. He read dozens of newspapers and magazines each week and watched all national news broadcasts in both English and French to monitor what kind of image he was projecting.

The sixth, and final, source of power for a PM is the ability to select, and dominate, the cabinet, which is the real executive of Canada. Cabinet members are usually prominent political figures. Unlike in the U.S., cabinet members do meet and decide on overall policy. Because they must be familiar with many different issues, from foreign, defense and economic policy, to the state's treatment of aboriginal peoples, they are normally "generalists," rather than specialists in one field. Nevertheless, the PM decides what the political agenda will be along with a sense of the cabinet on a particular issue.

Members of the cabinet cannot publicly criticize the PM due to the principle of "collective responsibility." This means that once a decision has been made, all members of the government are obligated to support it. The whole cabinet takes public responsibility for a policy, regardless of whether each individual member agrees with it. Even if cabinet member were to resign voluntarily, they are not permitted to reveal their grounds for doing so unless the PM freed them from the oath of secrecy they took on assuming office cabinet members are protected from removal by the House of Commons by the fact that if a single member were to lose the confidence of the House, then the entire government would have to resign.

Only once in Canada's history, in 1896, has a cabinet ever forced a PM to resign.

Much more important, the PM hires and fires cabinet members. Also, as evidenced by Prime Minister Justin Trudeau's removal of two former cabinet ministers, Jody Wilson-Raybould and Jane Philpott, he can unilaterally remove members from the Liberal caucus. Their resignations from the Liberal cabinet were principiated by what former solicitor general and minister of justice Raybould saw as undue influence from the PM office regarding a criminal case about a Quebec multinational business. That business was a SNC-Lavalin which was seeking a remediation agreement to pay fines and agree to other terms in order to end the prosecution against it which was based on corruption, the payment of funds to the Gaddafi family for contracts in Libya.

Both ministers were later dismissed from the Liberal caucus. This was a huge scandal where, due to cabinet confidentiality and solicitor-client privilege, former minister Raybould was only able to give a partial accounting of events and where due to cabinet confidentiality, former minister Philpott was also unable to "speak all of her truth" in public. The PM's office stropped a complete investigation by the House of Commons Justice Committee and the Ethics Committee.

This case raised serious concerns in Canada's legal community as it goes to the root of an independent justice system in Canada which means that all politicians must not attempt to influence Crown Prosecutors when they exercise their judgment after due deliberation and a final decision having been made. This would not preclude discussion prior to a final decision having been made by the Solicitor General but not thereafter. Clearly, the Canadian political system must follow the lead from the United Kingdom and separate the two portfolios of Minister of

Justice, a political position, and Solicitor general, an independent judicial position).

A PM can select how many members to include in the cabinet; in 1984 Mulroney chose 40 while Prime Minister Jean Chrétien appointed only 22 because he wanted to underscore his seriousness about tightening federal government operations. Paul Martin chose in 2004 to appoint 39 to his cabinet. In 2015, Justin Trudeau appointed 30 ministers; half were women, four were Sikhs, two were aboriginal, two were disabled, one is openly gay, and one was an Afghan female Muslim. Former Liberal leader Stéphane Dion was named foreign minister.

In a key duty, because a PM determines which assignments, or portfolios, cabinet members receive, these decisions can make or break political careers. A minister of state for fitness, for instance, will have far less visibility and influence than a justice minister. Also, some posts are extremely important but are so exposed to public scrutiny and criticism that they are considered to be professional suicide. The most prominent of these is the Ministry of Finance. Few PM were ever finance ministers. Recent exceptions were Jean Chrétien, who had been entrusted with all major portfolios at one time or other during the Trudeau era, and Paul Martin. Certain portfolios are traditionally reserved for specific regions: fisheries are usually cared for by someone from the Maritimes or British Columbia and agriculture is for a westerner. The finance minister is usually an MP from Ontario with good business connections.

Despite the power of PMs to select cabinet members, they must observe certain traditions which do restrict choices somewhat. Because Canada's major parties are large, they include members of diverse ideological persuasions. Most PMs try to include all such directions in their cabinets in order to maintain party unity. It is also a wise move for PMs to muzzle certain vocal critics from within their parties by including them in the cabinet and thereby throwing the blanket of collective responsibility over their heads.

A far more important restraint, though, is the "representation principle." This is natural for a country as geographically and demographically diverse as Canada. Although there are no hard and fast rules, most regional, provincial, territorial, social, and economic interests in the country are represented in the cabinet. Each province should have at least one representative, although tiny Prince Edward Island has often gone without one. If a ruling party did not elect a single MP in a given province, as was the case for years with the Liberal Party in the West and in Nova Scotia in 1997, then Senators from those provinces can be included in the cabinet.

The two giants in the federation, Ontario and Quebec, which have two-thirds of the seats in the House of Commons, usually receive about ten cabinet seats. These members are chosen from different regions and cities from within those provinces to make representation as dispersed as possible. Major cities like Montreal and Toronto usually have more people in the cabinet than do all the Atlantic provinces put together.

In Jean Chrétien's cabinet that was sworn in after his reelection victory in 1997, for example, there were 27 senior and eight junior ministers, called secretaries of state. Twelve were from Ontario and four, plus Chrétien, from Quebec. He appointed four of the 11 Liberal MPs elected in Atlantic Canada. In an effort to reach out to the restless western provinces, he tapped nine of the 15 Liberal MPs elected in the West.

In 2006, Stephen Harper named a cabinet of 27 ministers reflecting a broad geographic distribution rather than over-representing the West, from where the majority of his government's seats came. The Tories won none of the 48 seats in Montreal, Toronto and Vancouver. Yet, he wanted someone in his cabinet from Montreal, so he appointed an unelected Tory co-chairman, Michael Fortier, to the Senate and brought him into his cabinet as public works minister. In order to have someone from Vancouver, he lured David Emerson from the preceding Liberal Party cabinet, pronounced him a Tory and made him minister for trade and the "Pacific Gateway." Harper selected six women and two Asian-Canadians for his cabinet. Justin Trudeau named 15.

The "representational principle" obviously has its advantages and disadvantages. In a country as diverse as Canada, every tool of unity is beneficial. Cabinet members are expected to support the interests of their region and social group. This is particularly important because the Senate cannot effectively perform this function. Some critics of Canadian government have argued that the provinces have far too little influence over federal politics; the cabinet is a place where at least some attention is paid to their interests.

At the same time, some cabinet members are named as "political ministers," charged with the responsibility to help organize the provincial parties and to oversee patronage appointments in the provinces. This means that the central government tries to influence the provinces, just as the provinces try to influence it. Disadvantages also include the growth of the cabinet to accommodate so many representatives. Some people fear that this makes the cabinets unwieldy. Finally, a PM is unable to choose the best person for a particular job; it may be more important to select a person for a ministry because he is an English-speaking Quebecer rather than because he is an expert in the portfolio he is assigned.

A seventh source of a PM's power is the ability to command of a multifaceted staff. Since Pierre Elliot Trudeau became PM in 1968, two offices have grown enormously in power: the PMO and the Privy Council Office (PCO). He increased their size and importance in order to get policy recommendations independent of the more entrenched civil service. The PMO, made up of the leader's major advisers and aides, who are political appointees, not civil servants, became the more powerful of the two. Its members do everything from answering mail and making travel arrangements to making policy recommendations and ensuring governmental unity.

Many Canadians, including Brian Mulroney, criticized the size and power of the PMO, charging that it was too costly and undercut the power of the cabinet and Parliament. Once in power, though, Mulroney made it even larger, costlier, and more powerful. In 1985 it had 114 members, as opposed to 90 under Pierre Trudeau and 57 under John Turner. It included a special office and two aides for the PM's wife, Mila. More significant, the political operations of the office have been strengthened, employing 13 policy advisers, instead of the three under Pierre Trudeau. It had the added responsibility of reviewing all cabinet members' major press statements before they were released and also cleared all patronage appointments and senior hiring by cabinet members. Some critics in the opposition and bureaucracy charged that this powerful center had become almost like a presidential White House staff.

The PMO lost none of its power under Prime Minister Jean Chrétien whose popularity had always been bolstered by his image as a humble man of the people. Former top civil servant, Gordon Robertson, who served PMs from Mackenzie King to Trudeau, said in 1998, "the concentration of power in the hands of this prime minister is as great as I have ever seen it."

Traditionally, the PCO has been the clearinghouse and coordinating agency for proposals and ideas from the cabinet and various committees. The most important are cabinet committees, which are smaller than the full cabinet. They can discuss matters more informally before they are brought to the attention of the full cabinet. The names, membership, precise organization and functions of these committees change with PMs. They usually deal with such matters as priorities and legislative planning, federal-provincial relations, economic and social policy and government operations.

The work of cabinet committees was normally supported by about 350 civil servants and employees in the PCO who prepared and circulated documents to ministers and the committees. Moreover, the PCO provides clerical and record-keeping back-up to ministers. It used to be almost exclusively responsible for briefing the PM on matters that were about to be discussed by the cabinet. Chrétien selected a bilingual microbiologist, Jocelyne Bourgon, to be clerk of the PCO. The first woman to hold the job, she was responsible for over 200,000 civil servants.

In addition to selecting his inner staff, the PM can make at least 3,500 "order-in-council" appointments, including about 500 high-level positions, such as ambassadors, Senators, judges and heads of key government agencies. PMs are technically free to hand out patronage appointments as they please, but both Trudeau and Mulroney were frequently criticized for their lavish hand-outs. Mulroney had made a campaign promise to give Parliament some say in the process, but only after much public grumbling about his own appointment practices did he consent to a procedure whereby all-party parliamentary committees would be permitted to review all appointees' qualifications.

The largest reservoir of support and information for the PM is the federal civil service, which has grown so fast in modern times that now one million Canadians, or one out of ten persons of working age, are employed by a government at some level. One of 50 Canadians works directly for a federal department or agency. Since Confederation in 1867, the Canadian population has increased seven-fold while the civil service has increased a hundred-fold. This growth reflects the fact that Canadian government has become far more active in such fields as social welfare, the economy, education, and language rights. Many people are skeptical that such a gigantic body of workers can be effectively controlled by anybody. People are particularly skeptical about the possibility of controlling the many Crown corporations which are wholly or partially owned by the state and whose directors are appointed by the PM and his government. Few would doubt, though, that the PM has more influence over the civil service than any other Canadian.

At the head of each department is a cabinet minister. The minister brings with some aides who are responsible to him or her. Ministers are also assisted by some "parliamentary secretaries," who are MPs without cabinet seats. Since these latter positions are excellent opportunities for newer MPs to demonstrate their talent, a minister can usually count on good work from them. The second highest positions within ministries are the deputy ministers, career civil servant at the top of the

Canada

promotion ladder. They are so important that they are often referred to as "Mandarins," reminiscent of the wise and powerful advisers to the Chinese emperors.

Deputy ministers are appointed, and can be removed, by the PM. Even so, they are supposed to serve any government and are usually non-partisan, even though they are active participants in policy making. The deputy ministers have usually directed the day-to-day operations of the department for years, so their expertise is badly needed by the cabinet ministers who, most often, are not specialists in the field for which they are responsible.

When a government changes, PMs usually replace a few deputy ministers. They are merely transferred to other civil service posts, because they cannot be fired. Still, the number of such changes is usually low. For instance, after coming out of the wilderness of 16 years in opposition, the Conservatives, under Prime Minister Joe Clark, replaced only three deputy ministers. Far fewer heads roll in Ottawa after a parliamentary election than in Washington after a presidential election. There is no "revolving door" in Canadian politics.

Entry based on competitive examinations and promotion based on performance and bilingualism has placed severe limits on the spoils system. These criteria have helped to produce civil servants who, by comparison with most other countries, are efficient, impartial, and able. Civil servants are kept honest and incorruptible by being paid better than their counterparts anywhere else in the world. They have handsome fringe benefits, have almost complete job security, and can retire as early as age 55 with pensions indexed to inflation. A sign of the high quality of Canada's civil service is shown by the fact that few Canadians propose radical changes in it, even though some often complain, that the government has grown too large. Finally, to the disappointment of gossip columnists, financial and sexual scandals involving civil servants are almost unknown in Ottawa.

PARLIAMENT

Canada has a bicameral parliament, but unlike in the American system, both houses are not equal in power. The House of Commons is by far the more important chamber. In parliamentary elections, which must be held at least every five years, citizens who are 18 or older vote for an MP in each of 338 constituencies, called "ridings" and increased from 295 in 1997 and 301 in 2004 to 308 in 2006 and 338 in 2015. Voters in Canada do not vote directly for PMs; only voters in their own ridings vote for them.

SEATS IN THE HOUSE OF COMMONS

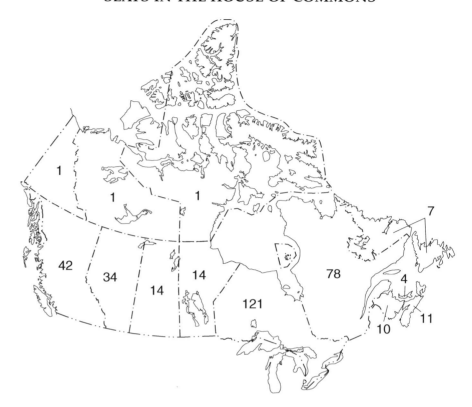

Counting the votes is not as complicated as in the U.S. Canadians have a uniform voting system in the entire country. Citizens vote with pencil and paper, marking an "X" next to the name of the desired candidate. All votes are counted by hand with results being known within hours, not weeks.

The system of election is the single member district or "first past the post," an electoral method now used only in the UK, the U.S., and New Zealand. The candidate with the most votes in each riding is elected, even if the individual wins fewer than 50% of the votes. This electoral system has the advantage of preventing many parties from gaining seats in Parliament, therefore enhances political stability. Insofar as one or the other of the large parties usually has a majority in the House of Commons, there has never been the need for a coalition government to rule in Canada. Even if one party does not win a majority of seats, the custom is for the one with the most seats to form a "minority government." This leads a precarious existence for a while, relying on votes from another party.

Some critics rightly point out that this electoral system enables the two larger parties to win a far higher percentage of parliamentary seats than the percentage of votes they win nationally. Elections are usually won or lost by a three to four percent shift to one party or the other.

If one focuses only on the parliamentary seats which are won or change hands, rather than on the popular vote, one gets an exaggerated impression of voter volatility; sweeps are seldom as massive as they seem. For instance, Mulroney's Tories barely received 50% of votes in all of Canada in September 1984 but won 211 out of the 282 seats in the House of Commons. In 1993 the PC Party won 16% of the votes but received only two seats; the Reform Party won 18% of the votes but captured 52 seats. The Liberals captured only 38% of the votes in 1997 but still won a majority of seats with 155. The same applied in 2011 to the Conservatives, who won only 39.6% of the votes, but secured a parliamentary majority with 167 seats. In 2008, the Greens captured 6.8% of the votes but not a single seat. in 2015, the Liberals garnered only 39.5% of the votes but won 184 of 338 seats.

The same thing can happen on the provincial level. In 1985 the Liberals won more votes than the Conservatives in the Ontario provincial elections. Because of the electoral system, the Conservative Party ended up with four more seats in the provincial legislature. Ontario's Liberals won only 46.5% of the votes in 2003, but captured 70% of the seats. In the 1998 Quebec provincial elections the Liberals won 43.7% of the votes but captured only 48 of 125 seats. The PQ received 42.7% of the votes but garnered 76 seats and remained the governing party. In 2015, the Liberals garnered only 39.5% of the votes but won 184 of 338 seats.

Almost never does a governing party win more popular votes than the combined opposition. For example, in 2000 the Liberals won a landslide victory of 173 seats, 57% of the total by winning 41% of the votes. If Canada had a proportional representation (PR) electoral system, the Liberals would have captured 123 seats, not a majority. In June 2004 the Liberals won 36.7% of the votes and 135 seats, 44% of the total; under PR it would have earned only 116 seats. The newly formed Conservative Party captured 29.6% of the votes and was awarded 99 seats, 32% of the total; under PR 92. The *Bloc Québécois* received 12.4% of the votes in Canada and 54 seats on 17.5% because it dominated Quebec; under PR it would have had only 37. Things were worse for the NDP, which won 15.7% of the votes, but earned a mere 19 seats, 6% of the total; under PR it would have had 49. It is understandable that smaller parties do not like this system.

Precisely because the largest parties benefit from it, it is unlikely that the system will be changed. During the 2015 campaign the Liberals promised to reform the electoral system, but there is little public support this proposition. Only 9% favored a complete overhaul. Indeed, as of 2019 it appears that this promise has been withdrawn, perhaps a wise decision by a government in power.

The distribution of seats is based on provinces' populations and is adjusted according to census figures. As of 2016 there are 338 seats in the House of Commons. Only Quebec's minimum of 75 seats are always guaranteed in order to protect the interests of the country's francophone minority; it now has 78. Ontario has 121 seats, a third of the total. Added together, both provinces' have about two-thirds of all the seats. The remaining seats are distributed approximately as follows: British Columbia 36, Alberta 28, Manitoba approximately 14, Saskatchewan 14, Nova Scotia 11, New Brunswick 10, Newfoundland 7, PEI 4, Northwest Territories 1, The Yukon 1, and Nunavut 1.

In 2011, the ruling Conservative government introduced the Fair Representation Bill, which raised the total number of seats by 30. Every ten years following a national census, redistricting changes the ridings' boundaries to reflect demographic changes. The constitution provides that no province can have fewer House seats than it had in 1986 or than it has in the Senate. This protects the smaller provinces. Alberta and British Columbia each received six more seats, Ontario thirteen and Quebec three.

Each province is represented fairly, but some ridings have more voters than others. For instance, cities, on the whole, are under-represented; in the 1979 election 81,000 persons voted in York–Scarborough, 45,000 in Vancouver Centre and only 28,000 in Gaspé, Quebec. The chief argument against making all districts equal in population is that some northern ridings would be even greater in size than they already are, thus making an MP's travel through the riding to keep in touch with his constituents almost impossible. In other words, some Canadians in such districts would be practically cut off from their government.

Election campaigns are much shorter and cheaper than in the U.S. For example, the 2000 campaign lasted only 36 days, but the one in 2015 went 78 days. Races are also more competitive. The chances for reelection were 72.5% in Canada and 98% in the U.S. Candidates for a House of Commons seat face a spending limit of about $50,000 and each national party must restrict its spending to about $8.5 million. The Harper government reduced the amount donors can give and eliminated public financing to the parties.

Salaries for the members Parliament are adjusted on the first of April each year. As 2017, members of the House of Commons earned $172,700 salary plus tax-free benefits, Senators, who by federal law must receive $25,000 less than members of the House of Commons, received $147,700 plus benefits for Senators. and cabinet ministers earned $255,300 plus benefits. According to the 2018 budget, the PM's salary is $347,400 plus tax-free benefits.

It is often said that money is the "mother's milk of politics." Yet, money cannot ensure victories. For example, the 1993 federal parliamentary elections, the Tories spent $10.4 million to win two seats, the Liberals $9.9 million for 177, the NDP $7.4 million for nine, the *Bloc Québécois* $1.9 million for 54, and the Reform Party $1.5 million for 52.

The physical layout of the House is similar to the British House of Commons. The governing party sits to the right of the robed Speaker, directly across from the opposition parties. The government and the opposition leaders occupy the center seats in the front rows on each side of the aisles. The latter are known as the "shadow cabinet" because each cabinet member has a counterpart in the opposition. The "shadow cabinet" is ready to take office at any time.

The fact that the two sides face each other across an aisle, which, by British tradition, is the width of two sword lengths, is intended to underscore the antagonistic relationship the government and the opposition have. Observers in the galleries notice, though, that this is only political, not personal, antagonism. MPs freely cross the aisle to chat with colleagues in other parties and it is entirely normal for an MP to stand up and publicly wish a member of an opposite party good health after a serious operation or illness. This also applies to the parties' headquarters staffs, which maintain cordial relations with their counterparts in other headquarters and even provide each other with complimentary tickets to their party conferences. The fact that domestic political opponents are not regarded as enemies is one reason why democracy has functioned so well in Canada.

The PM recommends the Speaker of the House of Commons from among his party's MPs, and since 1985 must be elected by the House. All MPs except party leaders and cabinet members are automatically considered to be standing for election unless they remove their names from the list. Individuals are usually prominent members of the governing party who were passed over for cabinet posts. The speakers in both chambers normally alternate between anglophones and francophones; in the House, the deputy speaker is always be a francophone if the speaker is an anglophone and vice versa.

By tradition, the PM and the opposition leader pretend to drag a resisting new Speaker down the aisle to the ornate Speaker's chair. This quaint custom was inherited from Britain. From the 14th century, the commoners' chosen spokesman risked the ire of the monarch and was sometimes even punished on reporting what the Commons wanted.

In Canada today, the Speaker is "punished" with a high salary of $255,300 in 2017, a rambling Kingsmere estate in the Gatineau Hills 15 kilometers or 10 miles from Ottawa, and a personal staff of about 15. This includes a chauffeur for his official limousine and a *maitre d'* to provide for the constant flow of visiting foreign members of Parliament who must be entertained. Most insiders would agree that the Speaker must earn these benefits. Speakers are expected to referee parliamentary debates impartially and even to call the PM plus the government to order when they seem to be playing fast and loose with the rules. The Speaker sets the tone of the daily debates and decides whether they will be spontaneous and scrappy or formal and stiff.

Former Speaker Gilbert Parent described the House as "like a huge animal. Sometimes it lies dormant. Sometimes you prod it and it will jump up and bite you, and it's a wise Speaker who knows when to prod and when to let it sleep." Finally, the Speaker must manage the Commons' staff of 3,000 aides, pages, police and janitors. Along with the House leaders, who are usually different from the national

Canada

party leaders in order that the latter can be absent from the Commons without disrupting the House's business, and whips, which each party selects, the Speaker is a crucial participant in shaping the House's law-making process.

The Speaker breaks tie votes in the House of Commons. On May 19, 2005, a no-confidence vote to determine whether then Prime Minister Paul Martin's government would fall resulted in a 152–152 tie. Speaker Peter Milliken, a Liberal, put the government over the top with his vote. This was the first time in Canadian history that a Speaker broke a tie in a vote of no-confidence. On October 12, 2009, Milliken became the longest-serving speaker in history.

Milliken stepped down June 2, 2011, after nine years in office when then Deputy Speaker Andrew Scheer of the Conservative party was selected in his place following his party's victory in the May 2011 federal elections. At age 32, Scheer was the youngest Speaker in Canadian history and the first to hail from Saskatchewan although he grew up in Ottawa. He cracked down on hecklers, time-wasters, and MPs who demonstrate rude behavior. He became Tory party leader in 2017. In December 2015, a Liberal from Nova Scotia, Geoff Regan, became Speaker, the first person chosen from Atlantic Canada for this post in almost a century. On December 5, 2019, Anthony Rota was elected by the House of Commons to be the speaker in the 43rd Parliament. He is a member of the Liberal Party and is the MP for the district of Nipissing-Timiskaming.

The House is free to establish its own working procedures and it is carefully examining and changing the way it does its work. Many MPs travel to and from their ridings on Mondays and Fridays. Its number of sitting days has declined gradually from as many as 163 days in a year to a low of just 105 in 2008. Traditionally, the average day would unfold something like this: when Parliament is in session, the usual day begins at 2 PM, 11 AM on Fridays, when the Speaker takes the chair and the sergeant-at-arms lays the mace, a gold-plated war club and symbol of the House's authority and of continuity in an ever-changing world, on the long table in front of the Speaker's chair.

The sergeant-at-arms is usually a mere adornment. However, in October 2014 the sergeant-at-arms became a hero when a Canadian-born Islamic jihadist fatally shot a soldier guarding the National War Monument outside Parliament, entered the building with gun blazing, and terrorized the MPs, who were meeting in their weekly caucuses. Kevin Vickers crept up on the assailant outside the entrance of the parliamentary library and shot him dead.

Anthony Rota,
Speaker of the House of Commons
https://lop.parl.ca/About/Parliament/speakers/hoc/sp-37Rota-e.htm

Vickers was rewarded with an ambassadorship to Ireland..

A woman trapped for hours in the parliament spoke for millions of her fellow citizens: "I never thought this would happen. This is Canada." On February 8, 2016, Vickers was presented with the Star of Courage along with six others involved in bringing the incident under control.

On March 15, 2019, Vickers announced he would run for the leadership of the New Brunswick Liberal Association to replace Brian Gallant. He was acclaimed as leader and the Liberal Party's executive board acclaimed Vickers on the recommendation by the leadership convention's steering committee on April 16, 2019, effective April 24, 2019.

After a few routine matters are completed, the question hour begins. This takes place from Mondays through Thursdays and is usually the liveliest part of the day, when the entire government and shadow cabinet are present, about 250 in all. This period, which lasts 45 minutes, is the most watched portion of each day in Ottawa. It is controlled by the opposition, which can pose any questions to any member of the government. Questions are intended to elicit information and often to embarrass the PM or cabinet members. One veteran MP confided, "the unwritten rule is never to ask a question unless you know the answer."

Sitting in his spectacular oak chair, the Speaker has a hidden computer screen in front of him with various camera angles to display the action in the House. In addition, the Speaker has a countdown clock

to help limit questions and answers to 35 seconds and keep things moving briskly so that as many MPs as possible can participate. Most have no involvement, limiting their role to standing, clapping, and cheering for their party while heckling and sneering at the other. So important is question hour for a government that Stephen Harper's cabinet became the first in history to meet every weekday after lunch to rehearse the ordeal together..

A few rules are generally observed. MPs are never to be addressed by their family names and all remarks are technically directed to the Speaker. Sometimes civility does break down. Former Prime Minister Pierre Trudeau once was likened to Hitler, a comparison that prompted the PM to invite the MP to step outside for a fight, one the MP declined. He was also compared to an organ grinder; whose cabinet members are like monkeys. Trudeau was a past master at repartee who dubbed opponents as "nobodies" and as "the honorable stinker." MPs can ask questions in either English or French, and the answers should be given in the same language, if the cabinet member can manage to do so.

The overall purpose of the rules is to keep the government responsible and responsive to the opposition and to the country. The answers the government gives during question hour are widely reported in the press. Since 1977 question hour has been televised. It is broadcast live in Ottawa from 2:15 to 3 PM, and in many parts of the huge country it appears at prime time. News programs frequently show excerpts. It is an opportune time for MPs to impress the folks back home, and the government must prepare in advance for potentially damaging questions. Question hour can be raucous at times. Asked in a 2010 poll if it had become so uncivil that it needed to be reformed, two-thirds of respondents said "yes, it's a daily embarrassment"; 21% admitted they had stopped paying attention, and only 14% said "this is politics—it's not meant to be pretty."

MPs do not pose questions to members of their own parties. Backbenchers, MPs who are in neither the government nor the shadow government, have that opportunity only in the weekly party caucuses, which are held behind closed doors and in which genuine debate occurs. The question hour is usually cut off promptly at 3 PM with the rest of day devoted to bills before a mostly deserted House. Former Prime Minister Stephen Harper, who was picked in 2012 as the best-informed MP, seldom bothered to speak in the House, except during question hour.

Most bills have been introduced by the government and must survive three separate readings in the House before they are sent to the Senate for consideration.

Senate Chamber
Public Archives Canada/PA34219

Debates are often lively and can be conducted in either English or French. Earphones with simultaneous translations are provided for MPs and spectators needing them. MPs are generally articulate and, as in Britain, feel free to bring humor into their remarks. About a third of the MPs are lawyers, with many of the rest drawn from business and the professions.

An increasing amount of legislative work is done in committees. This is in response to the growing legislative workload. The "Striking Committee" decides on the committees' membership although it takes its cues from the assignments agreed on by the parties themselves. There are "standing committees" which roughly correspond to the various cabinet portfolios such as the External Affairs and National Defence Committee.

There are usually 20 MPs on each standing committee, and the composition is determined by parties' proportionate strength in the House. These committees help refine and improve legislation, and they often call in outside experts to testify or provide opinions. Until the rules were changed in 2002, committees were never led by powerful and independent chairs who could defy their party's leadership and prevent legislation from ever getting

to the whole House. Chairs are now elected by the whole House rather than being appointed by the PM.

The party leaders' control on all MPs is so strong and their claim to party discipline so sure that the government's legislation will survive all the legislative hurdles, no matter what. Debates in the whole House are lively, but the outcome of votes is seldom in doubt so long as a government maintains its majority. If the government does not maintain its majority, then it can experience some real surprises. The Canadian political system hinges on a government elected by the people which can legitimize its program in Parliament and then enact it until voted out of office.

Senate

The upper house of Parliament, the Senate, was designed in 1867 to serve two purposes: to serve as a check against "hasty or ill-considered legislation" coming from the House of Commons and to represent regional interests in the federal government. Members of the Senate come from the various regions of Canada and have the constitutional power to veto or amend legislation but lacks the authority to bring down a government by defeating a bill.

As in so many other aspects of Canadian politics, powers on paper cannot always be exercised. In fact, the Senate has never performed the two functions given it in 1867. Canada's first PM, John A. Macdonald, swore that the Senate "will never set itself in opposition against the deliberate and understood wishes of the people." It has not dared veto legislation from the House of Commons since the Second World War. In fact, the Senate has rarely amended a House bill in such a way that its principle is touched. Its legislative role has deteriorated, and its debates are seldom reported in the news media. It is not even held in high esteem.

The first reason why the Senate is not held in high esteem is that it is an appointed, not an elected body. This means that its composition does not reflect the prevailing political power in the country. For example, in 1990 Liberals outnumbered Conservatives in the Upper House by two-to-one, even though the Liberals commanded only half as many seats in the House of Commons as the PC Party. Senators are appointed by the PM, not by the provincial governments. Because the Liberals ruled almost constantly throughout the 20th century, they understandably packed the Senate with their own people. Tory

Canada

Prime Minister Harper did the same in the 105-seat body. Appointments are almost invariably made on the basis of party loyalty and past service to the party in power.

A ruling party thus can dangle attractive patronage appointments to the Senate, which promise good pay until age 75 for work which need not be terribly taxing or time-consuming. One reporter observed, "being named to the Senate in Canada is a lot like winning the cash-for-life lottery." Other cynics have called an appointment "a taskless thanks."

Liberal Senator Andrew Thompson demonstrated just how cushy the life of a Senator can be. Claiming that his health would be endangered by Ottawa's winter weather, he spent most of his time at his home in La Paz, Mexico, attending sessions only 12 times from 1990 to 1998. Astonished critics computed that his pay amounted to about $43,000 per appearance, more than his secretary earned in a year. Senate records in 1997 revealed rampant absenteeism on the part of about two dozen other members and approximately a quarter of all Senators missed at least 40% of the chamber's sessions. A furious Prime Minister Chrétien stripped Thompson of his office space, secretary, travel privileges, and seat in the Liberal caucus. But the truant legislator could not be fired.

Unlike an elected MP, a Senator can seldom be held to account. An attempt was made in 2011 when a Liberal Senator, Raymond Lavigne, sent a staffer to chop down trees at his cottage and claimed more than $30,000 in work-related expenses during a three-month period in the preceding year. After years of resistance, every Senator's expenditures are now posted online and public criticism of expense accounts remains. In 2013 four Senators were caught claiming housing and travel allowances to which they were not entitled. The PM's chief-of-staff, Nigel Wright, had to resign when it was learned that he had given one of them a personal check to cover his $92,000 reimbursement and get him off the hook.

The trend has been to appoint people in the middle, rather than at the end, of their careers. An example of a Trudeau appointment was Ann Cools, who lost her bid for a seat in the House of Commons. A former student radical, who spent time in prison for her part in the destruction of a university computer in Montreal in 1969, she was quickly pardoned before being named to the Senate. The government can also ease a cabinet member gracefully out of governmental business by appointing the person to the Red Chamber, so named after the color of its interior decor. It can even appoint a member of the opposition party in order to free a riding of an unbeatable incumbent or to sow discord in the opponents' ranks. This does not mean that Senators are not talented people; it means that they need not be so as a condition of appointment.

Senators are chosen from the various regions of the country. The Fathers of Confederation gave equal representation of 24 members to Ontario, Quebec, and the Maritime provinces, 10 from Nova Scotia, 10 from New Brunswick, and 4 from Prince Edward Island. Newfoundland was awarded six when it entered the Confederation in 1949. The West was also given 24 Senators, with each of four provinces getting six. The Yukon, Northwest Territories, and Nunavut are also represented. Quebec's allotment must be selected from each of 24 Senatorial districts.

Unlike in the U.S., where all states are represented equally in the Senate, a provision that gives enhanced power to the smaller states, senate seats in Canada are distributed to provinces roughly on the basis of population. Even though appointees are residents of the various provinces, they cannot be said to "represent" them because they were appointed by the PM on the basis of their service to the party. No doubt, it is the absence of a true provincial voice in the federal governmental institutions in Ottawa that forced the provincial premiers to be so assertive about provincial rights and powers.

It cannot be said that the Senate performs no useful function. It does make minor amendments to bills that clarify some points. Some eminent lawyers or former premiers or cabinet members have the time to give a longer look at some bills in committee than the more harried MPs in the House have. Amendments made by the Senate are almost always accepted by the Commons, so long as those amendments are not seen as challenges to the deliberate will of the House. Senators are also invited to attend the weekly party caucuses with the MPs and try to influence their party's policies. The Senate has performed increasingly useful investigative work into a variety of topics ranging from defense policy to poverty and unemployment. It can thus sometimes produce useful reports much less expensively than could a Royal commission or task force, since its staff is already in place and Senators are already being paid. Finally, Senators are sometimes appointed to the cabinet.

For a long time there have been many voices saying that the upper house must be reformed. Over a half century ago the Quebec nationalist, Henri Bourassa, quipped that demands for Senatorial reform tend to break out "periodically, like other forms of epidemics and current fevers." The proposals have included allowing the provincial governments to appoint Senators, fixing the terms to, say, five, nine, or ten years, opening appointments up to a larger group of people than merely party loyalists, or changing its role in the legislative process. Unfortunately, these reforms do not get around the fact that an appointed body simply cannot enjoy the same legitimacy in the citizens' eyes as an elected one. Also, an increase in its governmental role could diminish the power of the PM, the cabinet, the House of Commons, and provincial governments. These power centers cannot be expected to be accommodating to any such proposals. This is especially true because there is nothing resembling a consensus over the functions the Senate could or should perform in the political system.

Controversies involving the Senate occur most frequently when different parties form a majority in each house. Thus, the public eye was again directed toward the Liberal-dominated Senate when it delayed approval of the Mulroney government's bills for months at a time. A seriously miffed Mulroney demanded a curbing or abolition of the Senate even though each time its assent was finally given. His ire came to a boil in the fall of 1988 when John Turner instructed the Liberal majority in the Senate, led by Allan MacEachen, to reject the Free Trade Agreement that his government had negotiated with the U.S. Although the Liberal majority shrunk through death or retirement since 1984 from 74 to 59, that was still enough to reject the bill. The Liberals knew that this would make it impossible for the Mulroney government to ratify the accord before the December 31, 1988, deadline and would therefore force the PM to call new elections which would serve as a kind of referendum on that landmark agreement.

This maneuver was perfectly legal, but some constitutional experts argued that it violated Parliament's unwritten conventions. There was no doubt about Mulroney's interpretation: "The leader of the Liberal Party has asked the Senate of Canada, a bunch of appointed people, to hijack the most fundamental rights of the Canadian House of Commons!" The tables were turned in 1994. The Conservatives, who had been reduced to only two seats in the House of Commons and whose remaining federal power base was in the Senate, used their upper house majority to overturn legislation that would have prevented Canada's election boundaries from being revised before the next federal elections. The Tories charged that this would have protected the seats of Liberal MPs.

In 1990, the question of whether an unelected Senate should have the power to veto legislation adopted in the elected House of Commons again grabbed headlines. When the Liberal-dominated Senate blocked passage of the government's highly unpopular value-added tax (GST), Mulroney appointed 24 new Tory Senators in one month. This included Nova Scotia's Premier John Buchanan, who was under investigation for financial impropriety and who became the first sitting premier to leave provincial politics directly for a Senate seat. This raised the total number of Senators to 112, eight more than normal. In order to do this, Mulroney invoked an almost forgotten procedure in the BNA, unused for 123 years, which empowers the British monarch, as Canada's head of state, to permit a PM to pack the Senate in order to break a legislative deadlock. When the Queen agreed to this, Mulroney had his majority.

The Liberal Senators reacted with an angry walk-out, a filibuster while court challenges were prepared and chaotic scenes on the floor of the dignified house which cast Canadians into disbelief: journalists were invited to enter the chamber floor; pandemonium broke out and vitriolic epithets were flung. One Liberal Senator called his best friend across the aisle a "despicable little bugger." After cool heads were prevailed, he went to his friend, embraced him, and apologized. Canadians rubbed their eyes and asked themselves again whether this institution, which many consider a constitutional relic, should be reformed or abolished. A poll at the time revealed that 80% favored reform.

Some provincial premiers, particularly those from the West and New Brunswick, have called for the election of Senators, but they often disagree on details. Alberta's former Premier Don Getty argued that western interests were being trampled by the Senate's central Canadian majority and called for a "Triple E" solution: an elected, equal and effective upper house, in which each province would have the same number of representatives. After a seat was vacated in 1987, Getty refused to nominate a replacement on the grounds that it should have been filled by election. In 1989 his government organized the first-ever Senatorial election, despite opposition from Ottawa. Mulroney took perhaps the most significant step. In the Meech Lake Accord of 1987 he struck a deal with the premiers by agreeing to give up his prime-ministerial prerogatives to appoint new Senators and instead to select them on an interim basis from a list of candidates agreed on with the provinces.

Then Meech Lake failed, as did the later Charlottetown accords. Because they failed spectacularly, Canadians shy away from attempting to change anything, including the Senate, by amending the constitution. Although 2013 polls showed that two-thirds of Canadians preferred Senatorial elections, and only a third, rising to 43% in Quebec, favored abolition,

any change would have to be incremental. A 2014 poll revealed that two-thirds think the Senate serves no "necessary and useful political function."

In 2006, Stephen Harper from Alberta violated the long-standing principle of his own western-based party by appointing unelected Michael Fortier to the Senate in order to have somebody from Montreal in his cabinet. Even so, he brought the upper house back into the heart of the debate over Canadian democracy, proposing significant reform of the Senate in 2006 but electing Senators and limiting their terms were not among his suggestions. Harper promised that his government would create "a new national process for choosing elected Senators from each province and territory."

Harper wanted to reform the Senate incrementally. In 2011 his government's Senate Reform Act was more specific, starting with nine-year non-renewable terms. Provinces and territories would be encouraged, but not forced, to conduct elections to produce lists of winners from which the PM could pick Senator. Thus, these would be "consultative" votes. Harper still looked for ways of redressing the kind of imbalance that allows New Brunswick and Nova Scotia to have 10 Senators each but provides mighty Alberta and British Columbia only six each.

Polls showed that three-fourths of voters care who gets appointed to the Senate and would like to see it reformed but they do not want a powerful American-like Senate which could introduce gridlock into Canadian federal politics. A majority supports term limits and election of Senators.

The prospects of successful reform are not good; 13 attempts since 1900 to reform the Senate failed. Harper, who called the Senate "a relic of the 19th century," admitted during the 2008 election campaign: "I'll be honest with you. I'm disappointed we haven't made at least some progress on Senate reform." He appointed 59 new Conservative members between 2008 and 2013, 18 in one day. These appointments finally gave his party a majority in the upper chamber. He enlarged that majority as more Senators retired. In a 2013 survey, three in five Canadians called Harper hypocritical for naming so many new Senators despite his public talk about reform. Yet efforts to reform the Senate are paying off. According to a 2019 Nanos poll, 77% of Canadians prefer a more independent appointment process.

The NDP, which became the official opposition in 2011, is traditionally staunchly anti-Senate and does not allow its members to sit there. former leader Tom Mulcair called it "an absurdity" and proposed that the chamber be converted to a daycare center.

Hoping to end partisanship and patronage in the upper chamber, Liberal party leader Justin Trudeau announced in 2014 that its 32 Senators would leave the party and sit as Independents. In the 2015 campaign he promised to introduce some form of independent selection process to propose nominees. Trying something new in 2016, Trudeau selected seven Senators from a slate of non-partisan candidates put forward by civic groups.

Any reform would require the approval of all provinces or seven provinces comprising at least half of Canada's population. When Harper asked the Supreme Court in 2013 whether his reform is constitutional and if the federal government can introduce it unilaterally or only with provincial approval, its answer was "no." Premiers would almost certainly oppose a new and more powerful Senate because it would replace them in Ottawa as the main voices of the provinces and regions in national affairs. Former premier Saskatchewan premier Brad Wall and former premiers Dalton McGuinty of Ontario, Gordon Campbell of British Columbia, Lorne Calvert of Saskatchewan, and Gary Doer of Manitoba, as well as the NDP and *Bloc Québécois*, favored abolishing the Senate altogether.

In the complex mechanism of Confederation, reform would diminish the importance of the provincial governments and those clubs of all premiers, the Conference of First Ministers, including the PM, and the Council of the Federation. There are many other problems: the convention that the upper house must normally pass bills the House sends to it would have to change. It was unclear how this transition might work when the chamber would be a mix of appointed and elected members Not until 2015 did forty-nine Senators reach mandatory retirement age. Fundamental Senate reform appears to be simply too complicated and too political for a federal government to address the issue.

The Senate stepped up to tackle such important issues as defense, Canada-U.S., and Canada-Mexico relations and health care reform. Finally granted $127,500 each for office and research expenses, Senators increasingly treat their positions as full-time jobs. One committee chairman, Michael Kirby, noted: "People forget that there is a lot of talent in the Senate."

THE LEGAL SYSTEM

Based on British common law and legislation, this section examines the two other key elements in Canadian criminal law is based on English common law. This means that the law is derived from previous

Canada

The Supreme Court Building in Ottawa

judicial decisions which together produce a fabric of rules, precedents, and their application to categories of situations. Common law is thus judge made law.

Criminal law involves such things as murder and theft which are considered to be crimes against the state even though they may be directed toward individuals. All criminal law is contained in the federal statute, the Criminal Code.. By contrast, civil law involves matters that are private to the individual citizen and have to do with property and civil rights, excepting divorce law which is governed by the federal Divorce Act.

Because the federal and provincial governments share responsibility for civil law, it differs from province to the next:

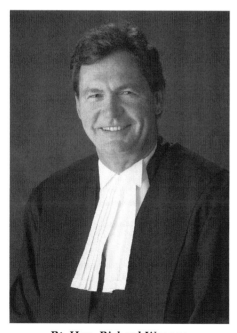

**Rt. Hon. Richard Wagner,
Chief Justice of the Supreme Court**
https://www.macleans.ca/politics/
the-other-political-son/

for example, each province has its own statutes dealing with education because this topic is a provincial responsibility under the Constitution Act of 1867. Quebec has retained its French Civil Code which means that its property or civil rights were established by law-makers, rather than by judicial precedent dealing with concrete cases and specific sets of facts.

Canada has a single court system organized hierarchically. There are three court levels: lesser provincial courts such as family courts; provincial courts composed of a provincial Supreme Court and superior, county, and district courts; and federal courts namely the Supreme Court and Federal Court of Canada. This organization is not as simple as it appears on paper, though. The federal and provincial governments share judicial functions and responsibilities. Insofar as the provinces have the power to determine the organization of their own court systems, there is considerable variation in the kinds of courts within the provinces. The federal government appoints all federal judges, meaning the PM, with the assistance of the minister of justice. There is no parliamentary confirmation of judges.

It should not be surprising to discover that the appointment of judges is, to some extent, based on political considerations. Any federal government would want to be certain that an appointee shares its general view on, for instance, gay marriage, defendants' rights or the distribution of powers between the federal and provincial governments. Judicial Advisory Committees in every province to vet nominees for the 1,100 federally appointed judge positions. During the Chrétien years, the Liberals filled these committees with their own party members.

Judgeships are been given to persons who had been active supporters or donors of the party in power. For example, half of the Liberal government's 2003

judicial appointments had donated to the party, 60% of those appointed in Ontario, Alberta, and Saskatchewan. Despite such politicization of the appointment process, the Supreme Court of Canada is not as ideologically divided as is its American counterpart.

The Canadian selection process relies more heavily than the American on the advice of peers in the legal profession. Traditionally, before the PM selects individuals, the justice minister and ministry, Canadian Bar Association, law societies, and provincial governments are consulted. Consequently, selections are based more on judicial abilities and peer respect than on personal opinions.

Change is in the offing, though. In 2004, former Prime Minister Paul Martin promised more public and parliamentary scrutiny of judicial appointments. When he appointed two women from the Ontario Court of Appeal, Rosalie Abella and Louise Charron, to fill vacancies on the Supreme Court, for the first time the justice minister defended the nominations before a parliamentary committee although the appointees themselves were not present. Abella is a well-known and outspoken advocate of feminist, minority, and gay rights causes. A judicial activist, she dismisses it as "unrealistic to say that judges should not impose their values or make law." It is "better to court controversy than to court irrelevance, and better to court criticism than to court injustice." Her appointment at a time of intense public discussion over same-sex marriage was significant.

Martin's last appointment to the Supreme Court before vacating office in February 2006 was Marshall Rothstein, a judge and former law professor at the University of Manitoba. He was renowned as the hardest working judge in the land, working seven days a week and refusing to hire clerks who did not do the same. For the first time in Canadian history, Rothstein was required to appear before an all-party panel of MPs for a televised grilling of his legal views. All was in English because he is the only justice who is not bilingual.

Former Prime Minister Harper wanted to strengthen the practice of allowing a parliamentary committee to interview potential justices. After all, justices are among the most powerful people in Canada and PMs choose people who may in the long run turn out to be more important than they ever will have been. This is because judicial decisions can change the country's social fabric; they can be so immense as to throws into serious question the whole notion of parliamentary supremacy. Nevertheless, when Stephen Harper tapped bilingual Nova Scotia judge Tom Cromwell to fill a Supreme Court vacancy in September 2008, he decided there was no time for the procedures he himself approved because he called an election two days later. Harper did not come back to it until he announced Cromwell's appointment on December 22. Cromwell was sworn in on January 5, 2009.

By 2016, Harper had appointed five of the Supreme Court's justices. As such, his government decided that an improved selection process should be firmly in place. Beginning in 2011, the justice minister invites members of the public, provincial officials, judges, and prominent lawyers to recommend long lists of candidates. A parliamentary panel composed of five MPs, including one each from the opposition New Democrat and Liberal parties, creates a short list of six candidates, from which the PM and justice minister pick two.

The two finalists then answer questions before an ad hoc House of Commons Committee, and the majority in parliament selects the judge. Harper explained that "overall, what you're looking for is record, experience, judgment, judicial temperament. These people sit on the bench a long time. We will choose very carefully." By 2013 Harper had appointed 439 judges to senior courts. Prime Minister Justin Trudeau tweaked this slightly in 2016 by choosing from a shortlist of bilingual jurists drawn up by worthies. Legislators can question, but not vote on, appointees.

One constitutional requirement with which few people quarrel is that three of the nine judges appointed to the Supreme Court of Canada, established in 1875, must be from Quebec. By law the three must be appointed from Quebec's court of appeal or superior court or be lawyers who work in the province. There is an unwritten tradition that the office of Chief Justice alternates between an anglophone and a francophone.

There was considerable controversy over Bill C-232, which parliament adopted in 2010, requiring all Supreme Court appointees to be fluent in both languages and be able to hear cases in both without the aid of an interpreter. The court had always been bilingual in the sense that anyone appearing before it could plead his case in either official language. Critics fear that this new requirement would dangerously reduce the pool of potential appointees, especially from the West. Harper ignored it in 2011 when he appointed the unilingual Michael Moldaver. The Court is just as sensitive about gender balance, so he tapped a second justice from the Ontario Court of Appeal, Andromache Karakatsanis, who is fluent in both languages and Greek.

In 1999, the first woman to be appointed Chief Justice was Beverley McLachlin. Born and educated in Alberta, she moved to British Columbia, where she became

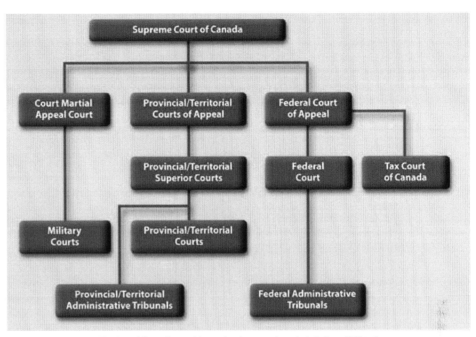

Retrieved from: https://www.justice.gc.ca/eng/csj-sjc/just/07.html

chief justice of the province's Supreme Court in 1988. She was appointed to the Supreme Court of Canada a year later. Also, in 1999, Louise Arbour, who won international recognition as head of the U.N. tribunal on war crimes, joined McLachlin on Canada's highest court by. Arbour resigned from the Supreme Court in 2004 to become the U.N. High Commissioner for Human Rights.

A former law professor, McLachlin is universally acknowledged for her intellect, scholarship, and persuasive powers as her Court produces an increasing number of unanimous decisions (82% in 2001). McLachlin takes a more cautious, centrist view of the law compared with her two predecessors, both of whom were regarded as activists. She is more deferential to Parliament and less open to charges of judicial activism although her court delivered some significant defeats to the government. In her words, "I'm not a politician. I'm not there to vote for this law or that. My job is to decide each case fairly, according to the law."

The formal powers of the Chief Justice are limited. The most important is to determine the size of the panel as five, seven, or nine judges to hear a case. However, people speak increasingly of the "McLachlin court." She is more available to the media and open to defending the court's actions in public. Chief Justice McLachlin retired after serving as Chief Justice for 17 years and 341 days in 2017. Prime Minister Justin Trudeau then appointed Justice Richard Wagner Chief Justice; he took office on December 18, 2017.

Gabrielle Giroday writing in the *Canadian Lawyer* magazine provided the

following information on Chief Justice Wagner.

Wagner, a graduate of the University of Ottawa's Faculty of Law, was called to the Quebec bar in 1980. He practised at Lavery, de Billy SENCRL / LLP (formerly known as Lavery, O'Brien and Lavery, Johnston, Clark, Carrière, Mason & Associés), from 1980 to 2004, when he was appointed to the bench at the Quebec Superior Court.

"There is a great deal of respect for Justice Wagner in terms of what he's done as a lawyer, his involvement in the community and his career as a judge. There was a lot of pride when he was appointed to the Supreme Court and all the much more so now that he's appointed chief justice," says Louis Charette, a partner at Lavery lawyers who worked with Wagner on construction and professional liability litigation files in the litigation team at the firm until Wagner was appointed to the bench in 2004.

Charette says Wagner brings a passion for the law but is more "reserved" in his approach than McLachlin.

"I think he's going to bring the same passion and rigour that Justice McLachlin brought, I think that's undeniable. In terms of his qualities he was passionate about what he did, he was rigorous and hardworking and that will continue. I think Richard is more reserved as a personality. Justice McLachlin had an ease with people and it was easy to speak with her. Justice Wagner is very reserved and perhaps that is a difference Canadians will see in terms of his approach in public speaking."

Wagner served as a judge at the criminal division, civil division and commercial

Canada

division until 2011, when he was appointed to the Quebec Court of Appeal.

Wagner's appointment ends months of speculation about who would take McLachlin's place at the court. On Dec. 18, he took an oath of office as chief justice.

"I have the utmost confidence in his ability to lead the highest court of Canada, an institution with a long and respected history of judicial independence and excellence," said Prime Minister Justin Trudeau, in a news release from the PMO.

"The judiciary, the legal profession, and all Canadians will be well served by his dedication to upholding the laws and Constitution on which this country is founded."

Emmett Macfarlane, an associate professor of political scienceat the University of Waterloo and author of *Governing from the Bench: The Supreme Court of Canada and the Judicial Role,* says in the short time Wagner has been with the SCC, he has carved out a reputation for being "straight-forward" and "clear."

"In some ways, it's the obvious choice. I also think it's the correct choice," he says.

According to Macfarlane, Wagner displays the potential for "consensus building" among the justices, similar to the retiring McLachlin. "It hasn't been that long since he was appointed to the court," says Macfarlane, who adds that in that time Wagner has shown he has a "collegial personality."

"He's very forthright in his public statements," says Macfarlane. Macfarlane says the other name most commonly floated as the potential Chief Justice was Rosalie Abella, but she faces a mandatory retirement in 2021, which could be problematic.

"This decision allows for a little bit of stability," says Macfarlane. He also said the decision to appoint Wagner follows a pattern of PM's elevating someone to the position of Chief Justice, who was appointed by a PM of a different partisan stripe. In this case, Wagner was appointed by former Prime Minister Stephen Harper.

"This is not a partisan institution," he says. He says an interesting issue to watch for will be if there are divisions that emerge amongst the justices in their decisions, as it's a "fairly young court."

The political nature of some appointments, aside, Canada holds firmly to the basic legal principle of the independence of the judiciary, a tradition inherited from Britain. This means that the government does not remove judge, even if it dislikes their decisions. Even though there are constitutional provisions for removing judges, no judge of any federal or provincial superior court has ever been removed since 1867. This principle of independence is also underscored by the appointment of

judges who can remain on the bench until they are 75.

Two other important principles are limited judicial review and judicial restraint. Canadian courts have the responsibility for delineating between federal and provincial jurisdiction. Therefore, the Supreme Court of Canada can determine which level of government has jurisdiction over which powers. The Court can rule that a parliament cannot enact a law because the authority for such issues resides with another legislature. That is, the Court can overrule laws but, unlike Parliament, cannot propose new ones.

The Canadian government can refer hypothetical questions, called a "reference," to the Supreme Court concerning the constitutionality of Constitution Acts or of federal or provincial jurisdiction and powers. Ottawa did this in 1997 when the Court responded no when asked whether Quebec had the right to declare independence from Canada unilaterally . The Court did so again in 2013 when asked if the federal government could reform the Senate without the provinces' approval. Such advisory opinions are issued in the form of judgments that have always been treated as binding.

The referee role in federal-provincial jurisdiction is only a limited form of judicial review. It is more than British courts have, but less than that possessed by the U.S. Supreme Court, which can deem any law null and void because it violates the constitution. Former Chief Justice Antonio Lamer noted: "Since the charter came into effect, we no longer only rule on cases. Now, we rule on the laws themselves."

Until 1949, some cases could be appealed from the Supreme Court of Canada to the Judicial Committee of the Privy Council, the highest court in Britain. Now the Supreme Court of Canada is indisputably the last court of appeal for Canadians. The country's courts have had a long tradition of "legal restraint," meaning that they have been hesitant to use all the powers the constitution had granted them. After 1949, though, the Supreme Court dealt increasingly with contentious issues, such as boundaries of free speech. Since the early 1970s, it has rendered important decisions such as that hanging is not "cruel and unusual punishment," that offshore minerals belong to the central government, that the provinces are free to censor entertainment, and that Quebec's ban on the use of English in the courts was unconstitutional.

The influence of the American model is clear. As James Snell, a Canadian history professor at the University of Guelph, noted: "There is no doubt that the high profile of the Warren court in the United States did influence us in terms of what we expect from the court. Canadian citizens

are now expecting them to make decisions that would before have been left to politicians." Former Chief Justice Brian Dickson also spoke about his American counterparts on the Supreme Court: "Increasingly, we look to their experience, not to follow it slavishly but simply as a starting point with which we may agree or disagree. They have made some mistakes that we don't have to make." There are two clear differences: unlike American high court justices, Canadian judges keep a low public profile and they are far more scrupulous in avoiding visible ideological partisanship. Their decisions rarely give evidence of justices' personal philosophies.

The Canadian Charter of Rights and Freedoms, enacted in 1982, gave the courts an additional watchdog role over citizens' rights. Some Canadians had thought that the tradition of "judicial restraint" would dissuade judges from becoming fully immersed in the legally difficult issues of individual rights. They were badly mistaken. The Charter of Rights has, in fact, greatly stimulated the activity of the courts and significantly changed Canadian political life in the process.

About half of the Constitution Act, 1982, was devoted to basic civil and political liberties. This Charter was a dramatic break from British and Canadian tradition. For a long time, Canadians believed that there was no need to write down basic individual rights because they were already adequately protected by Parliament and common law. There was therefore no mention of them in the BNA.

Over the years, though, there have been incidents that made some Canadians wonder whether their rights were indeed adequately protected. The 1914 War Measures Act struck many as perhaps allowing the government too many sweeping powers. The government could rule by decree, usurping the powers of both federal and provincial parliaments. In 1917 the government prohibited naturalized citizens of German origin from voting. Further, in 1960 the federal government passed a Bill of Rights, a normal legislative act which applied only to the federal government and which could have been invalidated by another simple act of Parliament. Just how little it could restrain the federal government was demonstrated in October 1970 when shocking kidnappings by Quebec nationalists took place. The Trudeau government invoked the War Measures Act and made membership in the *Front de Liberation du Québec,* Liberation Front of Quebec, illegal, then arresting those who had belonged to it before it was a crime to do so.

In the wake of a wiretapping scandal in 1986 involving the deputy PM, a legal commission reported that twice as many wire taps are permitted by Canadian

Canada

NATIONAL ANTHEM

O Canada! Our home and native land!
True patriot love in all thy sons command.
With glowing hearts we see thee rise,
The True North strong and free!
From far and wide, O Canada,
We stand on guard for thee.
God keep our land glorious and free!
O Canada, we stand on guard for thee.
O Canada, we stand on guard for thee.

 Canadian   Patrimoine
Heritage   canadien

http://www.pch.gc.ca

HYMNE NATIONAL

O Canada! Terre de nos aïeux,
Ton front est ceint de fleurons glorieux!
Car ton bras sait porter l'épée,
Il sait porter la croix!
Ton histoire est une épopée
Des plus brillants exploits.
Et ta valeur, de foi trempée,
Protégera nos foyers et nos droits.
Protégera nos foyers et nos droits.

Canada

judges than by American jurists. The report continued "It is astounding that this country has recorded on a per capita basis more than twenty times the number of authorizations [as] our massive American neighbor." Criticism of an overly-intrusive RCMP prompted the creation in 1984 of a special counterespionage agency, the Canadian Security Intelligence Service in order to reduce the RCMP's powers. In 1989 the second-ranking RCMP officer was forced to resign amid charges of political interference in two high-profile investigations involving a leak of the government's budget.

The Charter of Rights entrenches in the Constitution the rights of Canadian citizens, meaning that they cannot be done away with by a simple act of Parliament. The Charter, along with federalism, is yet another blow to the principle of "parliamentary supremacy." It applies to all levels of government while expanding Canadians' rights to include such things as equality of women and the right to use either of the two official languages.

In provisions, the Charter confers constitutional status to the guarantees in the 1969 Official Languages Act. Moreover, it spells out many of the same rights as are contained in the Bill of Rights which has been so important in the American political experience. Traditionally, Canada has placed more emphasis on group rights than have Americans. Yet, since the Constitution and Charter have been in place, legal scholars have noticed a convergence in the legal reasoning of the Supreme Courts of both countries when ruling on matters of rights. In this regard, former president of the Israeli Supreme Court, Aaron Barak, wrote in the *Harvard Law Review* that "Canadian law serves as a source of inspiration for many countries around the world" and may now be more influential than its American counterpart.

As in the U.S., Canadian courts must decide what the various freedoms mean in practice. Judges must give precise meaning to such phrases as "unreasonable search," "arbitrarily imprisoned," and/or "informed promptly." The Charter requires that any limitations on Canadians' rights must be "reasonable," but the courts must wrestle with the question of what kind of a line this draws. Further, the Charter affirms the existing aboriginal and treaty rights of native peoples even though its language is vague simply because there is no consensus in Canada as to the nature of these rights.

The courts have also found themselves in the middle of the emotionally-charged abortion question. In 1988 the Supreme Court struck down the restrictive federal abortion law as unconstitutional because it interfered with a woman's "bodily integrity." In July 1989 the Supreme Court of Quebec countered by ruling that the rights of the father and the fetus, which it considered to be a human being entitled to the right to life, must be respected. Following passionate debate across the country, though, the Supreme Court of Canada responded in August 1989 by permitting a Quebec woman to have an abortion after she had had one Trying to take the issue out of the courts, the Mulroney government received parliamentary approval in 1989 for a new law permitting abortion if one doctor believes a mother's health is threatened.

In 2003, the courts demonstrated how their interpretation of the Charter can affect sensitive social issues. The Supreme Court ruled that there is no constitutional right to smoke marijuana for recreational purposes, but left open the possibility that parliament could decriminalize it. In 2005 Canada became the first country in the world to approve a marijuana-based painkiller for multiple sclerosis patients. Attitudes against the recreational use of marijuana hardened when the Conservatives came into power in 2006. One of its first acts was to declare that the liberalization of the drug was a dead issue. Justin Trudeau's government legalized the recreational use of cannabis in 2018.

In June 2003, an appellate court in Ontario entered more controversial terrain by declaring that denying same-sex couples the right to marry violated their rights and offended "the dignity of same-sex relationships." Because the judgment took immediate effect, hundreds of gay couples rushed to Ontario, one-third of whom from the U.S., to marry. The then PM, Jean Chrétien, announced that the government would not appeal the decision, citing "an evolution in society."

In September 2003, then opposition leader Stephen Harper introduced a motion in Parliament that the Liberals overwhelmingly supported in 1999 defining marriage as the union of one man and one woman. This time it was narrowly defeated 137 to 132, a vote that accurately reflected the 50–50 split on the issue in Canadian society. Many Liberals said their switch was influenced by the case from Ontario. The PM, Jean Chretian, sent draft legislation legalizing gay unions to the Supreme Court to get an assessment of its constitutionality. Chief Justice Beverley McLachlin rebuked the government from for referring the matter straight to the court, which usually only addresses appeals of earlier orders. Nevertheless, with the Liberals split on the issue and constituting only a minority in parliament, the PM left the matter in the Supreme Court and appointed two new justices who might support same-sex marriages.

In 2003, the highest court rejected requests by religious and family groups to appeal the Ontario court ruling, letting it stand as the law of the land. Within a year gay marriage was legal in most Canadian provinces and territories. In 2004 the Supreme Court of Canada, acting on the government's request for a ruling on the constitutionality of eventual legislation, thought that same-sex marriage is consistent with the constitution and did not violate the rights of religious Canadians who desire to uphold the traditional definition of marriage. The Court did say that the guarantee

Canada

of religious freedom protects clergymen from being forced to perform same-sex marriages. In sweeping language, the court pronounced that the constitution "is a living tree which, by way of progressive interpretation, accommodates and addresses the realities of modern life."

The Alberta premier threatened to invoke the "notwithstanding," or opt-out, provision to prevent the order from taking effect in his province. Nevertheless, the Martin government vowed to pass a law permitting gay marriage, with all MPs except cabinet members free to vote according to their consciences. When it came to a vote in 2005, more than 30 Liberal MPs joined the opposition to reject the bill recognizing same-sex marriage. Many Canadians felt they had been railroaded on this. Still, polls indicated that those who opposed such unions would overwhelmingly accept the Conservative opposition's alternative of civil unions granting gays the same rights, benefits, and obligations as any married couples, with or without the title of marriage. By 2009, two-thirds of Canadians accepted same-sex relationships. In 2007 when Scott Brison became the first MP to marry a same-sex partner, two former PMs, Joe Clark and Paul Martin attended the ceremony.

In 2017, the PM apologized to gays who had been the victims of government discrimination, known as the "gay purge," granting them compensation. In that same year polls indicated that 85% of Canadians were willing to vote for a party led by someone who was gay.

In 2009, another unconventional form of family, polygamy, entered the spotlight. According to section 293 of the criminal code, polygamy is punishable by up to five years in prison. At this time, a poll revealed that 82% of Canadians opposed legalizing polygamy. When the government of British Columbia sought to end the practice in its borders, especially in a Mormon commune called Bountiful, where one former "bishop" had 26 wives and 108 children, in a lengthy decision in 2011 the province's highest upheld the prohibition against polygamy. The court reasoned that the inherent harms in polygamy justified limiting the religious freedom rights underpinning polygamy. Subsequently, in 2017, two men in Ontario, one of whom had 25 wives and 146 children in the first test of the 127 year old section 293 of the criminal code.

THE CHARTER OF RIGHTS AND FREEDOMS

The Canada and Constitution Acts had to be careful compromises in order to gain the backing of the provinces which, for

a hundred years, were unable to agree on these matters. Most provinces would agree to give the courts a clear mandate to strike down laws which violate the Charter only by securing a political safety-hatch in return but their officials wished to protect themselves from a flood of court cases attacking their laws.

In order to minimize the dangers of "judicial lawmaking," the Charter contains a clause in Section 33 which says that Parliament or the legislature of a province may expressly declare that their law would still operate "notwithstanding" or despite the Charter's provisions. When a legislature disregards a provision of the Charter, it must declare openly that it is doing so, and thereby bear whatever public onus such a declaration would cause; such non-compliance could only last five years but could be renewed.

Many Canadians were convinced that provinces would be hesitant to use this "notwithstanding" provision because that would be a public statement that they intended to deny rights guaranteed in the Charter. However, no sooner was the ink on the Charter dry when Quebec, which for years rejected the entire constitutional change and which fears that its efforts to make Quebec more French could be frustrated by the Charter, put a "notwithstanding" clause in all of its provincial laws. Quebec invoked the clause again in December 1988 to invalidate a ruling of the Supreme Court of Canada ruling restricting the province's French-only language legislation.

Many critics understandably see this escape-hatch as a serious weakening of the Charter. Yet, it is important to bear in mind that without such compromises, there would have been no Canada and Constitution Acts in the first place.

Since the Charter came into force in 1982, Canadian courts have been inundated with cases relating to individual rights. In the first two years alone, lower courts resolved more than 1,000 Charter-based cases, covering issues ranging from an accused person's right to counsel and Parliament's authority to keep stores closed on Sundays to anglophones' right to have their own schools in Quebec. Thousands more such cases are on the dockets. Of the 100 cases heard annually by the Supreme Court, constitutional cases are usually the most time-consuming. Canada's former chief justice, Brian Dickson, said in 1984: "When there is a breach of the fundamental rights and freedoms under the Charter of Rights, we have been given the right, the duty and the responsibility to deal with it—and it is our duty to strike [the violation] down."

In 1985, Canada entered yet another era when the so-called "equity clauses" of Section 15 of the Charter took effect.

This clause insures that every individual is equal before and under the law "without discrimination based on color, religion, sex, age, or mental or physical disability." Such protection had been postponed three years from the enactment of the Charter to give the federal and provincial governments sufficient time to amend any discriminatory laws or regulations. Capital punishment is outlawed even though 53% of respondents in 2009 approved of its use.

All provincial governments were slow to respond to this task, in part because they were not sure what precisely constituted discrimination. It was unclear whether age could be used for such questions as when a person may drive a car, consume alcohol, serve in the army, get married or be forced to retire or whether women be barred from combat roles in the military, and what "equal pay for equal work" means.

Section 1 of the Charter says that all of Canadians' rights and freedoms are subject "to reasonable limits prescribed by law," but it is unclear precisely what this means in concrete cases. The social and legal consequences of Section 15 remain unclear, but one thing which is certain is the revolutionary power that has been given to the Canadian courts. In the words of Brian Dickson: "The Charter has replaced parliamentary supremacy with constitutional supremacy." No wonder Brian Mulroney joked that one of the first things he intended to do with his new-born son was to enroll him in law school.

Ontario experimented with allowing Muslims to mediate some civil disputes by permitting tribunals that included imams, Muslim elders and lawyers to apply Islamic sharia law to family disagreements, inheritances, and/ or business and divorce matters. This possibility was provided for under the Arbitration Act of the Province of Ontario which grants religious and cultural groups the authority to resolve such disputes through private and binding arbitration. Catholics and Protestants never resorted to the act, but Jews had since 1991. By 2004 Muslim leaders had set up an Islamic Court of Civil Justice that had chosen arbitrators who had undergone training in sharia and Canadian civil law.

Much of the Canadian public was dismayed and incensed that such courts could be permitted to operate in a secular country. Even the Canadian Council of Muslim Women feared that they could undermine women's rights: "Sanctioning the use of religious laws under the Arbitration Act will provide legitimacy to practices that are abhorred by fair-minded Canadians, including Muslim women." Public opinion is enflamed by such a horrific crime in Quebec as the honor killing by drowning of three Muslim sisters and

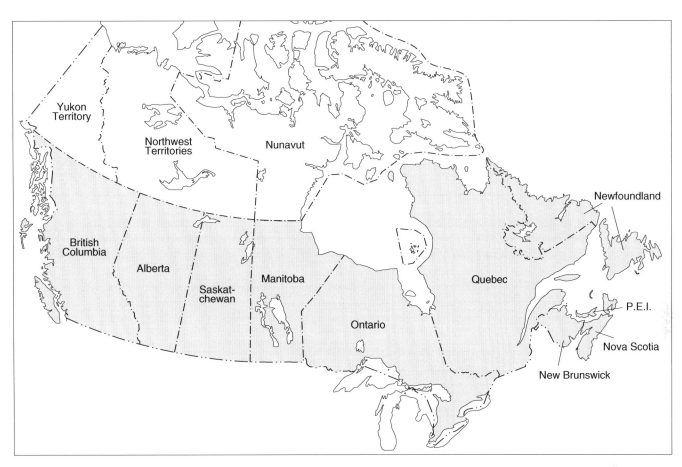

their aunt in 2011 who allegedly dishonored the family by dressing up, wearing makeup, and flirting with boys.

In June 2005, Quebec banned Islamic law. In the words of Premier Jean Charest: "It's important to send a very clear message that there is one rule of law in Quebec." In September 2005, there were demonstrations in a dozen Canadian and European cities against Ontario's legal experiment. The government in Toronto quickly scrapped the use of sharia law and moved to outlaw religious tribunals by Christians and Jews.

FEDERALISM AND THE PROVINCES

In 1867, the Fathers of Confederation intended to create a federation in which the central government would be more powerful than the provinces. The BNA therefore granted the provinces only restricted powers that would enable them to maintain their cultural identity, including powers over local government, property, social welfare, education, health, language, and culture. These were not exclusive powers, though, because the federal government was given the power to protect the educational rights of religious minorities, which meant primarily the English Protestants in Quebec and the Catholic francophones outside of Quebec. The BNA even spoke of "concurrent powers," such as agriculture and immigration, and contained a "supremacy clause" which made the central government's claim on these shared powers supreme.

The BNA granted a limited number of specific powers to the provinces. Conversely, it earmarked 29 kinds of powers for the federal government such as defense, finance, criminal law, transportation, postal services, coinage of money, banking, and Indian affairs. It also granted Ottawa the most lucrative sources of revenue. Unlike in the U.S. Constitution's Tenth Amendment, any powers not specifically granted to the provinces accrue to the central government in Canada. Further, the BNA contained a "declaratory power," which permitted the central government to usurp provincial powers if the reason for such action were "for the general Advantage of Canada or for the Advantage of Two or more of the Provinces." This power is seldomly used.

Ottawa can also "disallow" a provincial law within a year of passage, or can "reserve" such a law for federal governmental review before such a law goes into force. None of these powers has been exercised since 1961. The hefty central powers the founders built into the BNA explain why the regional units were called "provinces" rather than "states." The latter term denotes dignified sovereignty, while the word "province" implies a rural hinterland outside the limits of the metropolis. Almost everywhere else, "provincial" seems to be an insult. Yet over time, the provinces are entities that have drawn away some important powers from Ottawa and have become more powerful than American states.

Ottawa's power on paper is most impressive. Even so, political practice in Canada can differ greatly from documentary powers. While the founders fully intended to create a Canada with a stronger central government and weaker provincial governments than the U.S., the exact opposite has actually occurred. Today, Canadian provinces are considerably stronger than are American states and the provincial premiers are potentates whose strength can hardly be exaggerated. While it is true that the courts, including the Judicial Committee of the British Privy Council, tended to judge more often in the provinces' favor than in Ottawa's, the strengthening of provincial rights has come primarily from the provincial leaders themselves. In good Canadian style, change has come chiefly by custom and convention. Today's reality is the result of political accommodation,

Canada

Edmonton 937,845
Saskatoon 225,927
Winnipeg 671,274
Montreal 3,426,350
Calgary 951,395
Regina 192,800
Halifax 359,183
Vancouver 1,986,965
Toronto 4,682,897
Ottawa 1,063,664

Source: *Maclean's*

not judicial decision and constitutional change.

The forces of decentralization and centralization are always at work in Canada. Author Peter C. Newman put it this way: "Few land masses of such outrageous dimensions can withstand the tensions of democracy." The stresses and strains of stretching the rule of law across 88 degrees of longitude and 42 degrees of latitude virtually guarantee inefficient central government.

The powers of both levels of government have ebbed and flowed over the years. To summarize these evolutionary changes, because the provinces were quickly dissatisfied with their limited powers, they began almost immediately to strengthen their position through hard bargaining. Yet, two world wars, during which Ottawa ruled by means of expanded emergency powers, and the Great Depression in the l930s brought a resurgence of central powers. In the mid-1950s, though, the provinces reasserted themselves with a vengeance, first in Quebec, and then in the energy-rich West.

In the 20th century, Canada had become a predominantly urbanized country as provincial leaders faced the task of managing the growth of cities. The "minor powers" which the BNA granted provinces, such as social welfare, health, and education, became salient issues in a country that had become committed to expanding services in these areas. These maters now claim half the budgets of most provinces, requiring their leaders to put heavy pressure on Ottawa, with its greater taxing power, to help finance them. By the 1980s close to half of some provinces' budgets came from the federal government.

By means of a system that some authorities have called "co-operative federalism,"

the two levels of government share the cost of many programs. The usual practice for such cooperation is that Ottawa sends financial support such as for health insurance or pensions on the condition that the provinces' programs meet federal standards. Ottawa also sends some funds on an unconditional basis.

The dilemma remains: the constitution confers on provinces the responsibility for most public services, including justice, education, health, and the management of natural resources. Yet, the central government has more cash and can run up surpluses while the provinces struggle to pat for expensive services. Canadian politics is largely about chronic jurisdictional quarrels between different levels of government over transfers of money.

In the 1960s, provincial leaders even challenged the federal government's exclusive power to conduct foreign relations. Quebec created a department of intergovernmental relations which acts much like a foreign ministry and seeks to be represented in international conferences along with opening trade and cultural missions in a variety of foreign countries, including the U.S. and France. Many other provinces rapidly followed suit as Ontario alone maintains a dozen similar missions abroad. Prime Minister Pierre Trudeau set out to reverse the trend toward decentralization because the Constitution Act itself puts limits on the provinces' power to veto some constitutional amendments.

Of course, competition between Ottawa and the provinces is as old as the Confederation itself. The BNA granted the central government control over major 19th-century concerns, such as trade, banks, postal service and criminal law. Still, the provinces had control over matters that rose to greater prominence in the

late 20th and early 21st century such as health care and education.

The provinces accept money from Ottawa but resist federal intrusion into their jurisdictions. This is especially true of Quebec. Even Ontario has withdrawn from its traditional stance as the natural ally of Ottawa. Having been officially categorized temporarily as a "have-not" province, Ontario complains like the other provinces that it is being cheated by Ottawa politically and economically. It is a messy process. When asked in 2010 if federalism "has more advantages than disadvantages," 48% of respondents agreed, including in Quebec, and only 33% disagreed with 42% in Quebec joining this response.

Contemporary Canadian federalism involves close and frequent cooperation and negotiation between provincial and federal governments. This has been called "executive federalism" because the executive branches facilitate the highly interpenetrated relationships. Civil servants from both levels meet and talk by phone daily while cabinet members frequently meet to discuss common problems. Since the 1960s, the premiers and the PM meet in Conferences of First Ministers. These are convened and chaired by the PM.

Such "summit meetings" usually occur at least once a year although PMs often elect not to have them. former Prime Minister Harper never convened a meeting, but his successor, Justin Trudeau, organized a summit in March 2016. Much of the bargaining at these meetings occurs behind closed doors. To the participants it is known as "the Club," and civility is one of its most rigid conventions. According to one premier, "the clubby atmosphere of the gatherings puts tremendous pressures on each premier to conform." Such a situation discourages political head-on collisions although they sometimes occur. In 2004, the premiers began meeting semi-annually in the Council of the Federation, a forum that excludes the PM.

This form of "executive federalism" was seriously harmed by the failure of the Meech Lake Accord in 1990. Top leaders who were derisively dubbed "11 men in suits" made this agreement in relative secrecy. The result was a political disaster. Former Manitoba premier Gary Filmon learned the indelible lesson that if politicians indulge in top-down, brokerage politics, the voters will punish them. "When you look at the names and the faces that were associated with Meech Lake, every single person who signed that agreement was gone from office within a very few short years." Since 1990 federal-provincial agreements tend to be more painstakingly and publicly constructed over years of meetings and with much outside consultation.

The PM can decide whether to have more or fewer meetings with the premiers. Stephen Harper, who led minority governments from 2006–2011 and a majority until October 2015, chose to be as conciliatory as possible with the powerful provincial barons. He bought peace by increasing transfer payments by billions of dollars and avoiding policy clashes. Harper was careful not to intrude on spheres chiefly under provincial jurisdiction. However, by October 2015, when the Conservatives were voted out of power, Harper had not met the premiers as a group since November 2008. Prime Minister Justin Trudeau vowed to change this.

The federal cabinet has a Standing Committee on Federal-Provincial Relations and the Privy Council Office has a Federal-Provincial Relations Secretariat; both help prepare the PM and the PM's retinue for meetings. In addition to these conferences, the premiers and territorial leaders conduct an annual summer meeting among themselves, and frequently the Western or Atlantic premiers will gather. Starting in 2004 a Council of the Federation brings premiers and territorial leaders together twice a year. It has an Ottawa-based secretariat, and the federal government is not a member. Finally, bilateral meetings among premiers are a frequent occurrence.

PROVINCIAL GOVERNMENTS

Canada's provinces have governmental systems similar to that of the federal government in Ottawa except that none has an upper house. All have parliamentary systems meaning that the party leader with majority support in the legislative assembly forms the government led by a powerful premier. Don Braid, political columnist for the *Edmonton Journal* once described the premiers: "They recall the medieval barons who armed against the king while demanding his protection. Their interests are purely regional, but fate has given them a huge role in the national melodrama. On this stage they cavort like off-Broadway Falstaffs shoved into King Lear's shoes. And yet, their subjects love them for it." While premiers are important movers and shakers in Canadian politics, their strong regional power bases have always prevented them from rising to the pinnacle of Canadian political power in Ottawa. No premier has ever become PM of Canada.

The PM appoints a lieutenant governor in each province on the advice of the provincial premier; this person usually performs only ceremonial functions. In 2000 six of the ten lieutenant governors were women after then Prime Minister Chrétien appointed Myra Freeman, a sixth-grade Halifax teacher; she was the first woman and first member of the province's Jewish community to serve as the Queen's representative in Nova Scotia.

The members of the legislative assembly, called "MLAs" in all provinces but Ontario, Newfoundland and Quebec, where they are referred to as MPP, MHA and deputy respectively, are elected by the same kind of single-member district electoral system used in federal elections. There are three exceptions: on Prince Edward Island, MLAs are elected in two-member districts, with each voter casting two votes. Also, Nova Scotia has three such two-member districts and British Columbia seven. Three provinces have adopted fixed election dates. Each province establishes its own voter requirements for provincial elections. Thus, in British Columbia one must be age 19 to vote and in some provinces' citizens of the British Commonwealth and the Republic of Ireland are permitted to vote.

One of the provincial government's main responsibilities is to oversee local governments. Because the provinces are organized and granted authority by the provinces, their specific organization and responsibilities vary from one to the next. All provinces provide such services as elementary and secondary schools, to which 40% of the cities' budgets are devoted; such cultural and recreational facilities as parks, pools and ice rinks, libraries and art galleries; health and welfare including public health services, ambulances and welfare administration; housing for the aged and poor, and issuance of building permits, standards, planning and zoning; police and fire protection; public transportation and road repair; and a variety of utilities such as water, garbage collection, sewage, and electricity.

The cities' demands for more powers to cope with their responsibilities have fallen on deaf ears in provincial capitals. Even though the provinces have successfully demanded increased power from Ottawa, their premieres have stubbornly refused to share any of theirs with local governments. Nevertheless, the mayors of major cities such as Toronto, Montreal, or Vancouver can be powerful political figures in provincial and Canadian politics.

Of all the taxes Canadians pay, 50% goes to the federal government, 42% to the provincial governments, and 8% to the cities. To fund their activities, local governments rely primarily on provincial grants of 44%, property taxes of 34%, business taxes of 4%, plus sales and services of 8%. Cities find themselves continuously strapped for finances, made worse by budget cuts by the central government and high provincial debt. As demands for services have risen, property taxes can no longer cover municipal needs. With inadequate funding, cities, which generate most of the country's wealth, are experiencing deteriorating urban infrastructure and cuts in services. The debates over how to use limited funds does not seem to stimulate strong municipal electoral interest; voter turn-out averages only 30% in city elections, 68% in the 2015 federal elections, and 66% in the 2019 federal elections.

It has always been difficult to forge and maintain a unified country out of 13 different provinces and territories. This is

Harbor outside St. John's, Newfoundland

Canada

made particularly challenging because insofar as Canada's major parties are highly decentralized, they tend not to be strong in every part of the country. The parties can thus do little to help hold the country together. Insofar as the provinces have unique political scenes and problems and play such important roles in Canadian politics, it is worthy examining each in some detail.

NEWFOUNDLAND AND LABRADOR: Newfoundland and Labrador represent (Newfoundland) Canada's most recent province, having entered the Confederation in 1949 after a close vote in a referendum. In 2001 it was officially renamed Newfoundland and Labrador to recognize the latter's importance. In 2003 decades of negotiations culminated in agreement on a 29,000-square mile new Inuit-governed territory created in Labrador, called Nunatsiavut, "our beautiful land."

Newfoundland has the lowest percentage of French-speakers in all of Canada. French is the mother tongue of only 0.05% of the population, while 5% are bilingual. It also has its own dialect of English, having grown out of an archaic English spoken by seafarers and having been preserved by the province's relative isolation from the rest of Canada. So different is their language that a dictionary of Newfoundland English sells well. In it one can learn, for example, that a female companion was once called a "friendgirl." Heavily Irish, while a third of Newfoundlanders are Roman Catholic, in an effort to raise the educational level of their fellow citizens, in 1997 Newfoundlanders overwhelmingly voted to replace all church-run schools with a state-run educational system.

Newfoundland has faced knotty economic challenges, with the main one devastated fishing industry which its main source of employment in the over 700 communities around its 6,000-mile coastline. This occurred because in 1977 Canada declared a 200-mile limit in the sea and began subsidizing boats and fish processing plants, many of which now stand idle. Bowing to foreign and domestic political pressure, Canada banned the unrestricted

killing of seals thereby enabling the seal population to triple since the 1970s. Each animal consumes an average of 45 pounds of fish a day. This, as well as overfishing, combined almost to destroy the fish stocks, especially cod. Seal hunting with clear quotas is permitted annually as about 6,000 Canadians in outlying areas benefit from this part-time employment.

In 1989, Canada granted France the right to fish an extra 11,000 tons of cod from the waters off Newfoundland in return for its agreement to submit a dispute about the maritime boundaries around the French islands of St. Pierre and Miquelon, which have a population of only 6,000 and are located 16 miles off the coast of Newfoundland, to international arbitration. In 1992 an international tribunal awarded France only a fourth of the area it claimed. In 2009 France announced that it would file a new claim with the UN to an area of the continental shelf south of the two islands in an attempt to procure some of the oil and gas that is enriching Newfoundland.

Also in 2009, Ottawa slapped a moratorium on all northern cod fishing to allow the dwindling stocks to replenish themselves. This bitter decision sent thousands of fishermen and fishery workers into unemployment lines. Of the 42,000 who had once worked in the province's fishing industry, 27,000 were employed by 1999. Revenues from cod fishing had fallen from $136 million in 1988 to only $1 million a decade later. Former Premier Tobin acknowledged, "they know that the fish are gone, they know that the income support won't last forever."

In 2003, the federal fisheries minister announced the closure of most of

Hon. Andrew Furey
Premier of Newfoundland

the remaining Atlantic cod fishing industry because of the depleted stocks. Responding to former Premier Roger Grimes' angry demand for a constitutional change to give the province more control over the industry, former federal Liberal Party leader Stéphane Dion noted sadly: "No amendment would bring back the fish." There are some experts, such as George Rose of St. John's Memorial University, who think the cod will come back, but patience is needed.

There are some hopes that aquaculture, using the cold, unpolluted waters to raise seafood products such as scallops, salmon, mussels, whelk, and sea urchins, can provide work for some of them. In 1998 huge increases in crab and shrimp catches pushed the value of fish landings to an all-time high. Even so, the industry employs far fewer people, about 2,000 in

Government House, residence of the Lieutenant Governor of Newfoundland, St. John's

boats and 4,000 in processing plants, compared with about 18,000 in boats and up to 20,000 in plants earlier.

The EU agreed temporarily to suspend fishing in the area. When pirate fishermen from Europe continued to overfish the dwindling stocks, Canada acted in 1995. The government sent a frigate, fired a shot over the bow of a Spanish trawler outside the 200-mile fishing zone, boarded the vessel, and ordered it to St. John's. There officials found illegal nets on board and doctored records proving that the fishermen had violated international agreements. After much acrimony, a settlement was reached calling for closer monitoring and enforcement of fish catches. The then Fisheries Minister Brian Tobin, a former TV anchor from Newfoundland, became a national hero overnight. A year later he was premier.

In October 2003, Conservative Danny Williams, a former Rhodes Scholar, crusading lawyer, and multi-millionaire after selling his cable-TV business for $232 million in 2000, hence his nickname "Danny Millions," was elected premier with 34 of 48 legislative seats. He was scrappy, articulate and prone to the dramatic, and he has made a career out of tough talk and a knack for the well-chosen fight. His antics get Ottawa's attention. Williams faced a huge budget deficit, with $1 billion going annually to servicing a debt that amounts to $23,000 per person, Canada's largest. The population of 527,000 shrunk by 10% from 1994–2003 and is projected to plunge to 482,000 by 2035 despite the oil and gas boom. In only three years Williams turned his province's fortunes around.

In the 1960s great reserves of off-shore oil and gas were discovered in the Grand Banks. The Hibernia field on the edge of this trove, 200 miles offshore, contains large quantities of oil. The province fought a furious battle with Ottawa over who owns and controls those reserves. According to a 1984 ruling of the Supreme Court of Canada, the federal government owns offshore resources. However, in 1985, the Mulroney government signed an "Atlantic Accord" with Newfoundland, granting it most of the powers over the Hibernia field. In 1993, the federal government agreed to buy an 8.5% share in order that the project could continue and begin producing oil in 1997. The provincial government is trying to buy back that federal equity stake. It is Canada's highest producing field and helped make the province Canada's second-largest oil producer and for a while one of the richer "have" provinces.

The Terra Nova field, 20 miles southeast of Hibernia, produced its first oil in 2000 although its output did not materialize as expected. White Rose, in 2006, and other fields followed. The southern extension of Hibernia was delayed. Nevertheless, Newfoundland expected to receive as much as $4.9 billion in oil revenues for the eight years following 2005. That was not to be. Plunging oil and gas prices, as well as a collapse of the mining sector drove the government deficit close to two billion dollars and pushed the province's unemployment rate up over 11%, the country's highest. Oil and gas account for 30% of the economy, and one-third are employed by the provincial government.

Williams was determined to gain even more of the proceeds for his province, and he succeeded. In 2007 he risked a multi-billion-dollar deal with the oil companies by demanding a 4.9% ownership share in the Hebron offshore project and a generous royalty system. He signed a multi-year agreement with Chevron, ExxonMobil, Petro-Canada, and StatoilHydro to develop Hebron, located south of the lucrative Hibernia fields. He was guided by his simple principle of "no more give-aways," and he won. He had tapped the sense of aggrieved nationalism "the Rock," the province's nickname, pledging to make the half a million Newfoundlanders "masters in our own house."

Voters rewarded Williams richly with a landslide reelection victory in 2007. His party won almost 70% of the votes and all but four of the 48 seats. This was not necessarily good news for the federal Tories. Williams was the first premier to urge Canadians to vote for any other party but his own in federal elections because he believed a Conservative majority would be dangerous.

In 2002, a federal tribunal settled the 37-year boundary dispute between Newfoundland and Nova Scotia about 170 kilometers or about 105 miles, offshore. Newfoundland received 75% of the potentially oil-rich offshore region, known as the Laurentian sub-basin, which could hold nearly a billion barrels of oil. Nova Scotia was awarded only 16%, while the French islands of St. Pierre and Miquelon, home to 6,000 French citizens using euros, received 9%.

Leaders in St. John's bargained hard for maximum benefits from one of the world's richest nickel deposits at Voisey's Bay in Labrador's rugged interior. The mine has the potential of supplying 13% of the world's nickel. After years of negotiations the provincial government and two Aboriginal peoples, the 5,000 Inuit and 1,500 Innu, agreed to allow nickel mining at an open-pit site starting in 2006, while a pilot processing plant is built at Argentia. The project should create hundreds of permanent jobs, a hoped-for Can$11 billion in revenue for the government over 30 years, $255 million to the Inuit, who claim the land around the mine, and a percentage of the mine's profits to the two Aboriginal groups. A major problem is that it is so remote: there are no roads to it and sea ice closes it off for six months a year. Ice breakers must make a dozen trips per year to and from the mine. Premier Williams revived an earlier plan to build an 11 mile or 17-km tunnel under the Strait of Belle Isle to connect Newfoundland and Labrador's population of 28,000).

Newfoundland was Canada's poorest province and had its highest cost-of-living, lowest per capita income, and highest unemployment rate, 14.9% in 2017, more than double the national average of 5.9%. It also was heavily dependent on Ottawa, which in 2002 was the source of 39% of the province's revenues. In 2004–5, the central government sent $674 million or $1,304 per person in the form of federal equalization payments.

The situation changed for Newfoundland considering its rising oil revenues. Tens of billions of dollars poured into major developmental projects as the government surplus grew to $755 million in 2011. One unfamiliar problem emerged from this boom, an acute shortage of skilled labor in the midst of high overall joblessness.

In light of Newfoundland's prior condition, Ottawa awarded it equalization payments. These monies are designed to help poorer provinces that are less able to afford basic services so they can achieve an established standard. In 2009 Newfoundland joined Alberta, Saskatchewan, and British Columbia in not qualifying for such payments.

Canada

Williams quarreled with the federal government's view that Newfoundland's equalization payments should decline as revenues from offshore oil increase. He became popular at home, with an astounding approval rating of 92% by the time of his retirement in 2010 as his stand against big oil and his arguments that it's high time that Newfoundlanders be "masters of our own destiny" only heightened his popularity. However, he was unpopular everywhere else in Canada because of his insistence that Newfoundland receive every penny of its equalization funds while getting a bigger and fairer share of offshore oil wealth. Williams argued that this was Newfoundland's last and best chance to become a "have" rather than a perpetual "have-not" province. "This is our one shot. . . . We will invest in social programs, in infrastructure, we will lower our debt." He had already eliminated his province's budget deficit.

In 2009, the province still had a debt of $11.6 billion, the highest per capita in Canada. Nevertheless, Williams created the foundation for a more prosperous province, with housing prices soaring resulting in a shortage of affordable housing, higher wages, and lower unemployment. Williams continued to attract much investment capital to "the Rock," prompting local wits to call the province "Dannyland" or "Williamsburg." A film, *Danny*, portrayed his eventful life.

High unemployment continued to stimulate some emigration annually from Newfoundland to more lucrative pastures in Canada although increasing prosperity at home and hard times in the West reduced such movement. Three-fourths of those departing were between the ages of 15 and 34. According to the government of Newfoundland, out migration reached 2,700 in 2019. So many worked in the oil sand industry of Fort McMurray that locals jokingly called their town Fort McNewfoundland. The out migration was particularly distressing because Newfoundland's birthrate is Canada's lowest despite polls at the turn of the century citing its people as the most sexually active Canadians. Almost a half million Newfoundland emigrés live in southern Ontario and even have their own monthly newspaper, The *Downhomer*.

An enduring irritant is the 65-year contract which Newfoundland's former Liberal premier, Joey Smallwood, signed with Quebec in 1969. He needed Quebec's support of development loans to construct one of the world's largest hydroelectric plants at Churchill Falls, in the wilderness of Labrador. In exchange, Newfoundland agreed to sell Quebec almost all the electricity produced by the plant for 65 years at 1969 prices. There was no provision for renegotiating the contract. No one anticipated the skyrocketing of energy prices following the 1973 energy crisis.

Today, Quebec buys the Churchill Falls electricity for one tenth the prevailing market price and turns around and exports it to New England for ten times what it pays Newfoundland for it. Newfoundland loses $800 million annually. Quebec claims that its exported electricity actually comes from its huge James Bay project, and that Quebec uses Newfoundland's electricity at home. Few Newfoundlanders can accept that argument.

To rub salt into the wounds, Newfoundland has had to construct four additional power plants to supply its own electrical needs because it receives only a small portion of Churchill Falls' production. A much-trumpeted deal with Quebec to develop another hydroelectric project on the Lower Churchill River in Labrador collapsed in 2000. In 2005 Ontario and Quebec joined forces to bid for the development of the Lower Churchill River, one of the last remaining large untapped hydro-electricity sites in North America.

All efforts to renegotiate the original contract failed. The Supreme Court of Canada ruled that a deal is a deal. This issue seriously burdened relations with Newfoundland's western neighbor, giving Quebec political leverage. For example, when Newfoundland's premier announced his opposition to the Meech Lake Accord, Quebec Premier Robert Bourassa tartly responded that renegotiation of hydroelectric and other deals with Quebec would be easier in a climate of "cordial relations." Newfoundland continues to badger Quebec for a change to no avail.

That 1969 Churchill Falls deal still haunts the province. The boldness in negotiating high royalties and partial ownership in the Hebron field in 2007 offered the opportunity to put that painful and humiliating history behind them. The future holds even greater frustration regarding Churchill Falls. It was rediscovered that Quebec has the right to a 25-year extension of the contract at even lower pre-set rates after the current 44-year term runs out in 2016. Newfoundlanders groan that the new rate is "barely distinguishable from being free." A week before a new premier took office in December 2010, the province signed a $6.2 billion deal for a hydro mega-project on the Lower Churchill.

Williams was succeeded by his former minister of natural resources, Kathy Dunderdale. Not only was she Newfoundland's first female leader, but she entered the 2011 provincial election as the favorite in a field consisting only of women: Lorraine Michaels of the NDP and Yvonne Jones of the Liberals. Born one of 11 children of a trawlerman in Placentia Bay, Dunderdale never finished her degree at Memorial University in St. John's. Dunderdale worked her way up the political ladder, starting as a Liberal before switching to the Tories, and became Williams' right-hand person. Dunderdale was just as feisty as he was and became almost as popular: in 2011 she enjoyed Canada's second highest approval rating at 55%.

The economic shambles on the Rock opened the door for a Liberal landslide in November 2015. Dwight Ball, who called for more deficit spending, became premier, but retired from politics in 2020, replaced by Andrew Furey. In the election of 2021 (which had been delayed due to the global COVID-19 pandemic), Furey was returned to government with a majority of his own. The Rock has slipped to have-not status as oil royalties have declined by a third, the budget deficit grows, the economy shrinks, and megaprojects wind down.

Human residents share the island with 120,000 to 200,000 moose, the world's highest-density moose population that increasingly make nuisances of themselves. Brought from the mainland a century ago to help attract tourists and hunters to the then British colony, they

Hon. Tim Houston

The World Trade and Convention Centre, Halifax, Nova Scotia

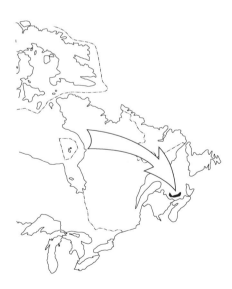

have no predators since the native wolf became extinct. Moose are unpredictable, can run 35 miles or 56 kilometers per hour, swim as fast as two grown men paddling a canoe, and worse, are inclined to wander out on highways at night and cause about 600 collisions each year. On a different note, sightseers were delighted in 2017 when a 15,000-year-old, 15-story iceberg bumped up against Newfoundland's shore.

NOVA SCOTIA: Like Newfoundland and Labrador, Nova Scotia staked great hopes on an economic resurgence stimulated by offshore energy resources, especially on the natural gas reserves in the Sable Island area 180 miles east of Halifax. With both offshore and onshore

facilities for producing and processing natural gas, it is the largest industrial undertaking in the province's history and Canada's biggest construction project entering the 21st century. Delivery of gas began in 1999, with New England as the principal market. There were hopes of even more gas outside the Sable development, but they have been disappointed by a series of dry wells and expired exploration licenses. Many analysts now conclude that there is not as much gas or oil as some had believed. Despite sizable investments offshore by energy giants, no oil was found.

In 2002, Nova Scotia lost an offshore boundary dispute with Newfoundland over possession of potentially vast reserves of gas and oil. Newfoundland claimed it had never signed a 1964 deal drawing a line. The financial stakes were raised for Nova Scotia in 2001 when Ottawa announced the closure of the Prince colliery, the island's last working underground coal mine. The province's Irving Shipbuilding yard supplies the navy with 15 frigates and eight Arctic patrol boats worth about $25 billion. Nova Scotia is the most populous of the four Atlantic Provinces but has one of Canada's oldest and most stagnant populations. It needs 10,000 immigrants to avoid a labor crunch.

In October 2013, the voters replaced the first NDP government in Atlantic Canada after a decade of Tory rule. Led by former Premier Darrell Dexter, who lost his own riding, the New Democrats came in third place winning only 26.84% of the votes, down from 45.26%, and 7 seats, down from 31. Riding on the coattails of popular federal Liberal leader, Justin Trudeau,

the Liberals emerged the big winners, led by Premier Stephen McNeil. Following McNeil's resignation in 2020, Iain Rankin became leader of the Liberals and premier, only to lose at the 2021 election. The Progressive Conservatives returned to power, with their leader, Tim Houston, becoming premier

PRINCE EDWARD ISLAND: The tiny, beautiful Prince Edward Island, which strives to maintain its unique culture and pace of life, saw the Tories end 10 years of Liberal rule in an electoral upset in 1996. The Liberal Party, whose former leader, Catherine Callbeck, had been the first elected female premier in Canadian history, captured only eight seats in the 27-seat Legislative Assembly.

Enjoying a 75% approval rating after three and one-half years, the Tories call new elections in 2000. The results were staggering. Running on the slogan, "Let's continue," they captured 58% of the votes and 26 of 27 seats. This was the Liberals' worst defeat in provincial history. Led in 2003 by Robert Ghiz, whose father Joe had been premier from 1986 to 1993, the Liberals did better, winning 43% of the votes, but only four seats. An astonishing 83% of eligible voters turned out to return the Tories to their third consecutive term.

Pat Binns became premier. His success was especially remarkable on an island where family connections can make or break a political career. Binns, born in Saskatchewan and having grown up in Alberta, first came to Prince Edward Island in 1970 on a student exchange program and married a local woman. Returning in 1978, he became a bean farmer and plunged right into politics. One of his Tory

Hon. Dennis King—Premier of Prince Edward Island

Retrieved from: http://www.peipc.ca/dennisking

Canada

Province House in Charlottetown, P.E.I., where the Canadian federation was born

colleagues noted: "Pat is the kind of politician they go for out here. He grew up on a farm, he always returns phone calls, he never loses his temper." He successfully met the unenviable task of helping PEI adjust to the shocks of steady reductions in transfer payments from Ottawa.

Under Robert Ghiz's able leadership, the Liberals won dramatic victories in both 2007 and October 2011. In 2011, voters again witnessed the effects of the single-member electoral system. With 51.4% of the popular votes, the Liberals won 22 seats. The Conservatives, led by Olive Crane, captured 40.2%, but garnered only five seats. The Greens, with 4.4%, and the NDP, with 3.2%, earned no seats in the legislature.

Ghiz, born in Charlottetown in 1974, became the country's youngest premier. He had studied political science at Bishops University in Quebec before going to Ottawa to work for the ruling Liberal Party. Ghiz ended up as Prime Minister Jean Chrétien's adviser on the Atlantic provinces, returning home in 2003 to compete successfully for the Liberal Party leadership. Liked for his collegial style and willingness to give credit to his team, Ghiz was succeeded as premier by Wade MacLauchlan.

Agriculture remains the island's main source of income, especially potato farming. Nevertheless, the number of family farms declined from around 5,000 in 1970 to only 2,200 in 2001, and most islanders work in offices. PEI was also the first province to provide internet access in all schools and public libraries.

In 1996, the last concrete span of the 13-kilometer, about 8-mile, Confederation Bridge was lowered into place, opening

on May 31, 1997. At a cost of about $25, cars can cross it in 12 minutes. This is Prince Edward Island's first physical link with the outside world since the ice age.

Fears of disrupting the island's peaceful style of living had erupted in 1987 when plans for this bridge across the frigid waters of the Northumberland Strait from Borden to Cape Tormentine, New Brunswick, were announced. In a 1988 referendum on the issue, 59% of voters approved the link with the mainland, despite protests from fishermen, ferry employees, and other islanders who feared that outsiders, particularly Americans, would be encouraged to buy up more land on their island.

In an effort to quiet the fear of voters, legislation was passed forbidding non-islanders from purchasing more than five acres without cabinet approval or from having a shorefront more than 50 meters or about 165 feet). In 2018, the Island Regulatory and Appeals Commission

conducted a major review to determine how land is owned by nonresidents and corporations. In 2016, people were required to live in the province for at least 365 days over a two-year period to be considered a resident instead of the prior six months. Som islanders believe that the bridge and foreign ownership threaten something fundamental to the psyche of residents, the sense that they are separate and different from the rest of Canada.

The Confederation Bridge attracts more tourists. In fact, Prince Edward Island's license plates feature the bridge instead of the pigtailed and freckled Anne of Green Gables, the island's most famous fictional resident and most popular tourist site. With a population of only 153,244 (2018) PEI already draws over one million tourists annually, outnumbering the islanders by almost ten to one. To boost its population, it avidly invites immigration. Ottawa rewarded the island for its royalist sentiments by providing $170,000 for tea parties, concerts, and picnics to celebrate Queen Elizabeth II's Diamond Jubilee in 2012.

In April 2019, voters ousted the Liberal government of Premier Wade MacLauchlan to a minority Progressive Conservative led by Dennis King. Interestingly the Green Party became the official opposition. Progressive Conservative won 12 seats, the Green Party 8, and the Liberal Party 6.

NEW BRUNSWICK: One of the New Brunswick's oldest political problems is how to accommodate the Acadian French minority. There are 242,000 French Acadians, only 8% of whom no longer speak French at home; they account for 35% of

Hon. Bryan Gallant

as the province's most vibrant economy, as the site for a Francophonie conference of leaders from 49 nations where a majority or sizable minority speak French. This was the first time a French president visited the nearly 290,000 Acadians spread out among the provinces of New Brunswick with 242,000 residents while Nova Scotia's 35,000, Prince Edward Island's 5,500, and Newfoundland's 2,300). In August 2005 tens of thousands of Acadians celebrated their survival of the deportation 250 years earlier.

Elephant Rock, Hopewell Cape near Moncton, was about 200 feet high until it collapsed in 2016.

the province's population. This is proportionately the biggest francophone community in any province outside Quebec. The Université de Moncton opened its doors in 1963 and rapidly became North America's largest French-speaking university outside of Quebec. For a while it was a hotbed of activism for bilingualism and equal rights for francophones. As life on New Brunswick improved, most of the anger disappeared. In 1969 New Brunswick became the only bilingual province in Canada as the government moved to make itself, courts, and public institutions bilingual. Francophone leaders, organized in such groups as the *Societé des Acadiens du Nouveau Brunswick*, pushed for faster progress.

The government's efforts to increase the number of bilingual civil servants, the bulk of whom are Acadian, aroused charges that unilingual anglophones could no longer be hired or promoted in government service, a claim that was incorrect. So angry were many anglophones that they pressed their demands through a New Brunswick Association of English-Speaking Canadians and a vocally anti-bilingual party, the Confederation of Regions (COR). COR's capture of 30% of anglophone votes risked inflaming language tensions, but in the 1995 elections it was wiped out of the legislature.

In a bid for language reconciliation, the Saint John Theatre Company adopted New Brunswick as the backdrop for its 2012 production of William Shakespeare's *Romeo and Juliet*. In the production Romeo's family spoke English while Juliet's spoke French.

During an Acadian world conference in 1994 author Antoine Maillet, whose play, *La Sagouine*, portrays Acadian resilience, could boast that "we don't need to fight for survival any more, we did it." Former Prime Minister Jean Chrétien savored the opportunity to take a swipe at Quebec separatists by complimenting Acadians for finding "concrete ways to live in harmony instead of remaining prisoners of old grudges." In 1999 he chose Moncton, which is on the verge of replacing St. John

New Brunswick's bilingualism still creates tension, bit it is now regarded as an asset instead of a liability. Moncton is the fastest-growing region in Atlantic Canada largely because it is bilingual. The percentage of anglophone children enrolling in French immersion courses is an impressive 11%, Canada's highest rate of such enrollment at the grade school level. New

Hon. Blaine Myron Higgs

Canada

**Baking bread in New Brunswick:
an Acadian village woman
in traditional garb**

Brunswick adopted language reforms to guarantee francophones more powers and rights, allowing them to attend French-language schools and receive health care in their mother tongue. Fifteen percent of anglophones are bilingual, compared with 71% of francophones.

In October 2014, 32-year-old Bryan Gallant, an athletic Moncton lawyer, became premier as his Liberal Party captured 43% of the votes and 27 of 49 seats. The Conservatives won 21 and the Greens 1. In 2018, Premier Gallant and the Liberal Party lost at the polls as Blaine Myron Higgs, the leader of the New Brunswick Progressive Conservative party became the 34ᵗʰ Premier of New Brunswick. He had been a member of the legislature since 2010 and served as Minister of Finance from 2010-2014 in the government of David Alward. Higgs' new government has 22 seats and on November 2, 2018 when combined with another party, the People's Alliance, passed a non-confidence vote against the Liberal Party minority government's 21 seats. At the 40th General Election since Confederation in 2020, Higgs was returned to government, this time with 27 seats, two more than required to form a majority.

The government faces unemployment of 10.2% as mines, mills, and an air force base closed. Further, the population is aging and the young are leaving. Services are more expensive in a province where half the people live in rural areas. Still, it sees a bright spot in exploration for shale gas deposits in the south as it finds itself in the middle of a sovereignty dispute with the U.S. over Machias Seal Island and North Rock, a tiny, rocky, treeless

uninhabited islands in the Bay of Fundy whose only inhabitants are 5,800 pairs of nesting puffins. Located almost equidistant between Maine and New Brunswick, these islands are the last land mass contested by Canada and the U.S.

QUEBEC: In 1985, nine years after it had ascended to power, the Parti Québécois (PQ) had to relinquish it. In 2007 it suffered an especially devastating electoral defeat, surpassed by two other Quebec parties. In a way, the PQ was the victim of its own success. French language and cultural rights within the province of 8.1 million inhabitants, and 70,000 French citizens, had been secured, and Canada had been prodded to become bilingual. Quebec had also modernized itself almost beyond recognition. As "masters in their own house," Québécois were ready to turn their attention more to personal achievement and to the down-to-earth problems of unemployment and economic revival. The PQ itself became divided over whether to cling to the dream of sovereignty. Neither the Tories nor the New Democrats are political forces in Quebec provincial politics.

Commenting on the Liberals' 1985 election victory, Lysiane Gagnon, columnist for *La Presse* of Montreal wrote: "Quebecers changed governments the way one changes banks—without passion, as a business decision. There are neither dreams nor exultation nor broken hopes." Dreams and passions were reawakened in 1987 when René Lévesque died of a heart attack. The emotional outpouring sparked comparisons of the charismatic spiritual father of the PQ and his successor, the aloof Pierre Marc Johnson. The latter's replacement in 1987 was future PQ premier, Jacques Parizeau, whose wit, energy, professorial air, and economic record were only outdone by his fervor for Quebec sovereignty.

The Quebec Liberals are staunchly pro-federalist. Consequently, Bourassa met many times with Brian Mulroney to negotiate the Meech Lake Accord. In 1987 he broke with almost a quarter century of Quebec tradition and hosted a banquet for the Queen, presiding over an enviable improvement in the economy of Quebec.

Bourassa's party had promised to relax restrictions on bilingual signs. However, in office Bourassa did nothing because the courts were reviewing the issue. After a temporary respite from language tensions, the flames were rekindled in 1988. The Supreme Court of Canada ruled that Bill 101 violated the freedom-of-expression guarantees in Quebec's own charter of rights by banning the use of non-French words on commercial signs. Nationalist groups immediately rose up against the Court's decision, showing just how volatile the language issue remains.

Wishing to avoid a confrontation with Quebec nationalists, Bourassa announced Bill 178, which prohibits English on outside signs while permitting it on inside signs, providing that French is used more prominently. He also invoked the so-called "notwithstanding clause" in the 1982 Constitution to prevent any further court challenge.

Bourassa saw this move as a compromise, but it pleased almost nobody and detonated the most serious English-French confrontation since 1980. Hardline *Québécois*, who were infuriated that English could again be used on some signs, demonstrated and threw fire bombs into the Montreal offices of the English-rights lobby group called Alliance Quebec, which later imploded in 2005 when the federal government cut off its funds. One young man climbed the large cross on top of Montreal's Mount Royal and sat there for 13 freezing hours in protest. Three anglophone cabinet members resigned, including Clifford Lincoln, who asserted: "rights are rights are rights. There are no inside and outside rights." Anglophone Quebecers felt betrayed and became uneasy again, while Anglophones all over Canada protested. Fears of emigration were reawakened. During the nine-year PQ rule, 140,000 left Quebec, and more than 400,000 departed over a two-decade span from 1976 and 1996.

The Meech Lake Accord was former Prime Minister Brian Mulroney's attempt to create harmony by granting Quebec the status of "a distinct society" and by protecting minority language rights everywhere in Canada; it also would have secured Quebec's ratification of the 1982 Constitution.

Its rejection angered Quebecers and reignited powerful nationalist sentiments. A saddened Hugh MacLennan, whose 1945 novel *Two Solitudes* chronicled the cultural divide between francophones and anglophones, mused in 1989, one year before his death, about his French-speaking countrymen: "I wish we could get along with them . . . I just don't know if they want us anymore." There remains much ignorance about Quebec. A 1989 study showed that only 5% of the stories in CBC or the *Globe and Mail* came from Quebec.

In making an unambiguous appeal for final and complete separation from Canada and in rejecting federalism of any kind as an option, which is why he rejected Meech Lake, the self-confident Parizeau differed from the humble populist, Lévesque, who always couched his pitch for sovereignty in the context of an undefined association with the rest of Canada. Parizeau, who speaks perfect English and has a doctorate in economics from the London School of Economics, argued that new social and economic conditions make independence more viable now. "I can rely on new strengths that Quebec did not have 20 years ago, when it was not at all obvious that Quebec entrepreneurs were capable of competing internationally. Now it is."

By improving the province's access to American markets, NAFTA further reduces Quebec's economic dependence on the rest of Canada. An independent Quebec would have to negotiate with Canada, the U.S., and Mexico to gain entry into the trilateral agreement. As an independent country it would be the U.S.'s sixth-largest trading partner. However, one of the most protected businesses in Quebec is the milk industry through a system of supply management which the federal government has had to, in part, open up to American competition due to the 2018 USMCA, which replaced NAFTA; a revised version of the USMCA took effect on July 1, 2020.

Both supporters and opponents of sovereignty rest their plans on economic prowess in Quebec. There have been some setbacks. The complex and expensive James Bay project was to be financed largely by exporting electricity to northeastern U.S. to supply cheap energy to companies lured into Quebec. Even so, the province suffered a severe setback in 1992 when its development plans collided with environmentalists and native claims. The 13,500 Cree living in Quebec maintained that the project is on their land and would poison their fish. Indeed, in 1912 the federal government devolved present-day northern Quebec, known to Indigenous people as Ungava, to the province as an administrative convenience.

The Crees' opposition to the James Bay project, which would reduce the flow in the Great Whale and other rivers, found support among American environmental groups. This resulted in New York State's cancellation of its power contract with Quebec, devastating news for the province. In 1994 Parizeau had to put the project on hold indefinitely. In 2002 the Cree agreed to drop their suits against the hydro plans on the Rupert and Eastmain rivers in perhaps the most important treaty signed with an Aboriginal group. They opened up their territory to mining, logging, and industrial development by Hydro-Québec. In return, Quebec paid the Cree a minimum of $3.5 billion over 50 years, granting them a say in any development in order to protect traditional hunting and trapping rights. This deal was calculated to create 8,000 jobs and increase electricity production by about 8%.

In 2011, the Quebec government announced an ambitious 25-year plan to develop a large part of its vast northern and Arctic region, an area where, in former Premier Jean Charest's words, "we have every resource imaginable." While industrial activity will be banned in some of the region, mining and industry will be allowed in other parts, all in close coordination with the local aboriginal populations. Not since the northern Alberta oil sands were exploited has there been such a grandiose attempt to develop the sparsely populated north. Charest argued that this "Plan Nord" will strengthen Canada's disputed claims to the Northwest Passage. It "is an affirmation of sovereignty." Charest's successor as premier, Pauline Marois, vowed to continue this project. Quebec created a sovereign-wealth fund, the Generations Fund, similar to Alberta's, into which royalties from mining and hydropower concessions, as well as profits from Hydro-Quebec, a provincially owned utility, can be deposited; it is managed by an independent agency.

An independent Quebec would have to face the prospect that the Cree and the Inuit, supported by Ottawa, would take back more than half the present province. Quebec's relations with its 60,000 aboriginal peoples, most of whom prefer to speak English, were already strained over their claims also to be a "distinct society." Quebec's aboriginals find their most compelling arguments in the PQ's rhetoric. Cree Grand Chief Matthew Coon Come asserts: "If Canada is divisible, so is Quebec," a concept endorsed by Prime Minister Chrétien in 1996.

Inuit leaders have also put Quebec on notice that "we are not coming with you on a journey toward independence," as Zebedee Nungak put it. The Inuit of the northern third of Quebec moved a step closer to

Cree lands

self-government in November 1999. They signed a political accord with Ottawa and Quebec setting up a commission to facilitate discussions leading to a government in their region called Nunavik. There are no roads linking Nunavik to the rest of the province. In an effort to bring the two parts closer together, the Quebec government is working on plans to construct roads to a few Nunavik communities. In 2016, the Quebec government announced a five-year, $100 million investment in municipal infrastructure.

Numerous anglophone groups in Quebec, supported by the federal government, picked up on the idea of partition if Quebec breaks away from Canada. Examples include the Quebec Committee for Canada and the Committee for a New Quebec. Both proposed that any area in which francophones are not prominent, including suburbs of Montreal, remain with Canada. PQ leaders dismissed such warnings and proposals as nonsense.

Parizeau shrewdly played on the frictions between Quebec and the rest of Canada in rejecting what he saw as a flawed federalism. His solution: a series of referenda to take over powers from Ottawa, on the way to a sovereign Quebec. The political equation was further complicated by the formation in the federal parliament of a *Bloc Québécois*, led initially by Lucien Bouchard. The PQ supported it in the 1993 federal elections rather than Mulroney's Tories, as it had done in the prior two campaigns. This cost Mulroney valuable backing in Quebec and enabled the *Bloc Québécois* to become the second-largest party and official opposition in Ottawa.

In 1994, Quebecers had their clearest choice ever. Gone was the fuzzy middle ground of "sovereignty-association" *à la*

Canada

Lévesque. The PQ now called for nothing short of separation, declaring that a victory would be interpreted as a mandate to have the National Assembly make a "solemn declaration" of Quebec's intention to become independent. The PQ would then approach Ottawa to negotiate terms and put the result to Quebec voters within 10 months of the election. A narrow plurality of Quebec's voters decided to give the PQ that chance.

The PQ noted with uneasiness that it received only 44.7% of the popular votes, compared with the pro-federal Liberals' impressive 44.3%. This bode ill for the referendum Parizeau had pledged to hold in 1995. Even if he could woo many of the 6.5% of voters who supported the *Action Démocratique du Quebec* (ADQ), led by Mario Dumont and composed of moderate former Liberals of a separatist tinge, he faced an uphill struggle. Bouchard, who lost a leg in 1994 to a frightening flesh-eating disease, began to express his opinion publicly that the separatist option should include close ties with Canada.

Quebec and Canada changed significantly since the referendum on Quebec sovereignty in 1980. The presence of the *Bloc Québécois* as the official opposition in the House of Commons gave separatism a new respectability and boost. Bouchard was able to persuade Parizeau and Dumont to agree on a "soft" referendum question calling for negotiating with Ottawa an economic and political partnership with an independent Quebec. The results of the 1995 referendum demonstrated that a majority of Quebec francophones supported that concept.

This is one reason why there was such an outcry throughout Canada in the midst of the 1997 federal parliamentary elections when Parizeau published his memoirs, *For A Sovereign Quebec*. In these memoirs, he admitted that he prepared to declare Quebec's independence immediately after a yes-vote in 1995, not after negotiations with Ottawa, as his party had proposed during the referendum campaign. Many think he deceived Quebec voters. In 2004 Parizeau published a letter in *La Presse* demanding that referenda be done away with and that the next PQ electoral victory be considered a mandate in itself to prepare for succession. Even within the PQ such ideas are scorned.

In the campaign, Parizeau stepped aside to allow Bouchard to energize it. A charismatic master of lofty emotion, he became a hero and savior in Quebec, the most popular figure since Lévesque. His oratorical skill brought separatists within a whisker of victory, winning 49.4% of the votes in a huge 94% turnout. This was 10 percentage points higher than in 1980. As in 1980, the difference was made by

Trompe l'oeil in Old Town Quebec

anglophones and immigrants, who voted overwhelmingly against independence, while 60% of francophones voted "yes."

Until the final days before the October 30, 1995, referendum the then Prime Minister Jean Chrétien chose to stand aloof from the debates in Quebec over separation, declaring that "I was elected not to talk about the constitution" and that "everybody knows where I stand. I come from Shawinigan. My province is Quebec. My country is Canada. My language is French. And they are all compatible." This aloofness was a serious blunder that hurt him in Canadian politics. Jean Charest was correct in saying that "winning a referendum doesn't mean you have solved the problem."

A confident Bouchard, who took over the premiership of Quebec from Parizeau in 1996, promised a new referendum by the year 2000, but had to back off from that. He defiantly rejected any option but sovereignty, asserting: "no one is going to get us into sterile discussions we've been having for 30 years. No longer will sovereigntists be begging for anything from the rest of Canada." This attitude guaranteed that Quebec would vigorously test Canada's fragile unity for many years. Perhaps Bouchard 's mother best captured the mood of many *Québécois* at that time: "I've never met an English-speaking Canadian. But I'm sure they are as nice as any other foreigners."

The Quebec economy, although vigorous in general, has Canada's highest per capita debt, highest tax burden (43% of

GDP, vs. 37.2% elsewhere), shortest work week, and oldest population, as well as aggressive unionization and a determined unwillingness to change its generous but expensive social system. The safety net used to be offered by the Church and large families, but that was replaced by the most interventionist government in North America. Quebec's GDP in 2020 was 43%, continuing a downward trend from a peak of 54.3% from six years ago. Business interests solidly oppose sovereignty with many withholding investments in the province until its political future was clarified. While investment grew by 2.7% annually in Quebec, the other provinces experienced a 4.2% rise. By 2007 Quebec's share of Canadian private investment declined dramatically from 23% in 1987 to below 18%.

Quebec economist Pierre Cléroux lamented: "we are not going in the same direction as the other provinces." University tuition was frozen for 13 years until Premier Charest vowed in 2007 to raise it slightly. Despite the freeze, Quebec had the lowest university attendance and degree-completion record in all of Canada.

The governing PQ resurrected the Commission to Protect the French Language, abolished in 1993, derisively known among anglophones as the "language police" or "tongue troopers" because of their linguistic repression. It pledged to enforce language laws strictly, which had been diluted since 1993 because of constitutional standoffs in the Supreme Court of Canada and international pressure, including from the U.N. English became permissible on outdoor signs, as long as it appeared at half the size of the equivalent French words. A Superior Court in Quebec upheld this law in 2000 when two anglophone storeowners erected signs featuring equal-sized French and English lettering.

In 2017, the legislature unanimously passed a non-binding resolution calling on shopkeepers to stop greeting customers with "bon jour hi" instead of "bon jour." A customer reportedly threatened a pet store owner for trying to sell a parrot that could not chatter in French. Yet, authorities permitted the use of "grilled cheese," "softball," and "drag queen."

The issue re-emerged after the PQ's electoral victory in September 2012. For 35 years the use of brand names by large American companies such as ostco, Walmart, Toys "R" Us, Best Buy, Pizza Hut, Linen Chest, Comfort Inn and some Canadian ones such as Canadian Tire were tolerated. They sued the province, which wanted to require the businesses to add a slogan or description in French to their signs indicating what they sell. Some avoided problems by changing their names in Quebec, such as KFC to PFK and Staples to Bureau en Gros.

English-speaking Canadians who move to Montreal can send their children to English-language schools, but francophone and immigrant parents are not permitted to do so. Quebec immigration ministry figures revealed in 2011 that two-thirds of immigrants to the province speak French. A slight majority of immigrants whose native tongue is neither French nor English now choose French over English.

Just how secular Quebec has become, especially in Montreal, was demonstrated in 1999 when the province replaced its Catholic and Protestant confessional school boards with 60 French-language, nine English-language, and three aboriginal boards. A constitutional amendment made its school system entirely secular.

This seems logical in a province where church attendance among Catholics stands at 15%, the lowest rate in North America. The average age of priests was nearly 65, with empty seminaries providing few replacements. While 88% of *Québécois* say they believe in God, less than a third assert that they believe in the God portrayed by the Church. Only 34% believe there is a hell, compared with 49% in the rest of Canada. Despite this secularity, Canada's cardinal and former archbishop of Quebec City, Marc Ouellet, was a leading candidate for the papacy in 2013.

The 1999 *MacLean's*/CBC Poll revealed that Quebecers value individual rights and freedom to define one's own morality more highly than other Canadians; 70% strongly believe no one has the right to impose morality on others as opposed to 52% in the rest of Canada, and 29% say they would support a 17-year-old daughter's decision to have an abortion, compared with 15% elsewhere. Sexual permissiveness is widespread, with 53% of births out of wedlock.

The province's share of Canada's population has shrunk from 27.9% in the early 1970s to 23.23% in 2016. While Quebec has one of the lowest birth rates in the western world, its situation is improving, and the province has gained a reputation as "parent-friendly. The first step was "bucks for babies;" parents were paid $500 and $1,000 for the first two offspring respectively; subsequent children brought in as much as $8,000. The next was 200,000 subsidized day-care places. This costs parents only $7 per day. A parental leave policy that allows parents to take almost a year off at up to three-quarters of their salary is North America's most generous.

The results are impressive: an 8% increase in the birth rate in 2006, and 2.6% in 2007. The fertility rate has risen to 1.66, which is higher than the national average, even if still under the replacement rate of 2.1. Yet, the Canadian Broadcasting Corporation noted that in 2015 the Quebec birth rate had dropped for the sixth straight year and that the average number of children born to a woman between 15 and 49 years of age was 1.60.

Former Language Minister Louise Beaudoin lashed out at what she called "rampant bilingualism" in the public service and proclaimed 30 new measures to send the message of "French first!" Civil servants are required to get permission from

Hon. Lucien Bouchard

superiors before making speeches in English. They may speak only French in meetings with Quebec-based companies and in dealing with the public by telephone or in person. The government no longer deals with Quebec-based companies that do not meet French language requirements in the workplace. More than eight of 10 francophones and over half of anglophones in Montreal already speak French on the job. All computer software must be available in French unless no French version exists.

In 1998, a new challenge emerged: Jean Charest resigned as federal chairman of the Progressive Conservative Party to assume the leadership of Quebec's Liberals. It was not easy for him to fight in Quebec for the cause of a united Canada. One cannot be so aggressive as to alienate the province's "soft nationalists," those who regard Canada as a sensible arrangement but give their emotional attachment to French Quebec. They are the voters who make the difference in provincial elections and referenda.

In 2001, Bouchard resigned as premier saying that he had failed to accomplish the PQ's dream of making Quebec an independent country. A decade later, in 2010, he remained extremely popular, but he had given up on Quebec sovereignty: "There's no referendum in sight, and I don't want any more defeats. . . . It remains just a dream."

Bouchard's successor was Bernard Landry. A former optometrist from Joliette, Quebec, Landry was drawn into the separatist movement by Lévesque's vision and charisma and has embraced the sovereigntist gospel most of his adult life: "I am convinced not only that Canada has no use, but that it has been harmful." He vowed that his government's priority

The late Dr. Jacques Parizeau

Canada

would be secession. However, Bouchard discovered that the province's foundering economy and a changed environment in North America made it necessary to put his pet project on the back burner. PQ party membership dropped to 65,000 although the party contended that the number is still close to 100,000.

In April 2003, a political earthquake occurred in Quebec. The PQ was buried in a Liberal landslide in provincial elections. Led by Jean Charest, the Liberals won a solid majority in the 125-seat National Assembly. The PQ under Landry, who predicted that Quebec would become a sovereign state within 1,000 days after his party's victory, fell to 33.2% and only 45 seats. It was hurt by Mario Dumont's ADQ, a center-right party that pledged to postpone referenda. Dumont described his party's goal as autonomy for Quebec while rejecting a complete rupture with Canada. "Old-fashioned separatism has little appeal for younger voters."

The turning point was a televised debate two weeks before the election in which Landry was unable to counter Charest's question why former Premier Jacques Parizeau was again blaming the loss of the 1995 referendum on "money and the ethnic vote," a code for Jews and immigrants. The PQ declined steadily thereafter.

Parizeau's reference to the importance of immigrants backfired, but it points to an important demographic development in Quebec that is distressing for the PQ. About one in ten voters in Quebec, as compared with 27% in Ontario, is an immigrant, and roughly 90% live in Montreal. With the birthrate plummeting, they make up a growing segment of the province's population. Although Quebec has for decades exercised its power to select its immigrants and to require that their children be educated in French, they feel little sympathy for the PQ's nationalist strivings. They have no stake in the historic English-French divide. But they have difficulties finding jobs.

Equally important is the fact that nearly 70% of the province's 918,000 anglophones are bilingual, an increase of roughly 12% since 1991; they do not fight against the language laws any more, and indeed the majority accepts them. The anglophones are willing to marry Quebecers outside their suburbs but overwhelmingly continue to support the Liberal party, Quebec's only outright federalist party. At the same, time more and more francophones believe that the goal to protect their language has been achieved. They are coming out of their Montreal ghettos. Teenagers are no longer inclined to speak the old *joual* dialect and often find English-sounding names for bars and restaurants "cool." The result is that more and more Quebecers are tired of

the old passionate language disputes, and this affects politics.

The long-term result of Bill 101 is that two-thirds of anglophones in Quebec are now bilingual, and more than half of those persons whose mother tongue is neither French nor English can now speak both. Francophones are no longer underdogs. When the bill was first introduced, the median income of anglophone households was 20% to 30% higher than the provincial average. Wealth is spread more evenly in today's Quebec. Sponsors of Bill 101 thought it would generate momentum toward independence, but it had the opposite effect. By demonstrating that such a radical reform was possible within Confederation, it deflated the separatist movement more than any measure Ottawa could have taken. Nevertheless, language remains a touchy subject in Quebec. Jean Charest exploited language fatigue, knowing that a political system based on the former lingual divisions was overdue for a shakeup.

Charest's Liberals were not helped by a damaging federal Liberal scandal that provided tens of millions of dollars in taxpayers' money to friendly advertising companies in the province to sway Quebec opinion away from independence after 1995. Most of the money was simply pocketed by the businesses. Yet, the *Québécois* were insulted that anglophone Canadians, who accuse them often unfairly of blatant corruption, would engage in such sordid tactics themselves. Even though the *Bloc Québécois* assured Quebec voters that a vote for it was not a vote for independence, the party benefited from the scandal in the 2004 federal elections. It captured 54 of the province's 75 seats, now 78 seats, and forced the federal Liberals into a minority government. In 2006 it slipped to 51 seats and only 42% of the votes, far short of the

majority it would need to secure independence for the province.

The 2006 federal elections caused a political earthquake in Quebec. The Conservatives gained a foothold in the province, rocketing from 9% to 24.6% of the vote as opposed the Liberals' 20.7%. By promising such things as flexible federalism, decentralization, and Quebec's own representation in international organizations such as UNESCO as well as by beginning practically every speech in Ottawa in French, Prime Minister Stephen Harper won a great deal of support, not just in Montreal, but in the eastern hinterland, including Quebec City, where nationalists were traditionally strong. Harper moved the Conservatives into the broad middle ground that formed after the federal Liberals and the separatists radicalized their positions between centralizing federalism and outright separation. The separatists no longer had an easily identifiable enemy.

It was ironic that *Québécois*, who had been unhappy during a 39-year period when PMs from Quebec ruled them for 36 years, were generally pleased with a western anglophone at the helm in Ottawa. Stephen Harper gave them much to be happy about. In 2006 he brought his entire cabinet to Quebec City to celebrate his close relationship with the people there; this was the first time since the 1950s that this had happened.

Later in 2006, Harper outmaneuvered both the *Bloc Québécois* and the federal Liberals to persuade an overwhelming majority in Parliament, including all four federal parties, to adopt a historic resolution declaring that Quebecers, not Quebec, "form a nation within a united Canada." Harper's words referred to a people, not a government or a state. Although this formulation had no constitutional significance and did not imply that Canada was

Quebec City in winter

a union of "two founding peoples," it was the first time Ottawa recognized the people of Quebec as a "nation."

Harper met with Premier Charest more frequently than with any other premier and more than any Canadian PM since the 1960s. Harper's 2007 federal budget corrected what he called "fiscal imbalance" by awarding an extra $2.1 billion transfer payment to Quebec, which already received $2.2 billion more each year from Ottawa than it contributed. He also steered a $900 million Strategic Aerospace and Defence Initiative to Montreal and permitted Quebec the prestige of occupying its own seat at UNESCO.

In November 2005, the PQ elected dashing young, 39 year-old André Boisclair as its new leader. He was the first PQ leader not belonging to the generation that had founded the party in the 1960s. Boisclair advocated a radical program for a quick referendum after the PQ returned to power, followed, "as soon as possible," by a unilateral "declaration of national sovereignty" if even the barest majority voted yes. He pledged to ignore the Clarity Act, parting with the party's former promises of a "partnership" with Canada and a year of negotiations leading to secession.

Boisclair's radical program was out of touch with the province's majority. To make things worse for the PQ, two of Quebec's cultural icons, playwrights Michel Tremblay and Robert Lepage, admitted in 2006 to have lost some of their faith in the separatist cause. In Tremblay's words, "it was a beautiful dream, and one must respect such dreams, but it will never be more than a dream if we keep looking at it in economic terms first." He remembered that "the driving force was our pride in being the beacon of francophone culture in America—not the economy."

The uproar and panicked bickering that followed revealed a real dilemma for the PQ. It had downplayed culture to broaden its appeal to include immigrant groups and not just francophones but had to assume power before it could achieve sovereignty. Yet, it had to soften its platform in order to win that power but lacked the strong mandate needed to proceed toward separation. It also competed in a greatly changed Quebec where language inequalities were eliminated. The PQ and Boisclair had trouble finding new arguments to fire up supporters for a new push for secession. This was especially hard with a conciliatory PM and a *Québécoise* governor general in Ottawa. The smoother the relations between Ottawa and Quebec, the greater the decline for the separatists. Prime Minister Harper astutely adjusted his policy to the shifting ground in Quebec politics.

François Legault

Noticing the PQ's disorientation and shaky leadership, the unpopular Premier Charest called an early election in 2007 in which his Liberal party lost its majority. This produced Quebec's first minority government since 1878. Even so, the PQ fared much worse, declining from 45 to 36 seats and only 28.3% of the votes, down from 33.2%. Both parties experienced their worst results since 1976, in the case of the Liberals, and 1970 for the PQ.

The primary victim of the PQ's electoral failure was Boisclair, who was promptly replaced as PQ leader by former social worker and former cabinet member in various PQ governments, Pauline Marois. Her condition for acceptance was that the party stop its squabbling over a timetable for a future referendum and get back in touch with the real-life concerns of many voters. A pragmatist, she argued that radicalizing the PQ "would be a recipe for marginalization, or even extinction."

The real surprise was Mario Dumont's conservative and moderately nationalist ADQ, which surged to within seven seats of Charest's minority government. A 36-year-old economics graduate from Concordia University, Dumont led a walk-out from the Liberal party in 1992 because it did not favor an independent Quebec. However, after the failed referendum in 1995, in which he gave lukewarm support for sovereignty, Dumont shifted his position between the extremes of federalism and hardline separation. By 2012 the coalition Avenir du Québec (CAQ) absorbed the ADQ.

According to an election-time poll in September 2012, only 28% of provincial voters supported separation, and 68% did not want another referendum. In another poll a month before the election, sovereignty ranked tenth on a list of priorities among Quebecers. In the wake of the fabulously successful Vancouver Winter Olympic Games in February 2010, fewer than a third of Québécois supported the notion of having their own Olympic team. That was wonderful news for Canadian unity. Support for sovereignty was at its lowest ebb in four decades. Although sovereignty is the PQ's raison d'être, it is an electoral non-starter.

Election year 2008 reflected this in Quebec. In the October federal elections, the Bloc Québécois won the most seats in Quebec, but saw its vote decrease by 4%, the second lowest in its history, after a campaign in which it did not say a single word about independence.

In Quebec's December provincial elections only seven weeks later, in which the economy was the main issue, the PQ, led for the first time by Pauline Marois, Quebec's first female leader, did better than predicted. One reason was that sovereignty was banished from her campaign. Marois noted in an interview: "We might well have a referendum someday. I'm keeping the door open." Her party captured 35.15% of the votes and 51 seats, while the ADQ crashed to only 16.35% of the votes and a mere seven seats.

Pauline Marois's cold feet about advocating concrete steps and timetables toward sovereignty made the PQ ranks restive. She earned a 93% endorsement as leader in the party's April 2011 national congress in return for allowing the hardliners to put language and sovereignty front and center again. If they get their way, Bill 101 would

Canada

have expanded to cover post-secondary schools and businesses with fewer than 50 employees would have to obey the French Language Charter. This was tricky terrain for the PQ: polls in 2011 indicated that two-thirds of Quebecers thought parents should have the right to school their children in the language of their choice.

These objectives also became grist for the May 2, 2011, federal elections, when the Bloc Québécois was practically wiped out in Quebec, losing all but four of its 49 seats. In the 2015 federal elections it fell below 20% of the votes in Quebec. Such near-extinction of the *Bloc Québécois* was the most startling sign of the change occurring in the province. Open intraparty warfare broke out within the PQ.

Jean Charest became the first Quebec premier since the 1950s to win three terms in a row. He won the majority he was seeking in the 2008 elections, with 42% of the votes and 66 of the 125 seats. His government was beset by scandals in the construction industry, though. Montreal seemed unable to deal with an endemic culture of corruption and organized crime that drove more and more citizens to the suburbs and increasing numbers of businesses out of the province.

When *Maclean's* published a cover story on October 4, 2010, calling Quebec "The Most Corrupt Province in Canada," Charest condemned such "Quebec bashing" and demanded an apology to Quebecers. The House of Commons expressed its "profound sadness at the prejudice displayed and the stereotypes employed by *Maclean's* magazine to denigrate the Quebec nation." Nevertheless, *La Presse* termed the claim "undeniable." Political columnist Vincent Marissal, supported this notion, writing that "every Quebec media outlet has drawn similar conclusions."

The corruption charges led to the resignations of the mayors of both Montreal and Laval while compelling an increasingly unpopular Charest to call for early elections September 4, 2012. He was helped by the distraction of six months of unpopular demonstrations by students protesting a doubling of university tuition, the lowest in Canada and half the national average. Tuition had long been kept low in order to encourage young Quebecers to study but few did so. A quarter of students drop out of high school and only 30% attend the university. About a third of students boycotted classes to oppose the increase. Striking students in Montreal harangued those who wanted to complete their courses, blocked roads, smashed windows, lit fires, tossed Molotov cocktails, vandalized government buildings, and clashed with police. The PQ allied itself with the protesters.

The PQ secured a narrow victory in the 2012 elections, winning 54 seats, up from 51, enough to form a minority government in the 125-seat National Assembly. Pauline Marois became Quebec's first female leader. The Liberals came within a whisker of overtaking PQ, capturing 50 seats, down from 66. Charest lost his own Sherbrooke seat he held for 28 years and resigned as party leader. ADQ fell on hard times and won only seven seats. It joined a larger grouping, the CAQ, the Coalition for the Future of Quebec, which won 19 seats. Led by Francçois Legault, this new party focused on education, health, culture, public finances, and a more efficient state, rather than Quebec sovereignty or Canadian unity. *Québec solidaire*, Quebec Solidarity, led by Françoise David, which believed the PQ drifted too far to the right, won two seats, up from one. The success of the smaller parties prevented PQ from winning a majority of seats.

A bloody incident on election evening served as a reminder of the passions language and independence can still rouse. Marois was in the middle of congratulating her supporters, vowing that "we want a country and we will have one!" when a hooded gunman entered the hall, screaming in French, "The English are awakening!" He shot two people, one of whom died. He then poured gasoline around the back door and set fire to the building as he fled. He was quickly apprehended.

In office Marois tried to wave the flag of sovereignty, declaring to the PQ's 90,000 members that Quebec's need for sovereignty had become an "emergency." The party was aware that it could not win elections by waving that banner. Marois' agenda included new restrictions on the public use of the English language, Bill 14, and on public displays of religious affiliation, known as the Charter of Quebec Values. It prohibits government employees from wearing "overt and conspicuous" religious symbols while on the job. This means no headscarves, hijabs, kippas, niqabs, turbans, and outsized crucifixes. It permitted small crosses and symbols. In 2017, women who provide or receive public services were prohibited from wearing face coverings. The most recent Quebec general election was held on October 1, 2018. The CAQ won 74 out of 125 seats, giving the party a majority and unseating the Quebec Liberal Party.

By way of background, in 2016 Quebec's Muslim population was 5.5%. In 2011 the percentage had grown to 3.1 % making the Muslim population much more visible. There has certainly been a backlash against all religious visibility in Quebec as the fruits of the Quiet Revolution continue to blossom in Quebec society.

This 2017 proposed law divided traditional Quebecers from new immigrants and multicultural Montreal, where most immigrants to Quebec settle, from the rest of Quebec. It also divided PQ members. Three former PQ premiers, including the late Jacques Parizeau, opposed it publicly. Nevertheless, Marois tried to use the issue in the April 2014 provincial elections to increase the PQ's poll numbers even though voters were more interested in the economy and in fighting corruption. Quebec ranked seventh out of the 10 provinces in terms of per capita GDP. The PQ and the Liberals, led by brain surgeon and former Quebec health minister, Philippe Couillard, entered the contest neck-and-neck, with the CAQ poised to capture many votes.

Polls suggested the PQ would win a majority of seats, but that was not to be. The PQ had hoped to ride to victory by the popular ban on religious symbols and to say as little as possible about a sovereignty referendum. After all, only a third of Quebecers wanted to separate from Canada. When one PQ candidate, billionaire media mogul Pierre Karl Péladeau, called for an independent Quebec and reinforced his point by pumping his fist in the air, he pushed the PQ campaign off a cliff. The PQ lead evaporated in an instant, and its results were a disaster. The Liberals captured 41.5% of the votes and 70 seats, an absolute majority. The PQ plummeted to 25.37% of the votes and only 30 seats. CAQ rose to 23% and 22 seats, while QS slipped in with 7.63% and 3 seats.

Despite being publicly associated with the PQ for only one year, Péladeau assumed the party leadership in the spring of 2015. The wealthy businessman related poorly to a core membership that was largely leftist and union-dominated. He alienated many members and caused a string of departures. Péladeau was mistaken in claiming that separatism was more alive than ever because it was a Baby Boomer dream that was less inspiring to young Québécois. After less than a year, Péladeau relinquished his leadership of the PQ and was succeeded by Jean-François Lisée, a former journalist and close advisor to Jacques Parizeau and Lucien Bouchard.

Couillard promised to concentrate on the real issues of concern to Quebecers and to bring them together rather than to divide them, as the PQ does. Separatism had been deflated as a political force in the foreseeable future. Throughout the campaign Couillard repeatedly made it clear: "We have a homeland—it's Quebec. It's the homeland of every Quebecer. And we have a country, Canada. We want it all! You won't take any of it from us! It's the homeland of every Quebecer. And we

have a country, Canada. We want it all! You won't take any of it from us!'"

Most recently, the government of Premier Francois Legault, leader of the CAQ who was sworn in on October 18, 2018, proposed a radical new law to promote Quebec secularism. The new law prohibits civil servants from displaying any religious symbols. The *Montreal Gazette* reported in March 29, 2019 the following. (Retrieved from: https://montrealga-zette.com/news/quebec/religious-symbols-what-you-need-to-know-about-que-becs-secularism-law).

The Legault government tabled a new secularism law Thursday that would prohibit the wearing of religious symbols at work for a variety of public-service employees. The law would also forbid people from delivering or receiving government services with their faces covered.

The law is based on the understanding that Quebec is a secular state, the government says. It comes after years of debate and controversy over the role of religion in Quebec.

Bill 21 will now be studied by a National Assembly committee before elected officials vote on it. The government hopes to have it adopted by the middle of June.

The law, known as an at respecting the laicity of the state, was enacted on June 16, 2019, and bans public employees including the minister of justice, attorney general, teachers, school principals and vice principals, Crown prosecutors, judges, police officers, labor arbitrators and court clerks from wearing religious symbols at work.

Employees currently working for the government are allowed to continue wearing religious symbols as long as they are in the job they hold as of Thursday. If they change jobs within the public service, they are no longer be able to wear their religious symbols. That means someone who is a teacher now but becomes a school principal loses the right to wear their religious symbol.

The law does not define what a religious symbol is. Immigration Minister Simon Jolin-Barrette said tattoos will not be considered to be religious symbols. He said employees will not be searched to

see if they are wearing hidden religious symbols.

The law bans people from delivering or receiving services with their faces covered from certain government agencies. They include members of the National Assembly, elected municipal officers, school board commissioners, people working at the National Assembly and for the provincial lieutenant-governor, police officers, some doctors, dentists and midwives and home childcare providers.

The law invokes the notwithstanding clauses in the Canadian and Quebec charters of rights to override religious rights.

The reaction across Canada has been immediate with the Prime Minister and others claiming that this is not an action consistent with Canadian values.

ONTARIO: Ontario has traditionally been Canada's political pivot and economic motor, despite the growth of the West, the ambitions of the Maritimes, and the assertiveness of Quebec. Ontario houses 38% of Canada's population and produces about a third of the nation's wealth. Toronto's massive economy alone is equal to or larger than that of every province. Former Premier David Peterson was once asked if he was uncomfortable

Toronto's Rogers Centre (formerly SkyDome), one of the most modern sports facility in the world   Photo: Ian Steer

Canada

about Ontario's becoming wealthier while other regions were suffering. He answered: "One of the things that keeps this country together is that everybody hates Ontario, and what keeps Ontario together is that everybody hates Toronto, and what keeps Toronto together is that everybody hates Bay Street" (Canada's Wall Street).

Ontario's its preeminence is being challenged by Canada's new economic power centers: Alberta, British Columbia, oil and resource-rich Saskatchewan, Newfoundland, and Labrador. Ontario does not play the kind of leadership role in Canada it once did. Although it is by no means a poor province, Ontario's economy has performed sluggishly for a long time and much of the troubled manufacturing and auto industry is within its borders. In the decade from 2001, its per capita GDP remained virtually unchanged. The surging West's combined GDP surpassed that of Ontario for the first time in 2008. Ontario embarrassingly received equalization payments as a "have-not" province.

Toronto's status as the country's premier city was challenged for the first time in over a century, this time by Calgary. Toronto has budget and infrastructure problems and its manufacturing sector is not in good condition, having shed 100,000 jobs in the five years up to 2008. Still, Ontario continues to attract 40% of all immigrants to Canada; 44% of its residents are foreign-born, well above the province's 27%. It also remains the country's financial center. Private wealth is pouring into art galleries, theaters and new museums as Toronto tries hard to retain its image as a "city on the rise."

Canada's largest province is not officially bilingual even though its government extends French-language services to Ontario's half million francophones, about 5% of the population). When a court in Ontario ruled that under the Charter of Rights francophones are entitled to an education in French, the province quickly complied. Toronto is the most ethnically diverse city in North America. In 2002 Ontario received its first Aboriginal lieutenant-governor in Canada: James Bartleman, a Minjikanig Indian and former Canadian ambassador to the EU.

In 1999, a reform compressed high school from five to four years while stressing more mathematics and science, a kind of pre STEM (Science, Technology, Engineering, and Mathematics) initiative. Since 2000, students are subject to a code of conduct that includes reciting the Oath of Citizenship and pledging allegiance to the Queen. Official hoped that the oath and code would instill respect for Canada and make schools safer. In 2001 vouchers were offered granting tax credits to parents who send their child to a private school.

Hon. Doug Ford, Premier of Ontario
Retrieved from: https://www.dailyxtra.com/
doug-fords-confusing-case-against-sex-ed-138583

For many voters the pace of the changes was too fast. In 1997 the provincial government stepped into a political minefield by introducing Bill 103. This unified the Toronto area's six municipalities and created a regional government of Metropolitan Toronto for a city of about 4.6 million. The idea was to eliminate inefficient redundancy in urban services while reducing the public payroll. Suddenly, signs reading "Vote No to megacity" appeared everywhere as three-quarters of voters opposed the merger in separate referenda in the six municipalities. The cost-cutting government ignored the results and enacted the reform.

In a 2007 referendum, voters turned down the proportional representation electoral system. Legislation now mandates that elections be held on fixed dates every four years, though. The defining issue in

the 2007 election's was the funding of religious schools. Ontario is the only province that pays the whole cost for attendance to Roman Catholic Schools, reflecting the fact that one-third of its residents are Catholic, but does not covers expenses for schools

of any other religion. Voters reelected the Liberal party in 2007 and again in 2011 albeit five seats short of a majority.

In 2012, Dalton McGuinty, Canada's longest-serving premier, suddenly resigned and handed the reins of power to Kathleen Wynne, not only the first female premier of Ontario but also its first openly gay leader. McGuinty became the sixth woman heading provincial governments in 2012; more than 87% of Canadians were served by female premiers at that time. McGuinty led her Liberal Party to its fourth consecutive victory, this time with an absolute majority.

Ontario's greatest embarrassment in 2013–14 was the self-destruction of Toronto's Tory mayor, Rob Ford, who became an international laughingstock. He came into office in 2010 on a populist wave of anti-elite suburban rage despite a well-known history of intemperate and profane outbursts. After months of denying allegations, Ford finally admitted to having smoked crack cocaine "probably in one of my drunken stupors." Ford showed up raging drunk at a function honoring Canadian soldiers, frequently drove drunk, assaulted his staff mentions, and entertained prostitutes in his city hall office. Since Ford had not been convicted of a crime, the city council was unable to take away his title, even temporarily but did remove most of his powers. Incredibly, Ford remained popular.

Ford vowed to run again for mayor in the October 2014 municipal elections. However, he was diagnosed with cancer and turned the candidacy over to his brother Doug. Emerging victorious was Conservative John Tory. A wealthy businessman, Tory personified the city as it imagines itself: smart, compassionate, clean-cut, and powerful. Ford passed away in 2016 at the age of 46.

In a surprise to many, the late Rob Ford's brother became Ontario's Progressive Conservative Premier Rob Ford on June 29, 2018. He secured the leadership of the Party after a political coup which saw the then leader, Patrick Brown facing allegations of "troubling conduct" and precipitously losing the support of his colleagues. Ford's campaign was built around conservative values of home, religion, the traditional family, and economic rationality after the huge deficits, identity politics, and education reform promulgated by the Ontario Liberal Party. The daunting economic and social challenges facing Premier Ford will not wait to be addressed and he has begun to move swiftly to seize the day.

MANITOBA: Manitoba was traditionally one of the few Canadian provinces in which there were real ideological differences between the two main parties that

Portage Avenue looking east to Main Street, Winnipeg   Photo: Henry Kalen

alternate in power: the NDP and the Conservatives. The divisions were created in the Winnipeg General Strike in 1919. Manitoba enjoys one of the country's highest economic growth rates and the lowest unemployment rate. Moreover, Manitoba has Western Canada's most diversified economy. It is increasingly shifting away from agriculture, constituting a mere 5% of its economy, and food-related industries into manufacturing, financial services, transportation, mining, and petroleum production. Sharing in the West's economic renaissance, this makes Manitoba well-equipped to deal with economic downturns.

Despite an $800-million expansion of the Red River floodway is designed to minimize the danger of flooding in the future, disaster struck in May 2011. The Manitoba government declared a state of emergency to deal with "unprecedented and historic" flooding of the Assiniboine River. About 2,000 people were displaced; 800 soldiers were sent to top up existing dikes, fortify unprotected properties, and deploy mobile flood protection equipment. It happened again in June 2014, necessitating assistance from the military. The year 2015 brought dangerous wildfires to all four western provinces.

On October 2009, Gary Doer passed the premiership to Greg Selinger, MLA from St. Boniface. Doer earned a Ph.D. from the London School of Economics and led the NDP to its fourth consecutive term in the 2011 provincial election. In 2014, Doer faced an open rebellion in his cabinet against his leadership, as five NDP cabinet members protested their inability to speak their minds.

Doer was named as Canada's ambassador to the U.S., a post that benefited

from his well-developed negotiation skills and the fact that he had been in the U.S. more than any other premier. He personally knew all four former governors in President Barack Obama's cabinet. Doer was replaced as Canada's ambassador on March 4, 2016 by David MacNaughton, the co-chair of the Liberal election campaign in Ontario.

The capital city of Winnipeg, where 60% of the province's population lives, is experiencing a worrying loss in population, especially by the young, educated and well-trained. In 2005 alone, 22,000 left Manitoba, the highest number since 1990, despite relatively low unemployment.

Hon. Heather Stefanson, Premier of Manitoba
Province of Manitoba, Office of the Premier

Enrollment has dramatically fallen in some neighborhood schools.

Winnipeg has the highest crime rate of any large Canadian city, double the national average. Manitobans' disposable income lags $2,400 behind that of Saskatchewan and $10,000 behind that of Alberta. Winnipeg has a growing indigenous population that experiences discrimination and poverty. *Maclean's* wrote that it is "arguably becoming Canada's most racist city." The indigenous account for 16.7% of the total population, 4 times the national average. However, it has a Métis Mayor (Brian Bowman) and a Museum for Human Rights in Winnipeg, the only national museum outside of Ottawa.

The question of extending francophone language rights in Manitoba has been an enduring problem with a long and bitter history. In the 1870 Manitoba Act that brought the province into the Confederation, guaranteed the use of French in the courts, legislature, and law. The percentage of anglophones climbed steadily and in 1890 the provincial government declared that English was the only official language. The once vibrant francophone population became gradually assimilated until, by the late 1970s, only about 50,000, or about 5% of the population, remained, scattered in 30 communities across the province conducting most of their daily affairs in English. Only in tiny Ste-Anne, near Winnipeg, did French survive as the main language. Due to immersion schools, adult language education, and offspring of marriages between anglophones and francophones, the number of French speakers doubled to over 100,000 by the end of the century.

In 1979, the Supreme Court of Canada invalidated the 1890 law as unconstitutional. This ruling raised serious questions about the validity of 4,500 provincial laws that were passed only in English. The then Conservative government in Manitoba began translating some of the laws. The issue took center stage in 1981 when a francophone lawyer from Winnipeg, Roger Bilodeau, challenged the constitutionality of a speeding ticket that was written in English only. Faced with the mind-boggling threat that a court might declare most of the province's laws to be invalid, the government worked out a deal with the *Societé Franco-Manitobaine*: 400 laws would be translated into French, at the federal government's expense, and some French language services in government agencies would be expanded. The government put the substance of this agreement into legislation and introduced it into the assembly.

The Conservatives in Manitoba were willing to allow the translation of 400 laws, but fought against any constitutional recognition of French as an official language in the province. Their opposition and a

Canada

deafening anglophone outcry against the legislation prevented it from being enacted. Francophone activists vowed to continue the long struggle in the courts. The situation was most uncomfortable for former Prime Minister Brian Mulroney, a bilingual Quebecer, whose firm support of French language rights was essential to his Conservative party's electoral chances in Quebec. Mulroney went to Winnipeg to argue strongly in favor of francophone rights, a move which alienated many Manitoban Tories.

The year 1985 witnessed a dramatic turn-around in Manitoba. The Supreme Court of Canada decided unanimously that all laws enacted in the province since 1890 were invalid. To head off legal chaos, the government engineered an agreement on a timetable for translating the existing laws. As a result, the entire French-language controversy wilted in importance and ceased for the time being to plague the province's political life.

The French language controversy reappeared in 1998 with a vengeance in response to Quebec's decision to disregard a Supreme Court ruling permitting English-language signs. Manitoba's government immediately announced that it would rescind its support of the Meech Lake Accord, a move that ultimately killed the accord. In 1992 the Supreme Court ordered the creation of a Manitoba-wide all-francophone school district in which 75% of the instruction would be in French. Perhaps a retired liquor board manager best captured the mood of more and more Westerners when he said: "Bilingualism is a bunch of horse manure. I don't accept this business of us being bilingual and Quebec being French only."

SASKATCHEWAN: Only seven decades ago, Saskatchewan, which is the size of Texas, depended almost entirely on a one-crop economy. One of Saskatchewan's few claims to fame was that all Royal Canadian Mounted Police are trained at a depot founded on a creek crossing known originally as Pile of Bones. It was made the capital of the Northwest Territories and soon thereafter renamed Regina after Queen Victoria.

Today Saskatchewan accounts for 40% of all cultivated land in Canada. Its average farm size has risen from 400 to 1,152 acres since 1936, producing 60% of Canada's wheat, 80% of its durum, a third of its oats and barley, and about a third of its oil seeds. Still, by 2005 agriculture represented only 7% of the province's GDP, down from an earlier 50%.

Saskatchewan also has impressive mineral resources, which now contribute more to its economy than does farming. It has oil, including bitumen-like oil sands in the northwest, which are part of the same geological formation as those found in neighboring Alberta. Oil-sands Quest from Calgary had, by 2008, invested $160 million in exploration of Saskatchewan's oil sands. The province became the ninth biggest supplier of oil to the U.S. In fact, the U.S. bought more oil from the province than from Kuwait.

Saskatchewan possesses natural gas and low-grade brown lignite coal as well as the world's largest carbon sequestration project near Weyburn. Six thousand tons of carbon dioxide emissions from a synthetic fuel plant in North Dakota are piped across the border each day and pumped underground. Saskatchewan has the world's largest recoverable supply of potash, over 40%, which is used for fertilizer. Backed by the federal government in 2010, Premier Wall blocked the hostile takeover of Potash Corporation of Saskatchewan, which had been privatized in 1989, by the Anglo-Australian mining giant, BHP Billiton. This would have been Canada's biggest-ever corporate takeover. BHP Billiton was already building the world's largest potash mine near the village of Jansen, 100 miles, or 150 kilometers, east of Saskatoon.

Saskatchewan has some of the globe's highest-grade uranium deposits,

Regina, with the Legislative Building (upper portion) set in beautiful Wascana Park

Scott Moe
Premier of Saskatchewan

producing more than one-quarter of the world's supply. Former Premier Brad Wall boasted: "We are the Saudi Arabia of uranium." Even so, Saskatchewan's industries cannot enrich uranium because Canada is not one of the few countries an international treaty permits to do so. In 1997, Saskatoon-based Cameco, the world's largest uranium processor, began to process nuclear material from former Soviet warheads as part of an international accord to reduce atomic weapons after the Cold War ended.

The province's dependence on the prices of grain and other commodities such as oil, potash, and uranium, means that its economy booms when prices are high and suffers when they are low. Prices were low for a long time, necessitating government overspending and a large deficit, which officials had to confront by slashing public spending and jobs, freezing wages, and selling off some of the province's largest publicly owned corporations, including Potash Corporation of Saskatchewan and the gas utility, SaskEnergy.

Saskatchewan had always been fertile ground for the NDP, which grew out of radical farmer movements that bloomed during the Great Depression. The NDP governed off and on for over a half century. It was the NDP which first brought socialized medicine to Canada and which became the model for Canadian Medicare. The province was shaken in 1988 when officials repealed a law requiring the use of both French and English in the courts and provincial assembly as well as the translation of all past and present laws into French. This upset Saskatchewan's

francophones who constitute 2.3% of the total population.

The NDP governed over a prospering province as its population was growing and stood at over one million. Saskatchewan agriculture was more diversified than ever. The number of oil and gas wells drilled rose steadily and its potash sector did well. The subsequent collapse of commodity and oil prices hurt Saskatchewan.

For a while the province was in deep trouble. After 1986, the number of small farms dropped by more than 20,000 because of shrinking farm subsidies, forfeitures, and drought. Many were bought up by large, intensive farm operations with hired management. The rural population was leaving the villages in droves and moving into Regina, Saskatoon, and neighboring Alberta. The overall population fell from 1,134,000 in 2002 to 994,843 in 2003. One saw abandoned buildings all along Saskatchewan's highways.

By 2018, Saskatchewan's population rose to about 1,620,000 with the fastest population growth and lowest unemployment rate of any province. A commodities-fueled boom brought greater prosperity to the entire province reversing the decades-long population exodus. Investments poured in. Perhaps most unexpectedly, Saskatchewan joined Alberta, British Columbia, and Newfoundland as "have" provinces, no longer entitled to federal equalization payments. Ontario slipped to embarrassing "have-not" status and had a per capita GDP lower than Saskatchewan's.

The inner city of Regina was in particular trouble because it was one of the poorest areas in urban Canada with almost a

third of its residents depending on government aid. Its poorest people are Aboriginals who are fleeing reservations and now constitute 42% of North Central Regina's population. While Statistics Canada reports that Aboriginals are doing better in most urban centers; Regina remains a conspicuous exception.

There were noticeable improvements by 2008, though. A new sense of optimism had taken hold in the city, as new

funding was found for youth employment and skills training programs and other initiatives. There was also greater interaction between city hall and the aboriginal community. Creeland Mini-mart, the downtown reserve's first business, began pumping gas and selling snacks. By 2011 Saskatchewan was booming economically as affordable housing and rental properties became extremely tight. Rent became a key election issue with one desperate new formation even naming itself "The Rent Is Too Damn High" party.

The last NDP premier was Lorne Calvert, a United Church minister, who grew up in a working-class neighborhood of Moose Jaw. In 2007 he faced a much strengthened Saskatchewan Party, which was created in 1997 by Tories who were joined by some Liberals and Reformers. It is the dominant conservative alternative to the NDP. Brad Wall, a young lawyer, moderated the party.

In the April 2016 election, Wall's Saskatchewan Party won a historic third term by a landslide, capturing 51, up from 49, out of 58, because it earned 63% of the votes, down from 64%. This was the best electoral results in the province's history. The NDP won only 10 seats, up from 9. Wall rode the wave of a booming economy and Canada's lowest unemployment rate at 5.9%. Following his victory Wall proclaimed: "After years of lagging behind the rest of the provinces, we are leading in so very many respects, and we are not going back." In 2016 Wall was the most popular premier in Canada, enjoying a 62% approval rating. Wall was the leader of the Saskatchewan Party and premier of the province from November 21, 2007 until February 2, 2018 at which time he retired and was replaced Scott Moe, a cabinet minister in the Wall government became premier. Moe won his own landslide electoral majority in the election of 2020, with the Saskatchewan Party winning 48 of the 61 seats in the Legislative Assembly.

Commenting on the province's rising fortunes, Jim Marshall, chief economist at the Saskatchewan Institute of Public Policy, said "we're not your father's Saskatchewan. It's a different place, and that's not well known."

In 2010, Saskatoon brought glory to the province by being named Canada's second "smartest" and second "most cultured" city, after Victoria and right above Regina, in *Maclean's* third annual ranking of Canadian cities. In terms of "social engagement," it topped the list. Thus, the city that has long been the brunt of jokes for being a hick town in the middle of nowhere emerges as a leading center of learning and culture.

ALBERTA: Alberta, named for Queen Victoria's husband, enjoys the fruits of its

Canada

The exciting Chuck Wagon Race during Calgary's once-a-year (July) celebration of the Old West called The Calgary Stampede

oil and gas wealth. Oil revenues swelled the province's treasury and the Alberta Heritage Savings Trust Fund, which is to be used toward the long-term development of the province and toward lightening Albertans' tax burden. Alienation and resentment in western Canada, so familiar in the nation's history, survives. There is little support for secession from Canada at this prosperous time despite a 2006 poll in the *National Post* showing that a third of western Canadians, and 42% of Albertans, thought the western provinces should explore setting up their own country. Basically, Albertans want the federal government to leave them alone. Alberta celebrated its 100th birthday in 2005.

In 1992, Ralph Klein, a former folksy environment minister and mayor of

Hon. Danielle Smith, Premier of Alberta

Calgary, began a 14-year run as premier. Son of a professional wrestler known as "Killer Klein," he was one of the most colorful figures in Canadian politics. A one-time high school dropout, he became a celebrated local TV reporter in the 1970s, known for his talent in getting stories from the street level. Klein cultivated contacts with biker gangs, prostitutes, and Indian groups. Sometime called "Red-neck Ralph" because of his undiplomatic language, he benefited considerably from his image as an extroverted down-to-earth man of the people. Klein passed away in March 2013 at age 70.

Klein launched "Ralph's Revolution" with his Albertan agenda dominating Canadian political debates. He demonstrated that governments can cut costs deeply and quickly and still post impressive victories. Klein was determined to resolve the financial crisis without raising taxes, making reductions in almost every kind of government service. By 1997 he reduced government expenditures by 20%, cut thousands of positions from the civil service, closed hospitals, and slashed welfare rolls. Alberta led Canada in deregulation and privatization as car licensing, liquor retailing and electricity distribution are in private hands.

Klein pushed through a law mandating a balanced budget and requiring that three-quarters of any budget surplus be used to pay off debt. Alberta has the lowest provincial personal tax rates, a flat-rate

of 10.5%, Canada's first, and is the only province without a provincial sales tax.

Alberta produces two-thirds of Canada's supplies of oil and gas. Fifty-four percent of its crude oil is derived from tar sands. These sources are under increasing scrutiny by its main customer: the U.S. Greenpeace succeeded in putting the oil sands on the green radar screen. And more recently, controversy is emerging between the government of Alberta and the Biden administration as the latter increases imports of oil from the Middle East rather than Canada.

Albertans dismiss the environmental threats, responding that if the Americans and Europeans do not want their oil, provincial leaders would commission a pipeline, called Northern Gateway, to the West Coast and ship it to China. Indeed, in 2009 state-owned Petro-China purchased a majority stake in two tar-sands projects. In 2012 the Canadian government approved the sale of Nexen, a tar-sands producer, to a state-owned Chinese oil company, CNOOC. Both the federal and British Columbia government approved of the transaction. There are local objections to Northern Gateway, though, especially from Aboriginal groups, to such a pipeline to the West Coast. Also, the government of British Columbia wants money for taking the risks presented by such a project. Both governments jointly appointed officials to work on a settlement of their pipeline differences.

Convention Centre, Edmonton, Alberta

The preferred pipeline was the Keystone XL which would take oil from Alberta to Texas and to refineries along the way. In 2015, President Obama rejected the project because of environmental concerns. While President Trump lifted the ban, it was reinstated by President Biden in January 2021. Albertans feel hemmed in, "landlocked." former Premier Redford made clear that other means of transport—rail, truck, river barge—are far more expensive and less safe than pipelines.

The Heritage Fund shrank to $15.3 billion by 2014. Sometimes no contributions were made or, worse, funds were raided when the government was short of cash. In order to manage the fund better, the Alberta Investment Management Corporation was set up in 2008 to run it on commercial lines.

Alberta's economy is helped in bad times because it has become increasingly diversified. By 2001 the energy sector represented only 21% of the province's GDP, down from 40% in 1985. The manufacturing, technology, service, and wholesale trade sectors are burgeoning. New industries are pouring in. Buoyed by a prosperous farm economy and rising oil and gas prices until 2014, the province outperformed the Canadian economy in every year since 1990 except one. Alberta has the highest per capita disposable income, the highest GDP per capita, and the highest rate of job creation in Canada.

The most visible sign of Alberta's dynamic economy is Calgary, the country's wealth magnet, second only to Toronto as a corporate head-office center. Toronto has 10 of the largest 20 Canadian companies' head offices, while Calgary has six, all oil and gas firms. Office space is the country's most expensive, and fossil fuel companies plus those doing business with them occupy three-fourths of these locations. Further, Calgary had the lowest unemployment rate of any major city.

Calgary boasts Canada's third most ethnically diverse population and the greatest number of post-high school degrees per capita. In 2010 Calgary voters elected the first Muslim mayor of a major Canadian city, Naheed Nenshi enjoys considerable popularity. Born of immigrant parents, he graduated from the University of Calgary and completed his graduate work at Harvard. The dynamic economy made Calgary a magnet for immigrants, ahead of Montreal, and almost a fourth of the residents are visible minorities. *Maclean's* ranked it third among Canada's "smartest" cities in 2010. Until the recession, the residential housing market in Calgary was booming.

Alberta built the finest public education system in Canada with its children regularly outscoring peers from other provinces and other countries, according to the 2007 PISA results, on standardized tests. In *Maclean's* annual college rankings in 2006, Alberta's sole university was rated number one in all of Canada, fifth in 2011. Alberta does need another university in light of its growth.

Albertans increased their tax-deductible charitable giving by more than 15% in 2006, thereby helping transform Calgary into an intellectual and cultural center as well as a business one. Yet, it is still one of the few North American cities of over a million residents that does not have an art museum. In 2016, Calgary opened the National Music Center which hosts events every day of the year.

The province faces serious problems. Canadians poured into Alberta at the rate of 100,000 each year, enough to create a medium size town. Its net migration in 2006 was 62,000, compared with Ontario's net loss of 34,000. This put severe strains on housing, government services and infrastructure, and the labor market. Calgary passed the one million mark in 2006, causing rush-hour traffic to slow to a trickle.

Fort McMurray, where the oil sands are located, needs new water and wastewater treatment plants, a new landfill, better and more roads and bridges and more nurses and doctors. The locals were wary of the boom all around them. One summed up the town's problems: "Too many single men, too much time, too much money, too much trouble." *GQ* magazine called it "a hellhole of testosterone and tattoos." The high wages also attracted drug dealers with drug abuse in the northern oil area is four times the average in the rest of the province. About 40% of oil workers test positive for cocaine or marijuana in job screening or post-accident tests. Economic hard times have befallen the city and lessened the intensity of these problems.

On another matter, during the summer of 2013, the country was shocked by images of flood waters overflowing the Bow and Elbow Rivers and spilling into Calgary. About 75,000 people had to be evacuated from the city. Three years later, in May 2016, Fort McMurray was engulfed by a such a large fire that all of 88,000 residents were ordered to evacuate. The blaze consumed entire swaths of the town and 2,400 buildings, but most of the city and the oil facilities north of town were saved. In dollar terms this was Canada's most destructive natural disaster.

Health-care reductions were temporarily scaled back due to festering unease about government spending cuts, dramatized by hospital workers' repeated walkouts. Then the government introduced Bill 11 which drew particularly sharp criticism. In order to reduce waiting lists and relieve pressure on the public health system, the legislation allows private clinics to perform all cataract surgery and many hernia,

Canada

foot, ear, nose, and throat operations. The expenses are fully covered by the provincial health-care plan. Critics contended that Alberta was, in effect, creating private hospitals, which are illegal in Canada, and was paving the way for American-style two-tiered health care. According to a 2006 survey, Alberta and British Columbia offer the best health care in Canada.

Alberta has a unique political culture. Oppositions are always weak with governments routinely reelected by huge majorities. During its existence, it has experienced only four changes of government. Each time an established ruling party was replaced by a new upstart.

Emerging in 2011 as Alberta's first female premier was Justice Minister Alison Redford, the preferred candidate of those who wanted to eliminate the "old boys' network." She entered the April 2012 elections far behind Danielle Smith's Wildrose Alliance in the polls, but was seriously underestimated and proved the pollsters wrong. Redford's Progressive Conservatives captured 44% of the votes and 61 seats in the enlarged 87-seat legislature.

Redford's premiership came to an end in 2014 when it was learned that she had sometimes used Alberta government aircraft for personal reasons. She was replaced by businessman Jim Prentice, who left a seven-digit salary to be premier. Knowing that the provincial economy was getting worse, Prentice called early elections in May 2015. The results were a disaster for the Conservatives, ending their 44 years at the helm. In a setting of large-scale layoffs, empty office towers, plunging house prices, and collapsing oil prices, the NDP surged to a landslide victory, winning 53 seats.

Rachel Notley, a labor lawyer and lifelong New Democrat, became premier. She vowed to change oil royalties, get tough on environmental protection, end coal-fired power generation, enhance aboriginal rights, and reduce the economic dependence on oil.

In April 2019, Premier Notley's NDP lost to the United Conservative Party of Alberta which was led by Jason Kenney, a former federal minister under the Harper government. His Party received 54.88% of the popular vote. The common belief is that Notley was liked personally. However, her policy of not supporting any but one of the three pipelines which were to move Alberta oil to tide water and her siding with the capping of Tar Sands emissions and acceptance of the carbon tax for Alberta, when combined with the terrible down turn in the Alberta economy, were a death knell to term as premier.

Because Kenny was aware of Notley's personal appeal, he fought the election claiming he was opposing the Trudeau-Notley coalition against Alberta jobs. The NDP countered with personal attacks against Kenny about his long-ago statements seen as being not supportive of the LGBTQ+ community and alleging that he used if not illegal, then at least improper, tactics to win the leadership of his party.

BRITISH COLUMBIA: Since the 1970s, British Columbia, with its 3.8 million inhabitants, has sometimes been referred to as "Lotus Land" because of its economic opportunities and relaxed and experimental life-styles. In Canada it conjured up images of a California in the North. British Columbia is the third largest province in size and population after Ontario and Quebec. About two-fifths of the province's people live in the greater Vancouver area. Facing Asia, its economic reach extends to the Orient.

In the May 2009, provincial elections the Liberals won a historic third straight victory. In a referendum at the same time, the complicated single transferable voting system was again rejected. The method is simply too complicated for voters. Christy Clark, a former talk radio host, became premier had been a scrappy former deputy premier, earning such descriptions as "pit bull" and "acid-tongued Liberal hellcat." Yet, she left politics for six years to be a good mother to her son.

Election day May 17, 2005 was a historic occasion: it was the first serving government in Canada to go to the polls on a date fixed by the legislature almost four years earlier. Henceforth regular elections in British Columbia are conducted every four years, depriving the governing party of the advantage of calling a vote at the most favorable time.

Citizens were also asked to vote on a complicated new electoral system, the single transferable method used in Ireland, which allows voters to rank all the candidates in their riding regardless of party. Those who end up with the most votes win. The measure barely fell short of the required threshold of 60% approval, winning 57%. Voters are excused for being somewhat baffled by their choice among 45 parties that registered for the elections including the Work Less Party of British Columbia, the Sex Party, the British Columbia Marijuana Party, the People of British Columbia Millionaires Party, and two separatist parties.

In the actual May 2017 election, the Liberals won the most seats, 43 of 87, but fell short of a majority. Voters in Vancouver, where half of the province's population lives, flocked to the NPD and Greens, which formed a narrow coalition government with New Democrat John Horgan as premier. This was the first time the Greens experienced real political power in North America. The election of 2020 saw Horgan increase his party's seats, from 41 to 57, with the Liberals the big losers, dropping from 41 to 28 seats. However, the Greens retained both of their seats.

The British Columbian dream has always had two Achilles heels: its dependence on natural resources and exporting. Although the province has experienced a transformation from a resource-based economy, now only 17% of its GDP, to a more service and manufacturing-based economy, it is still not fully prepared for today's global competition. Operating costs are high, which reflects elevated wages, living costs, and personal tax rates. Labor laws are restrictive and governmental regulation of the economy is excessive by North American standards. Taking pages from the success of neighboring Alberta's government, provincial leaders were pursuing tax cuts and privatizations.

In 2006, British Columbia and Alberta agreed to drop their interprovincial trade barriers and recognize each other's standards in more than 60 professions. This Trade, Investment, and Labour Mobility Agreement, called TILMA, is meant to save money and create jobs. Saskatchewan joined TILMA.

Thanks to China's insatiable appetite for natural resources, British Columbia is experiencing an economic upsurge with investment rising and unemployment falling. Chinese imports have saved its coal industry with its 25 billion tons of proven reserves. Three new mines have opened, bringing the total to nine in 2005. Copper, zinc, and molybdenum mining is booming, as is gas and oil production. British Columbia's lumber industry has found a new market in China. This resource boom brings prosperity to some of the province's poorer areas. British Columbia is well positioned for the future as North America increasingly looks toward Asia and as Ontario's manufacturing prowess is waning.

Crime

One export crop that is booming is B.C.'s marijuana, reputed to be three to five times more potent than Mexican or Caribbean varieties, including a popular variety called "B.C. bud." It is reported to be the province's most lucrative export crop, by 2008 worth from $5 billion to $7 billion each year, almost as much as the value of the province's tourist industry. It is estimated that the marijuana industry employs more people than do traditional sectors like forestry. The number of Canadians directly employed by the cannabis cultivation industry has increased by 250% in the past year according to Statistics Canada since the legalization of marijuana in October 2018. Canada has emerged as the dominant export of marijuana which Arcview Market Research and BDS Analytics estimated at 14.9 billion in sales for 2019. Despite the legalization of marijuana, the U.S. still treats it as illegal and ineligible for export. U.S. border officials estimate that marijuana smuggling increased tenfold from 1997 to 1999 and blame the upsurge partly on the leniency of B.C. courts. By 2008, Quebec had overtaken British Columbia both in terms of marijuana production and popularity among American consumers.

In July 2005, police shut down an elaborate 360-foot tunnel from a shed in Canada to a living room 300 feet inside the U.S. border in Washington state that was used to smuggle drugs. This was the first tunnel to be discovered at the Canadian one. Responding to requests by American investigators, Canadian authorities raided the headquarters of the British Columbia Marijuana Party, arresting its leader, Marc Emery, who had been operating a thriving mail-order business selling marijuana seeds over the Internet.

In 1999, the B.C. attorney general, Ujjal Dosanjh, a Sikh born in the Punjab state of India, became the first non-white to head a provincial government. He left India at age 17 for England. After four years there, he came to British Columbia in 1968 and earned a law degree. Canada's 400,000-strong Sikh community, concentrated in British Columbia and Ontario, produced an impressive list of leading Canadians. They included former Federal Fisheries Minister Herb Dhaliwal, figure skater Emanuel Sandhu, the federal Tory government's secretary of state for democratic reform Tim Uppal and the defense minister in Justin Trudeau's cabinet, Harjit Sajjan.

Because of their religion, some Sikh men have won the right in court to wear their beards and turbans while pursuing careers as Mounties or as boxers. Many, like Dosanjh, do not do that. In 1985 Dosanjh was attacked and beaten with an iron pipe by religious extremists angry because he had condemned their terror-based campaign for Punjabi independence. British Columbia is plagued by bloody Sikh gang warfare over drugs, money, and women in which most victims are Sikhs themselves. The Sikh gangs are Canada's most murderous.

In 2003, a Sikh separatist in Vancouver was incarcerated for five years after being the first to admit guilt in making the explosives for the 1985 bombing of Air India Flight 182 off the Atlantic coast of Ireland killing all 331 persons aboard, most of them Canadian. The dreadful deed, the worst terrorist act in Canadian history, was committed in revenge for the Indian

Hon. David Eby, Premier of British Columbia

army's storming of the Sikhs' holiest shrine, the Golden Temple, a year earlier. The publicity about this bloody behavior helps explain why only 30% of Canadians said in a 2009 poll that they had a positive view of Sikhism.

In April 2003, the trial of two other Sikh nationalists began in the Supreme Court of British Columbia. This was the culmination of one of the most exhaustive criminal investigations in Canadian history, hampered by mysterious deaths of witnesses and the unwillingness of Sikh immigrants to cooperate with investigators. This longest, most complex, and most expensive trial in Canadian history came to an end in March 2005 when the court allowed the two to walk free, concluding that the prosecution had not made its case. The verdict caused a public uproar when it was revealed that Canadian intelligence services destroyed vital evidence. After the trial, the government ordered further inquiries, first conducted by former Ontario premier, Bob Rae, and then by a retired Supreme Court judge. The inquiry released more documents that showed that Indian officials and Air India received frequent threat assessments in advance, but treated them with suspicion, ignoring the information.

A great deal of illicit trade is conducted by brutal immigrant gangs from India and elsewhere. More than half of their trade is inside the U.S., where they often exchange drugs for cocaine, firearms, and cash. They have also tapped the Japanese market. Vancouver's seaport is a point of entry for heroin and cocaine as the province has become a key hub in international organized crime, in part because Western Canada is positioning itself to be North America's most important commercial corridor to Asia. This is ideal for criminal gangs' operations.

Gang warfare in Vancouver goes beyond Sikh and Indian circles. In 2008, 37% of homicides in British Colombia were linked or

Aboriginal guide in UBC Museum before "Big Raven"

suspected to be linked to organized crime or street crime. Because the police department is understaffed, there are few arrests and prosecutions. More and more women gang members are involved in criminal activities. In all of Canada, women now make up about 6% of gang membership, 12% in British Columbia.

Perhaps it is not surprising that when *Maclean's* looked at Canada's most dangerous cities, 11 of the top 20 were in British Columbia. Police authorities rank Vancouver on a par with Los Angeles and New York in terms of being in the grip of crime syndicates. Their activities amount to about 7% of British Columbia's economy. Vancouver experiences 3.6 times as many breakings and entries as New York City, as measured per 100,000 inhabitants.

The lamentable neglect of the Eastside of Vancouver is the focus of city elections. A coalition of community activists, unionists, pragmatic leftists, and New Democrats, known as the Coalition of Progressive Electors (COPE) captured seats on the city council as well as the school and park boards. Voters decided that they had had enough of people dying of overdoses, disease, and murder in the Eastside. The new city leaders moved to create "safe injection sites," where intravenous heroin users could inject drugs bought elsewhere without the threat of arrest under the supervision of public health care workers who would offer them safe needles and counseling to change their lives.

In 2005 Vancouver launched North America's first trial of heroin maintenance: giving addicts free heroin on the condition they enter treatment. The battered Eastside remains the most concentrated pocket of poverty and crime in Canada, with up to 1,800 homeless in the

Canada

summer. In 2001 the Supreme Court of Canada found that maintenance and treatment programs pose no threat to public health or safety.

Vancouver became the first Canadian city to legalize marijuana as did neighboring Washington state. Vancouver's change was part of a movement advocating a more lenient approach to drugs until the Tories took power in Ottawa in 2006. Such legalization was in line with Canadians' attitudes about recreational marijuana; a 2006 poll indicated that 63% were in favor. In 2018 marijuana was fully legalized in Canada. The results from a Pew Forum Research Poll indicated that 52% of those approved of legalized marijuana while 41% disapproved.

Officials in both Vancouver and British Columbia promised in their winning bid for the 2010 Winter Olympics that they would build new housing and provide more services for the poor and homeless. Officials later confessed that they budgeted insufficient funds for these initiatives.

Environment and First Nations

British Columbians are statistically Canada's healthiest people. A mere 12%, 9% in Vancouver, are obese. Only 16% smoke, and British Columbia leads a group of provinces seeking to penalize the large tobacco companies for the health damage their products cause. Healthy living is a cultural trademark of the west coast.

One of major challenges facing the government of British Columbia was environmental. It approved continued logging in two-thirds of Clayoquot Sound on the Pacific coast of Vancouver Island. Since this is one of the world's last remaining rainforests, this action infuriated conservationists all over the world. Blockades and arrests along the logging roads kept the issue on the front pages until the government announced a plan to restrict logging and create new parks. The government found itself caught in the middle between the logging industry's demands for reducing some of the requirements of the province's Forest Practices Code, and environmental groups who view the code too lax to protect the forests. A new code was enacted to reduce the size of the blocks of trees cut during harvest, to force stricter environmental practices, and to increase the fees paid by forestry companies. This satisfied nobody, and protests continued.

To stimulate the logging industry, the B.C. government slashed logging royalties. The industry's new focus is the vast, largely undisturbed mid-coast forest between Vancouver Island and southern Alaska that contains a quarter of the world's remaining temperate rain forest.

Yet, loggers face a collision with Indian villages, a cross-border alliance of environmentalists, and the tourist industry, which greets a half million tourists each year, most from the U.S.

By contrast, almost everybody approved of the 1997 creation of the 10 million acre Muskwa-Kechika wilderness preserve in the northern Rockies, one of the largest conservation initiatives in Canadian history. Many North American environmentalists greeted this as an essential piece in a possible unbroken seam of protected land running from Yellowstone Park in the South through the Yukon Territory in the North, thus "Yellowstone to Yukon" or "Y2Y."

In 2000, four major logging companies and key environmental groups in British Columbia reached a landmark truce with regard to the Great Bear Rainforest. This rainforest is a remote temperate wilderness of thousand-year-old cedar trees, fjords, inlets, islands, glacial mountains, grizzly bears, and wolves. It is considered to be the world's largest unlogged temperate rain forest. Logging activity was postponed until an unusual alliance of loggers, environmentalists, native groups, and the government of British Columbia agreed in 2006 to create Great Bear Rainforest, a park along the Pacific coast from the mid-point of Vancouver Island to the Alaska border, twice the size of Yellowstone. This area remains off-limits to logging.

In 2007, the government of British Columbia unveiled a program to make the province "the continent's greenest spot." It would close down coal-burning energy plants and help create a Pacific Coast grouping of states and provinces to deal with climate change without waiting for their respective federal governments to act. British Colombia's carbon tax came into effect in 2008. It amounted to about 2.3 cents for every liter of gasoline. Because of its carbon tax, B.C. outpaced the rest of Canada both on emission reduction and GDP group according to Stewart Elgie, a professor of law and economics at the University of Ottawa. On April 1, 2019, B.C.'s rate was $40 per ton of carbon dioxide emissions, which translates to 8.89 cents per liter of gasoline. It's set to top out at $50 tons in 2021.

British Columbia's economic problems created an uproar over offshore oil and gas development. Muted for decades by moratoria, a panel of experts concluded in 2004 that restrictions were unnecessary.

Another challenge stems from 47 native claims to most of British Columbia's land. It was the only province officially to ignore a 1763 directive by the British Crown requiring land treaties to be signed with aboriginals. It never signed treaties with the approximately 160,000 aboriginal inhabitants, leaving legal title to most of the area in dispute. The government of British Columbia joined with the federal government to try to reach a settlement. Forty of the sixty British Columbia bands have joined the negotiation process.

There is widespread nervousness, even anger, among white British Columbians when the Indian bands begin tallying their losses in modern terms. One band, the Musqueam, claims all of downtown

Vancouver and most of its suburbs because their ancestors had hunted and fished there. In 1999 the Musqueam won judicial backing for a 74-fold increase in the land-lease rates it collects from householders in a Vancouver suburb. Residents say they face ruin. As such rulings engender opposition from non-aboriginal groups, bands ponder whether they might win more of their claims in court than in negotiations. The Supreme Court of Canada came to the rescue of the 73 leaseholders in 2000 by order that they pay an annual rent of $10,000, rather than the $23,000 the band had demanded. Band members were outraged.

In 1998 the government reached an agreement with the Nisga'a band, involving 772 square miles in the breathtakingly beautiful Nass Valley on the provinces northwest coast just south of the Alaskan panhandle. In return for relinquishing claims eight times that size, the 5,000 members received $190 million and extensive powers of government: taxation, land use, family, social and health services, police, courts, schools, language, and culture. Amid a storm of protest that the terms were too generous, the legislature of British Columbia approved the treaty in April 1999 as did the federal parliament at the end of the year. Another agreement in April 1999 awarded the Sechelt Indigenous people 2,000 hectares of land 50 kilometers northwest of Vancouver and a $42 million "prosperity fund."

Because British Columbia's Liberals opposed the model of self-government won by the Nisga'a in the 1998 treaty, former-Premier Campbell committed himself to put the native treaty process to a vote. In a July 2002 referendum an overwhelming percentage of voters gave the government a strong mandate to enter a "new era of reconciliation with First Nations." Voters made it clear, though, that private property should not have been subject to negotiation, parks should have been maintained for all British Columbians, and the inherent right of self-government was not on the table. Voters were further concerned that any aboriginal self-government should have the "characteristics of local government with powers delegated from Canada and BC." Only 36% of eligible voters participated in the referendum.

In 2009 the Nisga'a broke with their tradition of holding their land in common and to permit band members to own private property. Under Canada's Indian Act, aboriginals on reserves are usually given certificates of possession for their houses, which they rent, but they do not own; they cannot even use them as collateral for loans. This Nisga'a decision could have revolutionary implications.

The Canadian government hopes that the basic principles of British Columbia's prior agreements can be applied to negotiations not only with other bands there, but with such groups as Inuit in northern Quebec and the Algonquin band which claims the land in Ottawa on which the Canadian parliament sits. In an attempt to create a better atmosphere for negotiations, the government of British Columbia apologized in 2003 for its past treatment of indigenous peoples; it vowed to resolve unfinished land treaties, acknowledging that its institutions "failed aboriginal peoples across the province." It even admitted later that it had been wrong in the way the Nisga'a were treated and in 2006 announced "A New Relationship with B.C. First Nations."

Stephen Harper's federal government joined the British Columbia government to sign treaties with the Tsawwassen, Maanulth, and Yale First Nations that set a pattern for settling future land claims. These treaties will phase out reserve-based tax exemptions. Progress is being made on the huge backlog of other unresolved treaty claims. In 2012 the Tla'amin, a small tribe on the Sunshine Coast north of Vancouver, approved a deal for self-government, 20,564 acres of land, $30.5 million in cash and a share of natural-resource revenue. In 2014, the Supreme Court of Canada ruled that the Tsilhqot'in First Nation had title to 650 square miles of land, the first time it affirmed title to a specific parcel of land.

The business community blames such native-lands claims for the fact that BC attracted only half as much investment as Alberta during the 1990s. Yet, native leader Stewart Phillip responded that this was an unavoidable reality: "If any development does not enjoy the support of aboriginal people, then it's not going to happen."

A dispute over salmon fishing brought the governments of British Columbia and Canada into direct conflict with the U.S. After a 1985 treaty regulating the size of catches by American and Canadian fishermen expired in 1992, British Columbia claimed that Americans were catching too many salmon in U.S. and international waters, thereby preventing them from spawning in provincial rivers. To underscore its indignation, the provincial government announced that it would cancel a seabed lease to a navy weapons-testing base at Nanoose Bay that American submarines used for torpedo practice. Further, the provincial government suspended British Columbia's participation in about 50 agreements with neighboring American states on various topics.

In response, the U.S. Senate voted 81 to 19 for a resolution calling on the president to send the U.S. navy to protect American ferries. Before this was seriously considered, though, the Canadian government announced that the U.S. would not be forced from the testing base. By 2005 the number of salmon spawning in the Fraser River had fallen to about five million, fewer than half the expected number. The number was reduced due to higher ocean temperatures, overfishing, the destruction of spawning habitats, and, most controversially, diseases spread from open-pen salmon farms. The numbers continue to decline. This prompted federal officials to stop sockeye fishing. The Harper government announced in 2006 an inquiry into the collapse of the Fraser River salmon fishery and its opposition to "racially divided fisheries programs." Threats to the Fraser River continue today. One of the key issues is the Big Bar slide, which blocked salmon returning to key Fraser River tributaries such as the Stuart Quesnel and Chilco river systems.

One-quarter of British Columbia's population consists of immigrants. Some British Columbians are worried about an in-pouring of rich Chinese from Hong Kong, who were resettling their families and fortunes before mainland China assumed control of the colony in 1997. Canada actively tried to lure rich foreigners into the country so they could benefit the economy. Vancouver's Chinese population jumped from 30,000 in the 1960s to more than a quarter million today. Ethnic Chinese comprise a fifth of Vancouver's population; 61% of the children in the public schools speak English as a second language.

In the 1990s Chinese people from Hong Kong Chinese were entering at the rate of more than 100 per day. Even though migrants from other Canadian provinces outnumbered those from Hong Kong by eight to one, a backlash began against arose against them with some. Many natives accuse these Chinese of buying up British Columbia's prize real estate, such as the site of Expo 86, and driving up prices for the city's land and housing.

Vancouver's approximately 630,000 residents, 2,400,000 in the larger urban area, are expected to rise to 3.4 million by 2041, pay Canada's highest prices for property: in 2021 the average home cost more than 1.4 million Canadian dollars. Even though this amount declined slightly since 2018, these prices continue to drive away many families with children. This makes Vancouver's housing the third-least affordable among the world's major cities, exceeded only by Hong Kong, and Sydney, Australia. In an effort to hold down prices, the city's government levied a 15% property purchase tax on houses over $750,000 bought by foreigners.

Canada

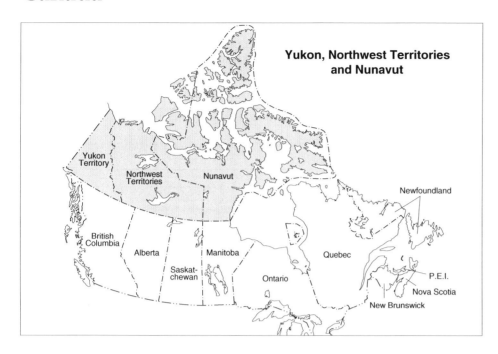

Yukon, Northwest Territories and Nunavut

THE YUKON, NORTHWEST TERRITORIES, AND NUNAVUT

As of 2018, the 35,874 residents of the Yukon, 44,541 inhabitants of the Northwest Territories (NWT), and the 38,396 people living in Nunavut took impressive steps toward self-government that they started in early 1970s. Yet, because these areas lack provincial status, they cannot unilaterally amend their constitutions, which are acts of the Canadian parliament that only the federal government can modify.

Northerners are becoming increasingly assertive, though, thereby making disagreements wider and more numerous. There are many unsettled land and mineral rights claims being made by native groups in the Yukon and Northwest Territories. As a condition for the separation of Nunavut from the NWT in 1999, all aboriginal claims were settled in Nunavut. Since the federal government receives lucrative royalties for resource extraction in the North, it is not easy for Ottawa to relinquish this power. All three depend on federal subsidies, amounting to more than $2,000,000,000 annually and accounting for 60% of budget revenues in the Yukon and Northwest Territories and close to 90% in Nunavut. Aboriginal groups also benefit from a host of other federal programs such as being exempt from taxes even though the Inuit must pay them.

All three territories have developed de facto responsible government. Put another way, the commissioners, formally the chief executives within the areas appointed by Ottawa and answering to the

British Columbia's former lieutenant governor, wealthy Vancouver businessman David See-Chai Lam, was Canada's first citizen of Chinese descent to occupy a vice-regal office. Lam, who donated up to $5 million to charitable causes each year, was an ideal man to help deal with this delicate and emotionally-charged issue. By 1999 the influx had slowed dramatically, as the number of immigrants dropped by about 30%. Also, the composition changed from wealthy Hong Kong investors to small business owners and young factory workers from Taiwan and China.

In February 2010, Vancouver and the nearby Whistler Resort hosted the Winter Olympics. Nervous organizers had to borrow money, import snow, look for ways to scale back on expenses, and make the event a little less spectacular than they had hoped. There were some miscalculations. One was the assumption that the 737 apartments in the Olympic Village, later named Millennium Water, could be sold without loss after the games finished. Given the economic recession, only half of the homes were sold at expected prices, and for a while the entire village had the air of a ghost town. The city had to assume the loan and sell the remaining apartments for about half the original prices, leaving taxpayers with a $200–$300 million loss. It is usually hard to lose money in Vancouver real estate; in 2011 *The Economist* again named Vancouver the most livable city anywhere.

From the moment three billion viewers tuned in to the opening ceremonies, it was clear that the Games would be among the best in history. Vancouver was the scene of spectacular Canadian athletic triumphs and an outpouring of Canadian pride.

More recently, the British Columbia government opposed the building of the Trans Mountain Pipeline from Alberta to the provincial coast. The federal government paid the original owner, Kinder Morgan 4.5 billion dollars for ownership of the pipeline after delays by British Columbia threatened that Kinder Morgan would walk away from the project.

Then Premier Notley threatened to shut off oil supplies from Alberta to British Columbia thereby triggering a gas shortage if its government continued to put impediments in the way of building the pipeline. The Federal Court of Appeal held that there had been insufficient consultation with Aboriginal groups in British Columbia and that the pipeline could not proceed until new consultation talks had been completed. It was, as one commentator said, a real mess. The federal government could use its disallowance power under the constitution and section 33 of the Charter if necessary to push the completion of the pipeline but it has chosen to start consultation rather than appeal to the Supreme Court of Canada or to take extraordinary legislative measures. However, on December 31, 2019, the Supreme Court of British Colombia granted an injunction barring member from the Indigenous nation from obstructing work on TransCanada's coastal gaslink pipeline from Burnaby, B.C to Edmonton, Alberta. Protesters continue to express frustration and Indigenous groups have 60 days to appeal the decision.

**Hon. Ranj Pillai,
Premier of Yukon**

Minister of Indian Affairs and Northern Development, accept the decisions made by the members of elected assemblies. Leaders, who call themselves premier, are selected by their legislative assemblies and are formally appointed by the commissioners. The commissioners behave like provincial lieutenant governors insofar as they do not overrule decisions made by the legislative assemblies.

Yukon

Self-government along the Canadian model proceeded fastest in the Yukon, the formal name of which was changed from Yukon Territory in 2002. The construction of the Alaskan Highway in 1942 brought thousands of immigrants into the Yukon, making the native population a minority. Because there are three times as many non-natives as First Nations people and Inuit in the Yukon, the demand for Canadian institutions was greatest there.

In 1978, party politics replaced a system of loose alliances with party discipline enabling the legislative system to operate more or less like any provincial government in Canada. Of course, it is no simple matter practicing democracy in a territory larger than France with only 16,000 registered voters, scattered in 17 ridings with as few as about residents in the smallest, Old Crow, many of whom are reachable only by airplane or dogsled, and in temperatures as low as minus-50 degrees centigrade on election day.

The government seeks to revive the declining mining industry while at the same time stimulating tourism, presently the Yukon's main industry, drawing 300,000 each year and diversifying the economy. In 2018, \$146.1 million, or 5.0% of Yukon's total GDP based on tourism. Gold production was only a tenth of what it was in its heyday, but the discovery of hard-rock deposits in 2011 sparked a gold rush. The 1997 closure of the lead-zinc mine at Faro, which had contributed a fifth of the Yukon's \$1 billion GDP, was distressing. A fascinating benefit of mining in the territory is that a treasure of ancient fossils tens of thousands of years old is uncovered as rock layers are blasted.

The social and economic challenges are daunting: almost a third of the workforce is employed by one of the three levels of government, and seasonal unemployment is high. As is true everywhere in the North, prices of products shipped in from the South, including food, are expensive because the Yukon has only about 160 working farms. The Yukon faces a severe housing crunch, as citizens oppose new housing developments at a time when Canadians are migrating to Yukon in great numbers to benefit from high-paying jobs in mining and government. The average price for a single-family home was a record \$455,000 in 2012, twice the price only six years earlier. As of 2020, the average cost was \$508,800. In Whitehorse, the capital the average price reached \$598,800 in 2021, up 13.9% from the previous year.

As dependent on Ottawa financially as the Yukon is, its leadership is gradually taking over more federal powers, such as resources, education, and health. In 2003, after 10 years of negotiations, Ottawa granted it control over its natural resources, one of the final steps on the road toward becoming a province. The two levels of government subsequently tangled over exploiting the Peel Watershed for its huge deposits of coal, gas, and minerals.

Disproportionately high levels of family breakdown and alcohol and drug abuse plague the Yukon. Even former Liberal leader Roger Coles was imprisoned in 1986 for cocaine trafficking. The capital city of Whitehorse, where 70% of the population lives, has a homicide rate 355% higher than the Canadian average. The good news is that the crime rate dropped more than 36% from 2000 to 2010. The crime rate in the Yukon dropped even further 2017-2018, from 183 to 170.34 according to Statistics Canada. In 2020, the Crime Severity Index had risen to 215.7.

In 1992, the Tories, who renamed themselves the Yukon Party to break ties with their unpopular federal counterpart, regained power but relinquished it to the NDP in 1996. The 2000 elections continued the game of musical chairs. For the first time since party politics were introduced to the Yukon in 1978, the Liberals won, as their leader, Pat Duncan, formed the government.

In 2002, she handed the reins of power to Dennis Fentie, leader of the Yukon Party. In May 2011, he made way for Darrell Pasloski, a Whitehorse pharmacist and community leader, who led the Yukon party to its third majority government in the 2011 provincial elections. While the 2016 elections produced a liberal majority, with Sandy Silver becoming premier, the 2021 elections produced a hung parliament, with both the Liberals and the Yukon Party capturing 8 seats. In April 2021, the Liberals formed a minority

Aerial view of Whitehorse, capital of the Yukon and home for two-thirds of the Yukon's inhabitants. In the foreground is the S.S. Klondike, a national historical site, which saw regular service from the 1930s until the early 1950s, carrying passengers and freight on the Yukon River between Dawson City and Whitehorse.

Canada

Hon. Caroline Cochrane
Premier, Northwest Territories

government with the New Democrats entering a formal confidence and supply agreement, for a total of 11 combined seats. Sandy Silver remained premier.

Northwest Territories

In contrast to the Yukon, native people constitute about 48% of the overall population in the Northwest Territories (NWT), a plural name that is likely to be singularized in the future. The various ethnic groups are not spread evenly over this gigantic region extending about 500,000 square miles and located mainly above the tree line. The population of the NWT consists of 52% non-aboriginal, 28% Dene, 9% Métis and smatterings of other aboriginals, speaking nine official aboriginal languages, including North Slavey, South Slavey, Cree, Chipewyan, Dogrib, Gwich'in, Inuvialuktun, plus English and French. One tenth are Inuvialuit or Western Inuit, who face daunting challenges because life expectancy is 10 years shorter than the Canadian average, the youth suicide rate is eight times higher, tuberculosis rates are 17 times higher, and dropping out of school is far more common than earning diplomas.

In 2003 a landmark agreement was reached with the 4,000 Dogrib Indigenous people who call themselves the Tlicho First Nation. Following the treaty with British Columbia's Nisga'a, this was only the second agreement that grants the inherent right to self-government to aboriginals. In the process they gained ownership of an area of 15,000 square miles, or almost as large as Switzerland, around Yellowknife between Great Slave Lake and the Great Bear Lake together with its natural

resources. Abutting a diamond industry from which it gains 2% of the royalties, and all from any future mines, the Tlicho could become one of the richest First Nation groups in North America; they make and enforce laws, collect taxes, levy royalties on mines, and regulate land use, education, family, and traditional medicine.

The NWT is a land rich in diamonds, oil, and gas with three operating diamond mines and many more planned. Diamonds now make up more than half of NWT's economic output. The last exhausted gold mine closed in 2005. One abandoned gold mine in Yellowknife, Giant Mine, contains deadly toxic arsenic waste, one of many sites that are the government's responsibility.

To facilitate traffic to and from mines, exploration, sites and remote communities, authorities build a thousand miles, or about 1,450 kilometers, of winter roads each year. The busiest runs about 280 miles or 420 kilometers northeast from Yellowknife, over more than 30 frozen lakes. Others run into neighboring Nunavut. An increasing problem is that global warming is shortening the time that trucks can cross ice, leaving mining operations short of the necessary huge construction equipment and vast quantities of supplies and fuel, which must then be flown in at great expense. Without the full use of these winter roads, the NWT's economic lifeblood is threatened.

Distance and the tenuous road conditions drive food prices up; a head of cabbage can cost $28, and a 24-pack of water can run $65. With prices like this, there can be no wonder why an estimated one-third of children go to bed hungry. Of course, global warming creates problems for the Inuit as they must deal with unpredictable sea ice that can be fatal, snowmobiles must take longer routes, and their buildings are weakened by melting permafrost.

The NWT is more self-sufficient and economically healthier than is Nunavut. The separation of Nunavut from the NWT in 1999 caused some economic suffering for the latter's gritty frontier capital, Yellowknife's population of about 19,500 as of the last available date accounts for the largest share of the NWT's estimated population of 45,136.

On a negative note, the NWT lost about 500 federal and territorial government jobs along with some of its much-needed transfer payments from Ottawa. It also suffers from a chronic shortage of doctors and nurses. From 2000 to 2010 the crime rate in the NWT rose by 35%. Aggravated assault in the capital of Yellowknife is more than 350% higher than the average in Canada. Yet, in the 21st century tourism, especially among Japanese, is thriving. Yellowknife's economy is robust, thanks in large part to

Hon. P. J. Akeeagok Premier of Nunavut

the mining boom. While Tiffany's has established a cutting and polishing factory in the town, housing remains tight while drug use and crime are problems.

The prospect of uranium deposits in the north has attracted even more interest in the NWT. In an effort to protect their territory and its Boreal Forest, a huge green swath across North America that is crucial for wildlife, native groups and the Canadian government agreed to move toward preserving an area four times the size of Yellowstone Park from diamond and uranium mining interests.

In the NWT's non-party system, the Legislative Assembly has the chance to review government leaders every two years. Since October 2019 the premier is Caroline Cochrane, who succeded Bob McLeod on his retirement.

By tradition, the NWT's is only one of two legislatures in all of Canada, the other being in Nunavut, that reaches decisions by consensus, rather than by party politics and majority votes. In fact, there is no formal opposition in the NWT legislative assembly. During sessions members use their own languages, with all remarks being translated into the other official languages from interpreter booths. For the time, being the NWT retains its name and territorial government. A new territorial constitution is being written and possible changes in the political system are being considered. During sessions members use their own languages, with all remarks being translated into the other official languages from interpreter booths. For the time, being the NWT retains its name and territorial government. A new territorial constitution is being written.

Nunavut

The Inuit, "The People," singular: Inuk, called "Eskimo" in Alaska, a term meaning "meat-eater" that these people resent, comprise 85% of the people in a definable area to the northeast of the NWT. In 1976 the Inuit Tapirisat of Canada, the national Inuit organization, asked that the former NWT be split in two. The result was the establishment of a new eastern Arctic territory named Nunavut, "Our Land," on April 1, 1999.

The Inuit disliked sharing power with people who have nothing culturally in common with them. Nunavut is much more homogeneous than the NWT. The Inuit, a gentle maritime people, have a different temperament than the NWT's mixture of "frontier mavericks and fractious aboriginal groups," as Maclean's described them. Inuit found many Canadian institutions alien, and considered Yellowknife to be too far away and too Canadian for their taste. For instance, one Inuit school supervisor in the Baffin region, located 2,500 kilometers and two time zones from Yellowknife, argued that the capital "is so far distant that I don't think they realize the impact of their decisions on our communities."

In 1982, the Inuit persuaded the territorial government to conduct a referendum in the NWT to determine whether there was popular support for such a division. The result was that 56% of voters supported the change. Inuit leaders made the division of the NWT the major item on their political agenda.

The breakthrough was made in 1992 when 54% of NWT voters accepted an agreement with the Canadian government. With a population of only 32,200 at that time, Nunavut's predominantly Inuit population, about 85% of its residents, extend over 772,000 square miles in the Eastern Arctic, almost entirely above the tree line. They are settled in 26 communities, which can be reached only by plane or ship. There are no road connections. The 300 kilometers or 200 miles of roads are mostly gravel streets within the communities and end at the last house, where the wilderness begins. There are only about 20 miles of paved highways. The population has grown 12.7% between 2011 and 2016, reaching 35, 944 in 2016. In 2021 the population was 39,285.

Perhaps the largest peaceful land settlement in history, the new territory comprises a fifth of Canada's land area, two-thirds of its coastline, and traverses three time zones. Nunavut is the size of California and Alaska combined. In Canadian terms, it is equivalent to British Columbia, Alberta, and the Yukon combined, or twice as large as Ontario.

Inuit received legal title to 136,000 square miles, mineral rights to 14,000 square miles, and $1,148 billion over 14 years. In return, the Inuit had to renounce their claim to another 640,000 square miles of ancestral terrain, possibly containing rich gas and oil fields, which remain Crown land. Nevertheless, the Inuit receive a share in federal royalties from gas, oil, and mineral deposits on Crown lands, as well as hunting and fishing rights over all of Nunavut. As one participant in the negotiations put it, "We're a small people, but we have big ambitions."

In a plebiscite to choose their capital, the Inuit selected Iqaluit, pronounced ee-KA-loo-eet, formerly called Frobisher Bay, a modern community on the southern tip of Baffin Island. Iqaluit is Canada's fastest-growing capital, with about 7,000 inhabitants as of 2019 but it is so small that there is no need for street names. Buildings simply have numbers.

Iqaluit launched the first Internet web site in the Inuktitut language, the first language for 70% of the territory's people. Along with English and French, it is an official language and the one that is used as much as possible in government. Fearing that Inuktitut will slowly die in the capital, then Premier Okalik ordered senior bureaucrats to learn the language if they want to keep their jobs. Laws are being drafted to make it Nunavut's working language by 2020. Television broadcasting is available in both Inuktitut and English. In Iqaluit one hears more English than Inuktitut, but the latter predominates in the 24 smaller communities. There is a local newspaper called the *Nunatsiaq News*.

Public school instruction is offered in Inuktitut, but parents may opt for English schooling. Increasingly, English is the language of choice among young Inuit, a matter of concern for elders. By 2015 only 63% of Inuit could speak Inuktitut. Instruction is given in Inuktitut until grade 3 or 4 then it tapers off and English is favored. There is also no universally recognized spelling and grammar for the Inuktitut.. In a 2006 poll, only 18% of students responded that they speak more Inuktitut than English in school. Part of the problem is a severe shortage of Inuktitut-speaking teachers. Only about a fourth of Inuit children graduate from high school causing Nunavut to have the lowest literacy rate in Canada.

Another problem is that two-thirds of Inuit children suffer some degree of hearing loss due to chronic ear infections. Teachers wear wireless microphone headsets to amplify their lessons in speaker-equipped classrooms. There is also an acute lack of dental care. Children with braces must fly south twice every two

Inuit camp, Baffin Island, Nunavut

Canada

months with a guardian for treatments; the average price to the government of each appointment is $25,806.

Nunavut Arctic College offers some academic courses in both English and Inuktitut, training teachers as well as instructing Inuit artisans who wish to diversify their products. In 2005 a joint effort of the College and University of Victoria trained 11 law graduates in order to afford the territory and its people more professional expertise rooted in native culture. In 2009 work began on an Inuit cultural school in Clyde River, which will have satellite campuses teaching cultural programs in Baker Lake and Igloolik. Since completion in 2011 the school provides full scholarships for 26 students age 18 or over. The school's name, *Piqqusilirivvik*, means "a place that has those things important to us" in Inuktitut.

The NWT and Nunavut each send one MP to the House of Commons in Ottawa and a Senate seat. Nunavut has an Inuit-controlled government with its own legislature, cabinet and court system, representing North America's boldest experiment to give a native group so much self-determination. In elections to their legislative assembly, many of the ballots must be dropped by planes into remote settlements. In the vote for the first legislature, held on February 15, 1999, 88% of eligible voters participated.

Under their nonpartisan political system, in which there are no parties and decisions are made by consensus, the 19 newly elected members meet for days after an election to choose their governmental leader. Their 19 seats are in a circle, not divided by an aisle to separate right and left, government and opposition, surrounded by symbols of their unique environment. The first item one sees on entering the premier's office is a huge polar-bear rug. The upholstery in the legislative chamber one floor below is of seal skin. The door handles are made of walrus tusk, and the shaft of the ceremonial mace that symbolizes legitimacy is the tusk of a narwhal, a small Arctic whale.

The premier must consult with all the Members of the Legislative Assembly (MLAs), not just the cabinet, which the MLAs, not the premier, select. They have become more comfortable with Westminster traditions, such as addressing all comments to the speaker. Still, there have been some critics of this unique government without parties and a loyal opposition. Critics contend that there is no mechanism for accountability, that deals involve too much pork-barrel politics, and that there is no way for voters to "send a message" to the government. Supporters respond that because the nonpartisan, consensual system is the Inuit way, it allows the most talented people in the entire legislature to form the government.

In April 1999, the one female and 18 male deputies selected lawyer Paul Okalik as premier. Easily reelected in 2004, his vision was "that we achieve the same standard of living as other Canadians and at the same time preserve our culture and language." Okalik personally experienced the troubles afflicting his entire Inuit people. Okalik was young enough to be the only premier in Canada still paying off his student loans when he took office. Okalik governed a young region with the continent's highest birth rate and where 40% of the population is under age 15 and half under 22; it is young men aged 15 to 29 who commit two-thirds of the crime. He also survived alcoholism, a term in prison, and a brother's suicide.

In November 2008, Eva Aariak succeeded Okalik as premier, serving until 2013. Peter Taptuna served from 2013 until November 2017, Paul Quassa until November 2018, followed by Joe Savikataaq, who took office on June 14, 2018. The current premier, P. J. Akeeagok, assumed office on November 19, 2021.

The rate of heavy drinking in Nunavut is three times the Canadian average, and a quarter of all babies are born with fetal alcohol syndrome. Only six communities, down from eight, are dry. The wet counties have three times the number of homicides and almost double the number of assaults. The head of Nunavut's RCMP said the root of all crime is "alcohol, alcohol, alcohol." Even in places where citizens have voted by plebiscite to prohibit alcohol, these decisions are undermined by bootleggers. This helps make the territories the most dangerous parts of Canada. From 2000 to 2010, the crime rate rose by 38%. The murder rate is ten times higher than the national average. Because jail space is so limited, Nunavut must pay

Dog team on the ice, Simpson Strait, Northwest Territories

to send some offenders to NWT to serve their sentences.

The suicide rate is seven times higher in Nanavut than the Canadian average. Young men are almost 30 times more likely to commit suicide with young women aged 15 to 24 are 36 times more likely to take their own lives than other Canadian women. Teacher Sheila Levy admitted: "suicide touches everyone here." In an attempt to combat this tragedy, a new mental health center was created in Iqaluit.

Drug addiction is epidemic in Nanavut. The lowest form of substance abuse, solvent sniffing, is 26 times more prevalent than in Canada as a whole; 20% of the people admit doing it. Aggravated assault is 1,033% higher, and sexual assaults are 1,270% more likely than in the rest of Canada. The rate of sexually transmitted disease is 15 times the national average.

A shocking dimension of this horrible crime rate in Nanavut is that some of the territory's political leaders show such bad examples. Levi Barnabas was given a cabinet post despite being convicted for sexual assault while he was Speaker of the House. James Arvaluk became education minister even though he served prison time for rape and assault, having beaten a former girlfriend so brutally that she needed 18 stitches to sew up her mouth and sustained permanent nerve damage. Lorne Kusugak was unanimously appointed to a cabinet post two months after being charged with sexual assault and trying to strangle his victim.

A major contributor to these lamentable social problems in Nanavut is the lack of work. The official unemployment rate in 2004 was 30% among Inuit. Yet, if one includes those who have given up looking for a job, the figure increases to an estimated 37% of Inuit. Due to the extremely high birthrate, many children will never find future jobs. By contrast, unemployment among the non-Inuit minority was only about 4%. Of the 2,789 jobs created in the territory's new public service by 2006, 45% went to Inuit, short of the stated goal of 50%.

Unemployment is especially serious because Nunavut has Canada's highest cost of living and lowest per capita income, a third of that in the NWT. In 2012 a bag of flour cost $33 and 10 pieces of chicken $61.99. It is small wonder that hunger is one of Nunavut's most persistent social ills. Nearly 70% of preschool children in Nanavut live in "food insecure" households. Some provide for their families by going outside the wage economy and engaging in hunting and fishing. The government encourages the consumption of local food such as seal, muskox and ground squirrels. It also subsidizes large-scale hunts to increase the food supply. A third of the residents receive welfare, more than three times the Canadian average. This does not go far for the 60% of adults who smoke; they pay $15 per pack. The government has launched an aggressive anti-smoking campaign.

Most jobs in Nanavut are related to government spending, which accounts for more than half of Nunavut's employment. What little private sector is in Nanavut depends directly on government projects such as construction. Only five communities exist in Nunavut where getting a job is a viable option. Not including the land-claim payments, Ottawa sends Nunavut 90% of the territory's revenues. Per capita handouts amount to $21,622 each year in addition to $40,000 per person in "compensation" payments.

Nunavut has a small tax base. It gets about five times as much revenue from tobacco taxes as from corporate income taxes. Lodging is a serious problem and is expensive: 83% live in government-subsidized housing. This situation stems from the 1950s when the federal government forced the nomadic Inuit to resettle in permanent communities, resorting to such brutal measures as shooting their dogs. In 1992 the Canadian government formally apologized to more than a hundred Inuit who, in the 1950s, had been forced to move from their northern Quebec homes to the desolate high Arctic settlements of Resolute Bay and Grise Fiord. The purpose was to assert Canadian sovereignty over the area where a U.S. military outpost was located.

Prospects for economic development are not encouraging. Nunavut has fewer developed resources than the NWT. The best hope for broadening the tax base is mining although extraction costs of many of its resources are prohibitively high. By century's end, three mines were producing lead, zinc, gold and silver. The first diamond mine opened, Jericho, just south of the Arctic Circle. Jericho is largely responsible for Nunavut's economic growth rate in 2006 of 5.8%, second only to oil-rich Alberta. Ottawa takes 95% of the revenue on mining riches and all three northern premiers want a bigger share.

A 1993 land claims settlement requires outside investors to draw up "impact benefit agreements" with local communities.

Mobility must be by air. This creates obstacles in developing the tourist industry. The federal government is committed to creating three new national parks in the territory and eco-tourism is rising. Still, with round-trip air tickets from Ottawa to Iqaluit costing over $2,000, tourism in Nunavut is for the well-to-do.

The Nunavut government engages in devolution talks with Ottawa while the premier meets independently of the Canadian government with the opposite number in Greenland. The topics of discussion include greater independence and control over natural resources. Greenland Air introduced direct flights between Nuuk and Iqaluit while Iqaluit and Nuuk co-hosted the hockey matches in the 2016 Arctic Winter Games.

Perhaps the highest-level tourists came to town in early February 2010: the finance ministers of the Group of Seven, the world's leading developed nations. Canada's choice of location was inspired by the wish to assert Canadian sovereignty in the Arctic and to take a stand against the European Union's ban on seal products. The ministers were invited to a "community feast" and served seal meat, caribou, char jerky, and muskox along with being given souvenirs of sealskin mittens and waistcoats. In August 2009, then Prime Minister Harper brought his entire cabinet to Iqaluit for a meeting as a part of a five-day visit to the Arctic. While in Iqaluit, cabinet members ate raw seal meat to take a swipe at the EU and to make a gesture of solidarity with the Inuit. Former Governor General Jean made the same gesture by eating a raw seal heart.

Most Canadians must experience the extraordinary light and sweep of the Arctic through films. The first Inuit-language feature in history, *Atanarjuat*, The Fast Runner, about an epic tale of love, jealousy, murder, and revenge, directed by Zacharias Kanuk, was greeted by rave reviews at the 2001 Cannes film festival. Award-winning Canadian filmmaker John Houston, who grew up in the Arctic and speaks fluent Inuktituk, turned his artistic talent to Nunavut. His *Songs in Stone*, about his Inuit art collecting parents in the North, opened in 1999. In 2001, Kanuk followed up with a documentary, *Nuliajuk: Mother of the Sea Beasts*, about a legendary sea deity by that name. No one can view these works without experiencing fascination for the Inuit imagination.

Canada

PARTIES AND ELECTIONS

Like any modern democracy, the Canadian political system could not function without parties. They recruit and select candidates, define issues which are important, educate voters about themselves and the issues, finance and fight electoral campaigns, put up governments which rule at all political levels, and provide well organized opposition parties, which continually remind the electorate of the governments' shortcomings. For the government, the party is an essential tool for maintaining cohesion and discipline among members and thus a parliamentary majority, and for the individual politician it is the ladder to power. For the political activist it is an important means for putting her ideas into practice, and for the voter it is an indispensable label for the set of politicians, policies, sympathies or interests.

Canadian parties emerged even before Confederation and were originally named and modeled after the two major British parties in the 19th century, the Conservatives and Liberals. For a while, they were loose coalitions of various factions with little discipline and almost no organization outside of parliament. By the end of the 19th century, though, they had changed considerably to conform to the nature of the Canadian state and society. They now have distinctive characteristics insofar as they are decentralized, which is exactly what one would expect in such a federal state. At the bottom is the local poll organization, and above that is the riding (district) organization, which selects the candidates for parliamentary elections.

Unlike in the United States, it is not necessary in Canada for a candidate to reside in the riding in which he runs. It is a fairly strong tradition, however, that the candidate be from the constituency. Occasionally higher party officials will ask a riding to allow a certain person to run in that electoral district. This is usually a party leader or cabinet member who desperately needs a parliamentary seat in order to be in a government or be a leader in the parliamentary opposition. An example of this was Brian Mulroney, who had never held an elective office before he was selected as Conservative party leader in 1983. In order to lead his then opposition party in the House of Commons, an MP from Nova Scotia agreed to give up his seat so that Mulroney could win it in a by-election. Since Mulroney had lived in the area as an undergraduate at St. Francis Xavier University, and since the riding organization calculated that it would doubtlessly benefit in the long run by lending a helping hand to a person who was likely to become the country's prime minister, it agreed to the move. However, the point must be reiterated: higher party bosses cannot simply "parachute" outsiders into ridings whenever they wish to do so. If the riding organization says "no!", then that is the answer. However, the leader of a party can stop someone from being a candidate for the party,

Parties also have regional and provincial associations. Most major parties maintain permanent provincial headquarters, which help the federal parties conduct campaigns during federal parliamentary elections. At the top is the national headquarters. Except for the headquarters in Ottawa and the provincial capitals, most of the lower party organizations more or less hibernate between elections. They remain ready to spring into action at a day's notice to wage electoral campaigns. The dates for these elections are never known long in advance. They are almost always determined by premiers and prime ministers to take place at their party's advantage. Provincial elections are never timed to coincide with federal elections. The national headquarters has a staff to support the party in a variety of ways. They hire issue consultants and pollsters, print literature and posters, and order campaign paraphernalia. They also plan party conventions, and generally serve the parliamentary party organizations in any way they can.

Party headquarters help raise money for campaigns. Elections have become very expensive, although Canadian candidates do not yet spend as much as their American counterparts. In 1963 Quebec became the first province to pass spending limits for campaigns. Some other provinces later followed suit and have a variety of spending ceilings. In 1974 the Trudeau government placed limits on federal election expenses. For example, in the 1988 elections, Canadian candidates were limited to spending a total of $6.6 million during the 51-day campaign, whereas American candidates spent $140 million in a campaign lasting two years.

Subsequent 2003 legislation also grants tax deductions for political contributions. Candidates who win more than 10% of the votes in their ridings recoup 60% of their expenses from the government. In addition, the federal government provides to candidates from recognized parties a certain amount of free broadcasting time. These contributions from state coffers have helped all the parties, particularly the NDP, which, unlike the Liberals and Conservatives, always had difficulty obtaining contributions from well-to-do individuals or corporations. It has had to rely more on dues from party members and affiliated labor unions than have the other two parties.

The volatility of public election finance was demonstrated in 2008, when a Tory budget provision that would have eliminated it almost brought the newly reelected minority government down. This seemed blatantly partisan since the Conservatives were in good financial condition while the other parties' finances were desperate. The measure was withdrawn. But in 2011 reductions in the maximum campaign contribution from $5,000 to $1,000 went into effect. This change prevented Liberals from fully tapping their

Federal Election 2021, Leaders Debate, Montreal, September 2, 2021: Prime Minister Justin Trudeau (Liberal), Yves Blanchet (Bloc Québécois), Jagmeet Singh (New Democratic Party), Erin OToole (Conservative Party), TVA moderator Pierre Bruneau.

Martin Chevalier/Le Journal de Montreal/Pool Reuters

stable of big donors. Federal election subsidies also began to be phased out from 2011 to 2015. Parties that received at least 2% of the votes received got a subsidy of $2.00 per voter.

Broadcasters are usually prohibited from announcing the results of federal elections in provinces where the polls have not yet closed. Thus, western Canadians would not be influenced in their voting by knowing how their eastern countrymen had voted. That rule was set aside by the Supreme Court in 2004 on the grounds that it is an infringement on the freedom of speech. Of course, the internet makes it impossible to black out results from being disseminated anywhere in Canada. But in 2004 and 2006 western Canadians could watch the returns in the east before deciding whether or how to vote.

Despite a kind of party structure that appears to be hierarchically organized from top to bottom, there are no powerful, country-wide parties that can hold the disparate governmental and party elements together and facilitate compromise or smooth out regional differences. No parties are powerful in all parts of the country; all have their fortresses and deserts. After 2006 the Liberals were weak in the West, the NDP had barely a toehold in the Maritimes, and until 1984 and again after 2006 there was almost nothing more depressing than being a Conservative (Tory) in Quebec. Also, regional parties can differ greatly from the national parties that bear the same names.

Although the overall organization is loose *outside* of legislative assemblies, the *parliamentary parties* are tightly bound and led. MPs or MLAs vote against their party leaders only at risk to their political careers. Indeed, as the SNC-Lavalin Affair demonstrated, those who do not support one issue, which is deemed highly significant to a Party, may be removed from the Party caucus and thus are no longer members of the Party in the House of Commons – being relegated to independent members or they may "walk the floor of the House of Commons" and join another party. Unlike their American counterparts, they seldom refuse to support their leadership, either for reasons of conscience, or to serve better the interests of their constituents in the ridings, or simply to hold their seats. Individual MPs make the concerns of their constituents known in their parliamentary caucuses, committees or debates in the whole House; they also serve their constituents in a variety of other ways.

The reason is that parliamentary democracy is practiced at every level in Canada is that governments stand or fall based on the legislative count – one member one vote. The stakes are therefore too high for a party to be indifferent to how its members vote. Such party discipline had been loosening over the years but as earlier stated, the SNC-Lavalin Affair has certainly changed things in the Liberal Party. When a government lacks a majority in parliament, as was the case for seven years after the 2004 elections, there is a lot of wheeling and dealing to win votes from other parties. Members of Parliament find themselves courted for their vote, and this can strengthen their political influence in parliament. Since the advent of multiparty politics after the First World War, Canada has had 12 minority governments compared with 15 majority ones. Some of those minority ones have been successful governments under such prime ministers as Mackenzie King and Lester Pearson and in the 21st century under Stephen Harper. The requirement to vote as the party leaders demand is lifted on votes of conscience, such as whether to legalize same-sex marriage.

A second major characteristic of Canadian parties is that they are democratic in at least two ways: they willingly relinquish power when they lose elections, and the selection of their leaders is decided on at national leadership conventions of delegates representing party organizations throughout the country. Only about a tenth of adult Canadians actually belong to a political party. But any member who wishes to be active in his local, regional or provincial party organization has the chance to influence the outcome of the leadership race. He or she can speak with aspirants for the national party leadership, who travel around the country soliciting support. The caucus pollings are a bit like primary elections among party activists.

At the party conventions, the candidates make speeches, and the voting is by secret ballot based on the majority principle. The first candidate to win a majority of the delegates' votes, a process usually taking multiple rounds of balloting, wins. In each round of voting a candidate is eliminated.

The losing candidates often openly symbolize their support for one of the stronger candidates by actually going over to that person's section in the stands to shake hands or embrace. Sometimes such gestures pay handsome political dividends. For instance, the first contender to cast his support to Brian Mulroney after the first ballot in 1983 was Michael Wilson, who later became finance minister. In 2006, he was named Canada's ambassador in Washington. The purpose of party conventions is not only to select new party leaders, but also to serve as pep rallies to boost party morale. They bring the party elite together with the grass-roots. Sometimes they also draft

Sir Wilfrid Laurier

or adopt party programs or platforms, which are usually statements of what the party would like to achieve in the best of all worlds.

Such conventions have a certain American air about them. Permeated with the smell of hot dogs and hamburgers and awash with Coca Cola and beer, they are noisy, colorful affairs, with a rainbow of hats, scarves, buttons and signs, and big bands playing such songs as "When the Saints Come Marching In" and "Glory, Glory Hallelujah." Before the candidates deliver their crucial speeches (invariably mixing French and English), their enthusiastic supporters march in carefully orchestrated parades around the convention floor, accompanied by bands playing such unlikely political tunes as "Chariots of Fire" (for the underdog, of course). Bono and Canadian singer Paul Anka performed at the Liberals' 2003 convention. The supporters of Stéphane Dion, who won the Liberals' leadership contest at their December 2006 convention in Montreal, pranced around the arena wearing green T-shirts with his name on them and reminding everyone of Dion's special expertise on the environment.

There are also plenty of unabashed expressions of patriotism, such as "this beautiful country," "the most fortunate cluster of people on the face of the globe" and *Vive le Canada!* In dizzying rounds of expensive receptions, dances (with plenty of rock music for the one-fourth to one-third of the delegates who are under age 25), barbecues and "chuck-wagon breakfasts," candidates have the opportunity to meet delegates directly. One major difference with American conventions, though, is that one does not always know for sure whom the Canadian delegates will select.

Programs and platforms seldom bind the party leaders, who must seek votes

Canada

and make policy. The reason for this is related to a third characteristic of Canadian parties: they are mass, non-ideological coalitions of many diverse groups. From the beginning, their goals are to win elections and divide the spoils of victory. Thus, they are pragmatic, practical and flexible.

Minor or regional parties in Canada usually began outside of legislatures as protest movements and therefore tend to be more ideological in their programs and orientation. The federal system, which fragments the political process, helps such parties to arise and provides them with smaller arenas that are less heterogeneous than Canada as a whole. In such smaller units with fewer groups to appease, it is more feasible to take a more partisan approach. A closer look at each of the major parties will help elucidate the differences that do exist among them.

The Liberal Party

The Liberal Party, which in its earliest days was called the Reform Party, was Canada's most successful federal party in terms of years in power. Indeed, this party's history is in many ways the history of Canada itself. It originally began as a combination of agrarian interests in Western Ontario, anti-clerics from Quebec and reformist elements from Nova Scotia and New Brunswick. The dominant Ontario group lent the entire party its nickname as "Grits," a term which derived from one of its founders, who reportedly said that the party wanted candidates who were "all sand and no dirt, clear grit all the way through."

Sir Wilfrid Laurier was the party's first great leader. By standing firmly against conscription during World War I, he was able to convert Quebec into a powerful pillar of the Liberals. Laurier succeeded in persuading many *Québécois* that Canadian-style liberalism was not as stridently anti-clerical as the European variety. He was thereby able to synthesize Canadian liberalism with French Canadian support. This synthesis has been one of the great strengths of the party. Liberals have traditionally appealed to Roman Catholics, Jews and other ethnic minority groups, and they generally have been more successful in patching together diverse groups and interests. As Christina McCall-Newman wrote in her book, *Grits,* the party forged powerful "alliances of elites," which was a "marvelously adaptable institution." In every generation, the Liberals succeeded in giving Canadians what they thought they wanted. The party also led Canada into the welfare era. In its Kingston policy conference of 1960, it pledged such innovations as universal medicare, minimum wages, old-age pensions, measures which

all major Canadian parties have come to support.

In the 1970s, the party began to stumble because of some important changes in Canadian society. Its base in Quebec was eroded by the struggle over separatism; in the eyes of many *Québécois*, the party no longer was the best vehicle for their aspirations. Clashes with the western provinces almost entirely eliminated the Liberal presence in that increasingly powerful region. The social welfare net was predicated on the assumption that the economy would continue to grow and that the federal government would always have handsome surpluses at its disposal. When the worst recession in 50 years began in the early 1980s, that basic assumption was wiped away. More and more Canadians began to wonder if liberalism was a viable economic doctrine any more.

Trudeau let the party machinery and base wither and seemed to become increasingly aloof and insensitive. He had greatly invigorated the party after 1968, but he became more and more unpopular and a growing liability for his party. The party was in the doldrums and needed a fresh start.

The Liberal Party had dominated federal politics for most of the 20th century, after Sir Wilfrid Laurier created a seldom beatable majority in 1896. By election year 1984 it had ruled all but 22 years in that century. Ruling parties suffer from the declining popularity of leaders, whom a party cannot dismiss gracefully after many years of good service. "Trudeaumania" had long-since disappeared.

Many Canadians still admitted that Trudeau had been, in some important ways, good for Canada after becoming prime minister in 1968. He was a highly intelligent, learned, flamboyant and

**Rt. Hon. Jean Chrétien,
former Prime Minister**

intriguing man. A completely bilingual Quebecer, he effectively confronted the specter of Quebec separatism by extending French language rights throughout Canada. The Liberal Party suffered in the West for this policy, but Canada's unity as a country was preserved. Trudeau's last government nationalized the constitution so that Canadians no longer have to request the British parliament to change it. He was also a very visible figure in the world arena. Some Canadians would say that he "put Canada on the map."

At the same time, many Canadians came to view him as aloof, arrogant, and condescending, a reputation that began to rub off on his party. Also, many saw him as an unpredictable politician who sometimes behaved childishly in public. His banister slides or public displays of "the finger" were neither widely applauded nor appreciated. Finally, he seemed to ignore his party's need for effective organization of sound finances. He stepped down in June 1984 and lived in active retirement in Montreal until his death in October 2000.

His passing ignited an outpouring of grief that his countrymen had never before experienced. Parliament adjourned, the Supreme Court closed its doors, and normally reserved Canadians wept openly. He had clearly retained a hold on the imagination and loyalties of millions at home and abroad. People from all over Canada waited in line at Parliament Hill in Ottawa to see and touch his casket. They left red roses, which he had always worn in his lapel. His coffin was loaded into a hearse, a 19-gun salute was fired, and it was put on a train to Montreal. Along the way it slowed in small towns, and people waved and threw red roses. His body lay in state again in Montreal's City Hall. The doors were left open until 4 AM, when the last mourners left. Eight Mounties dressed in scarlet carried his coffin to his grave.

All Canadian prime ministers have mountains named after them when they die. The only exception is John Diefenbaker, who had a lake in Saskatchewan named for him. When Jean Chrétien, who admired Trudeau as his own mentor, decided to change the country's highest mountain, Mount Logan, to Mount Trudeau, an immediate outcry was heard. William Logan had been a famous geologist who in the mid-19th century had overseen the first comprehensive geological survey of Canada.

John Turner replaced Trudeau in June 1984. The former served as prime minister for 80 days before leading his party in a disastrous electoral defeat in September 1984. The 1984 leadership convention pitted Turner against his chief rival in the

party, Jean Chrétien of Quebec. Chrétien was an extraordinarily versatile politician, having held virtually all the major cabinet posts. The 18th of 19 children (only nine survived), he grew up in an economically struggling family in Belgoville in northeast Quebec. After graduating from Laval University law school and practicing law in Shawinigan for a while, he went to Ottawa in 1963 as an MP who could barely speak English. He not only mastered the language, but he developed a good sense of humor. A childhood illness had left him able to move only one side of his mouth. But he shrugged this off, saying that unlike many politicians, he could not speak out of both sides of his mouth.

He became party leader in 1990. Chrétien's appeal for Canadian unity was popular in anglophone Canada, but he faced hostility in his native Quebec, where his brand of "renewed federalism" found little resonance. Seldom in history had the Liberals' fortunes been so low in Quebec.

Chrétien led his Liberal Party into the 1993 federal elections ahead of all other parties. No one could have anticipated how massive the Liberal victory would actually be. It won 41.2% of the votes and 177 of 295 seats, all but exterminating its traditional rivals. Chrétien became the first Liberal prime minister ever to win office without a majority of seats in Quebec, where it captured only 19 of 75. This was particularly remarkable considering the fact that Chrétien himself is a *Québécois*.

He entered the June 1997 elections both as the most popular prime minister since polling began a half century ago and as the first federal leader to reduce the budget deficit in modern times. Although his Liberals declined from 174 seats (and 40% of the votes) to 155 seats (and 38%) in the House of Commons, his government was able to hang on to a narrow majority.

The Liberals had expected to win the 2000 elections, but the magnitude of victory was especially gratifying: they captured 173 seats (up from 155) based on

41% of the popular votes. This provided Chrétien with a comfortable majority in parliament and the honor of being the first leader to form three straight majority governments since 1945.

In 2000 Liberals found themselves divided. Finance Minister Paul Martin and his followers made it known that they had waited long enough to take over the party's reins. Martin's and Chrétien's differences went back to their bitter leadership contest in 1990, which Martin lost, and to the Meech Lake controversy, which Chrétien opposed, and Martin supported. Martin had always been more accommodating to Quebec nationalists. The result was profound distrust between the two leaders. Chrétien resisted being pushed out.

By 2002 the party could no longer bear the public feuding. After Chrétien fired Martin in June, the Liberal caucus in parliament put enormous pressure on the prime minister to declare his intentions. He stepped down in December 2003. Martin assumed leadership of the party in the November 2003 convention.

In the June 28, 2004, elections the Liberals failed to capture their fourth parliamentary majority in a row and had to settle for a minority government. They captured only 36.7% of the votes and lost 37 seats, falling from 173 to 135. They did well in Atlantic Canada, fell far behind the *Bloc Québécois* in Quebec, saw their stranglehold in Ontario broken even though they still won the most seats, and did better than expected in the West.

The 2006 elections were a disaster for the Liberals, who were consigned to the opposition for the first time in a dozen years. They fell to 30.2% of the votes and only 103 seats. To no small extent, the outcome was as much a rejection of Martin and the Liberals as an acceptance of Harper and the Conservatives. A defeated Martin resigned as party head, leaving the Liberals leaderless and in disarray. They faced the dual task of choosing a leader and rebuilding their fractured and directionless party.

Its leadership convention took place in Montreal December 3, 2006, following a campaign that lasted almost a year. The most interesting contender was Michael Ignatieff. He is the grandson of Tsar Nicholas II's last minister of education, whose son landed in Montreal as a refugee in 1928. Michael, like his friend Bob Rae, was the son of a top-ranking Canadian diplomat, including an assignment as ambassador to the UN. He spent much of his youth abroad.

After graduation, he left Canada for three decades, earning a PhD in history at Harvard, writing 14 books, including his family memoir that won the Governor General's Award, and gathering seven

honorary doctorates. He lectured on genocide and ethnic violence in Britain and the U.S., ending up in a professorship of human rights at Harvard from 2000–5. In 2006 he won a seat in Toronto as a Liberal.

However, he proved to have serious skeletons in his closet. In countless articles in leading American newspapers, he had displayed what became known as the "pronoun problem": using the words "we" and "us" when referring to Americans. Many Canadians did not like that. He had supported the U.S. invasion of Iraq in 2003, and he continued to favor military action in Afghanistan. That left him in Canada with a reputation as a "hawk."

Often compared with Trudeau because of his scholarly nature and unusual path into politics, he lacked parliamentary and cabinet experience, and that showed. He made many gaffes in the campaign. His loss to Stéphane Dion on the fourth ballot 55% to 45% was as much a protest against the Harvard alien carpetbagger as a vote for Dion. The Conservatives soon picked up on this theme by running TV and Internet ads saying "Just Visiting" and contending that Ignatieff has no interest in Canada unless he can rule it.

For more than a century, every elected leader of the Liberal Party eventually became prime minister. History did not repeat itself. Dion came off as a cerebral ex-professor whose strong suit was not political organization. He spoke mangled English, and did not connect with people. He failed both as a party organizer and parliamentary leader. Indeed, under his stewardship the party had gone from $5 million in the bank to $6 million in debt. The Liberal performance in the October 2008 elections was a disaster. Its share of the popular vote fell to 26%, the lowest since the party's founding in 1867. It dropped from 103 to 76 seats.

Dion agreed to go. Ignatieff's only serious rival was his former roommate at the University of Toronto, Bob Rae, the former leader of the New Democratic Party of Ontario prior to becoming a Liberal, but he dropped out without forcing a leadership vote.

The May 2011 federal elections were such a calamity for the Liberal Party that wondered if it would ever recover.

The party and the nation were dumbfounded. The Liberals had fallen to less than 20% of the votes and a mere 34 seats. This was their worst result ever and the first time they were not among the top two parties. It had to relinquish to the NDP its position as official opposition in parliament. Ignatieff lost his own seat in Toronto and immediately resigned as party chairman to return to the classroom at the University of Toronto and Harvard.

Canada

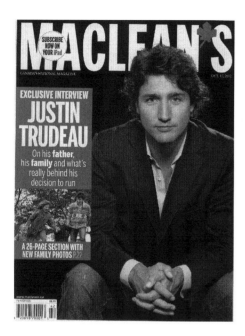

The party was left to ponder its continued relevancy and to face the many questions about its future and purpose. It selected Rob Rae as interim leader of the Liberal caucus in parliament. He chose not to seek the permanent leadership. He recalled the wisdom a former mayor of Toronto had imparted to him when he was just entering politics: "Bobby, in politics, you don't get what you deserve, you get what's coming to you." Any leader would have to be bilingual and know how to maneuver the party back into the political center.

The party chose an official party leader in April 2013. The frontrunner was Justin Trudeau, the son of Canada's longest-serving prime minister, Pierre-Elliot Trudeau.

Rt. Hon. Charles Joseph Clark

He moved many Canadians when he delivered his father's eulogy in 2000. When he threw his hat in the ring, Justin described his decision: "My father's values and vision of this country obviously form everything I have as values and ideals. But this is not the ghost of my father running for the leadership of the Liberal party. This is me." His father tended to be divisive whereas the son is conciliatory.

He admitted that the timing was not ideal. Age 40, he was 12 years younger than Stephen Harper and has two small children. His youth helps him attract young voters. He wished he had spent more time in parliament although former Prime Minister Jean Chrétien noted that Justin had been elected twice in his Papineau Montreal riding, which is overwhelmingly poor and francophone; "it's one more time than his father when he became leader." "Why am I doing this? Because I can, not because I want to. Because I must." Trudeau received 80% of the votes.

He holds a B.A. in English from McGill and a B.S. in education from the University of British Columbia. He did further graduate study in engineering and environmental studies. He taught English and math at two different Vancouver private schools. As an MP, he was responsible for the party's positions on youth, post-secondary education and amateur sport. He was considered very popular when first elected as Prime Minister but the bloom has somewhat faded off the rose. His party's imposition of a carbon tax, stress on identity politics, and the SNC Lavalin Affair with the, in effect, firing of a hugely popular First Nations Minister of Justice and Solicitor General Jodi Wilson-Raybould and former Minister of Health and Treasury Board member Dr. Jane Philpott, have dogged his time in 2019 as Prime Minister. Indeed, the Affair caused the prime Ministers friend and Principal Secretary, political advisor Gerry Butts, and the chief civil servant in the federal service, the Clerk of the privy Council, Michael Wernick, to resign. Thus, the idea that the Prime Minister was a feminist has been challenged due to his recent actions and with photographs of dozens of women turning their backs to him in the House of Commons in April 2019 as he addressed the Daughtress of the Vote, it appears that his "sunny days" motto is long gone. In October 2019, Trudeau was re-elected for a second term as Canada's prime minister, but as a minority government. Justin Trudeau went to the ballot box again in 2021 with a snap election in an attempt to regain a majority; the Liberal were returned to government, but with a second consecutive minority.

[1]

The Conservative Party

Until 2004 two parties of the right had offered the Liberals three federal election victories on a platter because they split the opposition vote. For example, in 2000 they won a combined total of 38% of the votes (to the Liberals 41%), but because of the effect of the single-member electoral system, they received a combined total of only 78 seats to the Liberals' 172. They were cutting each other's throats. But "uniting the right" was difficult because the Progressive Conservative Party (PC) and the Canadian Alliance had grown out of different traditions, appealed to different kinds of Canadians, and had much bad blood between them. A look at both pillars of the new Conservative Party shows why their merger in 2004 was difficult but necessary.

Progressive Conservative Party

The Progressive Conservative Party (PC), under the leadership of Sir John A. Macdonald and his Quebec partner, Sir George-Etienne Cartier (then "The Conservative Party"), had dominated Canadian politics for most of the first three decades of confederation. Macdonald revealed a strong partisan approach to politics: "I do not say that all Grits [Liberals] are horse thieves. But I feel quite sure that all horse thieves are Grits." The Conservatives (Tories) suffered devastating political setbacks in the 20th century because of their support of a military draft during the First World War and because they were in power when the Great Depression struck in the early 1930s. At times it seemed almost as if they had been condemned to permanent opposition in federal politics. They traditionally drew much support from Protestants of British ethnic origin, but they needed to broaden their base.

In 1968 their exclusion from Quebec was prolonged by the emergence of the *Parti Québécois* and its antagonist, Pierre Elliott Trudeau. To polish the party's image by underscoring its moderate course and acceptance of Canada's social welfare net, they changed its name to Progressive Conservative, words which are not a contradiction in terms. They did not allow the Liberals either to outdo them in welfare spending by very much or to shove them to the right on the political spectrum. In 1978 Trudeau said that the Liberal position was the "radical center." Six years later, the PC leader defined the position of his own party as "the extreme center."

In the late 1970s the PC's opportunity to regain power in Ottawa had come. The Liberals had been driven out of power in every Canadian province, and the PC captured control of most provincial parliaments. In 1976 Joe Clark, a young Albertan in his 30s, who had buckled down to learn

fluent French, came from behind to capture the party leadership. In 1979 he led his party to victory in the federal parliamentary elections. However, his minority government made some cardinal blunders that ensured that it would be short-lived. Despite the fact that the PC had failed to win a majority of seats in the House of Commons, Clark decided that his government would rule *as if* it had a majority. In other words, he decided on a bold political course, which included such controversial stands as moving the Canadian embassy in Israel from Tel Aviv to Jerusalem, delaying the opening of parliament, and driving a very hard bargain with Conservative-governed Alberta in setting oil prices.

In an important budget vote, he failed to count noses carefully and lost the vote. He thereby prompted a new election in 1980, only eight months after the last one. An electorate that was most unimpressed with Clark's leadership gave the Liberals a new lease on life and voted the Conservatives out of power. Constantly nipped at the

Rt. Hon. Brian Mulroney

heels by critics within his own party, Clark decided to silence them by calling for a new leadership conference in June 1983. The result revealed the magnitude of his miscalculation: he lost on the fourth ballot to his challenger, Brian Mulroney.

Although Mulroney had had a passion for politics since his youth, he had never held elective office before becoming party leader. The oldest son of an Irish working-class family, Mulroney was born in the mill town of Baie Comeau, a predominantly French-speaking community located 265 miles north of Quebec City. His father was an electrician who had to hold down two jobs to make ends meet for a family with six children. He was the first offspring of a working class family ever to become prime minister in Canada.

The biggest asset he derived from his family background was that he grew up speaking French with his friends and English at home. Thus, he had acquired that indispensable advantage of being completely bilingual from childhood. This lingual ability, combined with a deep understanding and sympathy for their concerns and fears, enabled him to break through the distrust that many Quebecers had borne toward anglophones for two centuries.

Mulroney became prime minister in 1984. In 1988 he was the first Tory prime minister since 1891 to receive back-to-back majority governments and the first prime minister of any party in 35 years to win two consecutive victories. The Tories won 43% of the vote (down from 49.9% in 1984) and 169 seats (down from 211).

In many ways Mulroney was a success. He changed Canada more profoundly than most of his predecessors because of his free trade, tax, and constitutional policies. As a party leader he held together a fractious mix of anglophone westerners and francophone Quebecers, with only a few defections. He was effective in foreign policy. But his popularity dropped to the lowest of any prime minister in a half century. He was widely mistrusted and disliked, partly because of his manner, which seemed affected and insincere.

Mulroney's reputation was not helped by scandals after leaving office in 1993. He faced allegations that he had received money from Airbus to lobby the government and Air Canada to buy the European planes. He sued the government and won an apology and $2.1 million payment. But in a sensational House of Commons ethics committee inquiry in December 2007, Mulroney admitted that he had indeed received between $225,000 to $300,000, probably Airbus money, from a disreputable jailed dispenser of bribes, Karlheinz Schreiber, a German arms industry lobbyist. The cash was slipped to

him in envelopes in hotel rooms, and he issued neither invoices nor receipts. Nor did he pay taxes on the money at the time but sensing trouble he paid them later. He went to great lengths to cover up the payments.

In his testimony to the committee, Mulroney admitted that he had shown an "error in judgment" and had made the biggest mistake of his life. A government enquiry found in 2010 that he had acted inappropriately by accepting the cash. However, he was soon working as a senior partner at the Norton Rose law firm in Montreal, was being feted for his accomplishments and was being sought out for his advice.

Mulroney was disliked because of unpopular policies, such as the Free Trade Agreement, Meech Lake, high interest rates, and the federal 7% goods and services tax (GST), which went into effect in 1991. He faced the twin threats of regional alienation and Quebec nationalism. The rejection of his constitutional reform in October 1992 forced him to make an unpleasant decision in the interest of his party.

Acknowledging his bleak electoral prospects, Mulroney announced in 1993 that he would step down after almost nine years as prime minister. He cleared the way for Kim Campbell, a former justice and defense minister from Vancouver, to take his place in June as party leader and prime minister and to lead the Tories in the October federal elections. Promising to "change the way we do politics in this country," she offered a refreshing candor in public, and her approval rating initially soared. In August 51% of respondents approved of her performance as prime minister. This was the highest rating for any prime minister in 30 years.

Campbell was an inept campaigner and committed so many gaffes that one cruel reporter wrote that she rarely opened her mouth except to change feet. Although it would have been very difficult for any Tory to have succeeded, given the Mulroney legacy which had spawned severe cynicism in voters' minds, she led her party to the worst defeat in the history of any Canadian party. A group of 25 Canadian historians judged her in 1996 to have been the worst prime minister in Canadian history. After lecturing at Harvard and writing her autobiography, *Time and Change*, she accepted the post of Canadian consul general in Los Angeles. In 2010 she tried her hand at comedy by appearing in promotional clips for a VisionTV sitcom, "She's the Mayor."

The PC experienced a meltdown from 154 to *two* seats in the House of Commons, on the basis of 16% of the votes. The former pillars of Mulroney's strength, Quebec and Western conservatives, crumbled, as

Canada

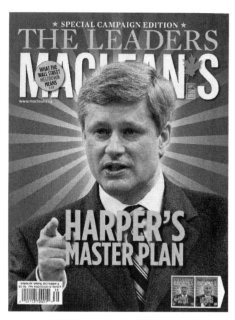

Rt. Hon. Stephen Harper

voters there streamed to the *Bloc Québécois* and the Reform Party, both protest movements committed to remaking the federal system.

Campbell relinquished leadership to the perfectly bilingual Quebecer, Jean Charest, whom she had narrowly defeated for the leadership in June and who was one of the two Tories to win a seat. During the 1995 Quebec referendum campaign, he displayed far more guts and effectiveness in pleading the federal case than did Prime Minister Chrétien and was the only federal politician who advanced his status during that painful struggle.

The party, which is called the Yukon Party in that territory and the Saskatchewan Party in that province, retained parliamentary influence only in the Senate. Their desperate situation gave rise to black humor: "Why did the Tory cross the road? To meet the other Tory!" Even one longtime Tory strategist remarked: "At least now we know the real meaning of the Conservative ad that said, Think Twice." Under the leadership of the most popular pro-federal politician in Quebec, Jean Charest, the PC fought its way back to respectability in the 1997 elections, winning 19% of the votes and 20 seats. It emerged as the strongest party in the Atlantic provinces.

In 1998 Charest resigned to become the Liberal Party leader in Quebec; in 2003 he became Quebec premier. He was replaced by ex-Prime Minister Joe Clark, who had yearned to return to politics. Since the debt-ridden party could not afford a leadership convention, its 87,000 members were invited to cast ballots. With half voting, he garnered 77% of the second-round votes.

He watched in 2000 as many Tories left the party to join the new Canadian Alliance that grew out of the Reform Party. The Tories were able to win a disappointing 12 seats in the House of Commons, based on 12% of the votes. This was the third consecutive devastating defeat. In only seven years the party had fallen from a majority government to a fifth-place party. It could no longer make its once-proud claim of being a truly national party able to speak for all Canadians in all walks of life. In 2002 Joe Clark told his party to select a new leader, and on June 1, 2003, it chose Peter MacKay in a dramatic convention. In 2006 MacKay became foreign minister and later defense minister.

The Canadian Alliance

The second pillar of the new Conservative Party is the Canadian Alliance, which had grown out of the Reform Party of Canada (RPC), led until 2000 by Preston Manning. Founded in 1987, this party viewed itself as carrying on the tradition of earlier western populist movements and promised to integrate its conservative philosophy with a commitment to the disadvantaged. It championed the cause of western Canada without advocating separation. It sought such constitutional changes as an elected Senate with equal regional representation and the possibility of recalling MPs whose performance is questionable to voters. It opposed bilingualism and special treatment for Quebec.

Manning spoke about "One Canada," meaning that Quebec should decide whether it wishes to be a part of Canada as an equal province; if it does not, it should leave. An anti-statist party, it sought a reduction in taxes, the size of government, and immigration. It also demanded more direct democracy in the form of referenda, recalls, and initiatives. Some observers saw its momentum as the "revolt of the middle classes."

It was so successful in exploiting western dissatisfaction that the party decided in 1991 to compete in elections everywhere but Quebec. Manning explained the party's momentum: "People are saying yes to Senate reform, . . . yes to a fair language policy and no to forced bilingualism, yes to candidates responsible to their ridings, no to central Canadian parties that tell their MPs how to vote." An avid student of the American Civil War, he saw the situation in his own country as similar to the U.S. before 1861. An insoluble problem leads to a totally new realignment of parties and the country. And it is an outsider, a "man of the people" from the West, who comes in and picks up the pieces. Whom might Manning have had in mind as Lincoln's Canadian equivalent?

The Reform Party demonstrated in the 1993 elections that it had become a major political force in Canada. It won 18.7% of the votes and 52 seats, narrowly missing becoming the official opposition in Ottawa. All its seats were from the West. One of its difficult challenges was to expand into eastern Canada. Manning was a folksy, mild-mannered man who sought more decorum in the House of Commons and modestly sat in the second row even though he had front-bench privileges. One of his first motions was to amend official bilingualism. Not surprisingly, the Liberal government and the separatist *Bloc Québécois* handily defeated this. Manning was not an effective parliamentarian.

The BQ and Reform Party actually had much in common, as Manning noted after meeting Lucien Bouchard over pancakes one morning: "I said we were discontented and wanted to reform the system, he said they were discontented and didn't think the system was reformable." In 1995 he told a gathering of conservatives in Washington: "The emerging political axis is: are you a traditionalist defending old systems . . . or are you a system changer? I would put us at the changing end. In Canada I would put the traditional parties on the system-defending end." The party capitalized on English Canada's frustration following the 1995 referendum on Quebec independence.

In the 1997 federal elections, the Reform Party dominated the western provinces, winning 60 seats (19% of the votes nationwide) and becoming the official opposition in parliament. Manning showed that he has become a force to be reckoned with in Canadian politics. The Liberal government's deficit cutting and law-and-order policies, as well as its tough approach toward Quebec, were influenced by Manning's popular appeals. His key political objective—to supplant forever the Tory party on the political right—was problematic, not least because Joe Clark adamantly rejected it. The Tory leader refused to attend Manning's "unite-the-right" convention in Ottawa in February 1999, calling it a "media event." No one denied the damage the two parties did to each other by competing in constituencies for the same voters. By fielding separate candidates, they cut each other's throats. But Manning wanted to change central Canada from the outside. Clark wanted to work with the center; he said: "I didn't grow up with the sense, ever, that the rest of the country was against me."

Manning became convinced that Reform was destined to permanent opposition if it remained trapped in the West and if Canada's conservatives remained divided. He was painfully aware that Reform and the Tories together had received as many

Hon. Pierre Poilievre, Leader of the Conservative Party of Canada

votes in the 1997 federal elections as had the victorious Liberals (38%). But by competing with each other, they had won only 80 seats to the Liberals' 155. Therefore, in January 2000 his party invited all interested Tories to join them at a conference to discuss unification. By a 75%–25% margin, the delegates voted to create a new, broader party, called the Canadian Alliance. It promised to make some concessions to the center, such as accepting Canada's official bilingualism. It actively raided Tory ranks, and by the middle of the year it had surged to 19% in the polls, leaving the panicked Tories behind at 9%.

Stockwell Day, Alberta's former treasury minister, was elected party leader in July 2000, defeating a stunned Manning by a crushing 2-to-1 margin. He had undergone a dramatic transformation since his days as a marijuana-smoking college dropout who worked as a fisherman, hearse driver, auctioneer, and butcher in a meat packing plant. He became a born-again Christian with a social agenda so conservative that *Maclean's* magazine put his photo on the front cover with the title, "How Scary?" He pledged to reduce the role of government.

In the 2000 elections, the Alliance was all but vanquished in Ontario, winning only two rural seats. This was especially disappointing for Day, who had figured that if Alliance and Conservative voters could unify under one banner in Ontario, a powerful challenge to the Liberals' unassailable federal dominance could be made. That hope was dashed. The Alliance captured 64 seats from Manitoba to British Columbia. Although the Alliance, under Day's leadership, consolidated its hold on the West and its position as official opposition in Ottawa, it did not emerge as a

national party that could serious threaten Liberal dominance in federal politics, despite its capture of 66 seats and a fourth of the popular vote nationwide.

In 2001 Day resigned, but he did not disappear. In 2006 his replacement, Stephen Harper from Alberta, who was only 43 years old at the time, put him in charge of the sprawling Department of Public Safety, the Canadian equivalent of the Department of Homeland Security. This had been created by the former Liberal government after September 11, 2001, to give a single minister control over everything from the RCMP and Canadian Security Intelligence Service, to running federal prisons and managing the border with the United States. He is praised for his front-bench survival skills.

An intelligent former policy adviser to Manning, Harper grew up in Toronto the middle-class son of an accountant. He moved to Alberta to do graduate work and has always lived a middle-class life in Calgary suburbs driving ordinary cars and earning a modest salary. Harper was not only a brilliant student, but a walking encyclopedia for hockey trivia who claims to have been writing a book on the subject. In fact, he wrote much of the party's early platform. He is an articulate campaigner in both official languages, a fiscal conservative, sure of his convictions, and an evangelical Christian without Day's public displays of born-again Christianity.

Harper demonstrated his negotiating skill throughout 2003 by building a bridge between the two rival parties on the right and then merging them to create a credible alternative to the Liberals. He persuaded the more centrist PC leader, Peter Mackay, that union was their only hope for electoral success. The two parties made the decision to form the Conservative Party in December 2003. The Alliance gave almost unanimous backing for the merger, but PC members had a more difficult time accepting it.

In March 2004 Harper defeated a neophyte politician—telegenic multi-millionaire heiress and Magna CEO, Belinda Stronach, who switched to the Liberal Party in May 2005—and former Tory health minister in Ontario, Tony Clement, for the new party's leadership. Harper declared: "My goal is not only to win an election. It's to create a natural Conservative majority in this country." He admitted that Quebec would be his party's toughest long-term challenge. There were defections, and fault-lines in the new party remained. Some prominent Tories refused to join. For example, Joe Clark not only refused to run for parliament again, but he hinted that he might support Paul Martin, "the devil we know." Many disgruntled Tories gravitated to the Liberals.

It takes a new party time to gel, and the Conservative Party was not yet a sturdy union when Prime Minister Martin called for new elections in June 2004. It was thrust into an election campaign without a full debate over policy. It still spoke with many contradictory voices. But the Conservatives performed reasonably well, showing in many ways more cohesion than the Liberals, who were licking deep wounds from Martin's bloody unseating of his old rival, Jean Chrétien. They captured 29.6% of the votes (down from the PC-Alliance combined total of 38% in 2000), but received 99 seats in the House of Commons, up from a combined 78. Most important, the Conservative Party now represented a viable political alternative for Canadians. In March 2005 Harper easily won a leadership review, receiving the support of 84% of the delegates at the party conference.

In the January 2006 elections the Conservatives won an impressive victory, securing 124 of 308 seats in the House of Commons on the basis of 36.3% of the votes. They won big in the West, where they got more than half of their seats, and all the seats in Alberta. Harper proudly proclaimed: "The West is now in." They broke the Liberal stranglehold on Ontario, winning 40 of its 106 seats. However, it was shut out in Toronto, Montreal and Vancouver.

Most dramatically, the Conservatives picked up 10 seats in Quebec, capturing 24.6% of the votes (up from 9%). Harper's openness to *Québécois* concerns, his budgetary gifts to the province, his talk of more flexible federalism, his frequent consultation with Quebec's Premier Charest, and his practice of beginning practically every speech in Ottawa in French, which he commands confidently, offer the prospect of even greater gains in Quebec. According to a 2007 poll, Harper received a good rating on his French from 81% of francophones.

The Conservatives rose steadily to almost 40% in the polls, but its numbers still did not translate into a parliamentary majority. He had to hang on to power in order to have a chance to achieve his real goal: to transform his party into a force capable of replacing the Liberals as the country's natural governing party due to their claim that only they can balance the interests of Quebec and the rest of Canada.

Nevertheless, Harper found himself in an agenda-setting position in Canadian politics. His disciplined control over the party left little room for sentiment or tolerance for failure. He is said to enjoy a comfortable family life that has changed little since his wife and their two children moved into the prime minister's residence. He is an accomplished amateur piano player who is a huge Beatles fan. When in 2009 his wife Laureen was the honorary

Canada

chair for a benefit at the National Arts Center in Ottawa, she turned to him for the starring role. He grudgingly agreed to wear a leather vest and cowboy hat and to accompany himself on the piano while he sang *With a Little Help from my Friends* and *I Need Somebody to Love*. The black-tie crowd loved it and gave him a standing ovation. Four years later he demonstrated his musical versatility at the Conservative convention in Calgary by performing with the Herringbone band, playing Stompin 'Tom Conners's The Hockey Song, as well as some Johnny Cash and BTO songs. The national media all reported the event with delight.

Although ceremonial duties are performed by the Governor General, a prime minister's wife has no official role. She is not officially the "first lady." In fact, Laureen Harper's only public cause is fostering homeless cats for the Humane Society. However, the fact that she is more outgoing and social than her husband is a political asset for him. He is often seen as stiff and arrogant, while Laureen, a farm girl from Alberta who rides motorcycles and hikes mountains, is viewed as more down-to-earth and fun-loving. She softens her husband's image. Having grown up in a political family, she has a sharp political sense. Many Conservatives call her Harper's secret weapon.

Ensconced in their sprawling new campaign headquarters in an Ottawa industrial park and with a winning election team intact after the 2004 and 2006 campaigns, Harper and his party were itching for an election fight. By September 2008 he decided to ignore his own law fixing parliamentary terms and to call new elections for October 14. He failed to win his majority, but his party did increase its popular vote to 37.6% and win 19 additional seats. Disappointingly, it made no gains in Quebec, winning only 22% of the votes.

Through daring, Harper survived an opposition attempt to unseat his government through a vote of confidence shortly after the elections. That would have created an unworkable three-headed government that would have offered neither stability nor popular legitimacy. There was outrage throughout Canada over the prospect that separatists, the BQ, might get their hands on the levers of power in a deal concocted with no respect for the ballot box. Harper instinctively knew this, and polls showed upwards of 60% of the public hostile to the coalition taking power.

The Conservatives continued to rule via a somewhat stronger minority government. However, his large lead in the polls at least temporarily evaporated when he prorogued (sent home) parliament a second time for two months until the throne speech on March 3, 2010. This

Jagmeet Singh

was a very unpopular decision. Although Harper claimed he needed time to "recalibrate" the budget, it appeared that he was preventing embarrassing documents relating to the treatment of detainees in Afghanistan from being discussed in a parliamentary committee. It seemed the government had something to hide.

Perhaps he was saved politically by the Winter Olympics in Vancouver. He was the chief fan for the victorious Canadian men's and women's hockey teams and basked in the glow of the thrilling sudden-death 3-2 victory of the Canadian men over their American rivals in the last event. Polls showed that he had widened his personal approval ratings over Michael Ignatieff during the Games, and shortly before the hockey final, 37% of voters favored the Conservatives compared with 29% for the Liberals. Only in Canada could this happen.

The Tories and Prime Minister Harper ruled for more than five years as Canada's longest-serving minority government. When the three opposition parties won a no-confidence vote in parliament on March 25, 2011, by a vote of 156 to 145, Harper jumped at the opportunity to call new elections in May that, he hoped, would give his government a stable parliamentary majority. He is a brilliant tactician who, in the words of the *Globe and Mail*, is "nasty, brutish—and competent."

He was not disappointed. The Tories captured 167 seats out of 308, based on 39.6% of the votes.

Harper's goal was to win a fourth federal election victory, something that had not happened since Wilfried Laurier about a century ago. He faced the October 2015 federal elections with confidence, but the results were a disaster for him and the Tory party. They lost 60 seats falling to 99. They slid to 31.9% of the popular vote. Only three provinces, including Saskatchewan, were still governed by a party associated with the federal Conservatives. Harper resigned as leader.

Not until May 27, 2017, was he replaced by a permanent leader. The decision was made by 85,000 party members, who listed the candidates in their order of preference. Emerging victorious from a field of 14 was 38-year-old Andrew Scheer from Saskatchewan. He campaigned on a platform to unify the party and establish intra-party consensus. A former Speaker of the House of Commons, he is likeable, experienced, and bilingual. On December 12, 2019, Andrew Scheer stepped down as the Conservative leader. Sources told the *National Post* that his resignation was because Scheer was using money from the Conservative Party to pay for his children's private school tuition. On August 24, 2020, the party chose Erin O'Toole as its new leader; he served as Leader of the Official Opposition until February 2, 2022, when he was removed by the party caucus and replaced by Candice Bergen.

The New Democratic Party
The most ideologically oriented Canadian party is the New Democratic Party (NDP), which is an offspring of the Cooperative Commonwealth Federation (CCF). The CCF was a protest party born in the prairies during the Great Depression that frontally attacked capitalism, "with its inherent injustice and inhumanity." Its famous Regina Manifesto of 1933 declared: "No CCF government will rest content until it has eradicated capitalism and put into operation the full program of socialized planning which will lead to the establishment in Canada of the co-operative commonwealth."

The NDP has nothing to do with two long-established parties miles to the left of it, which do consistently poorly throughout Canada. They are the Communist Party of Canada and a Maoist off-shoot called "Marxist-Leninists." The last Communist MP was elected in 1945, but his parliamentary career ended a year later when he was convicted of espionage.

The NDP has never been revolutionary in the sense that it would take power by force; it was always democratic and sought change by means of the ballot box. Since it always sought votes, it has watered down its program throughout the years. In 1961 it changed its name to the New

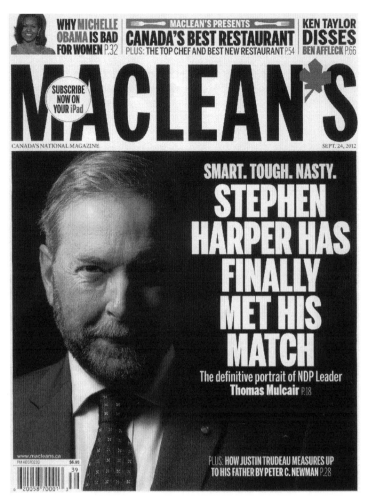

In the 1997 elections the NDP increased its voter harvest to 11% and 21 seats, mainly in the West. At its 1999 national convention delegates backed McDonough's demands by a 2 to 1 majority to move the party toward the political center. In the 2000 elections, the NDP won 8% of the votes and 13 seats, barely qualifying as an official party in Ottawa. McDonough was replaced in 2003 by Jack Layton, a charismatic PhD, fluently bilingual Toronto city councilor and former head of the Federation of Canadian Municipalities. He had a more ideological edge than his predecessor and was not above playing on latent anti-Americanism in Canada.

Layton reenergized the NDP and in the 2004 elections led it to its best result in a decade. Doing well in Ontario and the west, it more than doubled its votes nation-wide to 15.7% and jumped to 19 seats. Its platform called for increased government spending on healthcare and daycare, opposition to Canadian participation in America's missile defense, and especially the adoption of the proportional representation electoral system.

The NDP was the only party other than the Conservatives to improve its standing in the 2006 federal elections. Under the leadership of Jack Layton, who prefered the term "New Democrats" to the NDP acronym, it captured 17.5% of the votes and 29 seats. The NDP picked up a dozen seats in Ontario and 10 in BC. As usual, it was locked out of Quebec. It also had problems appealing to Asians and to other business-friendly immigrants. It did well in the 2008 elections, increasing its votes from 17.5% to 18.2% of the popular total and its seats from 29 to 37.

The NDP prepared well for the May 2011 elections. In an effort to attract Quebec voters, it advocated the separatists' view of the Canadian constitution as unfinished business.

Canadians were left reeling when the election results came in. The NDP captured 31% of the votes and 103 seats, 58 of which in Quebec, up from one in 2008. Because the NDP won seats in eight provinces, for the first time in its history, it became the official opposition in Ottawa and the dominant federal party in Quebec.

After the celebrations on election night were over, the party had to think hard how it would manage such a diverse and largely inexperienced group of MPs that included 58 Québécois, four McGill students (one of whom 19 years old, the youngest ever MP), an ex-communist, teachers and activists, with very few seasoned politicians among them; 19 of its MPs were under age 30. One new NDP MP, Ruth Ellen Brosseau, was working in an Ottawa student bar when a party

Democratic Party in order to broaden its appeal to non-socialists. However, tension remains between the impulses toward reform and toward electoral victory. It belongs to the Socialist International and remains the only successful social democratic party in North America.

The NDP found most of its support in urban areas in Ontario and the West. It also does well in rural western areas, where it pays attention to farmers' wants. It succeeds in labor union circles, which are a declining reservoir of voters. More men than women give their votes to the NDP. It was vulnerable to Liberals, who sometimes picked up the NDP's ideas, such as medicare, and wrote them onto their own banners. It is very vulnerable to surges of populist conservative parties. In the late 1950s, the Diefenbaker landslide wiped the CCF out nationally. Until the May 2011 elections, the NDP had always been disadvantaged by the single-member district electoral system. This prevented it from having as high a percentage of seats in the House of Commons as its overall popular vote.

In 1989 it chose the first woman ever to become leader of a national political party of any size in North America—Audrey

McLaughlin, a former social worker from the Yukon. She inherited a divided and aging party perceived as being adrift on policy and in serious danger of being shunted to periphery of Canadian politics. The western wings of the NDP moved towards the right to capture mainstream voters, but this disappointed many party members who viewed this pragmatic move as a betrayal of cherished social democratic goals.

In the 1993 elections it captured only 6.8% of the votes and eight seats. It won seats only in the west. McLaughlin admitted that in the rest of Canada, "what we have been putting forward has not struck a chord with many people. That's quite self-evident." The elections were the worst performance since the NDP's founding in 1961. Its Ottawa headquarters were sold, and most of its staff was laid off. While the buzzards circled, a new leader was selected in 1995: Alexa McDonough, a popular former social worker and 14-year leader of the tiny Nova Scotia NDP. Her selection followed a series of primaries among party members all over Canada intended to revitalize the party. She was chosen because she promised to unify the party's left and right.

Canada

Gilles Duceppe. Clever election slogan: A "clean" party in Quebec or Its "own" party in Quebec

desperate for candidates from Quebec asked her to run in a Quebec riding. She said yes, but she did not set foot in the riding during the entire six-week campaign. Instead she spent some of her time in Las Vegas celebrating her 27th birthday. Never mind, Brosseau cruised to victory over the incumbent by 7,000 votes. Brosseau displayed good French skills when she visited her riding after the election and went on to defy expectations in Commons, serving as the NDP's deputy agriculture critic.

Jack Layton had made the NDP electable by distancing it from the unions and guiding it toward the political center. He professionalized it much like Stephen Harper had done for the Conservative party. But he slept only one night in Stornoway, the opposition leader's residence in Ottawa. At the top of his career after one of Canada's most dramatic electoral performances, he died of prostate cancer on August 22, 2011. He was the first opposition leader to die in office in more than 90 years, since Sir Wilfried Laurier in 1919. Then Prime Minister Harper offered his family a state funeral in Toronto, a rare honor usually reserved for former prime ministers, governors-general and prominent cabinet members. For six days his country mourned for him.

Thomas Mulcair won a hard-fought election, mostly online, to succeed Layton as party leader. Mulcair grew up in Montreal, the second-oldest of 10 children in a devout Catholic family. He decided at age 14 to become a politician, and he was admitted to McGill's prestigious law school at 18. Although his family spoke English at home and all his education was in English, he polished his French language skills, especially by marrying a French visitor to Quebec, Catherine Pinhas. After the historic 1995 referendum on Quebec independence, Mulcair worked as the only Anglophone bureaucrat on the staff at the *Conseil de la Language Française* (referred to by critics as Quebec's "language police"). Mulcair served as environment minister in the province's Liberal government before switching to the NDP. He acquired the nickname "grizzly bear" for his quick thinking and sharp tongue.

Mulcair sought to shore up the NDP's strong newly won foothold in Quebec. He objected to the party's tradition leftist rhetoric and was determined to move the party toward the center. An example is its approach to the development of oil-sands, which the NDP always opposed. Mulcair declared that the party would be "a partner for the development of Canada's energy resources" although he opposed the Northern Gateway and Keystone XL pipelines. *MacLean's* picked him in 2016 as "parliamentarian of the year." MPs of all parties stood to applaud his service.

Mulcair's influence was significantly diminished by Justin Trudeau's ascent. As reflected by the October 2015 elections, Mulcair was no longer the politician on the opposition benches whom everybody was watching as the NDP dropped from 103 to only 44 seats and from 30.69% of the popular vote to 19.7%. Things became worse in 2019 and 2021, with party, led by its new leader, Jagmeet Singh, taking only 24 and 25 seats, respectively.

The NDP needed a new leader. Jagmeet Singh, whose Indian parents had immigrated to Canada, won the job decisively. A turban-wearing Sikh, he is a lawyer with a degree in biology.

Bloc Québécois

Until the 2011 federal elections, the political landscape was complicated by the *Bloc Québécois (BQ)*, composed originally in 1990 of a break-away group of nine Conservative and Liberal MPs from Quebec. Its first leader was Lucien Bouchard, formerly Canada's ambassador to France. The BQ captured 54 of the 75 seats in Quebec, the only province in which it competes. As the second-largest party in the House of Commons, the BQ became the official opposition. But Bouchard signaled the impermanence of his party in Ottawa by refusing to reside in Stornaway, the mansion at the disposal of the opposition leader. "We don't intend to settle in Ottawa. The presence of the *Bloc* in Ottawa is by definition temporary," he declared.

Most of its MPs were new to Ottawa: 48 of 54. Many spoke no English. As a group, the BQ caucus members have little in common other than their commitment to separation from Canada; they range from left-leaning union activists to moderate lawyers and conservative business owners. They were quick to learn how to operate in Parliament.

Bouchard was an eloquent and passionate speaker in both languages. While leader of the opposition, he made official visits to Paris and Washington to explain his party's separatist agenda. These caused outrage in the rest of Canada; the *Edmonton Sun* described his Paris trip as a "one-finger salute to the country." In 1994 he nearly died from a flesh-eating disease that cost him a leg. Rising from doom, he enjoyed considerable sympathy for his personal courage and support for his milder form of Quebec separatism that allowed for continued economic ties with Canada.

The day after the failed 1995 referendum on Quebec independence, Jacques Parizeau announced his resignation as premier. Bouchard agreed to leave his post as BQ leader and replace him as Quebec's premier in 1996. Gilles Duceppe, a former hospital attendant, Maoist union organizer

Fortunately, here, it's the Bloc

Canada

in his youth, and son of a famous Quebec actor, took over leadership of the BQ. He attributed his separatist leanings partly to having had to hear as a boy "God Save the Queen" played before hockey games.

Quebec nationalist sentiments has weakened considerably since the 1995 referendum, and Quebec sovereignty and constitutional reform has been put on the back burner. In April 2003 the PQ, on whom the BQ relies for organizational support, was ejected from power in Quebec. These developments hurt the BQ, a one-issue left-leaning party.

Its prospects looked dim until the 2004 elections gave it new life. After less than a year in power, the Quebec Liberal government under Jean Charest had become very unpopular. Then a government audit in Ottawa found that the federal government had since 1995 dished out about $75 million to advertising companies friendly to the Liberals to make anti-separatist propaganda in Quebec. Although most of the money had been simply pocketed with little or no work done, *Québécois* were deeply offended. After having cleaned up much of the corruption in their province, this "sponsorship scandal" had been perpetrated by hypocritical federalists in Ottawa.

The results were stunning. The BQ won 50% of the votes. Its 54 seats matched the party's best performance in 1993. Even Jean Chrétien's old riding was picked off by a BQ candidate. The party's slogan was clever: "*Un parti propre au Québec,*" meaning either "a clean party" or "its own party" for Quebec.

Duceppe said repeatedly during the campaign that a vote for the BQ was not necessarily a vote for independence, but after the election he declared: "*Québécois* form a nation. We haven't decided tonight to make Quebec sovereign, but we can say that Quebec has shown it has confidence in sovereigntists." In the run-up to the 2006 federal elections, he argued that an independent Quebec should have its own army and intelligence service, and he reminded Canadians in the televised debates: "Everyone common in Quebec knows Quebec is quite different from the rest of Canada. Not better, not worse. Plain different."

In the October 2008 elections, the PQ did not campaign under the banner of Quebec independence, and partly for that reason it was able to block any Conservative advance in the province. It lost one seat for a total of 50.

The BQ experienced near annihilation in the 2011 and 2015 elections, plunging from 47 to a mere four seats, too far below the requisite dozen to qualify as an official party in parliament. It remained as a powerless rump group.

Its membership declined by 17,000 to only 36,000 in 2012. Gilles Duceppe, the longest-serving leader on the federal stage, immediately resigned. Only the most militant advocates of Quebec sovereignty stuck with the BQ, while soft sovereignists and federalists switched to the NDP. Clearly many Quebecers are tired of the BQ and seriously asked themselves if they really wanted to be represented in Ottawa by a party that is in perpetual opposition. Many want to play a more constructive role in federal politics. The fact is that in its two decades of existence, the BQ failed to make a contribution to achieving the goal of separatist destiny. That is why it is a spent force. Federal elections in October 2015 demonstrated that yet again. It captured less than 20% of the votes in Quebec and only 4.7% countrywide. Of the ten seats it won, none was for Duceppe, who lost his riding for the second time. He resigned as leader.

In the October 2019 election, the *BQ* finished in second place in Quebec, taking 32 out of 78 seats, more than triple its haul of 10 in the last election. It achieved the same result in 2021. While the *BQ* was known in the 1990's as a party that would defend Quebec's sovereignty movement, today it is seen as a party that protects Quebec's interests. Yves-Francois Blanchet is the party's leader.

The Greens
One new party, the Greens, took heart from the ecological protest movement in Germany. In 1983 it formed a movement that views "economic growth as a problem, not as a solution." In 2004 it made its best showing, winning a respectable 4.3% of the votes, up from only .8% in 2000. This was too few to win a seat but enough to qualify for federal financing of $1.75 per vote. Rejecting the labels of "right" or "left," the party combines traditional environmental positions, such as banning nuclear power and genetically modified foods, with calls for corporate and income tax cuts. But it has gotten a gust of wind in its sails from the rise of climate change in Canadians' list of concerns.

The party's combative leader, Elizabeth May, is an American activist who left Smith College and accompanied her parents to Nova Scotia in 1972 in protest against the Vietnam War. May became a Canadian citizen in 1980, studied law at Dalhousie, added a Master Degree in Theology, and headed the Sierra Club of Canada for 17 years. The party has never been more popular since being led by May, who once

Canada

described herself as an "eco bitch." She is earthy and quick-witted. In fact, the Green party more than doubled its membership to 11,000 in only one year.

At the same time, though, Green support has not traditionally translated into votes, in part because the party lacks effective organization. May has not been able to cure the party's backbiting, infighting and defections, and members have differing opinions on whether they belong to a party or a social movement. "Deep greens" suspect all power and are committed to shaking up the status quo. May prefers to work with those in power. For example, she cooperated closely with the Liberals to get the Kyoto Protocol ratified.

By helping to put the environment at the center of Canadian politics, May has spurred all parties to show more ecological commitment. However, electoral success did not quickly materialize. Spurned by voters in Ontario and Nova Scotia, May moved to Saanich-Gulf Islands, British Columbia, to win her long-coveted seat in the House of Commons. Nobody worked harder to win one as May knocked on countless doors and handed out packages of sunflower seeds, the international Greens' symbol. May's efforts paid off, and she won the party's first seat; she won it again in October 2015 although she was the only Green to do so. However, the Green part's popular vote fell from 3.9% to 3.45%, its worst showing in a decade. Her party captured three seats in the 2017 provincial elections in BC and for the first time entered a government.

While she was re-elected to her seat with 54% of the vote in the 2019 election, Elizabeth May stepped down as leader following the 2019 election and, following an interim leader, Annamie Paul, an activist and lawyer, became leader of the party on October 3, 2020. Her tenure was short-loved. Failing to win her own seat in the 2021 election (although the Greens retained their two seats in the Parliament), she resigned as leader on November 14, 2021. Amita Kuttner, an astrophysicist, currently serves as interim leader. Elizabeth May continues to serve as the Green Party Parliamentary Leader in the House of Commons.

Maclean's named May the Parliamentarian of the Year in 2012; in 2013 she was recognized as the hardest working MP. The following year May was cited as best orator. May stands out in a parliament that placed only 45th in an international survey of women in national legislatures.

THE 2000 FEDERAL PARLIAMENTARY ELECTIONS

In 1993, Canadians experienced *three* prime ministers, matched only in 1896

Elizabeth May

and 1984. Peter C. Newman was right: "Governing Canada in the 1990s is a balancing act—like juggling wet fish while standing on a slippery diving board." The October 1993 elections had brought the biggest political upheaval in Canadian history. Turning against the Tory party of Brian Mulroney and his successor, Kim Campbell, the Conservatives fell to a humiliating two seats in the House of Commons. Rising from the debris were two new parties, the *Bloc Québécois* and the Reform Party. Both were committed to remaking Canadian

politics and the country itself. They battled each other in Ottawa over their sharply different visions of Canada's future.

Put in charge was the Liberal Party of Jean Chrétien, who had held every major portfolio during the Trudeau era. Chrétien became the first francophone Quebecer ever to win a majority in the House of Commons without taking a majority of seats in Quebec. This was repeated in 1997, when Liberals captured only 26 seats in Quebec. Chrétien barely hung on to his own seat in his paper mill hometown of Shawinigan against a fiery Quebec separatist.

Against the advice of his aides, he had called new elections for June 2, 1997, after only three and one-half years. The party squeaked through with a 155-seat majority in the newly expanded 301-seat House of Commons. This was the first time since 1953 that a Liberal prime minister had won back-to-back majorities. With the BQ and the Reform Party winning votes by presenting radically conflicting views of Canada, it was difficult for Chrétien to develop a national accord on Quebec. The cracks in the Canadian federation appeared to be wider than ever.

Most Canadians, including members of Prime Minister Jean Chrétien's own Liberal Party, were surprised when he called new elections for November 27, 2000, after only three and one-half years. Chrétien decision was widely criticized, but the results proved that it had been an astute one.

LIBERALS		CONSERVATIVES		BLOC QUÉBÉCOIS		NEW DEMOCRATS		OTHER	
SEATS	POPULAR VOTE	SEATS	POPULAR VOTE	SEATS	POPULAR VOTE	SEATS	POPULAR VOTE	SEATS	POPULAR VOTE
137	37.1%	95	29.5%	54	12.8%	21	15.2%	1	5.4%

AS OF MIDNIGHT EDT. FOR COMPLETE RESULTS, VISIT globeandmail.com

THE GLOBE AND MAIL

CANADA'S NATIONAL NEWSPAPER ■ FOUNDED 1844 ■ GLOBEANDMAIL.COM ■ TUESDAY, JUNE 29, 2004

The election: A last-minute revival in central Canada propels the Liberals to a minority. But the nation is deeply split, with the largely Conservative West still waiting its turn and Quebec in the Bloc's hands

Ontario rescues Martin

Paul Martin replaces Chrétien in 2004

The economy was strong, and both the prime minister's and his party's popularity were at their highest level since 1993. The aftermath of an emotional outpouring in the wake of Trudeau's death seemed to indicate that the time was propitious.

The major opposition party to the Liberals, the Canadian Alliance, had just been created in 2000, and its fresh and energetic leader, Stockwell Day, was untested in national politics. He had just won a seat in the House of Commons and was planning to spend the winter parliamentary session to raise money and his profile for the next election. Chrétien also needed to do much work in Ontario to expand his new party's presence there in order to break the Liberal stranglehold that had delivered to Chrétien 101 seats in 1997. Finally, Chrétien's role as party leader was being challenged from within by popular Finance Minister Paul Martin, who was visibly impatient for his turn to be prime minister. By calling a snap election, Chrétien caught Day off guard and forced Martin to demonstrate loyalty in the heat of battle. Winning big, Chrétien silenced calls for him to step down in favor of Martin. "I'm elected and I intend to serve my term," he said.

It was an acrimonious campaign, with personalities playing a more important role than policies. The Liberals succeeded in painting the witty and telegenic Day as a political radical who harbored a secret agenda to endanger important Canadian institutions, such as state-funded one-tier health care, gun control, no capital punishment, and a woman's right to have an abortion under certain circumstances. Even his fundamentalist Christianity, including his belief in creationism, was scorned. Faith is normally considered out of bounds in Canadian elections, but former Ontario Premier David Peterson remarked on TV that Day's creationist views brought his intelligence into question. Such comments made Day a subject of ridicule. Even Conservative leader Joe Clark, who was generally credited with having conducted the best campaign, asked publicly: "Do you trust Stockwell Day's agenda?"

Day turned the heat on the prime minister by accusing him of criminal conduct for securing a loan for a friend in his Quebec constituency. Day rejected Chrétien's characterization of his intervention as a "normal operation" that a representative performs for his constituents and called it "moral rot." Chrétien was cleared of the ethics allegations five days before the election, but the whiff of scandal hung in the air. All participants demonstrated acrimony. Chrétien suggested that the Alliance was out to "destroy Canada." Day once charged that the prime minister put the rights of pedophiles over those of children. Even NDP leader Alexa McDonough compared Day to a cockroach, while the Tories ran negative ads on TV accusing Chrétien of being a "serial liar." It is little wonder that many voters lost interest, and voter turnout fell from 67% in 1997 to 62% in 2000, one of the lowest in Canadian history.

The Liberals had expected to win the elections, but the magnitude of victory was especially gratifying: they captured 173 seats, up from 155, based on 41% of the popular votes. This provided Chrétien with a comfortable majority in Parliament and the acclaim of being the first leader to deliver three straight majority governments since William Lyon Mackenzie King accomplished that feat in 1935, 1940, and 1945. The victory also came embellished with some remarkable gains. In Quebec, where the prime minister was often dismissed as an unpopular federalist, the Liberals increased their seats from 29 to 37, all at the expense of the BQ, which fell from 44 to 37 seats.

These gains and the fact that Chrétien's unity-oriented party won as many seats as did the separatist BQ lent credence to the Chrétien government's hardline policy toward Quebec separatism. The Liberals retained their rock-solid domination of Ontario in federal elections by winning an overwhelming 100 seats, down only one from 1997. They also gained eight extra seats in the Atlantic Provinces.

The performance of the Canadian Alliance demonstrated the gaping divide between the East and West in Canada. It was all but vanquished in Ontario, winning only two rural seats. The party calculated that if only its voters and the Tories' voters could unify under one banner in Ontario, a powerful challenge to the Liberals' unassailable federal dominance could be made; that hope was dashed. The Alliance captured 64 seats from Manitoba to British Columbia, leaving only 14 to the Liberals. Such an outcome again raised the question about national unity and western alienation. Although the Alliance, under Day's leadership, consolidated its hold on the West and its position as official opposition in Ottawa, it did not emerge as a national party that could seriously threaten Liberal dominance in federal politics, despite its capture of 66 seats and a fourth of the popular votes nationwide.

Both the Conservatives and the NDP narrowly escaped extinction and barely won the required dozen seats needed for official recognition as parliamentary parties. Only by winning nine seats in the Atlantic provinces, four fewer than in 1997, were the Tories able to secure a disappointing 12 seats in the House of Commons, based on 12% of the votes. This was the third consecutive devastating defeat. In only seven years the party had fallen from a majority government to a fifth-place party. It could

Liberal government runs out of wind

Source: *Globe and Mail*

Canada

no longer make its once-proud claim of being a truly national party able to speak for all Canadians in all walks of life. The NDP also faced the prospect of spending the next few years on the fringes of Canadian politics. McDonough held on to her Halifax riding, but her party's seats in the Atlantic provinces dropped from seven to four. Overall, the NDP won 8% of the votes and 13 seats, barely qualifying as an official party in Ottawa.

The election campaign was rancorous and personal, with too little serious discussion of issues of importance to Canada's future, such as how the country could remain competitive in the world economy, what to do about the declining value of the Canadian dollar and how to fix the health-care system. Noting that the wrangling about counting votes in Florida had diverted Canadians' already low interest in their own vote, David Rudd, director of the Canadian Institute for Strategic Studies, remarked dejectedly: "Even Mexico is more exciting than we are. I suppose that is what you get when you are a country that is at peace with itself and with its neighbors."

THE 2004 FEDERAL PARLIAMENTARY ELECTIONS

For a decade Paul Martin had worked to become prime minister and to assemble a formidable political war machine to accomplish his goal. His ruthless unseating of Jean Chrétien in 2003 created a deep rift in the party, and his turfing out and ostracizing of the former prime minister's loyalists added to the bad blood. His heavy-handedness alienated many local Liberal officials and volunteers and left the party vulnerable to a newly united Conservative Party.

Shortly after he gained his coveted top spot, a scandal came to light revealing that $75 million of federal taxpayer money had been funneled to Liberal cronies' advertising firms to be used to undermine the separatist cause in Quebec. As Chrétien's former finance minister, Martin could not escape unscathed. The *National Post* called the scandal "the mother of all Achilles' heels." An Ipson-Reid poll in 2004 found that 61% of voters considered the Liberals corrupt, and only 36% believed their party deserved to be reelected. There was a strong feeling that the Liberals had been in power too long. *Québécois* were furious, and many western Canadians saw it as proof that the Liberals are a profligate party.

Martin's half-year in power had been largely directionless and ineffective, with no overarching new policy agenda. Nevertheless, strongly desiring his own personal mandate, Martin decided to call new elections for June 28. Although many of his advisers thought he had made a mistake, he feared that the scandal might cause even more damage to the party. His poll ratings were falling continually. Also for the first time in over a decade, there was a credible alternative to Liberal rule taking shape in the form of the newly merged Conservative Party. He could have waited another 16 months to call new elections, but the longer he hesitated, the more organized and prepared the new Conservatives would be. For the first time since 1993 Canada had a federal election whose result could not be predicted.

What followed was an ill-tempered and divisive campaign that produced a fractured parliament. There was a heavy dose of negative advertising. Harper tried to swing his new party toward the political center. But the outspoken social conservatism of some of his candidates and advisers fueled charges that Harper had a "hidden agenda," perhaps involving attempts to end abortion rights, alter the sacred medicare, abandon environmental treaties (especially the Kyoto Protocol on global warming) or align Canada more closely with U.S. foreign policy. It is impossible to disprove a "hidden agenda."

Harper fueled these suspicions in the final days of the campaign when he suppressed but refused to apologize for a press release from his party headquarters suggesting that Martin supported child pornography. Until the final week, Martin ran an incompetent and lethargic campaign, and the opinion polls showed the race as neck-and-neck. All three anglophone candidates speak tolerable to good French, and the general impression after the French- and English-language televised debates was that the Conservative leader, Stephen Harper, had done the best.

In the final days of the campaign Martin threw everything he had into the race, flying on the last day from coast to coast and dipping his feet into both oceans. When the votes were counted, the Liberals had succeeded in retaining power, but with a minority of seats in the House of Commons. One out of five voters changed his or her mind on the last day and decided not to take a chance on Harper's new party. Only 60.5% of voters decided to go to the polls, by far the worst turnout ever in federal elections. The Liberals captured 36.7% of the votes and 135 seats, twenty short of a majority. In general, the Liberals dominated Canada's bigger cities, while the Conservatives did well in smaller communities.

CONSERVATIVES		LIBERALS		BLOC QUÉBÉCOIS		NEW DEMOCRATS		INDEPENDENTS	
SEATS	POPULAR VOTE	SEATS	POPULAR VOTE	SEATS	POPULAR VOTE	SEATS	POPULAR VOTE	SEATS	POPULAR VOTE
122	36.5%	105	30.3%	50	10.4%	30	17.3%	1	0.6%

LEADING AND ELECTED AS OF MIDNIGHT EST. FOR COMPLETE RESULTS, VISIT globeandmail.com

THE GLOBE AND MAIL

CANADA'S NATIONAL NEWSPAPER ■ FOUNDED 1844 ■ GLOBEANDMAIL.COM ■ TUESDAY, JANUARY 24, 2006

HARPER'S THIN BLUE LINE

Tories win slim minority, Martin steps down, pizza Parliament looms

BY MURRAY CAMPBELL
AND HEATHER SCOFFIELD

Voters put an end to 12 years of Liberal government yesterday but left the victorious Conservatives under Stephen Harper with a very tenuous hold on government.

Helped by a dramatic breakthrough in Quebec and a slide of Liberal fortunes in Ontario, the Conservatives eked out a minority government that will make Mr. Harper, a 46-year-old economist, Canada's 22nd prime minister.

Liberal Leader Paul Martin said he would not fight another election although he would remain as an MP. He promised to consult his new caucus and the party leadership "in the coming days" to ensure an orderly transition to a new leader.

"We are Liberals," he told supporters in Montreal. "We will not lose faith, we will not lose hope or resolve."

Canadians appeared to be saying they were tired of the scandals that had plagued the Liberals under Mr. Martin during his 26 months as prime minister and were ready to give a tentative embrace to a Conservative Party that pledged to clean up government while cutting taxes and cracking down on crime.

"This has been a difficult and challenging day at the end of a long and challenging campaign," said Finance Minister Ralph Goodale, who was re-elected in Regina.

Even though he was denied a majority, the election represented a significant victory for Mr. Harper who was given little chance of success when he took over the Conservatives more than two years ago after a merger of the Canadian Alliance and the Progressive Conservatives.

And for the 67-year-old Mr. Martin, the results will kindle a debate

Laureen Teskey and her husband, Stephen Harper, leave for Calgary yesterday morning. Last night, the Conservative Leader became prime-minister-designate.

Canada

The Conservatives overall won 29.6% of the votes, as opposed to a combined total of 38% in 2000, and a respectable 99 seats compared with 78 in 2000. The Conservatives even broke the Liberal stranglehold on Ontario by winning 24 of 108 seats. Atlantic Canada proved to be a Liberal stronghold. Conservatives were disappointed not to have dominated the west, especially BC, more than they did. The NDP made spectacular gains, more than doubling its votes and winning 19 seats.

The biggest surprise was the strong showing of the separatist *Bloc Québécois* in Quebec. It is ironic that a shady financial tactic designed to weaken separatist sentiment in Quebec had precisely the opposite effect. The BQ captured half the votes and 54 of 75 seats, leaving only 19 for the Liberals. The vote was more a protest vote against the Liberals rather than a show of support for Quebec sovereignty. Nevertheless, separatists felt wind again in their sails.

A chastened but relieved Paul Martin admitted, "The message was unmistakable: Canadians expected, and expect, more from us as a party, and as a government we must do better, and we will." Without a parliamentary majority Liberals had to proceed carefully. Martin rejected the option of forming a coalition government, something that Canada has not had since the First World War. Martin instead chose to lead what he called a "stable" minority government, seeking parliamentary votes from different parties for different issues. The last minority government had been formed in 1979 and lasted only eight months. No minority government in Canadian history has survived more than two years, and the average is 18 months. This was to be the fate of the Martin government.

THE 2006 FEDERAL PARLIAMENTARY ELECTIONS

The outgoing Liberal government of Paul Martin was dogged and ultimately dealt a fatal blow by the ever worsening "sponsorship scandal" in Quebec. This involved federal funds directed to Quebec advertising agencies with close ties to the Liberal Party in order to weaken the separatist movement. When the official Gomery inquiry began hearing testimony in Montreal, the information was explosive. Advertising agency executives admitted to kickbacks, payoffs and payroll padding. One head of a firm received $30 million in government contracts and in return paid a "commission" of 17.5% in the form of false invoices and fake bills. Another ad executive secretly kicked back nearly a half million

dollars to Liberal Party accounts. He told how he made payments in envelopes left on restaurant tables and put party operatives on his payroll, including relatives of former Prime Minister Chrétien.

These revelations were a political bombshell and a death sentence for the Liberal government, especially in Quebec. Then opposition leader Stephen Harper asked publicly: "How can we continue to prop up a government that is under criminal investigation and accusation of criminal conspiracy?"

The Gomery inquiry explicitly exonerated Prime Minister Martin in November 2005 of any blame. The same was not the case for Chrétien and his aides, who were cited for "omissions" and "insufficient oversight" by allowing the slush-fund scheme to be set up and operated under his watch. A beleaguered prime minister ordered his Liberals to repay about $1 million in party contributions and sent the 686-page report to the RCMP for possible criminal investigations. The damage from this sleaze debilitated the Liberal Party and haunted Martin. The then opposition leader Stephen Harper gained enormous credibility for his call: "We have to clean things up."

Martin was forced to focus on survival instead of a clear direction for his government. A successful finance minister, Martin proved to be a disappointing prime minister. Dependent on the demanding and big-spending NDP for its continuation, Martin departed from his decade of careful financial management and doled out public funds with abandon. His minority government nevertheless lost a vote of no-confidence 171 to 133, and new elections were called for January 23, 2006. This was the first winter election in 25 years, and at 56 days, the campaign was long by Canadian standards.

Tory leader Stephen Harper would not allow himself to be painted again as a dogmatic social conservative. He presented an effective blend of traditional conservatism and reassuring moderation. Harper moved pragmatically toward the political center as he skirted around emotional social issues, pledged to uphold Medicare, ruled out any change in the abortion law, and tempered both his party's opposition to gay marriage and the Kyoto climate protocol. Instead, Harper focused on such things as cracking down on crime, reducing the sales tax, shortening waiting times for health care, giving parents money for child care and boosting defense spending.

Harper avoided foreign policy issues except for promising to improve relations with the United States, which he called "our best friends." This matter did provide some temporary excitement in an otherwise unexciting campaign. The U.S.

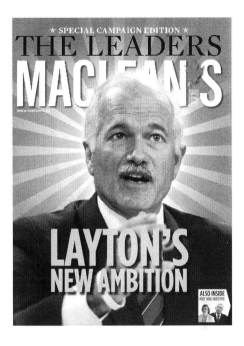

ambassador to Canada, David Wilkins, lost patience hearing Martin lecture the U.S. on the subject of greenhouse gas emissions when it was public knowledge that the U.S. was decreasing such emissions, while Canada's were growing. Wilkins made the untimely, if correct, statement: "It may be smart election-year politics to thump your chest and constantly criticize your friend and your No. 1 trading partner. But it is a slippery slope, and all of us should hope that it doesn't have a long-term impact on the relationship."

Martin, who in 2004 had campaigned for a "more sophisticated" relationship with the U.S., jumped on this intrusion into Canadian electoral politics and talked tough against the Yankees: "I'm not going to be dictated to," and "I'm going to call them as I see them." This flap bumped up Martin's poll numbers for a few days, and then they continued on their downward trajectory. When election day arrived, it was no longer a question of whether Harper's Conservatives would win, but whether they would be able to form a majority government.

Voters ended over 12 years of Liberal rule but brought in the country's second minority government in a row. The Conservatives won an impressive victory, securing 124 (up from 99) of 308 seats in the House of Commons on the basis of 36.3% of the votes (up from 29.6% in 2004). Thanks to a defection of a former Liberal minister from Vancouver, David Emerson (who later became foreign minister), the Tories actually command 125 seats.

The Liberals could hardly afford to lose any seats, having declined since 2004 to 30.2% of the votes, down from 36.7%, and only 103 seats, down from 135). To no

Canada

small extent, the outcome was as much a rejection of Martin and the Liberals as an acceptance of Harper and the Conservatives. A defeated Martin resigned as party head, leaving the Liberals leaderless.

What was remarkable about this comeback was that Harper's party made gains in all parts of this diverse country and became a national party again for the first time since 1993. Canada returned to a competitive system of two national parties.

The Conservatives won big in the West, where they received more than half of their seats in Alberta. Harper proudly proclaimed: "The West is now in." The election gives another nudge to the westward shift of Canada's political center of gravity. The Conservatives broke the Liberal stranglehold on Ontario, winning 40 of its 106 seats. However, none was in Toronto or Ottawa, nor in Montreal or Vancouver; it was shut out in these big cities. Its gains in Atlantic Canada were modest, but the post of foreign minister (later the defense ministry) was given to Peter MacKay to raise this region's visibility in the government. In fact, Harper gave his new cabinet geographical balance, even appointing his party co-chairman, Michael Fortier of Montreal, to the Senate so that he could have someone from Montreal in his cabinet.

Most dramatically, the Conservatives picked up 10 seats in Quebec, capturing 24.6% of the votes, up from 9%, ahead of the Liberals, who with 20.7%, and 13 seats, experienced one of their worst performances in Quebec since Confederation in 1867. It was headline news that many of those Conservative votes were won in nationalist strongholds in the eastern part of Quebec. The *Bloc Québécois* fell short of a majority of votes in Quebec, winning only 42% and slipping from 54 to 51 of the province's 75 seats. Not reaching the magical 50% mark, the BQ offered no prospect of a successful independence referendum any time soon.

Harper's openness to *Québécois* concerns, his talk of more flexible federalism, and his practice of beginning practically every speech in Ottawa in French, which he commands confidently, offers the prospect of even greater gains in *la belle province*. After becoming prime minister, he showered Quebec with attention, promising to recognize "the unique place of a strong, vibrant Quebec in a united Canada." Harper and his party were rewarded for this: within three months as prime minister, polls showed Tory support in Quebec reaching 34%, ahead of both the BQ and the Liberals.

The only other party to improve its standing was Jack Layton's New Democrats, which captured 17.5% of the votes and 29 seats (up from 19). The NDP picked

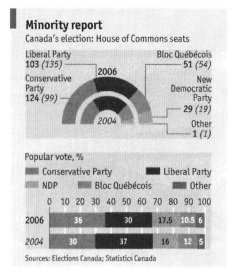

2006 Parliamentary Elections
Source: *The Economist*

up a dozen seats in Ontario and 10 in BC. As always, it was locked out of Quebec. Despite this strengthening, the NDP does not command the balance of power in Commons it did after the 2004 vote.

Normally a strong economy helps reelect incumbent governments, but that rule did not apply in 2006. Voters opted for a government that had not tarnished itself with corruption and not endangered its perceived moral right to govern in a democracy. Further, voters liked Harper's humility, self-deprecation, moderation and willingness to listen and learn. His first words as prime minister designate were: "Tonight, our great country has voted for change."

THE 2008 FEDERAL PARLIAMENTARY ELECTIONS

In September 2008 Stephen Harper took stock of his two and one-half years in power at the head of a minority government during which he demonstrated considerable skill in managing the House of Commons. Harper had been an innovator on Quebec's nationhood and his government was relatively free of scandals. Moreover, Harper put a dramatically new face on Canada's foreign policy. Analysts were writing that it had been a generation since Canada had had such an effective, ambitious and young leader. And the Liberal Party had just elected an ineffective leader, Stéphane Dion. Opinion polls indicated that no major aspect of his agenda bothered the voters and that a majority was within the Conservatives' reach.

Harper's ambition was for the Conservative Party to be the natural

governing majority in the country. He was confident in declaring elections for October 14, despite the law he himself had sponsored to have parliamentary elections at fixed times—thus not until a year later—and despite the fact that this would be the third time in little more than four years voters were called to the polls.

For the first three weeks, things went well for Harper's party, which maintained a steady 10-point lead. The situation then turned sour as the global financial crisis that started in the United States changed the mood in Canada overnight to one of foreboding. Canada's economy was relatively good compared with most other rich nations, but suddenly voters doubted Canada's ability to cope with the world downturn. A bewildered Harper came off as insensitive and out-of-touch when he argued that the crashing stock market offered "good buying opportunities." Haper mentioned no government spending to stimulate the economy and save jobs. The polls eroded, and the Conservatives found themselves fighting for their lives.

On election day only 59.1% of registered voters turned out, the lowest in history. The Conservatives increased their share of the popular vote slightly to 37.3%. This translated into 19 additional seats. This meant a somewhat stronger minority government, but not the hoped-for majority. The Tories consolidated their western base and picked up seats in suburban Ontario and the Maritime provinces. The Reform Party elements can be satisfied with the steady, incremental progress, slowly advancing eastward from British Columbia and Alberta election after election, now winning seats in suburban Ontario and

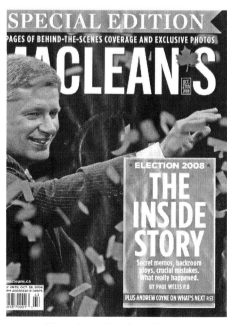

Victorious Stephen Harper

THE 2011 FEDERAL PARLIAMENTARY ELECTIONS

the Maritime Provinces. They see a majority in the future.

Their biggest disappointment was Quebec, where the Conservatives won only 22% of the votes and finished third behind the BQ and Liberals. The prime minister had made a serious misstep by making a snide remark about artists who receive government grants. Because many Québécois consider their culture to be the cornerstone of their nation, that was an insult with major symbolism. This rare Harper mistake prompted him immediately after the election to open the Francophonie Summit in Quebec City declaring himself "heir" to Samuel de Champlain and with a pledge of more funding for the international Quebec channel TV5. The *Bloc Québécois* made virtually no mention of Quebec sovereignty during the elections and was able to blunt any Conservative advance. It sacrificed one seat to win 50 of the 75 total Quebec seats.

Disaster befell the Liberals whose share of the popular vote plunged to 26.2%, their lowest since the foundation of the party in 1867. This was the third consecutive election in which their popular vote dropped. Their number of seats dived by a fourth from 103 to only 76. These included a mere seven seats in the entire West, while they lost their dominance of Ontario. The Liberal Party had become largely a Montreal-Toronto party with enclaves in Atlantic Canada. These results raise the serious question about whether it can even be considered a national party. This is a bitter realization for a party that had ruled Canada 55 of the previous 73 years.

Stéphane Dion had chosen to conduct a campaign based on an environmental plan called "Green Shift," that would include a carbon tax, just when Canadians were worrying primarily about the economy. The party's poor performance, along with Dion's clumsy attempt to defeat the government in a vote of no-confidence and take over the prime minister's role himself a few weeks after the election, cost him his leadership. Michael Ignatieff, whose popularity rivaled that of Prime Minister Harper, took the party's reins. Perhaps the only bright spot for the Liberals was the election of Justin Trudeau, son of the former prime minister, in suburban Montreal.

Canada now had a five-party system. The NDP finished no higher in the popular vote than it had in 2006 but did climb from 29 to 37 seats even as it remained as far as ever from its professed goal of replacing the Liberals as the government-in-waiting. The Greens, led by the hard-charging Elizabeth May, fell far below their inflated expectations but did increase their electoral support by 41%, winning 940,000 votes, or 6.8% of the total. Yet, this did not translate into any seats.

In one of the most dramatic federal elections in Canadian history, Canada returned to a three-party political system. The Tories and Prime Minister Stephen Harper had ruled for more than five years as Canada's longest-serving minority government. When the three opposition parties won a no-confidence vote in parliament on March 25, 2011, by a vote of 156 to 145, Harper jumped at the opportunity to call new elections in May that, he hoped, would give his government a stable parliamentary majority. Harper was a brilliant tactician who, in the words of the *Globe and Mail*, was "nasty, brutish—and competent" who correctly predicted that the Liberals and New Democrats would split the vote on the left and the Tories would dominate the center.

Harper was not disappointed as the results transformed Canadian politics. Voters responded to Harper's argument that parliament had become dysfunctional and that his government needed a majority to stop the "socialists and separatists," namely the New Democrats and Bloc Québécois, from endangering the economic recovery and the nation's security. Harper framed the election as a simple choice between a stable Conservative majority in parliament or a "reckless coalition" of Liberals, New Democrats and Quebec separatists as he steered away from social issues, such as abortion and gay marriage, which are controversial and polarizing vote-losers. Instead, Harper focused on the economy, lower taxes, stronger defense and tougher measures against crime.

The Tories captured 167 out of 308 seats, based on 39.6% of the votes. Only seven Tory incumbents lost their seats, compared with 82 from other parties. Although its votes fell below 40% in all of Canada, they totaled 50% in two-thirds of the country, revealing a formula for long-term success by the dominant party.

This was not just a victory. It was a realignment that could make the Conservatives the natural governing party in Canada, as the Liberals were in the 20th century. Their traditional Liberal opponent was crushed. Tory dominance of the West was strengthened: it won 54% of the votes in Manitoba, 56% in Saskatchewan, 67% in Alberta and 46% in BC. This was an average of 55% in the West, up by 9%.

The most stupefying were the Conservatives' gains in Ontario. In 2000 the Conservatives captured two seats; in 2011 they won 73 seats and 44% of the votes. This was the first time since 1984 they carried this most populated province. The

Conservatives even won 30 seats in greater Toronto, including that of Liberal leader Michael Ignatieff. Although they lost ground in Quebec, the Tories made inroads into the influential immigrant community, especially South Asians and Chinese.

There was thus a new governing coalition: the West plus Ontario, one that never existed before. This coalition was destined to grow as those two regions get about 30 more seats in the coming redistricting via the Tories' redistribution bill. The West now began at the Ottawa River as the Conservatives become Canada's dominant party.

The elections were such a calamity for the Liberal Party that some observers wonder if it could ever recover. Ignatieff had triggered the election in March 2011 by joining the NDP and separatist BQ in bringing about a vote of no-confidence against the Conservative minority government over an issue that voters seemed to care little about: contempt of parliament in concealing the true cost of prisons and new jet fighters. A February poll found that 51% of voters viewed Ignatieff unfavorably, while only 25% viewed him positively. The Conservatives branded Ignatieff as a carpet-bagging elitist, who had no clue about the struggle of ordinary Canadians. They were ready and itching for an election, but the Liberals were not.

By the time the votes were counted, the party and the nation were dumbfounded. The Liberals fell to less than 20% of the votes and a mere 34 seats, the party's worst result ever and the first time it was not among the top two parties. The Libera's turned to the left in desperation, but its voters gravitated to the Tories and New Democrats, who occupied the center. The Liberals lost big in Quebec because they could no longer pretend to be a bridge between the province and the rest of Canada. The Liberal Part was dead in the West and lost much of its foothold in Ontario as it had to step aside and allow the NDP to serve as the official opposition in parliament. Ignatieff lost his own seat in Toronto and immediately resigned as party chairman to return to the classroom at the University of Toronto. The party was left to ponder its continued relevance and to face the many questions about its future and purpose.

The NDP prepared well for the May 2011 elections. Party leader Jack Layton had just undergone prostate surgery and limped with a cane after hip surgery. Neither voters nor Layton could not know that he would die on August 22, 2011 but his party's campaign was anything but lame. In his eight years in charge, Layton overhauled the NDP and sharpened its electoral focus by throwing overboard policies that had cost the party votes in past elections. The NDP no longer spoke of a moratorium on new oil sands

Canada

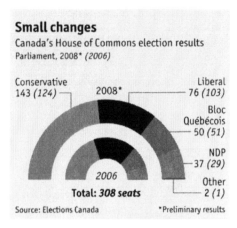
2008 Parliamentary Elections
Source: *The Economist*

development or marijuana decriminalization, and it called for tax cuts for certain businesses. Layton greatly improved the party's technical and fund-raising capabilities, and the party bought a downtown property in Ottawa for its headquarters.

To woo Quebec voters, the NDP advocated the separatists' view of the Canadian constitution as unfinished business as it supported a referendum standard for separation of 50 percent plus one vote. Additionally, the NDP proposed extending French-language protections to federally regulated industries. Yet, the party's biggest drawing card in Quebec was Layton himself: he was born in Montreal in 1950, grew up in Hudson, Quebec, and studied at McGill in Montreal, where he perfected the kind of relaxed, colloquial French that enabled him to perform best in the leaders' French-language TV debate. Layton not only emerged as a likeable street-smart Montrealer but also shined in the English-language debate.

Canadians were left reeling when the election results came in. The NDP captured 31% of the votes and 103 seats, 58 of which in Quebec, up from one in 2008, as it won seats in eight provinces. As noted, for the first time in its history, the NDP became the official opposition in Ottawa and the dominant federal party in Quebec. In fact, Layton was the first anglophone leader of a national party to win in Quebec when a francophone was heading another party, in this case Gilles Duceppe of the BQ.

Quebec voters have frequently demonstrated massive swings in elections. After the celebrations on election night were over, the party had to think hard how it would manage such a diverse and largely inexperienced group of MPs that included 58 Québécois, four McGill students, one of whom 19 years old, an ex-communist, teachers and activists, with very few seasoned politicians among them.

The BQ experienced near annihilation in the 2011 elections, plunging from 47

to a mere four seats, too few to qualify as an official party in parliament. The BQ remained as a powerless rump group. Gilles Duceppe, the longest-serving leader on the federal stage, immediately resigned. Only the most militant advocates of Quebec sovereignty stuck with the BQ, while soft sovereignists and federalists switched to the NDP. Clearly many Quebecers are tired of the BQ and seriously asked themselves if they really wanted to be represented in Ottawa by a party that is in perpetual opposition. Many want to play a more constructive role in federal politics. The fact is that in its two decades of existence, the BQ failed to contribute to achieving the goal of separatist destiny, resulting in its becoming a spent force.

Spurned by voters in Ontario and Nova Scotia, Green leader Elizabeth May moved to Saanich-Gulf Islands, British Columbia, to win her long-coveted seat in the House

of Commons. Nobody worked harder to win one as May knocked on countless doors and handed out packages of sunflower seeds, the international Greens symbol. May's efforts paid off, and she won the party's first seat. However, after 13 years of being the leader of the Green Party, on November 4, 2019, Elizabeth May stepped down as a follow through on a promise made to her daughter after the 2015 election, that the 2019 campaign would be her last. She remains the leader of the three-person caucus in Parliament.

THE 2015 FEDERAL PARLIAMENTARY ELECTIONS

Against a backdrop of a weakened economy, falling oil and resource prices,

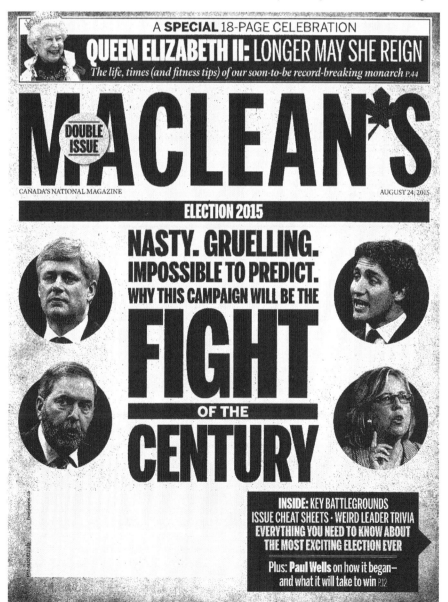

Situated halfway between the White House and the Capitol, the splendid Canadian Embassy is the only foreign mission permitted on Pennsylvania Avenue.   **Courtesy: Embassy of Canada**

controversy over Muslim religious headwear, declining popularity of a Conservative prime minister who had ruled for a decade, and the appearance of a charismatic young Liberal leader with a magic name, Canadians went to the polls on October 19, 2015, to elect a new federal parliament. Excitement was demonstrated by a turnout of over 68%, the highest since 1993. The campaign lasted a record 78 days making it the longest race in modern Canadian history. This was plenty of time for 43-year-old Justin Trudeau to disprove that he was "just not ready," as Tory politicians proclaimed and to move his Liberal party from third place to the top of opinion polls. Although he is not the towering intellect his father was, Justin was boosted by an outstanding TV debate performance, both in English and French. He was the clear winner and became Canada's 23d prime minister.

The Liberal Party staged a sweeping victory, its best showing since 1949. It won 39.5% (up from 19%) of the votes enabling it to advance from only 36 seats to an absolute majority of 184 out of 338 seats. This was the biggest seat gain in Canadian history as the Liberal Party captured every riding in Atlantic and Northern Canada, more than doubling its seats in Quebec to 45, winning a majority of seats there, and in Ontario. It even captured four seats in the Tory stronghold of Alberta, taking

two in Calgary. Trudeau maintained an optimistic and positive campaign and succeeded in helping bring about a generational shift to young voters. As dramatic as the result was, one perplexed BC voter said: "I see little real change with this election: another PM from Quebec, with central Canada politically controlling the country."

Many voters saw the election as a referendum on Tory leader Stephen Harper, was many Canadians viewed his 10-year rule as stern and divisive. Two-thirds of voters rejected Harper the polls, denying him a rare fourth consecutive victory, something that had not happened since 1908. Harper was not helped by the weak economy and came off as anti-Muslim by opposing so strongly a woman's insistence that she remain veiled during a ceremony in which she was to be sworn in as a new citizen. The Federal Court of Appeal dismissed his ban on the niqab in the ceremony.

The election was a calamity for the Conservatives as they lost 60 seats, falling to 99, from 39.6% of the popular vote to 31.9%. By the time the votes were counted, only one province, Saskatchewan, was still governed by a party associated with the federal Conservatives. Harper resigned as leader and was replaced by interim leader Rona Ambrose, an MP from Alberta who is forbidden from running for permanent leadership in the race that followed.

The NDP had a disappointing outcome, especially after briefly leading in the polls in the early days of the campaign. The dramatic gains the NDP made in the previous election were wiped away. Led by Tom Mulcair, the NDP dropped from 103 seats and 30.6% of the popular votes to 44 seats and 19.7%. Its largest provincial caucus remained in Quebec. Mulcair had to face a leadership review.

The Bloc Québécois (BQ) disappointingly captured less than a fifth of the vote in Quebec and only 4.7% of country-wide, a loss of 1.4%. Of the ten seats it captured, none was for leader Gilles Duceppe, who lost his riding for the second time resulting in his resignation as leader. The Greens, led by Elizabeth May, did no better, losing one of their two seats and falling from 3.9% of the popular vote to 3.45%. This was the Greens' worst showing in a decade. Other minor parties won 11 seats.

Compared to American campaign spending, the Canadian election was a bargain. Total spending by the parties and the candidates was $39 million for the Conservatives, $34 million for the victorious Liberals, and $27.5 million for the NDP. Canadian law prohibits labor unions and corporations from making political donations and establishes relatively low limits on personal donations.

The parliament that voters elected was as diverse as the country itself as it

Canada

containd 46 nonwhite members (14.2%), most of them immigrants. Aboriginals made up 3%. Women constituted 26% overall, but the Liberals alone elected 50, and half of the cabinet was female. The average age of the members of Parliament was 49.8 and 58.6% were elected for the first time.

Prime Minister Justin Trudeau made more than 200 promises during the campaign that keep parliament and his cabinet very occupied including more collegial relations within the cabinet and provincial leaders. He asserted that power would be less centralized in the hands of the prime minister and his father's goal of creating a progressive, multicultural and idealistic Canada would be restored. Trudeau said that his foreign policy would put more emphasis on humanitarian aid and peace-keeping, while military forces, including the combat aircraft bombing the brutal Islamic State, would be ended.

As Foreign Minister Stephane Dion noted, though, terrorists "are every-where" and Canada has to "fight with our allies." Orders for the purchase of F-35 fighter jets would be canceled. Relations would be improved with "our closest friend and partner, the United States." Stopping global warming and carbon emissions would be a much higher priority. Taxes would be lowered for the middle class, and pension improvements would be made. Government deficits would be maintained to pay for infra-structure improvements, including day care and affordable housing. Marijuana would be legalized. Senators would be appointed in a non-partisan way and the first-past-the-post British electoral system for the House of Commons would be re-placed by some kind of a new system.

THE 2019 AND 2021 FEDERAL PARLIAMENTARY ELECTIONS

Going into the 2019 federal election, the Liberal Party under Justin Trudeau continued to hold a majority, with 177 seats. Held on October 21, 2019, the Liberals returned to government, but with a minority, gaining 157 seats, 18 seats short of a majority, and 33% of the popular vote. The Conservative Party, while gaining 26 seats, and actually gaining a higher popular vote percentage than the Liberals (34%), still failed to fulfill expectations, and its leader, Andrew Scheer, soon came under pressure to step aside. Sheer did, in fact resign in 2020.

The New Democrats, the Official Opposition of Canada only four years ear-lier, continued to lose seats, dropping from 39 to 24, and garnered just under 16% of the popular vote. The Bloc Québécois (BQ) went from 10 to 22 seats, while the Green Party retained the 2 seats with which it en-tered the election. The erosion of support in Quebec, combined with fewer seats in the West and British Columbia, sealed the Liberal Party's fate. Without those key seats, a majority became impossible.

Nothing had changed by the time Trudeau called the snap-election in 2021, only two years into a five-year term. And the electorate punished the Liberal Party for the blatant attempt to gain the seats lost in 2019. Held on September 20, 2021, the Liberals went into the election with 155 seats and came out with 160, up only 3 from the 2019 result. The Conservatives held the 119 seats it entered with, as did the BQ (32) and the Greens (2). The New Democrats had a marginal gain of 1 seat, moving from 24 to 25. The regional vot-ing mirrored 2019. In the result, nothing changed: the Liberals and Trudeau contin-ued with a minority government, the Con-servatives formed the Official Opposition, and the BQ taking third party status. The New Democrats and the Greens held the left, barely, with 27 total seats.

It seems unlikely, given the current po-litical landscape, that any of the major parties can gain sufficient support across the country to be in a position to form a majority government. Indeed, since 2000, only twice have voters given a majority government—in 2011 to the Conservatives and in 2015 to the Liberals. Minority gov-ernment appears to be the norm for the regionally disparate national landscape found in Canada.

FOREIGN POLICY

Canada, in the upper half of the North American continent, shares a 5,335-mile border, including Alaska, with the United States. This fact makes each country vital to the other. Canada tried to expand its trade with Asia and view its own security as linked with that of Europe. Yet, Asia and Europe are located far away. Canada's shared values, economic well-being, and proximity to the United States require that it focus much of its foreign policy atten-tion on its southern neighbor.

Canada is involved in innumerable forms of cooperation with the United States. The Nations jointly administer the St. Lawrence Seaway, and their Interna-tional Joint Commission (IJC) has objec-tively and far-sightedly dealt with many environmental issues for years. Follow-ing a bilateral agreement in 1972, the IJC helped facilitate the cleanup of the Great Lakes, which contain 21% of the world's fresh water. A Permanent Joint Board on Defense coordinates the two countries' security relationship, and they are allies in the North Atlantic Treaty Organization (NATO) and in the North American Aero-space Defense Command (NORAD).

Polls have indicated that Americans are more willing to defend Canada in case of attack than they are to defend any other country. In 2004, 84% of Americans

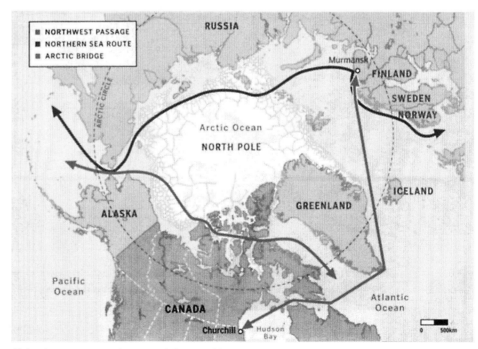

Shipping routes at the top of the world

supported their troops being sent to help Canada if attacked, and 75% of Canadians said the same about deploying their troops to defend the U.S. From 1984 to 1994, the top leaders of the two countries met each other at least annually, and the U.S. secretaries of state and Canadian ministers of foreign affairs met four times per year. By tradition, the first foreign leader with whom a new president should meet is the Canadian prime minister.

It was unusual that Bill Clinton waited almost two years to visit Ottawa in 1995. It was even more unusual that George W. Bush visited Mexico first after his inauguration in January 2001.

After his re-election Bush finally made his first bilateral visit to Canada, his third visit there overall, on November 30, 2004 in what was billed as an official, not state, visit. Breaking with precedent, Bush declined the invitation to address a joint session of parliament. Instead Bush delivered his main address in Halifax, Nova Scotia, in order to be closer to those Canadians who had helped thousands of American air passengers stranded after the September 11 terrorist attacks.

Each country is the other's most important trading partner and target for foreign investment. Every day close to US$2 billion in trade and travel pass over the border. Although it imports more from China than from Canada, the U.S. conducts more overall trade with the single province of Ontario than with either Japan or the entire European Union (EU); Canada trades more with California than with Japan. In fact, more international trade passes over the Ambassador Bridge that connects Detroit and Windsor than either the U.S. or Canada conducts with any other country in the world. Every province, except two in the Maritimes, has more trade with the United States than with other Canadian provinces. Overall, exports from Canada to the U.S. fell 1.7% in January 2020, mainly due to passenger cars and light trucks, but exports from the U.S. were up 1.6%, the first increase in five months (Statistics Canada, 2020). Canadian exports to the U.S. were $286.02 billion during 2020.

There always seem to be disagreements in the economic and trade field. In Washington there is a reservoir of good will toward Canada, even though there is often a need for American leaders to be reminded of what Canadians want. While the term is not used often any more, especially after former Prime Minister Chrétien's election in 1993, there is indeed a sort of "special relationship" between the two neighbors. If there were not, then Winston S. Churchill would not have been able to speak of "that long frontier from the Atlantic to the Pacific Oceans, guarded only by neighbourly respect and honourable obligations." It is now the world's longest thinly defended border.

Nevertheless, there are differences and difficulties between Canada and the U.S. Former Prime Minister Pierre Trudeau once said that 70% of Canada's foreign policy involves its dealings with the U.S. Far less of America's foreign policy attention is focused on Canada. Some observers have called that kind of relationship "asymmetrical" because Canada is more dependent on the United States than vice versa. The United States has ten times as many people and is economically and militarily more powerful and influential in the world than is Canada. Canada is a "middle power;" the United States is a "superpower." Canadians have problems getting their larger neighbor to pay attention to their concerns.

The Arctic and the Northwest Passage

The differences emerged in the uproar over the American Coast Guard icebreaker *Polar Sea's* voyage in the summer of 1985 through the Northwest Passage without Canada's permission. The U.S. has long held that those are international waters, while Canada's position is that they are territorial waters. At the 1987 summit meeting in Ottawa, Mulroney asserted unmistakably that Canada owns the northern waters "lock, stock and icebergs."

Leaders of both nations reached a compromise in 1988. The Arctic Cooperation Agreement (ACA) permits the U.S. and Canada to increase their collaboration in the region without prejudicing the legal position of either country. The ACA acknowledged American, EU, British, Russian and all other nations' reject Canada's claim that the waters are within Canadian sovereignty. No country questioned that Canada owns its resources or that it is sovereign over its Arctic islands. However, by requiring Washington to obtain Ottawa's consent for passages through the waters, which was always given, it hopes to prevent future incidents such as that caused by the *Polar Sea*. Canada and the U.S. agree that neither icebreakers nor nuclear submarines need permission to pass. When the U.S. announced in 2000 that its new polar icebreaker, *Healy*, would sail through the passage that summer, a team of Canadian navigators and pollution experts went along.

The passage is not yet a reliable commercial route, and until 2013 transit was limited chiefly to research or military craft. In that year the first container ship navigated the route from China. In 2016, no fewer than 25 ships transited. One, Capital Serenity, carried 1,070 passengers. Many more commercial vessels take the Russian-controlled Northern Sea Route along the Russian coast. Arctic ice has been declining by an area the size of Britain each year, twice as fast as the rest of the world. The U.S. Navy estimates that the North Pole will be ice-free by 2035; the UN estimate is 2050. Even so, commercial use of the Polar routes remains very expensive.

The routes are only open for a few months a year, and some ships must pay an icebreaker to accompany them. Because the waters are mostly uncharted, it is a problem getting insurance and securing rescue ships. The closest forward base is Halifax, a week's sail from the Northwest Passage. Once the ice is gone, the Bering Strait between Russia and the U.S. could rival the Persian Gulf and the Strait of Malacca in shipping importance. In 2008 Prime Minister Harper announced stricter registration of ships sailing through the Northwest Passage; all ships are required to report to Nordreg, the Canadian Coast Guard agency.

In general, it is tricky for Canada to determine whether to regard its southern neighbor as a friend or rival in the Far North. Former U.S. Ambassador to Canada, Paul Cellucci, once said he agreed with Canada's position on the passageway, he was quickly corrected by his successor, David Wilkins, who restated American insistence that the passage is an international strait. In 2006, Wilkins himself then slipped and called the passage "neutral waters," and the Canadian government jumped to correct his mistake. Wilkins' description was indeed at variance with the official American position, supported by the UK and others, that the waters are a "strait for international navigation."

A State Department official stressed that the U.S. prefers not to make a "big deal" of the navigation issue. The two partners agree to disagree about its legal status. But as a 2007 *Maclean's* poll reveals, 55% of American consider the Northwest Passage to be Canadian waters. This makes Americans the only people in the world besides Canadians, at 66%, to adopt this position. Consequently, it is important for Canadian politicians to be seen on the right side of this sovereignty issue.

Hours before calling a new election in 2008, Prime Minister Harper took selected members of his cabinet to the far North for three days to demonstrate his commitment to defend "Canada's Arctic sovereignty." In fact, after becoming prime minister in 2006, Harper made the Far North one of his signature issues, and he traveled there to inspect the military and its "Op Nanook" and Nunalivut exercises. Harper even held a rally in Yellowknife, Northwest Territories, during his 2011 election campaign.

In the summer of 2010 about 160 reserve soldiers were sent north to train near Yellowknife in "Exercise Sovereign Grizzly" as they helped set up the first reserve unit north of the 60th parallel. This

Canada

is part of the 20-year Canada First Defence Strategy, announced in 2008, emphasizing domestic defense, especially in the Arctic. He justifies this as "use it or lose it."

Harper's point was to demonstrate to the world that Canada's military forces can operate anywhere on Canadian territory. During the Second World War, the American ally had already demonstrated that it was possible to do that: in 1943 there were more Americans, 33,000 military and civilians, in the Canadian North than Canadians.

In 2009 Harper took the entire cabinet to the Nunavut capital of Iqaluit for a cabinet meeting and even required all the members to join him in eating raw seal meat to show solidarity with the locals. Harper also hosted a Group of Seven meeting of finance ministers in Iqaluit in February 2010 to underscore Canada's presence in the North. In fact, all Arctic powers are boosting their northern presence. Norway moved its operational command north of the Arctic Circle, and Russia is upgrading its northern fleet, which already includes more than 18 icebreakers.

Canadians fear that the issue of sovereignty could become more important because global warming continues to melt the ice to such an extent that thousands of ships from all nations could routinely traverse the ecologically vulnerable waterway. Arctic air is warming twice as fast as the atmosphere as a whole. This is especially worrisome because 90% of all goods in the world, measured by tonnage, are transported by sea. China's and India's rapid economic growth promises to increase the overcrowding of existing routes. In the 20th century, Arctic temperatures rose twice as fast as those in the rest of the world. If melting continues at its present rate, there will be no ice cover during the summer by the middle to end of the 21st century. Another powerful magnet is that the region is estimated to contain 13% of the world's undiscovered oil and a third of its gas.

The five various routes are a meandering set of channels through the Northwest Passage. They would offer a shipping channel between Europe and Asia 4,350 miles or 7,000 kilometers shorter than the route through the Panama Canal. For example, a ship traveling from Rotterdam to Yokohama would take 29 days to go around the Cape of Good Hope, 22 days via the Suez Canal, but only 15 days across the Arctic Ocean.

Two other Arctic shipping routes are also inviting: the Northern Sea Route (NSR) along the northern coast of Russia, which is already open part of the year, and the Arctic Bridge from Murmansk in Russia, around the southern tip of Greenland and into the Hudson Bay to Churchill, Manitoba, Canada's northern-most port. It was closed in 2016. As the summer ice melts, more and more ships sail through the Arctic waters. The alternative passages are more accessible than the Northwest Passage because only 10% of it has been charted, there is no infrastructure, and Canada's Arctic islands have special icing effects. The shrinking ice cap also makes mineral deposits more accessible. Some even predict a fishing bonanza, but scientists warn that a warming Arctic will not be full of fish.

A U.S. Navy study in 2002 reported that the ice cover has been shrinking by 3% per year. The Arctic Ocean could be ice-free in the summer by 2040. Western glaciers could shrink by 70% by 2100. As sea ice continues to melt, it can no longer deflect the heat away from land and water and so sped up the warming process. This scares Canadians, especially the Inuit, who urge Ottawa to assert its sovereignty over the waters of the Arctic Archipelago.

Canadians already claim that the 1982 Law of the Sea Convention gives them the right to regulate this area; as of 2019, the U.S. has yet to ratify the Convention but respects it in practice. The Canadian government ordered neither the promised powerful all-season ice-breaker nor the nuclear submarines needed to monitor the Northwest Passage and has no search-and-rescue helicopters permanently based in the North. Further, the Canadian government disbanded the one military unit

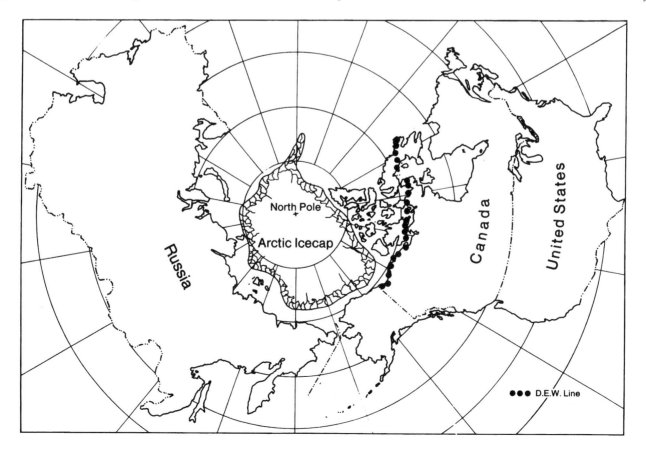

Une carrière militaire c'est différent!

The career with a difference

LES FORCES ARMÉES CANADIENNES
THE CANADIAN ARMED FORCES

capable of dropping onto the ice and has no deep-water ports north of Churchill, which is now shut down.

To underline its claims to sovereignty, Canada occasionally sends a coastal patrol boat into the passage during the summer, and every summer the Canadian Forces conduct joint army, naval and air exercises, called Op Nanook, in the Far North. The largest, conducted in 2011 near the hamlet of Resolute on Cornwallis Island, involving 1,200 troops, included a simulated rescue of passengers stranded on a grounded cruise ship. The relevancy of this exercise was soon demonstrated in August 2011 when a cruise ship was stranded in the Northwest Passage for two days until an icebreaker arrived. The vessel had hit a rock shelf, and the owner claimed that the Canadian government had not informed it about the shelf.

Following the practical principle of Arctic sovereignty, "use it or lose it," the Harper government promised to build three armed icebreakers, a deep-water port and a military training center in the Arctic. However, the number of icebreakers was scaled down to one.

While the ships are on hold, permafrost was broken at an abandoned mine in Nanisivik at the northern tip of Baffin Island near the entrance of the Northwest Passage to build a deep-water harbor that would allow Canada to refuel its military patrol ships. At Pangnirtung, with a population of 1,300 on the east coast of Baffin Island, a harbor for the small Inuit fishing fleet is being constructed. The Canadian government also made plans to refurbish an army facility in Resolute Bay in Nunavut to train soldiers year-round. Canada has only 120 year-round soldiers in the military bases to look after a northern region the size of Europe. These bases provide more resources to monitor traffic in the Passage.

In order to keep an eye on the entire Arctic region and to detect incursions, Canada has ordered from Northrop Grumman an unmanned spy aircraft (drone). This allows the kind of full surveillance not possible with the periodic Aurora CP manned flights and one Polar satellite. The Polar Hawk would enable Canada to take a photo of the whole Northwest Passage four times during a mission. The U.S. operates a similar drone over its own Arctic territory.

At Iqaluit the housing stock is being increased, and a research institute with a polar vessel is being constructed. A problem is that the maritime boundary between Alaska and the Yukon extending northward into a sliver of the oil-rich Beaufort Sea in the western Arctic has never been agreed. Canada protested when the U.S. sold leases for this disputed area.

In 2005 Canada became embroiled with Denmark over ownership of Hans Island, an uninhabited square-mile, or 1.6 kilometer, patch of Arctic rock of no strategic or economic value and of no influence on the maritime boundary between Greenland and Canada's northeast. The island is within the 12-mile territorial limits of both countries, which allows both to claim it. Although largely self-ruling now, Greenland still falls under Danish sovereignty. The minuscule island at one point is only 14.5 miles from Canada.

Reflecting how closely the rock could be related to other Arctic jurisdiction issues, Canadian troops followed by the then defense minister himself, Bill Graham, visited the rock to plant the flag and erect an Inuit stone marker. The Danes responded by sending a warship to back up their sovereignty over the island; they also planted their flag. Ottawa responded by dispatching a frigate to keep an eye on Danish fishermen. The two countries soon called a

truce and agreed to disagree over its possession. In an act of reconciliation, scientists from both countries proposed in 2007 that a joint weather station be built on the island. In December 2012 Canada and Denmark reached a formal agreement on the maritime border between Greenland and the Canadian Arctic. Hans Island is another dispute between Greenland and Canada. The status of Tartupaluk Island (called Hans Island) has been unresolved since 1973. However, as of May 2018 the Canadian-Danish task force on boundary issues are seeking to resolve a disagreement over the maritime border between the two countries. One of the resolutions they are considering is to name the barren island a shared sovereignty..

In the Arctic, two prominent trends are the speed with which development is going forward and the huge number of political, legal and technical questions that remain unresolved. Unlike the treaty-bound Antarctica, which is a land continent and not an ocean like the Arctic, there is no long-standing supranational body in the Arctic.

An Arctic Council, which in 2013 established its first permanent secretariat in the northern Norwegian city of Tromso, came into being in 1996 with eight members: the U.S., Canada, Denmark, Finland, Iceland, Sweden, Norway and Russia. Six non-voting representatives of cross-border indigenous Arctic peoples (such as Inuit, Sami, Athabaskan, Gwich'in and Aleuts), belong. There are more than 26 permanent observers joined later by many more countries, including China and India. No IGOs or NGOs are granted that status. Canada is wary of admitting the European Union because of the latter's ban on commerce in seal products, which is important for the Inuit. The Council began as a talk shop, but it became a decision-making body. Members have signed treaties on joint search-and-rescue missions and on cleaning up oil spills.

The starting gun for a scramble to claim chunks of the region was fired in August 2007 when Russia, using a mini-submarine, planted its flag on the ocean floor four kilometers below the ice of the North Pole. This daring move carried echoes of the Soviet launch of the first satellite, Sputnik, in 1957. In January 2014 Canada announced its intention to claim the North Pole, a surprising move that provoked a sharp response from Russia.

What is driving the polar countries is that according to the 1982 Law of the Sea, which is intended to regulate almost all human uses of the high seas, countries can claim an economic zone up to 200 nautical miles from their coast or even further if they can prove that the area in question is the extension of their own

Canada

continental shelf. This is the kind of claim Russia made by Russia with regard to the Lomonosov Ridge, which extends 1,800 kilometers or about 1,200 miles from the Russian coast to Greenland and Canada's Ellesmere Island.

The terms of the Law of the Sea require a country to make a claim within a decade of ratifying it. Russia's deadline was 2009, Canada's 2013, and Denmark's 2014. Because Washington has yet to ratify the Convention, the U.S. cannot make a claim. Canada is working together with Denmark and the U.S. to gather information needed to make the ultimate delineations.

In various ways Canada has little to worry about. No country is actually threatening to invade Canada's North. Although each Arctic state defines its own security policy to safeguard its sovereign rights, most members are allies in NATO and are unlikely to fire at each other. Norwegian Admiral Haakon Bruun Hanssen noted that the region is "probably the most stable area in the world." Legal norms are well established and all countries play by the rules. There is also no large or serious overlap of its claims in the Arctic and those of other contenders.

Falling oil prices and conflicts between Russian and NATO had by 2018 prevented an aggressive scramble for territory and resources in the Arctic. Even the Northern Sea Route was used by only 71 ships in 2013 and 53 in 2014.

Canada must be aware of potential conflict with its Inuit population who claim much of the Arctic coast as their traditional territory. Even so, the Inuit are not against development. However, they insist that development be on their terms, meaning that it respect the environment and provide them with a share of the benefits. They also have banded together in the Inuit Circumpolar Council (ICC), created in 1977 to strengthen their interests and demands.

Canadians are sensitive about maintaining their sovereignty and independence in the world, a sensitivity that is sometimes hard for Americans to understand. Despite all their resemblances, Canadians are *not* Americans and do not think like Americans in all matters of foreign and military policy. The two peoples' activities in world affairs are compatible but distinct.

International Organizations

There are various reasons for such differences. Canada is active in certain political arenas in which the United States is not. One is the British Commonwealth of Nations. Canada maintained close ties with Britain while it gradually cut the apron strings with the mother country. It was Canada's push for greater sovereignty as much as anything else that led to the Statute of Westminster in 1931. That

important act eliminated all pretenses that Great Britain made the foreign and defense decisions for the dominions or white-settled colonies. Canada actually helped to shape the kind of relationships with Britain that loosely bind together all Commonwealth countries.

Starting in 2012 Canada shares expenses and administrative duties with some British embassies. The UK offers Canada office space in its embassy in Myanmar while Canada returns the favor in Haiti. Canadian passports still contain instructions to go to the nearest British consulate in case of emergency in a country that lacks a Canadian mission.

Canada also is a leading member in the French Commonwealth of Nations, which loosely binds 49 countries that use French as their first or second language. This is dedicated chiefly to the survival of the French language. Canada's major purpose for supporting *La Francophonie* is to gain another forum for making its foreign policy presence known, as well as to indicate to the world Canada's bilingual character. Because of their bilingual status, the provinces of Quebec, New Brunswick, Ontario and Manitoba also have the right to send delegations. Another arena of special Canadian activity has long been francophone Africa, where Quebec has sought a more active Canadian role.

A further reason for differences is that Canada is a "middle power." It can neither project military power nor influence international politics, to the extent that the U.S. can. Therefore, Canadians are more inclined to focus on non-military or long-term economic developmental solutions to problems than are Americans, who despite the limits to their power can still project military force to many parts of the globe. Being a medium-sized power does not mean that Canada is of no consequence in world politics. To the contrary, Canada is far more important than one might expect for a country of only 35.5 million people.

Canada is a very active participant in international organizations. It was a founding member of the United Nations and is deeply involved in all aspects of the UN's work. With the largest combined coastline in the world, it took a strong interest in the law of the sea conferences. In 1997 the UN appointed a Canadian, Maurice Strong, to help coordinate the much needed administrative reform of that world body. In 1998 Canadian diplomat Louise Frechette was named the UN's first deputy secretary general in charge of reform issues. In 2004 Louise Arbour quit the Canadian Supreme Court to serve as UN High Commissioner for Human Rights until 2008. The head of the International Criminal Court (ICC) in 2005 was Canadian.

For the sixth time, Canada assumed a two-year term on the Security Council in 1999 but was rejected in 2010 for the first time since the UN's founding. The two western seats went to Germany and Portugal. It did not help that then opposition leader, Michael Ignatieff, said publicly that Canada had not earned such a prestigious position. Many member states do not like Harper's foreign policy, which gave outspoken support to Israel's government, closed embassies in Africa, and dragged its heels on climate change. Polls indicated that Canadians were indifferent to this setback: 38% said it did not matter, 42% that "it's humiliating and proves we're headed in the wrong direction," and 20% that "it's disappointing, but it shouldn't impact our policies."

The government had hoped that 2010 would be a year in which Canada would play an important role on the international stage. Canada is an important actor in the many international agencies that attempt to create and maintain global economic stability as it aids the World Bank, the International Monetary Fund (IMF) and the World Trade Organization (WTO). In 2000 Donald Johnston, a former Liberal cabinet member, was reelected to a second five-year term as secretary general of the Organization for Economic Cooperation and Development (OECD). He was the first non-European to hold the post.

Because of American insistence, Canada was in 1976 included in that select "group of seven" (G7) advanced industrial nations to meet periodically in "summit meetings" to discuss global economic issues at the highest level. When Russia participates, it is called the G8. In the 21st century that forum was enlarged to include major developing countries like Brazil, China, India and China, called the G20.

In the summer of 2010, Canada hosted both the G8 and G20 summits in Toronto. As always at such gatherings, thousands of anarchists, thugs, and advocates of myriad causes protested, and some turned violent, smashing shop windows, burning police cars and pelting the police with anything that can hurt. Toronto, which has always prided itself as a tolerant city, was shocked by the wanton criminality and destruction in the streets. There was an outcry in Canada about the $1 billion bill for security and clean-up and for what some viewed as overreaction by the police: about 1,100 demonstrators were arrested, including many bystanders, and 278 were ultimately charged.

In 1985, Canada hosted the first meeting in North America of the Organization of Security and Cooperation in Europe (OSCE), to monitor the progress of the so-called Helsinki Accords, signed in 1975 by 33 European nations and the U.S. and

Canada

Canada. Canad'a role in these accords indicates its interest in and importance for Europe. Then Minister of Foreign Affairs Joe Clark said in opening the conference, "Canada remains firmly convinced that a safe, prosperous and humane Europe is a cornerstone of a safe, prosperous and humane Canada."

Latin America

During the Cold War Canada was less likely than Americans to see the Soviet Union's hand in most Third-World conflicts. This meant that the U.S. had to do without Canada's support in dealing with such countries or regions as Grenada, Central America, or Cuba.

Canada never broke diplomatic and trade relations with Cuba. The Caribbean island has long been a sort of foil for Canada to demonstrate its foreign policy independence from the U.S. It is Cuba's largest trading partner, doing about a half billion dollars of trade each year, not including the sizable revenues from a steady stream of Canadian tourists. Canada is the island's largest source of foreign tourists. With a half billion in investments, it is also Cuba's largest foreign investor after Spain. In 1997, Canada reached an agreement with Cuba on a broad range of co-operation, including protecting human rights, combating drug trafficking and terrorism, and providing Cuba with food and medical aid. This was the broadest commitment yet by a major U.S. ally to work with the Castro regime. The House of Commons also signed an agreement with the Cuban parliament to exchange information and delegations.

Always sensitive to American attempts to place limits on its sovereignty, Canada strongly opposed the Helms-Burton Act, which denied travel rights in the U.S. to companies and individuals that benefit from expropriated property in Cuba. Ottawa dismissed Washington's preference for isolating Cuba, arguing that Canada's policy of engaging Cuba is the best way of achieving human rights and democracy in the long run.

In order to strengthen such "constructive engagement" in 1998, Chrétien became the first leader of a major Western country to visit Castro in Cuba in more than a decade. He made a personal appeal for the release of four prominent dissidents. When they were sentenced 11 months later, the prime minister felt betrayed and ordered a review of Canada's relations with Cuba. In December 2014 the U.S. government announced that it would restore full relations with Cuba. Although Canada did not participate in the negotiations, it hosted seven meetings in Toronto and Ottawa.

Not until 1989 did Canada join the Organization of American States (OAS), and it has still not signed its collective security agreement, the Rio Treaty. For many years Latin American governments had encouraged Canada to join the OAS in order to mitigate Washington's pervasive influence on the organization. But Ottawa had feared that full membership could limit its independence of action in the region and create a greater risk of putting its foreign policy at odds with positions taken by an OAS dominated by the U.S.

In 1989 Canada accepted a leading role in supporting a UN peacekeeping force in Central America. When the U.S. withdrew its peacekeeping troops from Haiti in 1996, Canada assumed command of the UN force through 1997. Its 750 troops were the key personnel in maintaining peace, training a police force, and improving the judicial system. In 2004 it sent peacekeeping forces to Haiti once again.

When Port-au-Prince, the capital of Haiti, was devastated by a powerful earthquake in January 2010, Canada's response was fast and generous, providing an emergency hospital, air transport and a wide variety of supplies. Canada's financial assistance was the largest per capita of any nation and the second largest in total dollars after the United States. The number of troops Canada deployed to help was nearly as many as it had fighting in Afghanistan. Successfully coordinating its effort was a new secretariat in the Foreign Affairs Department called START (Stabilization and Reconstruction Task Force), which is charged to make sure that all parts of the Canadian government work together in a crisis. Canada's close historical and cultural ties to Haiti center on the large Haitian immigrant community, especially in Quebec. Former Governor General Jean was the most prominent Haitian refugee.

Canada hosted the third Summit of the Americas, a gathering of 34 Western Hemispheric nations every three years, in Quebec in April 2001, where it supported creation of a Free Trade Area of the Americas (FTAA). It sponsored a "democracy clause" for FTAA that would penalize undemocratic regimes. However, little progress has been made for the FTAA. Prime Minister Harper's July 2007 trip through Latin America was a high-profile bid to intensify hemispheric development and trade. While Canada is increasing its two-way trade with Latin America, it amounts to less than 5% of total Canadian trade or 15% of that portion that does not involve the United States.

Through NAFTA Canada's ties with Mexico were significantly tightened. In 2005 it forged with the U.S. and Mexico the Security and Prosperity Partnership of North America (SPP). Its purpose was to facilitate closer cooperation to maximize the flow of goods and services across their borders while minimizing the passage of terrorists and illegal migrants. It aimed to continue North American integration where NAFTA left off. The "Three Amigos," the top leaders of all three member states, were to meet annually.

It achieved little beyond giving rise to countless conspiracy theories about a future "continental union" of all three countries. Of course, North America lacks the historical impetus that the Second World War had on European integration. Also, international terrorism, immigration and the violent drug war in Mexico have prompted Canada and the U.S. to strengthen their border enforcement. Canada imposed visa restrictions on Mexican visitors in 2009, a move that infuriated the Mexican government. The Obama and Harper governments found SPP too rigid and had little enthusiasm for it. They shut down its 20 working groups and cancelled the summits in 2010 and 2011.

Arms Control

Canadians push hard for arms control talks and once had a cabinet post in charge of disarmament affairs. In 1984, the government founded the Canadian Institute for International Peace and Security on the crest of strong public pressure for disarmament and a highly publicized and popular junket by Pierre Elliott Trudeau during his last year in office to world capitals in an unsuccessful attempt to stimulate greater support for the arms control process. Trudeau won the Albert Einstein Peace Prize for this, but his efforts were not appreciated in Washington. American officials saw this as a public relations gimmick to revive his party's declining popularity and as a hindrance to their own efforts to persuade the Soviet Union to negotiate seriously. The Mulroney government later closed the institute.

In 1997 Canada spearheaded the diplomatic campaign to negotiate an international ban on anti-personnel landmines, which killed more than 2,000 non-belligerents each month. In this "Ottawa Process," as the crusade was known, the government tapped a humanitarian tradition in Canadian foreign policy and endorsed the work done by Nobel Peace Prize winner Jody Williams and other private advocates, such as Princess Diana. Canada found huge support in world opinion. An American senator nominated Foreign Minister Axworthy for the Nobel Peace prize even though the U.S. did not support the ban. The Canadians detonated the remnants of their own stockpile, which had not been used since the Korean War and had long since ceased serving a tactical need for their armed forces.

Canada

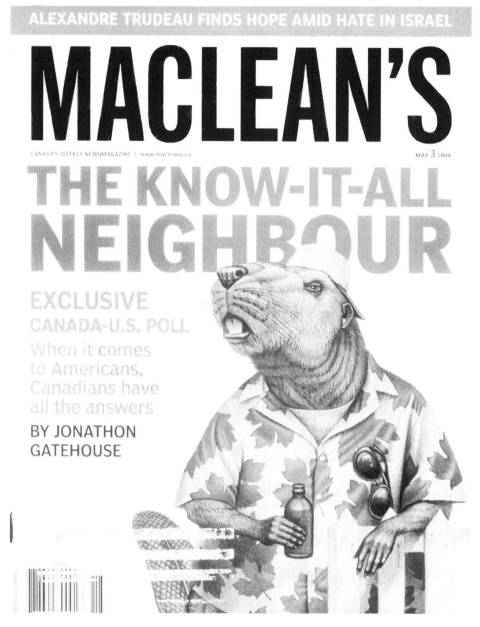

MACLEAN'S

CANADA'S WEEKLY NEWSMAGAZINE | www.macleans.ca

MAY 3 2004

THE KNOW-IT-ALL NEIGHBOUR

EXCLUSIVE
CANADA-U.S. POLL

When it comes to Americans, Canadians have all the answers

BY JONATHON GATEHOUSE

On December 3, 1997, delegates from about 100 countries met in Ottawa to sign the treaty, an example of Canada's "value-added" diplomacy that permits it to play a visible role in world affairs despite acknowledged limits on its resources. Axworthy explained: "With the new fluidity taking place [since the end of the Cold War], there is room for value-added diplomacy. We made a choice that other middle powers have not. We decided to stay global." The view of some Canadians that their country is a kind of "moral superpower" inevitably creates friction with the superpower to the south. Almost two decades later, the treaty's success was obvious: 161 countries had signed on, and deaths and injuries from mines had practically ceased, along with their use and production.

Quebec and France

In any country, domestic political factors strongly influence foreign policy. In Canada, the particularly fragile unity of the country has created difficulties. It has always made Canadians especially wary of what they might interpret as American threats to their sovereignty. Also, the threat of Quebec separatism revealed a potential Achilles heel. It forced Canada to turn its attention even more inwardly than before and to look nervously abroad to see how other countries, especially France and the United States, would respond to Quebec claims of independence.

In 1967, French President Charles de Gaulle gave public support to separatism by saying in a speech in Montreal, "*Vive le Québec libre*" ("Long live free Quebec") which infuriated his host, Prime Minister

Pearson. For a while it seemed as if the French government might even grant Quebec full diplomatic status in Paris, and, in some ways, it did indeed give Quebec's representatives, who outnumber Ottawa's diplomats, the trappings of such status. Such games were played as whose flag could be flown where, and there was some bickering over the titles which Quebec's representatives should be permitted to have. But France concluded, especially after Quebecers rejected sovereignty in 1980, that it should support a unified Canada and has subsequently done so.

In 1985 France's former Prime Minister Laurent Fabius, who went to Canada on his first official visit abroad as head of government, assured the Canadian government that while relations with Quebec were of great importance, "our ambition is vaster and aimed at all Canadians." He even offered a toast designed to undo the damage done in 1967: *Vive le Canada; vive la France!* The French government also turned a cold shoulder to the 10,000 Canadians of French ancestry who submitted a request for dual citizenship in 1989 on the occasion of the 200th anniversary of the French Revolution.

In 1994 *Bloc Québécois* leader Lucien Bouchard, who was once Canadian ambassador to France, made an official visit to Paris to demonstrate to Quebecers that independence would not leave them international pariahs. Bouchard's visit was not reported at all in the French media, and a reserved French foreign minister reminded him that France's position on the Quebec issue is "non-indifference but non-interference."

In 1997, Bouchard returned to the French capital as Premier of Quebec with a bevy of Quebec ministers and received a mixed report: President Jacques Chirac told him, in Bouchard's words, that "whatever road Quebec chooses, France will accompany it." However, ex-Prime Minister Lionel Jospin, who regarded Canada as an important ally in countering American cultural dominance in the world, was less enthusiastic, noting that any decision to recognize Quebec would have to take into account the Canadian government's assessment of the post-referendum situation.

At the 1999 Francophonie summit in New Brunswick, Chirac was restrained. He stressed that France and Canada are partners and that Paris has no wish to interfere in other countries' affairs. But a gaffe made by one of France's presidential candidates in 2007, Ségolène Royal, who said in a speech that Quebec should have the right to self-determination, demonstrated that there remains some ambivalence in Paris concerning Quebec's future in Canada.

On his returning to Canada, Bouchard found himself in a firefight over a

Canada

proposed agreement between the province and France to enforce child support settlements. Since Canada's constitution limits provincial governments' foreign relations to culture and commerce, Ottawa scuttled the deal because of the contractual language that treated Quebec as a sovereign country.

Even in the cultural sphere Ottawa resists any gesture that seems to treat Quebec as a sovereign state. In March 1999, Canada angrily pulled out of an international meeting of culture ministers in Paris after the French government issued a direct invitation to Quebec. "Only the government of Canada has the right to decide on the presence and representation of Canada and its constituent parts in our relations with other foreign states."

Quebec also tried hard to gain some form of special recognition from the U.S., but American leaders and diplomats were careful always to stress that the U.S. would deal only with Ottawa on diplomatic matters. They prevented Quebec from opening a kind of "embassy" in the U.S. and permitted only trade missions. Quebec has more than 25 representative offices throughout the world.

The consistent American view is that there should be only *one* Canada, not two. This was politely reiterated to Bouchard during his 1994 visit to Washington. U.S. officials expressed this more bluntly to a former American political officer and later ambassador at the U.S. embassy in Ottawa, David T. Jones, who wrote in a 1997 article in the *Washington Quarterly* that the U.S. could "live with" an independent Quebec. The State Department publicly called this statement "an outrageous, undisciplined act."

In order to shore up Canada's relationship with France in 2000, the former prime minister appointed his nephew, Raymond Chrétien, as ambassador in Paris. Quebec's Liberal Premier, Jean Charest, maintained much more cooperative relations with his fellow Liberal government in Ottawa after his election in 2003. At the same time, Chrétien traveled to Paris, flying the Quebec flag and acting like the government leader of a sovereign state. Chrétien initiated discussions to obtain for Quebec a greater presence in the international arena, especially in trade negotiations. "What we are aiming for is to be at the negotiating table with the federal government if the topic of discussion affects Quebec's competence. . . . As French speakers representing 2% of the population of North America, we have always felt the need to maintain external relations." Quebec did secure a seat in the UN Economic Social and Cultural Council (UNESCO), and it announced its desire for more such international memberships.

Charest returned to Paris in 2007 to meet with new French President Nicolas Sarkozy, who was openly pro-Canadian. Charest discovered that nobody talks about separation anymore. But this time he was working closely with the federal government to stimulate Europeans' interest in a transatlantic, Canada-EU free trade agreement. In April 2008, France's leading right-leaning newspaper, *Le Figaro*, described the PQ as "an empty shell" that has "sold its soul" by resigning itself to ruling only a Canadian province, not its own country.

In 2008 there was an unprecedented number of contacts between Canadian and French politicians due to the celebrations surrounding the 400th anniversary of Quebec City's founding. Immediately after the October 2008 elections, Harper raced to Quebec City to open the Francophonie Summit declaring himself "heir" to Samuel de Champlain and pledging more funding for the international Quebec channel TV5.

The prestigious French daily, *Le Monde*, lauded Governor General Michaëlle Jean, the great-great-granddaughter of French-owned Haitian slaves, during a May 2008 visit to Paris as an "almost Queen." Quebec nationalists fumed that she was being feted in France instead of Quebec Premier Jean Charest. President Sarkozy (2007-2012) antagonized them again in February 2009. After ceremoniously awarding Charest the Legion of Honor medal, Sarkozy added: "Do you believe the world, as it faces an unprecedented crisis, needs more divisions?" He favored "deepening in every domain the unique relation that links France to Quebec," but the best way to do that is "in harmony with the relation that France maintains with all of Canada." Quebec nationalists were stunned at such "lack of respect" and "contemptible epithets." PQ leader Pauline Marois was dumbfounded: "What are you talking about, Mr. President?"

Sarkozy was the first modern French president openly to oppose separatism. His successor, François Hollande, returned to the country's earlier official policy toward Quebec's future as "non-indifference and non-interference." Nobody knows precisely what this means. Hollande referred to *"une amitié et un cousinage."* roughly "Canadian friends and its cousins in Quebec". Hollande explained to ex-Prime Minister Harper, who was one of the first foreign leaders to congratulate him on his win, that France sees its relations with Quebec and all of Canada to be "parallel, harmonious and essentially synonymous" and that he has no intention of disrupting that state of affairs. Not to be left out, Hollande's conservative opponent, Jean-François Copé, conducted a charm offensive to Ottawa in early 2014.

Complex Relations with the United States

The Canadian domestic political system is complicated. The provinces are very powerful and can sometimes place limits on Ottawa's power. Of course, American states also have the power to act on their own in many matters. Therefore, both countries experience some difficulties in settling bilateral affairs, when state and provincial capitals manage to get into the act.

Canada's parliamentary system simplifies the conduct of foreign policy. Responsibility is clearer, and once the federal government establishes policy, there are fewer obstacles to its implementation than in the U.S. Canada's parliamentary committees in the House of Commons and Senate debate policy and hold hearings. They may also suggest amendments. But Parliament cannot thwart a policy to which the government has committed itself. No majority government that has negotiated a treaty needs to worry about whether Parliament will ratify it.

The American political system works differently. As in Canada, power is divided in a geographic sense. However, unlike in Canada, power is also separated in Washington, and this can create diplomatic nightmares for both American and Canadian leaders. Foreigners have every reason to be mystified by America's large, highly decentralized institutions, which wield power of their own and which often seem to be hostile to each other. Separation of powers is particularly troublesome for foreign policy: it is often impossible for a president to produce what he promises to foreign leaders.

The complicated and extensive interagency bargaining in Washington confuses many Canadians although they expend a greater effort to understand the U.S. system than Americans do the Canadian. The American political system enables relatively unknown persons of various professional backgrounds to rise to the highest national political offices through a painfully long and complicated electoral system, largely unfathomable to Canadians, and to many Americans as well.

Newly elected U.S. presidents such as Donald Trump may have had little experience in foreign affairs and yet have the power to select a multitude of foreign policy advisers, secretaries, and agency chiefs, many with little or no foreign policy background. Such a presidential "team" appears often to operate in an uncoordinated way, frequently sending off widely differing signals. This inevitably creates and fuels doubts about American leadership capabilities and the continuity of U.S. foreign policy. In 1996-7 it took 15 months for the Clinton administration finally to name a new ambassador to

Canada

Canada, Gordon Giffin, who lived most of his youth in Montreal and Toronto, and months more before the Senate confirm him to his post.

Canadians are particularly frustrated by the powerful U.S. Congress. It has undergone significant changes: the seniority system has weakened, and the number of committees and subcommittees has proliferated. Also, the workload has become so demanding that congressmen and senators are retiring earlier. Therefore, an increasingly high percentage of the legislators are new in Congress. At the same time, committee and personal staffs have grown enormously. What these changes have done is to take much of the power that used to be concentrated in a few key figures and to disperse it within Congress.

In this more decentralized, or, more positively, "democratized," Congress, legislative work has become more complicated. For instance, more than 40 congressional committees and subcommittees deal with the defense budget alone. Absent strong party discipline as in Canada, American congressmen and senators are more protective of their constituents' interests and can safely vote against their party leaders or the president if an issue of great interest in their districts or states is at stake. In December 2000, ex-Foreign Minister John Manley said that it would be easier to work with the new American President George W. Bush than with Congress: "It's always easier for Canada to deal with the United States when the administration has the strength to deal with issues and can expect congressional support."

Because the approval of the U.S. Senate, by a two-thirds vote, is needed for all treaties, the American upper house can even veto the most painstakingly crafted international agreement. Canadian governments have experienced how this fact can affect their bilateral relations with the United States. The East Coast Fisheries Agreement of 1979, the Tax Treaty of 1980 and the Pacific Salmon Treaty of 1983 were all victims of senatorial opposition. Also galling to Canadian diplomats and governments is the fact that after already making all the concessions it could to secure the president's or State Department's agreement, a president or secretary of state might come back to them and say that yet more concessions are needed in order to secure senatorial approval. Thus, Canada must sometimes go farther than halfway to get a ratified agreement, and that favors the United States.

In an attempt to get around this problem, Canada began to lobby directly in Congress in order to compete with the interest groups that were seeking to stymie agreements important to Canada. Allan Gotlieb, ambassador to the U.S. in the 1980s, wrote

in *The Washington Diaries* that "Americans just do not see us as different from themselves. When we do something different, Americans feel betrayed. They don't see us as foreigners but as perverse Americans."

Gotlieb changed the earlier standard practice of working only with the State Department and took his country's concerns directly to Congress and its powerful staffers. When calling on members of Congress, he remembers: "One always feels as though he is begging. One is. The challenge: how to beg and keep one's dignity." Gotlieb noted that diplomatic disputes often arise not as a result of White House decisions but from the rulings of unknown bureaucrats at federal agencies, which Canadian diplomats must not neglect. Gotlieb also worked with journalists: "I would never have dreamed of how important journalists are in Washington. My views were shaped by 20 years in Ottawa dealing with the semi-educated press corps there." Gotlieb concluded that his country has no friends in Washington, only interests. That might be changing: in 2006 a new congressional "Friends of Canada" caucus was created to focus on shared concerns.

In 2004 a new public advocacy and legislative secretariat was created in the Canadian Embassy, which includes provincial representatives, to lobby Congress more effectively. Alberta, which exports close to $90 billion in goods, mainly energy and food, to the U.S. annually, is the only province that runs a trade office out of the embassy. Quebec and Manitoba have their own lower-profile representatives to lobby on issues of interest. Quebec also has a tourism office elsewhere in Washington.

Former Ambassador Michael Wilson commented in 2007 that Canada's and Alberta's joint effort to influence the American government is good. Wilson wanted to demonstrate that the bilateral relationship goes much farther than merely dealing

Kirsten Hillman, Ambassador of Canada to the United States

with a few irritants and rises to the level of a global "partnership." This struck a positive note with an American diplomat: "It's exactly what we have wanted from Canada: a partner who will work with us together on the 96 per cent of international issues where our goals are the same: defeat terrorism, advance and consolidate democracy and good governance, prevent the proliferation of WMDs, promote economic development through open trade and development."

Canadians also rely on U.S. governors to advocate shared concerns in Washington. Gottlieb said "these governor relationships really matter because the states matter—that is increasingly where the problems come from. And if the governor is our friend, then we are closer to solving them." One governor who was a friend is Vancouver-born Canadian citizen Jennifer Granholm of Michigan. One of the oldest relationships is the Conference of New England Governors and Eastern Canadian Premiers. A major asset of former Manitoba Premier Gary Doer, who was appointed to replace Michael Wilson as ambassador to the U.S. in 2009, was that he had spent much time in the U.S. and knew personally all four former governors in President Obama's cabinet. Of course, mayors and city councils on both sides of the border work closely together.

It is rare that incivility is shown, as it was in 2013 over efforts to expand the plaza on the New York side of the Peace Bridge connecting Buffalo to Fort Erie in Canada. New York Governor Andrew Cuomo stooped to describing his Canadian counterparts in e-mails as "duplicitous" and their behavior as "deceitful, disrespectful and arrogant." Passions ran so high that the ambassadors on both sides had to step in and calm the parties down. The dispute was settled in June 2013.

It also began to try harder to influence the American public directly. In one case, the Canadians produced a film on acid rain to help educate Americans on its consequences for Canadian fish, trees, lakes and public monuments. Some American officials bristled at this attempt by a foreign country to go over their heads in an important diplomatic issue and appeal directly to the American people. U.S. officials temporarily banned the film, a move that predictably heightened Americans' interest in it and spurred them to jam halls in which the film was later shown.

Americans and Canadians have a great deal of practice in settling their disputes peacefully. When they cannot, they have taken their disputes to the International Court of Justice, agreeing in advance to abide by its decision. In 1984, the court rendered a long-awaited decision on a disputed maritime boundary in the Gulf

of Maine, giving Canada jurisdiction over about one-sixth of the rich Georges Bank fishing grounds. Canadians were unhappy with this outcome. The countries worked out an agreement as to what should be done to manage the fish stocks that cross the boundary and are caught by both countries' fishermen.

The two countries had a sovereignty dispute over Machias Seal Island and nearby North Rock, which are tiny, as Machias is 20 acres, rocky, remote and uninhabited islands in the Bay of Fundy. They have neither strategic significance nor oil and gas. Bird watchers go there to observe nesting Atlantic puffins. The disagreement stems from differing interpretations of the 1783 Treaty of Paris. Britain built a lighthouse on Machias Seal Island in 1832, and Canada has manned it ever since. Located almost equidistant between Maine and New Brunswick, it is the last land mass contested by Canada and the U.S.

The U.S.-Canadian Border

Even before the September 11, 2001, attacks, there was congressional clamor to tighten up controls along the U.S.-Canadian border. An Algerian with a fake Canadian passport was arrested at the border in December 1999 with enough material in his car to make four powerful bombs. Two other Algerians and a Canadian woman were apprehended at the border to Vermont five days later with traces of explosives that sniffer dogs detected. All were identified as members of a violent Algerian organization called the Armed Islamic Group (GIA).

Members of the U.S. Congress charged that Canada was "soft on terrorism." Months of intense diplomatic and political activity were necessary before a deal could be reached dropping the proposed requirements for Canadians to fill out time-consuming entry forms at the border like all other foreigners. Nevertheless, the U.S. added 600 new customs and special agents along the border, bringing the number to 2,200.

The September 11 attacks changed the way many Americans look at their borders, raising the urgency to secure them. Officials set out to apply technology to create a "smart border" to tighten security and thwart terrorists while keeping the 49th parallel open for the world's largest trading relationship. The longest undefended border became a bit more defended and more complex to traverse.

The challenge is daunting: a truck crosses the Ambassador Bridge between Detroit and Windsor every six seconds. This bridge, with an accompanying tunnel, is the cornerstone of the two neighbors' trade, especially that of Canada's export-dependent economy. Even a temporary closing of the 555-meter-long bridge, owned privately by the Manuel Mouroun family and its Detroit International Bridge Company, would be devastating to the two countries' $627 billion annual trade relationship (in 2010) and to Canada's economic future. That is why Michigan voters rejected a ballot initiative in 2012 that would have hindered the construction of a second bridge connecting Detroit and Windsor. It will be located about two miles from the Ambassador Bridge. It will be named the Gordie Howe International Bridge and will be built through a public-private partnership. Canada will bear most of the project's costs. By 2018, the highway on the Canadian side was completed, and Canada had obtained all the required approvals for the crossing.

About 70% of Canada-U.S. trade travels by truck, with 37,000 trucks crossing the border every day; 58% of these cross at only five border crossings—Ambassador Bridge, Sarnia, Fort Erie, Lacolle, and the Pacific Highway. Eight out of ten top crossing points are either bridges or tunnels and have become bottlenecks with long waits. Speed is increasingly important because of growing "just-in-time delivery." Trucks loaded with goods bound for either country are pre-cleared and sealed with electronic sensors that allow them to cross the border in fast lanes. The "Nexus" system of allowing "pre-approved frequent travelers" across the frontier was improved and reintroduced.

Before September 11, half the 126 official crossings were unguarded at night, but they are all protected 24 hours now. The U.S. Coast Guard stops all boats crossing the maritime border in the Great Lakes and escorts all oil and gas tankers. When U.S. Coast Guard vessels in American waters installed machine guns and conducted periodic live-fire exercises in 2006, an outcry was heard all around the lakes. Armaments in the Great Lakes are supposed to be limited, according to an 1817 treaty. Eighty American and Canadian mayors demanded that the shooting stop.

The Canadian-U.S. border has become more secure; it is not as open as it was before September 11. The number of Americans who cross the border dropped by 22% between 1999 and 2005. This hits Ontario the hardest, whose tourist trade is 95% dependent on Americans. BC and Alberta depend more on Asian visitors, and Quebec on Europeans. In the other direction, the opening in Canada of large American retail outlets like Wal-Mart, Best Buy, Pottery Barn and Home Depot, as well as growing internet purchasing, have contributed to the reduction of Canadian day-trippers into the U.S.

Canadian consumers have complained loudly about the fact that prices for American goods are still higher in Canada than across the border. One can see this in the two prices on book covers: the American price is always lower. The price difference is especially grating for automobiles: in 2007 a Lexus RX350 sold for $52,000 in Canada, but only $37,000 in the United States.

Source: *The Economist*

Canada

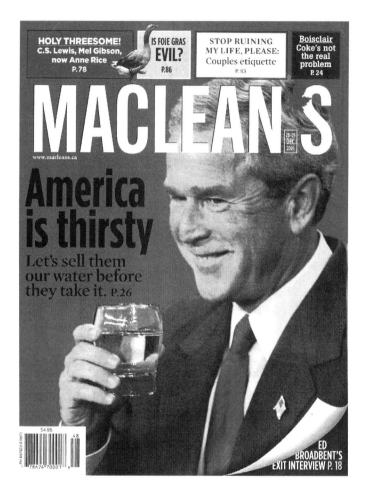

The stronger Canadian dollar and high Canadian gasoline prices helped drive many Canadians southward across the border for shopping. There they can visit certain chain stores, such as Macy's, Saks Fifth Avenue, J. Crew, Kenneth Cole, Anthropologie and Bath & Body Works, that have not expanded to Canada. Canadians can generally buy products in the U.S. for lower prices than they would pay at home. However, if they buy too much, they may be required to pay sales taxes and other duties when they reenter Canada. The greatest fear on both sides of the frontier is that the $2 billion daily two-way trade will be affected. Already old-style warehousing of goods is being reintroduced in many places to replace the efficiency of just-in-time delivery.

The main factor for slower border crossings is the fear of terrorist attacks; 44 government agencies on both sides have some jurisdiction over border matters, and that means slower crossings. Eight Canadian ministries alone have responsibility for some part of the border. The sprawling Department of Public Safety, the Canadian equivalent of the Department of Homeland Security, was created after September 11, 2001, to give a single minister control over everything from the RCMP and Canadian Security Intelligence Service, to running federal prisons and managing the border with the United States. In 2004 the U.S. began demanding fingerprints and photos at its borders for non-Canadian citizens between the ages of 14 and 80.

From January 2007 all airline passengers arriving in the U.S. had to show a valid passport. For the first time in history that was extended to land and water passengers on June 1, 2009, when the Western Hemisphere Travel Initiative came into effect. The disruption this requirement caused was reportedly modest even though there was a sharp drop in cross-border travel. However, relying on passports is a problem since only an estimated 34% of Americans over age 18 have one, compared to 54% of Canadians.

Where there is real worry, though, is that fire trucks and ambulances are delayed at the border, thereby hampering community-level cross-border cooperation. That already happened in 2008 when Quebec volunteer firemen speeding to a hotel blaze in upstate New York were held up so long on the border that the building had burned to the ground by the time they arrived on the scene. Nobody knows what may happen elsewhere in places like Stanstead, Quebec, and Derby Line, Vermont, which are, in effect, a single community. Not only do streets continue unguarded into the other country, but the joint opera house and library building is shared. Most of the interior is in Canada, but one can only enter the building from the U.S.. A black line on the floor runs through the library demarcating the two lands.

In the *Maclean's* 2003–04 year-end poll, 61% of Canadians approved of the idea of a North American perimeter. Prime Ministers Martin and Harper agreed that one of Canada's main challenges is to keep the American border open. After all, three-fourths of its exports head across the U.S. border, accounting for 52% of Canada's GDP.

Given the facts that a truck crosses the Canada-U.S. border every 2.5 seconds and that every minute more than US$1 million in trade passes across it, trade must be kept unimpeded. This is the rationale for the bilateral "Beyond the Border" trade and security plan of 2011–12. The main idea is that American customs and immigration officials will be physically stationed on the Canadian side of the border, and Canadian border officials on the U.S. side to screen people, trucks, and cargo before they cross into the other country. Both countries will share information about people crossing the border, facilitating trade and travel. As it stands, when goods cross the border, 45 authorities in the two countries require data.

Bilateral cooperation has been stepped up, with a growing exchange of intelligence information and criminal records, allowing U.S. law enforcement agents to retrieve records from the Canadian Police Information Centre, consultation on visas as Canada requires no visa for 52 countries, while the U.S. exempts only 32, and collaboration at foreign embassies to stop people smuggling from overseas. At the time of the September 11 attacks, only Canadians worked at the RCMP headquarters in Ottawa. Now Americans from four agencies are based there. Cooperation is reported to be "pervasive." The two countries have acted in concert to plug a hole at St-Bernard-de-Lacolle along the Quebec border with New York. It is now more difficult to arrive in New York with fraudulent passports and then scoot across the border to claim refugee status.

The Mexican and Canadian borders are still different. Whereas the Mexican border is normally divided by walls, the Canadian frontier is in most places no more than a ditch or a cleared area in a forest. By 2015 the U.S. stationed only 2,200 (up from 340 in 2001) border patrol agents along the Canadian border, compared with 18,600 along the shorter boundary with Mexico. Still, the U.S. is creating border security bases like it has along its

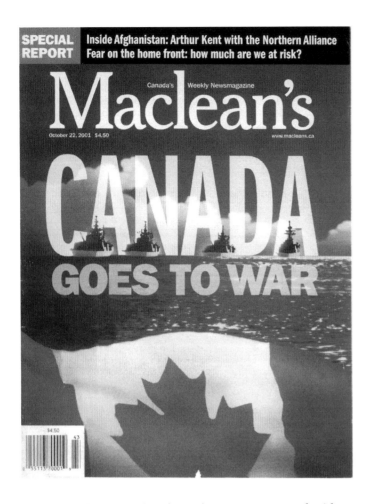

border with Mexico. Each equipped with two helicopters, an airplane, a high-speed boat, and a staff of about 70, the first was located at Bellingham, Washington, and Plattsburgh, New York, followed by bases near Detroit, Michigan, Grand Forks, North Dakota, and Great Falls, Montana.

President Obama's first homeland-security secretary, Janet Napolitano, wanted controls along the Canadian border to be brought in line with those on the Mexican frontier. She said she wanted everybody to realize that "this is a real border." There are plans to install heat-detecting sensors and additional cameras along the border. The U.S. also now uses aircraft with sensor arrays, thermal cameras, and unmanned surveillance drones to patrol parts of the frontier. Napolitano's replacement, Jeh Johnson, focused more on defense along the border, not the economic issues that matter to Canada.

Both countries are targeting potential terrorists and smuggling. The latter includes marijuana from Canada and cocaine and weapons from the U.S., as well as large amounts of cash in both directions. In order to deal with the dangers of such cross-border criminality, the 4,800 officers of the Canada Border Services Agency were armed with guns. The aim of such cooperation is an even more open and safe U.S.-Canada border.

Water Resources and Acid Rain

In 1909 the two countries signed and ratified the Boundary Waters Treaty to preserve the quality and quantity of their shared water, setting up an International Joint Commission to arbitrate disputes. In its century of existence, it has worked well; of 53 joint references, 51 were resolved by mutual agreement. Nevertheless, the two countries seem always to have ongoing disagreements over use of North America's water resources.

For decades American governments have been interested in a project to divert the waters of the Garrison River in order to direct water from the Missouri River basin into 250,000 acres of parched lands in northwestern North Dakota for irrigation purposes. North Dakota long wanted to drain millions of gallons of water from Devil's Lake, which has no natural outlet and is located 60 miles south of the Manitoba border, in order to prevent the rising lake from continuing to flood the surrounding countryside. The problem is that the spill-off waters might carry unwanted invasive species, parasites, disease, and

the high concentrations of sulphates, arsenic, phosphorus and other pollutants from Devil's Lake via the Sheyenne River into the Red River across the Canadian border into Lake Winnipeg. From there they could ultimately pass through Canadian rivers, most of which flow northward, into the Hudson Bay watershed.

Although the projects had actually been started, the determined efforts of environmentalist groups on both sides of the border, as well as the Manitoba provincial government, prevented for a while the projects from getting complete approval. Nevertheless, there continued to be support in Congress for them. After devastating floods along the Red River in North Dakota and Manitoba in 1997, the two countries agreed to work together to minimize future flooding.

In 2000, the North Dakota governor traveled to Manitoba to see firsthand the province's concerns and promised to consult with provincial leaders. A few months later the Manitoba premier and the governors of Minnesota and North Dakota met for the first time and reached an agreement to protect all citizens from Red River flooding. In the same year, Canada sent 200 firefighters to help weary Americans battle a hundred wildfires out of control across the Western United States. For the first time, the U.S. put a foreigner, a Canadian, in command of a unit battling a blaze.

Ultimately, patience ran out in mid-2005. North Dakota officials, who resisted Canadian requests to refer the issue to the commission, announced that the draining of Devil's Lake would begin. This kind of unilateral action could lead to difficulties for both neighbors. Half the 300 transboundary rivers flow southward into the United States. In 2005 Montana challenged BC's plans to mine coal under a vital riverbed. Good will can run thin. In a landmark cross-border pollution case, a Canadian company in BC, Teck Cominco, voluntarily agreed in 2006 to pay for any harm done to Americans or wildlife by the waste products its zinc smelter had dumped into the Columbia River and traveled downstream into the U.S.

With ten times Canada's population, the U.S. is in much greater need of water resources, and American eyes have often looked to Canada's supply as a long-range solution. Canada has always resisted the large-scale transfer of its water resources, though. Its leaders have noted that even though the Canadian Shield has abundant lakes and streams, its water is not easily replenishable. The fact is that the flow of rain, spring water and snowmelt that goes through Canadian waterways represents 7% of the world's renewable water supply.

Of Canada's 18 principal watershed systems, 15 provide less than 10% of their

Canada

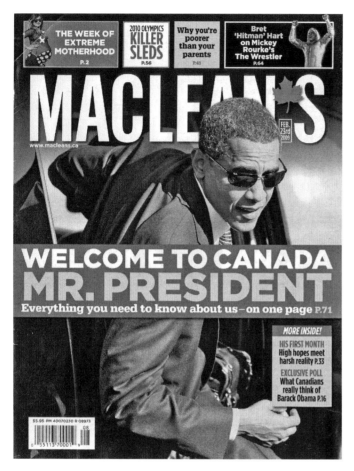

THE WEEK OF EXTREME MOTHERHOOD P.2

2010 OLYMPICS KILLER SLEDS P.56

Why you're poorer than your parents P.41

Bret 'Hitman' Hart on Mickey Rourke's The Wrestler P.64

MACLEAN'S
www.macleans.ca
FEB. 23rd 2009

WELCOME TO CANADA MR. PRESIDENT
Everything you need to know about us—on one page P.71

MORE INSIDE!
HIS FIRST MONTH
High hopes meet harsh reality P.33
EXCLUSIVE POLL
What Canadians really think of Barack Obama P.16

$5.95 PM 40070230 R 09973

annual renewable supplies to human usage. Canadians have also opposed large-scale diversion of water from the Great Lakes, which are shared by both countries. Although they have occasionally studied the possibility of siphoning off that water, the Great Lakes states agreed not to initiate any such scheme without Ontario's permission. Forty-five million, including 10 million in Ontario, get their drinking water from the Great Lakes.

In 2002 the International Boundary Waters Treaty Act went into effect banning the bulk removal of water from basins that straddle the border, particularly the Great Lakes. Actually, researchers who sought examples of economically viable ideas for bulk-water exports from Canada have found none. There are neither serious proposals nor realistic prospects for such exports to the U.S. Although NAFTA says nothing about water, ex-Foreign Minister Pierre Pettigrew, made clear: "Water is not a [tradable] good, it is a resource that needs to be managed."

One of the most stubborn problems of both countries was acid rain, pollution caused by the burning of fossil fuels and released into the air via high smokestacks that mixes in the atmosphere with nitrogen oxide from automobile emissions to form an acid moisture. This unhealthy

combination sometimes is then carried hundreds of miles before being brought back to earth by rain, killing trees, fish and other animal life and eating away at stone buildings and monuments. For a country whose people are rightly proud of its natural beauty and 10% of whose work force depends on tourism, this is a catastrophic ecological and economic problem.

Much of Canada's acid rain stems from plants in the U.S., particularly in the Midwest. Therefore, any solution to the problem must be an international one. American administrations tended to buy time by calling for "more research" on acid rain. Because of the salience of this issue in Canada, its leaders could not accept this and pushed for more concrete steps. The acid rain issue, which became a sort of litmus test for the two countries' relations, severely tried Canadians' patience.

In 1991 the two signed a landmark accord committing the two countries to curb emissions that cause acid rain and to reduce other pollutants. By 1995, acid rain levels had dropped significantly, and sulfur dioxide emissions had declined in the East by 40% since 1980. Still, work remains to be done on both sides. In 2000, the New York's Attorney General asked the President to put pressure on the Ontario government to clean up coal-burning plants

on the Canadian side that are destroying forests and causing respiratory problems in Buffalo and other border areas.

Prime Ministers and Presidents

Brian Mulroney came into office in 1984 determined to improve Canada-U.S. relations. Not since Lester Pearson and John F. Kennedy were in power in the early 1960s was there such a warm personal relationship between the leaders of these two neighbors and allies. Regular summit meetings forced Washington to confront Canadian issues promptly, instead of consigning them to the back burner. The invitation of Mulroney to address the U.S. Congress and to dedicate the newly completed Canadian embassy in Washington, the only foreign embassy to be permitted on Pennsylvania Avenue, demonstrated the two countries' good relations.

Mulroney had to pay a domestic political price for his relationship with Reagan and Bush. He reaped criticism for seeming too eager to please and to impress American presidents even though he was not afraid to say "no" when Canadian interests were at stake: he refused to withdraw from UNESCO, favored tough economic sanctions against South Africa, permitted Nicaragua to open a trade office in Toronto, and refused officially to endorse the Strategic Defense Initiative, or SDI. In fact, Mulroney publicly broke ranks with the U.S. more frequently than did either Pearson or Trudeau, whom President Nixon considered to be an "asshole," according to Watergate tapes. Mulroney merely concluded that a confrontational approach toward the U.S. is less effective than a more conciliatory style.

Former Prime Minister Chrétien decided that his approach toward the U.S. would be less enthusiastic and more formal. He had scorned Mulroney's pledge always to give the Americans the benefit of the doubt, joking that Mulroney would answer the phone from the president before it rang. Chrétien also announced after his election that, unlike Mulroney, he would not be going fishing with the president, fearing that he might end up as the fish. Chrétien played golf with Clinton, but he winced in 1997 when the president introduced him in the Rose Garden by saying that "I don't know of any two world leaders who played golf together more than we have." Chrétien had said in 1992: "Mulroney cares more about getting others to like him than about getting the things that Canada needs. Me, I understand that in politics there is no room for friendship."

Chrétien also knew that Canadian voters do not like overt reverence for the U.S. They have ambivalent feelings toward the U.S. and are alternately drawn

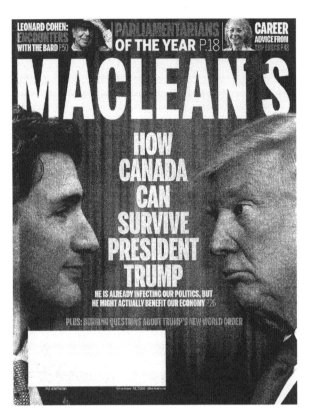

to and repelled by American might. Canadians prefer what the *Globe and Mail* called "affected standoffishness" toward Washington. Chrétien expresses that ambivalence well. A 1994 poll showed that 53% of respondents approved his management of the relationship with America, compared with 25% for Mulroney in 1992. Chrétien established comfortable rapport with President Clinton, meeting discreetly with him 16 times leading up to an official visit to Washington in April 1997, his first since taking office in 1993.

Chrétien described that rapport he had with Clinton as "good, and not cozy," treating him as an equal, not as the ranking world leader. Chrétien thus felt free in 1997 to expound to the leaders of Belgium and Luxembourg that Clinton's views on NATO expansion are "not for reasons of security" but "for short-term political reasons to win elections." As one Canadian political commentator noted, Chrétien's assertion that American foreign policies are driven by domestic interests are about as shocking as the reality that the same is true for Canada.

Chrétien offered swift support for important American policies and appreciated Clinton's pitch for a united Canada during the president's 1995 visit to Ottawa, repeated at the time of the Quebec referendum: "A strong and united Canada has been a wonderful partner for the United States and an incredibly important and constructive citizen throughout the entire world." But when he introduced Clinton

to Parliament, he said: "The Americans are our best friends—whether we like it or not." Moreover, Chrétien went out of his way in Washington in 1997 to underline the differences between the two countries, stressing the way Canada values such things as universal health care and gun control.

In Chrétien's words, "it's nice to have a big client like the United States, but you can't have just one. It wouldn't be a good business position." Nevertheless, the two countries' close economic ties and cordial relations remained essentially unchanged. Chrétien's foreign policy had been less outspoken about human rights, more aggressive about promoting Canadian exports and economic interests, and less generous with foreign aid (which it cut to only .28% of GDP by 2018 (the world's 15th highest, ahead of the United States' .21%).

Ex-Foreign Minister Axworthy crusaded visibly and energetically on the world stage under the banners of "soft power" and "human security" that emphasize values and human need. He stepped down in 2000 and was replaced by John Manley, who proclaimed that his first priority was to enhance Canada's privileged relationship with the United States. In September 2003 the government announced that seven new consulates would be opened in the U.S., and two consulates would be upgraded to consulate generals. Twenty honorary consuls would be appointed. Thus, representation in the U.S. grew from 15 to 22. Most new locations were in the Southeast, Southwest, and Midwest. This

reflects the government's concern about the shift of American political and economic power to the "Sunbelt" away from the northern states adjacent to Canada.

Prime Minister Paul Martin promised the same thing on taking power in December 2003 and even created a cabinet committee with himself as chairman to explore ways to improve relations with Washington. The business lobby in Ottawa, as well as many other Canadian leaders, encouraged Martin to continue in this direction. Martin appointed a heavy hitter as ambassador to the U.S.: Frank McKenna, former premier of New Brunswick. Despite serious disagreements with the American government over issues like Iraq, there was unease about being estranged from the United States without the backing of a rising regional block like the European Union. If one adds to this an inadequacy of military power, fewer funds for foreign aid, and a declining share of America's imports, Canada was worried about its influence in the world.

Martin shifted the locus for making important decisions on the Canada-U.S. relationship from the Department of Foreign Affairs and International Trade to the Privy Council Office (PCO). Martin's proposal to create a new Department of International Trade, separate from the Department of Foreign Affairs, was rejected by parliament in 2005. The Harper government decided in 2006 to keep the two together, thereby emphasizing the importance of trade with the U.S. After the September 11 terrorist attacks, responsibility for the bilateral border was transferred to the PCO.

Martin ordered major policy reviews in both foreign affairs and defense. In April 2005 the results, entitled "Now is the time to rebuild," were unveiled. The government pledged to bolster its diplomatic corps, beef up the military, and overhaul foreign aid in an attempt to reverse Canada's diminishing influence in foreign affairs. The prime minister asserted: "You cannot have a robust foreign policy if all you're prepared to engage in is empty moralizing." Concrete proposals included raising military spending by C$10 billion over five years, increasing the size of the armed forces by 5,000 to 67,000, instituting a central command, strengthening the special operations forces, purchasing more equipment, such as helicopters and ships, and creating a new emergency response team capable of dealing with disasters anywhere.

After his reelection in 2004, President George W. Bush seized the opportunity to reach out to Canada and to improve the tone of the relationship. With only two weeks' notice, he accepted Martin's invitation to Canada. In his December 1, 2004, speech in Halifax, he thanked all those

Canada

Canadians who "came out to wave—with all five fingers—for the hospitality." Bush expressed belated gratitude to those who had taken in stranded American passengers after the September 11 terrorist strikes in New York and Washington. Martin admitted that "it's not always easy to sleep next to the elephant," but he spoke a language Canadians like to hear: building multilateral institutions and making international cooperation a top priority. Bush and his Canadian counterpart displayed the warmest personal relationship at the top in over a decade.

Martin's successor as prime minister, Stephen Harper, publicly resisted any opposition efforts to paint him as a Canadian Bush, and he stuck up for Canadian interests whenever they were challenged, such as in the Arctic. Still, he vowed throughout his leadership of the Conservative Party to transform a bilateral relationship that had turned sour. Noting that Canada's access to the highest governmental circles in Washington had persistently eroded, he named as ambassador investment banker and former finance minister in the Mulroney government, Michael Wilson. The new ambassador promised a respectful but firm approach: "America is a neighbor. You don't throw snow on his driveway." When he left his post in the autumn of 2009, he noted that his best calling card in Washington was the fact that Canadian soldiers were fighting shoulder-to-shoulder with Americans in Afghanistan. "It was highly appreciated and highly admired." He was replaced by former Manitoba Premier Gary Doer.

Doer's American counterpart in Ottawa until 2013 also took office in 2009: David Jacobson, a Chicago-based corporate lawyer and top fund raiser for President Obama. Like most American ambassadors, Jacobson knew little about the country when he was appointed. But in order to understand this huge land, Jacobson embarked on an 8-week coast-to-coast road trip across Canada, avoiding airplanes and getting the feel of the terrain. Jacobson met all the premiers and as many Canadians as he could. H Jacobson successor, Chicago investment banker Bruce Heyman, made similar voyages.

Harper sent some positive signals to Washington: "Canada intends to be a player" and will advance "our shared values." He promised and delivered a large increase in defense spending, and he pledged to strengthen border and port security, renew NORAD, and continue his predecessor's policy of bolstering his country's efforts against the Taliban in Afghanistan. Harper embraced the American-led war on terrorism and asserted Israel's right to protect itself, daring to incur Turkey's ire

by calling the killing of Armenians in the First World War a genocide, something his American counterpart, Barack Obama, did not dare do as president. Harper discusses human rights with the Chinese to little avail. In fact, China's leaders lambasted him for his "disgusting conduct" in meeting the Dalai Lama in October 2007. Nevertheless, a 2007 poll revealed that a quarter of Canadians consider China the most important country to their interests.

Harper had seldom traveled outside Canada before becoming prime minister but showed a wide-ranging interest in international affairs. He quickly acquired the confidence to handle foreign policy himself without depending on career diplomats and enjoyed not having no subordinate on foreign policy. At the same time, Harper re-energized relations with Washington. He has his public's support in this. A survey published at the time he entered office showed a slim majority (54%) of Canadians wanting a foreign policy that would bring Canada closer to the U.S. But pollster Michael Adams says this message comes with a warning: "The minute you look like you're kowtowing, as far as we're concerned, you're toast."

The Canadian government is acutely aware of the traditional ambivalence many of its people show toward too extensive cooperation with the U.S. Ex-Foreign Minister Manley noted: "There are two rules in Canadian politics. The first is: don't be too close to the United States. The second is: don't be too far from the United States." In the aftermath of the September

11 attacks, Canadians wanted their leaders to emphasize the second rule.

That was not the case in 2003 when the U.S. led a coalition to end Saddam Hussein's rule in Iraq. Emotions were high, and three-fourths of the Canadian public favored the government's decision to stay out of the war. The media do make a difference, though. Canadians who get most of their news from U.S. television were three times more likely to support the war effort in Iraq. In a 2004 poll, 66% of Canadians said their attitude toward the U.S. had worsened since 11 September; 76% said this was because of their dislike of President Bush. Only 16% of Canadians would have voted for him. Half saw the U.S. as arrogant, bullying or dangerous, and two-thirds thought America's global reputation had worsened over the past decade. Americans did not reciprocate these negative feelings: 74% said their opinion remained unchanged after four years, and 12% said they had improved.

American diplomats in Canada revealed some mild irritation of Canadian attitudes in cables publicized by Wikileaks. One is the American perception that Canadians "always carry a chip on their shoulder," apparently because of their feeling that Canada "is condemned to always play 'Robin' to the U.S. 'Batman'." Another is "moral outrage, a Canadian specialty." One diplomat described "soul searching" in Canada about its "decline from 'middle power' status to that of an 'active observer' of global affairs, a trend which some Canadians believe should be reversed." The Americans marveled that

Canadian Soldiers in Afghanistan

"despite the overwhelming importance of the U.S. to Canada for its economy and security," candidates for parliament rarely mention anything about relations with the U.S. The U.S. is like the "900-pound gorilla": "overwhelming but too potentially menacing to acknowledge."

Thousands of Canadian fans booed the American national anthem before two Montreal Canadiens hockey games. Even a pee wee hockey team from Boston was booed and heckled. Such insensitive treatment of young Americans was so appalling to some Canadians that the team was invited back to Fredericton, NB, where it was treated with touching love and respect.

A stream of insults came from Canadian officials and MPs. The prime minister's communications director, Francine Ducros, called President Bush a "moron," a slip that cost Ducros her job. A Liberal MP was overheard to decry the "damn Americans, I hate those bastards"; Carolyn Parrish later apologized for that remark. However, a year later she lapsed into another anti-American tirade by stomping on a Bush doll during a nationally televised satire show. For this she was ousted from the Liberal parliamentary caucus. Another MP was reproached for declaring that the U.S. was leading "the coalition of the idiots" in Iraq. An NDP MP called Bush a "war criminal."

Some Canadians who actually met with President Bush had more complimentary memories of him. Bush was said always to have been well briefed. Former Liberal cabinet member, Anne McLellan, remembered that "he was a person easy to deal with. There is no artifice. He tells you exactly where he is coming from. There are not a lot of surprises—and there are benefits to that." No back-channels were needed to clarify statements or inferences.

Bush's commitment to NAFTA was never in doubt. By contrast, the Democratic Congress was more protectionist. During her campaign Democratic presidential candidate and later Secretary of State Hillary Clinton called NAFTA her husband's "mistake." Barack Obama sought electoral college votes by suggesting that it should be renegotiated. He dropped that pledge after his election, advocating only that the side agreements on labor and the environment should be brought into the main text of the treaty to ensure enforcement. As president he repeatedly emphasized his commitment to open trade between the two northern neighbors. President Donald Trump ordered the resumption of complicated NAFTA negotiations in 2017 and 2018.

President Bush was a more consequential president for Canada than were most of his predecessors. For instance, he created the Department of Homeland Security after September 11, 2001, spurring Canada to reorganize its own government by creating the equivalent Department of Public Safety. He rearranged North American defense by creating a Northern Command. This prompted Ottawa to create its own Canada Command.

Canadians hated Bush's infamous "axis of evil" term. Few were aware that it had been coined by David Frum, a Canadian author and pundit who spent 13 months as a speech writer for the American president. Perhaps even fewer know that one of America's hardest-hitting neo-conservative columnists, Charles Krauthammer, also hailed from Canada, as does Tea Party Texas Senator Ted Cruz. The latter's parents worked in Alberta's oil patch before moving to Texas when he was a child.

In 2008 Americans elected a president whom many Canadians greeted as the near-perfect political leader: Barack Obama. They celebrated his inauguration on January 20, 2009, with an outpouring of enthusiasm not even shown to a Canadian prime minister for decades. Busloads of admirers made the nine-hour trip from Toronto and Ottawa to witness his swearing in, and some Canadian schools interrupted their classes to enable pupils to watch the ceremony. For the eight years of the Bush presidency, Canadians felt a kind of moral superiority to Americans, but that almost completely changed with his successor.

By February 19, 2009, when he made his first foreign trip as president, to Ottawa, Obama enjoyed an approval rating in Canada of 82%, higher than in the U.S. where it was 64% and much higher than that of Prime Minister Stephen Harper at 38% and then opposition leader Michael Ignatieff at 42%. Obama was more popular in Canada than Harper would ever be.

From the time he stepped off Air Force One in Ottawa, Obama commanded nonstop TV coverage during his six and a half hours in the country. Canadians clustered on overpasses and along the road to get a glimpse of him, and he greeted 2,500 of them who had gathered outside the Parliament in freezing weather. Obama's welcome by Canada's first black governor general, Michaëlle Jean, was a historic moment for both nations.

Obama's charm never faltered, and he revealed a special attachment to Canada: that he has a brother-in-law who is Canadian and that two of his key staff people are from Canada. "And I love this country and think that we could not have a better friend and ally." An opinion survey at the time revealed that 41% of Canadian respondents desired greater ties with U.S., while 45% thought Canada should maintain the same level of relations. Only 9%

wanted the country to distance itself from its southern neighbor.

Within months, many Canadians expressed disappointment that the new American president appeared to be unresponsive to Canada's needs, soft on protectionism and supportive of legislation pending in Congress that could prevent Canadians from selling the oil gained from their western sands in the U.S., the destination for half of it. Obama eased some concerns when in August 2009 he approved a pipeline called the Alberta Clipper to carry 800,000 barrels of oil sands fuel a day to the U.S. Yet, that relief was slashed in 2015 when Obama rejected the much more important Keystone XL Pipeline that would bring Canadian crude all the way through the U.S. to the Gulf of Mexico. The Nebraska state government approved of a new route for the pipeline, and the State Department initially gave the green light, but died because of American environmental and domestic politics. In one of his first acts as president, Donald Trump lifted the ban that his successor, Joseph Biden reinstated on taking office in 2020.

Perhaps expectations had been too great. Magazine headlines began to read: "Canada's Biggest Problem: America" or "Barack Obama. Why He's Bad for Canada." In 2013 *Maclean's* characterized the two leaders' relationship as "growing mutual indifference and incomprehension." *Maclean's* reminded its readers that, though unpopular, "Bush was in fact a strong and committed supporter of many causes dear to our national interest, including trade, open borders and energy."

Donald Trump is unpopular in Canada. In 2019 New Research Co. poll found that 17 % of people think Trump's presidency was good for Canada, and 65% say it was bad or very bad. Conversely, another poll concluded that between 41% and 46% of Canadian conservatives would vote for Trump. An updated poll in 2020 from Maclean's showed that only 14% of Canadians would vote for Trump, while 86% support Biden.

Response to September 11 Terrorist Attacks

Canada's prime minister on September 11, 2001, Jean Chrétien, said at the time: "You know, the world will never be the same again," and he was right. The terrorist attacks against the World Trade Center in New York City and the Pentagon in Washington, D.C., gave Americans and Canadians a shared sense of vulnerability. Their feeling of security between two wide oceans disappeared. Foreign Minister John Manley, who became deputy prime minister and was named to lead a powerful new cabinet committee on national security, stated: "The towers in Toronto

Canada

are just as vulnerable. Canadians want to be safe, too." Not only did Manley show his solidarity with New Yorkers by signing up to run the New York marathon. He led his colleagues in assuming an unapologetic pro-American stance.

President George W. Bush's gaffe in failing to include Canada among 13 other countries he thanked in his September speech to Congress did not alter this. An embarrassed president later explained that the U.S. considers Canada a brother and saw no need to thank family. His ambassador to Ottawa, Paul Celucci, told the 100,000 Canadians who had gathered on Parliament Hill to honor the victims: "You are truly our closest friends." The 2002 annual *Maclean's*/CBC poll revealed that only a tenth of Canadians accept Bush's description of the relationship as "like family." The most frequent description (47%) was "friends but not particularly close"; 23% agreed with the formulation, "the best of friends"; 18% chose "cordial but distant," and only 1% described it as "openly hostile."

Canada's foreign policy shifted in the wake of the attacks from a primary preoccupation on trade and economics to fighting international terrorism. Prime Minister Chrétien vowed a few days after the attacks that Canada would "go every step of the way" with its American neighbors. His people seemed to agree: 84% of Canadians supported joining the U.S. fight against terrorism although only 23% wanted to see their troops directly involved in the fighting. A third favored closer ties with the U.S., compared with only 23% in March 2001. Manley captured the mood: "On the Hill when we had the memorial service, and people had their Canadian and American flags and tears running down their faces, you realized that when it comes to an event like that, forget the border. There is no border in the sharing of that experience."

Canada's assistance to its hard-pressed southern neighbor included a military contribution to the war effort in Afghanistan. It dispatched the largest fighting flotilla the country sent to sea since the Korean War to join American and British war vessels: three frigates, the HMCS Halifax, the HMCS Charlottetown and the HMCS Vancouver, a destroyer, HMCS Iroquois, one of its two supply ships, HMCS Preserver plus Sea King helicopters that staffed by more than 1,000 sailors. The air force sent three Hercules transport planes, one Airbus and two Aurora maritime patrol planes.

Canada dispatched 100 commandos from the secretive Joint Task Force 2. In 2004 President Bush awarded this elite commando unit a Presidential Unit Citation for "extraordinary heroism in action against the enemy" in rooting out Taliban fighters

from caves in Afghanistan. It was the first time since the Korean War in the early 1950s that Canadian soldiers received this rare and prestigious recognition.

Canada's airmen also served on NATO Airborne Warning and Control System (AWACS) crews that patrolled the American east coast. This was the first time since the Revolutionary War that the U.S. needed protection by foreign troops on its soil. A Canadian pilot could scarcely believe what he was doing: "I never, ever imagined that we'd be here. This place in the world that we're now trying to defend has always been the biggest boy in town. It has always been the U.S. protecting everyone else."

Few Canadians or Americans knew at the time that in the minutes before the first hijacked airplane slammed into the World Trade Center, it was senior Canadian officers on duty at NORAD headquarters that morning who gave permission to U.S. Air Force base commanders on the east coast to intercept the aircraft in terrorists' hands.

The neighbors introduced important steps to shift the overall protection of their territory to North American "perimeter security." The Canadian public supported these cooperative measures as long as they did not challenge their country's sovereignty or capacity to act independently.

Both populations support efforts to stop terrorism. When asked in a 2005 poll, 74% of Canadians and 86% of Americans favored closer collaboration to deal with this threat. Canadians were reminded in 2013 that terror can be homegrown. Canadian citizens, under instructions from al-Qaeda, were involved in an attempt to derail a passenger train between Toronto and New York, an attack on a natural-gas plant in Algeria that left 68 dead, and a pressure-cooker bomb attack outside the BC legislature in Victoria, reminiscent of the Boston Marathon bombing. A horrid reminder of the danger of home-grown terrorism occurred in October 2014, when a terrorist ran over two soldiers at a Quebec mall, killing one, and when another shot dead a guard outside of Parliament and terrorized thousands inside until he was killed. Both were Canadian-born converts to Islam who became radicalized jihadists. Both nations need a more integrated system of military and emergency responses in the event of a catastrophic attack or natural disaster, like Hurricane Katrina in 2005.

Canada was not interested in creating a jointly managed North American perimeter with a common approach to customs, trade, immigration, security and defense, and it worries about talk in the U.S. of registering all travelers entering and leaving the country, including Canadians. Still, Canada agreed in 2002 to allow U.S. troops to cross its border in the event of terrorist

attacks or natural disasters, and Canadian troops have the same right to cross into the U.S. When that happens, U.S. forces would serve under Canadian command while in Canada, and Canadian soldiers would be commanded by Americans while on U.S. soil.

In 2002 the U.S. created a new Northern Command to defend North America and coordinate military relations with Canada and Mexico. A joint task force called the "Planning Group," based at NORAD's Colorado Springs headquarters, was created with Canada to work on contingency plans to defend North America. Canadian leadership discussed a new command structure to match this Northern Command. It calls for the integration of the army, navy and air force into six regional commands answering to a single Canada Command headed by an admiral. A new expeditionary force would be created to respond to calls to intervene in failed states, and counter-terrorist special forces would be strengthened.

The common border is not the way Canadian diplomat Hugh Keenleyside defined it in 1929: "It is physically invisible, geographically illogical, militarily indefensible, and emotionally inescapable." It is more guarded today. Nevertheless, this frontier still has only one Border Patrol agent for every 16 miles, compared with the border with Mexico, which has enough agents assigned for one every 1,100 feet.

There is more intelligence sharing. For the first time ever, the FBI provides the RCMP access to its digital fingerprint database; no other foreign police force is granted such information. American law enforcement officers can now gain access to criminal records in the Canadian Police Information Centre. The Canadians introduced more tamper-proof passports and check background references more carefully before issuing travel documents. The partners ended "asylum shopping." They created a common set of standards for asylum and a common list of countries whose citizens must obtain visas before entering either country. Would-be refugees must apply for asylum in the first country they enter and cannot reapply in the other if they are rejected. Those entering at unguarded crossing are exempt from this rule.

Ottawa moved swiftly to erase any impression south of the border that Canada was tolerant toward terrorism. Canada's intelligence agency identified more than 50 terrorist groups that operate and raise money in the country. The government allotted $4.2 billion to fight terror and steered a vigorous anti-terrorist act through both houses of parliament that makes it illegal "to harbor a terrorist" or to collect money to carry out terrorism. Police were granted authority to use electronic surveillance against terrorists and to arrest and detain suspected terrorists without warrants.

Former Justice Minister Anne McLellan answered the objections of civil liberties groups by arguing that "reasonable limits" on citizens' rights "are justified in a free and democratic society." In February, 2007 Parliament voted 159 to 124 to allow two anti-terrorism measures to lapse since they had never been used. A week later the Supreme Court of Canada gave Parliament a year to fix a law allowing foreign terrorist suspects to be detained indefinitely without trial while awaiting deportation.

Canada acted energetically in detaining immigrants suspected of involvement in terrorism. In August 2003 it arrested 19 men who could have links with al Qaeda. Its spy agency, the Canadian Security Intelligence Service (CSIS), conducts only domestic security operations, relying on "liaison officers" to gather foreign intelligence from friendly governments. The CSIA does no spying overseas. The CSIS handed over to the U.S. an alleged al Qaeda operative accused in a plot to blow up the American and Israeli embassies in Singapore. These actions keep alive the debate about how the fight against terrorism can be made compatible with the Canadian ideals of tolerance, inclusion and the belief that immigrants should have the same rights as Canadian citizens. Prime Minister Harper underscored Canada's vigilance on terrorism during President Obama's first visit in February 2009: "I just want to make this clear to our American friends. The view of this government is unequivocal: threats to the United States are threats to Canada."

That terrorism is no idle threat to Canada was dramatically demonstrated in June 2006. Working closely together, the RCMP and CSIS uncovered a deadly plot by 18 homegrown Muslim terrorists in the Toronto area to launch a wave of truck-bomb attacks against the Toronto Stock Exchange, the Toronto office of CSIS, an undisclosed military base, and Parliament in Ottawa. The plotters intended to capture politicians and beheading the prime minister if he refused to order the withdrawal of Canadian troops from Afghanistan. Those charged came from a variety of Muslim countries, especially South Asia. Most were born in Canada, and the oldest plotter was an imam who reportedly spewed hatred of Canada in his sermons.

The operation began with police monitoring of internet chat rooms. Soon 400 intelligence and law-enforcement officers were involved in Canada's largest counterterrorist operation since the often-reviled Anti-Terrorism Act was adopted

after the September 11, 2001, attacks. The powers the act granted to the police were crucial in foiling the plot. The RCMP paid two civilian informants $4.4 million to help execute the successful sting operation. One, who received $300,000, was a young, charismatic Muslim with a taste for cocaine. The other, a Muslim businessman, was paid $4.1 million and is in the witness protection program.

Canadian authorities moved in when the group acquired three tons of ammonium nitrate fertilizer, one-third of the amount used in the 1995 Oklahoma City bombing. A Toronto mosque was burned in a backlash. But the roughly 2% of Canada's population that is Muslim, half of whom were born in the country, could be relieved that such a tolerant country did not blame them for the ghastly project of a small minority.

In 2008 charges were dropped against seven of the defendants. The evidence seemed to show that the group was more like a youth gang that loved inflammatory chatter. Even so, the plotters knew little about the means and methods of pulling off an effective attack. Some Canadians had begun to wonder if this entire incredible conspiracy had been fact or fiction. Subsequent testimony and convictions eliminated any doubts that it had been real and dangerous. In September 2008 a young man who had been only 17 years old at the time of his arrest was found guilty of knowingly participating in a plot to behead the prime minister. He was the first to be found guilty of terrorism since the anti-terrorist laws had been enacted in 2001.

In 2009 four more were tried for conspiring to ignite three explosions in southern Ontario. Three of them pleaded guilty, including the 24-year old ringleader of

the group, Zakaria Amara. His testimony revealed shocking incompetence. He underestimated the Canadian police, grossly exaggerated his chances for success, and placed faith in the wrong people, including two RCMP informants supported by numerous wiretaps. At his sentencing hearing in January 2010, Amara apologized to Canadians and especially his fellow Muslims for his "naïve and gullible" interpretation of Islam. He faced a life sentence since Canada has no capital punishment.

There have been other warnings about the political radicalization of some young Canadians. Two friends from a Canadian high school were killed while participating in a terrorist attack on an Algerian gas plant in January 2013.

Omar Khadr, who had been born in Toronto, was incarcerated at Guantánamo Bay, Cuba, at age 16 for killing an American soldier in Afghanistan. In September 2012 he was transferred to a Canadian maximum security prison.

In 2017 the Canadian government gave Khadr an apology and Can$10.5 million in damages. This was done quietly without the knowledge of the widow of Sgt. 1st Class Chris Speer, a US special forces medic who died in July 2002, 12 days after shrapnel hit him in the head during a raid on an Afghan compound in which Khadr was with a terrorist cell. Sgt. Speer's widow Tabitha Speer sued Khadr and received a 134 million-dollar US judgment against him. Although she has been unsuccessful to date in recovering against Khadr, many Canadians who are outraged at either the payment to Khadr or the fact that it is not subject to the claim by Ms. Speer, have joined together to provide financial assistance to Ms. Speer's family.

The Canadian intelligence service's web site asserted that "with the exception of the United States, there are more terrorist groups active in Canada today than in any other country in the world." That judgment was confirmed by documents found at Osama bin Laden's Pakistani compound specifically naming Canada as a worthy target for terrorism.

DEFENSE

Both the U.S. and Canada are blessed with oceans that insulated them from European and Asian conflicts and with a border between themselves that has not had to be defended for more than a century and a half. Therefore, military concerns were never paramount in either country until well into the 20th century. Yet, two world wars forced very different

Canada

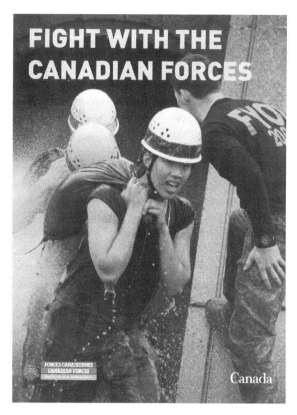

FIGHT WITH THE CANADIAN FORCES

FORCES CANADIENNES
CANADIAN FORCES

Canada

roles on them. With Europe in shambles and near poverty, and with the emergence of the Soviet Union as a dominant force in Europe and Asia, the United States was compelled to play a role as financial, military and political leader of the free world. This role brought increased military responsibility to the United States, and security concerns became very important in America's body politic.

Canada's military role remained minor, compared to that of the U.S.. Therefore, security issues have been much less important in Canadian politics. This low salience was reflected in Canada's low defense budgets, amounting to a mere 1% of GDP, the lowest in the Atlantic Alliance except Iceland and Luxembourg and lower than those of his liberal predecessors. The Harper government promised and produced in 2006 a hefty increase in defense spending that included US$13 billion in equipment purchases. By the May 2011 election, he raised defense spending by 27%, falling back to 1.5% annually after the election. His countrymen have supported this unprecedented increase, which was intended to "revive Canada's leadership in the world."

As in political and economic affairs, Canada is linked with and dependent on the United States in defense. Its close cooperation was first formalized in the Ogdensburg Agreement of 1940, before the U.S. had entered World War II. The Canadian government realized that Britain might be conquered and would therefore

be unable to defend Canada. The American government was concerned that the approaches to the North American continent might not be secure if Britain were indeed defeated. Therefore, Prime Minister King met with President Roosevelt to sign a permanent defense agreement. As with all good and lasting treaties, this one was firmly based on mutual interest. A year later at Hyde Park, FDR's New York estate, they agreed to pool their military production. The two countries' wartime cooperation was excellent.

Both nations sacrificed thousands of lives in the bitter global struggle but were spared the destruction of their own homelands and emerged from the war intact and richer than before. Both Canada and the U.S. were among the very few countries in the world that could positively contribute to the reconstruction of wartorn Europe. Both shared the view that the Soviet Union posed a threat to the democracies of Western Europe. Canada agreed that its own security was linked to that of Western Europe. Additionally, Canada wanted to forge military ties with Western Europe in order to counterbalance its necessarily tight defense links with the U.S. Canadian leaders were the first to make public statements about the need for a postwar Atlantic Alliance, and Canada became a founding member of NATO.

It is characteristic of the Canadian understanding of the world that its diplomats insisted on the inclusion of article II of the treaty, which underscored their

conviction that the Atlantic Alliance had to be more than a military alliance. This became known as "the Canadian article" and called for a pledge by members to strengthen free institutions and to encourage economic cooperation.

Canada never provided the personnel and equipment to which it had committed itself at NATO's birth. In 1969, the Trudeau government reduced its troop strength in Europe from 10,000 to 5,000, a decision that angered Western European allies, especially Germany. The fact is that Pierre Trudeau, who was despised by many soldiers, spent more on defense than any other prime minister since. His federal budget allotted 13.3% to the Department of National Defence (DND), compared with 8.7% under Harper until 2011. The Mulroney government raised the Canadian contingent in Europe to 7,800 troops.

The end of the Cold War prompted Canada to announce in 1992 the withdrawal of all its troops and airmen from Europe and the closure of its bases in Lahr and Baden-Soellingen. This was completed in 1994. Canada hosted German air force units that trained in Goose Bay, Newfoundland, and army artillery and armor units outside of Winnipeg. The Germans announced in 2004 that they were moving out of Goose Bay.

At home Canada maintains three land combat groups along with two squadrons of aircraft that could be flown quickly with aerial refueling to Europe for close support of NATO forces. Part of Canada's naval forces is also occupied in protecting the North Atlantic approaches. Canada regards NATO as a key part of its defense policy and earmarks 10,000 combat troops for NATO service. Ottawa confirmed at NATO's Prague Summit in 2002 that it would take part in the alliance's new 21,000-strong rapid-response force deployable to all parts of the globe to combat terrorism and contain outlaw regimes.

In 2006 a Canadian general, Ray Henault, occupied the key post of chairman of NATO's military committee; this was the highest NATO post ever held by a Canadian. In April 2009 then Defense Minister Peter MacKay was on the short list to become secretary-general of NATO. Although he lost out to Danish Prime Minister Anders Fogh Rasmussen, MacKay's near success demonstrated that a Canadian could one day occupy NATO's highest political office. This is particularly true since the Conservatives took power in 2006.

The Harper government intended to make Canada a responsible military partner, and Canada's participation in Afghanistan and Libya provide convincing evidence. He was aware of the criticism he gets from some Canadians who prefer to see their country as primarily a peacekeeping country. He responded: "When you're in a dangerous world and countries are from time to time called on to do things to deal with these dangers, if you don't have the capacity to act you are not taken seriously. Nobody takes your views seriously unless you can contribute to solutions . . . including military capabilities."

In an effort to raise the morale of Canadian soldiers and to reconnect with the country's rich military heritage, the Conservative government reintroduced the word "royal," which had been dropped in 1968 when the three branches of the services were unified, and all soldiers wore the same uniform. The Maritime and Air Commands are once again called the Royal Canadian Navy and Royal Canadian Air Force. The Land Force is again the Canadian Army.

Aa of 2019 Canada's navy consists of about 8,500n sailors and 5,100 primary reservists supported by 5,300 civilians. In 2007 Commodore Jennifer Bennett, who headed an Ontario private school, was given command of the country's 24 naval reserve divisions, a position her father held when she first joined the naval reserves 33 years earlier. She was the first woman to lead a Canadian naval formation

Canada's Pacific fleet is based at CFB Esquimalt on Vancouver Island with a larger fleet is stationed at CFB Halifax. Among its resources, the navy has 12 modern frigates, four submarines, seven support ships, 14 patrol and coastal combatants, and one diving support vessel. With 63 ships in 2019, the Canadian navy is proportionate to the British fleet of 74 commissioned ships and the U.S. navy's 282 combat vessels. Canada has no anti-mine or year-round icebreaking capability and is widely considered to be incapable of adequately protecting its huge coastline.

The Canadian navy has four patrol submarines, two on each coast. In October 2004, after three years of refitting and maddening cost overruns, one of the subs, the HMCS Chicoutimi, caught on fire during her maiden voyage, and the first Canadian seaman in 49 years died of smoke inhalation. All four subs were promptly docked until the cause of the tragedy could be determined. The inquiry cast no blame, but part of the subsequent $10–$15 million in repairs was devoted to making the electrical cables much more waterproof. Critics were quick to react, claiming that Canada had bought the outdated subs mainly to engage in cat and mouse training exercises with American nuclear submarines in the North Atlantic. Why, they asked, was $750 million (mainly in trade for the use of Canadian airspace to train British pilots) squandered when Canada could

Cheyenne Mountain, Colorado. Canadian and American soldiers at NORAD. NOTE: This operation was moved to nearby Peterson Air Force Base in 2006.

not afford to field armed forces capable of defending the country?

Canada had no reliable naval helicopters or submarine surveillance planes. By 2014, 14 of its Sea King helicopters had self-destructed, killing a dozen crew members. One crashed in 2003 while trying to take off from the deck of the HMCS Iroquois, a destroyer that was heading for the Persian Gulf. The navy could not find a replacement, so the ship had to leave without it.

In 2004 the government selected an American-led consortium, with Canadian participation, to build 28 new Sikorsky H92 Superhawk maritime helicopters for a price tag of Can$3.2 billion (US$2.4 billion). They can fly from the navy's frigates and used for anti-submarine, patrol, rescue and transport tasks. Delays stretched out for years. In 2013 the government threatened to scrap the deal and shop around for an alternative to the Sikorsky. All forces will benefit from the purchase in 2009 of 15 Chinook heavy-lift helicopters built by Boeing and originally scheduled for delivery in 2013. Canada had already received six used Chinooks from the Americans for use in Afghanistan. In 2015, new Cyclone helicopters began to arrive.

In 2011 the government announced a $35-billion investment in new warships and support vessels over the next three decades. Because many of Canada's existing ships are over 40 years old, keeping them operational is very expensive. Promised ships to patrol the Arctic are years behind schedule.

The land and air forces have been slightly better off. In 2019, Canada had more than 60,000 men and women in its

army and air force. Canada's army consists of about 23,000 men ans women plus 17,000 reservists. The air force consists of about 14,500 personnel on active duty, backed up by about 2,600 reservists and 2,500 civilians in support of 258 manned aircraft. Women can serve in all combat roles, including submarines. Between 2001 and 2011, 310 women filled combat roles in Afghanistan, and artillery Captain Nichola Goddard became the first female Canadian soldier to die in combat. In 2016, the first woman (Christine Whitecross) was promoted to three-star general, and Jennie Carigman was the first general to emerge from the combat arms.

There are more Canadians trying to get into the all-volunteer military than there are open slots. The result is that the military personnel are carefully selected and well trained. The main problem is in retaining experienced soldiers, not attracting raw recruits. In 2002 the Canadian Forces raised the mandatory retirement age from 55 to 60 in order to head off a manpower shortfall. Canadians fly the aging CF-18 fighter.

In October 2014 Canada began a deployment to Iraq, not Syria, to support the U.S.-led effort to defeat the brutal Islamic State. The mission involved six CF-18 fighters, 600 support personnel, two refueling planes, two surveillance aircraft, and 69 Special Forces to train Kurdish troops. The Liberals and NDP opposed this involvement although 57% of Canadians approved. Nevertheless, newly elected Prime Minister Justin Trudeau kept his campaign promise and ordered the fighter aircraft home because he wished to refocus Canada's military role to peacekeeping and humanitarian operations.

Canada

Canada's French Military College
Retrieved from: https://commons.wikimedia.org/wiki/File:Flag_of_the_Royal_Military_College_of_Canada.svg

The Harper government purchased 65 F-35 Joint Strike stealth jet fighters from Lockheed Martin and spend hundreds of millions of dollars helping to develop this plane. There was criticism about the sophistication of the plane and the increasing cost and wisdom of purchasing a one-engine plane for use in the remote Arctic region. The future use of surveillance drones to watch the entire Canadian Arctic also erodes the rational for the F-35. With a price tag of $45 billion over 42 years—much more than the government had promised—it would be the largest military purchase in Canada's history. In 2012 the government stopped funding the project and began to review alternatives to the F-35. A stopgap 18 F-18s will be purchased while the government decides on a permanent solution. In 2019, Canada bid for a F-18 Super Hornet, which will replace its fleet of CF18s, according to *Defense News.*

To save money, the air force had to retire an entire fleet of electronic warfare aircraft. When it decided to send peacekeeping forces to East Timor in Indonesia in 1999, the Canadian government had difficulty transporting them there because it had so little transport capacity that it was compelled to use its only supply ship to service its entire Pacific fleet. The first of its aging transport planes was forced to turn back to base three times because of malfunctions with its compass and tail rudder. Another 34-year-old C-130 Hercules aircraft managed to make the trip, but only by flying below 10,000 feet because of a faulty cabin-pressurization system. Canada subsequently ordered three large C-17 transport aircraft.

Canada is caught between the conflicting realities of declining defense budgets and increasing military conflict around the world. This was apparent in August 2000 when armed Canadian commandos in a dramatic high-seas seizure had to be dropped from a Sea King helicopter onto the deck of a private American freighter to take control of the ship that was transporting 590 military vehicles and 440 containers of small arms, ammunition, communications and surveillance equipment being shipped back on contract from Kosovo. The shipping company had refused to unload it in Canada until a private debt was settled. The capture was flawless, but the embarrassing thing was that the cargo amounted to about 10% of the Canadian army's entire supply of such equipment. A Canadian defense expert, David Rudd, remarked: "There is a definite mismatch between Canada's desire to remain a player on the world stage and the ability of the armed forces to carry it out. They are over-stretched everywhere."

The air force is acquiring new search and rescue helicopters. To hone their capabilities in the Arctic, Canada hosted joint exercises with American and Russian soldiers in 1995. It was the first time in 50 years that Russians trained on Canadian soil. NORAD had a joint exercise with Russia in 2010.

In 1993 the Canadian government created a secret counter-terrorist force called Joint Task Force 2 (JTF2). Well-trained and well-equipped with the latest high-tech weaponry, this commando unit, numbering 1,500 in 2010, is considered to be on a par with the best of Britain's and America's special forces. The JTF2 is especially trained for operations in extreme winter conditions, and in 2001 it was tapped for clandestine service in the Afghan war. The JTF2, which fights effectively alongside U.S. and other allied special operations forces, was granted a prestigious U.S. Presidential unit citation by the U.S. president. The former commander of U.S. Central Command, Gen. Tommy Franks, praised the Canadian soldiers: "They've done an absolutely wonderful job." "We are in their debt. We recognize our friends."

Canada's land forces are good. Because the White Paper designates peacekeeping as the Canadian Forces' main job in an unstable world, Canada acquired additional armored personnel carriers and other equipment needed for that commitment. It purchased 66 soft-armor Strykers, an 8-wheel troop carrier that is lighter and more mobile than tanks.

Public outrage over the murder of a Somali teenager and shockingly crude hazing rituals led to the disbanding in 1995 of the Canadian Airborne Regiment. It was replaced by three separate parachute companies, each serving as the nucleus for a new light infantry battalion. Canada is strained to maintain adequate units for peacekeeping. In 2017, there were only 112 soldiers on peacekeeping assignments.

In order to reduce costs, headquarters staffs were slashed by 50% and the top officer corps by 25%. The civilian workforce was trimmed from 33,000 to 20,000. The three services consolidated their headquarters in Ottawa. In 1999 the defense department endorsed a plan to sell off as much as 10% of its property and buildings to raise funds for equipment.

Sovereignty over the Arctic is enforced by 60 soldiers stationed in Yellowknife, backed by a 100-soldier reserve unit. They are supported by four ageing Twin Otter bush aircraft. The main ground force is 1,600 Canadian Rangers, 80% of whom are Inuit. They are a reserve force based in 165 remote communities composed largely of Inuit and Indians, including women who, transported by snowmobiles, provided by the Rangers themselves, and armed with pre-First World War Lee Enfield rifles and a toll-free 800 number to report any trouble, perform surveillance duty in the Arctic. Their mission is to fly the Canadian flag and assert sovereignty over remote Arctic areas and are the only arm of the military that uses its own transportation equipment, such as fishing boats and motorized canoes. The unit, which is organized in over 50 patrols in communities across the North, each limited to 30 members, is widely admired as demonstrated by the fact that there are waiting lists of Inuit hoping to join.

It is no surprise that Canada depends on its alliance with the United States. It is engaged in many forms of military cooperation. The two countries' security relationship is coordinated by the Permanent Joint Board on Defense. There is the Defense Production Sharing Agreement, which exempts Canada from duties and "Buy American" policies. By 2007 Canada had a $7 billion defense industry. Half of it came from sales to the U.S. military and 80% to all NATO allies. Much of the rest came from over 70 countries. In 2005 it was the world's ninth-largest seller of military weapons.

There is also cooperation in anti-submarine warfare (ASW). Since Canada is economically dependent on trading, it is crucial that the seas surrounding it be safe in times of crisis. It does have some ASW destroyers and some long-distance coastal aircraft, but it needs American air cover and nuclear attack submarines to deal with an enemy submarine threat, especially in the Arctic Ocean.

Perhaps the closest form of military collaboration is in the North American Aerospace Command (NORAD), created in 1957 and renewed again for five years in 2006, with a new emphasis on global surveillance from space. NORAD has a joint staff of American and Canadian officers. The only thing that distinguishes the Americans from the Canadians there is the patch on their sleeves. They formerly worked in a well-protected headquarters dug into Cheyenne Mountain in Colorado. But NORAD announced in 2006 the transfer of its surveillance operations to an office building a dozen miles away at Peterson Air Force Base. The mountain facility, composed of 15 underground buildings centered on the war room, is kept on "warm standby," meaning that it could be reopened within hours in case of emergency.

NORAD was a response to the threat posed in the 1950s and 1960s that Soviet bombers could fly across Canadian territory and into the North American heartland. In order to meet this threat, two lines of radar installations were stretched across Canada. The outermost line was called the Distant Early Warning Line (DEW), consisting of 31 radar stations scanning the Arctic region. The second, closer to the U.S. border, was the Pine Tree Line, consisting of 24 stations. Canada supplemented these radar lines with three all-weather fighter squadrons, which fly American F-18 aircraft, a training squadron, an electronic warfare squadron and space sensor units.

By the 1980s, these radar lines were obsolete. Low flying airplanes and cruise missiles could fly past them undetected. Also, the increasing importance of land- and submarine-based missiles (ICBM and SLBM), as opposed to manned bombers, made these radar defenses even less suited to present defense needs. The transition to missiles also made parts of NORAD's defense system, composed of interceptor aircraft and defensive missiles, obsolete. The collapse of the Soviet threat completed the process of obsolescence. The manned DEW stations were converted to unmanned ones.

Nuclear Weapons

The problems of creating a defense against potential air strikes from the Soviet Union were linked with a ticklish issue in Canada: the use of nuclear weapons. From the very beginning Canadians and their governments have been uneasy about any Canadian role involving atomic weapons. They assumed a commitment in the 1950s to arm their forces ear-marked for NORAD with such weapons for one major reason: in terms of destructive power, nuclear weapons are less expensive than conventional arms. Canadians hosted five kinds of U.S. nuclear weapons from 1950 to 1984: Mark IV air-dropped atomic bombs deployed for use by the Strategic Air Command bombers at Goose Bay; Bomarc surface-to-air missiles; Genie air-launched missiles on CF-101 VanDoo fighters; Falcon air-to-air missiles; and anti-submarine nuclear depth bombs at Argentia Bay, Newfoundland.

The Canadian government under John Diefenbaker stalled Canadian acceptance of nuclear weapons to be used with the military equipment it had purchased. He also hesitated to put NORAD forces, which still lacked nuclear warheads, on alert during the 1962 Cuban Missile Crisis, thereby greatly exacerbating his already strained relationship with President John F. Kennedy.

The leader of the opposition Liberal Party, Lester Pearson, put the issue squarely to the people by promising an end to Diefenbaker's wavering policy by "discharging the commitments [which Canada] has already accepted. . . It can only do this by accepting nuclear warheads for those defensive tactical weapons which cannot effectively be used without them but which we have agreed to use." By the skillful use of press releases that showed that the Canadian prime minister was not being entirely honest with his own people, Kennedy helped bring about Diefenbaker's defeat in the April 1963 election. The vote was, in part, an expression of Canadians' desire to honor their defense commitments and military cooperation with the United States. At the same time, the entire debate was an early reminder of how unenthusiastic and ambiguous Canadians have been concerning their country's part in a defense based on atomic arms.

In 1984, the Canadians deactivated their last nuclear warheads, replacing them with conventional ones. Canada still was linked with nuclear deterrence, though. Ottawa permitted experiments with a wide variety of nuclear-related weapons systems on Canadian territory, so long as they did not actually carry nuclear warheads. The

Helping earthquake victims in Kashmir   **Source:** *Maclean's*

Canada

Prime Minister Harper visits troops in Afghanistan

most controversial result was that Americans were permitted to test unarmed cruise missiles over Canada. Germany officials actually proposed such testing to their Canadian counterparts as a token gesture in support of the 1979 twin-track decision involving the deployment of medium-range nuclear missiles in Western Europe. Trudeau had committed himself in public to disarmament but accepted NATO's request because he was aware that Canada relied on nuclear deterrence for its defense and therefore had to accept some obligations because of that reliance.

These tests unleashed a loud debate and demonstrations throughout the country. A diverse "peace movement" began to gel. In 1994, the Canadian government grudgingly approved the continuation of U.S. cruise missile tests over Western Canada, but the U.S. announced that such tests are no longer needed. Canada still permits some forms of U.S. testing. In December 1999 it permitted the U.S. Air Force to test an unmanned aerial vehicle (UAV) called Global Hawk, which is used for intelligence purposes.

Remarks by former U.S. Secretary of Defense Caspar Weinberger on Canadian television during the Quebec summit meeting in 1985 to the effect that American nuclear weapons could possibly be sent to Canada during a crisis brought down a thunder of protest and prompted an official denial that there were any such plans. A similar outcry erupted over the question of whether Canada should participate in the Strategic Defense Initiative (SDI—dubbed "Star Wars"). Such

participation promised hefty contracts to Canadian industries, but the fear that it could unleash a new round of arms competition made it a "hot potato." In 1985, Mulroney announced his government's decision not to participate in SDI, but to permit private Canadians to accept contracts for SDI-related research.

Former Defense Minister Art Eggleton sought in 2000 to lay the groundwork for some kind of limited Canadian participation. He argued that it fits within NORAD and that failure to take part would deprive Canada of important space research and harm Canada's defense relationship with the U.S. While Canada was prepared to assume a certain role as a partner in nuclear deterrence, its leaders stressed that Canada is a nuclear-free country. It was adamantly opposed by the NDP, whose support Martin's minority government needed on certain issues.

In 2004 the Martin government quietly agreed that the joint U.S.-Canada NORAD operations center in Colorado Springs could share incoming missile information with NORTHCOM, the American command that will control the 40 interceptor rockets planned for Alaska, California and at sea. Therefore, technically the Canadians are already in although the Americans do not ask them for land or money for the system. In 2005 Ottawa announced that Canada would not take part in the planned North American ballistic-missile defense system. This decision could be reversed in the future.

There are not many influential voices in Canada calling for withdrawal from NATO

or NORAD. These alliances are supported by a solid majority of Canadians. Besides, there has always been an uncomfortable awareness that if Canada did not contribute to its own defense, the United States might defend Canada in its own way in time of crisis. Some have called this possibility an "involuntary American guarantee."

It is doubtful that any enemy would ever consider Canada and the U.S. as totally separate entities, one neutral and one belligerent, in time of war. The two countries are linked so closely economically that no enemy could attack the United States without also affecting Canada's vital interests. Also, Canada's location is so strategically important to the U.S. that no country could attack it without the a response from the U.S. Insofar as this is the case, Canadian governments have always considered it better to cooperate in North American defense arrangements in order to be able to influence or shape that defense. Such a calculation has been gruesomely called, "no incineration without representation." One of Canada's most distinguished diplomats, J.H. Taylor, noted that though many Canadians find it hard to accept, they are "one of the most secure countries in the world . . . defended by the United States in the act of defending itself, whether we choose to defend ourselves or not."

Defense Efforts

Responding to concern over sovereignty in the 1980s, the Mulroney government established a northern training center and five new fighter bases in the high Arctic. Canadians traditionally saw the primary threat to their *security* coming from the Soviet Union and its allies and the primary threat to their *sovereignty* coming from the United States. Both of these threats intersected in the Arctic. No longer is it true, as a Canadian officer said in the 1940s, "there's nowhere to go and nothing to do once you get there." It remains an unlikely theater for ground operations, but long-range aircraft and nuclear submarines posed major problems.

Located between both superpowers, the Arctic was the only ocean from which American nuclear subs could hit targets anywhere in the Soviet Union. The USSR was no less committed to the Arctic: half of its nuclear attack and missile-launching subs were deployed there. Soviet subs could trespass in Canadian waters to launch cruise missiles, to lay mines which could block sea access and exits from Canada, to ambush American submarines which might be moving through them, with or without Canada's consent or to pass to the North Atlantic, over which Canadian reinforcements would travel in case of war in Europe.

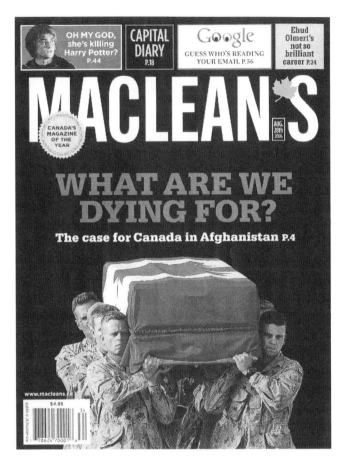

MACLEAN'S AUG. 28th 2006

CANADA'S MAGAZINE OF THE YEAR

WHAT ARE WE DYING FOR?

The case for Canada in Afghanistan P.4

www.macleans.ca

$4.95

The frightening thing for Canada is that it does not have a single ship capable of operating in the Arctic outside the summer months. Canada has neither all-season icebreakers nor minesweepers and lacks submarines capable of operating under the ice for more than a few days, even though a third of its territorial waters are covered by ice most of the year. Finally, Canada has no independent way of even knowing what is going on in the Arctic.

In 1989, the government announced budget cuts that canceled orders for more CF-18 aircraft, a new generation of frontline tanks to replace the aging Leopards, and the promised "Polar 8" icebreaker and fleet of nuclear-powered submarines capable of under-ice warfare. This stunning move led some critics to question the government's commitment to Arctic sovereignty. An exasperated Peter Newman wrote in *Maclean's:* "To have Arctic sovereignty protected by the only country [the U.S.] that challenges it means we have become squatters on our own land."

In 1991 Canada faced a dilemma about how to respond to Iraq's invasion of Kuwait. It was torn by conflicting traditions of participation in the Western alliance and of peacekeeping, and polls indicated that Canadians were unsure what

to do. The Mulroney government decided that it had to support its allies militarily while assuring Canadians that its participation had not compromised its ability to be a peacekeeper. President George H.W. Bush declared: "The American people knew from Day 1 where Canada stood. We are very, very grateful for that."

Canada sent its crack CF-18 Desert Cats fighter squadron to Bahrain; its 24 planes, refueled by a Canadian tanker based in Qatar, flew 2,700 combat missions. Canada also sent three ships to the Persian Gulf outfitted with weaponry cannibalized from half-completed replacement frigates. In all, 2,200 military personnel participated in the campaign, and for the first time in Canadian history, there was not a single casualty. Canada's Gulf operations captured the attention and admiration of a people normally indifferent to defense. As soon as the hostilities ended, the government dispatched hundreds of troops to the Iraq-Kuwait border as part of a UN peacekeeping mission.

In 1997, Canada won praise at home when it deployed 8,600 troops, three times the combined strength of its UN peacekeepers in Bosnia, Haiti, and the Golan Heights, to try to stop the flooding Red River in Manitoba, which drove 25,000 Canadians from their homes. This was the

country's largest single military endeavor since the Korean War. The military's image, tarnished by a series of embarrassments, was reversed by the sight of skilled helicopter pilots plucking desperate countrymen from their rooftops and of mudcaked troops standing in knee-deep water while tossing sandbags.

In 1998, the government mobilized 11,000 troops to help communities across eastern Ontario and southern Quebec, including Ottawa and Montreal, deal with a devastating ice storm and power blackout, called the "Ice Siege of '98." Ex-Defense Minister Eggleton said: "This is by far the biggest deployment in our history to deal with a disaster in Canada."

In 1992 the armed forces lifted the ban against homosexuals in the armed forces, following a court ruling that exclusion violated the Charter of Rights and Freedoms. While there is still a diminishing stigma attached to being gay in the forces, there was little resistance to the new rules. In fact, Pentagon officials had extensive consultations with their Canadian counterparts to discuss the relative success of this transition. Gay partners of Canadian soldiers receive spousal benefits with the first gay marriage at a Canadian Forces base taking place in 2005. In 2008 a Canadian Forces set up a recruiting booth at Toronto's gay pride festival.

By 2017 Canada was spending only 1.29% of its GDP on defense, half the average figure for its NATO partners. Most shocking to many communities was the outright closure of 30 military bases in Canada. The government did not have to take the blame for the 1994 American closure of its naval base in Argenta, Newfoundland, where unemployment was already 20%. A crucial installation during the Second World War, when 20,000 Americans were stationed there; it, too, fell victim to defense cuts following the end of the Cold War. This closing brought to public attention conflicting visions of what the government owes civilian employees, who have claim to much higher severance pay than in the U.S. Insofar as the employer of the 265 newly unemployed Newfoundlanders was the U.S. government, they grudgingly had to accept a far smaller good-bye package than their Canadian counterparts elsewhere.

Canadians suddenly developed a renewed interest in military matters after the September 11, 2001, terrorist attacks in New York and Washington. In the 2002 and 2003 *Maclean's*/CBC polls, two out of three Canadians agreed that "we must substantially increase the amount of money we spend on the Armed Forces" although 57% believed that the main purpose of the military should continue to

Canada

be peacekeeping. Eggleton argued: "The world is changing, and Canada must adapt its armed forces to the evolving military and security environment." Yet, a 2001 defense study by the Canadian Conference of Defence Associations concluded: "The Canadian Forces currently inhabit the worst of two worlds: conventional military capabilities are in decline; and new capabilities are unaffordable." Prime Minister Harper fulfilled his campaign pledge to raise military spending, with transport helicopters and planes as priority items.

Two military academies were closed: the Collège Militaire Royal (CMR) in St-Jean, Quebec, and the Royal Roads Military College in Victoria, BC, leaving only one military university, the bilingual Royal Military College (RMC) in Kingston, Ontario. The shutdown of the CMR was met by a thunder of protest in Quebec since it had been a major steppingstone for francophone Quebecers into the officer ranks. The government needed to reexamine not only its defense funds, but also its doctrine in a dramatically different world.

The Canadian Armed Forces underwent painful self-examination following a wave of bad publicity from peacekeeping missions in Somalia and Bosnia. In 1997 it was revealed that Canada's first female infantry officer, Captain Sandra Perron, had been the subject of discrimination, had perhaps been brutalized during training exercises, and had "never been totally accepted" despite her good performance record. In 1998, *MacLean's* published three lengthy reports about sexual assaults in the military that prompted many women to come forth with complaints. A scathing report in 2015 concluded that the military culture was hostile to women and that female soldiers were twice as likely as the civilian population to have been victims of sexual assaults. The situation does not seem to be getting better. According to *Statistics Canada* in 2018, the proportion of women in the Regular Force who were sexually assaulted (4.3% of the population) was about four times higher than that of men (1.1%).

The forces felt compelled to set up a sexual assault hotline and to join in encouraging female soldiers to tell their stories. They were swamped with charges of rape, including from 21-year veteran Deanna Brasseur, one of the first Canadian women to fly a CF-18 fighter. The Ministry of Defence released a damning report that described how women had faced assault, harassment and intimidation for the past decade. For the first time in its 40-year history, the renowned Snowbirds aerobatic squadron was assigned a woman commander, LTC Maryse Carmichael, in 2010.

Peacekeeping and Overseas Deployments

Canada used to be one of the world's most important sources of peacekeeping forces. In 1995 it opened the Lester B. Pearson Canadian International Peacekeeping Centre in Cornwallis, NS, to train soldiers in this kind of service, named after the former prime minister, who won a Nobel Peace Prize for his mediation efforts in the 1956 Suez Crisis. Pearson proposed that forces from nations not involved in the conflict help separate the belligerents. Since that time Canada has supported every peacekeeping venture which the UN has sponsored. Canadians have served in Palestine, Korea, Cyprus, Egypt, India, Pakistan, New Guinea, the Congo, Yemen, Lebanon, Nigeria, West Irian, Cambodia, Iran, Iraq, Kuwait, and East Timor.

In 2004 Canada had over 4,500 troops serving in a dozen trouble spots, including in Afghanistan and war-torn Bosnia, Kosovo, and the Ethiopian-Eritrean border. In 1997 Major General Lewis Mackenzie commanded all UN forces for four and one-half months in the former Yugoslavia. In 1993 Canada deployed 845 troops to Somalia to assist in a global rescue operation. In 1994 two Canadian generals commanded the UN peacekeeping contingent trying to create order in Rwanda's genocidal civil war. In 1996, Canada again took the lead in central Africa when the UN appointed the ex-Canadian ambassador to the U.S, Raymond Chrétien, as special envoy to deal with the war and refugee crisis. Canada sent 350 troops to prepare the mission. Its publicly visible peacekeeping operations were supported materially and diplomatically by the United States, a sign that they were in line with American interests as well.

Canadians solidly supported their country's involvement in the NATO bombing campaign against Yugoslavia in 1999 to try to bring a halt to ethnic cleansing of Albanians in Kosovo, sending 18 CF-18 Hornets equipped with precision-guided munitions to fly missions. Canadian pilots flew about 10% of the initial NATO strike missions and commanded half the ones in which they participated. It left 800 troops in Kosovo to try to stabilize that traumatized land. It continued to deploy 1,200 troops in Bosnia, turning over its role there to European allies in 2005.

Canada dispatched 800 ground troops to Macedonia to help enforce an eventual peace settlement. This was in line with ex-Foreign Minister Lloyd Axworthy's policy, which he called the "human security agenda" to help suffering individuals. Ex-Prime Minister Chrétien asserted: "As Canadians, as world citizens, we could not sit and watch as people are displaced, their homes looted and burned, and lives

taken away." Referring to peacekeeping, he added in 1999: "We are always there, like the Boy Scouts. Canadians love it."

Canada's peacekeeping experience in Somalia and the Balkans was sobering. The worst military scandal in Canada's post-1945 history occurred in Somalia, where a group of elite Canadian soldiers from the Airborne Regiment brutally tortured and killed a frail 16-year old Somali, who entered their camp looking for food. At least 16 other soldiers heard his screams and pleas but did nothing. This seriously tarnished the country's positive self-image as a peacekeeper, as well as the public image of the Canadian Forces themselves. The Airborne Regiment involved in this crime, for which nine soldiers were court-martialed, was disbanded in 1995 when videos were released showing soldiers making racist remarks and engaging in grotesque hazing rituals.

The follow-up inquiry delved deeply into the subtleties of how leadership and organization may have created the atmosphere in which such beatings could occur. They also had to deal with a 1993 occurrence in Bosnia in which Canadian troops were caught engaging in drunkenness, sex, black marketeering, and patient abuse at a mental hospital they were guarding. Officers must now undergo special training in military law, human rights, ethics, and public affairs before assuming command of their own units. In 2017, Canada adapted new rules of war: if a threat comes from Children, shoot first.

The challenges to peacekeepers have increased enormously. This is, in part, because of obsolete equipment. General Mackenzie called his overworked, under-armed and outgunned troops "the poor cousins when it comes to the budget, and they deserve better when we send them abroad to do our dirty work." Also, the days are over when peacekeepers serve at the invitation of a host country to monitor an existing peace. They must deal with belligerents who still want to fight.

Alex Morrison of the Canadian Institute for Strategic Studies noted that today's peacekeeping "is not playing with toys in a sandbox. It's what our men and women in uniform would surely call war." There is an unofficial distinction today between "peacekeeping," which involves wearing a blue UN beret and keeping two groups separate that want peace, and "stabilizing operations," which involves troops who can coerce belligerents with overwhelming military power. In 2017 only 112 Canadian forces were committed to nine UN missions; the rest of the soldiers deployed overseas were in the more dangerous second category. Ex-Defence Minister, and former general, Gordon O'Connor observed in 2006: "It is a shock for many people in our country that we're involved in something that is not blue helmets and no rifles."

Canada seemed to become a warrior nation, not a peacekeeping one although there was some nostalgia for the earlier role. A Canadian's opinion about the country's new role in the world is influenced by his party loyalty. Asked in 2012 if he or she is proud of Canadian's global reputation, 54% of Conservatives said yes, while 60% of Liberals and New Democrats said they were embarrassed by it. Three fourths of Conservatives were "proud of Canada's new military might, whereas 61% of Liberals and 68% of New Democrats were worried about it. Nevertheless, Canada's image abroad has not changed dramatically. In 2011 the Global Peace Index ranked it the eighth-most peaceful nation out of 153, up six places from the year before. Iceland placed first, and the U.S. 82d.

Canadians tend to have certain beliefs which feed their ambivalence about war: Canada is never the aggressor, never starts a war, and always fights someone else's conflict. Canada always goes to war as part of an alliance but has little influence on the strategy. At the same time, Canada is unlikely to be united in war, but when involved, its soldiers show uncommon courage.

Peacekeeping and other more robust military deployments create problems that Canada must confront. Repeated peacekeeping deployments pose severe hardships on soldiers and their families and produce burnout. This aggravates the problem of retention in the armed forces. At its peak in 1993, Canada deployed 4,641 peacekeepers worldwide. If one does not count its soldiers in Kosovo and Afghanistan, Canada had fallen by 2011 to 53th place of 115 nations in terms of total number of troops, police and observers involved in UN peacekeeping operations. Most were in Haiti and Sudan, and 13% were women. The U.S. placed 71st.

In 2019 Canada was the ninth largest contributor to the UN's total peacekeeping budget. Its foreign aid spending, .28% of GDP in 2020, compared with .19% for the U.S., also ranks 15th in the world as a percentage of GDP with the U.S. 22d; this is among the lowest within the OECD as a percentage of GDP. Canada spends more than 6.1 billion in foreign aid each year, but Conservative Party Leader Andrew Scheer plans to cut 25% of Canada's foreign aid spending "to help Canadians get ahead at home." However, not all Canadians agree with Andrew Scheer's plan. They fear that by cutting aid, Canada would be retreating from the world stage.

In 2004 Canada deployed 170 troops to Haiti to join with U.S., French, and Chilean troops to restore order on that strife-ridden island. Canada left 66 police officers until July 2007 to train the Haitian National Police while sending hundreds of soldiers and tons of supplies and an emergency hospital back to Haiti in January 2010 to help relieve the suffering after the catastrophic earthquake that devastated the capital of Port-au-Prince and killed tens of thousands of Haitians. Further, Canada permanently deploys 303 military personnel in the United States with Northcom and NORAD. It also maintains troops in Germany and Kosovo.

COVID-19 and the Economy

A virus of uncertain cause in China in December 2019 led to what is now called the COVID-19. This has affected 199 countries with the numbers of sick and dying increasing rapidly as this book heads to press.

The World Health Organization declared the virus a pandemic on March 11, 2020. According to the National Post, Minister Karina Goud says that Canada will spend 50 million to help the world's most desperate people fight COVID-19 because it is in the country's long-term security interest and because it is the right thing to do. Gould says the government must spend $50 million globally to protect Canada's future security and economic prosperity from a virus that knows no border.

On March 29, 2020, the federal [1] government assed an emergency COVID-19 bill with $52 billion of support to help workers, families, and employers to cope with the COVID-19. At the time of writing, COVID-19 continues to affect millions of people plus economies across the world. Vaccines are offering hope and the government is predicting that by the end of September 2021, everyone who wants a vaccine will have access.

Iraq

Canadian diplomats had worked in vain to achieve a compromise in the UN Security Council that would have avoided war with Iraq. Two days before the bombing in Iraq began in March 2003, Prime Minister Chrétien announced that no Canadian troops would fight because the war was not backed by a UN mandate. Opposition leader Stephen Harper of the Canadian Alliance publicly apologized to Americans, writing: "For the first time in history, the Canadian government has not stood beside its key British and American allies in their time of need."

Nevertheless, Canada left its more than 50 technicians and liaison officers at allied headquarters in Qatar, at sea with U.S. ships, and as exchange soldiers in U.S. units in Iraq. One was Major-General Walter Natyncyk, who had been seconded to the U.S. Third Armored Corps in Fort Hood, Texas, as deputy commander. When his unit shipped out to Iraq, Ottawa gave him the green light to go too. "The Canadian government sent me to Fort Hood, bottom line, to show in a tangible way the close affiliation between the U.S. and Canada."

Canadian soldiers in Iraq under the cover of various "liaison" programs are more numerous than some of the contingents in the coalition of the willing. Thus, in a December 2007 Maclean's poll that determined that Americans know more about Canada than any other people, the half of Americans who thought Canadian soldiers were fighting on their side in Iraq were not entirely wrong.

Canadians still make up the largest contingent of foreign nationals serving in the American military, and hundreds of them were in Iraq. A Canadian commodore commanded a flotilla of a dozen American, British, French, Italian and other nations' ships, including two Halifax-class frigates and the HMCS Iroquois destroyer, in the Persian Gulf in case of "an emergency." Canada also trained Iraqi police and troops in Jordan. In 2009 Canada dispatched a warship, Winnipeg, to the Indian Ocean waters off the coast of Somalia to be part of an international flotilla formed to combat down pirates.

Canada had delivered $215 (US$166) million in humanitarian and reconstruction aid to Iraq, and it distinguished itself as the fastest disburser of aid. It deployed a small mobile medical team to save lives in the recapture of Mosul in 2017. This quiet effort was far more than that of most nations explicitly backing the war. This is why Canada was hurt by the U.S. decision to grant primary contracts in Iraq only to allies who were supporting the war effort, thereby excluding Canadian companies. This slight was rectified when President Bush assured ex-Prime Minister Martin that Canadian companies could bid on a new round of contracts. Ottawa announced that it would send troops back to Afghanistan, thereby freeing American soldiers for operations in the Persian Gulf.

Tempers gradually cooled. Chrétien called on his countrymen to respect the American decision. He tried to explain his stand in the least offensive way, saying that he did not support the war effort, but hoped for victory, that he did not support regime change in Iraq, but was glad Saddam was gone. Chrétien's deputy, John Manley, made it clear that "at the end of the day, governments come and go, different people are in different offices, but at an institutional level we've got to make sure the continental relationship works."

Canada

Quebec singer Celine Dion was flown to the USS Truman to sing "God Bless America" to the troops. In 2005 she donated US$1 million to aid Katrina hurricane victims, while her government offered whatever assistance the U.S. might need. American ambassador Paul Cellucci, who had earlier expressed his "disappointment" in Canada's lack of support, joined in the conciliation: "We are friends, we are allies, we are neighbors, and we are family. And nothing is ever going to change that."

Asked why Canada first sent troops to Afghanistan, General Rick Hillier explained: "As a way to relieve the pressure of saying no to the Americans on Iraq." The Afghanistan deployment was therefore of major political importance for the Canadians, their most conspicuous contribution to the "war on terror" and was therefore significant in Ottawa's attempt to rebuild its credibility in Washington after refusing to participate in the 2003 Iraq war. The Canadian Forces felt a strong need to do something significant for the United States.

Afghanistan

Its major overseas military commitment was to Afghanistan. Ottawa offered 1,000 troops to join the UN peacekeeping force there in 2002. In 2003 it sent a battle group of 1,900 soldiers back to Afghanistan for a further one-year tour of UN duty and assumed command of peacekeeping forces in Kabul. By 2007 Canada's 2,500 soldiers constituted the fourth-largest contingent within the overall peacekeeping force of 32,800 NATO-led troops in Afghanistan. The combat contingent of its 2,830 forces was withdrawn in July 2011. But up to 1,000 were redeployed near Kabul to train Afghan security forces and police and to assist Canada's aid and reconstruction efforts. The Canadians weCanada'sre responsible for maintaining security in Kandahar, one of the most historically fractious and dangerous parts of the country. The Canadians left a great deal good works behind: a new road, 10 open schools. up from only one, and 600 trained Afghan police officers, up from 100.

In 2004 Canadian forces were commanded by Canadian General Rick Hillier, who was appointed a year later as chief of the defense staff. Hillier overhauled the structure of the Canadian military, restored its morale, and prepared it for a new era of combat missions abroad before his retirement in July 2008, appearing on TV regularly, gaining a level of fame theretofore unknown for a Canadian military officer. Hillier regularly took ice hockey players to visit the troops in the field. Moreover, Hillier expressed his view of military power in a very un-Canadian way: "We are the Canadian Forces and our job is to be able to kill people." The outspoken General Hillier's experiences with the Taliban left him convinced that they are "detestable murderers and scumbags."

The Afghan engagement enabled Canada to play its part in the post-September 11 world without being at the beck and call of the American president. By taking part in and even commanding the NATO force, which is acting with a UN mandate in Afghanistan, it showed and improved its military competence in difficult anti-insurgency warfare. For Prime Minister Harper, Afghanistan was the defining element in the new face for Canada in the world. He told troops at Kandahar Airfield: "Your work is also about demonstrating an international leadership role for our country."

At the same time, the government was careful not to imply that it was fighting in an "American war" as Canada interests that overlap with other Western nations and that are by nature global and threatened by a totalitarian ideology, represented by the Taliban. It was not easy for the Conservative government to make the point that its troops were serving under a UN and NATO mandate, not a U.S. one.

Its force is proving to be a workable alternative to the traditional blue-bereted UN peacekeeping missions. It is a display of what Ottawa calls "Three D" defense that also includes development and diplomacy. This engagement is Canada's dominant military commitment. Not since the Korean War has Canada been involved in such a large and dangerous wartime effort and suffered so many casualties, 158 deaths, half by roadside bombs, and 800 wounded. To put this in perspective, 211 Canadian police officers and firefighters were killed across Canada during the same period. This is proportionally higher than those of other NATO countries, including the U.S. Only the U.S. and UK suffered more total casualties.

The highest-ranking battle fatality was Colonel Geoff Parker, who had been slated to become NATO's deputy commander in Kandahar. The effort changed the public image of the Canadian Forces to an army engaged in full-scale combat and counterinsurgency warfare and gave the military a chance to transform itself into an efficient fighting machine.

Tragically, four Canadian soldiers were killed by friendly fire when an American F-16 pilot mistakenly dropped a bomb on them during a training exercise in Afghanistan. A high-level Canada-U.S. investigation concluded that the pilots had shown "reckless disregard" for the rules of engagement, but a subsequent American military hearing made a non-binding recommendation against court martial and criminal charges on the ground that administrative punishment would better serve "the interests of good order and discipline." The U.S. army awarded each of the four dead Canadian soldiers a Bronze Star.

Regrettably, this was not the last time such a tragic mistake occurred. In 2006, Canadian troops called in air support during a fierce engagement with the Taliban. But the U.S. jets mistakenly strafed the Canadian soldiers, killing one and wounding 30. The dead soldier was Mark Graham, a former Olympic sprinter at the 1992 Barcelona Games.

The war placed unknown strains on many of the Canadian soldiers who fought in Afghanistan. While on patrol in Helmand province, infantry captain, Robert Semrau, spotted a suffering enemy who he judged to be "98% dead." To end his suffering, he shot the man. But such mercy killing is a violation of the Geneva Conventions and the Canadian Forces Code of Conduct, which obligates soldiers to provide first aid to all casualties, friend or foe. Semrau, the first Canadian soldier to be charged with battlefield murder, was tried and convicted of disgraceful conduct, demoted and released from the army. His case captured the sympathy of thousands of Canadians and of many rank-and-file soldiers.

It is one of the largest donors to Afghanistan, providing $650 million in aid through 2007 and pledging over $1 billion more. This makes Afghanistan by far the largest recipient of Canada's bilateral aid. This assistance is the largest Canadian aid commitment ever made to a single country.

In 2005 the outgoing Liberal government decided to deploy 2,500 troops to Afghanistan to strengthen the anti-insurgency effort in the province of Kandahar, south of Kabul. They fought shoulder-to-shoulder with Americans, British, Dutch and other allies. In all, 37 allies contributed troops to the International Security Assistance Force (ISAF). In March 2006 it took command of the 6,000-strong multinational brigade that operated under aggressive NATO rules of engagement. This force included 100 elusive commandos from the elite Joint Task Force 2 unit. Canada paid for this deployment in lives because this was undeniably dangerous fighting. General Hillier called this "three-block war:" humanitarian assistance, peace support operations, and high-intensity conflict, all within a relatively small area.

Polls from 2007 to 2012 revealed that half the Canadians, 41% in 2012, thought the mission failed. The end of 2010, 53% of respondents in one poll responded that "it's time to get out." Only 31.6% thought Canada should stay. Many were appalled by the casualties and the brutality: one

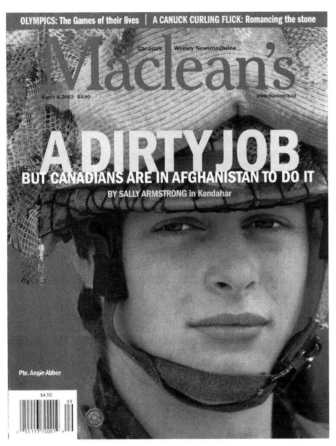

OLYMPICS: The Games of their lives | A CANUCK CURLING FLICK: Romancing the stone

Maclean's

Canada's Weekly Newsmagazine

March 4, 2002 $4.50   www.macleans.ca

A DIRTY JOB

BUT CANADIANS ARE IN AFGHANISTAN TO DO IT

BY SALLY ARMSTRONG in Kandahar

Pte. Angie Abbey

$4.50

purchase of transport helicopters, three new support ships, transport aircraft and 2,300 supply trucks. His government, which had budgeted $20.6 billion for defense in 2010, wanted to increase the full-time military force from 65,722 to 75,000 and add 10,000 more reservists, constituting 13% of the fighting forces in Afghanistan. However, by 2013 military talk was dominated by cost-cutting; the land force's operating budget shrank by 22%.

The fact that three generals with experience in irregular warfare in the Middle East and Afghanistan, Chief of Defence Staff General Rick Hillier, who stepped down in 2008 after more than three years at the top of the Canadian Forces, his chief of strategic planning, General Andrew Leslie, in 2007 Chief of the Land Staff, and General Walter Natynczyk, who replaced Hillier as Chief of the Defence Staff, had risen to top positions within the Canadian forces brought fresh thinking about modern war-fighting and about the need to reform Canada's military to be fit for more robust requirements. They restored the forces' morale and prepared them for a dangerous new era of combat missions abroad.

In 2012, General Tom Lawson, a fighter pilot, became Chief of the Defence Staff. In 2015 newly elected Prime Minister Justin Trudeau named Harjit Sajjan as defense minister. A turban-wearing Sikh, he was a highly decorated Afghanistan veteran and detective in Vancouver. Sikhs are known for their warrior culture. Between 2001 and 2014, more than 40,000 Canadian Armed Forces members served in the Afghanistan theater of operations with 158 Canadian of them dying in that conflict. The further sorrow is that on returning to Canada, many soldiers suf- fered post-traumatic stress syndrome. In a counter intuitive finding, though, the rate of suicide in the Canadian armed forces is higher among those who have not serve-din Afghanistan and elsewhere.

Harper staunchly supported the war effort to which the previous Liberal government had committed the country. His first foreign trip after becoming prime minister was to visit Canadian troops in Afghanistan for two days. In 2007 he defeated an opposition proposal in Commons to withdraw all Canadian troops. However, Harper could not extend the mission beyond 2011 without parliamentary approval, and all three opposition parties opposed that. There was a strong fear of an open-ended commitment. Harper did not need parliamentary approval to leave up to a thousand troops in Afghanistan to train Afghan security forces and to support humanitarian efforts.

Realizing that this war could go on for years, Harper ordered a substantial increase in military spending, to include the

captain was badly wounded in the head by a young man wielding an ax while attending a meeting of village elders.

One of the first political crises Prime Minister Harper faced in office was its return to the tradition of banning news media coverage of returning coffins from war and the flying of flags at half-staff to mark the death of troops. Harper argued that the families should be able to grieve out of the limelight, but critics accused him of not honoring the dead and forced him o back down. Harper telephoned the family of every soldier killed in action, so he was constantly reminded of the horror of that war.

The ensuing vigorous and emotional debate merely underscores Canadians' uneasiness over this enhanced role in Afghanistan and the government's nervousness about uncertain public support for the war. Some see an Iraq-like quagmire, the wrong cause in the wrong place. Canadians debated what the appropriate global role is for their country and military.

In late 2009 the Harper government was embarrassed by allegations made by a former diplomat in Afghanistan, Richard Colvin, that in 2006 and early 2007, Canadian soldiers handed detainees over to Afghan authorities knowing that the latter use torture and that they did not follow up on the detainees' welfare. Colvin called this practice "un-Canadian,

counterproductive and probably illegal." The Harper government allegedly ignored reports of this. When a parliamentary committee of inquiry demanded to see documents relevant to the case, Harper prorogued, or closed, parliament for two months, while Canadians were distracted by the Winter Olympics. It seemed to many that the government had something important to hide. This scandal overshadowed the entire debate of Canada's military role in the country. It eroded further Canadians' fading support for the war effort.

Harper staunchly supported the war effort to which the previous Liberal government had committed the country. His first foreign trip after becoming prime minister was to visit Canadian troops in Afghanistan for two days. In 2007 he defeated an opposition proposal in Commons to withdraw all Canadian troops. However, Harper could not extend the mission beyond 2011 without parliamentary approval, and all three opposition parties opposed that. There was a strong fear of an open-ended commitment. Harper did not need parliamentary approval to leave up to a thousand troops in Afghanistan to train Afghan security forces and to support humanitarian efforts.

Realizing that this war could go on foryears, Harper ordered a substantial increase in military spending, to include the

Canada

purchase of transport helicopters, three new support ships, transport aircraft and 2,300 supply trucks. His government, which had budgeted $20.6 billion for defense in 2010, wanted to increase the full-time military force from 65,722 to 75,000 and add 10,000 more reservists, constituting 13% of the fighting forces in Afghanistan. However, by 2013 military talk was dominated by cost-cutting; the land force's operating budget shrank by 22%.

The fact that three generals with experience in irregular warfare in the Middle East and Afghanistan, Chief of Defence Staff General Rick Hillier, who stepped down in 2008 after more than three years at the top of the Canadian Forces, his chief of strategic planning, General Andrew Leslie, in 2007 Chief of the Land Staff, and General Walter Natynczyk, who replaced Hillier as Chief of the Defence Staff, had risen to top positions within the Canadian forces brought fresh thinking about modern war-fighting and about the need to reform Canada's military to be fit for more robust requirements. They restored the forces' morale and prepared them for a dangerous new era of combat missions abroad. In 2012 General Tom Lawson, a fighter pilot, became Chief of the Defence Staff. In 2015 newly elected Prime Minister Justin Trudeau named Harjit Sajjan as defense minister. A turban-wearing Sikh, he was a highly decorated Afghanistan veteran and detective in Vancouver. Sikhs are known for their warrior culture.

Between 2001 and 2014, more than 40,000 Canadian Armed Forces members served in the Afghanistan theater of operations with 158 Canadian of them dying in that conflict. The further sorrow is that on returning to Canada, many soldiers suffered post-traumatic stress syndrome. In a counter intuitive finding, though, the rate of suicide in the Canadian Armed forces is higher among those who have not served in Afghanistan and elsewhere.

ECONOMY

By world standards, Canada is a rich country. Measured in terms of gross national product or GDP, the total value of the goods and services a country produces annually, Canada ranks eleventh in the world, despite the fact that it has only 37.06 (2018) million inhabitants. As visitors can easily see, the average Canadian has a standard of living as high as the average American. Enjoying the sixth highest per capita GDP in the Organization for Economic Cooperation and Development (OECD), often called a "rich man's club" of nations, Canadians live better than the Japanese, Germans and French. There is less visible poverty than in the U.S. Canadians are well clothed, housed, fed, educated and cared for.

The UN Human Development Report consistently ranks Canada as among the world's best places to live based on standard of living, life expectancy, and educational attainment, usually slightly above the United States (U.S). Because of its bountiful natural resources, many people have said that Canada was economically "a solution searching for a problem." However, there are occasional reminders that the large, complex Canadian economy has weaknesses as well as strengths.

Canada has a capitalist, free-market economy, although the state's hand in the economy is considerably greater than in the U.S. Canada's natural beauty attracts millions of tourists each year, mainly from the U.S. although that has slowed since the September 11 attacks; a million Canadians, or about one out of ten jobs, earn their living from the tourist industry.

Canada is a country richly endowed with natural resources of all kinds. Although only 5% of its total territory is arable, Canada possesses enough arable land to be one of the world's largest producers of food. For a long time, natural resources and agriculture were the pillars of Canada's economy. In the 18th and 19th centuries, Canada borrowed and attracted large amounts of capital from abroad, and it imported manufactured goods. It paid for imported goods with raw materials and grain.

In the 20th century, and especially after 1945, the Canadian economy changed considerably. Its services and manufacturing sectors now overshadow the resource and agricultural (primary) sector in terms of contribution to GDP and employment. Services in 2019 provided 71% of employment and 70% of GDP while industry was responsible for 22% of the jobs and 28% of GDP. Only 2% of employment and 2% of GDP were derived from agriculture. This sparsely populated country has a small domestic market of 35.5 million people. Canada must trade in order to maintain its prosperity; foreign trade with the U.S. alone generates 52% of its GDP, as opposed to less than 20% of the U.S.'. One out of three Canadian jobs is linked to trade. This dependence on the international market makes Canada particularly vulnerable to world-wide economic trends and protectionism.

The problem of dependence is compounded by the fact that its international trade is practically dominated by one country: the U.S. Every year Canada sells about three-fourths or 74% (2019) of its exports to the U.S., and approximately 64% (2019) of its imports must be bought from its only neighbor. The two countries' trade is roughly balanced over time. Until 2008, Canada relied on its trade surplus with the U.S. to pay for its trade deficit with the rest of the world. In 2007 China overtook Canada to become the largest source of American imports, and it is now the U.S.'s second-largest overall trading partner after Canada. China buys 4.3% of Canada's exports and provides 11% of its imports. Its trade with Canada doubled in the five years to 2011, and it continues to grow, amounting to nearly US$56.5 billion in 2019, according to the United Nations COMTRADE database on international trade. In 2020, exports to China grew 8.1% while declining internationally 11.9%. Imports from China grew 1.9% during this time.

Foreigners, especially Americans, own a large portion of its economy. The U.S. accounts for 64% of total foreign direct investment (FDI) in Canada and the European Union (EU) for only 29%. In 2000 Americans accounted for 75% of Canada's foreign ownership. Canadian FDI in the U.S. more than trebled between 1989 and 2002, growing to US$92 billion in 2002 and multiple times that by 2005. Half of its outbound foreign direct investment (FDI) goes to the U.S. and a fourth of it to the EU countries.

Because the Canadian and American economies are so tightly linked, when the U.S. sneezes, Canada catches pneumonia. *Maclean's* went even farther in 2008: "If the U.S. catches a cold, well, call up the undertaker." U.S. economic growth is too important and its ties to other economies too complex for the effects of an American downturn not to be felt beyond its borders. When the American economy slips into recession, the Canadian economy normally follows the same downward path, but it usually takes a little longer to recover. The good news is that when the U.S. economy booms, it can pull Canada along in its slipstream.

Lacking the size and diversity of the U.S. economy, Canada is normally not as resilient as the U.S. when faced with economic adversity. However, in the 21st century the high world demand for natural resources, especially oil, gas and mining,

Canada

gave the Canadian economy much needed stability and predictability. In the 1970s and 1980s, the dependence on the U.S. stimulated economic nationalism again, which has always been close to the surface of most Canadians. As reasonable as the calls for "Canada for the Canadians" seem to be, they brought serious problems to the Canadian economy.

On November 19, 2018, Canada launched its new $10 vertical note, which features the portrai of social justic icon Viola Desmond. She is honored as the first woman to appear on a Canadian bank note. In 2019. it was named Banknote of the Year by the International Banknote Society.

Geography has so closely linked the two countries' economies that cooperation, not conflict, is in their mutual interest. Also, Canada is too open a country, with too vulnerable an economy, to pursue a consistent policy of economic nationalism. The U.S. and Canada are each other's most important trading partners and form the world's largest bilateral trade relationship. Since the Free Trade Agreement (FTA) went into effect in 1989, the value of two-way trade had trebled by 2013, surpassing US$680 billion, making this the world's largest bilateral trading relationship. If services are added, the total is about $800 billion. Total trade equals $2 billion each day. In the process, the FTA has reoriented Canada's economic axis from east-west to north-south. Since 2000 trade with non-U.S. partners grew faster than trade with the U.S.

Trade with Canada is of increasing importance for the U.S.; a fifth of America's exports and 15% of its imports flow to and from Canada. One-third of all trans-border trade takes place within companies having a presence on both sides of the border. Cross-border trade supports 221,500 jobs in Michigan alone. The Canadian foreign ministry estimates that more than 7 million American jobs depend on Canada-U.S. free trade. America's trade with Canada is, in dollar value, about three times its trade with Japan. Canada's second largest partner is China, which provides 11% of Canadian imports. Canada runs a large trade deficit with it, and until the financial crisis of 2008, that was more than compensated by Canada's trade surplus with the rest of the world. By 2004, 400 companies had established a permanent presence in China, and in 2005 its trade with China soared by 40%.

The U.S. sells more to the single province of Ontario than to either Japan or all of Western Europe. Canada sells more to a single American company, Home Depot, than it does to all of France. Canada is the largest trading partner for 36 of the 50 American states, and Pennsylvania exports more to Canada than to its next seven markets combined.

Motor vehicles and parts represent 14% of Canada's manufacturing output and employ more than 150,000 Canadians, accounting for about 25% of U.S. merchandise exports to Canada and about a quarter of imports. Motor vehicles constitute 23% of Canadian exports to the U.S., and 90% of the vehicles and automotive parts manufactured in Canada are shipped south. In 2011 Canada produced 2.1million vehicles, or about 16% of the North American total. Thus, when the situation of the American automotive industry turns bad, as in 2008–9, this is shared by Canada, and production in Canada plummets. Windsor's jobless rate shot up to 14.4% during the recession, and two-thirds of the jobs lost were in Ontario, most of them in manufacturing. The second largest category of U.S. exports is electronics and telecommunications equipment.

Canada is the U.S.'s largest supplier of imported energy, oil, uranium, natural gas and electricity, sending 99% of its oil exports to America. Consequently, Canada it is vulnerable to the lack of pipeline capacity and an oil glut in America. Canada supplies 21% of U.S. imports of crude and refined oil products, amounting to more than 10% of America's overall oil needs. Over half of Canada's gas production is shipped to the U.S., accounting for 94% of its natural gas imports and 13% of its demand. Much flows through 31 pipelines that cross the U.S. border. Canada is the only country in the Group of Seven, except the UK, that is a net oil exporter. Its people consume per capita roughly twice as much energy as other developed countries. Both countries suffer similar problems, though: high labor costs although the unit cost of production is lower in Canada and a decline of traditional industries.

After this brief overview of the Canadian economy, it is worth looking more closely at its individual components and at the economic policies that the Canadian federal governments have pursued.

The Primary Sector

Any treatment of the Canadian economy must always begin with the primary sector. Throughout the country's history, raw materials and agriculture provided the foundation for Canada's development. Today this sector accounts for only 5% of the workforce and less than 8% of its GDP, and the agricultural portion now amounts to 2% of the value of Canada's total output. In terms of employment, 2% of Canadians now make a living from farming, and the corresponding figure for mining, lumbering, fishing and other forms of primary extraction is only about 2%.

These figures understate the importance of the primary sector for the overall economy. This element is the basis for much of Canada's manufacturing, such as wood and paper products, food and beverages and petroleum products. Even more significant is its contribution to Canada's export trade: about 60% of the country's exports leave in raw or semi-processed form, a high percentage for any developed country.

Canada can be thankful for its natural wealth. A problem with heavy reliance on the export of raw materials, though, is that their prices fluctuate widely on world markets. Therefore, a country becomes excessively vulnerable to the ups and downs of outside market forces. Unfortunately, this has often been the case with Canada. Things go well whenever the voracious demand in the U.S. and developing countries, especially China,

Earlier days in Battle Harbour, Labrador.

Courtesy: Mike Earle

for raw materials keeps the prices for Canada's metals, minerals, lumber and oil up. Canada's economy thrives when the prices of natural resources, especially energy, are high, which has been the case most of the time in the 21st century; it is hurt when prices go down.

Fishing

Most of Canada's earliest European visitors came to fish in the waters off its 241,402-kilometer, or 149,670 miles, coastline, and the success of early settlements in Canada depended greatly on the ability to maintain a subsistence fishery. Canada was once the world's leading exporter of fish and fish products. Canada's formerly rich fishing grounds, extending 200 miles off its coasts, contained 150 fish and shellfish species and was able to maintain more than 900 fish processing plants, which employed over 100,000 persons. Most of these plants were located in the Atlantic provinces. In Newfoundland alone, about l5% of the inhabitants found employment in fishing or fish processing.

In 1989 Newfoundland's dependence on a fishing industry was devastated by over fishing and dwindling stocks. A 2005 study concluded that stocks of adult cod off the North American coast had diminished by 96% since the fishing industry took off in the 1850s.

In 1992 Ottawa slapped a moratorium on all northern cod fishing to allow stocks to replenish themselves, thereby provoking a clash with France. The French claimed the right to fish in the Gulf of St. Lawrence because of their tiny island outposts, St. Pierre with a population of about 6,500 and Miquelon and its approximately 600 residents, located just 16 miles off the Newfoundland coast. Fishermen in both Newfoundland and the two French islands feared that French trawlers would further deplete codfish stocks in the Gulf. The feud was settled by treaty in 1995, a year in which Canada used its navy to see that earlier agreements would be respected. A further dispute between the two countries broke out in 2005 over rights to thousands of square miles of Atlantic seabed south of the islands.

The EU agreed temporarily to restrict fishing in the waters inside and outside the 200-mile zone in order to allow stocks to replenish themselves. When pirate fishermen from Europe, especially Spain, continued to overfish the dwindling stocks, the Canadians decided to act in 1995, sending a frigate to fired a shot over the bow of a Spanish trawler outside the 200-mile fishing zone, boarded the vessel, and ordered it to St. John's. There it found illegal nets on board and doctored records proving that the fishermen had indeed violated international agreements.

After a great deal of acrimony, Canada and Spain reached a settlement calling for closer monitoring and enforcement of fish catches. However, in 1998, the UN International Court of Justice decided that it lacked jurisdiction to settle the dispute. Canadians applauded the use of military force to support their national interests. In 2003 the federal government closed down most of the remaining Atlantic cod fishing industry.

Canada also was involved in a festering dispute with the U.S. over the fishing of fragile West Coast salmon stocks, which swim through Alaskan waters into Canadian waters to breed. Both sides accepted mediation, but those talks ended in stalemate in 1997. In June 1999 a landmark agreement was reached establishing a system of flexible catch quotas and a $140 million fund to protect spawning grounds. Aquaculture still threatens to make diplomacy irrelevant, though, despite the emotional tie that British Columbia has with wild salmon. More fish are produced on fish farms within the province than are caught in its waters. The number of wild salmon continues to decline, many from diseases contracted from salmon farms.

No beings overfish more than do seals. Bowing to foreign and domestic political pressure, Canada banned the unrestricted killing of seals, thereby enabling the seal population to triple since the 1970s to about six million on the east coast. Each animal consumes an average of 45 pounds of fish a day. This, as well as overfishing, combined almost to destroy the fish stocks, especially cod.

In order to reduce the seal population to a manageable level, the federal government began in 1994 to support the price of seal meat, which is used for animal feed. Seal over-reproduction and the need for employment in outlying areas are the reasons why people from Quebec and Newfoundland living close to thawing ice floes in the Gulf of St. Laurence are permitted each spring to engage in the world's largest seal slaughter for a few weeks. For those living in rural regions where work is sporadic at best following the disappearance of cod stocks, the hunt supplements their meager winter incomes. One sealer who pocketed $5,000 in one week noted: "When you make $25,000 a year, that's a big boost."

About 6,000 people benefit from seal hunting, and by 1997 they had quadrupled the size of their annual catch, despite the protests of animal rights activists. The largest seal hunt in a half century took place in 2004, with more than 200,000 taken in the first 36 hours. The rest of the 350,000 maximum was hauled in by smaller operations. The quota for 2006 was 335,000 harp seals, not the whitecoat seals, a tiny percentage of the overall population. The 2008 quota was 275,000 harp seals and 8,200 hooded seals. The killing of baby seals remains outlawed, but critics claim that it still happens and that most of the seals killed are only one or two months old.

The business is fraught with dangers. In April 2007, nearly 100 fishing boats became trapped in thick ice caused by a sustained dry Arctic wind. The crushing ice destroyed or damaged some of the boats, and only the country's largest icebreakers could free the boats and rescue the 450 stranded hunters. Due to global warming there are fewer suitable seals to hunt; premature thawing of the ice causes seal pups to fall through the ice and drown.

The sealers are harassed each step of the way by animal rights activists, such as Paul McCartney, Pamela Anderson, and Brigitte Bardot who find such an animal culling cruel. Tempers flare as both sides do what they think has to be done. Opinion polls in 2009 revealed that most Canadians agree with the celebrities: 51% found seal hunting "cruel and inhumane and should be banned;" another 17% regarded it as "ugly and brutal, but that's no reason to ban it." Only 25% had no objections and 7% "don't care."

A major blow to commercial harvesting was delivered in May 2009 by the European Parliament, which banned the importing or sale of furs and other seal products. Canadian officials immediately protested, pointing out that European fur farms growing minks and foxes kill more animals every four or five days than the entire annual hunt does in a year. But, a European animal rights spokesman called the ban the "final nail in the coffin." Products from subsistence hunts by Inuit and other indigenous peoples were exempted. To poke a thumb in the EU's eyes, the prime minister and his entire cabinet flew to Nunavut and nibbled appetizers of raw seal. Governor General Jean helped Inuit cut out the heart of a seal and then ate part of it raw. The parliamentary canteen in Ottawa even served seal meat for the first time ever.

Fur and Timber

Lucrative fishing possibilities had lured Europeans to Canada who then established contact with Indians. These native Canadians had very valuable goods to trade, furs. With its cold climate and rugged timbered terrain, Canada provides a natural habitat for a wide variety of fur-bearing animals, including beaver, wild mink, Arctic fox, muskrat, otter, coyote, timber wolf, red fox, marten and Canada lynx. As noted earlier, the fur trade dominated the Canadian economy from the early 1600s to the late 1700s, and it powerfully shaped the Canadian destiny.

Canada

Largest grain elevator in North America, Thunder Bay, Ontario

Unlike the fishing industry, which was restricted chiefly to the fringes of Canada, the fur trade directed European attention toward the north and the interior of the huge North American continent. The fur trade broadened the horizon of the early Canadians and provided the initial impetus to expand Canada "from sea to sea."

The fur trade was also an enterprise best conducted by huge trade monopolies, such as the Hudson's Bay and Northwest Companies. It therefore left in Canadians' mouths a good taste of large, state-sanctioned economic monopolies, which still differs somewhat from the American preference for purely private competitive firms. A negative consequence of the fur trade, though, was that for many decades it delayed both permanent settlement in the West and the development of Canadian manufacturing. Profits from fur could simply buy whatever foreign manufactures were needed. Although its significance for Canada's overall economy is minimal today, the sale abroad of raw Canadian furs continues. Despite protests by animal rights activists, the British army admitted in 2003 that it failed after twenty years of searching to find an artificial substitute for the traditional bearskin head-dresses worn most famously by guards at Buckingham Palace as only the pelt of the Canadian black bear can survive the 24-hour year-round onslaught of British weather.

An unintended consequence of the severe restrictions on the fur trade is that the traditional livelihood of many Aboriginals disappeared as they have had to replace their lost income by permitting oil, gas and mining into their previously unspoiled areas. This has contributed to environmental problems. Trappers once killed wolves to protect other animals in their traps. But the wolf population has soared, to the detriment of the caribou and buffalo herds. A national symbol, the beaver, has also multiplied dramatically to an estimated 20 million animals in Canada alone. In their avid pursuit of building dams, they have destroyed many trees and caused unwanted flooding of farmland.

Unlike the fur trade, the timber trade was favorable to settlement in Canada. Ships carrying timber to Europe had excess space for the return passage. Settlers could occupy such space very economically. Indeed, except during the American Revolutionary War, timber provided the first significant boost to the populating of Canada. In addition, timber was conducive to agriculture because logging operations left land cleared for agricultural use. Further, unlike the fur business, timber-work stimulated manufacturing as lumber had to be processed in sawmills, transported in vehicles larger than canoes and ultimately transformed into such goods as ocean-going vessels and furniture.

At the same time, the timber trade created a market for many kinds of metal tools. A fourth of Canada's territory is covered by forest. With 10% of the globe's total forest area, it is the world's premier exporter of timber and forest products and its third largest producer, with about 14% of the total world production. In a good year, almost 250 million trees are felled in Canada.

Four million trees are required to produce the newsprint for *The New York Times* in one year alone. Canada is the world's largest exporter of newsprint. A third of the world's newsprint comes from its forests. Unfortunately for the industry, declining newspaper sales worldwide, smaller newspaper formats, the transfer of many classified ads to the internet, and such modern practices as the "paperless office" have cut seriously into demand. Sales were also harmed by environmentalist policies of such publications as *Victoria's Secret*, which announced in 2006 that it would not print catalogues on paper manufactured from endangered Canadian boreal forests. Sales fell 8.5% in 2005 alone, and 31 pulp and paper mills in Canada (13 of them in Ontario) closed either entirely or partially.

The problem is that trees are being cut faster than they can be replenished. Moreover, mismanagement is so bad that millions of cut trees are cut are never transported out of the forests and are left to rot. To make matters worse, Canadian forests have been ravaged in recent years by acid rain, by fires which have destroyed about six times more forest area than loggers harvested, and by such pests as the spruce budworm, which defoliated about 185 million acres in the eastern half of Canada, and the mountain pine beetle, which kills more trees in BC than wildfires or logging. The latter, which can kill a mature tree in one year, is threatening to cross the Rocky Mountains and sweep across the entire northern continent.

The gradual destruction of Canada's most lucrative natural resource is particularly dangerous because it is Canada's largest employer, employing about 300,000 persons as loggers and as workers in sawmills and pulp and paper operations, primarily in outlying communities whose economic stability depends on it. Another 700,000 jobs exist because of it. In British Columbia, which accounts for 60% of Canada's lumber production, one in four persons is at least indirectly dependent on the forest industry. Thus, when this industry experiences hard times, as a result of a decline in the American construction industry, for example, the entire Canadian economy suffers. Canadians control about 75% of the country's total timber production.

For many years passions on both sides of the border were inflamed by a seemingly interminable dispute over softwood lumber. Canada consistently supplies about a third of the U.S. market. American companies claimed that Canadian producers receive illegal subsidies and should therefore be forced to pay countervailing duties (which amounted to 32% in 2001 and 10% in 2006). Canada retorts that it merely has a different system for granting rights to cut and that American producers are engaging in selfish protectionism. In a nutshell, 95% of the timber in the U.S. is privately owned and is sold by auction at market prices. In Canada, because the provinces own about 94% of the timber, they set the harvest levels and stumpage fees. American producers contend that the fees are below market prices and therefore constitute a subsidy, which is forbidden. Canadians rejected this argument.

In 1996 the two countries signed an agreement granting selected provinces fee-free access to the U.S. market for a certain volume of wood but requiring Canada to collect fees on anything above that level. When the agreement expired in

2001, the two countries again found themselves at loggerheads, so to speak. While waiting for the World Trade Organization (WTO) to rule on the dispute, mills in British Columbia, which account for half of lumber exports, and Quebec had to close, and thousands lost their jobs.

In 2002 the U.S. imposed countervailing duties averaging 27% on Canadian lumber exports. Although these duties hurt, the Canadian lumber industry concentrated its production in its most efficient mills thereby lowering average costs and strengthening the industry economically. This unexpected Canadian response hurt both American producers, who faced stiffer competition, and consumers, who must pay higher prices for protected lumber.

In May 2003 the WTO determined that Canada's stumpage is not an unfair subsidy, and a North American Free Trade Agreement (NAFTA) panel decided in September that the U.S. had not proven that Canadian softwood exports threatened to injure American lumber firms. In December the two countries reached a tentative agreement lasting three years that would limit Canadian producers to 31.5% of the U.S. market.

In another judgment in April 2004, the WTO rejected all of Canada's complaints against American anti-dumping duties on softwood lumber. Nevertheless, the deadlock continued, even after a NAFTA panel ruled yet again in September 2004 that Canada's softwood lumber exports are not subsidized, and the U.S. agreed to accept this ruling. A half year later the WTO established a dispute panel to investigate whether the U.S. has complied with its rulings against tariffs on Canadian softwood lumber. While Canada's annual softwood sales of $7 billion to the U.S. accounted for only about 3% of the trade relationship, the dispute took on oversized political symbolism.

The 20-year dispute seemed to be resolved in April 2006, the first foreign policy success of Prime Minister Harper's government. The U.S. lifted a 10% duty on softwood lumber and agreed to refund $4 billion of the $5 billion collected since 2002, paying about a half billion of the remainder to American softwood lumber producers. However, Canada agreed that if the price of lumber fell below a threshold calculated by a complex formula, or if a surge in exports occurred, it would levy an export tax to be retained by the Canadian provinces or quotas on Canadian shipments, or a combination of the two. Although this settlement departed significantly from the principle of free trade, Canadians greeted it.

In April 2009 the new Obama administration reintroduced a 10% duty on some lumber imports, claiming that the Canadians had not made amends for

violating the trade deal. In January 2011 American trade officials asked a London arbitration court to penalize exports from British Columbia arguing that the underpricing of timber from public lands was a subsidy. BC shrugged this off because the U.S. is not its only market now because its exports to China have increased. By 2011 its total sales to China and Japan exceed those to the U.S., which once bought two-thirds of BC's lumber. By 2011 that had fallen to only a third, thanks in part to its housing crisis. This endless dispute arose again in 2017 when Donald Trump became president and has yet to be resolved even under his successor Joseph Biden.

Agriculture

Agriculture provided the livelihood for a large portion of settlers to Canada. When, toward the end of the 19th century, strains of wheat were developed which could thrive in the northern climes of the Prairie regions, settlement in the Western part of Canada was greatly stimulated. This produced a strong demand for metal implements and manufactured supplies and a powerful additional incentive to complete the East–West railway. Newcomers could easily enter farming; a federal governmental homestead policy provided any farmer with 160 acres of land, provided that he lived on it and worked it for five years.

Such family-owned and operated farms remain the backbone of Canadian agriculture, despite the continuing tendency for farms to grow in size and decline in number. The average farm in Canada today is 540 acres; in the Prairie provinces they average over 900 acres. About 7% of the country's total land area is devoted to farming; most is within 300 miles of the U.S. border and is concentrated in only three provinces: Saskatchewan, which has 40% of it, Alberta and Ontario.

The relative importance of agriculture has declined in Canada, although it remains important in its export sector. In 1900 approximately 75% of Canadians

were engaged in agriculture; by 1946, this percentage had decreased to 29%, and today it is 2.4%. Its share in GDP has also declined dramatically, from 12% in 1951 to 2%. Nevertheless, agriculture remains important. About 40% of Canada's produce is exported, including about 85% of the wheat crop. Its major buyers are Japan, the U.S., the EU and China. In 2010 Canada sold three times more wheat to Asia than to EU countries.

Behind only the U.S., Canada is the world's second largest exporter of wheat, 60% of which is grown in Saskatchewan, alone accounts for nearly half of all agricultural export earnings. Canada possesses a fifth of the international market. Any precipitous fall in world wheat prices sends many Saskatchewan family farms into bankruptcy, as occurred at the turn of the century when the cost of production exceeded prices of grain. Also, the widespread rejection in Europe of genetically modified organism (GMO) foods has narrowed Canada's market. Only in North American markets can GMO foods be readily sold. In 2003, Canada joined the U.S. to challenge in the WTO the EU's ban on GMOs. Some Canadian farmers are trying to keep their crops free of GMO pollen in order to be able to sell to non-GMO markets.

Because of its agricultural prowess, Canada is a net exporter of food. However, this fortunate situation is due chiefly to wheat production. Canada runs a deficit in fruit, vegetables, nuts, honey, sugar, tobacco and other products, which may in the future cause Canada to become a net importer of food. Canadians face the same specter as do the American farmers: hard times at best, and bankruptcy at worst.

In 2003 cattle farmers, who sell $7 billion worth of beef each year, were shaken by North America's first case of mad-cow disease (BSE). A single cow in northern Alberta tested positive. The U.S., which normally accounts for three-fourths of all Canadian beef exports, and nearly 30 other countries temporarily sealed their

Canada

borders to Canadian beef, causing severe financial loss to Canadian farmers. Herds in all three western provinces were quarantined and slaughtered. The next shock came in December 2003 when a cow in Washington State also tested positive for BSE. It turned out that it had come from an Alberta herd. In 2007 a 13-year-old beef cow from Alberta was confirmed to have the disease, the 11th case since 2003. Ottawa opted for a partial ban of U.S. beef that was much less restrictive than the one Washington had imposed.

During 2004, the U.S. slowly opened its doors to boneless processed Canadian beef from young animals. President Bush said before his visit to Canada in November 2004 that the ban should be lifted, but the wheels of bureaucracy grind slowly and mysteriously in Washington. Despite the fact that another Canadian cow was found in January 2005 to be infected by BSE, the American door to Canadian cattle under 30 months of age was to be opened in March 2005. However, a federal judge in Montana ordered the border to remain closed. Two months later the U.S. Senate blocked the agriculture department's efforts to open the border and instead voted to block Canada's designation as a "minimal risk" region for BSE. In 2006 Bush vowed to end all BSE-related restrictions.

One product in which Canada does not run a deficit is beer. American beer drinkers have been thirsty for the Molson, Labatt, O'Keefe, and Moosehead beers and ales. In 1992 agreements were reached not only eliminating barriers that prevented beer brewed in one province from being sold in another but opening up the market to American beers. By 2004 the only Canadian-owned beer left after Labatt was bought by Belgium's Interbrew was Molson, which has over 40% of Canada's beer market. Yet, the beer that flaunted nationalism and came up with the rant, "I am Canadian," merged with Coors, the third-largest brewer in the U.S. It had already brewed and sold Coors in Canada. Canadian beers in the U.S. face stiff competition from the rapidly growing number of microbreweries and successfully challenging the old conventional wisdom that Canadian beer tastes better than the American variety.

Canadians purchase about half of California's exported wines. Canadian wines, 90% of which come from Ontario, particularly the Niagara area, and most of the rest from BC, have come into their own and have won hundreds of international awards. Canadian "ice wine" is an expensive dessert wine made from frost-bitten grapes of which Canada has become the world's leading producer. It has a national appellation, which enables it to be sold in the European Union (EU) but faces stiff competition from another Canadian product, cider or "apple ice wine," a beverage with 12% alcohol from Quebec. The domestic market for wine remains somewhat restricted because Canadians are not big wine drinkers although that is slowly changing. Canadians consume on average only 10 liters per year (one-sixth that in France and Italy), compared with 88 liters of beer.

As in other sectors of the Canadian economy, the state's hand has always been involved in agriculture. Since the Great Depression, marketing boards for various types of farm products have regulated markets. They have attempted to keep farm prices up in order to control the chronic problem of low and unstable agricultural prices. In the centralized "supply management" structure, dozens of federal and provincial government boards assign production quotas for dairy, poultry and other farm products.

Wheat growers typically had only one customer, the Canadian Wheat Board (CWB) monopolized the buying and selling of wheat and barley crops, as well as providing quality control. The CWB fixed a guaranteed price, and the government covered any losses. Founded in 1935, the CWB was the only marketer for Prairie grain destined for export or human consumption within Canada and was one of the world's biggest grain exporters. Farmers elected the majority of its 15-member board of directors and the federal government did not control or interfere in day-to-day operations.

The U.S. launched numerous formal complaints claiming that the CWB was a monopolistic state trading organization that broke global trading rules. Believing that farmers should be able to sell their crops freely, Prime Minister Harper moved to eliminate the CWB's "single desk" monopoly as of August 2012, a reform that had been advocated for decades.

The Western Grain Stabilization and the Agricultural Stabilization Act Programs are federal projects designed to enhance stability offering limited subsidies to save Canadian farmers. For example, in 1998, for every $100 of income for a Canadian wheat farmer, $9 came from government subsidies while an American farmer received $38 and a Western European $57.

Governmental protection of agriculture is not as great as in the EU or Japan, but there has been a tendency over the years for it to grow in Canada. As such, these efforts are perpetually surrounded by political controversy. American farmers resent high subsidies and tariffs up to 350% on dairy products. As a result of the tariffs on dairy imports, ranging from 200% to 300%, the Canadian consumer pays 63% more for milk than in the U.S. Quebec holds about half the dairy quota, and younger farmers resent having to pay hundreds of thousands of dollars to purchase a quota share when they go into business. Other farmers contend that without protection, their farms would be taken over by American conglomerates.

The potential Achilles' heel of Canada's agricultural breadbasket has always been transportation of grain from western sources to eastern markets or ports. Western farmers are dependent on the railroads, which take their grain to the port of Thunder Bay on the northern shore of Lake Superior where the grain is deposited in some of the largest grain elevators in the world from which it is loaded into ships and transported through the elaborate locks of Sault Ste. Marie and into the St. Lawrence Seaway system.

Mining

Canada is one of the world's major storehouses for minerals, ranking first in the world in mineral exports and third in terms of mineral production, behind the U.S. and Russia. Canada is the world's largest producer of asbestos, zinc, silver, nickel, and potash and the second largest of gypsum, molybdenum, and sulfur. Plus, Canada is one of the world's major producers of uranium, titanium, aluminum, cobalt, gold, lead, copper, iron, and platinum.

Canada exports of potentially deadly asbestos mainly to poor countries has come under increasing criticism within Canada, especially Quebec, where ca. 1,000 persons still make their living from asbestos mining. In 1981 a huge body of gold ore was discovered at Hemlo in northwestern Ontario. With improved mining technology, Canada is now extracting more gold than ever and is the world's third largest producer, after Russia and South Africa and tied with the U.S.

Diamond production in the Northwest Territories and Nunavut is increasing so dramatically that it has transformed that region into the world's third-biggest producer of high-quality diamonds with 11.4% of the world market, after Botswana's 26% and Russia's 17.8%. The boom has generated commercial and political interest in the Canadian Arctic not experienced since the 19th century. Most diamonds are shipped to London and then to Belgium. A Tiffany diamond-finishing center was established in Yellowknife.

Canada has the potential to threaten De Beers' century-old grip on the industry. For this reason, in 204 De Beers channeled almost half of its exploration budget to Canada. Further, De Beers signed joint ventures and partnerships while more than four-fifths of its holdings are in Nunavut, leading it to open a mine in 2007.

Canada's mineral wealth is distributed over virtually the entire country. This brings both advantages and disadvantages. It provides some economic activity to regions, especially in the North, which would be otherwise almost completely locked out of the country's economy. On the other hand, the costs of extraction and transportation are very high in the North. Also, mining operations sometimes create unfortunate collisions between the interests of mining companies, on the one hand, and environmental groups and native groups, on the other, whose lands and special rights are largely located in the North.

Industry and Services

For all of Canada's wealth in the primary or agricultural sector, it must be remembered that the country is no longer a rural society composed of farmers, trappers, lumberjacks, and fishermen.

Rather, Canada is a predominantly industrial, highly urbanized country with four out of five in its population living in cities as the largest ten cities produce 51% of Canada's GDP.

Only about 10% of Canada's GDP comes from its primary sector, even though much of its manufacturing is centered on processing primary products. Industry accounts for 28% of GDP, of which manufacturing and mining constitute about a fifth of GDP. Industry creates 22% of employment.

In terms of sales, the largest industry is petroleum and natural gas extraction and refining, followed by the manufacture of motor vehicles, pulp and paper, meat processing and iron and steel. The auto and paper and pulp industries are the leaders, as measured by employment. Over one million jobs depend on the resource sector, making it Canada's second-largest employer.

It is nevertheless true that the soaring world prices of energy and natural resources turned part of Canada's economy on its head in the 21st century as its engines of growth are no longer cars and high-tech industries, which were hurt by the nation's strong dollar and troubles in the North American auto sector, but energy and other natural resources, which by 2005 constituted more than 60% of its exports when imported components are subtracted. The same applies to employment. Young Canadians in rural areas, where jobs are available in oilfields, mines, and forests, have an easier time finding work than youth in big cities. Since 2000 the number of blue-collar jobs has increased faster than white-collar ones. In oil-rich Alberta the unemployment rate is below that in the rest of the country.

A particular characteristic of Canadian manufacturing is that it is highly concentrated in four ways. First, it is mainly located in the two largest provinces: Ontario and Quebec. Second, it tends to be concentrated in the hands of rather few firms. For instance, almost all brewing is concentrated in one company, and the same is true of cane and sugar beet processing. Fifteen of the top 40 industries in Canada had concentration ratios in the hands of single firms of more than 50%. Third, an unusually high percentage of Canadian manufacturing is in the hands of foreign companies.

A fourth, and final, reality is that much of Canada's manufacturing is done by industries that produce semi-processed primary products. Such industries are particularly vulnerable to competitors in developing countries, where labor costs are much lower. In 1970 the manufacturing sector provided 20% of Canada's GDP, but by 2014 that had shrunk to 13%. In part because of the higher value of the Canadian dollar, outsourced manufacturing has not returned to Canada as it is in the U.S. Canada has become the most expensive place in North America for manufacturing.

This is not to say that Canada lacks high-technology industries. In 2006 the World Economic Forum ranked Canada sixth in the world in terms of information technology; the U.S. was first. It produces such sophisticated products as guidance systems for missiles and "smart" weapons, space satellites, and robot arms for American space ships.

"Canadarm" was used on more than 50 shuttle missions, most spectacularly on the repair of the Hubble Space Telescope in 1993. In 1987 it had become the first international partner to reach an agreement on participating in NASA's space station project. In 1999 the company that produced "Canadarm" was sold to the American concern, Macdonald-Rotweiler. It supplied a sophisticated computerized manipulator arm, called "Canada Hand," that not only services spacecraft in the sky, but put together sections of the orbiting

Astronaut Julie Payette
(Governor—General of Canada, 2017–2021)

space station after the U.S. has ferried them into space. In return, Canadian researchers are able to use the full range of capabilities provided on the permanently manned space station. "Canadarm" was retired after NASA launched its last shuttle mission in July 2011, but designers are working on a "next-generation Canadarm."

Canada provides astronauts, such as Chris Hadfield. The U.S. Navy Test Pilot of the Year in 1992, he was the first Canadian to be a part of a shuttle flight crew, as opposed to a scientific team. He commented: "For a Canadian kid, this was just an impossible dream." In 2001 he became the first Canadian to walk in space, doing so twice to help deploy Canadarm2 on the international space station. However, without warning the robotic arm froze and refused to function. This was a dramatic breakdown because the entire multibillion dollar space station depends on the Canadarm2. Fortunately, it was a computer problem that was fixed a tense month later.

In 2010 Hadfield was chosen to lead a NASA underwater mission, which uses the ocean floor to simulate exploration missions to asteroids, moons and Mars; he then commanded the International Space Station for five months. During this time he shared his experiences by entertaining millions from space with musical performances with his acoustic guitar, many Twitter postings, and publicity stunts like demonstrating how to make a sandwich and brush one's teeth in space. At age 53 he announced his retirement at the Canadian Space Agency headquarters in Montreal.

In 1997 a Canadian born in Iceland, Bjarni Tryggvason, took part in an 11-day

Hard numbers

Rough diamond production, by value, 2005, %

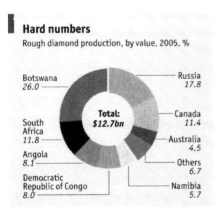

Botswana 26.0
South Africa 11.8
Angola 8.1
Democratic Republic of Congo 8.0

Total: $12.7bn

Russia 17.8
Canada 11.4
Australia 4.5
Others 6.7
Namibia 5.7

Source: *The Economist*

Canada

space shuttle mission. In 1999 Julie Payette (who later became the 29th Governor–General of Canada), was the first Canadian to fly to the international space station, and she returned in May 2009. Canada has a mini "Silicon Valley" clustered mainly around Ottawa. Nevertheless, some Canadians are worried that their country's manufacturing activities revolve too much around low-growth industries.

As in most economically advanced countries, the fastest growing sector in Canada's economy is the service one, in which no physical object is produced. If one includes all persons involved in wholesale and retail trade, finance, transportation, recreation and in the wide range of government services, including health and education, then three-fourths of all Canadians are employed in this sector; they produce 76% of GDP. According to the Economic Council of Canada, proportionally more people hold jobs in the civilian service sector in Canada than in any other economically advanced, western nation. This is this area in which most women who are moving into the employment market find jobs but it is also the sector that is hit hardest by unemployment.

Every economically powerful country has its own peculiar problems, vulnerabilities and dependencies. There is no denying that most countries on this earth would be delighted to have the kinds of problems that Canada has. Still, one should not lose sight of the fact that Canada does confront some real challenges, which include its large size, the tensions that plague federal-provincial relations, labor unions that are far more confrontational and ideological than their American counterparts, and heavy economic dependence on a single foreign country, namely the U.S.

Energy

Among Canada's plentiful natural resources are copious energy reserves of all kinds. It is self-sufficient in energy. This is a particular blessing given the fact that Canada is one of the world leaders in per capita energy consumption, even higher than the U.S. Canada is blessed with large reserves of fossil fuels. In the 21st century energy in all forms is Canada's number one export as it accounted for more than half its merchandise trade surplus with the U.S. Canada supplies 13% of America's natural gas needs and over 10% of its oil. Canada, with the world's second-largest oil and third-largest gas reserves, after the U.S. and Russia, is by far America's most secure and reliable source of imported energy, considering that the next suppliers, each responsible for 11%–12% of U.S. imports, are Mexico, Saudi Arabia, and Venezuela.

Artemis 2 Mission Specialist Jeremy Hansen
Courtesy of NASA.

Canada possesses almost a quarter of the world's fresh water and 7% of the planet's renewable water supply. The Canadian government, backed by 69% of the people, according to polls, refuses to export any of it to the U.S., which is dangerously short of water in some regions. It is not surprising that Canada is a major producer of hydroelectricity, which now supplies about three-fifths of its own electrical power needs.

Since 1901 Canada pumps much leftover electricity into American grids. New Brunswick sells power from its Point Lepreau nuclear plant to Maine, and Hydro-Québec has major contracts with New York and New England states. Hydro-Québec took over New Brunswick's power generating plants in 2010 and proceeded to move into the American Midwest market of 66 million people, where electricity rates are three times higher than in Quebec. Manitoba sells ten times more electricity to its American neighbors than to Saskatchewan, and British Columbia exports electricity as far as California.

Canadian electricity companies benefit from American federal legislation mandating electricity suppliers to increase their renewable energy sources by 20% by 2020. The country's vast clean hydroelectricity is in this category. Hydro-Québec is also investing heavily in wind power. Despite its green image, Quebecers are the second biggest energy consumers after Alberta, 31% of whose GDP is derived from oil and gas.

Canada is a major supplier of electricity to New York and Michigan. At peak times, especially in the winter, Canada buys electricity from U.S. utilities. In fact, it was a problem in one of Ontario's relay stations that caused the great blackout in 1965, which paralyzed the entire northeastern U.S. In 1997 Ontario Hydro and Hydro-Québec were told by American regulators that they must open their markets or lose cross-border sales.

The U.S. and Canada have developed an interconnected power grid that is so

tight that a problem at one power plant can cascade and cause a massive blackout. This happened August 14, 2003, when a breakdown in an Ohio power plant triggered automatic shutdowns of 100 generating stations, including 18 nuclear power plants, across Ontario and seven American states. It left 50 million Canadians and Americans, including 10 million in Ontario alone, without power. The blackout was six-times more extensive than the one in 1965. Officials on both sides of the border were left to confront estimates that up to $100 billion would be needed to modernize the North American power grid and increase its capability. In the previous decade, American demand for power increased by 30% while capacity grew by only 15%.

Canada produces a fifth of the world's uranium; 15% of its exports go to the U.S. In 2009 Canada had a total of 22 nuclear reactors, many of which are close to the end of their useful service. It had been two and a half decades since a new reactor was commissioned in either Canada or the U.S. Until 1999 Ontario relied on nuclear power for 60% of its electricity, compared with 13% for Canada as a whole and 20% for the U.S. Ontario had earlier announced that eight of its 18 reactors would be shut down after an internal study documented widespread management problems and years of inadequate maintenance and safety practices. This was a severe blow to the Canada Deuterium Uranium (CANDU) reactors, which had been touted as more versatile, cheaper to operate and safer than its competitors. In 40 years CANDU was able to make only 11 sales.

Ontario dominates Canada's nuclear industry but has been in turmoil since an earlier Conservative government in 1998 broke up the now defunct Ontario Hydro, a long-standing monopoly. The province now has less generating capacity than it had in the mid-1990s. The problems with Ontario's crumbling power generating system can almost certainly only be solved with more nuclear power in the future. In 2005 Ontario started up two reactors at the Pickering station east of Toronto and restarted two more later.

Environmentalists predictably vow to oppose any further plans to develop nuclear power. Although Ottawa has no say in how provinces supply their power needs, the Harper government supported an expansion of the nuclear option. Atomic power emits almost no greenhouse gasses; only the upfront cost of $5 billion for each nuclear plant is daunting. By 2007 public opinion in favor of nuclear had risen to 44% overall and 63% in Ontario, where people remember the 2003 power grid failure. However, Harper wanted the government out of the nuclear business as his government announced in 2009 that it would privatize the part of the state-owned Atomic Energy of Canada (AECL) that makes and services nuclear-power stations. This means the eventual extinction of CANDU.

Coal supplies only a tenth of Canada's overall energy needs. This is an environmental advantage. Canada is a net exporter of coal, selling more through Vancouver to Asia than it imports into eastern Canada from the nearby Appalachian fields in the U.S. Nova Scotia announced in 2001 that its last underground coal mine, the Prince colliery 25 miles north of Sydney, would shut down, ending a 280-year industry that had sustained a poor region. Ontario vowed to shut down its coal-fired power stations by 2009 although they provide a fifth of its electricity. Alberta is the only province still constructing coal-fired plants. Still Ottawa and Alberta spend heavily on carbon capture technology.

Coal is a major contributor to global warming, a climatic phenomenon whose signs are obvious in Canada: droughts in the prairies and melting sea-ice and permafrost in the North. Coal is responsible for a fourth of all of Canada's greenhouse gas emissions, while only about 5% are produced by the oil sands. This amounts to one-tenth of one percent of global emissions. In 2002 parliament ratified the Kyoto Accord, which obligated Canada to reduce its greenhouse gas emissions by 6% of its 1990 levels. The federal government had to fight to win agreement among provincial premiers.

Some argued that Kyoto is a costly fiasco that would mean mass layoffs. The earlier Liberal governments endorsed Kyoto but did almost nothing to meet its objectives. By 2009 gas emissions were 20.4% higher than in 1990. The government could have offset this by purchasing emission credits from countries, such as Russia, that have exceeded their targets. But handing billions of dollars over to countries like that for this purpose was hard to sell politically at home.

After assuming power in 2006 the Conservative government acknowledged the obvious fact that painful cuts in jobs and public spending would be necessary to achieve small benefit for the environment. Such a modification would also require wrenching life changes that many Canadians would not make.

Canada uses more energy than any other developed nation in the world except tiny Luxembourg and Iceland. Like their southern neighbors, Canadians burn a large amount of gasoline, which, although more expensive than in the U.S., is still half the price as in Europe. It does not help that global warming sounds good in a country that has long and bitter winters. Some growers, such as grape, maple,

corn, wheat and soybean farmers, would see their yields rise, and mining operations in the North would be easier and cheaper. Another bright note is that because of its low population Canada's overall emissions amount to only 2% of the world total.

The government reduced funding for the protocol in 2006 and dropped the targets. The U.S. refused to ratify the original Kyoto Protocol, but it nevertheless managed to reduce its greenhouse gas emissions because of its plentiful natural gas. With the U.S. and China outside of the protocol, the Conservative government announced in 2011 that it was pulling out of it, which every party has a legal right to do. Remaining in would have cost Canada multibillion dollar penalties for failing to comply with the emissions reduction targets. Harper argued that remaining in would have harmed Canada's energy companies without contributing much to saving the planet.

Canada's problems stem in part from the fact that 28% of its increased carbon dioxide emissions come from its oil production, especially from the oil sands, which is responsible for 5% of it. Since Canada produces only 2% of global emissions, the oil sands are responsible for only .1% of them. The Obama administration approved the construction of a 1,000-mile Alberta Clipper pipeline to carry 800,000 barrels a day of fuel from the vast oil sands into the U.S.. It was completed in 2014. An existing Keystone pipeline runs from Alberta to the oil crossroads at Cushing, Oklahoma.

Far more important was the fate of the proposed $7-billion 2,000-mile underground Keystone XL pipeline, which opened new capacity for Alberta's crude oil by extending from Cushing to the Texas Gulf Coast with connections to a network of pipelines and refineries elsewhere in the U.S. Since this crosses the U.S. border, the U.S. State Department had to approve. In 2010 it issued a favorable draft environmental impact statement and conducted public hearings along the proposed pipeline route, especially in Nebraska, where opposition was strongest. The pipeline company, TransCanada, submitted a revised route around the sensitive Sand Hills area, and the state's governor approved it in 2013.

The U.S. State Department then issued a new report concluding that the pipeline would have little effect on greenhouse-gas emissions, that extraction of oil from the oil sands would continue regardless, and that alternative transportation means by rail or truck would be even dirtier and more dangerous. It approved of the pipeline's new route all the way to Texas. It reiterated this judgment in 2014, reporting again that the pipeline would have little environmental impact. The final approval lay with President Obama, who hesitated to make a decision until he was certain that the project "does not significantly exacerbate the problem of carbon pollution." Vigorous domestic debate and resistance from environmentalists delayed the decision. Finally, in 2015, Obama vetoed the pipeline. One of newly elected President Trump's first acts was to give the go-sign for the pipeline in 2017. With the ban lifted, the work could be completed.

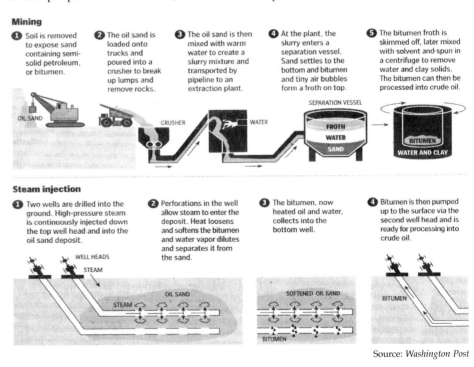

Mining

❶ Soil is removed to expose sand containing semi-solid petroleum, or bitumen.

❷ The oil sand is loaded onto trucks and poured into a crusher to break up lumps and remove rocks.

❸ The oil sand is then mixed with warm water to create a slurry mixture and transported by pipeline to an extraction plant.

❹ At the plant, the slurry enters a separation vessel. Sand settles to the bottom and bitumen and tiny air bubbles form a froth on top.

❺ The bitumen froth is skimmed off, later mixed with solvent and spun in a centrifuge to remove water and clay solids. The bitumen can then be processed into crude oil.

Steam injection

❶ Two wells are drilled into the ground. High-pressure steam is continuously injected down the top well head and into the oil sand deposit.

❷ Perforations in the well allow steam to enter the deposit. Heat loosens and softens the bitumen and water vapor dilutes and separates it from the sand.

❸ The bitumen, now heated oil and water, collects into the bottom well.

❹ Bitumen is then pumped up to the surface via the second well head and is ready for processing into crude oil.

Source: *Washington Post*

Canada

Progress has been made in reducing oil sand pollution, estimated to be 18% higher than conventional extraction. For example, more than 80% of the water is recycled, and some tailing ponds containing wastes are being reclaimed as green land. Steam is being increasingly used in extraction. Still, the proposed pipeline became a lightning rod for discontent about the environmental consequences, especially CO_2 emissions, of exploiting the oil sands in Alberta and elsewhere. Nine Nobel Prize laureates, including the Dalai Lama and Bishop Desmond Tutu, signed an open letter to Obama condemning the project.

The case for the pipeline was not helped by two oil spills in Michigan in 2010 and Arkansas in 2013. Further a spate of crude oil train derailments created doubts about the transport alternatives to pipelines. Crude oil shipments by rail have soared as pipelines fail to keep up with growing supply and pose greater danger and environmental destruction than do pipelines. This was made tragically clear in a small Quebec town, Lac-Mégantic, In July 2013, A runaway train carrying crude oil derailed and exploded, creating a fireball that destroyed the center of the city and killed 47 people, Canada's worst train accident in 149 years. Progress is being made in oil car safety.

Stephen Harper, who considered development of the oil sands as a national strategic priority, was furious about the decision by the president of the country he considered to be Canada's best friend and which is the destination for over 90% of Canada's oil and gas exports. Supported by Trudeau's Liberal government, extraction of oil from the sands continues.

The oil sands, which contain 97% of Canada's oil reserves, became a major political and diplomatic problem for the Conservative government. Canada became a pollution villain in the eyes of many environmental groups. An international Climate Change Performance Index for 2009 placed Canada 59th, one rung higher than Saudi Arabia. The Trudeau government takes a more aggressive role in combatting climate change, an approach favored by two out of three Canadians in 2016.

More than 900 American companies supply Canada's oil sands operations as it is making plans to expand its Asian market for petroleum. Pipeline projects are being considered to transport its oil westward to the Pacific coast for shipment to China and Japan. The most important and controversial is the 728-mile or 1,172 km Northern Gateway Pipeline from Edmonton. Disputes with dozens of aboriginal and green groups complicated and delayed these efforts. Law requires the government to consult indigenous people on such development projects. British Columbians support it 48% to 32%, but the BC government insisted on a share in the royalties and more money from Alberta to cover the risks of such a pipeline. The BC and Albertan governments negotiated over this, and the Harper government supported the agreement reached by the two provincial governments. However, the Trudeau government opposes this. The prime minister did approve the Kinder Morgan Trans Mountain pipeline carrying oil for export from the oil sands to the west coast in BC. Another possibility is Energy East, which would deliver oil by pipeline from Alberta to New Brunswick.

Canada is one of the few developed countries with the potential to be self-sufficient in both crude oil and natural gas, energy sources now supplying about 60% of its current energy consumption. Natural gas accounts for about a fifth of Canada's total energy. Canada is not only self-sufficient in natural gas but is able to export considerable amounts to the U.S. which itself is experiencing a gas boom. In 1999 a natural gas pipeline was completed that transports enough gas from northwestern Canada to Chicago to heat a million American homes each day.

A massive offshore natural gas deposit, estimated to be equal in size to all of the country's known gas reserves, was discovered in 2002 about 120 kilometers (80 miles) west of Vancouver Island in BC. The fuel is frozen in a thick layer of ice, and environmental concerns could postpone extraction for decades.

Until recently, most of Canada's known oil and gas reserves and production were in Western Canada, mainly in Alberta and Saskatchewan. Today 11 of the 13 provinces and territories, with Quebec and Nunavut being the exceptions, are energy producers and have more of a stake in the energy industry than as mere consumers. Thus, governments all over Canada have welcomed American investment in the Canadian oil and gas industries. During 2001 alone, more than $35 billion in Canadian assets fell into American hands. This brought foreign ownership to 48%, up from 33% in 1999, but below the 74% level in the late 1970s. Of course, energy investments flow both ways across the 49th parallel. Canadian oil and gas giants, such as PanCanadian Energy, Alberta Energy Company, and Nexen have extensive holdings in the U.S.

Canada is the world's sixth largest oil producer. With a 10% share, it is America's largest foreign source of imported petroleum products by far ahead of Mexico, Saudi Arabia and Venezuela. Oil furnishes almost 40% of Canada's own total energy needs. Now that Canada is able to extract oil from oil sands, a molasses-type substance also called tar sands, it has the world's second largest reserves after Saudi Arabia that are predicted to last for 40–50 years.

On the coast of British Columbia

ST. LAWRENCE SEAWAY

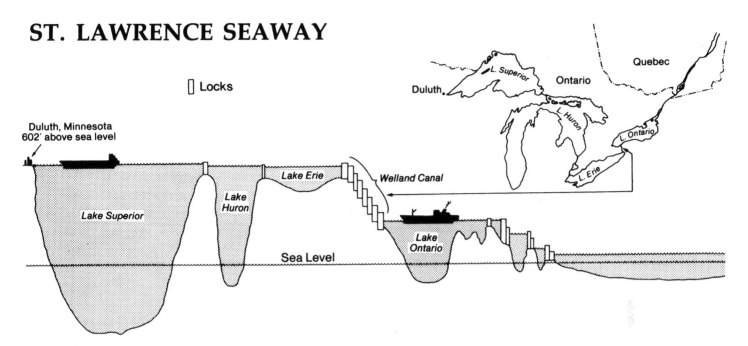

☐ Locks

Duluth, Minnesota
602' above sea level

Lake Superior

Lake Huron

Lake Erie

Welland Canal

Lake Ontario

Sea Level

L. Superior

Duluth

Ontario

Quebec

L. Huron

L. Ontario

L. Erie

Investments in the petroleum and gas industries poured into Canada, not only from the U.S. but also from countries including India, France and China. The Canadian government made a rare exception in 2012 by approving a $15.1 billion bid by China National Offshore Oil Corporation, a state-owned, as opposed to a privately-owned, Chinese oil company, for oil-sands producer Nexen. The sale means that China's government controls almost 10% of oil-sand extraction. Helped by tax and royalty breaks from the federal and Alberta governments, $51 billion in realized or promised investment in oil-sands development were made for the years 1996 to 2010.

The Athabasca oil sands in Alberta are the chief basis for Canada's energy optimism. They are found in an area about half the size of Colorado in central Alberta, and the formation extends into neighboring Saskatchewan. The commercial center is Fort McMurray with its peak population 88,000, in the northeastern corner of Alberta. Property values in this boom town shot up higher than in Toronto or Vancouver. Although a huge fire in 2016 consumed 2,400 buildings, it spared the oil facilities. The sands are estimated to contain the equivalent of some 300 times the known recoverable Canadian liquid oil reserves. Thanks to impressive technological advances in separating the oil from the sand, almost half (46%) of Canada's oil production comes from the sands. Huge investments poured in from Royal Dutch Shell, ExxonMobil and Total.

Almost needless to say, it presents a technological challenge to dig up raw oil sand using massive power shovels, or in a liquefied form using steam so that bitumen can be pumped to the surface. The process requires large quantities of water and natural gas to boil that water at a great environmental cost. Each barrel of oil produced requires two to five barrels of water and enough natural gas to heat a home for one to five days. Four tons of earth are dug up and the process emits lots of greenhouse gases as it produces two or three times as much carbon dioxide as does a normal well. However, progress has been made to reduce such pollution.

Oil sands production became profitable after the price of oil shot over $50 per barrel; the break-even point for new operations is considered to be $100 as compared to $30 to $65 for existing projects. Oil sand operations are expensive to start and take five to ten years to design. Once up and running, such operations have a 25–50 year lifespans with profit margins of about 15% compared to about 30% for conventional oil drilling. Yet, there are advantages: oil from the sands involves no exploration risk because it is definitely there.

Once up and running, the oil from sand production flows for 30 years or more. The crude oil that is extracted in this way is shipped to refineries in the American Midwest and on to Oklahoma and the Gulf coast. It is a hugely valuable future resource for Canada and the rest of North America. The collapse of world oil in 2014–15 hit Canada, especially Alberta, very hard: 40,000 workers were laid off, doubling the province's unemployment. Plunging oil prices dragged the Canadian dollar down as it lost 30% of its value. Canada's dream of becoming an energy superpower has been put on hold.

Other large potential reserves of oil and gas are believed to lie under the Arctic Ocean, especially Beaufort Sea, and under the Atlantic waters off the east coast of Canada. Prospecting and drilling off Canada's coast is expensive and dangerous as demonstrated by the capsizing of the oil rig Ocean Ranger, with 85 men aboard. Operations are also politically delicate, igniting serious disagreements between Ottawa and provincial governments over ownership and pricing of these resources.

Canada is encountering some difficulty in finding new, easily extractable, gas reserves, as gas in western Canada is being depleted. The resulting squeeze has heightened interest in two ambitious long-term projects to transport natural gas from Alaska and the Canadian Arctic to the lower 48 states. The all-Canada route would link new gas fields in the Mackenzie River delta to pipelines in Alberta and could provide almost 2% of American consumption. An even larger one extending from Prudhoe Bay in northern Alaska through the Yukon to the Alberta pipelines would yield even more. Both schemes face numerous environmental, technical and financial obstacles.

In 1984 North America's first tidal power plant began to churn out electricity at Annapolis Royal on the Bay of Fundy in Nova Scotia, where the tides are among the largest in the world. Despite its long coastlines, immense forests and bountiful sunlight and wind, these kinds of renewable resources made up less than 5% of Canadians' energy consumption. It will be many years before these kinds of renewable energy sources will make a truly significant contribution to Canada's energy requirements.

The COVID-19 pandemic has significantly affected the oil and gas industry. Canada sends almost all of its oil exports

Canada

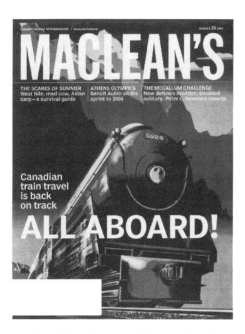

to the U.S. and tens of thousands of energy-sector workers are at risk at losing their jobs. The oil and gas industry has not been good over the past five years and has only gotten worse during the COVID-19 pandemic.

Transportation

As immense as Canada, given the distribution of its population, it should best be viewed as a snakelike country, more than 4,000 miles wide and only 75 to 100 miles deep. The major population clusters are separated not only by such physical barriers as the Gulf of St. Lawrence, the Great Lakes, the Canadian Shield, the Rocky Mountains and sheer distance; they are also separated by lingual barriers. Boston, New York City, Buffalo, Detroit, Chicago, Minneapolis and Seattle have always exerted an economic pull on Canadians as strong or stronger than that of other Canadian cities or regions. Therefore, Canada must expend enormous sums of money to bind that band of regions together that stretch east to west from coast to coast. From the beginning, constructing and maintaining roads and highways which cut through the Shield and the forests and which must withstand the hostile winter climate have been major undertakings. However, roads alone could never hold together the world's second largest country.

Canada was blessed with long coastlines and a fifth of the world's fresh water, all of which facilitated the cheapest form of transportation: by water. Nevertheless, a complicated and expensive canal system was required to bind these natural waterways together. None is as significant as the St. Lawrence Seaway, a grandiose project lining 56 ports that was undertaken jointly by Canada and the U.S. By means of seven

locks, stepping from Montreal to Lake Ontario and eight locks along the Welland Canal, ships can now reach waters 183 meters or 617 feet above sea level and 2,300 miles or 3,864 kms from the Atlantic Ocean to the head of the Great Lakes. Containing a fifth of the world's non-polar fresh water, the five Great Lakes are governed by the Boundary Waters Treaty of 1909, implemented by an independent bi-national joint commission, which has functioned without dispute or political intervention.

Due to successful cooperation between Canada and the U.S., and the local governments around the lakes, they are much cleaner than they were in 1978, when the cleanup was launched. Still, Lake Erie was afflicted anew by a huge thick and growing coat of toxic algae that appears every summer and which covers one-sixth of its waters while killing much of the marine life.

By the 1980s the St. Lawrence Seaway was losing much cargo traffic to barges down the Mississippi River and container traffic by rail to large Atlantic ports in the U.S. and at Halifax. Maintenance problems and the drop in American steel production have further threatened its major role as a seasonal carrier of grain, coal and iron

ore. The result has been severe financial losses. Nevertheless, this bilateral cooperative project, completed in 1959, was a welcomed change from the competition that had existed between the two neighbors from the beginning of the 19th century, with the U.S. always being a step ahead. The problems of proceeding by water from the St. Lawrence River into the Canadian West had been clear since the early part of the 16th century, when Jacques Cartier was rebuffed by the turbulent Lachine Rapids just west of what is now Montreal, thereby frustrating his efforts to find a Northwest Passage to the Far East.

When the fur trade with the Northwest was diverted to the Hudson Bay in 1820, Canadian planners began to devise a way somehow to bring grain from both the U.S. and Canada through the Great Lakes to Montreal. These designs were temporarily foiled by the American construction of the Erie Canal in 1825, which enabled Midwestern grain to be shipped through the Great Lakes to Buffalo or Oswego and then along a relatively inexpensive, two-way, all-season canal through the flat terrain of upstate New York into the Hudson River to New York harbor. In order to build a competitive Canadian canal system required enormous support from

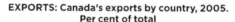

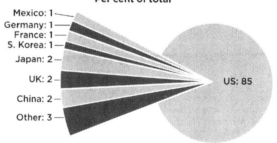

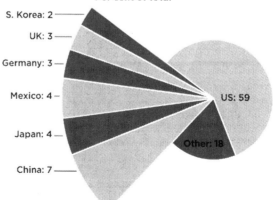

THE U.S. REMAINS our dominant trade relationship, but to prosper, Canada has to focus more on the rest of the world

Source: *Maclean's*

governments in both Britain and Canada, and it also required solutions to daunting technical challenges. The first was to soften the abruptness of the 300-foot drop from Lake Erie to Lake Ontario. As demonstrated by numerous adventurers who have gone over the Niagara Falls in barrels, there are certain risks involved with navigating that treacherous watery precipice.

No sooner had the construction of the Welland Canal in 1829 solved this problem when the energetic southern neighbors presented another challenge: they expanded their railroads at a dizzying rate. By 1850 they had over 9,000 miles of track laid, compared with only 100 miles in Canada. This necessitated another Canadian mega project to carve railways, through hostile country from the Atlantic to the Pacific, that were so expensive that the nation was strapped with a huge debt even before it became self-governing in 1867.

The government chartered what became the Canadian Pacific Railroad (CPR), bestowing ultimately on it 26 million acres of prime land, more than $100 million grants and loans and 700 miles of already-built railway in eastern Canada. Pierre Berton wrote in his books, *The National Dream* and *The Last Spike*, that the CPR tied Canada together "like a line of steel from coast to coast." "Our cities and towns popped up along it like beads on a string. Without it we would have developed vertically rather than horizontally. We became the nation we are because of the railroad."

The Canadian Rail Passenger Service or VIA, is heavily subsidized by taxpayers. Prior to establishing this service in 1977, rail passenger service had been provided almost wholly by the two Canadian systems, Canadian Pacific and Canadian National. Both are private since the government privatized CN in 1995. Most shares were bought by Americans and doubled their value in two years. CN's largest shareholder is Bill Gates, who possesses about 10% of its stock. To remain economically viable, CN shed 14,000 of its 36,000 employees and sold off a half billion dollars of real estate holdings, including the CN Tower in Toronto. It abandoned more than a quarter of its track. By 1996 it was earning a profit.

Seeking to cut costs, the CPR requested the government to take over its passenger operations, forgetting about the huge subsidies it had received from the government when it was built. The state's purchase of the passenger business left the CPR as one of the world's most profitable railways, with large holdings in the energy, shipping, trucking and hotel sectors. It moved its headquarters from Montreal to Calgary in 1996.

CP Rail and Canadian National, renamed CN North America with its headquarters in Montreal, entered the north-south freight market in a big way. CP Rail owns two U.S. railways, the Soo Line in the Midwest and Delaware and Hudson in the Northeast. CN North America formed an alliance with the Burlington Northern railway in the West. CN also allied with America's largest long-distance trucking firm, JB Hunt. After NAFTA went into effect, trains started running from Canada through the U.S. into Mexico. In 2000 CN and CP agreed to share track in Canada and the U.S. CN gained access to CP's New York, New Jersey and Pennsylvania networks, while CP began operating on CN's busy Toronto-Chicago main line. This agreement was historic for such traditional rivals. In 2012 the New York hedge fund Pershing Square Capital Management LP took a 12.2% stake in CP and installed an American boss. The oil sands have sharply boosted both companies' freight revenues. Trains bring supplies and carry out crude oil.

VIA was chartered and the passenger service was amalgamated into a single system calculated to save costs. However, as in the U.S., when it comes to calculating the cost of passenger service, railroad accountants are highly imaginative. The system provides vital service to areas with no roads which otherwise would not be accessible. A few smaller lines supplement this service. Combined, they reach such remote points as Mosoonee on James Bay, where there may be snowstorms in June, and Churchill on Hudson Bay, where polar bears plague the local dumps and trash bins. Canada is home to the world's largest polar bear population, numbering 15,000. In all, the system reaches 450 communities, but 85% of its revenues are generated in the Quebec City-Windsor corridor linking the major cities in Ontario and Quebec.

By 1989 the government had to face squarely the obvious problem that Via

simply was not sustainable. Federal subsidies had risen steadily, totaling $1.6 billion from 1992–7 with an increase of $402 million in 2000, and ridership had declined from 55.4 million passengers in 1945 to 6.4 million in 1988, less than 5% of total inter-city travel by all means of transportation. Half the track being used was originally built before 1914. Therefore, routes and subsidies were slashed. More than half of Via's service disappeared in 1990, to about 9.5 million kilometers, down from 19 million.

From 1990 to 1998, service had fallen from 810 trains per week to 396, and Via's job force had been slashed from 7,000 to 3,000. Some transcontinental service from Vancouver to Halifax and numerous regional routes, mainly in Central and Eastern Canada, remain. But its southern transcontinental route in the West on the Canadian Pacific was cancelled. Cuts created real hardships for travelers in many rural communities, where services disappeared entirely. Even so, healthy infusions of government money enabled a resurgent VIA in 2003 to offer 139 plush new passenger cars, 21 new locomotives, and renovated stations.

In addition to rivers, canals, lakes, and railways, there is an air link, the only tie to many points in the extreme Canadian North. Two privately-owned airlines competed: Montreal-based Air Canada and Calgary-based PWA, parent of Canadian Airlines International or CAI. Both struggled to survive. After their merger in 1999, Air Canada carried 80% of Canada's air passengers and got 90% of airline revenues.

The situation changed dramatically as no-frills discount carriers increasingly snatched market share. Air Canada's fell by 2004 to 51%, and Calgary-based WestJet, modeled on Southwest Airlines in the U.S., steadily increased its share by 2009 to 36%. It hopes to squeeze out Air Canada and control as much as half the domestic market one day. It also signed deals with international carriers to corner a greater share of the lucrative transborder business.

A variety of other low-cost carriers, such as Jetsgo in Montreal and Canjet Airlines of Nova Scotia, have grown rapidly and even started cutting into Air Canada's extensive cross-border network. All of these trends helped force Air Canada into bankruptcy protection in 2003 and into acrimonious litigation with WestJet over suspected industrial espionage. Victor Li, a Canadian citizen and son of a Hong Kong billionaire, acquired a 31% stake in Air Canada. In 2004 it emerged from bankruptcy. It flies smaller aircraft more frequently on domestic routes to compete with low-cost competitors, while expanding its more profitable international

Canada

routes. America's stricter visa requirements for transit passengers encourage more international passengers to fly over Toronto, Montreal and Vancouver, thereby benefiting Air Canada, enabling it to return to profitability. The rejuvenated airline selected Céline Dion as its main advertising voice.

In 1995 Canada and the U.S. signed an "open skies" agreement allowing their airlines access to any airport on the other side of the border at unregulated prices. For the first time in more than three decades, there is direct service between Washington, DC, and Canadian cities. In the five years after the agreement was signed, air passenger traffic between the two countries went up by two-thirds, as 24 U.S. cities began direct flights to Canada, and Air Canada tripled its American destinations to 45.

Federalism and Labor

A second major concern is the effect on the economy of federal-provincial controversies. Canada is a federal state in which the provinces are more powerful than are American states. The boundaries of jurisdictions between the governments in Ottawa and in the provinces have not yet been as sharply drawn as in the U.S.; the upshot is that these overlapping jurisdiction become very visible in economic disputes. The situation is made more difficult because the two levels of government have become much more economically interdependent since 1945.

In an attempt to even out the economic disparities among the various provinces and to demonstrate to all Canadians the benefits of being a part of Canada, no matter where in the country they might live, the federal government transfers some of its tax revenues directly to the provinces. These "transfer payments" are made on the basis of a hodge-podge of fiscal formulae, laws, regulations, subsidies and traditions, which support such activities as social welfare, health and education.

The allocation formulae inevitably cause serious disagreements between Ottawa and the provincial governments, some of which depend on such payments for half their budgets. Saskatchewan, Alberta and BC receive nothing. Transfers to newly rich Newfoundland and Nova Scotia were supposed to be reduced by 70 to 90 cents for every dollar of provincial revenue for their huge offshore oil and gas reserves. The Newfoundland government retained some of its support, though. An embarrassed Ontario moved into the "have-not" category. Since more than two-thirds of Canadians now live in a province receiving equalization

payments, the math no longer works. Ontario's have-not status threatens the sustainability of the system.

It is not clear that these transfer payments significantly improve poorer regions' basic economic structures; some of the Atlantic provinces remain relatively poor, and Alberta is the economic leader. Nevertheless, these transfers sometimes spark criticism from the U.S. because the assistance to exporting industries smacks of export subsidies forbidden by GATT international trade agreements. There are few policy areas where only one government acts.

Intense intergovernmental arguments are raging over transfer payments. The negotiations and compromising necessary to coordinate economic policies greatly delay solutions. In an effort to reduce the federal government deficit, the Liberal government made serious cuts in the transfer payments to the provinces. Between 1990 and 1998 the total value of such payments fell by 5.4%, leaving the provinces to serve more people with less money. In response, they cut services, including in health care, universities, and welfare.

Social welfare is almost entirely a provincial responsibility, with Ottawa providing only 16% of health care costs. Cash transfers to the provinces constituted about 10% of federal program spending in 1997. In 1999, then Prime Minister Chrétien and nine premiers agreed on a "social union" to provide a framework for more power sharing and cooperation on national social programs. Quebec's premier rejected the plan because it did not give Quebec the right to opt out of new federal programs and simply take its proportionate share of federal funding.

A third burden to the economy is the type of labor unions in Canada. Of course, employers' power in Canada needs the same kinds of organized employee checks as in other countries. Workers and civil servants have almost complete freedom to organize in Canada, and the unions perform an essential function of watching out for employee interests. Almost a third, 30%, of private employees compared with less than 10% in the U.S. of all wage-earners are unionized; further, 70% of members belong to unions affiliated with the Canadian Labor Congress (CLC). Private sector union membership in 2008 had declined to 16%, while 71% of public sector workers are unionized, comparable to the situation in the U.S.

As in the U.S., unions negotiate by workplace rather than across an industry. Canadian unions are a blend between American and British and have problems stemming from both connections. A further complication is that many union leaders in Quebec are nationalists who are willing to

use their economic clout to further their separatist or provincial political goals.

About half of the Canadian labor movement belongs to unions whose headquarters are in the U.S. and are extensions of large American unions. The AFL-CIO affiliates give their Canadian branches considerable autonomy, but Canadian unionists are nevertheless subject to pressures from south of the border. After a 1984 strike against General Motors of Canada resulted in a settlement more favorable than that received by American workers, Canadian United Auto Workers (UAW) director Robert White decided to sever Canadian auto workers from the American-based UAW. White no doubt hoped that other Canadian unionized workers would follow, but Canadian members of the United Steelworkers refused in 1985 to break their ties with their Pittsburgh headquarters.

The more militant tendency reflects the other labor heritage which Canadian unions share: the British one. As in the United Kingdom, Canadian unions are organized along craft lines. This means that a company must usually deal with multiple unions, rather than with only one. Consequently, if only one union strikes, an entire plant closes down. Canadian unionists tend to regard their American counterparts as too cowardly and too accommodating to employers.

Another difference is the ties unions have to political parties. Although most American unions like to support the candidates of the Democratic Party, it is a moderate, middle-of-the-road party. By contrast, the CLC is directly supportive of the New Democratic Party, much as British unions are organizationally linked to the British Labour Party. The NDP once wrote class conflict on its banner, and, therefore, Canadian unions share a tempered spirit of class conflict. The CLC is always forced to deal with governing parties in Ottawa and most provinces that it is trying to put out of power. This makes for considerable tension.

In Canada, the unions' political influence has declined, and their support by the general public is waning because they have shown themselves to be impotent in fighting unemployment. On top of their image problems, they are unable to attract white collar and service industry workers. As in the U.S., their traditional base, smokestack industries and mining, are losing jobs due to technological changes. An outgrowth of this more confrontational approach is that Canada has the third-worst strike record among western industrialized countries after Iceland and Spain. When Canadians strike, they tend to strike hard and long. The first national public-service strike in Canadian history almost paralyzed the country in 1991. The frequency of strikes, sometimes with the financial backing of hefty strike funds in the U.S., is one of the factors that make Canadian productivity lower than in the U.S. even though it outperforms the American neighbor in some sectors.

Economic Dependence

A fourth major economic issue with which Canadians have struggled since their inception as a self-governing people is their dependence on the outside world, especially on a single country—the U.S. With a relatively small domestic market, Canada must trade heavily abroad in order to maintain its citizens' high standard of living. Fifty-two percent of Canada's GDP is generated by foreign trade, and the bulk of that trade is with its neighbor to the south. In some sectors of Canada's economy, the dependence on foreign trade is much greater. For newsprint, the proportion is 88%; for wheat 85%, and for zinc 61%.

In 1972 the Canadian government decided to try a "third option" to impossible self-reliance and excessive dependence on the U.S.: to diversify its trade with countries other than the U.S., Canadians vigorously sought trade with the EU and Asia.

In 2009 Canada and the EU gave the green light to talks aiming at a trade agreement. Most trade between Canada and the EU was already tariff-free. What remained were farm products, which were the hardest to eliminate. The deal is more ambitious than the Canada-U.S. free trade agreement insofar as it included the provinces and sought to open markets in services, investment, and government procurement. The Comprehensive Economic and Trade Agreement (CETA), completed and put into effect in 2017, is Canada's most important trade agreement since NAFTA and now the USMCA.

China is Canada's second-largest trading partner, accounting in 2019 for $24.4 billion of its exports and $6.48 billion of its imports. The EU is also Canada's second biggest source of investment after the U.S. Ex-Prime Minister Harper hailed the EU as "the biggest deal our country has ever made." The deal opened access to a larger market than does NAFTA and is broad in its sweep as it not only eliminates 99% of tariffs on both sides of the Atlantic, but removes regulations and red tape on services and many other areas. The inclusion of the ten provinces as parties to the negotiations was something new. The CETA agreement had to be approved by all the provinces, the EU's 28 member states and the European Parliament.

The EU, the world's largest trading bloc, trades five times more with China than with Canada. Ottawa wants more of that trade for itself, and Canadians agree. A *Maclean's* poll in 2012 revealed that 72% of respondents believed that American dominance peaked in the 20th century. A third preferred China as the partner for future trade, 22% the EU, 15% India, and only 12% the U.S. While the U.S. remains Canada's main trading partner, popular enthusiasm for continental free trade has plunged from 80% at the turn of the century to 54% in 2012, even though 40% of total North American trade takes place within NAFTA, and Canada's GDP per person has grown faster over the two decades of NAFTA's existence than that of the other two partners. The government emphasizes that Asian trade would not supplant NAFTA but would take the country beyond it.

Canadian efforts to expand diversify trade in Asia bore some fruit. China is Canada's second-largest trading partner, with Japan in fourth place. However, Canada's trade with Asia is little more than 10% of that with the U.S. although it is growing faster. From 2006–2009, Canada signed eight bilateral trade agreements with other countries in a further attempt to lessen its dependence on trade with the U.S.

Vancouver, which is closer to Tokyo than to Halifax, NS, is North America's second busiest port after New York and handles more tonnage than all other Canadian ports put together. The seat of many banks, Vancouver aspires to become North America's gateway to Asia. Of course, the expansion of trade ties with Asia is a two-way street. The challenge to Canadian markets from China, South Korea, Taiwan, and other Asian countries with low labor costs and aggressive marketing strategies is as worrisome to Canada as it is to the U.S. This challenge from the Orient has given the two North American countries even more in common with each other and helped undermine the objective of the "third option."

Despite the efforts to diversify, Americans still buy and sell about three-quarters of Canada's exports and imports. American-Canadian trade constitutes the largest two-country trade relationship in the world. This trade tie is very important for the U.S., amounting to about a fifth of its exports and 15% of its imports, roughly the same volume of American trade with the entire EU. According to Canadian government estimates, about 7 million American residents are employed, directly or indirectly in the export trade with Canada, and the border states of Michigan, New York, and Ohio are particularly involved in such trade. Clearly, this vibrant trade relationship is mutually beneficial to both neighbors, even though American trade has an overall greater importance for Canada than *vice versa*.

Roughly two-thirds of Canada's $75 billion tourist trade depends on American travelers. Thirteen million American tourists annually and million more from other countries provide jobs for one out of ten Canadians. Due to a tightening of the border since the September 11 terrorist attacks, especially since passports are required since June 1, 2009, tourism from the U.S. slowed down.

Canadians are also ardent foreign travelers. At any given time during the winter, 5% of the Canadian population is vacationing in Florida. Two million Canadian "snowbirds" find their way there, and more than a million vacation in Mexico each year. Francophones have their own free newspaper, *Le Soleil de la Floride.* From early November until the first week in April, Monday through Saturday, all can listen to five-minute news broadcasts on about 20 Florida radio stations, "Canada Calling—the News from Home for Vacationing Canadians," anchored by long-time Toronto newscaster Prior Smith (website: www. canadacalling. com). He is kind to his American listeners by using inches, feet, Fahrenheit and "zee," not "zed."

Francophones tend to congregate on the Atlantic Coast, while anglophones prefer the Gulf Coast. In 1992 the Canadian Snowbird Association was formed and since 1994 Canadians gather in the Florida State Fairgrounds for a couple days in January and flaunt their being Canadian in a "Snowbird Extravaganza" which offers entertainment and a trade show; 80,000 attended in 1997. The yearning for a warmer climate also helped persuade a million Canadians to settle permanently in the Los Angeles area. By 2012 Canadian investors were not only snapping up distressed properties in sunny Phoenix, but they were the largest foreign buyers of American real estate, making up about a quarter of international purchasers.

A far more worrisome development than trade dependence, in the minds of many Canadians, has always been the high degree of foreign ownership of their country's economy. No other industrialized country has such a large portion of its economy in foreign hands, and certainly no other industrial country has such a great chunk of its wealth in the hands of *one* foreign nation. This is, of course, not a new problem. From the early 19th century on, investment capital, primarily British, poured into Canada to build canals and railways and to develop paper and mining industries. After World War I, the U.S. replaced Britain as the main source of capital. John A. Macdonald's "National Policy," which erected a tariff wall against foreign goods in order to encourage

Canada

manufacturing within Canada, had the unforeseen effect of encouraging foreign producers to scale that tariff wall by creating branch plants in Canada itself. That way, foreign companies could sell in the Canadian market and also, for a long time, even gain favored access to markets in the British Commonwealth due to the British Preferential Tariff. Thus, the high Canadian tariffs had at least two effects: first, they increased foreign ownership; second, manufacturing enterprises within Canada could relax behind the tariff shield, rather than strive for the kind of efficiency which would be required if they had been fully exposed to foreign competition.

In 1947 the discovery of oil in Alberta sparked huge foreign investments in the exploration and development of energy sources. Almost before Canadians realized it, foreign investments in Canada had increased by 800% between 1950 and 1975. At the same time, Canadians are investing more abroad, especially in the U.S., than foreigners are investing in Canada. Measured on a per capita basis, Canadian investment in the U.S. is twice as high as the American investment in Canada. In

1999 it owned 9% of total foreign direct investment (FDI) in the U.S., making it the fifth largest foreign investor, with the United Kingdom as first.

Statistics Canada figured that in 2005 FDI in Canada, primarily from the U.S., was worth $390 billion. By boosting a strong Canadian dollar, Canadian ownership of foreign companies, with the U.S. remaining the most popular place for Canadians to invest, was growing at an even faster rate, now worth $452 billion. In some sectors, such as machine manufacturing and metals, Canadians are already the leaders. Lured by many American chambers of commerce, Canadians are attracted by the political stability, the tax incentives, and the size and proximity of the world's largest market. Such Canadian giants as Alcan, Northern Telecom, Seagram, Bombardier, and Magna International bought companies in the U.S.

Some Canadians cynically refer to their country as a "branch-plant economy," the most important decisions for which being made in a foreign country. They argue American companies are like parasites, drawing huge profits out of Canada,

closing their Canadian subsidiaries whenever it pleases them, and saving most of the research and development for their American headquarters and plants. For example, in 2015 Target, which failed to satisfy Canadian tastes, announced the closure of its 133 stores in Canada employing 17,600 people, leaving gaping holes in some prominent shopping centers. In 2018 Sears announced the closure of its stores in Canada, costing 12,000 jobs.

The critics frequently overlook the fact that these American companies created thousands of jobs in Canada which otherwise would not have existed, introduce much future technology into Canada, and pay staggering amounts of taxes to the federal and provincial governments. In 2014, Burger King purchased financially strapped Tim Hortons, a national icon named after its ice hockey playing founder in 1964. It was the largest chain in Canada. Company headquarters were in Canada, where corporate taxes are lower, but it is managed from the U.S.

FIRA and the National Energy Policy, 1960–1985

By the 1960s, the question of foreign control over the Canadian economy had become an important and widespread political issue in that country. "Economic nationalism" exercised a formidable influence on Canadian politics from the late 1960s into the 1980s and became a considerable bone of foreign political contention between these two large neighbors. These fears prompted the creation of the Foreign Investment Review Agency (FIRA) to screen investment proposals by foreigners; such an agency actually came into existence in 1974.

FIRA was a red flag waved in the faces of foreign, mainly American, investors. While about 90% of all proposals were ultimately approved, a figure that climbed by 1983 to 97%, a fact that irritated many Canadian nationalists, applications were so expensive and time-consuming that many potential investors decided not even to submit them. In general, applicants had to be able to demonstrate that the American company's presence in Canada would be of "substantial benefit" to the Canadian economy. Moreover, approval often came with numerous conditions, known as "performance criteria" that could include a minimum of jobs to be created or of money to be invested or requiring foreign companies to purchase supplies in Canada, a standard which, on American prompting, was declared impermissible by the General Agreement on Tariffs and Trade (GATT), now enforced by the WTO. These "performance criteria" would not apply to Canadian companies, so a double standard was created.

FIRA and other economic nationalist policies did succeed in the sense that foreign control over the assets of all corporations in Canada did fall from 37% in 1971 to 16% by 1981. On the other hand, foreign investors found FIRA excessively intrusive and began to fear that the Canadian government might change the rules of the game after they had placed their money in Canada. Foreign investments began to dry up. At the same time, inflation and unemployment began to climb. In other words, FIRA coincided with the worst recession in Canada since the 1930s, and unlike in the U.S., Canadian nationalism always tends to become weaker in times of economic distress.

FIRA became a major target of the conservatives who were not ideologically opposed to such regulation of foreign investment, but who concluded that such restrictions seriously threatened Canadians' high standard of living. Therefore, within weeks of becoming prime minister in 1984, Mulroney renamed the agency "Investment Canada," giving it the mandate to encourage, not discourage, foreign investment. Mulroney assured Americans that "there shall be one game, building Canada, and one set of rules. These shall not be changed after the game has started to the detriment of any of the players."

Investment Canada screened only those direct foreign takeovers of firms with more than $5 million in assets. The government continued to watch any foreign investments in the cultural sector closely, though. Almost all Canadians, of whatever political persuasion, are very sensitive to any threat of foreign control over Canadian culture.

Energy was another sector of Canadian concern. In 1980, at the peak of Canada's lucrative production of oil and gas, the government made its most far-reaching economic move, designed to take control of at least 50% of its oil industry by the 1990s. The National Energy Policy (NEP) was a series of legislative acts that, through grants, tax write-offs and various incentives, favored Canadian owned or controlled companies. There were other odious aspects of the NEP, from the standpoint of foreign investors as it operated retroactively to confiscate some of the foreign oil companies' profits. This lowered the book value of the companies and therefore made them prime targets for being bought out by favored Canadian firms.

American businesses that felt forced to sell out did not receive what they considered to be a fair market price. Perhaps worse, the NEP contained a "back-in" clause. This clause required the transfer to the government-owned oil company, Petro-Canada or PETROCAN, created in 1976 with its headquarters in Calgary, of up to 25% of the value of an oil or gas well after a find was made on federal lands; indeed, all land in the Arctic region is owned by the federal government. This clause took no notice of the exploration costs of finding the oil or gas in the first place.

By world standards, the NEP was rather gentle. The nationalization of all foreign energy assets was never considered, even though Canadian provinces earlier had taken over direct control of certain other raw materials: Quebec took control of most of the asbestos industry, while Saskatchewan did the same with the potash within its borders.

The NEP did represent a changing of the "rules of the game" by violating the principle that discriminatory changes in rules should not be applied to foreign investments already in place. This is a dangerous practice for any country that is so dependent on foreign investment, as Canada has always been. Both the FIRA and the NEP moved Canadian-American relations into the spotlight and stimulated intense irritation in the minds of many Americans who had barely thought about Canada before, adding tension to the two countries' dealings. As Andrew Malcolm observed, "it signaled the end, if a formal conclusion was needed, of the quiet old boy network of handling bilateral relations."

The basic objective of the NEP, to "Canadianize" the bulk of Canada's own energy resources, was and remains popular in Canada. In fact, one of the reasons why the Tory Prime Minister Joe Clark was thrown out of office in 1980 was the fact that he wanted to return PETROCAN to private ownership. In one respect, the NEP was succeeding: by 1983, the percentage of the oil industry belonging to Canada had already risen to 35%, an impressive step toward the goal of 50%.

The timing of the policy could not have been worse. In the years leading up to the NEP, oil and gas prices steadily increased, but by the early 1980s, they declined significantly on world markets. This meant that the holdings and profits of PETROCAN and private Canadian oil companies also declined. The government had calculated that rising oil and gas prices would provide the revenues to buy back much of the foreign-owned oil industry. Instead, those prices fell, and interest rates rose to the stratospheric level of 21%.

Canadian oil companies learned that they created serious problems for themselves by going deeply into debt to buy foreign companies at what seemed at the time to be bargain prices. These companies were thrown into a serious economic crisis. The most celebrated case of a Canadian oil company that went on a wild spending and borrowing spree was Dome Petroleum.

By 1982 Dome Petroleum was on the verge of becoming such a financial disaster that it could have undermined confidence in the country's entire financial system if the federal government and the banks had not given it large amounts of aid to keep it from going bankrupt. By 1983 Dome Petroleum had to take huge losses to sell assets in a depressed market in order to remain solvent. The lowered price of oil, combined with foreign investors' fears of losing any more money in Canada, caused drilling operations in the country to dry up for a while, and it diverted much of that activity to the U.S. The resulting bust severely hit Alberta's economy and temporarily created the first *eastward* shift of population in many years.

The economic costs of the NEP and FIRA brought a political reaction as well. Their introduction roughly coincided with Canada's worst recession in a half century, during which unemployment climbed into double figures. These measures exacerbated Canada's economic woes and actually discouraged the achievement of self-sufficiency. More and more Canadians became convinced that they were more damaging than helpful to the nation in the long term. The debate that ensued did not revolve around matters of principle; Canadians by and large accepted the federal government's right to seek the objectives which FIRA and NEP sought. Indeed, no people can be faulted for wishing to gain control over their own economic resources, and thereby over their own destiny. Instead, the debate involved the question of what is prudent and necessary for Canada.

In Canada, protectionist sentiment is usually strongest in times of economic prosperity but the years leading up to FIRA and the NEP were boom years. In times of economic adversity, Canadians are more likely to look for ways to facilitate the international trade and the in-flow of foreign capital on which their prosperity has always depended. In the U.S., the opposite is true: protectionist sentiment tends to be strongest during threatening economic times and weakest during good times. In Trudeau's final years as prime minister, FIRA's provisions began to be slackened and streamlined, and more attempts were made to assuage the fears of foreign investors. The Conservatives pointed directly at these nationalist measures as villains partially responsible for Canada's hard times.

The Mulroney government moved quickly to dismantle the two programs since the Liberal government had designed them. Most of the teeth were pulled out of FIRA's mouth and the thrust was reversed

Canada

to encourage, rather than discourage, investment. FIRA was renamed "Investment Canada" and, in the words of one of its advertisements in foreign magazines, "the Canadian Government has placed the welcome mat out to foreign investors." By 1985 the Montreal and Toronto stock exchanges opened electronic trading links with the stock exchanges in Boston, New York and Chicago, facilitating the sale of a number of Canadian stocks to American investors.

In 1985 Mulroney signed an "Atlantic Accord" granting Newfoundland control over its offshore energy resources. He also signed a "Western Accord" with the premiers of British Columbia, Alberta and Saskatchewan that largely freed the Canadian oil industry from federal regulation. In a third step, Mulroney's government adopted a frontier energy policy known as the Canada Petroleum Resources Act, which meant less government intervention in federally-controlled northern and offshore areas. Finally, the government deregulated the natural gas market.

Government controls on the exporting and pricing of oil and natural gas have been abolished, and discrimination in tax treatment of exploration spending between Canadian and foreign firms was ended. These accords effectively spelled the end of the NEP. Canadian ownership in its oil industry declined to 42.1% by 1989, down from 47.9% in 1985. In 1991, 15% of PETROCAN's shares were sold to the public, and in 1995 the Chrétien government announced the sale of its remaining 70% stake and eliminated the 25% limit on foreign investment in PETROCAN. In 2009 it was acquired by Suncor Energy, which had pioneered the development of Alberta's oil sands.

In 2010 a rare rejection of private foreign investment in Canada took place. BHP Billiton, an Anglo-Australian mining company, made a $39 billion hostile takeover bid for PotashCorp of Saskatchewan. Premier Brad Wall called on Prime Minister Stephen Harper and his fellow Canadians to "stand up for Canada" by opposing this purchase. Canada possesses 53% of the world's reserves of potash, a strategic resource vital to food production. PotashCorp alone accounts for about a third of the world's supply of this food nutrient. They stopped the deal.

Out of 1,600 reviewed foreign purchase requests in the preceding 25 years, this was only the second time one had been turned down. Canada has always been among the world's most open countries to foreign investors although the OECD ranked it in 2011 one of the most restrictive places for foreigners to invest. Still, some sectors that remain off-limits to foreigners: banks, publishing, broadcasting, cable television systems, telecommunications, airlines and

one of Canada's two major railways. In 2011 the largest banks and pension funds launched a rival bid to prevent the London Stock Exchange from buying the Toronto stock exchange (TMX), regarded by most Canadians as a strategic asset. The new merger would be branded "Maple."

In light of the the Cornovirus pandemic, there has been a great deal of human suffering and major economic disruption. Global trade was already weak with merchandise trade volumes falling in the declining in 2019. In January 2020, China's decline in production has been felt around the world.

Free Trade Agreement

By 1985 the old, controversial issue of free trade with the U.S. again moved into political center stage. This debate has existed as long as Canada has been an independent country. When the British adopted a policy of free trade in 1846, the colonies of British North America entered into a Reciprocity Treaty with the U.S. This treaty facilitated free trade for many manufactured goods until the U.S. unilaterally abrogated it in 1866. This American move divided Canadians on the question of free trade with the U.S. for the next century and a quarter. After all attempts to reach some kind of agreement had failed, John A. Macdonald declared his National Policy of trade protection in 1878, asserting that "no great nation has ever arisen whose policy was free trade."

In the early 20th century the Canadian government had second thoughts about this. Prime Minister Laurier reflected on President William Howard Taft's comment and question: "Canada is at the parting of the ways. Shall she be an isolated country, as much separated from us as if she were across an ocean, or shall her people and our people profit by the proximity that our geography furnishes and stimulate trade across the border?" Laurier decided that his country should seek free trade, but Canadian voters had different thoughts and voted him out of power in the 1911 election, which was fought on that issue. The Conservative slogan, "No Truck or Trade with the Yankees!" was a potent one. The arguments for or against free trade have not basically changed since that time.

Two world wars greatly intensified the trade ties between the Canada and the U.S. and after the Second World War they entered sectoral free trade agreements with each other. In 1959 leaders created the Canadian-U.S. Defense Production Sharing Arrangement, which permits unfettered trade in military products. To the chagrin of Canadian peace groups, the government and industries seek to increase their contracts with the Pentagon in

order to have a larger share of American defense spending.

The second milestone in sectoral free trade was the 1965 Canadian-U.S. Automotive Trade Agreement which required the Big Three U.S. automakers to build as many cars in Canada as they sell there. It is responsible for the fact that a third of Canada's exports to the U.S. and more than a fourth of its total exports are in the form of finished vehicles and automotive parts. Auto ownership in the U.S. has reached an astonishing 99.8% in the U.S., compared with 68% in Canada, and 85% of all vehicles assembled in Canada are sold in the U.S. Ontario produced more vehicles than Michigan for the first time in 2004.

The Canadian Autoworkers Union announced in 2005 that 57,500 Canadians were directly employed by carmakers, 10,000 fewer than in 1998; 85% worked for the Big Three. The auto pact did not provide for free trade in replacement parts, tires, batteries, and used cars. In 2000 the WTO accepted Japan's and the EU's argument that the auto pact violates international trade guidelines. The Canadian government unsuccessfully appealed the ruling. Canada's auto industry was responsible directly or indirectly for more than a million jobs in Canada, 11% of the full-time work force. When the Big Three fell into crisis in 2008–9 and Chrysler entered bankruptcy protection in April 2009, many Canadian autoworkers found their employment terminated or curtailed, but the government came to the rescue and acquired Chrysler stock that Fiat was eager to buy.

The Mulroney government was more interested in free trade. Radically reversing the position which John A. Macdonald had taken a century ago, Mulroney asserted in 1984 that efforts to control trade and investment "ignored the basic lesson of our history, namely that free and unfettered access to world markets has been a boon to strong and dynamic economic growth." No doubt the massive Canadian surplus in the trade account with the U.S. helped change some Canadians' minds.

Canadians have always been afraid that free trade with the U.S. would kill their weaker, less efficient manufacturing companies. However, this fear was less justified in an era when Canadians are able to sell more manufactured goods to the U.S. than vice-versa. It also makes less sense at a time when both countries face their greatest trade challenges from Japan, China, and some third world countries, whose lower labor costs help them to undersell American and Canadian products in those two countries' home markets. These challenges give the U.S. and Canada a strong incentive to join efforts to tighten their own trade ties with each other.

Prime Minister Harper meets with Presidents Calderón and Obama in Guadalajara

The business community is almost unanimously in favor of free trade but the Liberal Party opposed completely it. Some provincial premiers, especially in Ontario, were fearful that an agreement could prevent them from subsidizing or otherwise favoring companies within their boundaries in order to save jobs. Organized labor, supported by the NDP, feared that free trade could destroy the jobs of many Canadian workers. Finally, cultural nationalists argued that such cornerstones of Canadian culture as film-making and book production would be killed by free trade.

In an attempt to assuage all these fears, Mulroney announced that essential Canadian economic, political, cultural, and social features were not negotiable. In a speech in Chicago he said: "Our political sovereignty, our system of social programs, our commitment to fight regional disparities, our unique cultural identity, our special linguistic character—these are the essence of Canada."

Mulroney argued that "the deal is a must for Canada," proceeding to negotiate and sign the Free Trade Agreement (FTA) on January 2, 1988. The following 12 months saw one of the most furious debates and outbursts of nationalism ever to grip Canada. It pitted proponents, who argued that the agreement would protect Canada against American protectionism, keep economic nationalism within Canada in check, and create jobs, against opponents, who feared that Canadian industry and culture would be crushed.

As the smaller European members of the EU or EFTA have seen, distinctive cultures can indeed survive within free trade organizations. Also, some sensitive areas of the economy were exempted from the agreement such as water, east coast fish, most agricultural products, and the "cultural industries."

Free Trade was the crucial issue in the 1988 elections. The fact that Mulroney's Tory government was returned to power was an important sign that Canadians had largely shed their economic inferiority complex toward the U.S. In 1988 both houses of parliament approved of FTA amidst uproarious attempts to show who was the most patriotic: opposition members sang "O Canada," while Tories waved the Canadian flag. The pact went into effect in 1989.

The value of bilateral merchandise trade jumped by 42% in the first four years of FTA's existence. Yet, criticism persisted that it brought job losses to Canada. The issue of subsidies continues to be an explosive matter even while cross-border trade and investment boomed. In 1994 some shoppers were induced to stay in Canada by a lowering of Canadian taxes on cigarettes, as well as by the opening of 136 Wal-Mart stores, purchased from Woolworth Canada. Each has a McDonald's restaurant inside and the trademark low prices, customer service "with a smile," and "greeter" at the door. Wal-Mart promised that 60% of the products in these stores would be produced in Canada. This was necessary at first because of the requirement that every package in Canada be labeled in French and English.

The retailing giant had to learn some hard lessons about doing business in Quebec. Wal-Mart distributed thousands of flyers in English only and sent letters to its middle managers in English, which were violations of the province's language laws. Another problem is the way Wal-Mart 's name sounds in Quebecers' ears. A columnist for *Le Journal de Montreal* claimed that "even uttering the word [Wal-Mart] is disgusting, like chewing an old Kleenex that was forgotten in the pocket of a winter coat."

Wal-Mart found itself in a legal thicket in 1997 when, fearing American legal action, it took a line of pajamas off its shelves produced in Cuba. This action was a violation of a Canadian law that forbids companies in Canada from complying with the American trade embargo against Cuba, with which Canada conducts normal relations. This incident merely demonstrated again how sensitive Canada is concerning its sovereignty *vis-à-vis* the U.S; Wal-Mart restocked the pajamas.

The Ontario Labor Relations Board ordered the company's store in Windsor to become the chain's first to have union employees. This did not happen, but in 2004 the Quebec Labour Relations Board approved the United Food and Commercial Workers (UFCW) union's bid to represent the 180 Wal-Mart employees in Jonquière, 250 miles northeast of Montreal. Wal-Mart responded a year later by closing the store, allegedly for economic reasons. Few people believed that explanation, and the union continued to recruit support from a dozen of the 44 stores in Quebec and at twice that number elsewhere in Canada.

In 2006 it faced a union showdown in St. Hyacinthe, 40 miles outside of Montreal, the only Wal-Mart store in North America with broad union representation. In 2009 a Quebec government arbitrator awarded employees at the store a labor agreement including a grievance process and seniority rights. Wal-Mart's struggle is greatest in Quebec, where about 40% of the workforce is unionized, the highest percentage in North America.

Despite such problems of adaptation, by 2005 Wal-Mart 2005 captured about 52% of the discount market. By 2014 it was Canada's largest retailer, not only taking business from other department store giants, such as Kmart, which has disappeared, Canada's traditional leader but now American-owned, Zellers with 28% of the market share, and "The Bay," a struggling dowdy department and discount chain that was sold in 2006 to an American company. By offering an 8% reduction in the price of a standard basket of department store goods and by winning customer loyalty through friendly service, it helped force Eaton's, a national institution, to seek bankruptcy in 1997, from which it emerged wounded later in the year; Eaton's market share had dwindled to 7% by 1999.

This was a bitter blow to many Canadians who for generations had grown up

Canada

mail-ordering from the Eaton's catalogue and staring at its magical Christmas season displays. Eaton's, which French language police forced to drop the English possessive from its signs in Quebec, failed to adjust to a new age of retail competition. In 1999 Sears Canada bought Eaton's corporate entity and 18 of its stores including six downtown stores and the flagship Toronto Eaton Center, which were renamed Eatons, without an apostrophe, and reopened in 2000 after an upscale makeover. The rest were turned into Sears stores. However, this business plan failed and in 2002 five of the remaining stores were converted to Sears outlets while two were closed. Eatons is no more.

Though vilified on both sides of the border, Wal-Mart's success is related to what it offers to areas, consumers, and employees. Most Canadian communities with outlets reached out to and embraced them. Thousands of small suppliers compete to get their products on Wal-Mart's shelves and new stores receive six to ten applicants for every available job. A 2004 survey by the Canadian Imperial Bank of Commerce of more than 1,800 small-business owners in Canada revealed that only 16% claimed to have been hurt by competition from large retailers like Home Depot and Wal-Mart, and 5% said they had benefited from them. The overwhelming majority contended that their presence had little or no impact on their businesses.

The American chains keep coming. In 2013 Target took over leases for up to 220 Zellers stores, the last major Canadian discount chain, which had been owned by the Hudson's Bay Company. This was its first expansion over the U.S. border, but it failed within a year. Safeway also pulled out of Canada in 2013. Other American businesses hoping to make up for declining sales at home by expanding to Canada are J. Crew, Nordstrom, Kohl's, and Marshalls. Hudson's Bay bought Saks.

Canadian firms, seeking lower tax rates, lower wages in anti-union states, and especially market penetration, are the fifth-largest purchaser of American assets, with 9% of the total foreign holdings. Canada's international competitiveness is enhanced by its being one of the cheapest places in the industrialized world to do business despite its high corporate taxes. In 2000 federal corporate rates began to be reduced from 28% to 21% over three years, below the U.S. level. By 2007 it stood at 15%. In 1999 the start-up and operating costs of a business were 7.8% lower in Canada than in the U.S. A World Bank/Harvard study in 2000 placed Canada at the top of the international list for the least amount of red-tape in setting up a business.

Canada's strengths are relatively high quality and inexpensive telecommunications, a good transport network, cheap fuel, low total business travel costs, and a lack of corruption. Housing prices used to be generally lower than in the U.S., but the average home in Canada was $449,142 in 2020, higher than in the U.S. Still 69% of Canadian households own their own dwelling. During the housing crash in the U.S. from 2008 on, house prices dropped more than 30% in the U.S. compared with only 8% in Canada. Canadians also have 2.5 rooms per person versus 2.3 rooms per person in America. However, one of Canada's weaknesses is that its manufacturers are only about 80% as productive as their U.S. counterparts.

The FTA helped reorient Canada's economy north–south rather than along the historical east-west lines. British Columbia looks increasingly to Washington and Oregon, Quebec to New York, the Maritimes to the American Northeast. A former Ontario premier said: "We have a stronger relationship with Michigan than any other jurisdiction around."

North American Free Trade Agreement

In 1991 negotiations the U.S. entered negotiations with its southern neighbor, Mexico, to have it sign on to NAFTA. Only a tiny fraction, about 4% of Canada's trade in goods and services was with Mexico. Yet, national leaders feared that the country court be adversely impacted by remaining on the sidelines, that its preferential access to the American market could be eroded, and trade and investment could be diverted. Canada thus joined the talks. The parties reached a trilateral agreement extending from the Yukon to the Yucatan creates an open market of then 435 million people, now almost 600,000,000 with an economic output larger than that of the EU. Proponents say that it increases growth and makes North America more competitive with Asian and European rivals, adding that it could be a step toward a Western Hemisphere free trade area.

The difficulty was to knit together three economies of vastly different sizes and stages of development and with huge disparities in per capita income; in 2007 this was about $41,640 in the U.S., $34,480 in Canada, but only $7,180 in Mexico. Negotiations were concluded in 1992 with the three countries' leaders signing NAFTA in December.

NAFTA, which took effect on January 1, 1994, was phased in over 10 years. In its first year, Canada's trade with the U.S. increased by 12% and with Mexico by 21%. Because U.S.-Canadian bilateral trade doubled from 1988 to 1999, few people in Canadian political circles criticize

the principle of free trade. An EKOS poll in 2002 found that three-fourths of Canadians supported free trade with the U.S., up from 30% in 1992. In 2003 two-thirds favored stronger economic integration with the U.S, and 57% even supported an economic union along the lines of the EU; 59% of Mexicans agreed while only 44% of Americans liked this idea. By 2013 Canadian support for NAFTA felle to 54%. NAFTA was oversold at its onset: it did not reverse U.S. trade balance, produce Mexican prosperity, or hold down migration to the U.S.

The strains of globalization have cut away at Americans' liking for free trade. Asked in 2007 if America has benefited from foreign trade agreements such as NAFTA, only 15% of Democrats and 20% of Republicans agreed. Hillary Clinton said in her campaign that NAFTA had "hurt a lot of American workers." Barack Obama vowed immediately to call the "president [sic] of Canada to try to amend NAFTA." When one of his staff met a Canadian diplomat in Chicago, though, telling him not to worry about such election rhetoric, the information was leaked and caused confusion in Canada. Both Prime Minister Harper and ex-Mexican President Felipe Calderón made it clear they would not support reopening the agreement. As president, Obama dropped the talk of reopening negotiations and limited his message to bringing side agreements on labor and the environment into the text of the treaty to make them more enforceable.

In the beginning, many Canadians had feared that closer integration with the American economy could threaten their social-welfare model, but that has not happened. Canadians are willing to pay the higher taxes needed to finance their generous public services. Nevertheless, conflicts continued over cultural products, wheat, potatoes, fishing, lumber, beer, steel and other things. Most trade disputes between Canada and the U.S. involve sectors shielded from NAFTA. These disagreements test the willingness of both countries to live peaceably within the rules they had accepted.

In 1995, Chile was invited to join. In 1996, Canada signed free trade agreements with both Chile and Israel, with which it conducts a modest amount of trade annually, about a half billion dollars each. In 1997, former Prime Minister Chrétien called for more bilateral trade agreements with Latin American countries, beginning with Brazil. Canada entered formal negotiations with Costa Rica in 2000, followed quickly by free trade talks with Guatemala, Honduras, El Salvador, and Nicaragua. A trade deal with Costa Rica was ratified in 2002, and a bilateral free-trade agreement was forged with Colombia in 2009.

Canada also proposed a NAFTA-EU agreement, then a Canadian-EU pact. The EU turned this down in 1999, but agreed in 2009 to begin talks. Discussions with Japan to forge a trade pact remained fruitless. The Canadian market is too small to tempt some non-North American partners. In 2001, Quebec City was host to 34 Western Hemispheric nations to launch the creation of a Free Trade Area of the Americas (FTAA). Canada is one of FTAA's strongest advocates, with a 2003 poll finding that 69% of Canadians supported it. But it had made little progress by the end of the decade.

It may be surprising that although Canada enjoys freer trade with its NAFTA partners, there are still sizable trade barriers between Canadian provinces. Such "balkanization" is cited as an important reason for sluggish productivity growth. Two of them, Alberta and British Columbia, became so frustrated with the lack of progress toward domestic free trade that in 2007 they created the Trade, Investment and Labour Mobility Agreement (TILMA). Within two years this eliminated most impediments to the free flow of trade, investment, and labor between them. An example of obvious improvement is that a hay wagon from one province that crosses the border into the other no longer has to have its bales restacked in order to comply with two different arcane transportation rules. The two neighbors are the country's fastest-growing region, with 7.7 million people and a GDP of CAN$400 billion. The agreement created Canada's second-largest economic unit after Ontario.

During the 2016 American electoral campaign, Donald Trump blasted NAFTA as "the single worst trade deal" the U.S. ever signed even though it has been a success with trade among the three partners almost quadrupling since 1994. But negotiations in 2017 and 2018 to update the treaty dealt with new problems left out of the earlier agreement, such as the web, e-commerce, and robust labor and environmental protections.

Strong State Role

The territorial size, low population, and hostile geography of Canada have always necessitated a greater degree of state intervention in the economy than was the case in the U.S. Canadians have always been less receptive to the notion of a *laissez-faire* market in which the government intervenes little and more receptive to strong government control than have Americans.

As Canadian economist Dian Cohen wrote in a column in *Maclean's*, "public policy and public enterprises to activate the policies in the absence of private initiatives are even more Canadian than the beaver and the Maple Leaf. It is ironic that we Canadians spend so much time looking for ways in which we differ from Americans but overlook the one crucial characteristic that has always set us apart—an almost blind belief in the virtues of public enterprise."

Even though they differ among themselves in matters of degree, all Canadian political parties are more supportive of a strong state hand in the society and economy than either the Democratic or Republican parties in the U.S. During his electoral campaign, Mulroney stressed the Conservative welfare tradition. Nevertheless, in its first economic policy statement the Mulroney government had to conclude that in Canada "government has become too big."

This welfare tradition cis visible in the large number of nationalized industries, or "Crown corporations," as they are called in Canada that can be found in virtually every aspect of Canadian life: in culture (Canada Council or the CBC, which was founded on the cry: "It's the state or The States!"); trade (earlier the Canadian Wheat Board); housing; transportation (St. Lawrence Seaway Authority, National Harbors Board); utilities (Atomic Energy of Canada, Eldorado Nuclear); industry (Sydney Steel Corporation); development (Canada Development Investment Corporation). Conversely, in the U.S., utilities are privately owned, but regulated by public commissions, in Canada they are publicly owned and operated.

At the top of Canada's financial world are five banks: the Royal Bank of Canada, the Bank of Montreal, the Canadian Imperial Bank of Commerce, the Bank of Nova Scotia, and Toronto Dominion Bank. Among all North American banks, all five of these are in the top 15 in market value. Although Canadian banks were not immune to the global banking crisis in 2008–9, their value fell less than in the U.S. but no bank failed. In 2008 the World Economic Forum picked the country's banking system as the healthiest in the world; U.S. banks were ranked 40th. Canada's big five control 93% of the assets of the 12 national banks. In 1998, the Canadian government blocked two proposed mergers among four of these giants, calling the links "an unacceptable concentration of economic power." It would have enabled only two banks to control 70% of all bank deposits, especially since U.S. banks are prevented from entering the Canadian market.

In general, Canada has relatively few multinational companies. On the Fortune 500 list of the world's largest companies in 2004, Canada's top entry was George Weston Ltd. in 240th place. While Sweden has Ikea and Finland Nokia, Canada does not have a single global brand.

Some Crown corporations have existed for a long time and are known to some Americans, such as the CBC, 70% of which were created since 1960. Some make a profit, but some of them are perennial money losers and are kept alive chiefly to save jobs; in fact, many were taken over in the first place because they were not able to survive on their own.

Second, Canada has a higher percentage of its GDP in government hands than does the U.S. Of course, defense spending is much greater in the U.S. although it rose in both countries. In 2019 it accounted for 1.3% of GDP in Canada. If one only looks at the civilian sector, then the differences between the two countries would be even greater. Canadians pay higher taxes and have fewer write-offs. Canadians cannot write off the interest they pay on home mortgages, whereas this is perhaps the greatest tax "loophole" in the U.S. Americans can even write off the charitable contributions they give to Canadian charities; Canada is the only country to which the U.S. extends this privilege.

The annual *Maclean's*/CBC polls from 1997 to 2002 revealed that Canadians were less inclined to look to the state to solve their economic problems than they once were: they accepted the message that government deficits must be reduced if the country's long-term prosperity is to be preserved. Canadians are willing to tolerate fundamental changes in the social safety net: 61% accept the evolution of private universities; 53% are resigned to having the government hand over some social services to charities; and 47% find the emergence of a two-tier, state and private, health-care system acceptable. On leaving his job at ABC in New York in 2001, Canadian Broadcaster Kevin Newman recalled a difference that remains between the two peoples: 56% of American adults do some form of volunteer work every year compared with 32% of Canadians.

The growing trend toward individualism was confirmed in the 2002 *Maclean's*/ CBC poll: 81%, compared with 71% three years earlier, thought they themselves, as opposed to government, labor unions or business leaders, were best able to take care of their economic interests. In 1997 Canadians gave then Prime Minister Chrétien his second majority in a row even after he declared that they "know that there is nobody who will have a magic wand and solve all the problems [just by] being there."

Health and Welfare

Another key issue is that Canada has a more extensive and expensive social welfare net than does the U.S. It is an ironic fact that many democratic countries that have

Canada

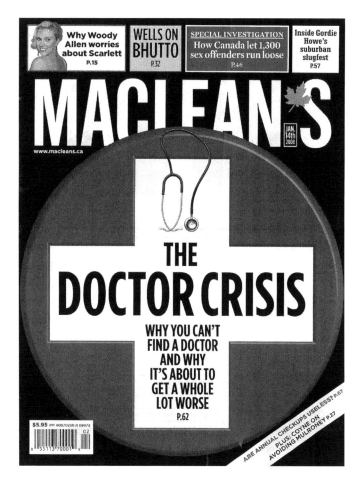

conservative, elitist political and social traditions also have developed broad nets of social welfare. This is the case with Britain, Germany, and Sweden as well as Canada. In the U.S., equality of opportunity for the individual has been a supreme value, requiring a weaker state that could not place restrictions on the individual. Canada always had a strong state, and when it became democratized, citizens demanded that it intervene on behalf of all of them to secure more *equality of results*. That is, Canadians demanded that the state redistribute the wealth of the country in order to diminish differences among its citizens.

The Great Depression that started in 1929 gave special impetus to this. As Keith Banting observed in his work, *The Welfare State and Canadian Federalism*, "during the last half century, the Canadian state has established a new set of social rights, a set of claims for protection from the insecurities of modern society. It is deeply embedded in the fabric of Canadian life." Social welfare spending in Canada now embraces such things as pensions, disability protection, unemployment insurance, child benefits, maternity welfare, subsidized housing, and free medical care.

Under the Canada Pension Plan, all Canadians have the right to receive a government pension on reaching retirement age. This pension includes an automatic entitlement, as well as supplemental benefits for those who can demonstrate need. Almost all employed and self-employed persons are compelled to contribute to this plan, and the payments are financed from the contributions and interest of the invested funds. Like the U.S. social security system, it is a pay-as-you-go system, meaning that current contributions are used to pay current retirees. Unlike America's system, Canada's has been on solid financial footing for at least the next three-quarters of a century. Under the Family Allowances Act of 1944, parents with children under age 18 living at home and with low enough incomes are automatically entitled to a monthly allowance of $29.95, which is taxable, for each child.

Canada's Medicare system, paid largely from tax sources, provides health care to any Canadian in needs. Patients choose their own doctors, who are not employed by the state, and they seldom see large hospital bills. "Medically necessary" hospital treatment and doctor services are paid out of taxpayer dollars making up 71% of spending on health care in 2003. However, other medical goods and services such as drugs dispensed outside hospitals, vision care, dental services and long-term care, are not always covered. About 30% of all health care spending comes from private pockets. Originally the federal government paid one half of the cost but cuts greatly reduced that share to only 16% of its health dollars, with the provinces paying more and more. Within federal guidelines, the provinces operate their own health systems.

Canadians like this system in principle; in 2010, 69% said they were proud of their health care system. Former Governor General Adrienne Clarkson called Medicare "a practical expression of the values that define us as a country." In 2004 a television contest to determine "the greatest Canadian" picked Tommy Douglas, the earlier Saskatchewan premier who pioneered Medicare; a *Maclean's* poll found that Pierre Elliot Trudeau is considered the greatest Canadian, either living or dead with 22% of the votes.

Polling figures in 2002 showed that 85% of Canadians considered their health-care system better than America's with 87% opposed making it more like that of the U.S. However, Canadians argue about its problems and demand more funding. In 2006 the World Health Organization (WHO) ranked Canada 30th in the world, ahead of 37th-placed U.S., in terms of quality of health services. A 2010 comparative study of seven developed countries placed Canada last in terms of effective care and timeliness of care, behind the U.S. The level of government spending per capita on health care twice as high in the U.S.: $7,290 vs. $3,895 in Canada. As in the U.S., the costs of health care have ballooned; by 2005 they had climbed by a third over the past decade.

Canadians say that health care is one of their foremost worries. In 2005, 86% told pollsters that health care was a very or fairly serious problem. In the 2006 federal elections Prime Minster Stephen Harper did not propose a sweeping overhaul of Medicare, but one of his five chief campaign promises were to guarantee shorter waiting times for services to help the two million Canadians on waiting lists. Yet, because this is a provincial responsibility, Harper was unable to fulfill his promise. Although the situation has improved, a quarter of patients, as opposed to 7% of Americans, waited more than four months for non-emergency, elective surgery.

Canada faces a crisis of spiraling health costs caused by higher pay and benefits for medical personnel, who constitute 7% of Canada's work force, soaring prices for high-tech medical equipment, and a growing number of older persons. To cope with the costs, hospitals everywhere have taken beds out of service, limited the operations performed, cut back on many services and purchases of high-tech diagnostic equipment, and reduced nursing and physician staffs. One result has been lengthening waiting lists and some highly publicized deaths of patients waiting for treatment or surgery. One exasperated patient claimed: "You could die before they know what's wrong with you!"

Asked in 2004 if their confidence in the health system was rising or falling, 6% of respondents said it was rising, and 47% said it was falling; 86% said there were not enough doctors and 81% not enough nurses. In 2005, only 23% of Canadians were able to see a doctor the same day they needed one. A 2014 survey of 11 prosperous countries placed Canada last when it comes to how quickly patients can get an appointment with a regular family doctor. Five million Canadians had no family doctor in 2011. Emergency rooms were maxed out. Part of the problem is that the new generation of physicians is no longer willing to work the many hours their predecessors did. This is related to the large number of women in the healthcare profession, who must juggle work and families: 80% of the workforce is female, as are 52% of physicians under age 35.

More and more Canadians wonder if their country can afford the popular publicly funded universal system that offers one of the highest standards of health care in the world. Few Canadians, even doctors, look to the U.S. for a solution although many Americans turn to the Canadian system as worthy of imitation. Health costs in the U.S. are rising even faster, and Americans pay a higher percentage of their GDP for medical care than do Canadians, even though millions of the former long had no medical protection at all prior to the passage of the Affordable health Care Act, commonly called Obamacare. Canadian doctors, who remain in the top 1% of all professional workers in terms of income, must devote a much smaller percentage of their earnings to malpractice insurance.

Canadians are seeing their drug medication prices rise because of a booming cross-border trade in pharmaceuticals. Drug prices are cheaper than in the U.S. because of the lower value of the Canadian dollar and because of price breaks from pharmaceutical companies negotiated by the Canadian government. Ottawa demands lower prices and threatens to strip away patent protection if the manufactures do not give in. Americans who need common medicines, which can often be half the price in Canada, flock across the border or use the internet to acquire at a discount the medications they need. Even many American city and state governments are turning to Canada to purchase

drugs although dozens of Canadian internet pharmacies refuse to fill such bulk orders. Thus, medicines mostly produced in the U.S. but intended for Canadians are being resold at a profit in the higher-priced American market. This tightens supplies and increases prices for Canadians. Former Health Minister Ujjal Dosanjh proclaimed: "Canada cannot be the drugstore of the U.S."

By almost any standard, the Canadian system keeps its citizens at least as healthy as does America's. A joint head-to-head survey in 2004 by Statistics Canada and the U.S. National Center for Health Statistics determined that the overall health status of both nations is remarkably similar. The study reported that Americans like their market-based health care system more than Canadians like their own Medicare, which costs less per capita. For-profit U.S. hospitals cost on average 19% more than publicly funded Canadian equivalents.

Life expectancy in Canada of 80.4 for men compared to 76.3. in U.S. and 84.2 years for women as opposed to 80.1 in U.S. At 84.3, Canada ranks 12th highest in the world for life expectancy as opposed to the U.S. which is 32nd at 81.6. Heart disease, the focus of much advanced American medical research, kills Canadians at a rate 20% lower than for Americans, despite similar dietary habits. Americans are more obese: 33% of women and 31% of men, compared with 19% of women and 17% of men in Canada; 36% of Canadians are merely "overweight," and 8% of kids are obese. At just over five feet eleven, the average Canadian-born male is nearly an inch taller than his American counterpart. More Canadians smoke regularly, but the disparities between the health of rich and poor are more pronounced in the U.S.

The Canadian approach to health care is that it cannot be left to market forces. In 2001 Canada became the first country to allow terminally ill patients to grow and smoke their own marijuana to alleviate their pain as long as they obtain a doctor's certificate. The Canadian government also began gearing up to supply patients and researchers. In 2018 this was extended to recreational use of the drug. Almost two-thirds, or 63%, of Canadians told pollsters in 2006 that they favored legalization. A government report revealed in 2004 that marijuana use in Canada had nearly doubled in the previous 13 years. A law was enacted in 2016 permitting people with terminal illnesses to end their lives with the assistance of a doctor or nurse.

A basic principle in health care benefits, as well as in other benefits such as family allowances, is universality, meaning that all Canadians can receive them, regardless of wealth and/or income. During his 1984

electoral campaign, Mulroney called such universality "a sacred trust." The daunting costs of the social welfare system caused his government to reconsider after the election, but public pressure on the government was so great that Mulroney was forced to back off from any attempt to tamper with this fundamental principle.

The soaring costs and federal cuts sparked demands that fundamental changes be made in health care and the welfare system. In 1994, Ontario ended health coverage for thousands of foreign students and immigrants with temporary residence authorization. Some provinces refuse to cover bills for Canadians visiting from other regions of Canada. Provinces imposed three-month waiting periods before new residents can be covered, and coverage abroad was limited. Specified operations, such as vasectomy reversals, that were once paid, are no longer free.

In 2004 Ontario imposed a new healthcare tax while removing coverage for physiotherapy, chiropractic and eye tests. In the same year Vancouver's St. Paul's Hospital contracted out 947 publicly funded surgeries to three private clinics. Private health care had already slipped into the door. In 2004, almost a third of all money spent on health care had been paid for out of private pockets. Private clinics were springing up everywhere.

The ground was thereby set for the kind of private services and insurance approved by the Supreme Court in a landmark ruling in June 2005. The Justices struck down a law from Quebec that banned private medical insurance and ordered the provincial officials to enact a reform within a year. The Court ruled that long waits for various medical procedures violate patients' lives and freedom and that prohibitions on private health insurance were unconstitutional when the public system failed to deliver "reasonable services."

The Supreme Court of Canada's judgment generated calls for more private clinics and insurance in multiple provinces beyond Quebec, which already had about 50 private health clinics even before the court decision. While there were dozens of such clinics in Alberta and BC, they were primarily limited to services not covered by Medicare.

Polls in 2004 indicated that Canadians are very wary about their health-care system and were open to change as long as there is no resort to higher co-payments and personal wealth to get timely care. A year later 59% of respondents supported the Supreme Court's order; a further 59% expressed their support for Alberta's proposal permitting payment out-of-pocket for service enhancements, like better prosthetic joints; and a majority believed that private insurance would reduce

Canada

waiting times and have a positive effect on Medicare as a whole.

BC and Alberta led the way to more private care. The BC government considered a system in which it would pay for essential treatment delivered in both public and private clinics and hospitals. Albertans are discussing legislation to permit doctors to practice simultaneously in private and public institutions and to permit the construction of private hospitals. Even the widely-read weekly newsmagazine *Maclean's* devoted an entire issue on May 1, 2006, to advising Canadians on all the private care offerings in their country.

The level of care varies from region to region and from city to rural locales. Attempting to eliminate the federal deficit, Ottawa took billions of dollars out of the system, amounting to an 8.7% reduction from 1985–95. This left the difficult decisions to the provinces, which passed many of them on to local governments. The federal government thereby abdicated its right to insist on maintaining national standards. In effect, there is no longer a national Medicare system.

Because Ottawa was under intense pressure to return to the provinces the money it had taken from health care, so in 2000 the federal budget boosted such spending by 25%.

The biggest health scare in 2003 was the spread of a mysterious respiratory disease, Severe Acute Respiratory Syndrome, or SARS, to Canada. Due to its close links with China, Toronto became the population center most affected by the deadly virus outside of Asia.

The WHO thought it necessary to issue a travel advisory twice for Toronto, an embarrassing and economically damaging move the city's mayor called outrageous. Toronto accounts for 20% of Canada's economic growth and tourism is the city's second-largest industry after finance. SARS seriously blemished Toronto's image as a safe place to visit and live even though the city won praise for the way it handled the crisis. The illness claimed 31 lives in Toronto, 44 in Ontario. An investigative commission issued a report in 2007 that SARS spread due to a shoddy public health system and inadequate safety practices insofar as almost three-fourths of the victims became infected in clinics and hospitals.

In 2004 British Columbia experienced an outbreak of an avian influenza, which was fortunately not the kind that could infect humans and animals. Nevertheless, 38 countries, including the U.S., imposed bans on poultry products from BC while 19 million chickens, turkeys, and other poultry had to be killed to prevent the flu from spreading.COVID-19 is the latest outbreak to affect the Canadian health care system.

According to IBISWorld, the challenge for Canadian hospitals is that they are already functioning at a 100% capacity rate or more for the last 20 years. With the increased number of affected people needing health care because of the COVID-19, hospitals will be even more overcrowded and come with added challenges.

The erosion of the Canadian health system shows the risks of making health care dependent on taxes. When budget deficits must reduced, and political pressure makes tax increases impossible, health and welfare programs become targets for cuts. The earlier Reform and Alliance Parties' success since 1993 demonstrated the appeal in Canada of attacking government waste and abuse by overhauling social programs and holding the line on taxes.

The rapid rise in Canadian taxes from 31.6% of GDP in 1980 to 36.8% in 1999, compared with 29% in the U.S., provoked a near tax revolt. The difference is particularly pronounced in income taxes: at middle-income levels, Americans pay about half the income tax Canadians owe. Yet 40% of Canadians pay no income tax at all, and the lowest rate is 15%. Those in the top income bracket pay from 39% in Alberta to 48% in Quebec, compared with a top of 37% in the U.S. The high taxes have driven wealthy Canadians, such as singer Shania Twain, billionaire

Michael DeGroote and auto magnate Frank Stronach, to establish residency in lower tax jurisdictions, such as Bermuda or Switzerland. In 2008 the federal goods and services tax fell to 5%.

While Canadians remain devoted to their safety net, they are demanding that their governments end what seems to be a built-in incentive for those who resort to welfare and unemployment. In 1999, Ottawa responded by providing a modest tax break. This was continued in 2000, when the federal government announced sweeping tax cuts, indexing tax brackets to inflation to eliminate "bracket creep," and increasing child tax benefits. Canadians often find welfare policy models in the U.S. In 2007 the federal government proposed a Working Income Tax Benefit to make work more appealing than welfare. This is practically a carbon copy of America's Earned Income Tax Credit.

There seems to be an emerging consensus that many social programs have failed to solve the problems of those who need them most, while bestowing benefits on many for whom they were never intended. From 1981 to 1995 the number of Canadians on social assistance doubled. Some programs have perhaps even hurt those whom they were designed to help by fostering dependency. Provincial leaders are clamoring for the right to

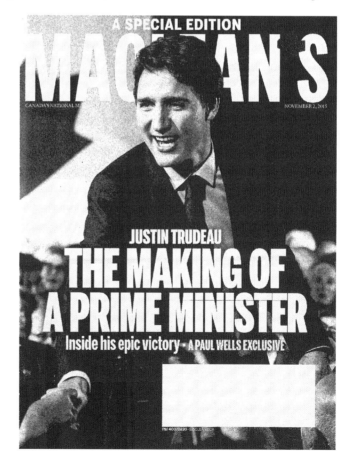

introduce their own reforms while demanding more federal assistance to pay for them.

Called for reforms seem to undermine a fundamental tenet of Canadian federalism, uniform standards of social services across the country. Because many Canadians regard their social security net as one of the country's hallmarks which helps define their national identity, any attempt to overhaul it arouses fierce opposition and intense struggles among competing interests. With a half-trillion-dollar national debt hanging over their heads, though, politicians find it harder to sweep the problems under the rug.

Canada's social welfare system has not eradicated poverty. As in the U.S., the gap between rich and poor continues to widen. This development challenges deeply held assumptions about Canada as a place where U.S. style extremes of wage and income distribution do not exist and where the safety net is adequate for all. More than one in ten Canadian adults and children lived in 2014 below the poverty line, defined as a household in which income is half the national median; 17.9% live in low-income households. That proportion has remained steady over the preceding 25 years. In 2013 UNICEF ranked Canada in the bottom third of rich countries in regard to relative child poverty.

About 235,000 Canadians are homeless, including families with young children. The number of people using food banks was 900,000 in 2010, a 9% increase in one year and 92% increase from 1991–2001. Single mothers are especially hard hit: a federal report in 2001 concluded that it took 75.4 weeks of work, the equivalent of 1.5 full-time jobs at an average wage, to cover a family's basic expenses. Specific goals announced in the 1980s to eliminate child poverty by 2000 are no longer mentioned.

The number of homeless persons who trudge with their few belongings from soup kitchen to hostel has doubled in Canadian cities since the 1980s. Observers estimate that at least 100,000 people lack shelter on any given day. Despite the magnitude of social welfare benefits and income guarantees, Canadians are still vulnerable to the ups and downs of the economy. Poverty has not been a major political issue in Canada, probably because it still does not have a high enough visibility to prompt the government to try to act on it.

The federal and provincial governments share responsibility for social welfare policy; it has therefore become a major source of conflict between Ottawa and the provinces. These issues have been at the heart of many a struggle concerning the distribution of power among the various governments of Canada. Social welfare spending was a major contributor

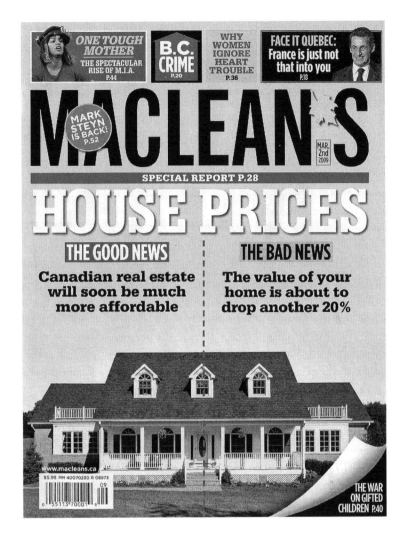

to staggeringly high federal and provincial budget deficits. As the federal and most provincial governments balanced their budgets, welfare spending declined.

Transfer payments sustain public services in all "have-not" provinces. Only British Columbia, Alberta, and more recently Saskatchewan and Newfoundland, qualify as "have" provinces. The preponderance of "have-not" provinces threatens the sustainability of the system. Newfoundland has used some its new-found oil and mining wealth to reduce its poverty rate in half to 6.5%. Ontario slipped into the "have-not" category, but it is unlikely to remain there. Beginning in 1996 federal transfer payments to the provinces for social programs were converted into block grants and reduced by 4%. Provinces, most of which try to balance their budgets, are severely indebted and have no alternative to reducing their services.

COVID-19 Crisis

Almost needless to say, the coronavirus disease of 2019, commonly known as COVID-19, that rocked the global community, had a major impact in Canada. In response to the crisis, officials in the Public Health Agency of Canada continue to work with their counterparts in the provinces, territories, and international partners, including the World Health Organization, as they continue to monitor the situation with a focus on containment outbreak and preventing its further spread. In addition, Canada's Chief Public Health Officer remains in close contact with provincial and territorial Chief Medical Officers of Health to ensure that cases of COVID-19 are identified rapidly and managed in order to protect the health of Canadians.

As of May 12, 2020, the government of Canada reported that there were 3,784,278 confirmed COVID-19 cases in the country resulting in 39,877 deaths and 3,472,555 people who recovered. In addition, 59,791,354 COVID-19 tests were taken and 84,609,785 doses of vaccine administered.

Trucker's Strike

Unhappy with the Canadian government's vaccine mandate that required

Canada

truckers who crossed the border into the United States to be inoculated against COVID-19 or be subject to two-week quarantines, truckers created what they called the "Freedom Convoy" to demonstrate their unhappiness. As a result, in January 2022, truckers obstructed border crossings while others engaged in noisy demonstrations in various cities. The convoy finally came to an end when Prime Minister Justin Trudeau invoked the Emergencies Act for the first time in Canadian history, thereby allowing police to move against, and arrest, hundreds of protesters in late February.

Current Economic Situation

The accumulated national debt, including provincial debt, stands at $1.4 trillion (2016/17) sharply up from $833 billion between 2007 and 2008. The COVID-19 pandemic will likely create a global recession as countries shut down non-essential businesses and lock down their citizens. In 2021, combined national and provincial debt is up 65.2% and is expected to climb to $2 trillion by the end of 2021.

At the time of this writing, the federal deficit could spike to $113 billion and the unemployment rate could hit 15%. Paying the interest on this debt is one of the federal government's largest single expenditures, greater than its spending on health care, family allowances, old-age pensions and social assistance combined. When the indebtedness of the 10 provinces is added, the total debt is larger than the economy itself. This is high among industrialized nations, and from a third to half of that debt is in foreign hands. Canada succeeded in eliminating its budget deficits after 1998, but in 2018 it stood at 1.7% of GDP. The victorious Liberal government promised to run deficits for multiple years to modernize the country's infrastructure.

Due to the global financial crisis that began in 2008, the government was forced in the fiscal year of 2009-10 to end 12 years of budget surpluses. By 2009 the economy had shrunk by an annualized rate of 3.4%, a year later by 1.2%. However, Canada's recession was the mildest downturn in three decades, and by 2018 annual growth was 3%, slightly higher than America's 2.3%. Inflation was 1.4% in 2018. Unemployment sank to 5.9%, higher than 4.1% in the U.S.

Eight thousand jobs were lost when the postal service ended door-to-door letter deliveries in 2018 to concentrate on package deliveries. City dwellers will have to pick up their mail at community mailboxes. Apartment inhabitants must get their mail in their buildings, and country folks continue to use their rural mailboxes.

None of Canada's banks collapsed during the great recession with the then governor of the Bank of Canada, Mark Carney, earning much of the credit for this and the rapid return of the economy to growth. In July 2013 Carney became the Bank of England's governor, arguably the most influential unelected post in Britain. He is the first foreigner to head Britain's central bank in its 318-year history.

By 2012, while American housing was still in the doldrums, the Canadian housing market was soaring on low mortgage rates to a record high median home price of $300,000, up 83% from 1999. Vancouver, which *The Economist* selected in 2011 as the world's most livable city, with Toronto and Calgary also ranked in the top five, was the most expensive housing market, with an average house price in 2017 of around $1 million and $2.5 million in Westside, followed by Toronto at $916,500). About two-thirds, or 69%, of Canadians have their own homes. Recently, in 2018-19 the BC government has taken measures to slow down the real estate market which has caused a significant reduction in home sale prices in Vancouver. In Alberta, the inability to move oil to market has slowed the housing market.

High world prices for oil and gas were a boon for the country with the world's second largest oil reserves and helped increase Canada's diplomatic and economic influence in the world. For instance, these high prices elevated Canada to a higher priority in the eyes of the U.S. government.

Productivity is lower in Canada. In 2007 output per man-hour was 79% of America's, and there are reasons for this. In general, the U.S. economy remains more productive in part because of its investments in technology and education. Canada spends less than half as much on research and development;

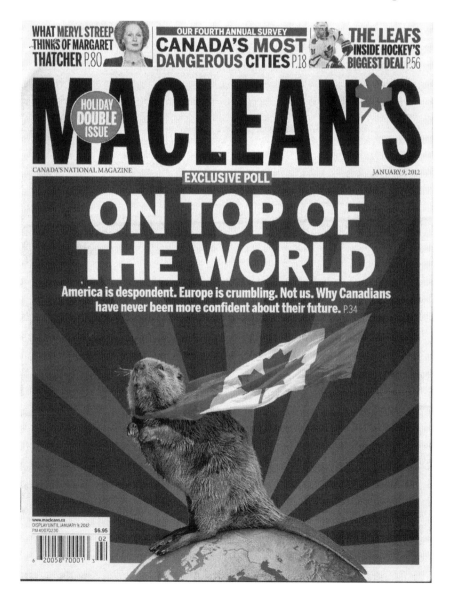

business investment in R&D especially lags. Canada devotes less on higher education and training; since 1993 the U.S. increased the annual spending on education by 3.3%, compared with .2% for Canada. Investment per worker in machinery and equipment, especially in information technologies, is only 60% of the American level.

The productivity gap is partly explained by the facts that the average Canadians work 69 fewer hours per year, taking 3.9 weeks of vacation compared with two weeks for their American counterparts. Moreover, Canadians retires earlier at age 61. In the World Economic Forum's annual rankings of most competitive countries, Canada had slipped from sixth in 1998 to tenth in 2008.

Measured in terms of per capita GDP, Canada's living standard is one fifth below that of the U.S. Using purchasing power parity, the gap is 13%. However, this may be changing: Canadian median incomes rose 20% between 2000 and 2010 to $18,700, putting Canadians equal to Americans. Canadians live in slightly smaller houses of about 2,000 vs. 2,434 square feet, but each Canadian has on average 2.5 rooms compared with 2.3 in the U.S. Nevertheless, in 2007 only 19% of Canadians thought that Americans had a better standard of living than they did; 53% did not think that a gap would make any difference in their lives. An impressive 72% were satisfied with their living standard as it was.

That satisfaction did not necessarily extend into the future. In a 2007 poll, 45% of Canadians did not believe the next generation would be able to afford a better standard of living, and only 26% thought it would continue to get better.

Canada tried to rebrand its economy in the 1990s as high-tech. Yet, the contemporary foundation of its economy is a familiar one: natural resources, particularly oil and mining, albeit technologically sophisticated. When world, and especially Chinese, demand keeps commodity prices high, Canada can look forward to a strong economy. One thing Canadians had to get used to was the gradual disappearance of their penny. In other words, because it cost more than one cent to make a copper penny, the last one was struck in May 2012.

FUTURE

In 2017, Canadians celebrated the 150th birthday of their country. A SES survey (SES Research was a Canadian public opinion and research company established in 1987 and later renamed Nanos Research) in 2005 revealed that, despite

The White House from Washington, DC
By Shealah Craighead. https://www.flickr.com/photos/whitehouse/44300765490/, Public Domain. https://commons.wikimedia.org/w/index.php?curid=74766604

their political differences, Canadians and Americans think much more alike about important things and are, in fact, closer than one might think. They want to work closely with each other on such matters as counter-terrorism and still define their two nations more by their similarities than by their differences. Asked which country is most like their own in terms of human rights, Canadians picked the U.S. more than any other at 43% while 51% of Americans chose Canada.

Canadians are as determined as ever to preserve their sovereignty and their independence of action. Still, they accept the need for greater security along the border, increased police cooperation with U.S. authorities, common policies on immigration and refugees, and even restrictions on some of their personal freedoms in order to meet the terrorist threat.

Canadians have a developed sense of social justice as most support same-sex marriage and allowing gay and lesbian couples to adopt children. Also, in 2016 after much debate and litigation, the House of Commons amended the Criminal Code of Canada to allow for Medically Assisted Dying. It also decriminalized the recreational use of marijuana. Canada legalized the use of marijuana in 2018.

This social liberalism points to an increasingly self-confident country. These social issues join gun control and universal one payer health care in solidifying a Canadian sense of, to some degree, separateness from the U.S.

Dramatic changes have taken place in Quebec. *Québécois* seem to accept Canada more than they used to as only 2% of them considered national unity a major issue. As the most socially liberal Canadians, the majority of *Québécois* approve of gay marriage, abortion, and the legalization of marijuana:

69% endorsed the statement that they are proud of what Canada is becoming "because it shows what a socially progressive and diverse country, we live in." The figure in the rest of Canada was 54%.

A major reason for this unprecedented *Québécois* embrace of Canada is the confidence they now have that their language and culture are more firmly entrenched than ever before. In the 2011 and 2015 federal elections, the separatist *Bloc Québécois* was wiped out in the province, winning only ten lonely seats in the House of Commons, far short of the number required to constitute an official parliamentary party. The *Bloc Québécois* is divided over how bold to be in seeking a separate Quebec. When the issue became dominant for it in the April 2014 provincial election campaign, it spelled disaster for the party, which was thrown out of government. Independence remains unlikely in the foreseeable future.

In the October 19, 2015, federal elections, Justin Trudeau of the Liberals generated a lot of enthusiasm for his party, which until April 2019 retained a consistent lead in the polls since becoming prime minister in November 2015.

Canada had done well under Harper's economic stewardship. It suffered a milder recession, a gentler housing decline and much lower unemployment than the U.S. The country benefited from a well-regulated banking system, growing Asian markets and reasonably good world prices for Canada's natural resources.

The opposition has two new leaders: Conservative Andrew Scheer and New Democrat Jagmeet Singh. Although the Liberals remain in the lead 35% to 33%, the gap is narrowing. Asked about their preferred Prime Minister, Trudeau scored 45%, Scheer 21%, and Singh 9%. Two-thirds

Canada

of Canadians rate the Liberals as good at representing Canada internationally.

As of February 2019, though, a Nanos poll found that as far as Canadians were concerned, the leader of the Green Party, Elizabeth May, was most ethical, followed by the leader of the progressive Conservative Party, Andrew Scheer, followed by Liberal Leader and Prime Minister Justin Trudeau, and New Democratic Party Leader, Jagmeet Singh. As stated earlier in this volume, the bloom appears to be off the rose for the Prime Minister.

There is tension with President Trump having scrapped NAFTA for the United States–Mexico–Canada Agreement (USMCA).

Its fighter jets and one frigate participated in NATO's enforcement of a no-fly zone over Libya. It also sent a large military transport aircraft to support the French anti-terrorist operation in Mali. It supports its allies' diplomacy in Syria, and it sent planes and 69 Special Forces to support the allied fight against the Islamic State in Iraq. Newly elected Justin Trudeau announced the withdrawal of the combat aircraft. The government will continue persistently to assert Canadian sovereignty in the Arctic.

Looking forward, Canada will keep its door open to refugees and more than 300,000 immigrants each year; this amounts to 1% of its population, 80% of whom will become citizens. Canadians will continue to worry about Islamic terrorism. Reform of the electoral system has fallen along the wayside for lack of popular support. Prime Minister Trudeau's political honey moon is over despite his popularity: 61% of respondents agree that he possesses the qualities of a good political leader.

Maclean's 2012 annual poll found a nation that was proud and confident about the future. An overwhelming majority (86%) agreed with the notion that their country is "the greatest in the world"; 97% of Tory voters agreed. Asked if their country is heading in the right direction, 63.5% of Canadians answered yes, while a meager 17% of U.S. voters answered in the affirmative. Was their country the best place to raise a family?: 87% of Canadians but only 61% of Americans thought so. Only 17% of Canadians thought they could get better work in their southern neighbor.

A decade later, in the midst of a great deal of uncertainty in Canada and the world, a Matus Public Poll published in the *Toronto Star* in February 2022 revealed a different picture. According to the poll 66% of Canadians fear for the future in light of the Trucker's Convoy, as 82% thought that the protests never should have been allowed, fearing that there is no longer a common ground for civil discourse. Let us hope that with COVID-19 on the wane, the world situation will sort itself out, this result is an aberration, and that Canada's future will be bright.

Web Sites and Bibliography of Key English-Language Books

WEB SITES

https://budget.gc.ca/2022/home-accueil-en.html

https://comtrade.un.org/ (United Nations Comrade Database-detailed global trade data)https://covid19tracker.ca/ https://premier.novascotia.ca

www.cbsa.asfc.gc.ca (Canada Border Services Agency) https://www.canada-population.net/ontario-population/

https://www.canadapopulation.net/quebec-population/

https://www.ctvnews.ca/canada/freedom-convoy-protest-how-did-we-get-here-1.5772901, n.d.

www.defensenews.com (Global website and magazine about the politics, business and technology of defense, serving senior military and industry decision-makers.)

www.dfait-maeci.gc.ca (Foreign Affairs and International Trade)

https://www.canada.ca/en/canadian-heritage/services/official-languages-bilingualism/publications/statistics.html

http://www.eco.gov.yk.ca/stats/pdf/real_estate_q219.pdf (Yukon Bureau of Statistics)

https://www.gov.nl.ca/premier/www.gov.nl.ca/fin/economics/pop-overview (Newfoundland)

https://www.ibisworld.com (research on industries worldwide)

http://www.mapleleafweb.com/main.shtml (Central site for Canadian affairs)

https://www.ntassembly.ca/meet-members/mla/caroline-cochrane

https://nunatsiaq.com/stories/article/nunavut-premier-talks-1st-week-on-the-job/

https://www.worldatlas.com/articles/religious-composition-of-canada.html

https://worldpopulationreview.com/canadian-provinces/british-columbia-populationlop.parl.ca/About/Parliament/speakers/hoc/sp-37Rota-e.htm

www12.statcan.gc.ca/census-recensement/index-eng.cfm

www.150.statcanada.com (Stats Canada)

www.canoe.ca and www.Yahoo.ca (Canadian search engines)

www.canadianembassy.org (This site is a key source containing a search engine, an issues menu, many links, a virtual reference desk and a virtual tour of the Canadian embassy in Washington.)

www.ambassadeducanada.org (All of the above functions in French)

www.usembassycanada.org (Site for US embassy in Ottawa with reports and information)

www.canada.gc.ca (General Web site for information on Canada from the Canadian government. See links.)

www.cbc.ca (Web site for the Canadian Broadcasting Corporation. This is an excellent current source for all aspects of Canadian news, with numerous links. See also www.cbc.ca/newsworld/)

www.ctv.ca (Broad Canadian reporting)

www.radio-canada.ca/nouvelles (French-language news)

www.elections.ca (election results. Phone: 1-800-463-6868)

www.pm.gc.ca (Web site for Canadian prime minister's office. By substituting the first letters of other ministries, access to other ministries' Web sites can be gained. See below.)

www.fin.gc.ca (Web site for Canadian Finance Ministry)

www.strategis.ic.gc.ca (Industry Canada)

www.dfait-maeci.gc.ca (Web site for Department of Foreign Affairs and International Trade)

www.cfp-pec.gc.ca (Web site of Canadian Centre for Foreign Policy Development. See many links. For peacekeeping, add: /peacekeeping/menu-e.asp. For additional links, add: /y2k. For magazine, add: /Canada-magazine)

www.cbsa.asfc.gc.ca (Canada Border Services Agency)

www.cic.gc.ca (Citizenship and Immigration Canada)

http://www.mapleleafweb.com/main.shtml (Central site for Canadian affairs)

www.canschool.org (Web site for many aspects of Canadians in the World)

www.citizens.ca (Site for information relating to who Canadians are; description of people)

www.gov.nu.ca (Site for Nunavut)

http://parkscanada.gc.ca (Parks Canada site)

www.travelcanada.ca

www.liberal.ca (Liberal Party site)

www.conservative.ca (Conservative Party site)

www.ndp.ca (National Democratic Party site)

www.bloc.ca (Bloc Québécois party site)

www.greenparty.ca (Green Party site)

www.un.org (Web site for United Nations. Many links.)

www.nato.org (Web site for NATO. Many links.)

www.chatelaine.com (Web site for *Chatelaine* weekly Canadian magazine. In English and French.)

www.macleans.ca (Web site for *Maclean's* weekly Canadian news magazine)

www.macleans.ca/news/canada/the-safest-and-maybe-most-honest-places-to-live-in-canada/ (Poll on safest places to live in Canada)

www.mh-education.com (*Maclean's* educational Web site. See links.)

www.mercer.com (Quality of life)

www.GlobeAndMail.ca (Respected Canadian national newspaper)

www.nationalpost.com (Respected Canadian national newspaper)

www.torontostar.com (Respected Canadian national newspaper)

www.ottawa citizen.com (Respected Canadian national newspaper)

www.montrealgazette.com (Respected Canadian national newspaper)

www.winnipegfreepress.com (Respected Canadian national newspaper)

www.vancouversun.com (Respected Canadian national newspaper)

www.ledevoir.com (Respected Quebec French-language newspaper)

www.candacalling.com (Prior Smith's five-minute Canadian newscasts)

www.cyberpress.com (Canadian news)

www.iam.ca (Humorous Web site for Molson beer's Canadian nationalism commercial)

www.economist.com (Respected British news weekly with some coverage of Canadian affairs)

www.chicagotribune.com (Respected U.S. newspaper with some coverage of Canadian affairs. Named best over-all US newspaper online service for newspapers with circulation over 100,000.)

www.csmonitor.com (Respected U.S. newspaper, *Christian Science Monitor*, with some coverage of Canadian affairs. Named best overall US newspaper online service for newspapers with circulation under 100,000.)

www.nytimes.com (Respected U.S. newspaper, *The New York Times*, with some coverage of Canadian affairs)

www.washingtonpost.com (Respected U.S. newspaper with some coverage of Canadian affairs)

www.washingtontimes.com (Respected U.S. newspaper with some coverage of Canadian affairs)

www.canada.plattsburgh.edu (The Center for the Study of Canada at the State University of New York Plattsburgh maintains the major Web site for Canadian Studies. E-mail address: CANADA-ACSUS@Plattsburgh.EDU. Search also for Association for Canadian Studies in the U.S.—ACSUS.)

philippe.premont@dfait=maeci.gc.ca (New-scan E-mail of Weekly Canadian news summaries)

http://www.eco.gov.yk.ca/stats/pdf/real_estate_q219.pdf (Yukon Bureau of Statistics)

www.gov.nl.ca/fin/economics/pop-overview (Website for Government of Newfoundland)

https://trading economics.com/Canada/imports/china (An online platform that provides historical data, economic forecasts, news, and trading recommendations)

https://www.arctictoday.com/in-the-battle-for-sovereignty-of-a-disputed-arctic-island-canada-and-denmark-use-

Bibliography

whisky-and-schnapps (An individual news site reporting on the arctic)

https://www.bbc.com/news/world-us-canada-42586638 (British Broadcast Corporation poll on passports)

www.angusreid.org (Angus Reid Institute is a national, not-for profit organization commissioning research and opinion polls on issues that matter to Canada)

www.univcan.ca/universities/facts-and-stats/tuition-fees-by-university/ (Universities Canada)

https://comtrade.un.org/ (United Nations Comrade Database-detailed global trade data)

www.defensenews.com (Global website and magazine about the politics, business and technology of defense, serving senior military and industry decision-makers.)

https://www.ibisworld.com (IBISWorld provides trusted industry research on thousands of industries worldwide)

I. GENERAL

Beach, Richard, ed. *O Canada, Its Geography, History and the People Who Call It Home.*

2nd rev. ed. Plattsburgh, NY: Center for the Study of Canada, 2000.

Berton, Pierre. *Why We Act Like Canadians. A Personal Exploration of Our National Character.* Toronto: McClelland and Stewart, 1982.

——. *Hollywood's Canada.* Nd.

Black, Peter. *Canada Matters: Chronicles of a Northern Neighbour.* Plattsburgh, NY: Center for the Study of Canada, 2002.

Ricker, Darrell and John Wright. *What Canadians Think.* Toronto: Doubleday, 2005.

Callwood, June. *Portrait of Canada.* Garden City, NY: Doubleday, 1981.

The Canadian Encyclopedia, 2nd ed., 4 vols. Edmonton: Hurtig, 1988.

——. *The Canadian Pocket Encyclopedia.* Vancouver, BC: CanExpo, annual edition.

Center for the Study of Canada. *Occasional Paper Series.* See also its annual *Teaching Canada.* Its 2002 volume (21) is entitled *Canada & The World.* Plattsburgh: State University of New York. (Phone: 518-564-2086).

Crowley, Jason Clemons and Niels Veldhuis. *The Canadian Century. Moving Out of America's Shadow.* 2010.

Dermer, Jerry, ed. *The Canadian Profile. People, Institutions, Infrastructure.* North York, Ont: Captus Press, 1992.

DePalma, Anthony. *Here: A Biography of the North American Continent.* New York: HarperCollins, 2001.

Gould, Karen, Jockel, Joseph T. and Metcalf, William, eds. *Northern Exposures. Scholarship on Canada in the United States.* Washington, D.C.: Association for Canadian Studies in the United States, 1993.

Hobson, Archie. *The Cambridge Gazetteer of the United States and Canada. A Dictionary of Places.* New York: Cambridge University Press, 1995.

Joyce, William W. and Richard Beach. *Introducing Canada. Current Backgrounders, Strategies, and Resources for Educators.* Washington D.C.: National Council for Social Studies, 1997.

Malcolm, Andrew H. *The Canadians.* New York: Times Books, 1985.

Mathews, Robin. *Canadian Identity. Major Forces Shaping the Life of a People.* Ottawa: Steel Rail Educational Publishing, 1988.

Metcalfe, William, ed. *Understanding Canada. A Multi-disciplinary Introduction to Canadian Studies.* New York: New York University Press, 1982.

Olive, David. *Canada Inside Out: How We See Ourselves/How Others See Us.* New York: Bantam, 1996.

Pryke, Kenneth G. and Soderlund, Walter C. *Profiles of Canada.* Toronto: Copp Clark Pitman, 1992.

Richler, Noah. *This is My Country, What's Yours?* Toronto: McClelland & Stewart, 2006.

Roste, Vaughn. *The Xenophobe's Guide to the Canadians.* London: Oval Books, 2004.

Sabin, Louis. *Canada.* Mahwah, NJ: Troll Associates, 1985.

Sherman, George. *O Canada. Its Geography, History and the People Who Call It Home.* Plattsburgh, NY: Center for the Study of Canada, 1994.

Taras, David, et al. *A Passion for Identity.* 2nd ed. Scarborough, Ont: Nelson, 1992.

The 1997 Corpus Almanac & Canadian Sourcebook. Don Mills, Ont.: Southam Magazine & Information Group, 1997.

II. BIOGRAPHIES AND AUTOBIOGRAPHIES

Ayre, John. *Northrop Frye.* Vintage Books, 1990.

Boyden, Joseph. *Extraordinary Canadians: Louis Riel and Gabriel Dumont.* Toronto: Penguin, 2009.

Brown, R.C. *Robert Laird Borden: A Biography.* 2 vols. Toronto: 1975, 1980.

Cayley, David. *Northrop Frye in Conversation.* Donn Mills, Ont: Anansi, 1992.

Charlesbois, Peter. *The Life of Louis Riel.* Toronto: NC, 1975.

Chretién, Jean. *Straight from the Heart.* Toronto: Key Porter, 1985.

——. *My Years As Prime Minister.* 2007

Clarkson, Adrienne. *Heart Matters.* Toronto: Penguin, 2006.

Cohen, Andrew and J.L Granatstein, eds. *Trudeau's Shadow. The Life and Legacy of Pierre Elliott Trudeau.* Toronto: Vintage, 1999.

Creighton, Donald. *The Old Chieftain.* (Classic biography of Macdonald). 1955.

——. *John A. Macdonald.* 2 vols. Toronto: Macmillan, 1968.

Delacourt, Susan. *Juggernaut: Paul Martin's Campaign for Chrétien's Crown.* Toronto: McClelland & Stewart, 2003.

Diefenbaker, John G. *One Canada.* 3 vols. Toronto: Macmillan, 1975–1977.

English, John. *The Worldly Years of Lester Pearson 1949–1972.* Toronto: Alfred A. Knopt, 1993.

Ferns, Henry and Ostry, Bernard. *The Age of Mackenzie King.* Toronto: James Lorimer, 1976.

Flanagan, Thomas. *Louis "David" Riel: Prophet of the New World.* Toronto: University of Toronto Press, 1979.

——. *Harper's Team: Behind the Scenes in the Conservative Rise to Power.* 2007.

Foran, Charles. *Extraordinary Canadians: Maurice Richard.* Toronto: Penguin, 2011.

Fraser, Graham. *PQ: Réne Lévesque and the Parti Quebecois.*

Garr, Allen. *Tough Guy: Bill Bennett and the Taking of British Columbia.* Toronto: Key Porter, 1985.

Gillen, Mollie. *Lucy Maud Montgomery.* Markham, Ont: Fitzhenry Whiteside, n.d.

Gwyn, Richard. *The Northern Magnus. Pierre Trudeau and Canadians.* Markham, Ont.: Paper Jacks, 1981.

——. *John A.: The Man Who Made Us.* (About John A. Macdonald). 2007.

——. *Nation Maker.* Second volume of Gwyn's 2007 book above. 2011.

Hadfield, Chris. An Astronaut's Guide to Life on Earth. 2013.

Harcourt, Michael, with Wayne Skene. *A Measure of Defiance.* Vancouver, BC: Douglas & McIntyre, 1996.

Ignatieff, Michael. *True Patriot Love. Four Generations in Search of Canada.* Viking Canada, 2009.

——. Fire and Ashes. Failure in Politics. Cambridge, MA: Harvard University Press, 2013.

Johnson, William. *Stephen Harper and the Future of Canada.* Toronto: McClelland and Stewart, 2005.

Lam, Vincent. *Extraordinary Canadians: Tommy Douglas.* Toronto: Penguin, 2011.

Lavigne, Brad. Building the Orange Wave: The Inside Story Behind the Historic Rise of Jack Layton and the NDP. Douglas & McIntyre. 2013.

Lévesque, Réne. *Memoirs.* Toronto: Cross Canada Books, 1986.

Levine, Allan. *Toronto: Biography of a City.* Toronto: Douglas & McIntyre. 2014

McNaught, Kenneth. *A Prophet in Politics. A Biography of J.S. Woodsworth,* Toronto: University of Toronto Press, 1959.

MacDonald, L. Ian. *Brian Mulroney. The Making of the Prime Minister.* Toronto: McClelland and Stewart, 1987.

MacNeil, Robert. *Looking for my Country. Finding Myself in America*. Toronto: Vintage Canada, 2002.

Martin, Laurence. *The Antagonist: Lucien Bouchard and the Politics of Delusion*. Toronto: Viking, 1997.

Martin, Paul. *Hell or High Water*. 2008.

McIlroy, Thad, ed. *A Rose is a Rose: A Tribute to Pierre Elliott Trudeau in Cartoons and Quotes*. Toronto: Doubleday, 1984.

Morison, Samuel Eliot. *Samuel Champlain, Father of New France*. Boston: Little Brown, 1972.

Mulroney, Brian. *Where I Stand*. Toronto: McClelland and Stewart, 1983.

Myers, Mike. *Canada*. Toronto: Doubleday Canada, 2014

Neatby, H.B. *William Lyon Mackenzie King*. 3 vols. Toronto: 1963, 1976.

Nemni, Max and Monique. *Trudeau Transformed: The Shaping of a Statesman, 1944–1965*. Translated by George Tombs. 2011.

Manning, Preston. *The New Canada*. Toronto: Macmillan, 1992.

Pearson, L.B. *Mike: The Memoirs of the Rt. Hon. Lester B. Pearson*. vol. I, 1897–1948; vol. II, 1948–1957; vol. III, 1957–68. Toronto: 1972–75.

Pelletier, Gerard. *Years of Impatience*. New York: Facts on File, 1984.

Pickersgill, J. W. *My Years with Louis St. Laurent*. Toronto: 1975.

Pratte, André. *Extraordinary Canadians: Wilfrid Laurier*. Toronto: Penguin, 2011.

Radwanski, George. *Trudeau*. Agincourt, Ont: Signet, 1978.

Rae, Bob. *From Protest to Power: Personal Reflections on a Life in Politics*. Toronto: Viking/Penguin, 1996.

Richards, David Adams. *Lord Beaverbrook*. Toronto: Penguin Group (Canada), 2008.

Ross, Catherine S. *Alice Munro*. Toronto: ECW Press, 1992.

Saul, John Ralson. *Extraordinary Canadians: Louis Hippolyte LaFontaine and Robert Baldwin*. Toronto: Penguin, 2010.

Sawatsky, John. *Mulroney. The Politics of Ambition*. Don Mills, Ont: Stoddart, 1991.

Schull, J. *Laurier: The First Canadian*. Toronto: 1966.

Stanley, G. *Louis Riel*. Toronto: 1963.

Sweeny, A. *George-Etienne Cartier: A Biography*. Toronto: 1976.

Thomson, D. *Alexander Mackenzie: Clear Grit*. Toronto: 1960.

Thomson, D.C. *Louis St. Laurent: Canadian*. Toronto: 1967.

Troiano, Edna. M. *Uncle Tom's Journey from Maryland to Canada: The Life of Josiah Henson*. Charleston, SC: The History Press. 2019.

Trudeau, Justin. *Common Ground*. 2014.

Trudeau, Pierre Elliott. *Memoirs*. Toronto: McClelland and Steward, 1993.

Urquhart, Jane. *Extraordinary Canadians: L.M. Montgomery*. Penguin Group (Canada), 2009.

Young, B. *George-Etienne Cartier: Montreal Bourgeois*. Montreal and London: 1981.

Penguin Group (Canada) launched in 2008 a three-year *Extraordinary Canadians* series, edited by Ralston Saul and composed of 20 Canadian biographies by notable Canadian novelists and authors. The biographies are lively and important stories told by talented writers, not ponderous academic works.

III. HISTORY

Allan, Ralph. *Ordeal By Fire. Canada, 1910–1945*. Toronto: Doubleday, 1961.

Anderson, Fred. *Crucible of War. The Seven Years War and the Fate of Empire in British North America, 1754–1766*. Toronto: Vintage Books, 2001.

Baldwin, Douglas and Odnyak, Emily. *Canada's Political Heritage*. Regina: Weigl Educational Publishers, Ltd., 1985.

Bailyn, Bernard. *The Barbarous Years: The Peopling of British North America, 1600-1675*. 2012.

Beal, Bob and Macleod, Rod. *Prairie Fire. The 1885 North West Rebellion*. Edmonton, Alb.: Hurtig, 1984.

Bercuson, David J. *Canada and the Burden of Unity*. Toronto: Copp Clark Pittman, Ltd. 1985.

Berger, Carl. *Contemporary Approaches to Canadian History*. Toronto: Copp Clark Pittman, 1987.

Bernier, Serge. *The Royal 22e Regiment, 1919–1999*. Montreal: Art Global, 2000.

Berton, Pierre. *My Country. The Remarkable Past*. Toronto: Seal Books, 1979.

——. *The Invasion of Canada 1812–1813*. Toronto: McClelland and Stewart, 1980.

——. *The Great Depression, 1929–1939*. Markham, Ont: McClelland Stewart, 1990.

——. *Marching as to War. Canada's Turbulent Years 1899–1953*. Toronto: Doubleday Canada, 2001.

Bird, Harrison. *Attack on Quebec: The American Invasion of Canada 1775*. New York: Oxford University Press, 1968.

Black, Conrad. *Rise to Greatness: The History of Canada From the Vikings to the Present*. Toronto: McClelland & Stewart, 2014.

Bothwell, Robert and Drummond, Ian, and English, John. *Canada Since 1945*. Toronto: University of Toronto Press, 1989.

Bourrie, Mark. *The Fog of War: Censorship of Canada's Media in World War Two*. 2011.

Boyko, John. *Cold Fire. Kennedy's Northern Front*. 2015.

Broadfoot, Barry. *The Pioneer Years 1895–1914. Memories of Settlers Who Opened the West*. Toronto, Garden City, NY: Doubleday, 1976.

Brown, Craig. *The Illustrated History of Canada*. Toronto: Lester, 1991.

Buckner, Phillip A. *The Transition to Responsible Government: British Policy in British North America, 1815–1850*. Westport, CT: Greenwood, 1985.

Budiansky, Stephen. *Perilous Eight: America's Intrepid War with Britain on the High Seas, 1812–1815*. 2010.

Bumstead, J.M., *The Peoples of Canada, 4th ed*. Vol 1: *A Pre-Confederation History. Vol 2: A Post-Confederation History*. Don Mills, Ont: Oxford University Press, 2014.

Butler, Rick and Carrier, Jean-Guy, eds. *The Trudeau Decade*. Toronto and Garden City, NY: Doubleday, 1979.

Canadian History. A Readers Guide. 2 volumes: *Beginnings to Confederation*, ed. by M. Brook Taylor, and *Confederation to the Present*, ed. by Doug Owram. Toronto: University of Toronto Press, 1994.

Canadian Broadcasting Corporation. *Canada: A People's History*. A 16-part film documentary series, 2001.

Careless, J.M.S. *Canada. A Story of Challenge*. Rev. ed. Toronto: Macmillan, 1970.

Carroll, Joy. *Wolfe and Montcalm. Their Life, Their Times, and the Fate of a Continent*. Buffalo, NY: Firefly Books, 2004.

Clarkson, Stephen and McCall, Christina. *Trudeau and Our Times. The Magnificent Obsession*. Vol. 1. Markham, Ont: McClelland and Stewart, 1991.

Cohen, Andrew. *Lester B. Pearson*. Penguin Extraordinary Canadians, 2008.

Conrad, Margaret and Finkel, Alvin, et al. *History of the Canadian Peoples*. 2 vols. Toronto: Copp Clark Pitman, 1993.

Conrad, Margaret. *A Concise History of Canada. 2 vols*. New York: Cambru=idge University Press.

Constain, Thomas B. *The White and the Gold. The French Regime in Canada*. Toronto and Garden City, NY: Doubleday, 1970.

Cook, Ramsey. *The Voyages of Jacques Cartier*. Toronto: University of Toronto Press, 1993.

Cook, Tim. *Vinny: The Battle and the Legend*. 2017.

Cross, Michael S. *A Biography of Robert Baldwin: The Morning-Star of Memory*. 2012.

Dempsey, Hugh A., ed. *The CPR West. The Iron Road and the Making of a Nation*. Vancouver, BC: Douglas and McIntyre, 1984.

Douglas, W.A.B. and Greenhous, B. *Out of the Shadows: Canada in the Second World War*. Rev. ed. Toronto: Dundurn Press, 1993.

Ehret, Matthew J.L. & Saunders, Richard. *The Untold History of Canada: The Forgotten Struggle for Progress*. Toronto: Canadian Patriot Press: 2019.

Finkel, A. *Business and Social Reform in the 1930s*. Toronto: 1979.

Bibliography

Flanagan, Thomas. *Riel and the Rebellion: 1885 Reconsidered.* Saskatoon, Sask.: Western Producer Prairie Books, 1983.

Francis, R. Douglas and Smith, Donald B. *Readings in Canadian History.* Vol. 1: Pre-Confederation. vol. 2: Post-Confederation. 4th ed. Toronto: Harcourt Brace, 1994.

Francis, R. Douglas, et. al. *Origins: Canadian History to Confederation. Destinies: Canadian History Since Confederation.* 2 vols. 2nd ed. Toronto: Rinehard Winston, 1992.

———. *Readings in Canadian History.* Vol. 1: Pre-Confederation. vol. 2: Post-Confederation. 4th ed. Toronto: HBJ-Holt, 1994.

Fraser, Blair. *The Search for Identity. Canada: Postwar to the Present.* Garden City, NY and Toronto: Doubleday, 1967.

Gilbert, A.D., et al. *Reappraisals in Canadian History.* 2 vols. Scarborough, Ont: Prentice-Hall, 1993.

Granatstein, Jack. *Who Killed Canadian History?* 1999.

———. *The Greatest Victory: Canada's One Hundred Days, 1918.* 2014.

Gray, Charlotte. *Gold Diggers.* 2014 (About the Klondike gold rush).

Gruending, Dennis. *Great Canadian Speeches.* Markham, Ont: Fitzhenry and White, 2004.

Gwyn, Richard. *Nation Maker.* 2012. (Two-part biography of Sir John A. Macdonald).

Hagan, John. *Northern Passage. American Vietnam War Resisters in Canada.* Cambridge, MA: Harvard University, 2001.

Hardy, W.G. *From Sea Unto Sea. The Road to Nationhood 1850–1910.* Toronto and Garden City, NY: Doubleday, 1970.

Harris, R. Cole and Warkentin, John. *Canada Before Confederation. A Study of Historical Geography.* New York: Oxford University Press, 1974.

Hayes, Derek. *Canada: An Illustrated History: An Illustrated History, Revised and Expanded.* Toronto: Douglas & McIntyre, 2017.

Historica-Dominion Institute. *We Were Freedom.* Contains 65 gripping oral histories by Canadians in World War II. 2010.

The Illustrated History of Canada. Markham, Ont: Fitzhenry Whiteside, 1988.

Jasanoff, Maya. *Liberty's Exiles. American Loyalists in the Revolutionary World.* New York: Knopf, 2011.

Lanctot, G. *Canada and the American Revolution, 1774–1783.* Toronto: 1967.

Lane, Barry. *Canadian Pacific: The Golden Age of Travel.* Fredericton: Goose Lane Editions, 2015.

Levine, Allan. *King: A Life Guided by the Hand of Destiny.* 2011.

Lussier, Antoine S., ed. *Louis Riel and the Métis.* Winnipeg: Pemmican, 1983.

Mackay, Donald. *The People's Railway. A History of Canadian National.* Vancouver: Douglas McIntyre, 1992.

Masters, Donald C. *A Short History of Canada.* Huntington, NY: Krieger, 1980.

McFadden, Fred, ed. *Origins. A History of Canada.* Markham, Ont: Fitzhenry Whiteside, 1988.

McInnis, Edgar. *Canada. A Political and Social History.* Toronto: Holt, Rinehart and Winston, 1982.

McNaught, Kenneth. *The Pelican History of Canada.* New York: Penguin, 1982.

Moore, Christopher. *The Loyalist Revolution, Exile, Settlement.* Toronto: McClelland and Stewart, 1994.

Morchain, Janet. *Search for a Nation.* Markham, Ontario: Fitzhenry and Whiteside, Ltd., 1984.

Morton, Desmond. *A Short History of Canada.* 5th rev. ed. Toronto: McClelland and Stewart, 2001.

———. *A Military History of Canada. From Champlain to Kosovo.* Toronto: McClelland and Stewart, 1999.

Morton, W.L. *The Canadian Identity.* 2nd ed. Toronto: University of Toronto Press, 1972.

Neatby, Blair. *The Politics of Chaos: Canada in the Thirties.* Toronto: Macmillan, 1972.

Newman, Peter C. *The Canadian Establishment.* 2 vols. Toronto: McClelland and Stewart, 1975 and 1981.

Silver, A.I. *An Introduction to Canadian History.* Toronto: Canadian Scholars' Press, 1993.

Sherman, George. *The Canada Connection in American History. A Guide for Teachers.* 3rd rev. ed. Plattsburgh, NY: Center for the Study of Canada, 1994.

Sprague, D.N. *Canada and the Métis, 1869–1885.* Waterloo, Ont.: Wilfrid Laurier Press, 1988.

Stanley, George F.G. *The War of 1812: Land Operations.* Toronto: Macmillan, 1983.

———. *The Birth of Western Canada. A History of the Riel Rebellions.* Toronto: University of Toronto Press, 1992.

Taylor, Charles. *Radical Tories: The Conservative Tradition in Canada.* Toronto: Ansi, 1982.

Taylor, Alan. *The Civil War of 1812.* 2011.

Thompson, John H. *Canada, 1922–1939. Decades of Discord.* Toronto: McClelland and Stewart, 1985.

Vance, Jonathan. *Maple Leaf Empire: Canada, Britain, and Two World Wars.* 2011.

Waiser, Bill and De Brou, Dave, eds. *Documenting Canada. A History of Modern Canada in Documents.* Saskatoon, Sask: Fifth House, 1991.

Weisbord, Merrily. *The Strangest Dream. Canadian Communists, the Spy Trials, and the Cold War.* Toronto: Lester Orpen Dennys, 1983.

Wise, S.F. and Brown, R.C. *Canada Views the United States: Nineteenth-Century Political Attitudes.* Toronto: Macmillan, 1976.

Zaslow, M., ed. *The Defended Border: Upper Canada and the War of 1812.* Toronto: 1964.

IV. POLITICS

Adams, Michael. *Fire and Ice: The United States, Canada and the Myth of Converging Values.* Toronto: Penguin, 2003.

Archer, Keith, and Alan Whitehorn. *Political Activists. The NDP in Convention.* New York: Oxford University Press, 1998.

Atkinson, Michael M. *Governing Canada. Institutions and Public Policy.* Toronto: Harcourt Brace, 1993.

Bell, David and Teppermann, Lorne. *Roots of Disunity. A Study of Canadian Political Culture.* Rev. ed. New York: Oxford University Press, 1992.

Bickerton, James P., Gagnon, Alain-G., and Smith, Patrick J. *Ties that Bind. Parties and Voters in Canada.* New York: Oxford University, 1999.

Bickerton, James P. and Gagnon, Alain-G. *Canadian Politics. An Introduction to the Discipline.* Peterborough, Ont: Broadview Press, 1994.

Blair, R.S. and McLeod, J.T., eds. *The Canadian Political Tradition. Basic Readings.* Scarborough, Ont: Methuen, 1987.

Boydell, Craig L., and Connidis, Ingrid Arnet. *The Canadian Criminel Justice System.* Toronto: Holt, Rinehart Winston, 1982.

Brodie, Janine. *Women and Politics in Canada.* Scarborough, Ont.: McGraw-Hill Reyerson, 1985.

Brooks, Stephen, ed. *Political Thought in Canada. Contemporary Perspectives.* Richmond Hill, Ont.: Irwin, 1984.

———. *Canadian Democracy.* 3rd ed. New York: Oxford University, 2000.

Cairns, Alan C. and Williams, Douglas E. *Constitution, Government and Society in Canada.* Toronto: McClelland and Stewart, 1988.

Cairns, Alan C. *Charter Versus Federalism.* Montreal: McGill-Queens University Press, 1992.

Cameron, Duncan and Smith, Miriam, eds. *Constitutional Politics.* Toronto: James Lorimer, 1993.

Cheffins, Ronald I. and Johnson, Patricia A. *The Revised Canadian Constitution.* Scarborough, Ont: McGraw-Hill Ryerson Hill, Ltd., 1986.

Conklin, William E. *Images of a Constitution.* Toronto: University of Toronto Press, 1989.

Cook, Ramsay. *Canada, Quebec and the Uses of Nationalism.* Toronto: McClelland and Stewart, 1986.

Courtney, John C., ed. *The Canadian House of Commons.* Univ. of Calgary Press, 1985.

Dawson, R. MacGregor and W.F. Revised by Norman Ward. *Democratic Government in Canada.* Toronto: University of Toronto Press, 1989.

De Palma, Anthony. *Here: A Biography of the New American Continent.* 2001.

Doern, G. Bruce, Leslie A. Pal and Brian W. Tomlin, eds. *Border Crossings. The Internationalization of Canadian Public Policy.* New York: Oxford University Press, 1996.

Donaldson, Gordon. *Eighteen Men: The Prime Ministers of Canada.* Toronto: Doubleday, 1985.

Eagles, Munroe, et al, eds. *The Almanac of Canadian Politics.* 2nd ed. New York: Oxford University Press, 1996.

Flanagan, Tom. *Waiting for the Wave. The Reform Party and Preston Manning.* Don Mills, Ont: Stoddart, 1995.

Forbes, Hugh Donald, ed. *Canadian Political Thought.* Don Mills, Ont.: Oxford University Press, 1985.

Franks, C.E.S. *The Parliament of Canada.* Toronto: Univ. of Toronto Press, 1987.

Gerecke, Kent, ed. *The Canadian City.* Montreal: Black Rose Books, 1993.

Gollner, Andrew B. and Salée, Daniel, eds. *Canada Under Mulroney. An End-of-Term Report.* Montreal: Véhicule Press, 1988.

Goldenberg, Eddie. *The Way It Works: Inside Ottawa.* 2006.

Granatstein, J.L., et. al. *Sacred Trust: Brian Mulroney and the Conservative Party in Power.* Toronto: Cross Canada Books, 1986.

Grant, George. *Lament for a Nation. The Defeat of Canadian Nationalism.* Ottawa: Carleton University Press, 1982.

Higgins, Donald J.H. *Local and Urban Politics in Canada.* Agincourt, Ont: Gage, 1986.

Jackson, Robert J. and Jackson, Doreen. *Politics in Canada. Culture, Institutions, Behaviour and Public Policy.* 4th ed. Upper Saddle River, NJ: Prentice-Hall, 1998.

Kealey, Linda and Sangster, Joan. *Beyond the Vote. Canadian Women and Politics.* Toronto: University of Toronto Press, 1989.

Kernaghan, Kenneth, ed. *Public Administration in Canada.* 5th ed. Toronto: Methuen, 1985.

Knopff, Ranier and Morton, F.L. *Charter Politics.* Scarborough, Ont: Nelson, 1991.

Lagassé, Phillippe. *The Crown and Parliament.* 2015.

Landes, Ronald G. *The Canadian Polity: A Comparative Introduction.* 2nd ed. Scarborough, Ont.: Prentice-Hall, 1987.

Langford, J. Stuart. *A Practical Guide to the New Canadian Constitution.* Toronto: Canadian Broadcasting Corporation, 1982.

Leach, Richard H., ed. *Reshaping Confederation: The 1982 Reform of the Canadian Constitution.* Durham, NC: Duke University Press, 1984.

Levine, Allan. *Scrum Wars. The Prime Ministers and the Media.* Toronto: Dundurn Press, 1993.

MacIvor, Heather. *Women and Politics in Canada.* Peterborough, Ont: Broadview Press, 1994.

Manfredi, Christopher P. and Rush, Mark. *Judging Democracy.* Peterborough, Ont.: Broadview Press, 2008. This is a comparison of the Canadian and American Supreme Courts.

Manfredi, Christopher P. *Judicial Power and the Charter.* 2nd ed. New York: Oxford University, 2000.

McKenna, M.C. *The Canadian and American Constitutions in Comparative Perspective.* Calgary: University of Calgary Press, 1993.

McKercher, William R., ed. *The U.S. Bill of Rights and the Canadian Charter of Rights and Freedoms.* Toronto: Ontario Economic Council, 1983.

McKercher, Asa. *Camelot and Canada* (about Kennedy and Diefenbaker). 2016.

McMenemy, John. *The Language of Canadian Politics. A Guide to Important Terms and Concepts.* Rev. ed. Waterloo, Ont: Wilfred Laurier University Press, 1993.

McRoberts, Kenneth, ed. *Misconceiving Canada. The Struggle for National Unity.* New York: Oxford University Press, 1997.

———. and Patrick J. Monahan, eds. *The Charlottetown Accord, the Referendum, and the Future of Canada.* Toronto, 1993.

McWhinney, Edward. *Canada and the Constitution 1979–1982: Patriation and the Charter of Rights.* Toronto: University of Toronto Press, 1982.

Megyery, Kathy, ed. *Women in Canadian Politics.* Toronto: Dundurn, 1992.

Milne, David. *The New Canadian Constitution.* Toronto: James Lorimer, 1982.

Monahan, Patrick. *Politics and the Constitution. The Charter, Federalism and The Supreme Court of Canada.* Agincourt, Ont: Carswell, 1987.

Morton, Desmond. *The New Democrats 1961–1986.* Toronto: Copp Clark Pitman, 1986.

Morton, E.L. *Law, Politics and the Judicial Process in Canada.* 2nd ed. Calgary: University of Calgary Press, 1992.

Pal, Leslie A., ed. *How Ottawa Spends 2000–2001. Redefining the Federal Role.* New York: Oxford University, 2000.

Pal, Leslie and Taras, David, eds. *Prime Ministers and Premiers. Political Leadership and Public Policy in Canada.* Scarborough, Ont: Prentice-Hall, 1988.

Pammett, J., et al. *The Absent Mandate: The Politics of Discontent in Canada.* Agincourt, Ont.: 1984.

Peacock, Anthony A., ed. *Rethinking the Constitution.* New York: Oxford University Press, 1996.

Penner, Norman. *From Protest to Power. Social Democracy in Canada 1900–Present.* Toronto: James Lorimer, 1993.

Perlin, George, ed. *Party Democracy in Canada. The Politics of National Party Conventions.* Scarborough, Ont: Prentice-Hall, 1988.

Pike, Corinna and Christopher McCreery. *Canadian Symbols of Authority: Maces, Chains and Rods of Office.* 2011.

Rathgeber, Brent. *Irresponsible Government: The Decline of Parliamentary Democracy in Canada.* Dundurn Press, 2014.

Romanow, Roy J. and Whyte, John D. *Canada . . . Notwithstanding.* Toronto: Methuen, 1984.

Russell, Peter H. *Leading Constitutional Decisions.* 3rd ed. Ottawa: Carleton University Press, 1982.

———. *The Judiciary in Canada. The Third Branch of Government.* Scarborough, Ont: McGraw-Hill Ryerson, 1987.

———. *Constitutional Odyssey. Can Canadians Be a Sovereign People?* Toronto: University of Toronto Press, 1993.

Simpson, Jeffrey. *Faultlines. Struggling for a Canadian Vision.* Scarborough: HarperCollins, 1993.

Snell, James G. and Vaughan, Frederick. *The Supreme Court of Canada.* Toronto: University of Toronto Press, 1985.

The L-Shaped Party: The Liberal Party of Canada, 1958–1980. Toronto: 1981.

Wearing, Joseph. *Strained Relations. Canadian Parties and Voters.* Toronto: McClelland and Stewart, 1988.

Wells, Paul. *Right Side Up. The Fall of Paul Martin and the Rise of Stephen Harper's New Conservatism.* Toronto: McClelland & Stewart. 2007.

———. *The Longer I'm Prime Minister. Stephen Harper and Canada.* Random House Canada, 2014.

Whitehorn, Alan. *Canadian Socialism. Essays of CCF-NDP.* Don Mills, Ont: Oxford University Press, 1992.

Woods, Shirley E. *Her Excellency Jeanne Sauve.* Toronto: Cross Canada Books, 1986.

Wilson-Smith, Anthony. *Double Vision: The Inside Story of the Liberals in Power.* Toronto: Doubleday, 1996.

Wright, Robert. *Trudeaumania.* 2016.

V. FEDERALISM, REGIONALISM, PROVINCIAL POLITICS AND NATIVE PEOPLES

Alfred, Taiaiake. *Peace, Power, Righteousness. An Indigenous Manifesto.* New York: Oxford University, 1999.

Bibliography

Anderson, Alun. *After the Ice: Life, Death and Geopolitics in the New Arctic.* Washington: Smithsonian (Virgin Books), 2009.

Archer, Keith, and Young, U., eds. *Regionalism and Party Politics in Canada.* New York: Oxford University, 2000.

Asch, Michael. *Home and Native Land: Aboriginal Rights and the Canadian Constitution.* Toronto: Methuen, 1984.

Banting, Keith and Simeon, Richard. *And No One Cheered. Federalism, Democracy and the Constitution Act.* Toronto: Methuen, 1983.

Banting, Keith. *The Welfare State and Canadian Federalism* 2nd ed. Montreal: McGill-Queen's University Press, 1987.

Barman, Jean. *The West beyond the West. A History of British Columbia.* Toronto: University of Toronto Press, 1993.

Bennett, A., et al. *Inuit of the North.* Markham, Ont: Fitzhenry Whiteside, n.d.

Berger, Thomas R. *Northern Frontier, Northern Homeland.* Vancouver: Douglas McIntyre, 1988.

Bolger, F.W.P., ed. *Canada's Smallest Province: A History of P.E.I.* Charlottetown, P.E.I.: 1973.

Bone, Robert M. *The Geography of the Canadian North.* Don Mills, Ont: Oxford University Press, 1992.

Bothwell, Robert. *Canada since 1945. Power, Politics and Provincialism.* Toronto: University of Toronto Press, 1982.

Brym, Robert J., ed. *Regionalism in Canada.* Richmond Hill, Ont.: Irwin, 1986.

Byers, Michael. *Who Owns the Arctic.* 2013.

Careless, J.M.S. *Toronto to 1918. An Illustrated History.* Toronto: James Lorimer, 1985.

Cassidy, Frank, ed. *Aboriginal Self-Determination.* Lantzville, BC: Oolichan Books, 1991.

Coates, Kenneth. *Aboriginal Land Claims in Canada.* Toronto: Copp Clark Pitman, 1992.

Conway, J.F. *The West: The History of a Region in Confederation.* Toronto: James Lorimer, 1983.

Cox, Bruce Alden, ed. *Native People, Native Lands. Canadian Indians, Inuit and Metis.* Ottawa: Carleton Univ. Press, 1987.

Crowe, Keith J. *A History of the Original Peoples of Northern Canada.* Rev. ed. Montreal: McGills-Queens University Press, 1991.

Dickerson, Mark O. *Whose North? Political Change, Political Development, and Self-Government in the Northwest Territories.* Vancouver: University of British Columbia Press, 1992.

Dickason, Olive P. *Canada's First Nations. A History of Founding Peoples from Earliest Times.* Markham, Ont: McClelland Stewart, 1992.

Duffy, R. Quinn. *The Road to Nunavut. The Progress of the Eastern Arctic Inuit Since the Second World War.* Montreal: McGill-Queen's Univ. Press, 1988.

Elias, Peter D. *Development of Aboriginal People's Communities.* North York, Ont: Captus Press, 1991.

Ellis, Richard. *On Thin Ice: The Changing World of the Polar Bear.* New York: Knopf, 2009.

Forbes, E.R. and Muise, D.A., eds. *The Atlantic Provinces in Confederation.* Toronto: University of Toronto Press, 1993.

Francis, R. Douglas and Palmer, Howard, eds. *The Prairie West. Historical Readings.* 2nd ed. Edmonton, Alb: University of Alberta Press, 1992.

Frideres, James. *Native People in Canada: Contemporary Conflicts.* 3rd. ed. Scarborough, Ont: Prentice Hall, 1988.Friesen, Gerald. *The Canadian Prairies. A History.* Toronto: University of Toronto Press, 1984.

Friesen, John W. *The Cultural Maze: Complex Questions on Native Destiny.* Calgary: Temeron Books, 1991.

Gallant, Melvin. *The Country of Acadia.* Toronto: Simon Pierre, 1985.

Gibbins, Roger. *Regionalism. Territorial Politics in Canada and the United States.* Toronto: Butterworths, 1982.

Giraud, Marcel. *The Métis in the Canadian West (Le Métis Canadien).* Translated by George Woodstock. Edmonton: University of Alberta Press, 1986.

Griffiths, N.E.S. *The Acadians: Creation of a People.* Toronto: McGraw-Hill Ryerson, 1973.

Hamilton, John David. *The Arctic Revolution. Social Change in the NWT 1935–1993.* Toronto: Dundurn Press, 1993.

Hiller, J. and Neary, P., eds. *Newfoundland in the Nineteenth and Twentieth Centuries.*

Ibbitson, John. *Promised Land: Inside the Mike Harris Revolution.* 1997.

Johnston, Wayne. *The Colony of Unrequited Dreams.* (Novel about Joe Smallwood and Newfoundland) NY: Anchor Books, 2000.

Lauritzen, Philip. *Oil and Amulets: Inuit—A People at the Top of the World.* St. John's, Newf.: Breakwater Books, 1983.

Lemon, James. *Toronto Since 1918. An Illustrated History.* Toronto: James Lorimer, 1985.

Levine, Allen. *Toronto: Biography of a City,* 2014.

Little Bear, Leroy, et al, eds. *Pathways to Self-Determination. Canadian Indians and the Canadian State.* Toronto: University of Toronto Press, 1984.

Long, Anthony and Boldt, Menno. *Governments in Conflict? Provinces and Indian Nations in Canada.* Toronto: University of Toronto Press, 1989.

Malone, Greg. *Don't Tell The Newfoundlanders: The True Story of Newfoundland's Confederation with Canada.* 2012.

Melnyk, George, et. *Riel to Reform. A History of Protest in Western Canada.* Saskatoon, Sask: Fifth House, 1991.

Milne, David. *Tug of War. Ottawa and the Provinces under Trudeau and Mulroney.* Toronto: James Lorimer, 1986.

Molyneux, Geoffrey. *British Columbia. An Illustrated History.* Vancouver: Polestar, 1992.

Morley, J.T. *Secular Socialists: The CCF/NDP in Ontario, A Biography.* Montreal: McGill-Queen's University Press, 1984.

Morrison, R. Bruce and Wilson, C. Roderick, eds. *The Native Peoples.* McClelland Stewart, 1986.

Morse, Bradford W., ed. *Aboriginal Peoples and the Law. Indian, Métis and Inuit Rights in Canada.* Ottawa: Carleton University Press, 1984.

Morton, W.L. *Manitoba: A History.* 2nd ed. Toronto: 1967.

Neary, Peter and Hiller, James, eds. *Twentieth Century Newfoundland: Explorations.* St. Johns: Breakwater, 1993.

Nikiforuk, Sheila Pratt and Wanagas, Don, eds. *Running on Empty. Alberta After The Boom.* Edmonton: NeWest Press, 1987.

Olling, Randy and Westmacott, Martin, eds. *Perspectives on Canadian Federalism.* Scarborough, Ont: Prentice-Hall, 1988.

Ormsby, M. *British Columbia: A History.* Toronto: 1968.

Palmer, Hans and Tamara, eds. *Peoples of Alberta. Portraits of Cultural Diversity.* Saskatoon, Sask: Western Producer Prairie Books, 1985.

———. *Alberta: A New History.* Markham, Ont: McClelland Stewart, 1990.

Patterson, E.P., III. *The Canadian Indian: A History since 1500.* Don Mills, Ont.: 1972.

Peterson, Jacqueline and Brown, Jennifer, eds. *The New Peoples: Being and Becoming Métis in North America.* Winnipeg: University of Manitoba Press, 1984.

Purich, Donald. *Our Land, Native Rights in Canada.* Toronto: James Lorimer, 1987.

———. *The Inuit and Their Land. The Story of Nunavut.* Toronto: James Lorimer, 1993.

Rasporich, A.W., ed. *The Making of the Modern West.* Calgary: University of Calgary Press, 1984.

Ray, Arthur. *I Have Lived Here Since the World Began.* General Publishing, 1996.

Riggs, A.R. and Velk, Tom. *Federalism in Peril.* Vancouver: Fraser Institute, 1992.

Robinson, J. Lewis. *Concepts and Themes in the Regional Geography of Canada.* Vancouver: Talon Books, Ltd., 1983.

Rocher, François and Smith, Miriam. *New Trends in Canadian Federalism.* Peterborough, Ont: Broadview Press, 1994.

Ross, Sally and Deveau, Alphonse. *The Acadians of Nova Scotia.* Halifax: Nimbus, 1992.

Saywell, John T. *The Office of Lieutenant-Governor.* Toronto: Copp Clark Pittman, Ltd., 1985.

Smiley, D.V. *Federal Condition in Canada.* Toronto: McGraw-Hill Ryerson, 1987.

Stelter, Gilbert A. and Artibise, Alan F.J. *The Canadian City. Essays in Urban and Social History.* Ottawa: Carleton University Press, 1984.

Taylor, John H. *Ottawa. An Illustrated History.* Toronto: James Lorimer, 1986.

Trudeau, Pierre Elliott. *Federalism and the French Canadians.* Toronto: Macmillan, 1968.

Tuohy, Carolyn J. *Policy and Politics in Canada. Institutionalized Ambivalence.* Philadelphia: Temple University Press, 1992.

Tupper, Allan and Gibbins, Roger. *Government and Politics in Alberta.* Edmonton: University of Alberta Press, 1992.

Weaver, R. Kent, ed. *The Collapse of Canada?* Washington, D.C.: Brookings Institution, 1992.

Webb, Melody. *Yukon. The Last Frontier.* Vancouver: University of British Columbia Press, 1993.

White, Graham. *The Ontario Legislature. A Political Analysis.* Toronto: University of Toronto Press, 1989.

———. and Levy, Gary, eds. *Provincial and Territorial Assemblies in Canada.* Toronto: Toronto University Press, 1989.

White, Randall. *Ontario 1610–1985. A Political and Economic History.* Toronto: Dundurn, 1985.

Wiseman, Nelson. *Social Democracy in Manitoba: A History of the CCF-NDP 1932–1977.* Winnipeg: University of Manitoba Press, 1984.

Woods, Jr., Shirley E. *Ottawa.* Toronto: Doubleday Canada Ltd., 1985.

Wotherspoon, Terry and Satzewich, Vic. *First Nations: A Struggle for Equality.* Scarborough, Ont: Nelson, 1992.

Zellen, Barry. *Breaking the Ice. From Land Claims to Tribal Sovereignty in the Arctic.* Lanham, MD: Rowman Littlefield, 2008.

VI. FOREIGN AND DEFENSE POLICY

Andrew, Arthur. *The Rise and Fall of a Middle Power: Canadian Diplomacy from King to Mulroney.* Toronto: James Lorimer, 1993.

Bercuson, David. *Significant Incident: Canada's Army, the Airborne, and the Murder in Somalia.* Markham, Ont.: McClelland & Stewart, 1996.

——— and J. L. Granatstein. *Dictionary of Canadian Military History.* Toronto: Oxford University, 1992.

Blanchard, James. *Behind the Embassy Door: Canada, Clinton and Quebec.* 1998.

Bothwell, Robert. *Your Country, My Country. A Unified History of the United States and Canada.* 2015.

Cellucci, Paul. *Unquiet Diplomacy.* Toronto: Key Porter, 2005.

Clarkson, Stephen. *Canada and the Reagan Challenge.* Toronto: James Lorimer, 1982.

Cohen, Andrew. *While Canada Slept. How We Lost our Place in the World.* Toronto: McClelland and Steward, 2004.

Cooper, Andrew F. *Tests of Global Governance. Canadian Diplomacy and United Nations World Conferences.* Washington: Brookings, 2004.

Cuff, Robert D. *Ties that Bind: Canadian-American Relations in Wartime from the Great War to the Cold War.* Toronto: Hakkert, 1977.

Curtis, Kenneth M. and Carroll, John E. *Canadian-American Relations. The Promise and the Challenge.* Lexington, MA: Lexington Books, 1983.

Cutler, A. Claire and Zacher, Mark W., eds. *Canadian Foreign Policy and International Economic Regimes.* Vancouver: University of British Columbia Press, 1992.

DeFede, Jim. *The Day the World Came to Town: 9/11 in Gander, Newfoundland.* 2003.

Dewitt, David B. and Kirton, John J. *Canada as a Principal Power. A Study in Foreign Policy and International Relations.* Toronto and New York: John Wiley, 1983.

Diubaldo, Richard J. *A Study of Canadian-American Defence Policy, 1945–1975: Northern Issues and Strategic Resources.* Ottawa: Department of National Defense, 1978.

Doran, Charles F. and Sigler, John H., eds. *Canada and the United States.* Scarborough, Ont.: Prentice-Hall, 1985.

Douglas, W.A.B., ed. *The Royal Canadian Navy in Transition, 1910–1985.* Vancouver: University of British Columbia Press, 1988.

Downton, Eric. *Pacific Challenge. Canada's Future in the New Asia.* Don Mills, Ont: Stoddart, 1986.

English, John and Hillmer, Norman, eds. *Making a Difference? Canada's Foreign Policy in a Changing World Order.* Toronto, Lester, 1992.

Flaherty, David and McKercher, William. *Southern Exposure.* Scarborough: McGraw-Hill Ryerson, Ltd., 1986.

Fox, William T.R. *A Continent Apart.* Toronto: University of Toronto Press, 1985.

Gotlieb, Allan. *Washington Diaries.* 2006.

Granatstein, J.L. *Canadian Foreign Policy. Historical Readings.* Rev. ed. Toronto: Copp Clark Pitman, 1992.

———. *Torwards a New World. Readings in the History of Canadian Foreign Policy.* Toronto: Copp Clark Pitman, 1992.

———. and Hillmer, Norman. *For Better or For Worse. Canada and the United States in the 1990s.* Toronto: Copp Clark Pitman, 1992.

Grant, Shelagh. *Polar Imperative: A History of Arctic Sovereignty in North America.* 2011.

Griffiths, Franklyn, ed. *Politics of the Northwest Passage.* Montreal: McGill-Queen's Univ. Press, 1987.

Gwyn, Richard. *The 49th Paradox: Canada in North America.* Toronto: McClelland and Stewart, 1985.

Haglund, David. G. and Sokolsky, Joel J. *The U.S.-Canada Security Relationship.* Boulder, CO: Westview Press, 1989.

Haycock, R.G. and Hunt, B.D. *Canada's Defence.* Toronto: Copp Clark Pitman, 1993.

Hillier, Gen. Rich. *A Soldier First: Bullets, Bureaucrats and the Politics of War.* 2009.

Holmes, John W. *Life with Uncle. The Canadian-American Relationship.* Toronto: University of Toronto Press, 1981.

Honderich, John. *Arctic Imperative. Is Canada Losing the North?* Toronto: Univ. of Toronto Press, 1987.

Jockel, Joseph T. *Security to the North. Canada-U.S. Defense Relations in the 1990s.* East Lansing: Michigan State University Press, 1991.

———. *No Boundaries Upstairs. Canada, The United States and the Origins of North American Air Defence, 1945–1958.* Vancouver: Univ. of British Columbia Press, 1987.

——— and Sokolsky, Joel. *Canada and Collective Security. Odd Man Out.* New York: Praeger, 1986.

Jockel, Joseph T. *Canada and International Peacekeeping.* Washington, D.C.: Center for Strategic and International Studies, 1994.

Keating, Tom. *Canada and World Order. The Multilateralist Tradition in Canadian Foreign Policy.* Markham, Ont: McClelland Stewart, 1993.

Kirton, John. *Canadian Foreign Policy in a Changing World.* 2007.

Laxer, James. *Stalking the Elephant: My Discovery of America.* New York: Viking, 2000.

Mahant, Edelgard E. and Mount, Graeme S. *An Introduction to Canadian-American Relations.* 2nd ed. Toronto: Methuen, 1989.

Martin, Lawrence. *The Presidents and the Prime Ministers. Washington and Ottawa Face to Face: The Myth of Bilateral Bliss 1867–1982.* Markham, Ont.: Paper Jacks, 1984.

McQuaig, Linda. *Holding the Bully's Coat: Canada and the U.S. Empire.* Toronto: Doubleday, 2007.

Middlemiss, Danford W. and Sokolsky, Joel. *Canadian Defence. Decisions and Determinants.* Toronto: HBJ/Holt, 1989.

Molot, Maureen Appel, and Hampson, Fen Osler, eds. *Canada Among Nations 2000.* New York: Oxford University, 2000.

Bibliography

———. eds. *Canada Among Nations 1999. A Big League Player?* New York: Oxford University, 1999.

Morton, Desmond. *A Military History of Canada From Champlain to the Gulf War.* Markham, Ont: McClelland Stewart, 1992.

Munton, D. and Kirton, J. *Canadian Foreign Policy.* Scarborough, Ont: Prentice-Hall, 1992.

Nossal, Kim Richard. *The Politics of Canadian Foreign Policy.* 2nd ed. Scarborough, Ont: Prentice-Hall Canada, 1989.

Orvik, Nils, ed. *Canada and NATO.* Kingston: Queen's University Press, 1982.

Pearson, Geoffrey A.H. *Lester B. Pearson and Crisis Democracy.* Ottawa: Carleton University Press, 1993.

Porter, Gerald. *In Retreat: The Canadian Forces in the Trudeau Years.* Ottawa: Deneau and Greenberg, n.d.

Preston, Richard A. *To Serve Canada. A History of the Royal Military College Since the Second World War.* Ottawa: University of Ottawa Press, 1991.

Reflections from the Past. Perspectives on Canada and on the Canada-U.S. Relationship. Plattsburgh, NY: Center for the Study of Canada, 1991.

Rosenblum, Simon. *Misguided Missiles.* Toronto: James Lorimer Company, 1985.

Shiels, Frederick L. *Ethnic Separatism and World Politics.* Lanham, MD: University Press of America, 1984.

Simpson, Jeffrey. *Star-Spangled Canadians: Canadians Living the American Dream.* New York: HarperCollins, 2000.

Stacey, C.P. *Canada and the Age of Conflict: A History of Canadian External Policies, 1867–1921,* vol. 1, and *The Mackenzie King Era, 1921–1948,* vol. 2. Toronto: Macmillan, 1977.

———. *Arms, Men and Governments: The War Policies of Canada, 1939–1945.* Ottawa: 1970.

Stein, Janice Gross and Lang, Eugene. *The Unexpected War. Canada in Kandahar.* Toronto: Penguin, 2007.

Thomas, David, ed. *Canada and the United States. Differences that Count.* Peterborough, Ont: Broadview Press, 1993.

Thompson, John Herd and Randall, Stephen J. *Canada and the United States. Ambivalent Allies.* Montreal: McGill-Queens University Press, 1993.

VII. QUEBEC

Arnopoulos, Sheila McLeod and Clift, Dominique. *The English Fact in Quebec.* Montreal: McGill-Queen's Univeristy Press, 1980.

Beach, Richard. *Alliance or Alienation. Québec & Canada as the Century Turns.* Plattsburgh, NY: Center for the Study of Canada, 2000.

Behiels, Michael D., ed. *Quebec Since 1945. Selected Readings.* Toronto: Copp Clark Pitman, 1987.

Bercuson, David. *Deconfederation: Canada Without Quebec.* Toronto: Key Porter, 1991.

Bernier, Luc. *From Paris to Washington: Quebec's Foreign Policy in a Changing World.* Washington, D.C.: Center for Strategic and International Studies, 1994.

Bourhis, Richard Y., ed. *Conflict and Language Planning in Quebec.* Clevedon, Avon, England: Multilingual Matters, 1984.

Center for the Study of Canada. *L'Americanité des Québécois.* Plattsburgh, NY, 2002.

Clift, Dominique. *Quebec Nationalism in Crisis.* Montreal: McGill-Queen's University Press, 1980.

Coleman, William D. *The Independence Movement in Quebec 1945–1980.* Toronto: University of Toronto Press, 1984.

Conologue, Ray. *Impossible Nation: The Longing for Homeland in Canada and Quebec.* General Publishing, 1996.

Dickinson, John and Young, Brian. *A Short History of Quebec.* 2nd rev. ed. Toronto: Copp Clark Pitman, 1993.

Dodge, William, ed. *Boundaries of Identity. A Quebec Reader.* Toronto: Lester, 1992.

Drache, D. and Perin, R. *Negotiating with a Sovereign Quebec.* Toronto: James Lorimer, 1993.

Eccles, W. J. *The French in North America, 1500–1782.* Rev. ed. Markham, Ont: Fitzhenry Whiteside, 1998.

Fidler, Richard. *Canada, Adieu? Quebec Debates its Future.* Latzville, BC: Oolichan Books, 1991.

Fitzmaurice, John. *Quebec and Canada: Past, Present, and Future.* New York: St. Martin's, 1985.

Fournier, Pierre. *The Quebec Establishment. The Ruling Class and the State.* Montreal: Black Rose Books, 1988.

Ganon, Alain G., ed. *Quebec: State and Society in Crisis.* Toronto: Methuen, 1984.

Gilbert, Paula Ruth, et al. *Women Writers in Quebec. Essays in Honor of Jeanne Kissner.* Plattsburgh, NY: Center for the Study of Canada, 2002.

Griffin, Anne. *Quebec. The Challenge of Independence.* Cranbury, NJ: Associated University Presses, 1984.

Guindon, Hubert. *Tradition, Modernity, and Nationhood. Essays on Quebec Society.* Toronto: University of Toronto Press, 1989.

Hero, A.O., Jr. and Balthazar, Louis. *Contemporary Quebec the United States.* Lanham, MD: University Press of America, 1988.

Jacobs, Jane. *The Question of Separatism. Quebec and the Struggle over Sovereignty.* New York: Vintage Books, 1981.

Lachapelle, Guy. *The Quebec Democracy. Structures, Processes and Policies.* Toronto: McGraw Hill Ryerson, 1993.

Laczko, Leslie S. *Pluralism and Inequality in Quebec.* New York: St. Martin's, 1994.

Leonard, Jean-François and Leveillee, Jacques. *Montreal after Drapeau.* Montreal: Black Rose Books, 1988.

Lévesque, Réne. *My Quebec.* Toronto: Totem Books, 1979.

Levine, Marc. *The Reconquest of Montreal: Language Policy and Social Change in a Bilingual City.* Philadelphia: Temple University Press, 1990.

McRoberts, Kenneth. *Quebec. Social Change and Political Crisis.* 3rd ed. Toronto: McClelland and Stewart, 1988.

Milner, Henry. *Politics in the New Quebec.* Toronto: McClelland and Stewart, 1978.

Moniere, D. *Ideologies in Quebec: The Historical Development.* Toronto: 1981.

Nardochhio, Elaine F. *Theatre and Politics in Modern Quebec. A History.* Edmonton: University of Alberta Press, 1985.

Nish, C. *The French Regime.* Scarborough, Ont.: Prentice-Hall, 1965.

Ouellet, Fernand. *Economy, Class, and Nation in Quebec.* Toronto: Copp Clark Pitman, 1991.

Parizeau, Jacques. *For a Sovereign Quebec.* 1997.

Poliquin, Daniel. *Extraordinary Canadians: René Lévesque.* Penguin Group (Canada), 2009.

Quinlan, Don. *Images of French Canada.* Markham, Ont: Fitzhenry Whiteside, 1988.

Reid, Scott. *Canada Remapped. How the Partition of Quebec Will Reshape the Nation.* Vancouver: Arsenal Pulp Press, 1992.

Richler, Mordecai. *Oh Canada! Oh Quebec! Requiem for a Divided Country.* Toronto: Penguin, 1992.

Robinson, Sinclair and Smith, Donald. *Practical Handbook of Quebec and Acadian French.* Toronto: Anansi, 1984.

Roussopoulos, Dimitrios I, ed. *Quebec and Radical Social Change.* Montreal: Black Rose Books, 1988.

Saywell, John. *The Rise of the Parti Quebecois 1967–1976.* Toronto: University of Toronto Press, 1977.

Shaw, William F. and Albert, Lionel. *Partition. The Price of Quebec's Independence.* Montreal: Thornhill, 1980.

Trofimenkoff, Susan Mann. *The Dream of Nation. A Social and Intellectual History of Quebec.* Toronto: Gage, 1983.

Vallieres, Pierre. *White Niggers of America.* Toronto: McClelland and Stewart, 1971.

———. *The Impossible Quebec. Illusions of Sovereignty-Association.* Montreal: Black Rose Books, 1988.

Wade, M. *The French Canadians*. 2 vols. Rev. ed. Toronto: 1975, 1976.

Walker, Douglas C. *The Pronunciation of Canadian French*. Ottawa: University of Ottawa Press, 1985.

VIII. ECONOMY

Anderson, F.J. *Natural Resources in Canada. Economic Theory and Policy*. Toronto: Methuen, 1985.

Armstrong, Muriel. *The Canadian Economy and Its Problems*. 4th ed. Scarborough, Ont.: Prentice-Hall, 1988.

Brodie, Janine. *The Political Economy of Canadian Regionalism*. Toronto: Harcourt Brace Jovanovich, 1990.

Caloren, Fred, ed. *Is the Canadian Economy Closing Down?* Montreal: Black Rose Books, 1988.

The Canada-U.S. Economic Relationship. Plattsburgh, NY: Center for the Study of Canada, 1991.

Crane, David. *The Next Canadian Century. Building a Competitive Economy*. Don Mills, Ont: Stoddart, 1993.

Doern, Bruce and Toner, Glen. *The Politics of Energy. The Development and Implementation of the NEP*. Toronto: Methuen, 1985.

Fallis, George. *The Costs of Constitutional Change*. Toronto: James Lorimer, 1993.

French, Richard and van Loon, Richard. *How Ottawa Decides: Planning and Industrial Policy-Making 1968–1983*. Rev. ed. Toronto: James Lorimer, 1984.

Fry, Earl H. *Canada's Unity Crisis. Implications for U.S.-Canada Economic Relations*. Washington D.C.: Brookings, 1992.

Globerman, Steven and Walker, Michael. *Assessing NAFTA*. Vancouver: Fraser Institute, 1993.

Hoebing, Joyce, et al. *NAFTA and Sovereignty*. Washington, D.C.: CSIS Press, 1996.

Howlett, Michael, Netherton, Alex, and Ramesh, M. *The Political Economy of Canada*. 2nd ed. New York: Oxford University, 1999.

Ismael, Jacqueline S., eds. *Canadian Welfare State. Evolution and Transition*. Edmonton: Univ. of Alberta Press, 1987.

Langdon, Frank. *The Politics of Canadian-Japanese Economic Relations, 1952–1983*. Vancouver: University of British Columbia Press, 1983.

Laxer, James. *Leap of Faith. Free Trade and the Future of Canada*. Edmonton: Hurtig, 1986.

Leslie, Peter. *Federal State, National Economy*. Toronto: Univ. of Toronto Press, 1987.

Levant, Ezra. *Ethical Oil: The Case for Canada's Oil Sands*. 2011.

Levi, Michael A. *The Canadian Oil Sands: Energy Security vs. Climate Change*. Washington, DC: Brookings, 2009.

Muirhead, B.W. *The Development of Postwar Canadian Trade Policy*. Montreal: McGill-Queen's University Press, 1992.

Naylor, C. David, ed. *Canadian Health Care and the State*. Montreal: McGills-Queen's University Press, 1992.

Pomfred, Richard. *The Economic Development of Canada*. 2nd ed. Scarborough, Ont: Nelson, 1992.

Pritchard, Robert S., ed. *Crown Corporations in Canada*. Toronto: Butterworths, 1983.

Rea, Kenneth. *A Guide to Canadian Economic History*. Toronto: Canadian Scholars' Press, 1993.

Safarian, A.E. *The Canadian Economy in the Great Depression*. Toronto: 1970.

Sarlo, Christopher A. *Poverty in Canada*. Vancouver: Fraser Institute, 1992.

Schott, Jeffrey J. and Smith, Murray G., eds. *The Canada-United States Free Trade Agreement: The Global Impact*. Washington, DC: Institute for International Economics, 1988.

Sitwell, O.F.G. and Seifried, Neil R.M. *The Regional Structure of the Canadian Economy*. Toronto: Methuen, 1984.

Vogt, Roy, et al. *Economics. Understanding the Canadian Economy*. 4th ed. Toronto: HBJ-Holt, 1993.

Watkins, M.H. and Grant, H.M.K. *Canadian Economic History*. Ottawa: Carleton University Press, 1993.

IX. CULTURE AND SOCIETY

Ashworth, Mary. *Children of the Canadian Mosaic. A Brief History to 1950*. Toronto: Oise Press, 1992.

Backhouse, Constance and Flaherty, David H, eds. *Challenging Times. The Women's Movement in Canada and the United States*. Montreal: McGills-Queens University Press, 1992.

Baker, Maureen, ed. *The Family: Changing Trends in Canada*. Scarborough, Ont.: McGraw-Hill Reyerson, 1984.

Balkind, Alvin, et al. *Visions/Contemporary Art in Canada*. Vancouver, B.C.: Douglas and McIntyre, 1983.

Berkowitz, S.D., ed. *Models and Myths in Canadian Sociology*. Toronto: Butterworths, 1984.

Berry, J.W. and Laponce, J.A., eds. *Multiculturalism in Canada. A Review of Research*. Toronto: University of Toronto Press, 1993.

Bibby, Reginald W. and Poterski, Donald C. *The Emerging Generation*. Irwin Publishing, Inc., 1985.

Bibby, Reginald W. *Restless Gods: The Renaissance of Religion in Canada*. Don Mills, Ont.: Stoddart, 2002.

Bird, Michael. *Canadian Folk Art. Old Ways in a New Land*. Don Mills, Ont.: Oxford University Press, 1983.

Bolaria, B. Singh, ed. *Social Issues and Contradictions in Canadian Society*. Toronto: Harcourt Brace, 1991.

Brannigan, Augustine. *Crimes, Courts, and Corrections: An Introduction to Crime and Social Control in Canada*. Toronto: Holt, Rinehart Winston, 1984.

Buchignani, Norman. *Cultures in Canada: Strength in Diversity*. Regina, Sask.: L.A. Weigl Educational Associates, 1984.

Burnet, Jean and Palmer, Howard. *Coming Canadians. An Introduction to a History of Canada's Peoples*. Markham, Ont: McClelland Stewart, 1988.

Burnett, David and Schiff, Marilyn. *Contemporary Canadian Art*. Edmonton, Alb.: Hurtig, 1983.

Canada in Film and Video. Plattsburgh, NY: Canadian Film Distribution Center (phone: 1-800-388-6784), annually updated.

Chacko, James. *Cultural Sovereignty: Myth or Reality*. Windsor, Ont.: University of Windsor Press, 1986.

Cédilot, André and André Noël. *Mafia Inc.: The Long, Bloody Reign of Canada's Sicilian Clan*. 2011.

Clandfield, David. *Canadian Film*. Don Mills, Ont: Oxford Univ. Press, 1987.

Clarkson, Adrienne. *Room for All of Us*. Allen Lane, 2012.

Colombo, John Robert. *Canadian Literary Landmarks*. Willowdale, Ont.: Hounslow, 1984.

———. *Contemporary Canadian Photography. From the Collection of the National Film Board*. Edmonton, Alb: Hurtig, 1984.

The Dictionary of Canadian Quotations. Don Mills, Ont: Stoddart, 1991.

Crean, Susan and Rioux, Marcel. *Two Nations: An Essay on the Culture and Politics of Canada and Quebec in a World of American Pre-eminence*. Toronto: James Lorimer, 1983.

Cross, Michael S. and Kealey, Gregory S., eds. *Modern Canada. 1930–1980s. Readings in Canadian Social History*. vol. 5. Toronto: McClelland and Stewart, 1984.

Driedger, Leo, ed. *The Canadian Mosaic. A Quest for Identity*. Toronto: McClelland and Stewart, 1978.

———. *Ethnic Canada: Identities and Inequalities*. Mississauga, Ont.: Copp Clark Pitman, 1987.

Elliott, Jean Leonard, ed. *Two Nations, Many Cultures. Ethnic Groups in Canada*. 2nd ed. Scarborough, Ont.: Prentice-Hall, 1983.

Feldman, Seth, ed. *Take Two. A Tribute to Canadian Film*. Richmond Hill, Ont.: Irwin, 1984.

Forcese, Dennis and Richter, Stephen, eds. *Social Issues: Sociological Views of Canada*. Scarborough, Ont.: Prentice-Hall, 1982.

Forcese, Dennis. *The Canadian Class Structure*. Scarborough: McGraw-Hill Ryerson, Ltd., 1986.

Francis, Daniel. *The Imaginary Indian. The Image of the Indian in Canadian Culture*. Vancouver: Arsenal Pulp Press, 1992.

Bibliography

Friesen, John W. *When Cultures Clash. Case Studies in Multiculturalism.* Calgary, Alb.: Temeron Books, 1993.

Frye, Northrop. *Divisions on a Ground: Essays on Canadian Culture.* Toronto: Anansi, 1982.

Globerman, Steven. *The Immigration Dilemma.* Vancouver: Fraser Institute, 1992.

Haas, J., et al. *Shaping Identity in Canadian Society.* Scarborough, Ont.: Prentice-Hall, 1978.

Harper, Stephen. A Great Game. The Forgotten Leafs & The Rise of Professional Hockey. 2013.

Herberg, Edward N. *Ethnic Groups in Canada. Adaptations and Transitions.* Scarborough, Ont: Methuen, 1988.

Huang, Evelyn and Jeffrey, Lawrence. *Chinese Canadians.* Vancouver: Douglas McIntyre, 1992.

Joy, Richard J. *Canada's Official Languages. The Progress of Bilingualism.* Toronto: University of Toronto Press, 1992.

Kallen, Evelyn. *Ethnicity and Human Rights in Canada.* 2nd ed. New York: Oxford University Press, 1995.

Kallmann, Helmut, et al, eds. *Encyclopedia of Music in Canada.* 2nd ed. Toronto: University of Toronto Press, 1992.

Knowles, Valerie. *Strangers at Our Gates. Canadian Immigration and Immigration Policy, 1540–1990.* Toronto: Dundurn Press, 1992.

Kymlicka, Will. *Finding Our Way. Rethinking Ethno-cultural Relations in Canada.* New York: Oxford University Press, 1998.

Link, Eugene P. *The T.B.'s Progress. Norman Bethune as Artist.* Plattsburgh, NY: Center for the Study of Canada, 1991.

MacNeil, Robert. *Burden of Desire.* A Harvest Book, n.d.

Marchak, M. Patricia. *Ideological Perspectives on Canada.* 3rd ed. Scarborough, Ont: McGraw-Hill Ryerson, 1987.

Marchand, Philip. *Marshall McLuhan: The Medium & the Messenger.* Cambridge: MIT Press, 1998.

Miles, Angele and Finn, Geraldine, eds. *Feminism in Canada. From Pressure to Politics.* Montreal: Black Rose Books, 1982.

Morris, Peter. *The Film Companion. A Comprehensive Guide to More than 650 Canadian Films and Filmmakers.* Richmond Hill, Ont.: Irwin, 1984.

Murray, Joan. *The Best of the Group of Seven.* Edmonton, Alb: Hurtig, 1984.

Nemiroff, Diana, et al, eds. *Land Spirit Power. First Nations at the National Gallery of Canada.* Ottawa: National Gallery of Art, 1992.

Porter, John. *The Measure of Canadian Society: Education, Equality, and Opportunity.* Ottawa: Carleton Univ. Press, 1988.

Reid, Dennis. *A Concise History of Canadian Painting.* 2nd ed. Don Mills, Ont.: Oxford University Press, 1988.

Rooney, John F., Jr., et al, eds. *The Remarkable Continent: An Atlas of the United States and Canadian Society and Cultures.* College Station, TX: Texas A&M Press, 1982.

Ross, Jeffrey Ian, ed. *Violence in Canada. Sociological Perspectives.* New York: Oxford University Press, 1996.

Shek, Ben-Z. *French-Canadian and Quebecois Novels.* Oxford: Oxford University Press, 1991.

Story, G.M. et al, eds. *Dictionary of Newfoundland English.* 2nd ed. Toronto: University of Toronto Press, 2002.

Tippett, Maria. *By a Lady. Celebrating Three Centuries of Art by Canadian Women.* Toronto: Penguin, 1992.

Trofimenkoff, Susan Mann and Prentice, Alison, eds. *The Neglected Majority. Volume 2. Essays in Canadian Women's History.* Toronto: McClelland and Stewart, 1985.

Webber, James D. *Reimagining Canada. Language, Culture, Community, and the Canadian Constitution.* Montreal: McGill-Queen's University Press, 1993.

Webster, Judith. *Voices of Canada. An Introduction to Canadian Culture.* Burlington, VT: Assoc. for Canadian Studies in the United States, 1977.

X. FICTION LITERATURE

Atwood, Margaret. *Surfacing.* Toronto: McClelland and Stewart, 1972.

———. *Lady Oracle.* Toronto: McClelland and Stewart, 1976.

———. *Life before Man.* Toronto: McClelland and Stewart, 1979.

———. Survival: A Thematic Guide to Canadian Literature.

———. ed. *The New Oxford Book of Canadian Verse in English.* Don Mills, Ont: Oxford Univ. Press, 1982.

———. and Weaver, Robert, eds. *The Oxford Book of Canadian Short Stories in English.* Don Mills, Ont: Oxford Univ. Press, 1988.

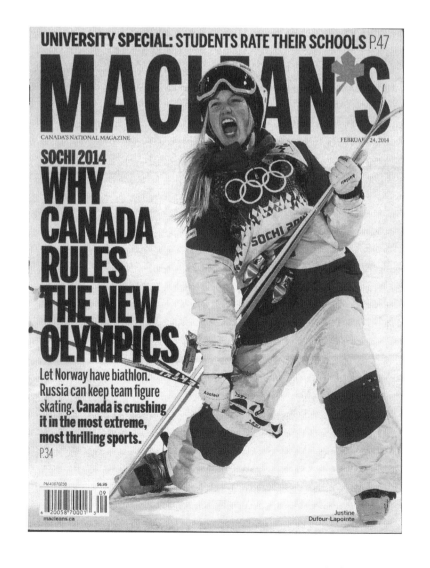

———. *Alias Grace.* 1996.

———. *The Blind Assassin.* New York: Doubleday, 2000.

———. *The Year of the Flood.* Bloomsbury, 2009.

Carrier, Roch. *La Guerre, yes sir!* Trans. Sheila Fischman. Toronto: Anansi, 1970.

Davidson, Arnold E. *Coyote Country. Fictions of the Canadian West.* Durham, NC: Duke University Press, 1993.

Gustafson, Ralph, ed. *The Penguin Book of Canadian Verse.* Markham, Ont.: Penguin, 1984. Toronto: Anansi, 1972.

Hebert, Anne. *Kamouraska.* Trans. Norman Shapiro. Toronto: Musson, 1973.

Hemon, Louis. *Maria Chapdelaine.* Trans. W.H. Blake. Toronto: Macmillan, 1921.

Keith, W.J. *Canadian Literature in English.* Toronto: Copp Clark Pitman, 1985.

———. *Literary Images of Ontario.* Toronto: University of Toronto Press, 1992.

Kirby, Peter. *The Dead of Winter.* 2012. (A first crime novel in a setting of colorful and gritty Montreal).

Leacock, Stephen. *Sunshine Sketches of a Little Town.* Toronto: McClelland and Stewart, 1970.

Lecker, Robert and David, Jack, eds. *The New Canadian Anthology: Poetry and Short Fiction in English.* Scarborough, Ont: Methuen, 1988.

Lee, Dennis. ed. *The New Canadian Poets. 1970–1985.* Toronto, Ont.: McClelland and Stewart, 1985.

MacLennan, Hugh. *Two Solitudes.* Toronto: Collins, 1945.

McCombs, Judith and Palmer, Carole. *Margaret Atwood. A Reference Guide.* New York: G.K. Hall, 1991.

Montgomery, Lucy Maud. *The Alpine Path. The Story of My Career.* Markham, Ont: Fitzhenry Whiteside, n.d.

New, W.H. *A History of Canadian Literature.* Chicago: Ivan R. Dee, 2000.

Norris, Ken. ed. *Canadian Poetry Now. 20 Poets of the '80s.* Toronto: Anansi, 1984.

Nowlan, Michael, ed. *A Land, A People.* St. John's, Newfoundland: Breakwater Books, Ltd., 1986.

Perkyns, Richard, ed. *Major Plays of the Canadian Theater 1934–1984.* Richmond Hill, Ont.: Irwin, 1984.

Roy, Gabrielle. *The Tin Flute.* Trans. Hannah Josephson. NCL, 1957.

———. Translated by Patricia Claxton. *Enchantment and Sorrow. An Autobiography of Gabrielle Roy.* Toronto: Lester Orpen Dennys, 1987.

Toye, William, ed. *The Oxford Companion to Canadian Literature.* Don Mills, Ont.: Oxford University Press, 1983.

Wagner, Anton, ed. *Contemporary Canadian Theatre. New World Visions.* Toronto: Simon Pierre, 1985.

Wasserman, Jerry, ed. *Modern Canadian Plays, Revised Edition.* Vancouver: Talon Books, 1986.

Weaver, Robert, ed. *Canadian Short Stories.* Fourth Series. Oxford University Press, 1985.

Wiebe, Rudy. *The Temptations of Big Bear.* Toronto: McClelland and Stewart, 1973.

———. *The Scorched-Wood People.* Toronto: McClelland and Stewart, 1977.